AMERICAN CRITICAL ARCHIVES 12
Willa Cather: The Contemporary Reviews

The American Critical Archives is a series of reference books that provide representative selections of contemporary reviews of the main works of major American authors. Specifically, each volume contains both full reviews and excerpts from reviews that appeared in newspapers and weekly and monthly periodicals, generally within a few months of the publication of the work concerned. There is an introductory historical overview by the volume editor, as well as checklists of additional reviews located but not quoted.

This volume offers a broad sampling of the immediate reaction to the appearance of Willa Cather's volumes of poetry, fiction, and criticism. While most reviews are from the major national journals and newspapers in major cities, some reviews show the responses in Nebraska, New Mexico, Quebec, and other locales where Cather's works are set. The reviews are often flattering, sometimes angry, sometimes so careful in their dissection of Cather's work that they are worthy of study themselves. This collection shows forty-five years of intelligent attention to one author's life's work.

Margaret Anne O'Connor teaches English and American Studies at the University of North Carolina, Chapel Hill. She has written and lectured extensively on Willa Cather.

The American Critical Archives

GENERAL EDITOR: M. Thomas Inge, Randolph-Macon College

1. *Emerson and Thoreau: The Contemporary Reviews*, edited by Joel Myerson
2. *Edith Wharton: The Contemporary Reviews*, edited by James W. Tuttleton, Kristin O. Lauer, and Margaret P. Murray
3. *Ellen Glasgow: The Contemporary Reviews*, edited by Dorothy M. Scura
4. *Nathaniel Hawthorne: The Contemporary Reviews*, edited by John L. Idol, Jr., and Buford Jones
5. *William Faulkner: The Contemporary Reviews*, edited by M. Thomas Inge
6. *Herman Melville: The Contemporary Reviews*, edited by Brian Higgins and Hershel Parker
7. *Henry James: The Contemporary Reviews*, edited by Kevin J. Hayes
8. *John Steinbeck: The Contemporary Reviews*, edited by Joseph R. McElrath, Jr., Jesse S. Crisler, and Susan Shillinglaw
9. *Walt Whitman: The Contemporary Reviews*, edited by Kenneth M. Price
10. *Langston Hughes: The Contemporary Reviews*, edited by Tish Dace
11. *Mark Twain: The Contemporary Reviews*, edited by Louis J. Budd
12. *Willa Cather: The Contemporary Reviews*, edited by Margaret Anne O'Connor

From "Four American Women: Portrait Drawings by Walter Tittle," *Forum*, 76 (October 1926), 557–61.

Willa Cather

The Contemporary Reviews

Edited by
Margaret Anne O'Connor
University of North Carolina, Chapel Hill

CAMBRIDGE
UNIVERSITY PRESS

For James and Roberta Woodress
Pioneers

PUBLISHED BY THE PRESS SYNDICATE OF THE UNIVERSITY OF CAMBRIDGE
The Pitt Building, Trumpington Street, Cambridge, United Kingdom

CAMBRIDGE UNIVERSITY PRESS
The Edinburgh Building, Cambridge CB2 2RU, UK
40 West 20th Street, New York, NY 10011-4211, USA
10 Stamford Road, Oakleigh, VIC 3166, Australia
Ruiz de Alarcón 13, 28014 Madrid, Spain
Dock House, The Waterfront, Cape Town 8001, South Africa

http://www.cambridge.org

First published 2001

Printed in the United States of America

Typeface Sabon 10/12 pt.   *System* QuarkXPress [BTS]

A catalog record for this book is available from the British Library.

Library of Congress Cataloging in Publication data
Willa Cather : the contemporary reviews / edited by Margaret Anne O'Connor.
p.   cm. – (American critical archives ; 12)
Includes index.
ISBN 0-521-39287-X (hardback)
1. Cather, Willa, 1873–1947 – Criticism and interpretation.   2. Women and
literature – United States – History – 20th century.   I. O'Connor, Margaret Anne.
II. Title.   III. Series.
PS3505.A87 Z9353 2001
813'.52 – dc21   00-031252

ISBN   0 521 39287 X   hardback

Contents

Series Editor's Preface

The American Critical Archives series documents a part of a writer's career that is usually difficult to examine, that is, the immediate response to each work as it was made public on the part of reviewers in contemporary newspapers and journals. Although it would not be feasible to reprint every review, each volume in the series reprints a selection of reviews designed to provide the reader with a proportionate sense of the critical response, whether it was positive, negative, or mixed. Checklists of other known reviews are also included to complete the documentary record and allow access for those who wish to do further reading and research.

The editor of each volume has provided an introduction that surveys the career of the author in the context of the contemporary critical response. Ideally, the introduction will inform the reader in brief of what is to be learned by a reading of the full volume. The reader then can go as deeply as necessary in terms of the kind of information desired—be it about a single work, a period in the author's life, or the author's entire career. The intent is to provide quick and easy access to the material for students, scholars, librarians, and general readers.

When completed, the American Critical Archives should constitute a comprehensive history of critical practice in America, and in some cases England, as the writers' careers were in progress. The volumes open a window on the patterns and forces that have shaped the history of American writing and the reputations of the writers. These are primary documents in the literary and cultural life of the nation.

M. THOMAS INGE

Preface

Willa Cather: The Contemporary Reviews collects reviews of only those book-length works by Willa Cather that she herself prepared for publication. Reviews included here appear in their entirety unless lengthy references to other works reviewed or repetitious plot summaries required deletions. Such omissions are indicated by ellipses in this text. Obvious typographical errors have been silently corrected, but inconsistencies between British and American spellings and punctuation remain. Wherever possible, complete bibliographic information has been given in the title lines to individual entries. In several cases, however, the items reprinted are from scrapbooks or clipping files, and I have identified these files as my source.

The lists of reviews reprinted here and provided at the end of each section as "Additional Reviews" are not comprehensive, but they do provide a representative sampling of the response to Willa Cather's work in the local, regional, national, and international English-language press.

Acknowledgments

I am greatly indebted to the scholarship and scholars referred to in the notes to the Introduction to this volume. In addition, Phyllis Martin Hutchinson and James Schroeter laid a careful groundwork for all subsequent bibliographic studies of the works of Willa Cather. More recent bibliographers John J. Murphy and Marilyn Arnold had access to an early version of the materials collected here when producing their extremely useful volumes for G. K. Hall— *Critical Essays on Willa Cather* (1984) and *Willa Cather: A Reference Guide* (1985). This collection has profited immensely from their refinements.

I wish to express my gratitude to the Research Council of the University of North Carolina at Chapel Hill, which has provided a grant toward fees and other production costs for this volume. Long overdue thanks in print is due the University of North Carolina at Chapel Hill for funding a research trip early in this project to visit libraries housing Cather materials all over the country. I returned with many unindexed reviews from some of the regions in which Cather set her novels and found a lively interchange of ideas going on beyond the publishing world of New York. Indeed, many of these reviews from the provinces seemed to be direct responses to the cosmopolitan voices and values represented in the newspapers and journals from New York that appeared on the first day of publication of any Cather work. Such bounty came at a price, however; reviewers' names, dates, and specific places of publication of these local commentaries had sometimes shaken loose from the reviews themselves. Professors Cynthia Bland, Patricia Terry, Lincoln Hall, Candace LaPrade, Dean Michael Dressman and his wife Fran applied their research skills to helping to solve these and other such mysteries during their graduate school days in Chapel Hill. Thanks also to an army of friends and helpers: Frances Coombs, Kieran J. O'Connor, Dorothea Lehmann, Ginger Elsmore, Gina Makalek, Patrick O'Neill, Dorothy Scura, Frederick T. Griffiths, and Marilyn Scott Linton. Mary Carroll Smith, Diana Rosen, Diane Cousineau, Nancy Joyner, Linda Wagner-Martin, and most especially Connie Eble provided expertise and moral support that made the completion of this project possible. My thanks also to Professor M. Thomas Inge, Julie Greenblatt, Andrew Beck, Russell Hahn, and other editors at Cambridge University Press for making molehills out of mountains of problems.

I would also like to acknowledge the newspapers, journals, and individuals listed below for permission to reprint reviews: Francis Talbot, S. J., "Willa Cather Eulogizes the Archbishop," September 24, 1927, reprinted with permission of *America* Press. Courtesy of the *Chicago Tribune* Company, reviews by Fanny Butcher, ©1923 to 1948. All rights reserved. Arthur Dygert Bates, "History and Romance in Old Quebec," reprinted by permission from the September 9, 1931, issue of the *Christian Century*, ©1931 by the *Christian Century* Foundation. C. R. W., "Miss Cather's Latest Novel," ©1923, "Three Stories of the West," ©1932, K. C. Kaufmann, "Truncated Destiny," ©1935, Michael Williams, "Miss Cather's New Novel," ©1940, and Horace Reynolds, "A Bit of the Old Gleam," ©1948, are reprinted with permission from the *Christian Science Monitor*. The *Des Moines Register* gives permission for the inclusion of reviews by Donald R. Murphy of *One of Ours*, *Shadows on the Rock*, and *Obscure Destinies*, as well as Helen Cowles Le Cron on *Shadows on the Rock* and Elizabeth Clarkson Zwart on *Not Under Forty* ©1922, 1931, 1932, and 1936. The National Council of Teachers of English gives permission for inclusion of two review essays originally published in the *English Journal*: Percy H. Boynton's "Willa Cather" of June 1924 and Granville Hicks's "The Case against Willa Cather" of November 1933. Two reviews from the 1923 issues of the *Freeman* appear courtesy of The Foundation for Economic Education, Inc. With the permission of the *Kansas City Star*, reviews ©1925 to 1936 appear. All rights reserved. Two reviews copyrighted 1927 and 1936 are reprinted with the permission of the *Los Angeles Times*. Eighteen reviews published from 1923 through 1948 appear with the permission of *The Nation*. Thirteen reviews from *The New Republic* are included with their generous permission. Ten reviews from the *New York Herald Tribune*, ©1925, 1926, 1927, 1931, 1932, 1933, 1935, 1936, 1940, 1948 are reprinted with the permission of the New York Times Company. "Recent Poetry: Various Publications of Mr. Richard Badger of Boston," June 20, 1903, is the first of 27 reviews reprinted from the *New York Times* and the *New York Times Book Review*, ©1903, 1905, 1912, 1913, 1915, 1918, 1920, 1922, 1923, 1925, 1926, 1927, 1931, 1932, 1933, 1934, 1935, 1936, 1940, 1948. Copyrighted by and reprinted with the permission of the New York Times Company. Reviews by Robert M. Coates and Hamilton Basso are reprinted by permission of *The New Yorker Magazine*, Inc., ©1931, 1932, 1948. All rights reserved. Two additional reviews from *The New Yorker* of 1932 and 1940 appear with the permission of their author, Clifton Fadiman. The *North American Review* and the University of Northern Iowa extend the courtesy of permission to publish reviews by Lloyd Morris, Herschel Brickell, and John Slocum. Six reviews from *Time* magazine appear with the permission of the Time Life Syndication: "Long an Apprentice," "Empty House," "Pride's Bed," "Buckskin Beatitude," "Home-Grown Parnassian," and "Pre-War Tale," ©1923, 1925, 1926, 1927, 1931, 1940. The *Omaha World-Herald* gives permission to publish eight editorials and reviews appearing from ©1918 to 1948. The *Union-News* and *Sunday Republican* of Springfield, Massachusetts, grant permission for the reprinting of seven reviews appearing in its pages from ©1922 to 1948. A review by Edward Killoran Brown in the *University of Toronto Quarterly* of 1936 appears courtesy of his son Deaver Brown. Attempts have been made to locate all copyright holders of reviews reprinted. All originial publication information is acknowledged at the beginning of each entry in the body of this text.

Introduction

Addressing the *Newsweek* readership of 1938, Sinclair Lewis offered an alphabetized list of the most prominent novelists of his day: Sherwood Anderson, Gertrude Atherton, Margaret Ayer Barnes, Louis Bromfield, Pearl Buck, James Branch Cabell, Erskine Caldwell, Dorothy Canfield, Willa Cather, John Dos Passos, Theodore Dreiser, James Farrell, William Faulkner, Edna Ferber, Scott Fitzgerald, Ellen Glasgow, Ernest Hemingway, Joseph Hergesheimer, Fannie Hurst, Kathleen Norris, Mary Roberts Rinehart, Upton Sinclair, John Steinbeck, Ruth Suckow, Booth Tarkington, Thornton Wilder, Harry Leon Wilson, Thomas Wolfe. Having compiled this list of current contenders for the title of "greatest American novelist," Sinclair Lewis named his choice for "the One Greatest"—Willa Cather.[1] Nobel laureate Lewis himself would probably have been on any short list his contemporary readers would have considered, but tastes have trimmed him and at least twenty others from the group of writers who are read and talked about using such superlatives today.

Sixty years after Lewis's generous assessment, Willa Cather remains secure as a major American writer of the twentieth century. The last two decades also have brought a flood of interest among biographers, bibliographers, and literary critics in general, many of whom write of the importance of Cather's immediate reception.[2] Contemporary readers may well choose a different novelist from Lewis's list for "the One Greatest," but no one can dispute Cather's prominent place in the literature of today.

This collection of contemporary reviews shows great disparity in the responses to Cather's works, even to those works most admired today. As her first critics, the most discerning contemporary reviewers not only respond to the work under scrutiny, but also try to create a context within which these works can be better understood. They compare works to classics, to the issues of the time, and to works by other writers of the same period. Cather's reviewers were increasingly likely to compare a new work to her own well-received earlier writings.

When Willa Cather's first book-length work, *April Twilights*, appeared, her friend George Seibel reviewed it favorably for the *Pittsburgh Gazette*. Despite its paternalistic title, "A Pittsburgh Poet's Volume of Verse,"[3] the review offers several stern appraisals and advice for changes. Few as they were, other reviews did not take the thin volume published by a Boston vanity press so seriously. When a substantially changed volume came out in 1923 under essentially the same title, the context for critical reception had changed immensely. After a decade of growing recognition for her prairie novels, including a Pulitzer Prize in 1922, Cather was reviewed as a novelist–poet.

By the time Willa Cather began her career as a novelist in 1912, she was familiar with reviewing from several different perspectives. As a student at the University of Nebraska, she reviewed theatrical and musical performances as well as books for the campus and Lincoln newspapers. After graduation, she moved to Pittsburgh to become the managing editor of the *Woman's Home Monthly*. Here, too, Cather often wrote reviews and features, sometimes under pseudonyms.[4] When she later moved to New York City to become managing editor of the socially conscious muckraking magazine *McClure's*, she had already published a collection of poems and another of short stories. At thirty-nine she found herself as a first-time novelist in the more vulnerable role of author, not reviewer. It is clear that Cather followed reviews closely, occasionally responding to issues brought up in her personal correspondence and in print.[5] Her handwriting scrawled across clippings and summaries of reviews shows, for instance, how closely she monitored British response to her work, in particular.[6]

Surveying the contemporary reviews, some generalizations about Willa Cather's critical reputation can be drawn. No one book serves as the single work epitomizing her accomplishment. Cather's acclaim came relatively late in life, came slowly, came under attack, and is still under reappraisal.[7] Almost universally, locale is a strong emphasis in the responses to her early work. Whether tied to Cather's biography or to the settings of the works, locale continues to play a strong part in the critical reaction to Cather's works throughout her career. Many regions can and do claim Willa Cather as a resident—the Virginia of her birth, Nebraska of her youth, Pittsburgh of her early adulthood, the American Southwest, France and Canada of her travels, and Manhattan, which was her home for more than forty years. Reviewers from these regions make demands on Cather as a product of their various environments; they want accuracy, sympathy, and even loyalty from the author.

The Roman Catholic press, too, regularly reviews Cather's works as if she were a coreligionist. Cather converted from the Baptist to the Episcopal Church in 1926, and she never became a Catholic, though her novels on the church in North America, such as *Death Comes for the Archbishop* and *Shadows on the Rock*, led many reviewers and general readers to think so.

In the early stage of her career as a novelist as reviewed in the national press, Cather's works are championed not by the established arbiters of taste but instead by reviewers and journals that are encouraging the new, the revolutionary in terms of subject matter as well as style. *Alexander's Bridge* is admired for its psychological portraits, its restrained style, and the metaphorical power of the image presented in its title. Perhaps because of its international settings or perhaps because the dust jacket suggests such a comparison, several reviewers discuss Cather in the light of Edith Wharton.

Grounds for comparison change with *O Pioneers!*. One of the earliest and most complete reviews was by novelist Floyd Dell in the Chicago *Evening Post*. In a response to *O Pioneers!* titled simply "A Good Novel," Dell uses Cather and her achievement in this novel to challenge the Eastern seaboard literary establishment: "The book provides an opportunity for the American Academy of Arts and Letters to justify its existence," he suggests. *O Pioneers!* is "touched with genius," he argues, and "worthy of being recognized as the most vital, subtle and artistic piece of the year's fiction."[8]

Another early champion was Baltimore's H. L. Mencken, who includes reviews of Cather's first five books of fiction in the pages of *Smart Set*. Though he had been one of many who found *The Song of the Lark* flawed in the conventionality of its plot, he finds much more to admire in the stories in *Youth and the Bright Medusa*. He triumphantly declares: "They are stories that lift themselves completely above the level of current American fiction, even of good fiction. They are the work of a woman who, after a long apprenticeship, has got herself into the front rank of American novelists, and is still young enough to have her best writing ahead of her." In a pattern to be repeated by many later reviewers, Mencken uses the opportunity presented by reviewing one book to renew his enthusiasm for an earlier work: "I can call *My Antonia* to your attention once more. It is the finest thing of its sort ever done in America."[9]

Mencken abruptly shifts from broad praise for Cather's novels, however, with the appearance of *One of Ours*, Cather's first novel with the new publishing house begun by Blanche and Alfred Knopf. A close look at the response to this single work suggests the variety of critical communities reacting to and thus affecting the reception of this and other Cather works.

Overall, the twenties were the years of Cather's greatest critical and financial success despite her experimentation in form and subject matter, which found detractors. Willa Cather was later to choose the year 1922 as the one in which "the world fell apart,"[10] a statement that proved prescient on many levels, national and international, political and literary. On a personal level, the year meant for Cather a break with the more revolutionary voices in the reviewing community nationally and more open criticism in Nebraska than she had encountered before. Reviewers fault her as a writer, as a woman, as disloyal to her roots; and in Britain, she is criticized for being all too American. Yet this is the one Pulitzer Prize–winning novel of Cather's career, and supportive reviews praise both the quality of writing and the handling of subject matter in the novel.

One of Ours caught the attention of the national reviewing community in a way that her earlier works had not. A son of Nebraska lost in the war was a topic of immediate concern. Critics compare the novel to depictions of the war in Dos Passos, to headlines, to personal losses felt by American families much like the one pictured in Cather's novel. The value of the novel, its plot, landscapes, characters, and style come under scrutiny, but the assumption that the novel attempts to be a justification of American sacrifices in the war eventually becomes the major focus of reviewers' comments. Taken together, the reviews record a public debate that argued in hindsight the pros and cons of American involvement in the Great War. *One of Ours* received the Pulitzer Prize in 1923, causing discussion of the novel to linger in book review pages of newspapers and in the literary digests for an unusually long time. Mencken's earlier high praise turns to sawdust when *One of Ours* appears in September of 1922. Praising her realistic evocation of prairie life in the first half of the novel, Mencken finds nothing to admire once the hero, Claude, sails for France: "The war she depicts has its thrills and even its touches of plausibility, but at bottom it is fought out not in France but on a Hollywood movie-lot. . . . There is a lyrical nonsensicality in it that often glows half pathetic; it is precious near the war of the standard model of lady novelist."[11]

Unpublished responses form another gauge of Cather's contemporary reception. After *One of Ours* received the Pulitzer Prize, untried novelist Ernest Hemingway wrote his friend Edmund Wilson a now-famous letter that—perhaps coincidentally—accuses Cather's novel of exactly the same failings that Mencken had listed. He adds touches of professional jealousy and sarcasm in his own assessment of the novel: "Prize. Big sales. People take it seriously. Wasn't that last scene in the lines wonderful? Do you know where it came from? The battle scene in *The Birth of a Nation*. I identified episode after episode. Catherized. Poor woman she had to get her war experience somewhere."[12]

On the home front, in Lincoln, Rev. Wilbur Theodore Elmore preached a lengthy sermon at the First Baptist Church, which Cather had attended in her first year at the University of Nebraska. Rev. Elmore defends the ministry in general and local ministerial students and ministers in particular from the unflattering caricatures of these types he sees in the novel. The *Nebraska State Journal* chooses to publish a complete transcription of the sermon, suggesting a high level of local interest. Rev. Elmore says Cather is "very much one of ours." He is appalled, however—and he expects his congregation to share his indignation—at the picture of the spiritless, vacuous world he sees in the novel's depiction of Lincoln as much as in the small Nebraska prairie towns. "Not one Christian home is shown," he laments. And he asks, "Is this true to life? Are our Christian mothers dwarfed by their faith?"[13]

On the national level, Henry Seidel Canby, the editor of the "Literary Review" section of the *New York Evening Post*, features *One of Ours* with

Sinclair Lewis's *Babbitt* in an editorial titled "Two Americas." He misses the "spirit" of *My Antonia* and laments that "Cather has succeeded in making the farm not only dull for the farmer but for the reader as well." He much favors *Babbitt*, as is shown perhaps by his invitation to Lewis to review Cather's novel at length in the same issue (Carl Van Doren reviews *Babbitt*).[14] Although Lewis, too, sees flaws, he concludes by suggesting the effect of this novel on the role of the critic: "There are books which it is a joy to attack; lying books, mawkish books, pretentious dull books, the books which stir a regrettable but natural spirit of deviltry, a desire to torture the authors, and a desire to keep people from reading them. *One of Ours* is quite the opposite. It makes the reader, for a moment of modesty, hope more for its success than for the authority of his own judgment."[15] A month later, the negative portions of Lewis's review attract a lengthy rejoinder from one of Cather's readers. At two thousand words, this "Letter to the Editor" is longer than the Canby and Lewis columns combined. The writer, Marion Ponsonby, methodically retraces Lewis's argument against the novel and concludes as politely as possible that "Mr. Lewis simply has not got the intuitional equipment for understanding Miss Cather, although he has an uncanny intuition for public psychology!"[16]

Yet another defender appears in the pages of the "Literary Review" a month later, one of Cather's students from a writing course taught at Breadloaf the preceding summer. Lorna R. F. Birtwell[17] has praise not for the professional critics but for Ponsonby's letter: "Here, at last, was a finely sensitive response to one of our most significant books, in place of an attempt to superimpose the preconceived and rather trite notions of the critics on a work whose distinction it is that it escapes from just such grooves as they would mark out for it." Birtwell avoids offering her own reading of the novel; instead she mentions literary and journalistic figures beyond Canby and Lewis in the *Post*'s "Literary Review" embroiled in the controversy over the novel, detractors such as Heywood Broun in the New York *World*, Gilbert Seldes in the *Dial*, and Ludwig Lewisohn in the *Nation*.[18] Perhaps it is Birtwell's focus on critics rather than on taking sides with regard to the value of the novel itself that prompts Cather to write to Birtwell only two days after her comments appear in the "Literary Review." Since Cather's testamentary restrictions make it impossible to quote directly from her letters, a paraphrase will have to serve here to show her response to the controversy, a response that says much about her public reaction to reviews throughout her career. Cather's letter is essentially a thank-you to Birtwell for saying what Cather herself had been thinking. She suggests that the real problem these critics have with *One of Ours* is that they liked *My Antonia* so much that they wanted her to write the same book again, a feat Cather compares to having a trained dog go through its paces. One particularly galling fact about these critics' present enthusiasm for *My Antonia* is that, from Cather's perspective, none of them cared about the

1918 novel until it had been out for at least two years. Their first reaction was that it was structureless, she says, and perhaps *One of Ours*, too, will be reappraised later. As for now, the novel is selling quite well and interest in it has raised sales of her earlier works. Overall, Cather says, it's not really important what critics say, although it's pleasant when they are admiring. To care too much about the positive or negative reviews would affect a writer's quality of life. According to Cather, if she experiments in technique or treatment, she finds the critics are perplexed and annoyed. Thanking Birtwell again for an instructive massing of evidence that puts the critical debate into a new perspective, she says that practically all the negative arguments given against *One of Ours*, particularly that it was dull, had been offered against *My Antonia* as well. The critics, for the most part, preferred *The Song of the Lark*.[19] As this final comment would suggest, Cather saw the major competitor for a new novel's success to be earlier works by the same author.

On the international level, Gerald Bullett responds to both the awarding of the Pulitzer Prize and the British publication of *One of Ours* with understated, if not damningly faint praise. For Bullett, Cather's femininity is less an impediment to her ability to write of the war than is her nationality. He finds the "literary qualities" of the novel "far from despicable" but predicts that British readers, who have had such a prolonged and agonized war experience, will become impatient with this American piece of "topical fiction." His final bitter quip suggests that no author however gifted, American or European, could write successfully about the war as far as he was concerned: "But the War having spoiled so many lives, it seems a pity to let it spoil our novels as well."[20]

Throughout the twenties, several prominent critics of major magazines and national newspapers followed Cather's career with enthusiasm. Her college friend Dorothy Canfield Fisher, novelist and eventually member of the Book-of-the-Month Club board, was one of many regular and invariably supportive reviewers of Cather's work in these years. Fanny Butcher of the *Chicago Tribune*, H. S. Canby and Stuart P. Sherman of the *Saturday Review*, and H. W. Boynton of the *Independent* would with regularity respond positively in print within days of the announced publication of a Cather volume. Among admirers, the word "masterpiece" appears, though it is often applied retrospectively to refer to *My Antonia* and the other prairie novels of a decade earlier. While *A Lost Lady* wins the title from several important critics, others, like E. F. Edgett, declare it only to be a skeleton of a novel. *The Professor's House* is a fragmented novel, according to some, suffering from the lack of a sturdy skeletal structure and a break in narrative continuity. Writing of *Death Comes for the Archbishop* in the Catholic monthly *Commonweal*, Michael Williams is unabashedly partisan and concludes his review by writing, "I consider it the duty of Catholics to buy and read and spread Willa Cather's masterpiece."[21]

During the Depression years, leftist critics codify a strain of negative response begun in the twenties. Among the most strident voices, Granville Hicks, Clifton Fadiman, and Lionel Trilling declare that Cather has not turned out to be the realist that critics of the teens had valued her for being. Archer Winsten gathers the threads of reviewers' complaints in order to reject them in "A Defense of Willa Cather," but as a comparison of titles suggests, his most direct effect appears to have been prompting Granville Hicks to compose "The Case Against Willa Cather." Hicks argues in his retrospective of Cather's career that she is an overrated escapist who had never adequately presented the economic struggle of the Midwestern immigrants whose lives she was famous for depicting.[22]

Negative criticism in the 1930s went beyond ideological differences between Cather and the leftist critics who accused her of escapism. In the popular press, too, there were some bitter words. A brief reaction to *Lucy Gayheart* in *Time* magazine reads: "The story of a small town musician who fell in love with a famed singer; a weepy book in which five of the important characters die like flies in the last few chapters."[23] Not surprisingly, the main character was often compared to the strong female characters in her earlier novels, particularly Thea Kronborg in *The Song of a Lark*. As her first novel set in Nebraska in more than a decade, *Lucy Gayheart* was a return to the locale of Cather's greatest successes, but the young aspiring accompanist lacked the will or the talent to succeed that Thea and Cather's other early strong women characters showed. Only the true diehards in the Cather reviewing camp offered strong praise: Dorothea Lawrance Mann in the *Boston Evening Transcript*, Fanny Butcher in the *Chicago Daily Tribune*, Howard Mumford Jones in the *Saturday Review of Literature*, and Charlotte M. Meagher for *Commonweal*.

Not Under Forty, the title of Cather's only collection of essays, was intended to define the expected readership for the work. Like her poetry and short story collections, these essays were only sparsely reviewed and seemed merely to provide reviewers an opportunity to talk about her achievement as a novelist. Lionel Trilling's important review essay in the *New Republic* does not mention *Not Under Forty*; instead it surveys her entire career as a novelist in order to chronicle "the subtle failure of her admirable talent."[24]

Cather's final novel is set in the Virginia of her birth. Set in 1856, *Sapphira and the Slave Girl* recounts a piece of family history: the family schism caused by slavery. Southern historical novels were in vogue in the late thirties, as seen in the continuing popularity of the work of Ellen Glasgow, the spectacular popular success of *Gone With the Wind*, and critical fascination with and confusion over *Absalom, Absalom!* Even Clifton Fadiman, an earlier Cather detractor, offers tepid praise for what Cather does well in the novel: "Willa Cather bucks the trend, swims upstream, walks by herself, and does very nicely, thank you," he begins.[25] Grudgingly, he notes that she writes with subtlety and restraint, avoids familiar stereotypes, and has the authority of her personal experience as a focus. Yet Fadiman manages to bring up the absence of affect in the characters' interactions that had troubled him in his earlier reviews of her work. By contrast, earlier detractor Morton Dauwen Zaubel calls *Sapphira* Cather's "best book in thirteen years," which is probably more a disparagement of the novels of the 1930s than a ringing endorsement of the novel at hand.[26]

Fifteen months after Willa Cather's death in April 1947, *The Old Beauty and Others* appeared as her last unedited text. Like the response to the three collections of stories she had written earlier, there were far fewer reviews than there were for her novels. Most reviewers chose to tie the stories to eulogistic tributes to Cather—but not all. In a prepublication notice in the *Library Journal*, Helene Scherff Taylor finds the stories "contribute nothing to the stature of Miss Cather as a distinguished artist," and she laments the "lack of literary maturity and the grace of expression" that she finds in Cather's earlier and best work.[27] Writing of the title piece, Margaret Marshall suggests "Miss Cather would have done better with her story, one reflects, in her untired days."[28] Fanny Butcher and Lloyd Morris are predictably more reverential in their discussions; yet still a recognition of waning powers and better days remembered underscores these and most of the other reviews.

Cather's contemporary reviewers spoke for their personal tastes, their interest groups, their religious denominations, their regions, their stations in life, and they fought among themselves over the stature of individual Cather works. A broad collection of the reviews no doubt says as much about the health and vitality of the reviewing community as it does about the specific literary works reviewed. In this respect, Willa Cather was truly fortunate. The reviews of the works of Willa Cather provide insights as thought-provoking today as when they were first in print. They still have much to tell Willa Cather's readers about her work.

Notes

1 Sinclair Lewis, "The Greatest American Novelist," *Newsweek*, 11 (3 January 1938), 29.
2 One of the most thorough of such surveys can be found in John J. Murphy's and Kevin A. Synnott's essay "The Recognition of Willa Cather's Art," which serves as the introduction to *Critical Essays on Willa Cather*, John J. Murphy, ed. (Boston: G. K. Hall, 1984), pp. 1–28.
3 26 April 1903, section 2, p. 4.
4 Cather's early journalism, including her reviews, has been gathered in *The Kingdom of Art: Willa Cather's First Principles and Critical Statements 1893–96*, Bernice Slote, ed. (Lincoln: University of Nebraska Press, 1966), and *The World and the Parish: Willa Cather's Articles and Reviews, 1893–1902*, William M. Curtin, ed., 2 vols. (Lincoln: University of Nebraska Press, 1970). See also M. Catherine Downs's *Becoming Modern: Willa Cather's Journalism* (Selinsgrove, PA: Susquehanna University Press, 1999).
5 Stephen Tennant includes four such responses in *Willa Cather on Writing: Critical Studies on Writing as an Art* (New York: Knopf, 1949), pp. 3–32, and Alfred A. Knopf characterizes her personal reaction to reviews as part of his recollections of their warm professional

relationship in "Miss Cather," in *The Art of Willa Cather*, Bernice Slote and Virginia Faulkner, eds. (Lincoln: University of Nebraska Press, 1974), pp. 205–24.

6 Scrapbooks at the Willa Cather Pioneer Museum in Red Cloud, Nebraska, were compiled with materials from Carrie Miner Sherwood, one of Cather's childhood friends; annotations by Cather call attention to reviews she finds most valuable (see the *Willa Cather Pioneer Memorial Newletter*, 4:1 [1960], 1). Since Joan Crane in *Willa Cather: A Bibliography* (Lincoln: University of Nebraska Press, 1982) offers citations to specific reviews and references to individual Cather letters when establishing publication dates for specific editions of Cather's works, her work is extremely useful for gauging Cather's reactions to her reception.

7 See Sharon O'Brien's overview of Cather's critical reception in "Becoming Noncanonical: The Case against Willa Cather," *American Quarterly*, 40 (1989), 110–17.

8 Chicago *Evening Post*, 25 July 1913, p. 9.

9 "Chiefly Americans," *Smart Set*, 63 (December 1920), 140.

10 Preface to *Not Under Forty* (New York: Knopf, 1936).

11 "Portrait of an American Citizen," *Smart Set*, 69 (October 1922), 141.

12 Letter of 25 November 1923, *Ernest Hemingway: Selected Letters, 1917–1961*, Carlos Baker, ed. (New York: Scribners, 1981), p. 105.

13 *Nebraska State Journal*, 19 February 1923, p. 6.

14 *New York Evening Post* "Literary Review," 16 September 1922, p. 21.

15 "A Hamlet of the Plains," *New York Evening Post* "Literary Review," 16 September 1922, p. 23.

16 "Across a Chasm," *New York Evening Post* "Literary Review," 21 October 1922, p. 138.

17 See Lorna R. F. Birtwell, "Remembering Willa Cather," *Woman's Press* (November 1948), pp. 8–10.

18 *New York Evening Post* "Literary Review," 25 November 1922, p. 254.

19 27 November 1922, Butler Library, Columbia University. Willa Cather's letters have not been published, nor can they be quoted directly due to testamentary restrictions. The most thorough and carefully documented use of these letters appears in James Woodress's *Willa Cather: A Literary Life* (Lincoln: University of Nebraska Press, 1987).

20 "America's War Novel," *Spectator* (London), 131 (3 November 1923), 661.

21 "Willa Cather's Masterpiece," *Commonweal*, 6 (28 September 1927), 92.

22 See Archer Winsten, "A Defense of Willa Cather," *Bookman*, 74 (March 1932), 634–40, and Granville Hicks, "The Case against Willa Cather," *English Journal*, 22 (November 1933), 703–10.

23 *Time*, 26 (12 August 1935), 56.

24 "Willa Cather," *New Republic*, 90 (10 February 1937), 10.

25 *New Yorker*, 16 (7 December 1940), 103.

26 "The Tone of Time," *Nation*, 151 (7 December 1940), 576.

27 *Library Journal*, 73 (1 September 1948), 1192.

28 *Nation*, 167 (2 October 1948), 376.

APRIL TWILIGHTS

APRIL TWILIGHTS

POEMS BY

Willa Sibert Cather

ARTI ERI-
ET TATI

Boston: Richard G. Badger

The Gorham Press: 1903

George Seibel, "A Pittsburgh Poet's Volume of Verse," *Pittsburgh Gazette*, 26 April 1903, section 2, p. 4

Publishers complain that the public does not buy poetry, and the public murmurs that publishers rarely print any poetry worth buying. Which is cause and which is effect would be a question difficult to answer. Certain it is that the most successful volume of verse does not bring its author a moiety of what a moderately successful novel would. Certain it is that a poor novel is a venial thing, like the measles, while a poor book of poetry is an unpardonable sin. Sinners are many and some sit in high places. All the more welcome is a book of genuine poetry in unpretentious guise, unheralded by sounding bugles, but singing its way straight to the heart of every one who looks within its covers.

Willa Sibert Cather, whose *April Twilights* is the book I mean, is not unknown to Pittsburghers, being one of them. Some of her poems have appeared in the magazines, but their author is even better known there by some short stories of subtle psychology and poetic style. This volume of verse is almost entirely fresh, uncontaminate of the types—and fresh in another sense—no faded garland from gardens of other singers. As one reads these fragrant lyrics one feels a "leafy luxury" that breathes through no herbarium.

There is an echo, but an echo afar and faint, as if Sappho whispered from the Leucadian rock or old Catullus sang to Lesbia on olive-silvered Sirmio. Most of the poems have a perfection of form that reminds one of Gautier and is surpassed by no living English poet except perhaps William Watson.

There are a few defective rhymes, like "thyme" with "thine" and "spray" with "quay" but they are only a few. There are a few verses that run on painful feet, as: "Playfellows who would fulfill" but they are only a few. There are a few unmelodious conjunctions of harsh syllables, as "dust-stopped," but they are only a few. Usually the verse rolls smoothly on, immaculate and musical.

Take one of the sonnets and hold it against the light, for the sonnet has ever been the despair and coronation of poets, and mark how each of its fourteen facets emits a ray of richness, until you seem to see a double rainbow whose combined hues shine as one perfect chrysolite. The sonnet I mean is "Aftermath," and but for a doubtful accent in the first line is perfect:

Can'st thou conjure a vanished morn
   of spring,
   Or bid the ashes of the sunset
   glow
Again to redness? Are we strong to
   wring
   From trodden grapes the juice
   drunk long ago?
Can leafy longings stir in Autumn's
   blood,
Or can I wear a pearl dissolved in
   wine,
Or go a-Maying in a winter wood,
   Or paint with youth thy wasted
   cheek, or mine?
What bloom, then, shall abide, since
   ours hath sped?
   Thou art more lost to me than
   they who dwell
In Egypt's sepulchres, long ages fled;
   And would I touch—Ah me! I
   might as well

Covet the gold of Helen's vanished
head,
    Or kiss back Cleopatra from the
    dead!

There is no misty grandeur in this, as
in Keats' sonnet on Homer, but a lucent
magic—moonbeams asleep on violet beds
or cloud-isles drifting through a hollow
sky. Certainly any poet might be proud of
this, or of its sister sonnet, "On Cydnus,"
which evokes the splendorous vision of
Antony and Egypt's queen:

The dream of all the world was at his
feet:
    Her eyes were heavy with the
    night of fate,
    When, from the purple couch
    whereon she sate,
She rose, and took a jewel that was
meet
For a queen's breast, where royal
pulses beat—
    A milk-white pearl, her milk-
    white bosom's mate,
    Dropped in the golden chalice at
    his plate,
And to his lips held up the nectar
sweet
    And bade him drink the cup of
    destiny.
How shall he pledge again? by what
emprise
    A chalice find that holds a
    kingdom's fee?
Perchance in that charmed liquor he
descries
    A madman, raving while his
    galleys flee,
    Who casts a world into the wine-
    dark sea.

The simile of Antony's world for
Cleopatra's pearl, so richly broidered here
in silken words, is one of the most beautiful and striking in the range of recent

poetry. It takes one back to "the spacious
days of great Elizabeth." On the other
hand, many of Miss Cather's stanzas
exhale the cloying sweetness which the
poets of that era borrowed from Petrarch
and the Rosardists. The manner, or man-
nerism, of Suckling and Herrick and
Donne is in verses such as these:

Alas, that June should come when
thou didst go;
    I think you passed each other on
    the way;
And seeing thee, the Summer loved
thee so
    That all her loveliness she gave
    away;
. . . .
Beggared herself of morning for thine
eyes,
    Hung on thy lips of every bird the
    tune,
Breathed on thy cheek her soft
vermillion dyes,
    And in thee at the singing heart of
    June.

Such conceits, however, are so rare
that we marvel at their exquisite setting
and forget the artificial ring. Simple and
sensuous is the usual strain of these
verses—a rich wine diluted with dreamy
tears, and "with beaded bubbles winking
at the brim." Only a single line I found
that was not crystal-clear: "Comeliest
his of sacrifice" [in "Provençal Legend"].
One wonders where that poor possessive
pronoun wandered from, and what it
is doing there. Perhaps it was put in by
the same compositor who has queered
classical geography with the River Cyndus
[the first edition had this incorrect spelling
in the Table of Contents and title of
poem].
    Aside from this single inversion, Miss
Cather's verse is direct and simple. And
simplicity is the true touchstone of all

poetry, of all art. Not the tangled thicket of thought, the overshadowing fronds of phrase, but the tall palm, chiseled out of the forest, takes men's eyes. Miss Cather disdains luxuriant words, and with homely Anglo-Saxon syllables paints pictures that will not fade. One can almost see the red glow, hear the hearty voices, in "The Tavern":

In the tavern of my heart
  Many a one has sat before,
Drunk red wine and sung a stave,
  And, departing, come no more.
When the night was cold without
  And the ravens croaked of
    storm,
They have sat them at my hearth,
  Telling me my house was warm.

The lyrics, "I Sought the Woods in Winter" and "Thou Art the Pearl," the song of "The Hawthorn Tree," the ballad of "The Night Express," illustrate this restraint, this temperance. There are poets who are dictionary topers. Rosetti used to dig up rare, succulent words and write poems around them, as one might make a waistcoat for a pearl button or build a house for a bronze door-knocker. There is no trace of this in these poems of Miss Cather's; even when she treads upon Swinburne's holy ground she wisely refrains from his fanfarons and flourishes. Take the poem, "Winter at Delphi," theme and spirit and rhythm of which have much in common with Swinburne's "Last Oracle." Miss Cather's verse runs:

Cold are the stars of the night,
  Wild is the tempest crying,
Fast through the velvet dark
  Little white flakes are flying.
Still is the House of Song,
  But the fire on the hearth is
    burning;

And the lamps are trimmed and the cup
  Is full for his day of returning.
His watchers are fallen asleep,
  They wait but his call to follow,
Ay, to the ends of the earth—
  But Apollo, the god, Apollo?

This is poetry, but "London Roses" isn't. Not even the catalogue of streets—"Holland Road, High Street, Bayswater" is poetic. Perhaps there is nothing about London that is [so] poetic as the prairie dawn or the birches of Wyoming, which inspire two of Miss Cather's loveliest nature lyrics. Her feeling for nature is everywhere vital and near—it is not a printed and perfumed nature, and one knows 'tis but a slip of the calendar when she lets daffodils bloom in summer.

Next to the love of nature, a spirit of haunting melancholy pervades the book. Take the lament for the vanished god, unresponding, unreturning, there is an undertone of pensive sadness, from the first poem in which a heartbroken maiden asks her "grandmither" to make room in the grave, to the last "Envoi." If she sings of the "Mills of Monmartre," it is to see the yellow grain ground into dust; if she sings of May and buds and roses and bees she sees "the dead under all." It is not a morbid grief, but a pensive sorrow, an "April Twilight" shadow hovering o'er a bank of flowers. Sometimes its expression wears a robe of words that fits like old FitzGerald's verse on Omar's Persian thought, thus in the "Envoi" I have already named:

Where are the loves that we have
  loved before
When once we are alone, and shut
  the door?
No matter whose the arms that held
  me fast,
The arms of Darkness hold me at the
  last.

No matter down what primrose path
    I tend,
I kiss the lips of Silence in the end.

Miss Cather has certainly produced a noble and notable little volume to enrich our poetic poverty. It is a volume that will go through many editions if it meets with the appreciation it deserves. It is a volume that will firmly fix her literary reputation, now confined to the ephemeral pages of magazines where even a prolific author is lost in the crowd.

"New Books,"
Nebraska State Journal,
18 May 1903, p. 6

Richard C. Badger of the Gorham Press, Boston, publishes *April Twilights*, a collection of poems by Willa Sibert Cather, formerly dramatic critic on this paper and later of the staff of the *Lincoln Courier* and of the *Pittsburg Leader*. It was only last week that *The Journal* announced the "arrival" of Miss Cather in the literary world through the offer of the McClure publishing house to back her future ventures in fiction and general literature. Some of these poems have heretofore appeared in the magazines while others are new to the reading public but as a collection they are unique and possess a quiet charm very appropriately suggested in the title. *The Journal* hails her first book with delight and feels sure that it is but the harbinger of many future achievements of her facile pen. A very interesting sketch of her life on a ranch in southwestern Nebraska and later in Red Cloud where she ran wild some years before beginning her school education that was completed at the state university accompanies the announcement of the publisher.

"Recent Poetry:
Various Publications of
Mr. Richard Badger of
Boston," New York
Times Saturday Review
of Books and Art,
20 June 1903, p. 434

Although Miss Cather is not always quite certain of her accented syllables and is perhaps overfond of lilting measures for a poet with so much insight to the sadder side of human experience, it is impossible to read her more successful pieces without recognizing the firm and delicate conception underlying the musical and suggestive phrasing. There is no doubt that with the gain of facility and assurance, of power over her plastic material, and of the discipline given by long practice she will be able to express those hidden relations of human souls which for the short and crude vision have no existence and which are infinitely interesting to those who are curious concerning the life beyond the obvious. One more quotation, to show the quality of her metaphor in presenting a familiar feeling. We venture to predict that in later editions of the poem the word "despoil" will replace "defile" in the penultimate line:

THE TAVERN

In the tavern of my heart
    Many a one has sat before,
Drunk red wine and sung a stave,
    And, departing, come no more.
When the night was cold without
    And the ravens croaked of
        storm,
They have sat them at my hearth,
    Telling me my house was warm.

As the lute and cup went round,
    They have rhymed me well in
        lay;
When the hunt was on at morn,
    Each, departing, went his way.
On some walls, in compliment,
    Some would scrawl a verse or
        two,
Some have hung a willow branch,
    Or a wreath of corn flowers
        blue.

Ah! my friend, when thou dost go,
    Leave no wreath of flowers for
        me;
Not pale daffodils nor rue,
    Violets nor rosemary.
Spill the wine upon the lamps,
    Tread the fire and bar the door;
So defile the wretched place,
    None will come, forevermore.

Edith M. Thomas, "Recent Books of Poetry," *Critic*, 43 (July 1903), 81

That *musis ámicus*,—the befriender of the yet uncommissioned troubadour,—the muse yet uncrowned,—we refer to Mr. Richard Badger,—has rendered no truer service than in introducing this shy, wistful, and winsome singer who here puts forth her maiden effort, under the suggestive title, "April Twilights." There is no small degree of skill shown in the fingering of her plaintive pipe; and ever and again we hear in her songs that which comes to our ear as the true "lyrical cry." A touch of sisterhood between herself and that lately stilled, impassioned voice

of song—Mathilde Blind—is felt on reading

    I have no house for Love to shelter
      him.

Though the singer of *April Twilights* exclaims, in a touching little *l'envoi*, "'Tis Loneliness that loves me best of all," we bid her take heart of grace; for she may yet win for her muse many a golden friend in the goodly companionship of the poets.

William Morton Payne, *Dial*, 35 (16 July 1903), 40–1

Miss Willa Sibert Cather is a new writer, and *April Twilights* is the title of her first book. The title has no particular significance, unless it suggests the subdued tone of her tranquil musings. "Prairie Dawn" is pretty enough to quote.

    A crimson fire that vanquishes the
      stars;
    A pungent odor from the dusty sage;
    A sudden stirring of the huddled
      herds;
    A breaking of the distant table-lands

    Through purple mists ascending, and
      the flare
    Of water-ditches silver in the light;
    A swift, bright lance hurled low
      across the world;
    A sudden sickness for the hills of
      home.

Of such exquisite description there is much in Miss Cather's collection; there are also engaging reflections from the world of books, the history and the legend of the ages.

"Minor Verse from Boston," *Academy and Literature* (London), 65 (18 July 1903), 57–8

There is some tenderness, some music, and some originality. Nowhere does the verse reach a high level, but it is seldom bathetic and never silly. Miss Cather, too, can get a lilt into her lines which has something of the real singing quality. We quote from "The Hills [sic] of Montmartre": ["Mills of Montmartre" is quoted in its entirety.]

Boston Evening Transcript, 12 August 1903, p. 16

The verses in *April Twilights* have scarcely any interest beyond the writer's personal circle, but they contain two bits of genuine sentiment. "The Night Express" is a picture of the iron horse which stirs the restless hearts of village boys, and taking them out into the great world, at last, in death brings them home again. The other poem, "The Namesake," invests our Civil War period with reality, as it depicts the soldier who lies dead on a Southern battlefield.

"Glimpses of Present Day Poets," *Poet Lore*, 14 (Winter 1903), 113–15

Miss Willa Sibert Cather, whose delightful volume of poems entitled *April Twilights* was recently published was born near Winchester, Va., in 1876. When she was ten years old, the family moved to a ranch in Southwestern Nebraska, and for two years the child ran wild, playing with the little herd girls, and visiting the Danes and Norwegians, who had settled there as farmers.

During the ranch period and for some time after, Miss Cather did not go to school at all, and her only reading was an old copy of Ben Johnson's plays, a Shakespeare, a Byron, and *The Pilgrim's Progress*, which later she said she read through eight times in one winter. The first two years of her course at the University of Nebraska, where she graduated in 1895, were spent in the hardest kind of study, but then she discovered herself and began to write a little. She edited a creditable college magazine, and did remarkably discriminating dramatic criticism for the *Nebraska State Journal*. Later she wrote for the *Lincoln Courier*, and in 1896 she came to Pittsburg, where she was for several years on the staff of the *Leader*, doing clever dramatic and literary criticism in addition to her regular work.

Miss Cather's first story "Eric Hermanson's Soul," a study of the effect of western climatic conditions on the Scandanavian temperament, was translated into German and republished by The Dresden Critic, Eugene Von Sempsky.

All of the verse published in Miss Cather's volume, *April Twilights*, has been done within the last five years. Her early effort was all toward prose, her verse always being incidental and usually accidental. "Grandmither Think not I Forget," the best poem of the collection, was never retouched after the first writing.

Miss Cather has contributed prose and verse to various American periodicals. Her latest story, "A Death in the Desert," published in *Scribners*, shows that her feeling for western atmosphere has in nowise diminished. She has also completed a series of short stories, all of which are studies of artist life.

The following poems are Miss Cather's favorites:

["Grandmither, Think Not I Forget," "Mills of Montmartre," and "The Hawthorn Tree" are reprinted.]

Rafford Pike, *Bookman* (New York), 19 (April 1904), 196

Miss Willa Cather writes very well indeed, as may be seen from the following lines, entitled "Prairie Dawn":

A crimson fire that vanquishes the
    stars;
A pungent odor from the dusty sage;
A sudden stirring of the huddled
    herds;
A breaking of the distant table-lands
Through purple mists ascending, and
    the flare
of water ditches silver in the light;
A swift, bright lance hurled low
    across the world;
A sudden sickness for the hills of
    home.

In the next poem, however, she begins with this line: "Can'st thou conjure a vanished morn of spring" [from "Aftermath"].

It is obvious that Miss Cather has confounded the pronunciation of "conjure" in one sense with the pronunciation which it bears when used in quite another. Also we might suggest that when writing about mills of Montmartre it is scarcely necessary to give the reader a foot-note explaining about the Moulin Rouge. Presumably Miss Cather is not writing for persons who need that particular sort of information.

Percy A. Hutchison, "Modern Verse Cut Loose from Literary Tradition," *New York Times Book Review*, 13 May 1923, p. 7

As it happens, three volumes of lyric poetry of high excellence have followed so close on the heels of Dr. Strachan's study [*The Soul of Modern Poetry* (New York: George H. Doran Co., 1923)] that they may well be reviewed in the light of his discussion. One volume is by an American, *April Twilights*, from the pen of the novelist Willa Cather. . . .

The quest of beauty is the predominating feature of Miss Cather's strangely haunting verses, several of which were published some years ago, but have long been out of print. And in her passionate desire to ensnare and fixate beauty, whether of thought or emotion or surroundings, there is evident the nostalgic wistfulness which Dr. Strachan finds so poignant a quality of modern poetry. One can open the book at random for illustration. It is evident on every page, it is evident in this lyric called "Autumn Melody" [quoted].

Miss Cather runs true to Dr. Strachan's study in another respect also. She projects her poetry into the commonplaces of life—rather, she finds the poetry that is inherent therein. Thus she writes of "Prairie Spring" and "Macon Prairie," of a "Street in Packingtown," and of going home by "The Burlington Route."

Into the poem "Street in Packingtown" (Chicago)... there enters another element to which Dr. Strachan calls attention, and that is the place occupied in modern verse by what is ugly, by what is evil in modern life. Miss Cather's poem is of a Polack child, unkempt, cruel, who is torturing a stray and half-starved cat.

> He twists the cat and pays no heed.
> From under a pale shock of hair
> Neither resentment nor surprise
> Lights the desert of those eyes—
> To hurt and to be hurt; he knows
> All he will know on earth, or need to
>   know.

How is the acceptance of such a subject, with such bald, unmoral treatment of it, to be reconciled with the statement that modern poetry is mainly concerned with its quest for beauty? Dr. Strachan solves the dilemma thus: "The only justification for sincere and realistic treatment in literature of ugliness and evil is in order to display it in all of its sheer and defiant hostility to the central harmony of the universe."

But for the moderns this "central harmony" is not—as was for Browning—a moral harmony. It is a harmony of beauty. In a world fully alive to beauty—unified by beauty, as the poet seeks to unify it—there would be no such spectacle as this of the gamin Polack and the unfortunate cat. Of course, if one pursues this reasoning, beauty and goodness are seen to be one; but Dr. Strachan does not pursue the thought, for it is evident that he finds the modern poet content to exhibit the defiance of the ugly and the evil, and to leave the solution of the problem to the individual thinker.

"Willa Cather's Poems," *Boston Evening Transcript*, 20 June 1923, p. 4

The disappointment that came when trying to read *One of Ours* is entirely wiped out by this collection of Miss Cather's verses. In the daintiest of bindings that somehow suggests April twilights, have been gathered together the poems she wrote some twenty years ago, also some entirely new poems, and many reprinted from *Scribner's*, *McClure's* and the *Century Magazine*.

"Grandmither, Think Not I Forget," is of poignant beauty. It is a simple tale made epic in the telling. The sorrow following the last line is cleared away by the first lines of the very next poem, "Fides Spea":

> Joy is come to the little
>   Everywhere:
> Pink to the peach and pink to the
>   apple.
>   White to the pear.
> Stars are come to the dogwood.
>   Astral, pale:
> Mists are pink on the red bud
>   Veil after veil.

Then sharp contrast again, of "Great Hearts Frozen Dumb," in all this beauty of little things.

10

One could quote indefinitely the sheer music and beauty of these poems. "Poppies on Ludlow Castle" has the touch of Swinburne, but the newer form of verse is found in "A Silver Cup." Nowhere, however, does Miss Cather sacrifice to modern cheapness of thought or disdain of the laws through the fulfilling of which only can beautiful things be created. Every line in this slender volume bears the mark of the craftsman who will be satisfied with nothing less than perfection and of the artist whose gift is very great.

Mark Van Doren, "Literature and the Land," *Nation*, 116 (27 June 1923), 753–4

In the novels of Willa Cather one comes home to an epic poet, to a great writer who deals simply and profoundly with love, age, separation, death, heroes, gods, and the land. No end of passion is there, and no end of reality. But her "Poems," so printed and so called, are not great. The themes of *April Twilights*, a volume now recalled from a twenty years' silence and somewhat enlarged, are the familiar ones; the abundant poetry is not here. It seems perfectly obvious that Miss Cather was wise in abandoning verse for fiction. She was not built to go at any but a prairie pace. Rhythm and rhyme were never fully effective in her hands; they retarded rather than sped her as she thought. At least our reading is made slow by such unnecessary artificialities as "yearneth," "in the purple gloaming," "young lads a-chasing," "parsons a-praying," and "children their kites a-flying"; and our attention is distracted by mechanics

everywhere. Miss Cather could hardly write a book that was not distinguished, and *April Twilights* is distinguished by feeling and observation; but a poem like "Spanish Johnny" reminds us of *The Song of the Lark*, and the reminder is fatal.

Eunice Tietjens, "Poetry by a Novelist," *Poetry*, 22 (July 1923), 221–3

This is a book of poems by a great literary personality, who well deserves the Pulitzer prize—but not by a great poet.

Willa Cather is, to my thinking, one of the few authentic voices among the prose writers of today. Her novels and short stories are as sweeping and indigenous as her own western prairies, as full of hope and heart-break as the immigrants she knows so well, and as pathetically courageous as the flame of youth in city slums. Her stories are unforgettable. They etch themselves into your consciousness and you can no more escape them than you can escape your own memories. They are an integral part of this our mother country.

But Miss Cather is not at heart a poet. She is not at home in the medium. Much of herself comes through, as is inevitable since she has so much to give. The same humanity, the same sense of drama, the same directness of vision are in this book which are in her prose. And they are almost as hard to forget. Eighteen or twenty years ago I read several of these poems, two in particular, "Grandmither, Think Not I Forget," and "The Tavern," and as I read them now they are as familiar as old friends.

Yet now, examining them in the cold light of later knowledge, I see that I have loved and remembered them because of the humanity, not because of the poetry. And this is not alone because they are in the manner of another day. In 1903, when this book was first published, English poetry had not undergone the cleansing and revivifying that has since come to it. Conciseness was not a virtue; rue and rosemary, minstrels and Helen of Troy were still legitimate lyric symbols. And it is inevitable that we should find them here. Yet if the form alone stood between Miss Cather and the reader accustomed to the idiom of today, the second part of the book, in which she speaks a later language, should reveal her as an authentic poet. But to me it does not.

She is simply not at home in the medium. Her thinking, for all its directness, is cramped and clouded by the song element, not released by it. Take this, called "Prairie Spring," and one of the most successful of the new poems.

> Evening and the flat land,
> Rich and somber and always silent;
> The miles of fresh-plowed soil,
> Heavy and black, full of strength and
>   harshness;
> The growing wheat, the growing
>   weeds,
> The toiling horses, the tired men;
> The long, empty roads,
> Sullen fires of sunset, fading,
> The eternal, unresponsive sky.
> Against all this, Youth,
> Flaming like the wild roses,
> Singing like the larks over the plowed
>   fields,
> Flashing like a star out of the twilight;
> Youth with its insupportable
>   sweetness,
> Its fierce necessity,
> Its sharp desire;
> Singing and singing,
> Out of the lips of silence,
> Out of the earthy dusk.

This is a vivid enough picture, with a real enough grasp of the substance of poetry to make a fine poem. But somehow it doesn't.

Yet for all this, the book is welcome, for it reveals a less known phase of a great literary personality. And some of these poems, especially the earlier ones, will surely be remembered when another twenty years have added themselves to the first twenty, for their human drama and their sympathetic understanding of the stuff of life.

John Gould Fletcher, "Three Women Poets," *Freeman*, 7 (18 July 1923), 452

[Compared to ranking Elinore Wylie's *Black Armour*,] it is much easier for the critic to place Miss Cather's achievement. The main bulk of her [Cather's] book is simply pretty sentiment; very neat, very light, very slight and occasional poetry. She is one of those whom it is easy to read and forget about, as Mrs. Wylie is one who is difficult to grasp and disquieting in later effect. Miss Cather's book contains, as far as I am able to judge, but one good poem. This is "Macon Prairie," a work whose almost infantile simplicity of technique is redeemed by an absolute fidelity to vision. In my opinion "Macon Prairie" deserves a place in every comprehensive anthology of American poetry.

To descent from Miss Cather's book to the next woman-poet on my list is to make a long step down. [In *Sea Change*] Miss Muna Lee is obviously convinced of the importance of her feelings. Unfortunately she says nothing that has not been said before, and better, by hundreds of other poets, masculine and feminine. . . .

William Rose Benet, "The Voice of the Thrush," *New York Evening Post Literary Review*, 28 July 1923, p. 860

Willa Sibert Cather's first published book was this same *April Twilights* which is now reprinted with the additional inclusion of later poems. Upon Miss Cather's present position as an American novelist it is surely unnecessary to comment. She has established herself as a literary artist.

Years ago, when Miss Cather was associated editorially with *McClure's Magazine*, I took great pleasure in the occasional poems of hers that appeared in that magazine. Through the present volume I have searched in vain for one of them, a haunting soliloquy of Sappho. But another I have found again, "Autumn Melody." "Autumn Melody" is either pure lyrical poetry or else I do not know what pure lyrical poetry is. Its only blemish seems to me the repetition of the word "sleep" in the second verse.

> In the autumn days, the days of
> parting,
> Days that in a golden silence fall,
> When the air is quick with bird-
> wings starting,
> And the asters darken by the
> wall;
> Strong and sweet the wine of heaven
> is flowing,
> Bees and sun sleep and golden
> dyes;

> Long forgot is building-time and
> blowing,
> Sunk in honeyed sleep the
> garden lies.
> Spring and storm and summer
> midnight madness
> Dream within the grape but
> never wake;
> Bees and sun and sweetness—oh, and
> sadness!
> Sun and sweet that reach the
> heart—and break.
> Ah, the pain at heart forever starting,
> Ah, the cup untasted that we
> spiked
> In the autumn days, the days of
> parting!
> Would our shades could drink it,
> and be stilled.

And on the opposite page appears "Spanish Johnny," a simple, vivid, memorable song.

Elsewhere in the book I have discovered but few measures as appealing as these. "Grandmither, Think Not I Forget" has the flavor of all good folk-song. "Evening Song" is another of the lyrics I have always remembered. But "Thou Art the Pearl," the song to the troubadour, and like efforts are too stale in manner. Indeed, some of the poems in Part I are altogether negligible when one considers what Miss Cather can do at her best. "The Palatine," the poem that begins Part II, is rather hackneyed; but "A Likeness," written after seeing the portrait bust of an unknown in Rome, succeeds despite its slight reminder of the work of Robinson. Native memories, "The Swedish Mother," "Prairie Spring," "Macon Prairie," "Going Home," convince one chiefly that Miss Cather speaks most individually of her Nebraska in prose and not in poetry.

As a whole, *April Twilights* is but a slight pendant to her outstanding work in prose. There are but four or five poems I myself should save. Yet these are of such merit and at least two of them are so truly lyrical that their author appears fortunate. The genuineness of her early stilled lyrical gift is undeniable. And having heard the thrush once—after all, even if all thrushes are not as wise as the one in Browning's poem—why expect the repetition?

David Morton, "Poems Collected and Selected," *Bookman* (New York), 58 (September 1923), 76

Willa Cather, author of the 1923 Pulitzer Prize novel, has an individual gift for achieving the simple clarity of classic song. *April Twilights*, a book of poems running to less than seventy pages, and embracing selections from an earlier volume of the same name, with about a dozen new poems, is chiefly interesting for its examples of this medium for the communication of delicate feeling. Her titles betray an interest in classical themes and countries, and her method and language have the gesture and accent that suit. The western prairie country, in landscape and mood and history, is a theme which divides attention with the Old World in the author's subjects, and is the occasion of poetry less artistically satisfying, but sometimes moving. *April Twilights* is not verse of large proportions nor of profound movement, but many of the poems in the volume are pleasing, and some are wrought in a fineness and sureness, both of feeling and execution, that recommend them for rereading and preservation. "Grandmither, Think Not I Forget" and "Paradox" and "Thou Art the Pearl" lack the distinction of feeling

and treatment that mark some of the poems, and are out of place in the company of such excellent pieces as "Lament For Marsyas," "A Likeness," and "The Poor Minstrel." "Macon Prairie," a combination narrative and character study, paints a vivid picture that is tragic, heroic—and memorable.

Dial, 75 (October 1923), 400

[*April Twilights*] consists largely of verses reprinted from an earlier volume with the same title. It was the epilogue to that first voyage to Europe from which the poet returns with a portfolio of classical memories: Antinous, Delphi, poppies on Ludlow Castle, the dialect of Robert Burns, and finally the expected Envoi, which like the others is perfecly imitated, quotable, dead. Her later verses are American, even Nebraskan in their subjects, but their form is equally and coldly perfect. They give the impression of being cast, accurately, into a mould which was not intended for them; they lack redeeming inconsistencies and never vary from a pattern which is fixed by the first line. It might have been Miss Cather who inspired Boileau to write: "*Un style trop égal et toujours uniforme / En vain brille à nos yeux, il faut qu'il nous endorme*" [A style too even and always uniform sparkles in vain before our eyes since it inevitably lulls us to sleep].

Harold G. Merriam, *Frontier* (Missoula, Montana), 4 (March 1924), n.p.

The first part of this volume is lyrics, written before 1903. In these poems there is *almost* clean rhythm, *almost* genuine lyricism; there is *almost* sudden beauty; but never any of these things *quite*. The lyrical spirit is best caught in "Fides, Spea," which is a beautiful poem. The second part, written in Miss Cather's later years, has finer strength and surer workmanship. The poems are reflective and narrative, and in "Macon Prairie" there is epic solidity. The poem is masterly, and should be treasured by Americans as verse genuinely reflecting the early American spirit. In it is the same spirit that gives her novel *My Antonia* its power. In the later poetry there is more emotional conviction and less argument.

"The Poetic Pilgrimage," *Morning Post* (London), 12 September 1924

This American poetess is better known as a novelist, who sees life full of sudden splendours—"bright shoots of everlastingness"—and writes prose with something of the *curiosa felicitas* of Thomas Hardy. Two-thirds of the contents of this, her sole verse-book, was published in 1903, and, apart from the refreshing lack of any tendency to the "cosmical style" that was so common in the American verse of that era, is interesting as having been her apprenticeship to a sense of form and of the *mot juste*—even the making of bad verse will help the young writer, better than any other intellectual exercise, to avoid verbiage and a fatal fluency! These early pieces, which caused her to be hailed as the poetess that should come, are often tragical in intention, touched with the pessimism peculiar to young things, being the shadow, so to speak, of their towering confidence in the future. A young girl, vexed by a love forbidden, resorts to her grandmother's grave and envies her cold immunity from passion:

> Grandmither, gie me your clay-cold
>   heart that has forgot to ache,
> For mine be fire within my breast and
>   yet it cannot break.
> It beats an' throbs for ever for the
>   things that must not be—
> An' can ye not let me creep in an'
>   rest awhile by ye?

Again, she contemplates the bust of Antinous, and asks that weary head which set the fashion in statuesque beauty for a century of inward decline:

> Did the perfection of thy beauty pain
>   Thy limbs to bear it? Did it ache
>   to be
> As song has ached in men, or passion
>   vain?
>   Or lay it like some heavy robe
>   on thee?

It is in the young days of tragical interrogatives and dark forebodings that Beauty, not Truth, seems the sole consolation, and there is a youthful sincerity in the last stanza of "I Sought the Wood in Winter":

> "How sure a thing is Beauty,"
>   I cried. "No bolt can slay,
> No wave nor shock despoil her,
>   No ravishers dismay.

Her warriors are the angels
 That cherish from afar,
Her warders people Heaven
 And watch from every star.
The granite hills are slighter,
 The sea more like to fail;
Behind the rose the planet,
 The Law behind the veil."

To go back twenty years to the verse one wrote in youth is to meet a stranger and envy his (or her) strange efflorescence of anguished unreason. Seeing the slow, solemn imagery of spring in the vast meadows of her Middle West, this still undaunted poetess sets against it the vision of her incredible younger self:

Against all this, Youth,
Flaming like the wild roses,
Singing like the larks over the plowed
 fields,
Flashing like a star out of the
 twilight;
Youth with its insupportable
 sweetness,
Its fierce necessity,
Its sharp desire;
Singing and singing
Out of the lips of silence,
Out of the earthy dusk.

Once more, imitating this evanished self, she questions the mute, marble faces of the Rome that was and views with a tolerant disdain the Augustan deities:

The Antonine booted and mounted
 In his sun-lit, hill-top place,
The Julians, gigantic in armour,
 The low-browed Claudian race.

But the sight of these arrogant symbols of departed power only prompts the question: "Who could have hoped for the West?" Twenty years from now, it may be, she will tolerate and despise the American autocrats, the Schwabs and Rockefellers and Fords and the rest. But now she has

seen them again and again, the wonder-cities of the Old World are not so much to her as the old immigrants' trail across the fertile wilderness (now all meted out in tilled maize-fields) of Nebraska, or even a mean street in Packingtown (Chicago), where a grey creek willow survives from the days before men made a desert and called it a city. American-born, she has, at any rate, succeeded in Americanising herself.

Times Literary Supplement (London), 18 September 1924, p. 573

Miss Cather has combined here verses reprinted from an early volume with those of a more recent date. She has done it to her own profit and her own loss. The earlier verses suffer through conjunction with the later, of which at the same time they heighten the significance. They are melodious, but their art is still for the most part only verbal, while their absorption in the theme of beauty long withered under pagan skies, of youth laid away by death from the sun and the wholesome air, of winter that treads malignly on the heels of spring, is only the more sentimental for its easy grace of expression:—

Woe is me to tell it thee,
Winter winds in Arcady!
Broken pipes and vows forgot,
Scattered flocks returning not,
Frozen brook and drifted hill,
Ashen sun and song-birds still;
Songs of summer and desire
Crooned about the winter fire;
Shepherd lads with silver hair,
Shepherd maids no longer fair.

Plainly here Miss Cather's exclamation of woe was no more than a polite acknowledgment to the past for supplying her with so touching a subject to embroider. There are only two poems in the first part of her book which can compare with those of the second, a vignette entitled "Prairie Dawn" and some vernacular verses beginning "Grandmither, think not I forget." In these there is an effort after personal vision and personal emotion to which the technique takes second place. This is true of all her later verses. She still dreams of the past, but she renews it with realism. Rome is no longer a book of legends to be decorated, but a dark life to be re-imagined; autumn now excites a deeper and a truer melody, while an urchin in a street in Packingtown, Chicago, has more to tell her than Marsyas "among the lamented dead." Her handling of metre too is freer and more closely related to natural impulse, while beauty is no longer a fading fire, but a perpetual "recognition":—

> The old volcanic mountains
> That slope up from the sea—
> They dream and dream a thousand
>   years
> And watch what-is-to-be.
>
> What gladness shines upon them
> When, white as white sea-foam,
> To the old, old ports of Beauty
> A new sail comes home!

Alice Hunt Bartlett, "The Dynamics of American Poetry—XI: Emily Dickinson—Willa Cather—Robert Hillyer," *Poetry Review* (London), 16 (1925), 405–14

Willa Sibert Cather gives us from her own knowledge of American life, and we may depend on her pictures, in which we find a Virginia background and a father who exhibited pioneer blood and crossed the Alleghannies and the Mississippi Valley to settle in the West, and on a ranch in Nebraska, when Miss Cather was but nine. From such neighbours as the little girl found in the sparsely settled country, Scandinavians, Russians and Bohemian farmers, she must have made her first world contacts.

The nearest school was at Red Cloud, and there she received her only schooling until she entered the State University and graduated at nineteen, going at once to Pittsburgh, where she was employed on the *Pittsburgh Leader* as telegraph editor and dramatic critic. On this paper she had her first experience in writing, and shortly after published her first book of verse, *April Twilights* (Badger, Boston, 1903), a slim book of poetry filled with her woods in winter, white birches, evening songs and laments, legends and taverns and hawthorne trees, the night express and rose time.

[. . .]

Miss Cather writes me:

I am afraid you will have a hard time proving that I have been an "effective force in American poetry." I do not take myself seriously as a poet. However, since you ask me which ones of my poems I prefer, I will tell you some of them. "A Likeness," "A Silver Cup," "Going Home," and "Macon Prairie," I think are the best ones. I believe "Spanish Johnny" is most popular.

[These poems are appended, along with "In Rose Time" and "L'Envoi."]

Joseph J. Reilly, "A Singing Novelist," *Commonweal*, 13 (25 February 1931), 464–6

Just seventeen years ago on a Boston bookstall marked "Your choice, ten cents," I chanced upon a slender brown volume. It contained thirty-five poems, all brief, and bore the copywright date, 1903, beneath the legend: "Boston, Richard G. Badger, The Gorham Press." I had already made the acquaintance of the author in a collection of little-known short stories which were distinguished by so rare a touch and so keen a flavor of life that I at once predicted great things of her future. To meet her thus in the guise of a poet, came with a shock of surprise. I had not dreamed that she had that gift of song.

To chance upon this stranger volume was a joy, but to discover it on a bargain shelf, its fortunes so sadly fallen, brought a sigh. Today however I sigh no more, for its fortunes have risen mightily. Cinderella has shaken the dust of the chimney-corner from her feet and is numbered among the elect. That slender volume now occupies a place in special catalogues which are devoted to rare items and to first editions.

What was this little treasure trove? A paper label (with orange-colored decoration) pasted to its modest brown cover bears the title, *April Twilights,* by Willa Sibert Cather.

In Miss Cather's prose is a distinction equaled (but not surpassed) by two other American novelists, Edith Wharton and Thornton Wilder. Similarly, in these poems, is a distinction delicate and difficult to analyze but unmistakable. It clings to every one of them like a fragrance. It is in such single lines as that which calls a melody at night "Tender as dawn, insistent as the tide," or that which tells of a Roman emperor who spent on a favorite "Honor and treasure and red fruits of war"; but in the finest of these poems it is all pervasive like the scent of lavender in old lace. Here is a typical instance in which the seventeenth-century Herrick lives again:

Alas, that June should come when
    thou didst go;
I think we passed each other on the
    way;
And seeing thee, the summer loved
    thee so
That all her loveliness she gave away;
Her rare perfumes, in hawthorn
    boughs distilled,
Blushing, she in thy sweeter bosom
    left,
Thine arms with all her virgin roses
    filled,
Yet felt herself the richer for thy theft;
Beggared herself of morning for thine
    eyes,
Hung on the lips of every bird the
    tune,
Breathed on thy cheek her soft
    vermilion dyes,
And in thee set the singing heart of
    June.
And so, not only do I mourn thy
    flight,
But summer comes despoiled of her
    delight.

A deeper passion than Herrick's lies below the surface of that sonnet, but passion in these poems is never hectic nor unrestrained, never overreaches itself or leaves one with a sense of exhausted emotions. It is not that the love motif is rare in *April Twilights*, but that love is here (as Mrs. Craigie once said it was with the Celt) a sentiment rather than a passion. The note is soft, not insistent; it is reminiscent of the spirit rather than of the body; it is acquainted little with triumph, much with tears. In "Thou Art the Pearl" is the rare note of triumph, but it is toned down to give one a sense of the lover's awe, kneeling and adoring, in the presence of beauty and its mystery:

I read of knights who laid their
    armor down,
  And left the tourney's prize for
    other hands,
And clad them in a pilgrim's somber
    gown,
  To seek a holy cup in desert lands.
For them no more the torch of
    victory;
  For them lone vigils and the
    starlight pale,
So they in dreams the Blessed Cup
    may see—
  Thou art the Grail!

An Eastern king once smelled a rose
    in sleep,
  And on the morrow laid his scepter
    down.
His heir his titles and his land might
    keep—
  The rose was sweeter wearing than
    the crown.
Nor cared he that its life was but an
    hour,
  A breath that from the crimson
    summer blows,
Who gladly paid a kingdom for a
    flower—
  Thou art the Rose!

A merchant man, who knew the
    worth of things,
  Beheld a pearl more priceless than
    a star;
And straight returning, all he hath he
    brings
  And goes upon his way, ah, richer
    far!
Laughter of merchants of the market
    place,
  Nor taunting gibe nor scornful lips
    that curl,
Can ever cloud the rapture on his
    face—
  Thou art the Pearl!

In mentioning the Celt and his love as a sentiment rather than a passion, I do not mean to imply that there is a Celtic strain in Miss Cather, although these poems encourage the surmise. For often the Celtic note appears, elusive enough in all truth and yet not to be missed. Listen for it in "In Media Vita" whose first stanza runs thus:

Streams of the spring a-singing,
  Winds o' the May that blow,
Birds from the Southland winging,
  Buds in the grasses below.
Clouds that speed hurrying over,
  And the climbing rose by the wall,
Singing of bees in the clover,
  And the dead, under all!

It is that last line which does it, coming like sudden tears after laughter, and revealing memories which are too poignant to forget.

Here is another instance, a little more Celtic in tone though not in sentiment:

Grandmither, gie me your still, white
  hands, that lie upon your breast,
For mine do beat the dark all night
  and never find me rest;
They grope among the shadows an'
  they beat the cold black air,

They go seekin' in the darkness, an'
   they never find him there,
     An' they never find him there.

Lacrimae rerum! In nearly all the poems in this slender volume the tears of things are near. The "sad earnestness" which Newman found in Horace flows like an undercurrent through lyrics that are but too aware of life and summer, of roses and love. Sometimes this sadness is mingled with languor, as if tears had left the singer no strength for rebellion or had brought her to acquiescence at the last. Sometimes it is touched with hopelessness, as if aspirations and golden dreams had perished beyond the power of any magic to restore them. Sometimes it is wedded to a yearning tenderness that goes as deep as any passion, as in "I Have No House for Love to Shelter Him," "The Poor Minstrel" and this sonnet, "Eurydice":

[Quoted]

Sometimes the note of sadness springs from a piercing sense of the soul's loneliness. It is a dominant note with certain rare individuals even as unlike as Newman and Joseph Conrad, and Browning has let one of his lovers give voice to it unforgettably in "Two in the Campagna." For all of us, whether we will or no, the hour strikes when we find ourselves alone, in spirit even more utterly than in body. There are recesses of the soul where none may follow and where not even love's self may find the way. It is in such an hour as this that Miss Cather writes "L'Envoi":

[Quoted]

In "The Encore" a poet is praised for a song. But the praise is belated; it was withheld from him in the day when he sought it and deserved it most, in the hour of his first fine careless rapture; it is given to him now that his golden note is fled and his glad confident morning gone

forever. The song they laud now was "done lang syne and was its own delight."

At least two of Miss Cather's poems are colored by an irony more sad than bitter whose implications go deep. In "Paradox" the night is made beautiful by a song; surely, such melody is the voice of Ariel, "proud prince of ministrelsy." In its witchery

The heart of night and summer stood
   confessed.
   And I rose aglow and flung the
     lattice wide—
Ah jest of art, what mockery and
   pang!
   Alack, it was poor Caliban who
     sang.

When I came piping through the
   land,
   One morning in the spring,
With cockle-burs upon my coat,
   'Twas then I was a king:
A mullein scepter in my hand,
   My order daisies three,
With song's first freshness on my
   lips—
   And then ye pitied me!

In all her poems Miss Cather avoids subtleties, symbols, abstractions. She has the true poet's eye for the concrete and the true novelist's interest in men and women. It is the heart which lures her, love, tears, dreams of dear but unforgotten yesterdays, revolt against blindness to beauty, a sense of the essential loneliness of life. Even when Miss Cather conjures up a scene known to history for two thousand years she envisions it as the drama of human hearts that yearn, and yearning, know passion and folly. Here is one of the most perfect poems in *April Twilights*, in which, for a golden moment, Anthony and his Egypt flit from out the eternal shadow:

The dream of all the world was at his
  feet:
  Her eyes were heavy with the night
  of fate,
  When, from the purple couch
  whereon she sate,
She rose, and took a jewel that was
  meet
For a queen's breast, where royal
  pulses beat—
  A milk-white pearl, her milk-white
  bosom's mate,
  Dropped in the golden chalice at
  his plate,
And to his lips held up the nectar
  sweet
  And bade him drink the cup of
  destiny.
How shall he pledge again? by what
  emprise
  A chalice find that holds a
  kingdom's fee?
Perchance in that charmed liquor he
  descries
  A madman, raving while his galleys
  flee,
  Who casts a world into the wine-
  dark sea.

Even in the two poems of nature
presented in *April Twilights* it is the
human note, expressed in "Prairie
Dawn," implied in "White Birch in
Wyoming," that gives to each its poignant
beauty. Here is "Prairie Dawn':
[Quoted]
Even when Paris is sung "pillared with
pride, the city of delight," with her "fields
elysian," her "towers of Notre Dame,"
her "silver Seine," we are to understand
that her glory lies not in her loveliness but
in the souls that toiled and wrought and
thought for her and of whose ideal of
beauty she is as a symbol:

Wherever men have builded hall or
  fane

Red war hath gleaned for her and
  men have slain
To deck her loveliness. I feel again
That joy which brings her art to
  faultless flower,
That passion of her kings, who, reign
  on reign,
Arrayed her star by star with pride
  and power.

April Twilights appears in current
booklists and in modern garb. But while
it contains a few new poems it omits, alas!
a round dozen from the original edition
of 1903. I state this because I have quoted
here (in whole or in part) six of these
"outcasts" as among the best examples of
Miss Cather's gift. It might seem unchival-
rous to remark that poets are often uncertain appraisers of their own verse; instead
let it be conceded, that critics, however
well-intentioned, are nevertheless notori-
ously perverse.

[Irita Van Doren,] *New York Herald Tribune Books*, 4 June 1933, p. 4

Every novelist probably wishes to write
poetry and nearly every poet, at one time
or another in his life, tries to write a
novel. The two mediums of expression
allow outlet for two very different types
of feeling. Poetry, especially lyric poetry—
and this is the type Miss Cather writes—
is the vehicle for personal emotions, for
personal responses to beauty. In writing a
novel one must be more impersonal, must
project one's own intensities only in such
characters as might, realistically and dramatically, have those intensities. The characters in time begin to act for themselves;

they separate themselves entirely from their author. In the modern novel, in particular, emotion is usually held in restraint. Direct expression of it is seldom possible.

Miss Cather's novels are built up architecturally; they have the quality of a fine and carefully chiseled piece of sculpture. The theme of each is carefully and artistically worked out. Everything is bent to that end. There is very little place for the novelist's own feelings or attitude, save as her sensibilities are the glass through which all is seen. Probably, therefore, it is with relief that Miss Cather turns to poetry, knowing full well that she will never be so important a poet as she is a novelist; feeling that, like Browning, she would like to find, if possible, another art in which to express her very self. Because she is an artist in words she can write musical and perfectly patterned poetry; because she is expressing herself directly and understands human feeling she can convince us of her sincerity. And this, despite the fact that she tends always to use, in verse, a more romantic diction, a more literary turn of phrase and less original style than she commands as a prose writer.

The first group of poems in *April Twilights* was published under the same title in 1903. These are young poems, poems entirely of lyrical feelings clothed in the traditional form and language of poetry. The second group of poems is quite different. In these Miss Cather returns to her own background, the prairie land of the Middle West. The manner and method of the novelist have come over, to some extent, into poetry. Here are dramatic monologues, narratives, lyrics, such as characters in her novels might speak or sing. Here are stories of her own pioneer ancestry. Here the personal emotion is put into the mouth of a character. The literary language of the early poems has dis-appeared. The smooth, singing mold of the earlier poems gives way to a rougher and more direct verse. No literary dreamworld is the background. The setting is the prairies and their strange and sometimes harsh beauty. All in all, the later poems are far better, far more authentic than the earlier. Not Arcadian winter but Macon Prairie is Miss Cather's correct setting. And the many readers who are interested in Miss Cather's prose will wish to read in *April Twilights* the songs of the people whom they have seen in the novels.

Eda Lou Walton, "New Books of Poetry," *New York Times Book Review*, 11 June 1933, p. 5

This new book of poems by the novelist Willa Cather is in part a reprint of *April Twilights*, poems printed in 1903, and in part a new group of later lyrics. Most of Miss Cather's earlier poems are romantic lyrics; the later poems are more realistic and dramatic narratives and songs of the Middle Western scene, the background from which Miss Cather drew her first novels. All the early lyrics seem to be emotional outlets for the more personal moods of the author, whose unique work as a novelist prevented her from the personal outcry. All the later poems indicate that the novelist's understanding of character, situation and drama is now functioning in poetry as well as in prose.

In the poem "Macon Prairie" (Nebraska), Miss Cather tells a story of her own aunt, a pioneer woman whose spirit was toward the conquest of new lands even more intently because, in seeking them, she must die. In "Prairie Spring" we get the Middle West: "Singing and singing,/ Out of the lips of silence,/ Out of the earthy dusk."

Another poem, called "A Silver Cup," tells of the poet's desire to return to romantic youth, the emblem of that youth. "Poor Marty" is a lament for Martha, the old kitchenmaid, by her fellow-servant, the stableman. "The Swedish Mother" is a monologue by another Nebraska woman. And all of these poems are very different indeed from the neatly and musically patterned purely romantic poems of *April Twilights* in 1903.

It seems as if, in poetry, Miss Cather, having shaken off all her literary influences, all of the reminiscences of poetry she once read, has returned to her childhood and girlhood setting. The later poems are, in consequence, far more interesting than were the somewhat imitative earlier poems. Willa Cather has always written well. Her poetry has always had music and beauty of language, but the earlier poems lacked the individuality and distinction which are so apparent in her novels. These later poems take on some of the same overtones of character that are constantly appearing in her prose fiction.

"Willa Cather's Poetry," *Boston Evening Transcript*, 14 June 1933, p. 2

Poetry and Willa Cather fail to contact, somehow. If you mention the two in the same breath to most people, you will be met by a puzzled frown. "I didn't know she wrote poetry." Yet her contributions have appeared within recent years in *Scribner's Magazine, McClure's Magazine* and the *Century Magazine.* And long before her reputation for faithfully chronicling pioneer America had gained a reader in every household, in fact as far back as 1903, a thin volume of verse titled *April Twilights* was published. It was her first work to reach print.

To this collection has been added a second group, and a four-page "lament for Martha, the old kitchenmaid, by her fellow servant, the stableman—The servants are not Negroes, but 'poor whites'—(Old Virginia)," which has not previously appeared. This plaintive "Poor Marty" would readily lend itself to the minor chords of the Western ballad, as the following lines may testify:

> On a moonlit winter night
> Marty made her kitchen bright.
> Wiped the pot-black from her hand
> For before her Lord to stand.
>
> Little had she here to leave,
> Naught to will and none to grieve.

The atmosphere of the piece provides naive charm to the completeness of the picture. A simplicity of expression immediately sets this poem apart—and the same might be said of the entire contents—in a day when verse is veiled in obscurity.

Although kind words were offered by a reviewer in the *Transcript* when a similar edition was published in 1923, the two poems chosen for special mention in August, 1908,—"The Night Express" and "The Namesake"—do not appear.

Checklist of Additional Reviews

Rafford Pike, *Bookman* (New York), 17 (July 1903), 542.

Jeannette L. Gilder, *Chicago Tribune*, 23
  May 1903, 9.
Criterion, 4 (October 1903), 53.
Book News, 22 (December 1903), 541.
Pendragon, "A June Parade of Poets
  under the Reviewer's Eye," New York
  World, 24 June 1923, p. 19E.

Booklist, 19 (July 1923), 327.
Wisconsin Library Bulletin, 19 (July
  1923), 410.
"Willa Cather Turns to Poetry,"
  Minneapolis Journal, 18 June 1933.
*Pratt Institute Free Library Quarterly
  Booklist*, Autumn 1933, p. 35.

THE TROLL GARDEN

THE
TROLL GARDEN

BY

WILLA SIBERT CATHER

A FAIRY PALACE, WITH A FAIRY GARDEN ; . . . . .
INSIDE THE TROLLS DWELL, ... WORKING AT
THEIR MAGIC FORGES, MAKING AND MAKING ALWAYS
THINGS RARE AND STRANGE   CHARLES KINGSLEY

NEW YORK
McCLURE, PHILLIPS & CO.
MCMV

Miss Cather takes the title of her book from Charles Kingsley: "A fairy palace with a fairy garden;... inside the trolls dwell,... working at their magic forges, making and making always things rare and strange."

In this collection of seven stories the author has shown a great deal of deep feeling and real ability, but many of the stories are too ambitious, and seem to be more the work of promise than of fulfillment. One wishes, while reading them, that Miss Cather would eschew the complex psychological attitude which she so frequently displays, and would stick to the simpler and more sincere.

"Flavia and Her Artists," holding up to ridicule that senseless toadyism to genius which obliterates entirely any appreciation for real worth which has not already been accepted by the world, is perhaps the best story in the collection, although the simple pathos of "The Sculptor's Funeral" gives emphasis to the belief that Miss Cather would show wisest judgment in choice of simple subjects. There is something about "The Garden Lodge" which rings shallow in spite of the pathos in which it is enveloped, and the same might be said of "A Death in the Desert." Nevertheless, the little book contains some excellent work between its covers, and is well worth while if only as an olive branch of promise.

I took up a little book of stories the other day without special interest in its contents, and found that after reading the first story I was impelled to go on to the second, and so on, until I had read the last and still wished there were more. Willa Sibert Cather is a new name to me, and *The Troll Garden* is evidently her first book. She derives her title from the following passage from Charles Kingsley, which appears on the title-page: "A fairy palace, with a fairy garden;... inside the trolls dwell,... working at their magic forges, making and making always things rare and strange." A troll in modern folklore is, according to the dictionary, a familiar and friendly, but often mischievous dwarf. I suppose the title is intended to indicate the vein of psychological inquiry which the author has worked in disclosing the things rare and strange which happen in her peculiar studies. For they are peculiar, these stories; that is to say: each story deals with a phase, a situation, a mood, a temperament which is out of the beaten track, which bares the soul to the ironic humor or mocking circumstance or mischievous fate that has played havoc in a life, estranged or bereft or divorced it from its kind. Nor can it be said that the author depends on the abnormal or unusual for her telling effects. The poignancy of the pathos in her appeal comes home swiftly and directly through our understanding and recognition of the truth as we have sometimes observed it in a similar or familiar guise. There are but seven stories in the volume, but each one wrests a tragedy from the commonplace, and leaves a distinct impression of dramatic power. In style and manner, in psychological force and insight, these stories bear some family resemblances to Mrs. Edith Wharton's earlier work, but the author of *The Troll Garden* has an individuality of her own and a distinctive style. I don't believe any short story ever moved me more than did "The Sculptor's Funeral." The name of Willa Sibert Cather is worth remembering.

"Notes on New Novels," *Dial*, 38 (1 June 1905), 394

It is the glamour of the artistic temperament that leads Mrs. Willa Sibert Cather to name her collection of short stories *The Troll Garden*. Seven truly entertaining studies of somewhat abnormal human nature fill the little book, and leave abundant food for reflection. The first possesses subtlety, being an account of a woman who runs after celebrities of various sorts, is grossly insulted by one of them, and yet persists in blundering on, a subject for mirth to her enemies and of pity to her friends. "The Sculptor's Funeral," which follows, is quite as vivid in its abruptness of contrast, the bringing home to a sordid little western village of the body of a distinguished artist affording the opportunity for contrasting noble artistic ideals and the crassest commercialism. Taken as a whole, the book indicates more than usual talent for close delineation.

Independent, 58 (29 June 1905), 1482–3

A group of seven short stories quite out of the ordinary, indigenous in matter, foreign in manner, the sort that one would recommend strongly but not widely among his circle of acquaintances. In style they remind one of Maupassant, but much more of the Russians. Is there something after all in the out-of-fashion climatic theory of literature that stories from the Great American Desert should have the savor of the steppes? For the best-pictured scenes in the volume are of our own arid region. Western Kansas and Nebraska and Southeastern Wyoming are described, not only with minuteness, but with feeling. Miss Cather was transplanted from the Shenandoah Valley to a ranch in Southwestern Nebraska about 10 miles north of the Kansas line when she was only nine years old and, until she went to the State University at Lincoln, she was in touch with pioneer life and can interpret its privations and rawness. But, like Hamlin Garland, she sees only one side of it: the drought, the drudgery, the isolation and despair. She has missed what William Allen White has caught: the push, the humor, and the indomitable and fantastic hopefulness. These are quite as characteristic of the life of the plains as the side of the shield she sees, and until she catches that too her work is defective. Two of the Western stories, "The Sculptor's Funeral" and "A Death in the Desert," and "Paul's Case," a study in juvenile morbid psychology, unfortunately too true to life, are the strongest of this collection, but there is promise of something greater in them all.

"Chronicle and Comment," *Bookman* (New York), 21 (July 1905), 456–7

Miss Willa S. Cather, whose book *The Troll Garden* has caused a good deal of discussion, began her literary career, like many authors, at an early age. When eight or nine years old, according to a man who knew her as a child in Virginia, she not only wrote a play, but arranged and supervised its performance with remarkable effect. Shortly after that period her family took her to Nebraska, where she lived for a while a healthful, quite unliterary life, spending most of her time in the open on horseback. Graduating at the University of Nebraska, she became correspondent for several newspapers, wrote, and in 1903 published, a volume of verse called *April Twilights*, and then took to writing the stories which have now been gathered in book form. In Pittsburg, where Miss Cather is living there was a foundation of fact for the incident around which she built her story of "Paul's Case." Two boys employed by a firm that managed a large estate ran away with two thousand dollars. They were found at the Auditorium Hotel in Chicago about ten days later, their money gone, and they were brought home. The papers were full of the affair for a time, but as one of the boys was a minister's son, and as the money was refunded, the firm did not prosecute. This story, of all the stories in the book, comes nearest to being based on actual occurrences; so that Miss Cather's psychology is all the more a remarkable attainment. There may be deduced a certain endorsement of her accuracy from the fact that concerning these accounts of hers of abnormal artistic personalities she receives in her mail a regular succession of such outpourings as have caused her to exclaim, "I never knew before there were so many madmen at large." Miss Cather herself is a hard-headed, clear-visioned, straight-forward young woman.

Bessie du Bois, *Bookman* (New York), 21 (August 1905), 612–14

The Troll Garden is a collection of freak stories that are either lurid, hysterical or unwholesome, and that remind one of nothing so much as the coloured supplement to the Sunday papers. The characters with the possible exception of Laird in "The Sculptor's Funeral," and Paul in the last and best of the stories, "Paul's Case," are mere dummies, with fancy names, on which to hang epigrams. The author has confined her attention wholly to what William James somewhere calls "the ash-heap of the human mind"—the thoughts and feelings that come to all of us when the pressure of the will is low, the refuse and sweepings of the mental life. Here and there are very striking passages, but they are not so much suggested by the story as sought out and worked up with the deliberate intention of saying something impressive, something warranted to thrill. For instance, in the little sketch entitled "A Wagner Matinee," a pioneer home in the West is described. Desolate and unsightly it is to the last degree, with the four dwarf ash seedlings, where the dish cloths were always hung to dry before the kitchen door. The story seems built around those dish cloths.

The following passage illustrates admirably both the strong and the weak points of the author. It is from "The Garden Lodge," the story of a woman whose early years have been passed in a sordid struggle with poverty, brought on by the extravagances of an "artistic" father and brother. By dint of merciless self-control she has attained wealth and place, and entertained for a month, at her husband's house, a world-famous singer, for whom she conceives in middle life the passionate love denied to her girlhood. It is of him the author is speaking:

> D'Esquerre's arrival in the early winter was the signal for a feminine hegira toward New York. On the nights when he sang, women flocked to the Metropolitan from mansions and hotels, from typewriter desks, schoolrooms, shops and fitting rooms. They were of all conditions and complexions. Women of the world, who accepted him knowingly, as they sometimes took champagne for its agreeable effect; sisters of charity and overworked shop-girls, who received him devoutly; withered women who had taken doctorate degrees and who worshipped furtively through prism spectacles; business women and women of affairs, the Amazons who dwelt afar from men in the stony fastnesses of apartment houses. They all entered into the same romance; dreamed, in terms as various as the hues of phantasy, the same dream; drew the same quick breath when he stepped upon the stage, and, at his exit, felt the same dull pain of shouldering the pack again.
>
> There were the maimed, even; those who came on crutches, who were pitted by smallpox, or grotesquely painted by cruel birth stains. These, too, entered with him into enchantment. Stout matrons became slender girls again; worn spinsters felt their cheeks flush with the tenderness of their lost youth. Young and old, however hideous, however fair, they yielded up their heart—whether quick or latent sat hungering for the mystic bread wherewith he fed them at this eucharist of sentiment.

Miss Cather knows her world thoroughly —the selfish, sensual world of song. Of another singer she writes (in "A Death in the Desert"):

> Adriance always said not only the right thing, but the opportune, graceful, exquisite thing. His phrases took the colour of the moment and the then present condition, so that they never savoured of perfunctory compliment or frequent usage. He always caught the lyric essence of the moment, the poetic suggestion of every situation. Moreover, he usually did the right thing, the opportune, graceful, exquisite thing—except when he did very cruel things—bent upon making people happy when their existence touched his, just as he insisted that his material environment should be beautiful; lavishing upon those near him all the warmth and radiance of his rich nature, all the homage of the poet and troubadour, and when they were no longer near, forgetting—for that also was a part of Adriance's gift.

The girl who is dying is one of the "forgotten things," but one does not take her death seriously. She will get up and come back to the footlights if there is the slightest applause.

"Paul's Case" leaves the fervid atmosphere of concert-hall and studio and frankly enters the Pittsburgh High School. Paul wears a red carnation in his buttonhole when he comes to beg for readmission, after a week's suspension, and everything about the boy matches the red carnation. One day at the blackboard his English teacher had attempted to guide his hand. "Paul had started back with a shudder and thrust his hands violently behind him. The astonished woman could scarcely have been more hurt and embarrassed had he struck at her." His father, though by no means poor, thinks that a boy should be earning something, and so he has put him to act as usher at Carnegie Hall. Here Paul found his real world, nothing else matters. He regularly lost himself in the music. The soprano, though a stout German woman and the mother of many children, was to Paul a "veritable queen of Romance." He followed her carriage to the hotel and caught a glimpse of bright lights and fresh flowers, and then went home, through the slush, to "the pictures of George Washington and John Calvin and the framed motto, 'Feed My Lambs,' which had been worked in red worsted by his mother." One feels all the hopeless, benumbing, bourgeoise surroundings, the smell of cooking, the lemonade in a red glass pitcher brought out to the "stoop" of a Sunday afternoon, the men going to work early in the morning with the "combings of children's hair hanging to their coats." Then—an eastbound train was ploughing through the snow. Arriving in New York, Paul bought the softest silk underwear, street clothes and evening clothes, all the things he had so longed for, and then was driven to the Waldorf, where he took rooms for a week. He missed one thing in his sitting-room, and sent the boy for flowers. At dinner he watched the people, and, holding his champagne glass between his thumb and middle finger, wondered "that there were honest men in the world at all." So the precious days slipped by. He read in the paper that his theft had been discovered. He crossed the ferry and floundered through the snow on the railroad track far out into the country.

The sound of an approaching train awoke him, and he started to his feet, remembering only his resolution, and afraid lest he should be too late. He stood watching the approaching locomotive, his teeth chattering, his lips drawn away from them in a frightened smile; once or twice he glanced nervously sidewise, as though he were being watched. When the right moment came he jumped. As he fell the folly of his haste occurred to him with merciless clearness, the vastness of what he had left undone. There flashed through his brain clearer than ever before the blue of Adriatic water, the yellow of Algerian sands.

He felt something strike his chest, and that his body was being thrown swiftly through the air on and on immeasurably far and fast, while his limbs were gently relaxed. Then because the picture-making mechanism was crushed, the disturbing visions flashed into black, and Paul dropped back into the immense design of things.

One feels rather defrauded that the author has omitted to say what came next: it would have been so easy to go on. If it was her highest aim to say unusual things, we think she has succeeded up to the measure of her hopes. Few, even of those who take what she herself calls a "doctorate degree," could do it better. We would, however, suggest that the form *rares aves* (p. 9) is not sanctioned by the Latin dictionary. And of all the quotations we remember to have seen, Dante's line "And in the book we read no more that night," quoted in "A Death in the Desert," comes in most grotesquely. Indeed, the "purple patches" of learning in the book, like the thrills, seem sewed on here and there, with one eye closed to get the effect.

Reader Magazine, 6 (September 1905), 477

In *The Troll Garden* Willa Sibert Cather shows herself mistress of the art of catching and photographing the crucial moment. In the ordinary phrase, this is a book of short stories. More accurately described, it is a collection of mood pictures with just enough events to give them life and setting. They are singularly vivid, strong, true, original, and they have withal a richness of quality, one might almost say of timbre, like a contralto voice. They are bits of life transmuted into art by the alchemy of a fine imagination; all will recognize their fidelity, some will delight in their charm. In atmosphere they are thoroughly modern, finding inspiration in week-end house parties, the emotional personalities of artists of all types, the poetry of Browning and the music of Wagner. The reader who has in himself some echo of the artistic impulse will find *The Troll Garden* strongly appealing to him. Its nimble fancy and temperamental style of treatment will mean much to those to whom they mean anything.

Critic, 47 (November 1905), 476

There is real promise in these half-dozen stories—studies, in reality, of different phases of the artistic temperament. The extremes are shown in the striking "Sculptor's Funeral" and in "The Case of Paul" [sic]—a sympathetic study of one form of sin to which "temperament" is liable.

Doubtless the best of the group is the opening story—"Flavia and Her Artists," which is good—very good. With Flavia's type we are, alas, familiar; she is of the race of climbing, would-be social powers that prey upon genius, as intent and skilful in her chosen field as a Wall Street broker on stocks or a good bird dog on the quarry. Clever, exceedingly clever in exhibiting herself clad in a kind of appliqué culture—impressions obtained at second hand but with no more capacity for fellowship, no more community of feeling with a true artist than a hen has with a skylark. Utterly different, but pathetically true to life, is the "Wagner Matinee."

Miss Cather has sincerity, and no small degree of insight. In fact when she writes her novel one may venture to predict it will be far too good to be among the "best sellers" of the month.

Mary Moss, *Atlantic Monthly*, 97 (January 1906), 48

... Mr. Huneker's stories seemed so far above the average that only after embarking upon Miss Cather's *The Troll Garden*, did I realize his temptation to be almost too clever. This young lady is fully as clever, even more so, I suspect, but she is so much in addition that no single quality predominates to the hurt of an harmonious whole. Not one of these six stories but is full of observation in which a keen eye for accessories merely aids the expression of a deep feeling for meanings. Each little vignette is a delicate and complete study of some phase of an artist's nature in contact with the outside world. I am tempted to point out in detail the tenderness of "The Sculptor's Funeral," the insight of "A Garden Lodge," the humor of "Flavia's Artists," the sympathy of "A Death in the Desert," with its incidental touches of that wisdom which, although only a repetition of world-worn facts, is ever new when it comes as personal revelation to any one of us. Miss Cather's discoveries, though seldom gay, are always colored with gentleness, as when she says, "Discerning people are usually discreet, and often kind, for we usually bleed a little before we begin to discern." Each story is entirely reasonable, probable, happening any day under our unseeing eyes. No new ground has been broken, yet they are fresh, unhackneyed. They reassure you on the point that true imagination does not depend upon fantastic flights; it may even, as in "Paul's Case," play upon an unpromising schoolboy in a back street. For cultivation and distinction of style, Miss Cather may even rank with Mrs. Edith Wharton, but she is far more sympathetic, far deeper; not in the sense of being obscure,—she is above all simple,—but deeper in feeling; yet she occupies your mind as fully, looking out upon the passing show with much discernment, with humor, and with a sense of beauty. Although her stories are short and unpretentious, they seem to me quite the most important in recent American fiction, and I hasten to note that the author hails from a part of the country which our grandmothers used to call "the West."

Mary K. Ford, "Some Recent Women Shortstory Writers," *Bookman* (New York), 27 (April 1908), 152–3

No one who has watched the development of our magazine literature can help being impressed by the number of women concerned therein, and also by the high average of their work, their diversity of talent, and their general literary skill. And this is peculiar to America, for, although in France the short story has reached a degree of excellence unsurpassed elsewhere, yet it is the work of men; there are few women who have sought that method of literary expression. And while England has had a continuous line of notable women writers since the days of Jane Austen, yet it was as novelists that they gained their fame, there are hardly any short story writers among them. . . .

In this country . . . there has been, during the last fifty years, an array of women short story writers which, beginning with authors like Rose Terry Cooke, Harriet Prescott Spofford, and Elizabeth Stuart Phelps, has continued through names of varied degrees of excellence, down to those of women like Mrs. Deland and Edith Wharton, whose only similarity is the sterling quality of their work.

Women ought to be among the best writers of short stories, especially of those modelled upon the French style, the story of character rather than that of incident, the successful seizure of an emotional moment, of a phase of thought; and there are writers who, like Mrs. Wharton and Miss Cather, are particularly good in that line. But it is more in character study that the American women excel, and for which material is offered them in the great diversity of type found in this country, material which has been so admirably dealt with in Alice Brown's studies of New England life, Myra Kelly's sketches of Jewish school children and Ruth McEnery Stuart's silhouettes of Southern life.

The great number of periodicals published here, with their incessant demand for short stories, is perhaps responsible for the number of women who are now writing them, but it does not account for the high quality of their work. Ever since the publication in 1863 of Mrs. Spofford's remarkably good volume of stories, *The Amber Gods*, there has been a long line of women writers, fully equal to the men of their calling, and those who are coming to the front now are keeping up the standard.

Among the best of these younger writers is Miss Willa Sibert Cather, a Western woman by birth, who not long ago gave up a position as a school-teacher in Pittsburgh in order to accept one on the staff of *McClure's Magazine*.

In her book of short stories, infelicitously named *The Troll Garden*, Miss Cather shows a wonderful aptness in seizing a decisive moment and, with a few touches, deducing from it a whole character, sometimes an entire life. Such a story is "The Sculptor's Funeral," where the body of the great artist is brought back to his native place for burial, and where we learn from the talk of the watchers, uncomprehending men to whom the palm on the coffin means nothing, just what his early life was, what he had to struggle against, his weaknesses and his faults; and after Jim Laird, once the sculptor's school friend, now the clever, unscrupulous, drunken lawyer, has risen to his defense, we know not only the character of the artist, but that of every man in the room. Such also is "A Death in the Desert," the story of the singer, dying at her brother's ranch in Wyoming, with the recollection of her brilliant career, her longing for New York and all that it represents to her, and her bitter memories of her fickle lover, all eating into her heart; and such is the story of "Paul," the young degenerate with a sort of inarticulate longing for beauty which he gratifies by means of a week of luxury at the Waldorf on stolen money; all of these show the author's keen perception of emotional value as well as her skill in character drawing.

ALEXANDER'S BRIDGE

ALEXANDER'S BRIDGE

BY

WILLA SIBERT CATHER

BOSTON AND NEW YORK

HOUGHTON MIFFLIN COMPANY

The Riverside Press Cambridge

1912

"Novels Worth Reading," *Outlook*, 100 (20 April 1912), 849

A story of more artistic quality [than Dorothy Canfield Fisher's *The Squirrel Cage*] is Miss Cather's *Alexander's Bridge*. A volume of short stories from the same hand several years ago gave promise of the fine skill which stamps this first long story as a piece of exceptionally well-conceived and well-written fiction. Miss Cather has gone far, and will go farther.

New York Times Book Review, 12 May 1912, p. 295

Bartley Alexander, in Miss Cather's story, is a famous engineer and builder of bridges. He is a forceful, energetic, fiery person, who wants all the birds he has in his hands and all there are in the bushes also, and wants them all at once. And when he is well up on the ladder of success, at the beginning of the story, Prof. Wilson tells him how he had always expected to see him drop in a crash and clouds of dust. "And another curious thing, Bartley," he says, "is that I don't feel it any longer. I am sure of you." And then the story all grows out of the crack and the threatened crash that after all were inevitable. A woman who was not his wife was the cause of it. The story is told with a good deal of charm and skill. There are dramatic situations, much clever conversation and some graphic description. Miss Cather has a faculty, which deserves special mention, of catch-ing and describing in terse refined phrase the salient features of personality both mental and physical.

"Explaining Her Novel: *Alexander's Bridge* Has Nothing to Do with Whist," *Sun* (New York), 25 May 1912

Willa S. Cather has been kept busy denying that her novel *Alexander's Bridge*, which was recently published by Houghton Mifflin Company, has anything to do with whist. "The only kind of bridge in the story," she says, "is a cantilever bridge. No, it isn't an industrial novel either. It does not give any more information about bridge building than it does about whist. In fact it doesn't give information about anything. Do I believe in the industrial novel that does give information? Certainly, but that is one kind of a story; this is another.

"This is not the story of a bridge and how it was built, but of a man who built bridges. The bridge builder with whom this story is concerned began life a pagan, a crude force, with little respect for anything but youth and work and power. He married a woman of much more discriminating taste and much more clearly defined standards. He admires and believes in the social order of which she is really a part, though he has been only a participant. Just so long as his ever-kindling energy exhibits itself only in his work everything goes well; but he runs the risk of encountering new emotional as well as new intellectual stimuli.

"Is Alexander himself meant to be a portrait of a noted New York architect? Not at all. He was not suggested by any one person. He simply has some of the characteristics which I have noticed in a dozen architects, engineers and inventors.

"Is the actress in the story meant to be much like Hilda Trevelyan? Certainly not. Miss Trevelyan is a different sort of person. I tried, however, to give the actress in this story certain qualities which I have found oftener in English actresses than in our own."

Outlook, 101
(4 June 1912), 317

There is strength in the dissection of character in this tragic tale, set in everyday surroundings and circumstances, but the strength is devoted to portraying the one-sided, hopeless, uninspired struggle of an unsymmetrical nature against the odds imposed by blind fate. Alexander failed in living the life he should have lived because of recognized weaknesses for which he was not responsible, and against which, so we are impressed, it was impossible for him to battle successfully. Alexander's bridge collapsed, causing tremendous loss of life, because Alexander was limited to insufficient material by the building commission. In effect, neither disaster was Alexander's fault; both are laid at the door of an outside superior, indifferent power. About this grim core the author weaves with great artistic skill a fine and unusual story, brilliant in its reflections of character and life, and admirably restrained and graceful in form and diction.

"Books," *McClure's Magazine*, 39
(July 1912), 360

Alexander's Bridge, by Willa Sibert Cather, is the story of a great engineer who has reached the crisis in his life when success and responsibility have begun to fret and weary a restless, energetic nature inherently impatient of restraint. Alexander tries to shake himself free, to go back to the time when life was at its highest, most adventurous pitch. He rebels against life, and life defeats him. The story is a love story, for it is through his relations with two women, Winifred, his wife, and Hilda, a young Irish actress, that Alexander learns to know himself. His pursuit of Hilda, begun in a spirit of adventure, grows into a destroying obsession. It yields him intoxicating moments of delight, in which he recaptures the sense of youthful freedom and power; but it torments him more and more with the consciousness of an ever-growing breach in his own inner integrity. The situation is developed with a dramatic skill that holds one's absorbed attention throughout. It is a story of brilliant and unusual power.

Independent, 73
(4 July 1912), 47

...We sometimes doubt whether it is a compliment after all to be likened in literary style to Mrs. Wharton. What it means is that in a book of that quality there is a deal of introspection and little outward action. Willa S. Cather's *Alexander's Bridge* is the story of an engineer of note. It analyzes a double-headed lover, and just when the man is tortured most, he meets his death on one of his own bridges. Psychologically there is some feeling to the story. There is also some good writing. But, as a novel, it all seems rather futile.

Living Age, 274 (20 July 1912), 192

In *Alexander's Bridge*, her first novel, Willa S. Cather has given the world an exceedingly finished piece of work, and a story which haunts the memory. Bartley Alexander was a builder of bridges and a man of power. He was one of those men who are destined to hear two distinct and separate calls in their lives, and to be forever uncertain which of two paths they should have taken. The situation is treated with subtlety, in a manner at the same time restrained and penetrating. The descriptions of Alexander's home in Boston and the London of his visits remind one of fine engravings and possess a charming atmosphere. It is unusual to find a book with so vital and intense a theme, handled with such refinement and distinction. Struggle and tragedy are always near the surface, but there is no hint of sordidness, and the pathos is never unrestrained. The story does not startle the reader into new lanes of thought, but awakens him gradually to the consciousness of a new possession.

Athenaeum (London), 31 August 1912, p. 217

Though sad, this story is interesting—chiefly as a psychological study. Alexander, as a student in Paris, fell in love. He afterwards went to America, became famous, and married. His one-time love also achieved fame as an actress. Their meeting, Alexander's discovery that the past still holds him, and his death are all told with some force.

"Literature and Art," *Current Literature*, 53 (September 1912), 337–8

American writers of fiction seem to group themselves into the crude and purposeful, the frankly and engagingly commercial, and—the "lesser Henry Jameses." To the last-named group, some of the reviewers think, belongs Willa Sibert Cather, the remarkable young poet and story writer whose first long work in prose, *Alexander's Bridge*, is now given to the public in book form. A "condensed novel," the Boston *Transcript* calls it; but rather is it a long short story, almost perfectly fulfilling Poe's requirements of brevity and unity. "The little book suggests a portrait group," says a writer in the Louisville *Courier-Journal*, "whose personages are presented with such intensity, with such feeling for character, as to make the canvas lose a moment its static quality, the figures seem but caught a moment in the scene of a drama." The psychology is so delicate, according to the Providence *Journal*, and the story in its way such a rare bit of fiction that "only readers as finely sensitive as the author will appreciate it." Miss Cather is a realist and a psychologist, and she possesses a highly developed faculty of using words, whether in poetry or prose, with exquisite fitness. "There are wordy writers sometimes called great," says the New York *World*, "to whom should be taught the lessons which *Alexander's Bridge* may teach of the power and blessedness of simplicity." Miss Cather's most notable successes thus far in the short story have dealt with American subjects touching on social psychology. *Alexander's Bridge* is evidently founded on the spectacular collapse of the great cantilever bridge in Canada several years ago—a titanic disaster in bridge building. But it was not Miss Cather's intention to make her story an industrial exposure. "Do I believe in the industrial novel that does give information?" she said recently to an interviewer. "Certainly, but that is one kind of a story; *Alexander's Bridge* is another, This is not the story of a bridge and how it was built, but of a man who built bridges." Nothing could better emphasize Miss Cather's individualism and her determination to use social and industrial conditions for her own purposes as an artist. Alexander's bridge—the greatest undertaking of its kind in the world—collapses because of insufficient material, the niggardliness of a building commission, altho "according to all human calculations" such a thing "simply couldn't happen." But all this serves only as a mighty symbol of the man's own moral nature, which collapses because of a like hidden erotic weakness. "There were other bridge-builders in the world, certainly," writes Miss Cather, "but it was always Alexander's picture that the Sunday Supplement men wanted, because he looked as a tamer of rivers ought to look. Under his tumbled sandy hair his head seemed as hard and powerful as a catapult, and his shoulders looked strong enough in themselves to support a span of any one of his ten great bridges that cut the air above as many rivers." Yet the greatest of these collapses, causing sad loss of life; and Alexander goes down with it, leaving not only the wife who loves him and whom he loves with a romantic devotion, but a charming young actress in London to mourn him. "There was no shock of any kind; the bridge has no impetus except from its own weight. It

lurched neither to right nor left, but sank almost in a vertical line, snapping and breaking and tearing as it went, because no integral part could bear for an instant the enormous strain loosed upon it."

Margaret Sherwood, *Atlantic Monthly*, 110 (November 1912), 683

One finds in *Alexander's Bridge* a welcome contrast to the over-emotional tales. In this study of passion, involving the lives of two women and the test of a man's faith, there is a steady and harmonious development of plot and of character, a dignity and reticence in the treatment of the dramatic scenes. The author's workmanship is deft and skillful, and the swift, clean stroke tells on every page.

H[enry] L[ouis] Mencken, "A Visit to a Short Story Factory," *Smart Set*, 38 (December 1912), 156–7

Alexander's Bridge, by Willa S. Cather, has the influence of Edith Wharton written all over it, and there is no need for the canned review on the cover to call attention to the fact—the which remark, let me hasten to add, is not to be taken as a sneer but as hearty praise, for the novelizing novice who chooses Mrs. Wharton as her model is at least one who knows a hawk from a handsaw, an artist from an artisan. The majority of beginners in this our fair land choose E. Phillips Oppenheim or Marie Corelli; if we have two schools, then one is the School of Plot and the other is the School of Piffle. But Miss Cather, as I have said, is intelligent enough to aim higher, and the thing she offers must be set down a very promising piece of writing. Its chief defect is a certain triteness in structure. When Bartley Alexander, the great engineer, discovers that he is torn hopelessly between a genuine affection for his wife, Winifred, and a wild passion for his old flame, Hilda Burgoyne, it seems a banal device to send him out on his greatest bridge a moment before it falls, and so drown him in the St. Lawrence. This is not a working out of the problem; it is a mere evasion of the problem. In real life how would such a man solve it for himself? Winifred, remember, is in Boston and Hilda is in London, and business takes Bartley across the ocean four or five times a year. No doubt the authentic male would let the situation drift. In the end he would sink into the lean and slippered pantaloon by two firesides, a highly respectable and reasonably contented bigamist (unofficially, of course), a more or less successful and satisfied wrestler with fate. Such things happen. I could tell you tales. But I tell them not. All I do is to throw out the suggestion that the shivering of the triangle is far from inevitable. Sometimes, for all the hazards of life, it holds together for years. But the fictioneers are seldom content until they have destroyed it by catastrophe. That way is the thrilling way, and more important still, it is the easy way.

Aside from all this, Miss Cather gives a very good account of herself indeed.

She writes carefully, skillfully, artistically. Her dialogue has life in it and gets her story ahead. Her occasional paragraphs of description are full of feeling and color. She gives us a well drawn picture of the cold Winifred, a better one of the emotional and alluring Hilda and a fairly credible one of Bartley himself—this last a difficult business, for the genius grows flabby in a book. It is seldom, indeed, that fiction can rise above second rate men. The motives and impulses and processes of mind of the superman are too recondite for plausible analysis. It is easy enough to explain how John Smith courted and won his wife, and even how William Jones fought and died for his country, but it would be impossible to explain (or, at any rate, to convince by explaining) how Beethoven wrote the Fifth Symphony, or how Pasteur reasoned out the hydrophobia vaccine, or how Stonewall Jackson arrived at his miracles of strategy. The thing has been tried often, but it has always ended in failure. Those supermen of fiction who are not shadows and dummies are supermen reduced to saving ordinariness. Shakespeare made Hamlet a comprehensible and convincing man by diluting that half of him which was Shakespeare by a half which was a college sophomore. In the same way he saved Lear by making him, in large part, a silly and obscene old man—the blood brother of any average ancient of any average English taproom. Tackling Caesar, he was rescued from disaster by Brutus's knife. George Bernard Shaw, facing the same difficulty, resolved it by drawing a composite portrait of two or three London actor-managers and half a dozen English politicians.

O PIONEERS!

O PIONEERS!

BY

WILLA SIBERT CATHER

"Those fields, colored by various grain!"
MICKIEWICZ

BOSTON AND NEW YORK
HOUGHTON MIFFLIN COMPANY
The Riverside Press Cambridge
1913

Gardner W. Wood, "Books of the Day," *McClure's Magazine*, 41 (July 1913), 199

The West seems inexhaustible. Here is a totally new kind of story come out of the prairies—*O Pioneers!* by Willa Sibert Cather. There have been plenty of realistic studies of the West, but this book is not a study—it is the West in action, a great romantic novel, written with striking brilliancy and power, in which one sees emerge a new country and a new people.

Miss Cather's story deals with the Norwegian and Bohemian pioneers who planted the first seed on the prairies east of Colorado. Alexandra Bergson, a young Swedish girl, is left, at the age of eighteen, to take care of her mother and three younger brothers, and to hold the homestead which her father has vanquished at the cost of his life in the dark early days of the Divide. The figure of this young girl, steadfast, unflinching, self-contained, with her fierce pride and her uncompromising idealism, dominates the whole book. Alexandra is triumphant womanhood—a sort of Nebraska Valkyr, with the daring and confidence of one who carries a new message. The forces of the New World have freed her from the old tradition of woman as a dependent drudge, pouring out her life in self-sacrifice and submission. In the quarrel between Alexandra and her brothers, Oscar and Lou, blindly contending for the proprietorship of their sister, are like voices of another generation, repeating a magic formula that has lost its power.

There is another heroine in the story—little Marie Shabata, the Bohemian girl, beautiful, eager, impulsive, so full of "go" that she can dance all night and drive a hay-cart for her cross husband next morning; too young and high-spirited to step aside and let her life go past her. Frank Shabata, her handsome, sullen husband, resents the youth and gaiety of his young wife; embittered himself, he finds something exasperating in her eager responsiveness to life; and Marie turns to young Emil Bergson.

Throughout the story one has the sense of great spaces; of the soil dominating everything, even the human drama that takes place upon it; renewing itself while the generations come and pass away.

E. U. S., "*O Pioneers!* A New Heroine and a New Country Appear," *Boston Evening Transcript*, 16 July 1913, p. 18

A new heroine and a new country appear in *O Pioneers!* Miss Cather's second novel. The story is created from the sturdy lives of the Scandinavian and Bohemian pioneers of the Middle West, and is filled with courage, endurance and final triumph. The publisher's announcement aptly characterizes it as "the very voice of those vast plains between the Missouri River and the Rocky Mountains, and of the hope and faith and power that made that country what it is today." . . .

The novel has great dramatic power; it is deep, thrilling, intense—and this intensity comes through the simplicity—one might almost say severity, of treatment. The reader, surfeited by the many-paragraphed conversations of the ordinary novel, finds his imagination unusually roused by the magnificent sufficiency of the book. The subject is not one which can be expressed in a pen and ink sketch; it needs the broad brush lines—and in such a way has Miss Cather treated it. Yet there is great delicacy of touch, particularly in the descriptive passages in which Marie and Emil—her lover and Alexandra's brother—appear. . . .

That Miss Cather knows and appreciates her people is self evident. It would be impossible for anyone who had not lived on unbroken farm land, who had not seen these purposeful immigrants, to catch so completely the spirit of a foreign race renewing the old ideals in a strange country. *O Pioneers!* has many missions: it is a disclosure of the splendid resources in our immigrant population; it is the revelation of a changed and changing country; it is, indirectly perhaps, an embodiment of the feminist theory; and, finally, it is more than worth reading for its literary value.

New York Tribune, 18 July 1913, p. 8

It takes many kinds of novels to reflect our world. With a steady hand this author holds up the mirror of fiction to a people of our land little, if at all, seen therein before: the Scandinavian and Bohemian pioneers of the more western Middle West. In her clear, smooth glass, we see these Old World pioneers adapting themselves to new conditions, identifying themselves with the prairie soil and becoming a voice in our national life. They yoke the great, unconquered lands, become rich and influential citizens of the farming country, today as rich as the

plains of Lombardy, and their sons captain the football teams of the state universities. This is a novel of considerable substance. The breath of the vast plains between the Missouri River and the Rocky Mountains is in it, and the character of a people of intelligence and sinew. Dramatic appeal there is also. There are two strongly contrasted heroines: the steadfast Swedish girl, Alexandra Bergson, endowed with the good business ability of her race and with an independent spirit which suggests the Swedish women leaders in the movement for the emancipation of their sex, and the bright, wayward and tragic little Bohemian, Marie Tovesky. Marie's love story has much color, both dark and light.

"One Sunday, late in the summer after Marie's graduation, she met Frank at a Bohemian picnic down the river and went rowing with him all the afternoon. When she got home that evening she went straight to her father's room and told him that she was engaged to Shabata. Old Tovesky was having a comfortable pipe before he went to bed. When he heard his daughter's announcement he first prudently corked his beer bottle and then leaped to his feet and had a turn of temper. He characterized Frank Shabata by a Bohemian expression which is the equivalent of stuffed shirt."

Altogether, this is a novel to be enrolled among the more solid of those in the summer reading kit.

Floyd Dell, "A Good Novel," Chicago Evening Post, 25 July 1913, p. 9

This book provides an opportunity for the American Academy of Arts and Letters to justify its existence. One of the functions of an academy—a function which the recently created British Academy has not hesitated to assume—is the discovery and recognition of genius. A committee including Bernard Shaw not long since selected a certain prose work for the honor of a prize, as containing that specific and peculiar promise which attaches to the early productions of genius. Well! It would be a gratifying result of the enterprise of our American academicians if a committee headed by W. D. Howells should discover this novel by Willa Sibert Cather. It has that specific and peculiar quality. It is touched with genius. It is worthy of being recognized as the most vital, subtle and artistic piece of the year's fiction.

Why is it all that? I despair of being able to show why. The book does not deal with any of the large ideas which rightly enough agitate this generation. It has no palpable finesse of style. It does not stun nor dazzle. It only tells the story of a girl and her younger brothers who live on a Nebraska farm: the story of their struggle with a stubborn land which almost crushed them to death before it suddenly smiled and yielded; the story, moreover, of such friendship and love as came, sometimes with wistful autumnal sweetness and again with tragic passion, into their lives. It is not an extraordinary story. Everyone knows a dozen like it.

The book opens rather unpropitiously in the little town of Hanover, anchored on a windy Nebraska tableland, and "trying not to be blown away." The Swedish and Bohemian farmers who are engaged in the fierce and almost despairing effort to reclaim the land from its prairie wildness—it was thirty years ago—are in to trade at the general store. Among them is the girl Alexandra, a fine, resolute, man-minded, thoughtful young creature, with her little brother Emil; and Carl Lind-strum, a thin, frail boy with an artist's sensitiveness and skepticism in his face; and the little Bohemian girl, Marie Tovesky, a pretty child with a coaxing little red mouth and eyes with golden glints in the brown iris.

These are seen for a moment in a setting of men drinking raw alcohol to protect themselves against the cold, and women pinning red shawls about their heads, and all talking loudly in a room reeking with tobacco smoke and kerosene. Then they set out, and the town vanishes behind them "as if it had never been." Alexandra goes back to the side of a father who is dying in the shadow of debt and failure, to her brothers to whom she must bear the difficult part of a mother, to a friendship that is cut short by separation, and to the terrible struggle with the land.

That is all there is in the whole first part of the book. And yet one does not stop reading. There is something in her calm yet vivid narrative that seems so profoundly true, a faithfulness not merely to the exterior of life, but to its intimate soul, that it has an extraordinary zest. And there is something more. One feels thru this narrative the spirit of the author, and comes to trust oneself completely in her hands. It is a spirit, an attitude toward life, that in its large and simple honesty has a kind of nobleness. Life, the course of events, as traced by such a mind, loses the taint of commonplace and becomes invested with dignity.

So one follows the story, seeing the struggle with the land, carried on inexorably by Alexandra against the poorer judgment and the feebler will of the two older boys, her brothers, at last successful: the gray prairie turned into a vast checkerboard of wheat and corn. The two older boys are married. Emil is away at college. Alexandra has a big house, in which the most interesting room is the kitchen, where three pretty, young Swedish girls chatter and cook and pickle and preserve all summer long. To be sure, they always wasted a good deal of time getting in each other's way and giggling at each other's mistakes. But, as Alexandra had pointedly told her sister-in-law, it was to hear them giggle that she kept three young things in her kitchen; the work she could do herself, if it were necessary.

Alexandra is unmarried. When Carl, after all these years, comes to see her, he is a painter, and in the eyes of her staid and prosperous brothers a vagabond. In his own eyes he is that, too. "Our landlady and the delicatessen men are our mourners," he says, "and we leave nothing behind us but a frock coat and a fiddle, or an easel, or a typewriter, or whatever tool we got our living by. All we have ever managed to do is pay our rent, the exorbitant rent that one has to pay for a few square feet of space near the heart of things. We have no house, no place, no people of our own. We live in the streets, in the parks, in the theaters."

But Alexandra sees more clearly the values of his life and the one he left behind. "I would rather have Emil grow up like that than like his two brothers. We pay a high rent, too, tho we pay differently. We grow hard and heavy here. We don't move lightly and easily as you do and our minds get stiff. If the world were no wider than my cornfields, if there were not something besides this, I wouldn't feel that it was much worth while to work. No I would rather have Emil like you than like them."

As for Emil, he has grown up into a handsome young man. He is a nice boy, and when he finds himself falling in love with Marie, the Bohemian girl, who is now the young and pretty wife of Frank Shabata, he goes away to Mexico City, thinking to make matters all right that way. . . . Alexandra reads his letters to Marie. "Marie knew perfectly well that Emil's letters were written more for her than for Alexandra. They were not the sort of letters that a young man writes to his sister. They were both more personal and more painstaking. . . . In short, they were the kind of letters a young man writes to a woman when he wishes himself and his life to seem interesting to her, when he wishes to enlist her imagination in his behalf."

Marie had eloped with Frank Shabata, who had dressed to hit the eye and was the desire of every Bohemian girl in the district. In a few years his gayety had turned to sullenness, his bravado to black misanthropy. In particular, he was jealous. He would nurse vague grievances in his mind until he grew capable of furious rages. He had little sympathy for his wife's attempts at friendship. But Marie met the situation with what seemed an inexhaustible fund of good fun. Carl Lindstrum, looking at her dancing eyes, thought to himself, "What a waste. She ought to be doing all that for a sweetheart. How awkwardly things come about."

As for Carl, he goes away, seeking a fortune in the Klondike. Alexandra's brothers are afraid she is going to marry him. "Can't you see he's just a tramp and he's after your money? He wants to be taken care of, he does." Alexandra says: "Well, suppose I want to take care of him. Whose business is it but my own?" Even Emil, just starting off for Mexico, couldn't see why she should want to. He wouldn't, of course: his sister was 40. And Carl will not accept happiness on these terms; off to the Klondike he goes.

Emil returns, and the dangerous friendship with Marie is recommenced. It is here, in conjunction with a remarkable restraint, that the writer's sympathy is most limpid-clear in its showing of life. It is the story of Youth. . . . One turns back to the little poem set in between the title page and the table of contents, telling of the somber land and the unresponsive sky—

Against all this, Youth,
Flaming like the wild roses,
Singing like the larks over the plowed fields,
Flashing like a star out of the twilight;
Youth with its insupportable sweetness,
Its fierce necessity,
Its sharp desire,
Singing and singing,
Out of the silence,
Out of the earthy dusk.

A song too soon, too tragically ended. But of that ending nor of the delayed happiness of Alexandra and Carl, I shall not go on to speak. Either I have conveyed some sense of the richness, the charm and the dignity of this novel, or I have not. But I have done all I can, and—now it [is] up to the Academy.

Frederick Taber Cooper, *Bookman* (New York), 37 (August 1913), 666–7

O Pioneers! by Willa Sibert Cather, is quite as local in theme and in characters as any volume that Mr. Fox ever wrote. It is a study of the struggles and privations of the foreign emigrant in the herculean task of subduing the untamed prairie land of the Far West and making it yield something more than a starvation income. Miss Cather has an unquestioned gift of observation, a keen eye for minute details and an instinctive perception of their relative significance. Every character and every incident in this slow-moving and frankly depressing tale give the impression of having been acquired directly through personal contact, and reproduced almost with the fidelity of a kodak picture or a graphonola record. And yet the net result strikes one, on second thought, as rather futile. . . . Now, the story of how Alexandra fought her battle and won it might have been well worth the telling; but this is precisely the part of her history which Miss Cather has neglected to chronicle. Instead, she has passed over it in leaps and bounds, and when we once more meet Alexandra, it is in the midst of prosperity, with all her brothers save the youngest happily married, her land increased by hundreds of acres, all yielding fabulous harvests, and Alexandra herself on the threshold of her fortieth year, and, with all her success, keenly conscious of the emptiness of her life, the craving for the love of husband and of children. Of course, it requires no keen guess-work to foresee that the young neighbour of her youth will ultimately return and the discrepancy of their ages will be forgotten. But somehow the reader cannot bring himself to care keenly whether the young neighbour returns or not, whether Alexandra is eventually happy or not,— whether, indeed, the farm itself prospers or not. The conscious effort required to read to a finish is something like the voluntary pinch that you give yourself in church during an especially somnolent sermon. The book does have its one big moment; but it is due to an incident that lies outside of the main thread of the story. Alexandra's youngest brother falls in love with Marie Shabata, the wife of a big, hot-tempered Bohemian; and one night the two forget discretion and are found in the orchard by the infuriated husband, who wreaks prompt vengeance. The swift, sharp picture which follows has a touch of Maupassant in it.

He did not see anything while he was firing. He thought he heard a cry simultaneously with the second report, but he was not sure. He peered again through the hedge, at the two dark figures under the tree. They had fallen a little apart from each other, and were perfectly still—no, not quite; in a white patch of light, where the moon shone through the branches, a man's hand was plucking spasmodically at the grass.

But this incident, perfect as it is by itself, lies outside the main story, outside the history of the conquest of prairie land. And for that matter, the whole volume is loosely constructed, a series of separate scenes with so slight cohesion that a rude touch might almost be expected to shatter it.

Chautauguan, 11 (2 August 1913), 203

In this tale of the Nebraska prairies Miss Cather has chronicled the history of a family of Swedish immigrants from the time of the death of the discouraged father, worn out in his youth by struggle with the unyielding land, to the triumphant success as a farmer of his daughter, Alexandra. The plot is slender. As far as Alexandra is concerned the tale is a chronicle of effort marked by but few outstanding incidents or situations. The younger brother brings into the story the love element and the tragedy. But the characters are new in American fiction, carefully differentiated and very much alive. The younger brother and the pretty Bohemian young woman whom he loves; his best friend, Amedee, and the French lads who leap and run and turn off the

lights so that they may kiss their sweethearts in the dark before the priest can turn them on again; the "innocent" old man; Alexandra's jealous brothers—all are drawn with the skill of an accurate observer touched by imagination and insight.

Outlook, 104 (2 August 1913), 767

This honestly wrought story of the Swedes and Bohemians of our Middle West is the same kind of book as was Miss Comstock's *Soddy*, of which we spoke some time since. It is a clear picture of the life of pioneers in a country at first bare and unfertile, but under right treatment richly responsive. The author evidently studied this immigrant life close at hand. There is character in her work as well as descriptive quality.

Celia Harris, *Lincoln Sunday State Journal*, 3 August 1913, p. A7

Early last fall a story by Willa Cather in *McClure's Magazine* startled a good many of us into remembering that there are other ways of looking at the west than the slangily humorous, the obviously picturesque or the drearily realistic ways of prevalent fiction. "The Bohemian Girl" was a story of the prosperous Scandinavians and Bohemians of our rich Nebraska farm country of today, now that the older generation has conquered the prairie and the younger generation has leisure to be temperamental. It was a rare, troubling, important story, for while it was warmly appreciative of its own middle-western soil, it was at the same time reflective of the intellectual and poetic influences of northern Europe. One saw Nebraska under a brilliantly quivering, modern light. Miss Cather's Swedes and Czechs, for all their Americanism, sent one across the sea to their melancholy or complacent or passionate brothers in European literature. Her style, like her Nebraskans, was both American and European.

The effect was beautiful but disturbing. One wondered just where "The Bohemian Girl" would lead Miss Cather. For after all, in interpreting America, even a European neighborhood in America, it would be a bad thing to let oneself be possessed by a European mood. It was evident that this was a transition story. She had not only found a new vein of material but in developing it she was showing a surer sense of life than she had shown before. "The Bohemian Girl" had all of her old stylistic brilliancy, her old sympathy with intellectual rebels and appreciation of human exotics; but in addition it had a new sympathy with the simpler types of human character and a feeling for productive land that is more usual in older countries than in the United States where apple orchards are given away as subscription premiums. Miss Cather has sometimes seemed hampered by an inclination to write of people who have what we rather sweepingly call the artistic temperament. She has always had a directness of outlook and an intellectual vitality which would seem to demand a wider human field. Of the younger writers she has been one of the few who have allowed themselves to produce slowly and to keep their artistic seriousness. And in "The Bohemian Girl" there were unmistakable signs that she was casting off those shackles of temperament which have kept her from coming into her own high place.

O Pioneers! Miss Cather's new novel of the Nebraska prairie, is an answer to most of the speculations which "The Bohemian Girl" aroused. She is in no danger of exoticism. The book is so deeply, unaffectedly American in style and inspiration that it may disappoint some of Miss Cather's readers by its very simplicity. It stirred me like a trumpet call.

It is a story of the taming of the prairie by the Nebraska pioneers. It tells of the courage and endurance and faith which struggled with a hostile waste, held to it, believed in it and changed it into the smiling, benignant mother land that it is today. In *O Pioneers!* the prairie is given an energy of its own. At first it resists man savagely; then it tries his faith; then it yields to him; then it blesses him. Through all the circumstances of the story one is conscious of the prairie; of the frozen ridges of winters; of the fresh brown furrow of spring; the rabbits that bob across it; the forces that wait under it.

The book produces an extraordinary effect of reality. It is at once homely and beautiful and strange. Its characters seem in true relation not only with their own prairie soil and sky but with those older home soils from which they originally came. There are many people in the book, and they are all drawn with comprehending tenderness. Miss Cather has stripped her style of cleverness, and has found a new warm simplicity of phrase.

The story begins in the early eighties on the Nebraska divide near the West Blue. John Bergson, a Swedish pioneer, is about to die, just as he has paid off the last of the mortgages on his homestead after eleven years of mischance. He has a wife and two well-grown sons, but he places the family under the leadership of his daughter, Alexandra, a girl of twenty. They have six hundred and forty acres of land and a log house. Their neighbors are foreign Americans like themselves—Swedes, Germans, Bohemians—nearly all unused to farming. Everybody is living roughly and toiling harder than people should.

Through the next ten years of struggle with prairie cold and prairie drouth and the tough prairie sod—those years which are so recent and sharp a chapter of the state's history that even now in the days of our prosperity there are a good many Nebraskans who do not like to look back and read it—through all that time of crop failure and bank panic, the tall, strong, steadfast girl, Alexandra Bergson, stands out as an embodiment of the pioneer faith that made Nebraska. When the disheartened are leaving the state by trainloads she mortgages the farm and buys more land. She could no more have run away from the prairie than her Viking ancestors could have run away from the sea. She sells the live stock and buys more land. She puts every dollar she can save or borrow into land. She does not work any harder than her neighbors—not half so hard, perhaps, as her plodding brother Oscar or her feverish, discontented brother Lou, but she has intelligence and faith. And so it is due to her that when the lean years are over the Bergson holdings are the richest in that part of the state and that the youngest brother, Emil, can go to the university at Lincoln and wear becoming tennis clothes and have leisure to taste the bitterest happiness and the most destructive pain.

Alexandra's youth is singularly unselfconscious. It is very sensible and cheerful and very lonely. Her one friend, Carl Linstrum, a sensitive, gentle German boy, moves away at the time when all the conquerable folks are fleeing. She is occupied most of the time with housework and stock reports and borrowing money from banks, but her nature grows steadily richer. She is like the prairie. She cannot be spoiled by the machinery of life. Prosperity only makes her golden.

When she is forty she lives in a big white house on the old homestead site. Her mother is dead. Oscar and Lou are married and on farms of their own. Emil is fresh from the university; he is having a full chance, Alexandra has seen to that. He can take his time and follow an unhampered career. She is glad to think that all of her work and Oscar's and Lou's have resulted in such a splendid well mannered boy. Alexandra is a great farmer. She is also a beautiful woman. But she has no idea how wonderful she is. No one knows that but Carl Linstrum, who has come back from New York, sensitive and self depreciatory as ever, to visit his old playmate. She has almost no consciousness of sex—or rather it lies so deep that it has never been stirred. It is never stirred in the book except in a strange, recurring dream which she does not understand.

She drives from one of her farms to another, managing them all. She sits at the head of her table with her farm hands and listens to their frank disapproval of her silo. She stands up for her rights against Oscar and Lou who are jealous of her superiority. Once a year she has for a visitor, Mrs. Lee, Lou's mother-in-law, a jolly old Swedish philosopher who likes to stay with Alexandra because she can have a toddy at bedtime, sleep with all her windows shut and run about the barns in Emil's boots. For friendship Alexandra has her neighbor, sulky Frank Shabata's gay hearted young wife, Marie, whose brown eyes have dancing points of yellow light "like the yellow bubbles which rise in a glass of champagne."

So unconscious is Alexandra of human passion that she lets Emil and Marie Shabata walk into what in the yellow newspapers is the commonest and most melodramatic of human tragedies. As Miss Cather tells it, it is the song of tragic youth.

Alexandra's own story moves quietly; it is merely part of the history of the evolving race. She marries Carl Linstrum without knowing that she does not love him and probably journeys with him to serene old age without once finding it out. She is a great relief in an age that is obsessed by the idea of sex. Her deepest, most personal experiences have been what others would call impersonal. Her struggle has been with the natural forces of a new, unbroken country. She has become part of the prairie. In comparison with pulsating Marie Shabata, sullen Frank, introspective Carl and all the other astonishingly vivid folk of this life-like book she seems like a great, calm, kindly, elemental fact. She could not possibly be dramatized. She creates her impression by triumph of actual existence, by character and that individual coloring which the inner life gives to a personality. She is infinitely restful, infinitely mysterious and infinitely lonely.

It is curious that in this almost passionately American book which takes its title from the most exaltantly American of poets, there are, as I remember it, just three characters whom one could even remotely suspect of being of native stock. One is Fuller, a real estate agent, who does not even have a speaking part; another is a little drummer who once meets Alexandra on the street and exclaims, "My God, girl, what a head of hair!" The third is a pale young penitentiary convict named Bertie. In Miss Cather's melting pot there are Swedes, Norwegians, Germans and French but there is no sign that native Americans played any personal part in the lives of these pioneers from the old world. Now, Nebraska lands were first taken up in large part by union soldiers released

from the civil war, and by enterprising young men from the eastern states; the foreign immigrants came later. And I can not help thinking that in a community where people of many nationalities were neighboring so naturally, where Swedes were going to French Catholic fairs, and Bohemians were telling Russian fortunes and being buried in Norwegian cemeteries—in such a neighborhood, which can be found only in a new, wonderful, forward moving country, I am sure there were a few friendly American farmers rubbing shoulders with the rest. I wish that Miss Cather had put one or two of these into *O Pioneers!* For the book breathes of Nebraska. It is impossible to take it as an isolated story. And I am jealous of the fact that the native Americans have not a single significant representative.

Living Age, 278 (30 August 1913), 576

Approbation from the late Sarah Orne Jewett was praise indeed, not easily earned or lightly bestowed, but evidently her favorable criticism of Miss Willa Sibert Cather's early work was not won by the flattery of imitation. Miss Jewett loved to show the beauty of quiet, unpretentious souls following the trivial round, accepting the common task. Miss Cathers likes to exhibit the fine quality of a nature almost unconscious of self; living only to guide others, to save them from themselves, to compel them to conduct their fortunes wisely, incessantly active and operative to the utmost limit of its influence. Probably the traits which especially won Miss Jewett's admiration were that Miss Cathers's charity is ready to pardon all sins and that she never preaches, no matter how great the temptation. Through her novel *O Pioneers!* move a beneficent woman and a girl whose very loveliness is mischievous, and even deadly, and about them seethes the motley assemblage of European immigrants that peopled so many parts of the Nebraska of thirty years ago, and Miss Cathers makes their history a message of enlightenment, to those whose imagination has not sufficient force to perceive all that is implied in chronological tables and statistics. Many an old Colony may envy the young State its chronicler in fiction.

Athenaeum (London), 2 (September 1913), 252

In early days many of the pioneers in the North-West of America were hard put to it; their knowledge of the land was scanty, and only gained by bitter experience, while droughts and epidemics were apt to swallow up their slender resources. Ruined and disheartened, many of them returned to the large towns and their old business. The more hardy, who managed to struggle on, were, however, in after years amply rewarded, and it is with such as these—and in particular with a Swedish family—that this story is concerned.

The father, broken in health by continued misfortune, but still firm in his faith in the ultimate possibilities of the land—Nebraska is the actual scene—dies, adjuring his daughter and his three sons not to give in. For a time ill-luck still dogs the community, and the two elder brothers—the youngest is but a boy—seeing their neighbours one by one drop out of the fighting line, begin to despair. They are hard workers, but destitute of imagina-

tion and opposed to change. Despite this their sister rallies them, economizing, experimenting, improving. In time the family becomes prosperous; but the youngest has a tragic lot, in depicting which the author has put in some of her best work, though the most interesting character-study in the book is undoubtedly that of the sister. Altogether it is a well-balanced, workmanlike story.

Richard King, *Tatler* (London), no. 636 (3 September 1913), 284, 286

Sometimes, as I stand crushed and rather stifled in the lifts of the city tube stations, I am astonished at the number of "dead" men and women who surround me. They are not ugly, their expression is not bad; it is simply unemotional—flat. Their faces simply say Clapham-Bank, Bank-Clapham, every day of their lives. Their tragedy, too, is not that they are suffocated but simply that they are commonplace and content. I wonder whether they have ever felt the call of the wilds, been goaded to flight by the coming of spring, ever loved not wisely but too well, been damned and risen again from this mount of ashes. I wonder, too, whether their hearts would stir at all at reading the description of the prairie spring which prefaces Miss Willa Sibert Cather's fine new story, *O Pioneers.*

["Prairie Spring" is quoted here.]

... As a story *O Pioneers* is distinctly interesting—interesting not only for the vivid pictures it gives of this wild, lonely Canadian [sic] life, but for the many beautiful descriptions of scenery scattered all through the book. One seems to feel the clear, fresh breezes of the prairie blowing across the face as one reads of the rolling hills of golden corn, the fierce storms of winter, the semitropical loveliness of summer. The characters, too—these pioneers—all stand out vivid, arresting, alive. They are real men and women doing great things. The whole story smells of the open-air life, of big ideals, big successes, big failures. It is a book to read and enjoy, and to read again.

Nation, 97 (4 September 1913), 210–11

Few American novels of recent years have impressed us so strongly as this. There are two perils by which our fiction on the larger scale is beset—on one hand a self-conscious cultivation of the "literary" quality, and on the other an equally self-conscious avoidance of it. The point may be illustrated by the work of two "late" novelists of native force, Frank Norris and David Graham Phillips. There was no doubt about the Americanism of either of them, so far as their subject-matter was concerned. It was the newer Americanism which has displaced the New Englandism of our nineteenth-century fiction. These men saw American life on a larger scale. Its scope and variety, its promise rather than its accomplishment, absorbed them. The big spaces and big emotions of Western life seemed to them far more interesting and more significant than the smug theory and languid practices of society in the smaller sense of the word. But Norris could not forget the books he had admired, and died before he had out-grown the influence of the French masters of "realism." Phillips, on the other hand,

failed to shake off the pose of the plain blunt man, who thinks that the amenities of life are symptoms of weakness and that all Harvard men are snobs.

Now (in writing this story at least) it is the same big primitive fecund America which engages Miss Cather's imagination. She dwells with unforced emotion upon the suffering and the glory of those who have taught a desert to feed the world. The scene is laid in the prairie land of thirty years ago. The settlement to which we are taken is of some years' standing. The rough work has been done, the land cleared and broken up, sod homesteads built, crops planted—and then (the great test of courage and faith in that land) a succession of dry seasons. The weaker have already abandoned their claims, or lost them by mortgage. Only here and there a strong heart, like that of the heroine of the story, refuses to be discouraged, persists in believing that country has a future. Her father, though defeated, has died in this faith, bequeath-ing it to her; so that when the stupid brothers wish to give up the fight, it is she who insists not only upon holding the land they have, but upon buying every acre they can in the thinning neighbor-hood. The years justify her, bringing wealth to her and to her beloved country. She prospers beyond her dull and penny-wise elder brothers, who nurse a grudge against her accordingly. Her heart she lav-ishes upon her younger brother, the baby of the family, and she procures for him the advantages of education which will give him a larger horizon, more flexible inter-ests, than her own. He is a fine lad, manly and responsive, but youth and circum-stance prepare a dreadful end for him and for the hapless object of his love. The familiar matter of "rural tragedy" is here. Whether its detail is dwelt upon too ruthlessly is a question which readers will decide according to temperament and individual taste. To us the treatment of the episode seems justified by the mood of tragic emotion which underlies it. As for the bereaved sister, if loneliness has shadowed her youth and tragedy darkened her maturity, there still remains the quiet fulfillment of a long-dreamt-of happiness. The sureness of feeling and touch, the power without strain, which mark this book, lift it far above the ordinary product of contemporary novelists.

"A Novel without a Hero," *New York Times Book Review*, 14 September 1913, p. 466

The hero of the American novel very often starts on the farm, but he seldom stays there; instead, he uses it as a spring-board from which to plunge into the mysteries of politics or finance. Probably the novel reflects a national tendency. To be sure, after we have carefully separated ourselves from the soil, we are apt to talk a lot about the advantages of a return to it, but in most cases it ends there. The average American does not have any deep instinct for the land, or vital consciousness of the dignity and value of the life that may be lived upon it.

O Pioneers! is filled with this instinct and this consciousness. It is a tale of the old wood-and-field-worshipping races, Swedes and Bohemians, transplanted to Nebraskan uplands, of their struggle with the untamed soil, and their final conquest of it. Miss Cather has written a good story, we hasten to assure the reader who cares for good stories, but she has achieved something even finer. Through a direct, human tale of love and struggle and attainment, a tale that is American in the best sense of the word, there runs a thread of symbolism. It is practically a novel without a hero. There are men in it, but the interest centres in two women— not rivals, but friends, and more especially in the splendid blonde farm-woman, Alexandra.

In this new mythology, which is the old, the goddess of fertility once more subdues the barren and stubborn earth. Possibly some might call it a feminist novel, for the two heroines are stronger, cleverer and better balanced than their husbands and brothers—but we are sure Miss Cather had nothing so inartistic in mind. It is a natural growth, feminine because it is only an expansion of the very essence of femininity. Instead of calling *O Pioneers!* a novel without a hero, it might be more accurate to call it a novel with three heroines—Alexandra, the harvest-goddess, Marie, poor little spirit of love and youth snatched untimely from her poppy-fields, and the Earth, itself, patient and bountiful source of all things.

Sewanee Review, 21 (October 1913), 509–10

If the great Middle West has ceased to be a field for the novelist in tales of Indian adventure and cowboy daring, it still contains fruitful subjects for the pen of the writer with sympathy and insight who, in the westward movement of the great hordes of foreign immigrants, can discover material as romantic and as historically valuable as that recorded in Cooper's *Prairie* and Irving's *Astoria*. In this romance of the modern West by Miss

Cather the author has broken new ground and reveals herself as a writer with insight into character, narrative skill, descriptive power, sense of proportion, and charm of style. In a few briefly and vividly sketched scenes revealed through the eye and heart of one that knows and loves the region, the writer makes us feel the atmosphere of the vast prairie and interprets it to us through its effect on the characters. There is no torturing of words, no forcing of the mood; all is done without conscious effort and with artistic restraint and reserve. The story deals with that medley of Scandinavian, Bohemian, German, and French immigrants who, with no experience in farming, crowded to the western prairies in the early seventies and sought to wring a livelihood from a reluctant soil. Each racial type is clearly depicted with its special customs and views of life, and the earlier generation is contrasted with the later,—the American in the making. The characters, however, are more than mere types; they are individuals who grow, and whose contrasted temperaments and training lead inevitably to a conflict in which the woman is the victor, triumphing by virtue of her superior common sense, her stronger will, her clearer vision, her greater courage, her firmer faith in the future of the country. Thus subtly the feminist theme is made prominent at the expense of the men, who are all singularly devoid of strength and initiative. As a consequence, the chief point of weakness in the story is that Carl, the lover of Alexandra, notwithstanding his self-abnegation, fails in the end to render himself altogether worthy of such a splendid woman, who in spite of herself has to do most of the wooing.

Miss Cather's story of Western pioneers is practically a novel without a hero, but it makes up for that omission by having three heroines. There are men in the book, but the interest centres on two women, not rivals, but friends—the splendid blonde farm woman, Alexandra, and Marie, poor little spirit of love and youth snatched untimely from her poppy fields. And, as much heroine as they themselves, looms large the earth, the land, patient and bountiful source of all things.

The average American does not have any deep instinct for the land or vital consciousness of the value and dignity of the life that may be lived upon it. But *O Pioneers!* is filled with this instinct and this consciousness. It is a tale of the old wood and field worshipping races, Swedes and Bohemians transplanted to the uplands of Nebraska and of their struggle with the untamed soil and finally their conquest of it.

It is a good story, a direct, human tale of love and struggle and attainment, a tale that is American in the best sense of the word. A thread of symbolism runs through it, in which the goddess of fertility once more subdues the barren and stubborn earth. This attitude of the author toward the soil gives her story an unusual interest and significance, since it is so directly opposed to our characteristic American feeling toward the land. For we are prone to consider it, in both our life and our fiction, as a sort of springboard from which to jump into other and more congenial modes of living.

Checklist of
Additional Reviews

P. A. Kinsley, "Trials of the Pioneers
Recounted in Novel," Philadelphia
Record, 9 August 1913.
Booklist, 10 (September 1913), 34.
Zoe Akins, *Reedy's Mirror*, 11
December 1914, p. 6.

THE SONG OF THE LARK

THE SONG OF
THE LARK

BY

WILLA SIBERT CATHER

" It was a wond'rous lovely storm that drove me ! "
LENAU'S *"Don Juan."*

BOSTON AND NEW YORK
HOUGHTON MIFFLIN COMPANY
The Riverside Press Cambridge
1915

James L. Ford, "Miss Cather's Story of a Prima Donna from the Western Desert," *New York Herald Tribune*, 9 October 1915, p. 8

There is so much of life, of action, of character study in this new novel by a steadily growing author that, paradoxically, one is of the opinion that the book would have been even more engrossing if she had condensed it somewhat. But the long novel has become the fashion of the day again, and, after all, Miss Cather's heroine and all the people whom she passes on the way to her goal are worth our while. . . .

This American lark of Norse-Swedish ancestry holds the centre of the stage. It is her growth in musical intelligence and feeling and aspiration, but also her development as a woman, that constitutes the central interest of the story. And, later on, there is added to this the hardening of character which a professional career, with its titanic labor, its self-denials and self-assertions, its heart-breaking delays and disappointments, its intrigues and jealousies brings.

Of Miss Cather's vivifying touch in describing the life of the West of a quarter of a century ago nothing need be said since the publication of *O Pioneers!* The scene and atmosphere of the second phase of her heroine's progress deserve a special word, however. Here we have a notable picture of the beginnings of music in the Middle West in the days of Theodore Thomas, a period of crudities, of gropings, of false enthusiasms and much bad art admired for its very faults, a period of saengerfests, choral societies and amateur soloists, of atrociously bad oratorio singers, but also a period of sincere endeavor, high devotion and steady advance. The episode among the ruins of the Hopi Indians has already been referred to; and, last of all, there is the opera house from the other side of the curtain.

Thea Kronberg's path upward is crowded with well-studied characters and scenes, which almost invariably have a wider cultural and social historical connotation. It is not in these passages, valuable and interesting in themselves, that must be sought the overgreat length of the book. That lies mostly in the endless conversations of Thea's two admirers—the Colorado desert doctor, become a mine owner, and the German-American multi-millionaire brewer. Miss Cather has ventured more ambitiously than ever before, and, if she has not quite achieved the great musical novel at which she undoubtedly aimed, she has certainly given us an animated, living picture of a period in the history of music in America, and a most interesting songbird heroine.

F. A. G., "A Woman's Climb from Nebraska to the Stage," *Boston Evening Transcript*, 13 October 1915, p. 22

One of the identifying qualities of genius seems to be that it "takes its own where it finds it." Often, as the biographer and the writer of vital fiction have revealed the lives of the greatly gifted, the taking is seen to be a ruthless process, whether consciously or thoughtlessly conducted. Thea Kronborg, whose life from early childhood to womanhood, is the subject of Willa Sibert Cather's *The Song of the Lark*, was a genius, and what she took from four men and her mother, though never with deliberate selfishness, for Thea was no "Tante," is the theme of an uncommonly interesting novel. Miss Cather's style is admirable; she writes straight-forward, lucid narrative without purple patches or arid wastes. *The Song of the Lark* is a story to read and not to "skip." If the reader is not interested in character development there is little for him in this tale, since its action is not dramatic. Its gripping power lies in the reaction of Thea Kronborg's temperament upon the wise and courageous mother and also upon the generous men who made her development possible.

Little Thea, in the opening chapter, is saved from pneumonia by Dr. Archie, the physician of the small Nebraska town in which she was born, and her good friend for many long years. . . . Thea, one of seven children in a poor clergyman's family, was given her chance to study music and her opportunity for work and privacy through the unselfishness and wisdom of her mother, who had the insight to know that her daughter was an unusual child. Thea's childhood was normal and wholesome; she bore her share in the family life tending her smaller brothers, suffering under her father's prosy sermons and enduring the Friday night prayer meetings with the rest of the community and getting her delight out of the music lessons she took from the peculiar Professor Wunsch, who had settled down in Moonstone after a precarious existence and who later made a stormy exit from it—but not until Thea had been made to realize something of what she wanted in life, and not until she had obtained from him all the knowledge his tired brain had left to give.

The devotion of another man made Thea's studies in Chicago possible and led to the discovery through a disinterested and brilliant teacher that her power lay in her voice and not in her fingers. In Chicago, too, she met the man who was to teach her what love and passion meant, to waken her through suffering to womanhood. Thea suffered and struggled and above all she worked. Therefore she conquered and sang Sieglinde from the stage of the Metropolitan. If Thea suffered in reaching her goal she also was the more or less unwitting cause of suffering in others. The mother who had made so much possible for her died longing for her daughter's presence which was denied because Thea was making her debut in Dresden—another of the sacrifices in the making of a genius. And a genius we are convinced Thea is. She is not one of the shadowy heroines whom novelists label with various attributes. Miss Cather has created a flesh and blood woman. . . .

An epilogue reveals the marriage of Thea and reverts to the little town of Moonstone which saw her beginnings and is left prattling of her successes. *The Song of the Lark* is an extremely able piece of writing and Miss Cather has succeeded remarkably in that which she attempted to do: "to deal only with the simple and concrete beginnings which color and accent an artist's work and to give some account of how a Moonstone girl found her way out of a vague easygoing world into a life of disciplined endeavor. Any account of the loyalty of young hearts to some exalted ideal, and the passion with which they strive, will always in some of us rekindle generous emotions." Sorry indeed must be the condition of one in whom Thea Kronborg's struggle would not stir some answering pulse. And perhaps Miss Cather would ask no better tribute than this response.

H[enry] W[alcott] Boynton, "Varieties of Realism," *Nation*, 101 (14 October 1915), 461–2

If one were to ask me for an example of sound and creative realism, I could suggest nothing better, among all the attempts which have been made within recent years, than Miss Cather's new story. *O Pioneers!* was a book of uncommon sincerity and power. This strikes even deeper, and will, we think, carry farther. One episode—Thea's three weeks' relation with Fred—will attract more attention from a certain class of readers than all the rest of the story. It is novel in fiction rather than in fact, and has here, convention to the contrary, the place which such episodes have so frequently in real life: it *is* an episode, important, but not determining or even focal.

In this book Miss Cather also has attempted that most dangerous of feats—to trace the genesis of genius. How many prima donnas alive have recent novelists alleged in vain! They were either merely pretty women forced to pretend that they were the idols of two continents, or viragos under the same compulsion. The roots of genius, its growth as a creative force (as against a factor of public "stunts")—how often have they been successfully studied in literature? Thea Kronborg we believe in. She triumphantly refutes the legend of the invertebrate artist. She becomes a great singer not only because she is born with the gift, but because she has the strength to develop it. And (the distinctive idea in the book) that strength of hers is rooted in the soil. To Moonstone, the little Colorado town in which her childish life had once appeared so limited—to her mother, her Mexican friends, poor old Wunst—to the place itself, the ground upon which it stood, the air it breathed, Kronborg the great singer was to trace back the stream of her powers, as to an only possible source. "Nearly all my dreams, except those about breaking down on the stage, or missing trains, are about Moonstone," she says to her old friend Dr. Archie. "You tell me the old house has been pulled down, but it stands in my mind, every stick and timber.... That's the house I rest in when I'm tired...."

And these people of Miss Cather's!—not an artificial or strained figure among them—Thea's mother, her rather disagreeable family, Archie, Fred Ottenburg, Harsanyi the pianist, Bowers the time-serving singing teacher—they are all actual persons of our acquaintance; and they all have their natural places in the action, quiet as it is. It is a story of something better than suggestiveness and charm—a thing finished, sound, and noble.

Hamilton Wright Mabie, *Outlook*, 111 (27 October 1915), 525

The Song of the Lark is the story of the unfolding of a great natural talent, the pursuit of a vocation from limited conditions to freedom of opportunity and expression. A Swedish girl, born in a frontier mining town has a gift for music which is recognized by two or three friends while it is still a blind instinct with her. She is a crude, repressed, unhappy nature in a community which does not help her to understand herself, and therefore keeps her tongue-tied and rebellious. The story of her childhood is told in great detail; her first serious education in Chicago is described, as is her later and broader training in Germany. Her final success is blurred by too great elaboration of the conditions under which the singer must win popularity. The title is not justified by Thea Kronborg's character and career. She has a great gift, and she rises above adverse conditions and sings her song; but the aerial joy of the lark is not in her. She fights her way to the upper air, but her ascent is not a "winged victory;" it is a resolute, stubborn achievement.

Miss Cather has written two broadly contrasted stories of unusual quality— *Alexander's Bridge* and *O Pioneers*! The latter is admirable in a freedom which does not sacrifice solidity of construction. *The Song of the Lark* shows ample ability, but it is too long and too heavily burdened with details which direct the reader from the song to the cage from which the singer finally escapes.

Arthur Guiterman, "Rhymed Reviews: *The Song of the Lark*," *Life*, 66 (28 October 1915), 822

Where Colorado sunsets fade
  On strangely—colored sand—
    formations,
A little Scandinavian maid
  Grew up with secret aspirations.

A girl to make the heart rejoice
  Was Thea, child of Kronborg,
    preacher;

Yet no one dreamed she had a voice
  But poor old Wunsch, her music
    teacher.

To town she went (Chicago, Ill.),
  By laudable ambition fired,
And strove to warble, chant and trill
  Until she grew immensely tired.

She needed rest like anything;
  And so in Mexico she tarried
With Ottenburg, the Brewer King;
  Alas, the naughty man was
    married!

Afar she fled, and learned her art
  So well in cities trans-Atlantic
That when she sang a Wagner part
  Her New York audience went
    frantic.

No operatic voice, they said,
  Was ever grander, richer, truer.
And when his crazy wife was dead
  She married Ottenburg, the Brewer.

It seemed to me, I must confess,
  That Thea, growing more artistic,
Declined in charm and loveliness;
  Achievement made her egoistic.

I like the pages best that tell
  Of things that proved to be her
    molders,
Her childhood friends, and what
  befell
    Among the desert sands and
    bowlders.

New York Times Book Review, 31 October 1915, p. 420

Miss Cather's new novel is a history rather than a story—the history from childhood to womanhood of one who was destined to become a great singer.

... But this is the history of Thea's beginnings, not of her triumphs; of how a "Moonstone girl found her way out of a vague, easy-going world into a life of disciplined endeavor." The discipline, often self-imposed, is, however, there from the very first. . . . The very leisurely method of narration gives abundant space for every little detail of Thea's daily life and environment from her eleventh to her twentieth year. Moonstone, the canyon in Arizona where the ancient people, the cliff dwellers, once lived and from which Thea got a sense of antiquity, of history, and the early, pathetic reaching out of humanity toward something it could feel but very dimly; Chicago, Harsanyi's studio, and at last New York, when, after ten years in Germany, Thea returns as the great singer, to meet and struggle against the petty malices and jealousies of the Opera House—all these are well and clearly pictured.

It is a very ambitious book, this novel of Miss Cather; big, mature, carefully and conscientiously worked out. Thea herself is an admirably drawn character, and most of the people we encounter while following her career—the career she strove so hard to attain, sacrificing other things and people to it with a certain steady calm ruthlessness—are real human beings. Her mother and Tillie are especially well done, and ought each to have at least a paragraph to herself. The style is clear and occasionally forceful, the descriptions vivid and full of color. *The Song of the Lark* is interesting and decidedly worth reading.

Frederick Taber Cooper, *Bookman* (New York), 42 (November 1915), 323

The Song of the Lark, by Willa Sibert Cather, is one of those volumes about which opinions may quite honestly differ. To the reader who appreciates a pleasant style, a keen observance of the little things of life, and an indulgent understanding of plain, simple souls, her portraiture of the daily, plodding routine of a Methodist minister's family in a remote Colorado town will bring a few hours of quiet but very genuine enjoyment. On the other hand, any one who demands action, a strong, well-knit plot carefully worked out with an ever-watchful eye for the greatest economy of means, will feel a growing irritation at the placid, casual manner in which things happen, the patient acceptance of life that characterises her people, the phlegmatic temperament of the Swedes, who play a dominant part in the story. Reduced to its simplest elements, this is the history of Thea Kronborg, from her early childhood in the town of Moonstone, until in ripe young womanhood she returns from her musical studies abroad, achieves fame in Wagnerian roles, and marries a Chicago millionaire, who has the wisdom not to interfere with her professional career. Stated in this form, this story has a rather familiar ring: the poor but worthy young woman with a latent artistic talent, which some man, more or less disinterested, helps to develop, recurs at fairly regular intervals. In the present case a slight novelty is introduced by making the benefactor a wealthy benefactor, a wealthy engineer, who secretly loved her, abiding his time until she should be old enough for marriage, and died leaving a life insurance policy in her name. But, as already intimated, the interest of Miss Cather's story is only secondarily in the plot. She has created a group of real persons; she takes us into their home and makes us share in their joys and sorrows, with a quickening sympathy such as we give to our friends in the real world. And that is a gift that is perhaps quite as rare as a genius for plot-building.

H[enry] W[alcott] Boynton, "The Great Novel Is Only a Dream but a Chapter in It Is Willa Sibert Cather's *The Song of a Lark*," *New York Evening Post*, *The Literary Review*, 13 November 1915

One reason why the Great American Novel remains a mirage lies in the extravagant nature of our demand upon it. If I ask you what is the Great English Novel, or the Great French Novel, or the Great Russian Novel, using the familiar capitals to express a similar requirement, the absurdity of the thing is evident enough. There is simply no such article to be produced. No nation has any single work in any field of art, so colossal, inclusive, and conclusive, as to give it anything like complete utterance. For if we are to follow the analogy of our own stock phrase, the thing we must look for abroad is a novel of absolute Russianism, or Gallicism, or Briticism—a sort of supreme picture which shall exhaust the meaning of its subject. And of course this is impossible. The greatest of fictions—*Anna Karenina, The Comedy Humaine*—what you will—can only make their contributions to the national store. The only sensible thing to say (it has been said perhaps often enough!) is that every sincere and organic novel created by an American is a chapter in the Great American Novel. Personally, I am not looking for anything more nobly indigenous than *The Scarlet Letter*, or *The Rise of Silas Lapham*, or *The Song of the Lark*.

The younger novelists of whom I am to have something to say in this and following articles, all seem to me to be representing different aspects or impulses of Americanism as well as of art. I do not see why we should care to have them all trying for the same thing in the same way—especially as we have a very vague notion as to what the best thing and way ought to be.

If I do not believe in the great American novel, certainly I do not believe in a novel without a country. On the contrary, I firmly believe that the finest and biggest fiction (or art of any kind) has consciously or unconsciously its roots in the soil. This does not mean that our finest prospect is necessarily our own back yard, or that "local color" is a thing worth pursuing for its own sake, or that there is any use whatever in striving, however honestly, to be indigenous. But it does mean that the character and quality of genius (I don't say talent) are largely determined by physical sources and early impressions of scene and atmosphere.

This idea is finely embodied in the latest novel of Willa Sibert Cather. Thea Kronborg, the Swedish-American girl who learns to sing to the world, always traces her strength back to her early home in the Colorado desert. It is not that she has been exceptionally happy there, it is not that she has found there uncommonly inspiring conditions. It is simply that she has lived there, and that in that place her own personality has first become aware of itself and of the world. Now it is clear that there is a good deal of Miss Cather's own experience in this, and it may be worth while to outline that experience as a whole, so that we may understand the sources of her work.

It is an experience which an Englishman would call typically "American." Willa Sibert Cather was born in Virginia. The Siberts were Norwegian, and the Cathers of Irish blood, but both families had been Virginian for some generations. It was not Virginia, however, which bred this personality, but the prairie country of Nebraska. Miss Cather's father took up a ranch there when she was nine years old. The few settlers in the neighborhood were chiefly Scandinavians and Bohemians. They greatly excited the interest of the eager child from Virginia. She seems to have lost no time in trying to get at the human nature half-hidden behind their strange speech and manners. She went among them with something deeper than the ardor of a journalist looking for copy, won their confidence, and learned much. She has said of this experience: "I have never found any intellectual excitement more intense than I used to feel when I spent a morning with one of these pioneer women at her baking or butter-making. I used to ride home in the most unreasonable state of excitement; I always felt as if they told me so much more than they said—as if I had got inside another person's skin. If one begins this early, it is the story of the man-eating tiger over again—no other adventure ever carries one quite so far." The Cathers were themselves pioneers; the life and the atmosphere of the prairie gave the girl her earliest and most permanent "saturation," to use Henry James's favorite phrase.

There was no school on the Nebraskan prairie, but there was a high school at Red Cloud, from which Miss Cather went on to the State University. On her graduation (at nineteen) she at once attacked the world with success. She spent several years on the editorial staff of a Pittsburgh daily and several years more as a teacher of English in a Pennsylvania high school. Her first book of verse, *April Twilights*, made little more stir than such books commonly do, but not long after a volume of short stories, *The Troll Garden*, reached a wider public and led to her becoming, in 1906, an editor, and a little later managing editor, of *McClure's Magazine*. In a New York office she found no time for writing, and three years ago she gave up editorial work and became a free lance. Three novels, *Alexander's Bridge* (1912), *O Pioneers!* (1913), and *The Song of the Lark* (1915), have more than sufficiently justified her.

Before *Alexander's Bridge*, Miss Cather had written only short stories. This first novel was short, but not, as so often happens in such cases, a mere elongated tale or novelette. It is the story of a crucial episode in the life of a strong man. Alexander, an American engineer, in the hour of his prime, is forced to make an ancient choice between the wife of his bosom and the charming actress who has been a comrade of his youth in Paris. The action takes place chiefly in New England and in London—not major scenes in Miss Cather's own life. The story is brilliant and interesting, but lacks the imaginative power and scope of its two successors. The writer was slow in getting command of the materials which were most vivid in her consciousness. She had written some short stories in the remembered Nebraskan setting, but to her own dissatisfaction. They did not ring true. "It is always hard to write about the things that are near your heart," she comments.

"From a kind of instinct of self-protection, you distort them and disguise them." It was Miss Jewett (to whom *O Pioneers!* is inscribed) who set her on the right track, the track of perfect simplicity and sincerity.

In *O Pioneers!* is the prairie life of her youth, with its material and social problems, its problems, too, of the melting pot, as constant if not as exigent as in the cities, yet hardly touched upon elsewhere in our fiction. Alexandra Bergson, like Thea Kronborg in *The Song of the Lark*, is a Swedish-American. In both is the clear blood of a strong race, well used to the battle with nature, and both are great lovers of freedom. Both have an immense capacity for single-hearted devotion. Yet they are very different types: in a way they represent the two possible types of feminine greatness. Alexandra's is almost infinitely the commoner—fortunately, on the whole. Hers is the greatness of character applied to service; she has all the virtues of the pioneer woman. Left an orphan upon the land, with a family of younger brothers, she brings them up and holds them to their post. Her triumph is to have done her part in the development of the adopted country she loves, and, more narrowly, to have made good her foothold there.

Thea Kronborg represents the rare type of the woman artist, born almost with a sense of her calling, and making her way steadily, against all obstacles, or by means of all obstacles, towards the perfect fruitage of her genius. True interpretations of this type are almost rarer than the type itself. As I have said elsewhere, "Thea Kronborg we believe in. She triumphantly refutes the legend of the invertebrate artist. She becomes a great singer, not only because she is born with the gift, but because she has the strength to develop it. And (the distinctive idea in the book) that strength of hers is rooted in the soil. To Moonstone, the little Colorado town, in which all her childish life had once appeared so limited—to her mother, her Mexican friends—poor old Wunst—to the place itself, the ground upon which it stood, the air it breathed, Kronborg the great singer was to trace back the stream of her power as to an only possible source."

In both of these books, which are works not of promise but of maturity, a single sex episode is treated as quietly as if such episodes were not conventionally an object of leering solicitude, or at least of strained attention. Miss Cather's frankness is not that of a superior person consciously giving a spade its right name; it is that of a sensible and wellbred human being speaking of perfectly natural things. In the hands of such a writer, who possesses also imagination of a high order, realism and the ideal, Americanism and humanity may be nowhere at odds. Nay, in such hands even "workmanship" becomes of appreciable value!

Edward E. Hale, *Dial*, 59 (25 November 1915), 496–7

Miss Cather's *The Song of the Lark* appears to be one of the biographies—childhood, education, love-affair or affairs, whatnot else—of which there are not a few nowadays. This time it is the story of a singer, as Mr. Beresford's last book is the story of a novelist, Mr. Dreiser's of a "genius" at painting, Mr. Maugham's of one who was not a genius. But the form is not much,—in fact, here it is not even a form (not even, like Logic, is it a dodge): it is hardly more than an excuse. Why tell us so much and no more?

Why not tell everything? Why ever Miss Cather or any other novelist would tell us that there must be just so much,—no more, no less. The theory has been that such a book is to be the account of life (or a life) just as it is. That gives reason for anything. But here is a book where theories of form go for little. "It was a wondrous storm that drove me on" says the title-page, doubtless with truth. Miss Cather wants to give the soul of the artist, the sense of art,—that something so impossible and so inevitable, which never explains itself, never philosophizes, is perhaps never even conscious of what it is. Here we have a fine realization of the artistic nature, a picture which stands for itself in its own way. Method and form are of little importance in so successful an achievement.

So one need not say much about the realistic touch. To tell the truth, though there is much record of picture and event, there is much also that is not in that manner at all. Miss Cather explains a good deal. Often she shows us life and lets us get the impression; but often for some reason she does not do that, but merely tells us what the impression should be. She not only analyzes, as they used to say, but she explains,—as, for instance, that Thea found faithful friends in these good women, and that no musician ever had a better wife than Mrs. Harsanyi. There is much that is seen, but there is much that is not seen at all, and that with no apparent reason. Sometimes it is one way, sometimes another. One cannot understand the method. Why sometimes tell the fact and sometimes explain? Why sometimes skip and sometimes not?

In spite of all this, one must take the book on trust, as far as I can see. One might perhaps understand these matters with more study, or with more appreciation. But understanding is likely to be the perfunctory task of the critic. The first thing to do is to get the experience; and then understanding and criticism, and so on, may be left to themselves. And for anyone who will have it, here is certainly an experience such as one has all too rarely,—even though there be several hundred novels this year and among them a number that are excellent. Is it (as hinted) the experience of an upland garden in the windy dawn when the world seems young? I have never been in such a place, nor have I ever heard the song of the lark,—at least not of the "unbodied joy whose race is just begun." It is not so much the feeling of life that I get here, as the sense of something much less common than life: namely, art as it exists in life,— a very curious and elusive thing, but so beautiful, when one gets it, that one forgets all else.

Living Age, 287 (27 November 1915), 576

The musical heroine of to-day in no way resembles the musical hero, as pictured by E. Sheppard in "Charles Auchester." She is not poetic, either in thought or in behavior, and, although she treats her art seriously, she has no illusions about it, and manages herself, body, soul and spirit, as coolly as she would discipline a valuable dog. Miss Willa Sibert Cather portrays such a type in *The Song of the Lark*, and makes it exceedingly interesting. Thea Kronborg, reared in a Colorado town, and petted by a few persons of rather extraordinary quality, grows up with a firm determination to make the best of her voice, and to extract the highest attainable price from the world in payment for its notes. She desires both fame and love, but most of all she longs for perfection in her art, and works for it in the dogged Scandinavian fashion, striving also to become a good accompanist, and in the interval necessary for her education, she supports herself by teaching music, and by singing in church choirs and at funerals. Such is the thread by which Miss Cather connects the history of the adventures and the development of many persons, Mexican, German, Swedish and American, making each in turn the object of the reader's close attention, and not scorning the most absurdly intimate details. The fault of the book lies in the author's toleration of verbal vulgarisms which should be left to streetboys and yokels. Its merits are apparent in vivid description of phenomena, from sand-storms, to choir-fights, and personages ranging from cave-dwellers to toddling babies. The faults are easily amended, and it is to be hoped that Miss Cather will soon eliminate their weakening influence from her vigorous work. A writer as strong as she cannot afford to have defects in her armor.

youth in Moonstone, the little Colorado town. Miss Cather is a close and sympathetic observer. The book has many characters, each of whom is a distinct personality, and Mrs. Kronborg, the hapless young lover, Ray Kennedy, and the odd, romantic, unattractive Tillie, become to us real people whom we like. The various scenes and incidents are graphically depicted. Exceptionally good is the epilogue, in which we are brought back to Moonstone to see Tillie living a glad, proud life on the triumphant career of her famous niece, who has finally severed all bonds of union with the place of her birth.

Miss Cather's manner is remarkably virile and effective. When her people speak it is because they have something to say; and she has a faculty for giving, without apparent effort, an unexpected turn to the commonplace that deprives it of that character. Her powers require the wider scope of some subject of broad human significance: with such an inspiration she could accomplish things not easily forgotten.

Catholic World, 102 (December 1915), 396–7

Although Miss Cather's latest novel is also her best, it is not so by virtue of its central theme. This story of the realization of a girl's ambition to be a great singer shows her as too self-centered to arouse any warmth of feeling for her; and the author's methods are not sufficiently meticulous to gain a place for Thea Kronborg in the gallery of chefs-d'oeuvre by the masters of analysis. Our interest is less with her than with the people about her, especially in her years of childhood and

"Diminuendo," New Republic, 5 (11 December 1915), 153–5

It seems a far journey back to the rare imaginative quality of O Pioneers!, the story by Miss Cather of young life in the Nebraska prairie with its beautiful and tragic denouement. O Pioneers! had a warm unity of tone, a youthful wistfulness, that made it appealing. One could scarcely believe it was not the work of a writer who was going to do great things in that imaginative realism which our current American fiction still so stupidly lacks. The appearance of dramatic imagination in any form in this country is something to make us all drop our work and run to see. It is the thing to keep straining our eyes for. One hoped that the adulation which greeted Mr. Poole's timid *The Harbor*, where the imagination was swabbed on from the outside rather than run as a vital current through the veins, would encourage more of the younger novelists to let themselves go, and stir us by a representation of life that is fearlessly bathed in a glow of youth and generous ideals. This is why it is so disappointing to find Miss Cather, with her rare promise, running now prudently to cover.

It is difficult from *The Song of the Lark*, to reconstruct that lyric preface to the former book, the "Prairie Spring," which sang the very theme of the book, and made at least one Dakotan youth quite weak with homesickness. This very title suggests a play to sentimental chords on the style of the unspeakable "Rosary." One could forgive it perhaps if the song of the lark were actually the *leitmotif* of the story. But it is not. Thea Kronborg sees the picture in the Chicago Art Museum, feels that it is her picture. "The flat country, the early morning light, the wet fields, the look in the girl's heavy face," were "all hers." But never again does either Miss Cather or Thea think of the picture, and the imagination simply refuses to relate the tense and golden Thea, ambitious, quiet, and a little fierce, to the placid and thickly knit girls of Breton's popular canvas.

The suspicious rift of artistic defect which this title discloses continues to widen through the story. Miss Cather's imagination seems acceleratedly to miss fire, until the last two parts seem an act of laborious creation, carried through after the author is really bored with her

story. The early chapters—the little Swede girl's childhood in the Colorado town, her quaint pastoral family, the old musician, her early musical studies in Chicago—are delightfully done. So are scenes like the Mexican dance, where Thea's artistic soul rises against the disapproving conventionality of the little town. There is air and sun in the Arizona cliff summer. All this is real because it is part of the Thea that Miss Cather is writing about, and part of Miss Cather's own assimilated experience. It is warm with the hard little golden fire that was at Thea's heart, and which drove her on and on in her quest.

In this fair and self-centered girl with her passion for her music, with that clutch at her soul which held her aloof from every environment, that urge which impelled her to realize her very self though it meant shutting out the whole world, Miss Cather had a great story. Such a story could have been a crescendo of interpretation, with the contrast between the inner clutch and the conventional appeals of life made ever more inescapable. But Thea's actual success limps very badly. The inner fire becomes smothered in wearisome objective detail of the operatic life and the uninteresting friends that she does not really need. The story could have worked up to the climax of Thea's cool flight to Mexico with the young Ottenburg, Thea inexorably true to her art, taking passion as an interesting but indispensable incident of life. There the story could have broken off with a leap. Our imagination would have easily supplied the finished career. Miss Cather does not mean to spell deterioration for Thea, and yet so unskilful is the handling of these later chapters that it is almost impossible to find in the bourgeoise Madame Kronborg the same Thea, with her "loyalty of young hearts to an exalted ideal, and the passion with which they

71

strive." In the inscrutable epilogue Miss Cather seems simply to throw to the winds what she is trying to do. Her story was the progress of a peculiarly arresting youthful talent. The epilogue acts as if she were writing a sociological treatise of the town of Moonstone, Colorado, in which every last citizen of the girl's early environment is to be accounted for to the anxious reader.

Yet few novels give so tell-tale a pattern of the difficulties that beset the imaginative writer, and the narrow way that must be walked. Miss Cather would perhaps be shocked to know how sharp were the contrasts between those parts of her book which are built out of her own experience and those which are imagined. Her defects are almost wholly those of unassimilated experience. The musical life of this opera singer who has so fascinated her she has admired, but she has not made it imaginatively her own. She has contented herself with the fascination and has not grasped the difficulty of reading herself into this other life and making it so much hers that the actual and the imagined are no longer separable. This is almost the whole cunning of the novelist's art. O Pioneers! was artistic because it was woven all of a piece of imaginatively interpreted experience. Its charm made one want to put Miss Cather's next book among that very small group of epics of youthful talent that grows great with quest and desire. But in that little library one cannot give even temporary place to The Song of the Lark. Resentment of this unpleasant fact is perhaps the greatest compliment one could pay to its author's genuine talent.

Henry Louis Mencken, "Cinderella the Nth," *Smart Set*, 48 (January 1916), 306–8

Cinderella the Nth—There is nothing new in the story that Willa Sibert Cather tells in *The Song of the Lark*; it is, in fact, merely one more version, with few changes, of the ancient fable of Cinderella, probably the oldest of the world's love stories, and surely the most steadily popular. Thea Kronborg begins as a Methodist preacher's daughter in a little town in Colorado, and ends as Sieglinde at the Metropolitan Opera House, with a packed house "roaring" at her and bombarding her with "a greeting that was almost savage in its fierceness." As for Fairy Princes, there are no less than three of them, the first a Galahad in the sooty overalls of a freight conductor, the second a small town doctor with a disagreeable wife, and the third Mr. Fred Ottenburg, the *Bierkronprinz*.

But if the tale is thus conventional in its outlines, it is full of novelty and ingenuity in its details, and so the reading of it passes very pleasantly. Miss Cather, indeed, here steps definitely into the small class of American novelists who are seriously to be reckoned with. Her *Alexander's Bridge* was full of promise, and her *O Pioneers!* showed the beginnings of fulfilment. In *The Song of the Lark* she is already happily at ease, a competent journeyman. I have read no late novel, in fact, with a greater sense of intellectual stimulation. Especially in the first half, it is alive with sharp bits of observation, sly touches of humor, gestures of that gentle pity which is the fruit of understanding. Miss Cather not only has a desire to write; she also has something to say. Ah, that the former masked less often as the latter! Our scriveners are forever mistaking the *cacoëthes scribendi* for a theory of beauty and a rule of life. But not this one. From her book comes the notion that she has thought things out, that she is never at a loss, that her mind is plentifully stored. I commend her story to your affable attention—at least the first half of it.

The Puritan.—One hears, in *The Song of the Lark*, too little of old Kronborg, the father of Thea, a one-horse Methodist preacher in a one-horse town. To me, at all events, there is endless fascination in such a man. What American novelist will first depict and interpret the Puritan? (I do not mean the Puritan Father, for that has been attempted by Hawthorne and others, but the Puritan of today, the neighborhood uplifter, the advocate of harsh laws, the bitter critic and reformer of his brother over the fence.) There is a brilliant flashlight picture in the second chapter of E. W. Howe's *The Story of a Country Town*, but it is no more than a flash. Frank Norris was the man for a full-length portrait, but he was too much intrigued by the romance of commerce to give his attention to it. Perhaps Dreiser will some day undertake it. He has the capital advantage of being of un-Puritan blood, of having no race sympathy to overcome. But he lacks, alas, the bitter wit, the hand for satire. The Puritan is not to be dealt with calmly and scientifically but savagely, joyfully, with gusto. What a job the Hilaire Belloc of *Emmanuel Burden* might have made of him! But that Hilaire Belloc, alackaday, is now no more! . . .

The Shy, Shy Girls.—Before parting from Miss Cather, let us join in praising her for a rare sort of courage: she gives the exact date of her birth in *Who's Who in America*. Do I spoof? Nay. Very few of our literary girls do it. Is Mrs. Atherton 27 or 72? You will never find out from that gaudy red volume, though the fact that she is a *g. g. niece* of Benjamin Franklin is duly set forth.

Another fair fictioner tells us that her father was the son of a sister of a president of the United States, but neglects to tell us how long she has been a student in the school of human experience. Yet another confesses that she has been "engaged in literary work since 1895," but doesn't say how old she was when she began. Yet another is careful to give the quite undistinguished occupation of her deceased husband, but goes no further with her confidences. Glancing through these humorless, telegraphic autobiographies, one happens upon various naif and chatty things. One lady says that she has been to Europe five times; another that she writes about "women's capacity and potentiality"; another that she has "made a specialty of geography"; another that she has four children; another that she is a Colonial Dame; several boast bravely that they are unmarried; more than one admits having contributed to *The Smart Set*, and even to *The Atlantic Monthly*. But none of these talkative girls tells us her age! . . . Lest I be accused of foul injustice, or worthy ladies be wrongfully suspected, let me add that most of the gentle authors whose work is comparable to Miss Cather's are quite as honest as she is. For example, Miss Mary Johnston, Miss Ellen Glasgow, Mrs. Wharton, Mrs. Watts . . . four names are enough. In this field, indeed, reticence seems to be in indirect ratio to accomplishment.

Times Literary Supplement (London), 20 April 1916, p. 188

Innumerable stories have been written round the lives and exploits of artists, and especially of musicians. *The Song of the Lark*, by Willa Sibert Cather makes one more; it is a good one more, not so much because of anything startling in the matter or style, with the exception of some of the American vernacular, which is surprising indeed, but because of the perception with which the simple influences in an artist's life are traced.

The first part of the book (there are six parts and an epilogue) gives a picture of life in the small Colorado town of Moonstone, some twenty-five years ago; the pettiness and kindness, the formality and the freedom of the people, and their surroundings make a sympathetic background to the portrait of little Thea Kronborg, the child of the Swedish pastor and his wife. Even in childhood Thea is conscious of a longing within herself, a power which she does not understand, but which is precious to her and which sets her apart, making her either attractive or repellent to her family and friends. It is felt by her mother, who, being a wise woman, can love and stand aside, by her sisters and brothers, who are not wise and are annoyed, and by others with whom she comes in contact; the railwayman who loves her without understanding her, the doctor for whom she incarnates a romantic symbol, the drunken German piano teacher who shares her unconscious artistic standard, the wayward "Mexican Johnnie" who loves music as flowers love the sun, and later the musical brewer magnate Ottenburg, whom she eventually marries. It is the piano teacher, in spite of his miserable state, who first awakens Thea's insight and leaves with her when he disappears upon his downward way a precious legacy in an old German copy of Gluck's *Orphée*.

The second part of the book takes Thea to Chicago, where her development is helped by a disinterested musician, Harsanyi. One wonders how many of the musical characters are real people, for the outline of Theodore Thomas, the conductor, makes one suppose that others also are portraits. It is in her piano lessons with Harsanyi that Thea, by chance, reveals her voice and also the harshness of her big untutored nature; and the author is truthful and spares Thea none of the difficulties which beset such a nature. The story is developed with a great many details. And at the end of the long book Thea Kronborg has become not only a great singer but a great artist; she even makes of the part of Fricka something

> so clear and sunny, so nobly conceived, that she made a whole atmosphere about herself . . . Her reproaches to Wotan were the pleadings of a tempered mind, a consistent sense of beauty. In the long silences of her part, her shining presence was a visible complement to the discussion of the orchestra.

It certainly takes a very great artist to do this. But though the author goes faithfully through a number of Thea's Wagnerian *rôles*, including an unrehearsed emergency appearance as Sieglinde in Act II of *Die Walküre*, one feels that it might have been enjoyable to hear more of that part of her character which made her love "Che faro" even at the expense of some of her triumphs in New York.

Commonweal, 15 (24 February 1932), 475

This is a reprint of the most interesting of Miss Cather's early novels. Between the limpid unity of *My Antonia*, which marks the coming-of-age of her artistic form, and the less certain, more casual and inclusive narration of *The Song of the Lark*, which preceded it by three years, there is a definite artistic gap. But this earlier book shows the full richness of the material from which such a flawless selection was made in the later one. It gives us, in plentitude, that atmosphere of Western post-pioneer life (this time in Colorado), unmellowed yet sharply flavored and distinct, that magical sense of the quality of common people so much more like identification than the outside process of perception, which are ingredients in the classic history of Antonia; and it gives us possibly the strongest of Miss Cather's heroines. Thea Kronborg, the Swedish girl who goes through all sorts of vicissitudes social, financial and moral, in order to become a great singer, is marked by nature with a rugged granite quality which shows harsh and unyielding beside the graces of a Marian Forrester, the life-enkindling warmth of an Antonia, the gentle civility and sweetness of a Cécile. But she has the authority of a powerful will, and a purity of artistic devotion, which make her a unique personage, even in this gallery.

Times Literary Supplement (London), 26 November 1938, p. 758

The Song of the Lark, first printed in America in 1915 and reviewed in these columns on April 20, 1916, has long been recognized, despite serious structural faults and a definite fading of interest towards the end, as outstanding among its author's earlier works. Miss Cather, her publisher declares, has now rewritten it, though revision would seem the better term for so relatively slight a process of minor omission and occasional retouching of lesser psychological brush-strokes. In all essentials the story of a poor country girl's rise by persistence and good fortune to operatic success remains unchanged, its Colorado and Arizona backgrounds and its characterization as superb, its machinery as noisily creaking, as ever. The undated Preface was written in 1932 and appeared in an edition issued in that year.

Checklist of Additional Reviews

Elia W. Peattie, Chicago *Tribune*, 9 October 1915, p. 10.
Open Shelf (Cleveland), 15 October 1915, p. 89.
Wisconsin Library Bulletin, 11 (November 1915), 329.
Independent, 84 (15 November 1915), 272.
Booklist, 12 (December 1915), 136.

MY ANTONIA

MY ÁNTONIA

BY

WILLA SIBERT CATHER

Optima dies . . . prima fugit
VIRGIL

WITH ILLUSTRATIONS BY
W. T. BENDA

BOSTON AND NEW YORK
HOUGHTON MIFFLIN COMPANY
The Riverside Press Cambridge
1918

New York Times Book Review, 6 October 1918, p. 429

Nebraska is the scene of Willa S. Cather's new novel, the central character being a young Bohemian girl, Antonia Shimerda, the daughter of immigrants. Her father and mother came to Nebraska, where they had bought a farm out in the prairie from a fellow countryman, who cheated them badly. Jim Burden, who tells the story, is an American boy, living with his prosperous grandparents on their big farm, which, as distances go in that country, is not so very far from the Shimerdas' place. Jim's grandparents befriend the Shimerdas, and it is Jim himself who teaches Antonia English. A large part of the book is given over to an account of the work and play of these two during the year when Jim was about 10 and Antonia about 14.

There is a carefully detailed picture of daily existence on a Nebraska farm, and indeed the whole book is a carefully detailed picture rather than a story.

[. . .]

The book is full of sketches of farm life, of plowing, reaping and thrashing, of the difficulties of feeding cattle in winter, and all the routine of husbandry. Antonia is a true daughter of the soil, thus described: "She had only to stand in the orchard, to put her hand on a little crab tree and look up at the apples, to make you feel the goodness of planting and tending and harvesting at last." There are other immigrants in the book besides the Shimerdas—Norwegians, Danes, Russians, etc.—and the ways of all of them are more or less fully described. They are all, to some extent, pioneers, the period of the book being that in which the first foreign immigrants came to Nebraska.

"My Nebraska Antonia," *Sun* (New York), 6 October 1918, section 5, p. 1

There is a special genius of Memory. Where it exists it is capable of accomplishing what no other genius can reach. The classic modern example of it is Joseph Conrad's story "Youth"—a thing of terrible poignancy, of wonder and tears. If a writer is so blessed as to be able, only one or two times, to recapture the past and rekindle the ancient fires he will leave a name remembered and loved from generation to generation.

Of living American writers there is particularly one who has this great gift. Willa Sibert Cather, writing *O Pioneers*! made an indelible impression upon the minds of those who read that novel, an impression which was merely confirmed with satisfactory completeness by her own confession afterward. . . .

What Willa Cather got out of her childhood was a wonderful awareness of the few people about her and of the soil they struggled upon and of the struggle itself, as desperate as that of the lonely swimmer to keep afloat in mid-ocean. This soil was an ocean, an illimitable ocean of tall red grass, forever billowing in the wind so that the visible earth appeared as restless as horizonless waters.

"As I looked about me I felt that the grass was the country, as the water is the sea. The red of the grass made all the great prairie the color of wine stains, or

79

of certain seaweeds when they are first washed up. And there was so much motion in it, the whole country seemed somehow, to be running."

The words are Jim Burden's and the perception is that of a ten-year-old set down for the first time in the plains of the middle West. But the picture cinematographed on a woman's brain and projected on the pages of Willa Cather's new book, *My Antonia*.

The most extraordinary thing about *My Antonia* is the author's surrender of the usual methods of fiction in telling her story. Time and again as you read the book it strikes you what an exciting novel Miss Cather could have made of it if she had wanted to plait the strands of her story into a regulation plot. But she renounces all that at the beginning in a brief introduction.

The introduction acquaints us with Jim Burden, a New York lawyer of wealth and reputation, whose youthful fortunes were much advanced by his marriage with the only daughter of a distinguished man. There appears never to have been love in that marriage. Only one woman ever really influenced Jim Burden's life or kindled his imagination—Antonia Shimerda, later Antonia Cuzak—a Bohemian girl who had been his playmate in their childhood on the Nebraska prairie. Miss Cather asks us to accept the story of Antonia as set down by Burden. It is a series of memories exclusively; it has continuity and it has development; but it has not and could not have any of the plot or suspense which could so easily be managed by telling the story in ordinary fashion. It would have been so easy for the author to have told her tale herself and to have matched Antonia against the woman who became Mrs. Burden; the complete contrast between the two would have been dramatic enough in all conscience, and the struggle in Jim Burden could have

been made wholly plausible. Then why didn't she do it that way?

Because to have done it that way would have branded her narrative as purest fiction in the mind of every reader; a comfortable sense that none of this ever had happened would have gone with you all the way through the book absorbing as it would have been. But now you are positively uncomfortable from page to page with the conviction that all of this happened! By deliberately and at the outset surrendering the story teller's most valuable perogatives Miss Cather has won a complete victory over the reader, shattering his easeful assumption of the unreality of it all, routing his ready-made demand for the regulation thrills and taking prisoner his sense of what is his rightful due. It is as if General Foch were maneuvering. The strategy is unfathomed and the blow falls in a most unexpected quarter. You picked up *My Antonia* to read a novel (love story, of course; hope it's a good one) and find yourself enthralled by autobiography.

What vivid autobiography it is we cannot indicate adequately. For a great part of the book Antonia (the Bohemians accent the first syllable of the name strongly, and this should be remembered in pronouncing the title)—for perhaps half of the book Antonia stands out not much more distinctly than a half dozen other people. The reader is puzzled to understand why she should mean so much to the boy Jim Burden. It takes the last fifty pages, we suspect, to make it clear just what she meant and how deeply, even as it took the sight of her and her children, after an interval of some twenty years, to make this clear to Jim himself.

The real interest of the narrative pending the final and moving disclosure of Antonia Cuzak, the interest and the rich delight of it, the heaped up satisfaction, lies in the simple and perfect picture of pioneer life. It lies in the figure of old Mr. Shimerda, a sad and stricken aristocrat, and in the account of his ghastly death. It lies in the figures of Jake and Otto. It rests in the portraits of Jim's grandfather and grandmother, of Pavel (or Paul) and Peter, the Russians, and their dreadful story. Mr. Shimerda, kneeling before the lighted Christmas tree on which all the colored figures from Austria stood out in the candle flame; Otto, cheerily carpentering Mr. Shimerda's coffin: Peter and Pavel and the bridal night in Russia which was also the night of the wolves; Crazy Mary, chasing Lena Lingard with a corn knife to "trim some of that shape off her"; Lena with her violet eyes, giving away her heart when she feels like it but never losing her head; Blind D'Arnault, the negro musician, and his strange story; the revelations regarding the satyr, Wycliffe Cutter; a performance of *Camille* in Lincoln, Nebraska; the worldly success of Tiny Soderball— these are the raw materials of romance, but the very substance of actuality. They need only to be skilfully related, and in handling them as Cather does unfailingly well. Nor is her accomplishment easy; murder, suicide, debauchery and occurrences that were not only unvarnished but unvarnishable are quite as much a part of what she has to handle as the happy, domestic scenes natural to childhood. She is no feminine Zola, fortunately; without any smirch of realism she achieves the happiest reality. A young writer who wants to deal honestly and yet inoffensively with a variety of difficult things can learn big lessons from reading this book.

Seven weeks ago, in reviewing on this page Gene Stratton-Porter's *A Daughter of the Land*, we quoted the aspiration of the heroine of that novel to become the mother of at least twelve children. Afterward a writer in *Reedy's Mirror* poked fun at this; the mother of twelve would be an impossible heroine in fiction, he seemed to think. The point was rather ignorantly taken. It might reasonably be argued that any mother of twelve (in these days, at any rate) must be so exceptional as to deserve not merely a fictional but a biographical eminence. But as a matter of fact, Mrs. Porter was herself one of twelve children; and it is very evident from her account of her mother that Mrs. Stratton would have been a striking figure in fiction, perhaps too unusual to be believed in readily. As if further to controvert the jester in *Reedy's Mirror* we have Antonia Cuzak.

And, by the way, at the Cuzak farm there must now be a red-bordered flag, and the stars, in the heart of it must form a glorious constellation.

"Two Portraits," *Nation*, 107 (2 November 1918), 522–3

... [In *Camilla* Elizabeth] Robins affects the deliberate, elliptical, smooth-spoken post-Jacobite manner that appears to attract so many of the current women story-tellers, Mrs. Wharton leading the way. It touches snobbishness at both ends. It is too niggling and high-heeled for much real usefulness on this side of the water. A writer like Miss Cather is as clear of it as of the man-in-the-street patter of the magazine story-tellers (snobbishness at its nadir). Her style has distinction, not manner; and it is the style of an artist whose imagination is at home in her own land, among her own people, which happens to be a democratic land and a plain people. She has a strong feeling about this—that we cannot get away from our sources. One recalls how this is enforced in *The Song of the Lark*—how we were made to understand that Thea Kronborg's genius sprang from the soil of her birthplace. And one recognizes how directly this story, like *The Song of the Lark,* springs from Miss Cather's own soil. She was born in Virginia, but her childhood was passed on her father's ranch in Nebraska. During her most receptive years her nature was responding to the charm and mystery of the prairie, and also to her human setting. The pioneer neighborhood was mainly peopled by Scandinavians and Bohemians. Their exotic character and ways became a part of the child's America. Her three novels are stories of women: two of them Swedish-American girls, and the third, Ántonia, the child of a Bohemian immigrant. This is and professes to be (despite the publishers who inconceivably declare it "a love-story") nothing more or less than a portrait of a woman. The Shimerdas are a poor Bohemian family who have taken up a little Nebraskan farm. The father, a man of sensitive feeling, devoted to his own land, has come to America at the insistence of the vulgar and ambitious mother. He finds nothing to live for here, and takes his own life not long after their arrival. The girl Ántonia has his fineness of nature but a vigor and steadfastness also, of body and spirit, which fit her for conquest of life. Not in Thea Kronborg's way, by genius infallibly journeying upward, but by the commoner road of a strong and simple character not to be submerged by circumstance. We do not so much hear her story told as go with her upon her humble triumphant way, as farmhand, hired girl, woman befooled and deserted by the father of her first child, and at last as happy wife and drudge of a commonplace good little man of her own race, and mother of a great brood of healthy and rewarding offspring. Our guide upon this quiet pilgrimage is

the American who has been Ántonia's neighbor and playmate in childhood, and whose love for her, in his years of "success" in the great world, remains a feeling of peculiar depth and unlessening inspiration. In some sense, after all that has come between them, she is still "his Ántonia." "She was a battered woman now, not a lovely girl; but she still had that something which fires the imagination, could still stop one's breath for a moment by a look or gesture that somehow revealed the meaning in common things. . . . It was no wonder that her sons stood tall and straight. She was a rich mine of life, like the founders of early races." A notable portrait, rendered too quietly, perhaps, to catch the eye of the seeker for color and movement of the picturesque or dramatic order, but worthy to stand with *The Song of the Lark* among the best of our recent interpretations of American life.

C. L. H., "Struggles With the Soil," *New York Call Magazine*, 3 November 1918, p. 10

Antonia is not the conventional heroine. She never becomes an heiress, she uncovers no spy plot for the government, she never even dreams of the life of a Red Cross nurse, and she is no adventuress. She is a stalwart Bohemian peasant girl, grows up on a windy and barren Nebraska farm and helps her parents till the soil and make it fruitful.

We follow her through a difficult and picturesque childhood, see her emerge into a glowing and vital young womanhood, and by the end find her where such a vigorous and elemental person should be—on her farm, surrounded by a family of nine or ten children.

No less vivid and stirring than Antonia herself is the physical background of the story. The long and bitter winters, the scorching summers, the vast stretches of uncultivated prairies, the hard struggle against poverty and actual starvation—these things are described with a simplicity and directness that give us a real feeling of the actuality. We read much of the struggles of the foreigners in our big cities. This book gives us a picture of the grim and determined fight for life and prosperity of the vigorous foreigners who have settled in the West and helped to make it a land of fruitfulness. The story is a fresh and sincere piece of work.

Booklist, 15 (December 1918), 107

The prairie is the background for this narrative of the fortunes of a Bohemian girl as they were observed by an American boy who grew up on a neighboring farm and in the little Nebraska village. Stark realism gives a haunting quality to two grim scenes; others are not so grim but just as vivid. The whole gives an intimate friendship for the quiet, strong, simple Antonia with her own charm and power from childhood to contented middle age as the mother of her prairie children. It will not appeal to as many readers as *The Song of the Lark*.

H[enry] W[alcott] Boynton, *Bookman* (New York), 48 (December 1918), 495

Miss Cather is an accomplished artist. Her method is that of the higher realism; it rests not at all upon the machinery of dramatic action which is so right and essential for romance. Her *Song of the Lark*, a triumphal story if there ever was one, lacked the rounded artifice that lures a big public—lacked, above all, the conventional "happy ending." So does *My Antonia*, which, even more frankly a portrait than its predecessor, is a portrait of a woman.

Miss Cather has owned as among the most vivid of her experiences on the Nebraska ranch of her childhood, her impressions of the Scandinavian and Bohemian settlers who were among her neighbors. Thea Kronborg in *The Song of the Lark* was of Swedish parentage. Antonia is a Bohemian girl on a Nebraska ranch. Her father, a musician and dreamer, has no heart in the new life and presently kills himself as the only way out. The mother and the elder son are ambitious and unscrupulous. Antonia is the one well-rounded member of the family: somehow she joins her father's sensitiveness to the sturdiness of her mother, and contributes that magic something of her own that is necessary to transmute mere characteristics into personality.

She is not infallible or protected by a special Providence, does not push forward to an obvious success or happiness. On the contrary she passes her first years of grown girlhood as a farm worker, becomes a "hired girl" in the neighboring town, runs away with a flashy drummer who deserts her before the birth of her child, and later marries an undistinguished and not especially successful farmer of her own race. But she is unconquerable; and she lives through everything to transmit that superb health and courage of mind and body to a great family who are bound to make their worthy contribution to America. It is in this guise, as "a rich mine of life, like the founders of early races", that we see her fulfilled and justified.

Clearly, the effectiveness of such a portrait depends in an unusual sense upon the skill of the painter. Casual as her touches seem, no stroke is superfluous or wrongly emphasized; and we may be hardly conscious how much of the total effect of the portrait is owing to the quiet beauty and purity of the artist's style.

Randolph Bourne, "Morals and Art from the West," *Dial*, 65 (14 December 1918), 557

... Let us turn aside to a novel so different that it seems impossible that it could have been written in the same year and by an American from the same part of the country as William Allen White. Willa Cather has already shown herself an artist in that beautiful story of Nebraska immigrant life, *O Pioneers*! Her digression into *The Song of the Lark* took her into a field that neither her style nor her enthusiasm really fitted her for. Now in *My Antonia* she has returned to the Nebraska countryside with an enriched feeling and an even more golden charm of style. Here at last is an American novel, redolent of the Western prairie, that our most irritated

and exacting preconceptions can be content with. It is foolish to be captious about American fiction when the same year gives us two so utterly unlike, and yet equally artistic, novels as Mr. Fuller's *On the Stairs* and Miss Cather's *My Antonia*. She is also of the brevity school, and beside William Allen White's swollen bulk she makes you realize anew how much art is suggestion and not transcription. One sentence from Miss Cather's pages is more vivid than paragraphs of Mr. White's stale brightness of conversation. The reflections she does not make upon her characters are more convincing than all his moralizing. Her purpose is neither to illustrate eternal truths nor to set before us the crowded gallery of a whole society. Yet in these simple pictures of the struggling pioneer life, of the comfortable middle classes of the bleak little towns, there is an understanding of what these people have to contend with and grope for that goes to the very heart of their lives.

Miss Cather convinces because she knows her story and carries it along with the surest touch. It has all the artistic simplicity of material that has been patiently shaped until everything irrelevant has been scraped away. The story has a flawless tone of candor, a naive charm, that seems quite artless until we realize that no spontaneous narrative could possibly have the clean pertinence and grace which this story has. It would be cluttered, as Mr. White's novel is cluttered; it would have uneven streaks of self-consciousness, as most of the younger novelists' work, done impromptu with a mistaken ideal of "saturation," is both cluttered and self-conscious. But Miss Cather's even novel has that serenity of the story that is telling itself, of people who are living through their own spontaneous charm.

The story purports to be the memories of a successful man as he looks back over his boyhood on the Nebraska farm and in the little town. Of that boyhood Antonia was the imaginative center, the little Bohemian immigrant, his playmate and wistful sweetheart. His vision is romantic, but no more romantic than anyone would be towards so free and warm and glorious a girl. He goes to the University, and it is only twenty years later that he hears the story of her pathetic love and desertion, and her marriage to a simple Bohemian farmer, strong and good like herself. . . .

My Antonia has the indestructible fragrance of youth: the prairie girls and the dances; the softly alluring Lena, who so unaccountably fails to go wrong; the rich flowered prairie, with its drowsy heats and stinging colds. The book, in its different way, is as fine as the Irishman Corkery's *The Threshold of Quiet*, that other recent masterpiece of wistful youth. But this story lives with the hopefulness of the West. It is poignant and beautiful, but it is not sad. Miss Cather, I think, in this book has taken herself out of the rank of provincial writers and given us something we can fairly class with the modern literary art the world over that is earnestly and richly interpreting the spirit of youth. In her work the stiff moral molds are fortunately broken, and she writes what we can wholly understand.

N. P. D[awson], "Miss Cather's *My Ántonia*," *Globe and Commercial Advertiser* (New York), 11 January 1919

Verily, some authors make the life of the reviewer a very pleasant one. Last week it was Mr. Hergesheimer; this week it is Willa Sibert Cather. In *My Antonia*, Miss Cather multiplies many times the genius of one of her first novels, *O Pioneers*, another story of Nebraska and the middle west, with the American pioneers and foreign settlers. It has the fascination of Mr. Hudson's *Far Away and Long Ago*, and the striking originality of Conrad's *A Personal Record*. The only book we can recall that approaches it in the truthfulness and charm of its descriptions of the prairie country is a book published some years ago called *A Stepdaughter of the Prairie*.

But here we are writing of Miss Cather's book as if it were autobiography and not a story. Like most works of art, it is probably both. Miss Cather has the gift of remembering, and the equally important gift of forgetting, what is not important. She is a genuine realist. Her passion for the truth is apparently as great as her aversion for mere writing. If she is ever tempted to indulge in fine writing, she seems to follow the advice of the one who said, "be bold and murder your darlings." Nor does this mean that Miss Cather's narrative has any of the dullness and flatness and ugliness generally associated with realistic writing. With manifest fidelity to scene and character, and apparent simplicity and naturalness in the telling of the story, it is at the same time shimmering with romance and excitement. She can tell a bigger snake story, and a more horrifying one than Mr. Hudson: while her story of the Russian bride thrown to the wolves is as picturesque, shall we say, as Mr. Conrad's story of his heroic great-uncle who was with Napoleon and ate the Lithuanian dog. There are stories within stories, all as neatly unfolding as a set of Chinese boxes. There are many characters—living, breathing people.

But it is the description of the country itself that will perhaps most impress the reader, especially the reader who knows. It may be wondered if there is something in what Miss Cather says in her opening chapter about the freemasonry of people who come from the same parts of the country. If this is true, as we are inclined to think it is, some tears may well be felt for the new internationalism. A child's idea of Heaven is a place just like home. In an introduction, in which she cleverly and with art explains the male medium of her story-telling, Miss Cather says:

> We were talking about what it is like to spend one's childhood in little towns like these, buried in wheat and corn, under stimulating extremes of climate: burning summers when the world lies green and billowy beneath a brilliant sky, when one is fairly stifled in vegetation, in the color and smell of strong weeds and heavy harvests; blustery winters with little snow, when the whole country is stripped bare and gray as sheet iron. We agreed that no one who had not grown up in a little prairie town could know anything about it. It was a kind of freemasonry, we said.

Well, the country is here in all its variety; hot summer nights when "you can hear the corn grow," and not only winters that bluster, but winters that are real with the "big blizzard," when the snow is "spilled out of heaven, like thousands of feather beds, being emptied"—such feather beds as Mrs. Shimerda, the Bohemian woman, used to keep her roast goose hot in.

On the train carrying the small boy from Virginia to Nebraska to make his home with his grandparents—the same train bringing the Bohemian family with "my Antonia," we read that "the only thing very noticeable about Nebraska was

that it was still all day long Nebraska." There was nothing but land. In fact, it seemed "not a country at all, but the material out of which countries are made." "The grass was the country as the water is the sea," and the grass had "so much motion in it that the whole country seemed somehow to be running."

Bits of description such as these are not only incredibly vivid, but are poetic and excite the imagination. . . . It is a story of great truth and great beauty. More than this, it is interesting and will be enjoyed by those who never heard the corn grow or saw a prairie-dog town either.

Independent, 97 (25 January 1919), 131

To those who appreciate style in fiction, and for that quality alone can enjoy a story that has neither exciting plot nor swift action, Miss Cather's new book, *My Antonia*, will make strong appeal. With sympathy and understanding she tells a tale of youth and courage in the red grass region of Nebraska, when that part of our country was being settled by a large foreign immigration. The simple tale of growth centers about a Bohemian girl and an American lad, but Antonia is the main character. The story of her development thru the hardships of frontier life is full of human appeal and the fascination of the making of Americans from the foreign born.

H[enry] L[ouis] Mencken, "Sunrise on the Prairie: VII," *Smart Set*, 58 (February 1919), 143–4

Two new novels, *My Antonia*, by Willa Sibert Cather, and *In the Heart of a Fool*, by William Allen White bear out in different ways some of the doctrines displayed in the earlier sections of this article. Miss Cather's book shows an earnest striving toward that free and dignified self-expression, that high artistic conscience, that civilized point of view, which Dr. Brooks dreams of as at once the cause and effect of his fabulous "luminosity." Mr. White's shows the viewpoint of a chautaqua spell-binder and the manner of a Methodist evangelist. It is, indeed, a novel so intolerably mawkish and maudlin, so shallow and childish, so vapid and priggish, that its accumulated badness almost passes belief, and if it were not for one thing I should be tempted to spit on my hands and give it such a slating that the very hinges of this great family periodical would grow white-hot. That thing, that insidious dissuader, is not, I lament to report, a saving merit. It is something far different: it is an ineradicable suspicion that, after all, the book is absolutely American—that, for all its horrible snuffling and sentimentalizing, it is a very fair example of the sort of drivel that passes for "sound" and "inspiring" in our fair republic, and is eagerly praised by the newspapers, and devoured voraciously by the people. One may observe this taste sadly, but it is rather vain to rail against it. The leopard is chained to his spots, and the dog to his fleas. This is the aesthetic echo and reflection of Christian Endeavor

and the direct primary; this is what the public wants. And this is why the English sniff when they look our way.

I shall not afflict you with the details of the fable. It is, in essence the usual and inevitable thing of its kind. On the one side are the Hell Hounds of Plutocracy, and their attendant Bosses, Strike Breakers, Seducers, Nietzscheans, Free Lovers and Corrupt Journalists. On the other side are the great masses of the plain people, and their attendant Uplifters, Good Samaritans, Poor Working Girls, Inspired Dreamers and tin-horn Messiahs. These two armies join battle, the Bad against the Good, and for 500 pages or more the Good get all the worst of it. Their jobs are taken away from them, their votes are bartered, their women are debauched, their poor orphans are turned out to starve. But in the third from the last chapter someone turns on a rose spotlight, and then, one by one, the rays of Hope begin to shoot across the stage, and as the curtain falls the whole scene is bathed in luminous ether, and the professor breaks into "Onward, Christian Soldiers" on the cabinet-organ, and there is happy sobbing, and an upward rolling of the eyes and a vast blowing of noses. In brief, the finish of a chautauqua lecture on "The Grand Future of America, or The Glory of Service." Still more briefly, slobber.

It is needless to add that Dr. White is a member of the American Academy of Arts and Letters. Nor is it necessary to hint that Miss Cather is not. Invading the same Middle West that engages the Kansas tear-squeezer and academician, and dealing with almost the same people, she comes forward with a novel that is everything that his is not—sound, delicate, penetrating, brilliant, charming. I do not push the comparison for the mere sake of the antithesis. Miss Cather is a craftsman whom I have often praised in this place and with increasing joy. Her work, for ten years past, has shown a steady and rapid improvement, in both matter and manner. She has arrived at last at such a command of the mere devices of writing that the uses she makes of them are all concealed—her style has lost self-consciousness; her feeling for form has become instinctive. And she has got such a grip upon her materials—upon the people she sets before us and the background she displays behind them—that both take on an extraordinary reality. I know of no novel that makes the remote folk of the western prairies more real than *My Antonia* makes them, and I know of none that makes them seem better worth knowing. Beneath the swathings of balderdash, the surface of numskullery and illusion, the tawdry stuff of Middle Western *Kultur*, she discovers human beings embattled against fate and the gods, and into her picture of their dull struggle she gets a spirit that is genuinely heroic, and a pathos that is genuinely moving. It is not as they see themselves that she depicts them, but as they actually are. To representation she adds something more. There is not only the story of poor peasants, flung by fortune into lonely, inhospitable winds; there is the eternal tragedy of man.

My Antonia is the best American novel since *The Rise of David Levinsky* [by Abraham Cahan, 1917], as *In the Heart of a Fool* [1918] is probably one of the worst. There is something in it to lift depression. If such things can be done in America, then perhaps Dr. Brooks, if he lives to be 85, may yet get a glimpse of his luminosity. But what else is there to bolster up that hope? I can find nothing in the current crop.

H[enry] L[ouis] Mencken, "Mainly Fiction," *Smart Set*, 58 (March 1919), 140–1

The Cather story, *My Antonia*, was reviewed somewhat briefly in this place last month. It well deserves another notice, for it is not an isolated phenomenon, an extraordinary single book like Cahan's *The Rise of David Levinsky*, or Master's [sic] *Spoon River Anthology*, but merely one more step upward in the career of a writer who has labored with the utmost patience and industry, and won every foot of the way by hard work. She began, setting aside certain early experiments, with *Alexander's Bridge* in 1912—a book strongly suggesting the influence of Edith Wharton and yet thoroughly individual and newly thought out. Its defect was one of locale and people; one somehow got the feeling that Miss Cather was dealing with things at second-hand, that she knew her personages a bit less intimately than she should have known them. This defect, I venture to guess, impressed itself upon the author herself. At all events, she abandoned New England, in her next novel, for the Middle West, and in particular for the Middle West of the last great immigrations—a region far better known to her. The result was *O Pioneers!* (1913), a book of very fine achievement and of even finer promise. Then came *The Song of the Lark* in 1915—still more competent, more searching and convincing, better in every way. And now, after three years, comes *My Antonia*, a work in which improvement takes a sudden leap—a novel, indeed, that is not only the best done by Miss Cather herself, but also one of the best that any American has ever done, East or West, early or late. It is simple; it is honest; it is intelligent; it is moving. The means that appear in it are means perfectly adapted to its end. Its people are unquestionably real. Its background is brilliantly vivid. It has form, grace, good literary manners. In a word, it is a capital piece of writing, and it will be heard of long after the baroque balderdash now touted on the "book pages" is forgotten.

It goes without saying that all the machinery customary to that balderdash is charmingly absent. There is, in the ordinary sense, no plot. There is no hero. There is, save as a momentary flash, no love affair. There is no apparent hortatory purpose, no show of theory, no visible aim to improve the world. The whole enchantment is achieved by the simplest of all possible devices. One follows a poor Bohemian farm girl from her earliest teens to middle age, looking closely at her narrow world, mingling with her friends, observing the gradual widening of her experience, her point of view—and that is all. Intrinsically, the thing is sordid—the life is almost horrible, the horizon is leaden, the soul within is pitifully shrunken and dismayed. But what Miss Cather tries to reveal is the true romance that lies even there—the grim tragedy at the heart of all that dull, cow-like existence—the fineness that lies deeply buried beneath the peasant shell. Dreiser tried to do the same thing with both Carrie Meeber and Jennie Gerhardt, and his success was unmistakable. Miss Cather succeeds quite as certainly, but in an altogether different way. Dreiser's method was that of tremendous particularity—he built up his picture with an infinity of little strokes, many of them superficially meaningless. Miss Cather's method inclines more to suggestion and indirection. Here a glimpse, there a turn of phrase, and suddenly the thing stands out, suddenly

it is as real as real can be—and withal moving, arresting, beautiful with a strange and charming beauty. . . . I commend the book to your attention, and the author no less. There is no other American author of her sex. now in view, whose future promises so much. . . .

"Paper Dolls or People?" *Chicago Daily News,* 12 April 1919

Some books are written about paper dolls—cleverly designed and smartly painted and dressed, but flat. Close the book and they lie quietly between the pages until some young person takes them down ten years later and says, "How quaint!"

My Antonia, by Willa Sibert Cather, hasn't a paper doll in it. The people come out of it as you read it and refuse to be put back on the shelf with the book. They go about your work with you, and presently it seems as if you had known them well for a long time.

This quality of realness is important because *My Antonia* tells of the west, and there are novels in uncounted numbers about a pasteboard west, full of gaily colored "cut-out" cowboys shooting up towns, sugar plum western girls and torn paper blizzards. It is a west manufactured by writers who thought they had to make-believe or their stories would not be interesting, and it can be done perfectly by a man who was never outside New York. When it is done it isn't half as important as one of Grimm's fairy tales that doesn't even pretend to be real.

Willa Cather lived in Nebraska when she was a little girl. It was a west that the conventional wild west novels never hint at. Homesteaders were coming into the state from the east and from all over Europe. The prairie flowers were no more varied than the families whose claims cornered and who got their supplies and their mail from the same raw little town.

Bohemians and Russians, Virginians and Norwegians, found themselves neighbors. While they built their dugouts and turned under the sod for their first corn they had to learn each others' racial and individual peculiarities.

Sometimes they clashed tragically. Czech and Austrian found each other antagonistic; slow Swede and fiery Bohemian loved each other to their own hurt. Oftener each discovered that the other was marvelously human and like himself.

Under the common necessity of co-operating in house-building and harvesting and educating their children, something very like an informal league of nations resulted. In an amazingly short time the community became American, with common interests and a common language, but with possibilities of varied development that no thoroughbred race could by itself exhibit.

Not since the early colonial times when Spanish, Dutch, English and French were shouldering each other off the American coast has there been opportunity for such racial contact and interplay.

Miss Cather has had the rare good sense to see that the west of the old romantic yarns is dull and shoddy compared to the west that she understands and loves, and she has given us three novels of the west that stand alone in American literature.

O Pioneers, The Song of the Lark and My Antonia can be compared only with each other. They are wise and humorous and often beautiful, but, above all, real; and of the three My Antonia is most generous of its riches.

It is packed with the feel of the country. A scant paragraph sets you out on the plains, and the breadth of the wind that billows the long grass never leaves your face. The fragrance and color and significance of a whole fruiting orchard rises from another.

The people going about their heavy work and their adventurous play are not conventional bohunks and dagoes; they are not even conventional fathers of families or rascally money lenders or handsome girls. They are real people. You find yourself saying, "If I had lived out there these folks would actually have been my neighbors." And you proceed to wonder which of the girls you would have fallen in love with.

It is this trustworthiness that makes My Antonia and its companion books of extraordinary importance.

If you are looking for light on the minds of the people who are conducting absorbing political experiments on the western plains this winter; if you are homesick for a far-sweeping, simple country; or if—and that is most likely— you want to brush away stiff-jointed literary puppets and live for a while with real people, you will read and give thanks for My Antonia.

C[arl] E[ric] Bechhofer, "Impressions of Recent American Literature— IV," *Times Literary Supplement* (London), 23 June 1921, pp. 403–4

Every traveller to New York is assured by his friends there that he must not take that city as fully representative of America. He is warned that New York, a cosmopolitan centre, and the whole New England country (Boston, &c.) are not the real America at all; if he wants to find that, he is told, he must go inland, into that huge expanse, filled with innumerable towns and villages, which is known as the "Middle West." The student of literature is similarly told to direct his attention to the literary output of Chicago and the other Middle Western centres; the New York writers, he is told, are not as fully representative of the country as those who spring from its centre. The visitor may feel that this concern is exaggerated and that, whatever its deficiencies, New York is probably as representative of America as London, say, is of England; the claims of Manchester, for example, may occur to him as a parallel to those of Chicago. But, however this may be, it is certainly necessary to emphasize the claims of the Middle West to consideration in treating of the more recent literature of America.

The most interesting figures in contemporary American prose writing who belong definitely to the Middle West are Theodore Dreiser, Edgar Lee Masters, Willa Cather, Sinclair Lewis, and Sherwood Anderson. Of Dreiser's novels, which are the major part of his part, it is unnecessary to speak at length here, especially since a complete edition of them is expected to appear shortly in England. His erratic, prolix and yet monumental style is so American, so completely typical of the vast country from which he comes, that he is as much a cultural as a literary figure. Let anyone compare his first book, *Sister Carrie*, which was cut down to half its original size before appearance by some unknown editor, with any of his later works, and the difference will at once be seen between Dreiser as he would be, were he a European writer, and what he is as an American, not to say, a Middle

Westerner. An early incident in his life is typical of the man. He was once obliged to take the post of editor of a series of "dime novels" for a New York publishing house, and was given a number of long novelettes to reduce to a more economical length; the method he adopted was to split the manuscripts in two and write a new ending to the first part and a new beginning to the second, thus making two novelettes where there had before been only one. (The publishers, needless to say, were delighted at this doubling of their material.) As Mr. Mencken has pointed out in a sympathetic study of Dreiser's work—it may be mentioned that he was the prime mover in the protest movement against the suppression of Dreiser's *The Genius* at the instance of the Society for the Suppression of Vice— Dreiser has no notion whatever of such sophistications as verbal economy.

[. . .]

An English publisher would probably feel justified in cutting Dreiser's manuscripts and also, perhaps, would venture a protest against the amount of *clichés* that disfigure his writings. But these defects are characteristic of the man. An interesting glance at Dreiser's psychology may be gained from reading those works of his which are not novels, for example, his travel-books, *A Traveller at Forty*, in which he describes a tour in Europe; *A Hoosier Holiday*, an account of an automobile journey from New York to his early homes in Indiana; and his curious *Plays of the Natural and the Supernatural*. American friends who have helped me to form these impressions tell me that they find *A Hoosier Holiday* the most revealing of Dreiser's books; but for the English reader this place must be taken by *A Traveller at Forty*. On every page of his experiences in England, France, Italy, and Germany, one finds a touch of his naïve, broad, cumulative personality. He tells us of the tips he gave on board ship, and how he forgot to pack his rug, and similar trivialities, side by side with his reflections upon life in general and his often very interesting wayside encounters and conversations. With the last there is no need to concern ourselves here, but one must mention his occasional philosophic observations and his comparisons between Europe and America.

[. . .]

The key to so much that is Dreiserian is to be found in his racial ancestry. As he tells us in the same book, he had a German father, and his mother was of Pennsylvania Dutch extraction. "I am not English but radically American." This is indeed the essence of the man and of what he stands for in contemporary American life. He is the unconscious mouthpiece of the non-English population of America. The traditions of the leading cultural class, the Anglo-Saxon New Englanders, are strange and unsympathetic to him, as he is to those who hold them. He is essentially the voice of revolt against the English tradition in America, the representative of the vast, bewildered, latently powerful immigrant races that do not understand or do more than pretend to appreciate the current standards of American civilization. He stands for the Continental young America of the Middle West.

He is no longer a solitary voice. In the works of Miss Willa Cather the reader will find, expressed certainly in a very different manner, an emphasis laid upon other non-English American classes, the Scandinavian and Bohemian settlers. Miss Cather herself began her career in the Middle West. Her first stories were sent to a New York paper; and she was invited by a sympathetic editor to join its staff. Since then she has published several novels and collected a couple of volumes of short stories. Her first novel was *Alexander's Bridge*, quite a short book

dealing with Boston and London life; it is of no great importance. Soon after she began to write novels dealing with the early Swedish and Bohemian settlers in the Nebraska prairies, of which the best are *O Pioneers!* and *My Antonia*. Recently she has collected some of her previously published short stories dealing chiefly with artistic circles in New York, and they have appeared under the title of *Youth and the Bright Medusa*. Of her books, those dealing with the immigrants in Nebraska are by far the best. *O Pioneers!* describes the life of a Swedish settler's daughter and the tragic love of her brother Emil for a beautiful Bohemian girl, Marie Tovesky. *My Antonia* (the accent is on the first syllable of the name) is a tale told by Jim Burden, a lawyer from the Middle West. Taken to the West as a child, he travels on the same train as a family of Bohemian immigrants, the Shimerdas, who have a daughter Antonia. The two children grow up together amidst the hardships of the settlers' life. Their ways part at last; poor Antonia is seduced by a scoundrelly Irish railwayman, but afterwards she marries a decent farmer of her own people and has a family of fine, healthy children. It is a simple tale, but full of charm and interest; besides Antonia's own experiences, we read of those of other Bohemian girls, her friends, who, though despised by the Anglo-Saxon inhabitants of the country (but not by their young men), succeed none the less in bringing a certain Continental atmosphere of gaiety and vitality into the arid existence of the Middle West. There are many excellent descriptions of life and people in the two books—of the French fair, for example, in *O Pioneers!* and of the Bohemian family, some Russian settlers, and a blind negro musician in *My Antonia*.

[. . .]

It is Miss Cather's high achievement in

these two books that she has brought out the beauty and the majesty of her country; as Dreiser in his works has shown us its strength and its bulk. To read their books is to be made to understand what racial contrasts and incongruities are contained in modern American life, until at last the old idea of the "melting-pot" seems less a romantic fact than a prosaic aspiration. The immigrants may change, as Miss Cather shows them to do, their national songs and dresses for vulgar rag-time ditties and ugly "waists," but there are certain spiritual qualities that they cannot lose.

Nebraska State Journal (Lincoln), 9 October 1921

The *Red Cloud Argus* has the following concerning a Nebraskan who has become famous in the world of letters:

It always gives us much pleasure when some reader of the *Argus* here on a visit calls at the office for a friendly chat because of the feeling that those who read the paper and those who are charged with its preparation belong to one big family. Naturally we were especially pleased when last Friday Miss Willa Cather, whose address is New York City, but who is at home in Red Cloud, New York, London, Paris, or any other city on earth in which she happens to be, called at this office for that reason. Miss Cather is enjoying a several weeks' visit with her parents, Mr. and Mrs. C. F. Cather.

While her work has called her to other scenes Miss Cather told us that there is not any place in this world that is more interesting to her than Red Cloud. She came here from Virginia with her parents when a child and here grew to womanhood, graduating from the local high school. During part of her course she wrote school items for the *Argus*, which may have been her first contributions to the public press. In those days she was often called upon to stay in her father's office while he was at the courthouse making abstracts or was out of the city on other business. She had her own desk in the office, and here she did much studying and writing. But the matter which she deems of greatest importance in this connection was the acquaintance formed with leaders in the life of the community who, calling to transact business with her father, remained to visit with her, telling her of personal affairs in the way that grownups will disclose to a child, matters which they would not disclose with a mature person. Often she accompanied Dr. Damerell or Dr. McKeeby on their long trips into the country, and listened with childish admiration as they talked on a variety of subjects from their personal experiences. There were no trained nurses here in those days, so sometimes she was called upon to assist them with surgical operations. In the best homes of the city she was always a welcome visitor. Red Cloud had many men and women of exceptional ability. Miss Cather looks back to her association with these as one of the brightest and most helpful periods of her life.

But the time came when it was necessary that she leave her home and friends. Greater opportunities in other places called her. Times were hard in Nebraska. Her father had acquired large holdings of land, but these were not producing enough revenue to pay the taxes. She could not be contented to stay here and depend upon her parents for support. But the thought of leaving her family and friends who meant so much to her, was almost too much and she confessed during her visit the other day that at one time she was actually on the point of giving up, when some words of timely counsel from Mr. and Mrs. O. C. Case gave her new courage and led her to go on with her plans for self-improvement.

The interest which has been felt by Red Cloud people in *My Antonia*, many of the scenes of which are laid in this city, led us to turn the conversation to that subject. Three characters of the story Miss Cather said, were intended as comparatively faithful pictures of citizens of Red Cloud about 1888 or 1890. These were the author's grandparents, whose charertistics made a deep impression upon her youthful mind when she first came here from Virginia, and Mrs. J. L. Miner—the Mrs. Harling of the book, in whose home she was frequently a guest. In the first draft of the story the picture of Mrs. Harling was of a very different character. While the manuscript was being revised by the author, news came to her of Mrs. Miner's death. So profound an impression did this make upon her, and so active were the memories of old times brought to mind by the news that she made changes in some parts of the book in honor of her friend of early days.

Another character in the book, she informed us, was in part a picture of a former Red Cloud man and in part of a man she had known in the east. For some reason, she said this treatment of a character is a very natural one for an author to give. We inquired if this were not because the life of the average person is so commonplace that a faithful delineation of him alone would not make interesting reading. Miss Cather wholly disagreed with this view. She contended that the average person has just as interesting emotions and experiences as public personages. She knew Red Cloud people whose experiences were no less intense and thrilling than those of the public personages with whom she was well acquainted. She found people here just as interesting as those she met in London and Paris, altho in a different way. She summed up the matter by saying that if a person is wide awake and not self centered he can see those interesting things in the life of those about him.

My Antonia has been translated into a number of different languages, has had a very large sale. Miss Cather is very familiar with the French tongue, and was able to revise the manuscript after the translator had completed his work in that language. This gentleman was very scholarly man and in the main did excellent work, but he was a little handicapped by never having lived in the prairie states. Miss Cather found that when he came to the word "gopher" at various places in the book he had used the French word meaning "mole." This might have passed among the French readers had it not been for a passage where the gophers were spoken of as playing in the sun.

Miss Cather writes of Nebraska, not from any sense of duty, but because her early life was so bound up with this commonwealth that this part of the world is of greatest interest to her. She has just completed a new book, some of the scenes of which are laid in this part of the state.

Harry Hanson, "The First Reader: *My Antonia* Revised," *The World* (New York) [Summer 1926]

The publication of a new and revised edition of *My Antonia*, by Willa Cather is as much an event in the world of books as if a new work by this author were spread upon the records; moreover, it gives an opportunity for directing attention to the fact that few books of the last ten years have surpassed it in originality, in truth and in vitality. It belongs to the basic foundation of our new literature.

But the reader may well ask: "How revised?" What has Miss Cather done to it? Can an author touch up a masterpiece? It is true that George Moore's revisions have gained in felicity; but even so, did the man of sixty have the right to tinker with the work of the man of twenty? And Miss Cather, whose painstaking attention to detail is well known—what of her?

So we may say at the outset that Miss Cather has left the body of the story untouched but rewritten the introduction, in which she meets Jim Burden and prepares to hear his tale of Antonia. And the Houghton, Mifflin Company has increased the white margin a bit, and made some other changes, but left the plates after Chapter I alone. Let us fall to.

This examination may prove profitable to students of writing; it may also mean an excursion into an author's mind.

Miss Cather's original opening sentence read: "Last summer I happened to be crossing the plains of Iowa in a season of intense heat, and it was my good fortune to have for a traveling companion James Quayle Burden—Jim Burden, as we still call him in the West."

Her revised opening reads: "Last summer, in a season of intense heat, Jim Burden and I happened to be crossing Iowa on the same train."

Score one for the author.

Then comes the story of Jim Burden's wife. The author explains in the original edition that she sees little of Jim Burden in New York,—that he is a busy man; moreover, "I do not like his wife."

Then in the original edition Miss Cather embarked on a description of the wife and her activities. She gave her name, told how she was jilted by her cousin, and that "she gave one of her town houses for a Suffrage headquarters, produced one of her own plays at the Princess Theatre, was arrested for picketing during a garment-makers' strike," etc. On the next page followed a characterization of Jim Burden—his faith in the West, his ability to raise money for new enterprises and his passion for hunting and exploring. We learned about Jim that "his fresh color and sandy hair and quick-changing blue eyes are those of a young man, and his sympathetic, solicitous interest in women is as youthful as it is Western and American."

It is here that Miss Cather has made the most drastic changes. The description of Jim's wife must have seemed superfluous to her, for she has boiled it down to one paragraph. She drops the specific and adheres to the essentials of her character. The keynote of the wife's personality is retained: "She is handsome, energetic, executive, but to me she seems unimpressionable and temperamentally incapable of enthusiasm."

The reference to her activities with Suffrage workers (already becoming history), theatres and the like is now revised to these general terms: "She finds it worth while to play the patroness to a group of young poets and painters of advanced ideas and mediocre abilities."

When the author approaches Jim Burden she exercises similar economy. The specific traits of his character are brought down to two or three generalizations. He has a romantic disposition, loves the country—"his faith in it and his knowledge of it have played an important part in its development." We are not to be sidetracked by the troubles of Jim Burden and his family.

Throughout the introduction Miss Cather has taken out the "dates," and worked for essentials. The new introduction is shorter than the old by three pages.

The physical changes in the new edition are slight, but may be worth noting for the use of collectors. Assuming that the collector has read the book—and Mitchell Kennerley, I believe, has known some who actually did read books—he will observe that the new edition stands a quarter of an inch higher on the shelf and that this gives a wider margin to the page. The story is no longer by Willa Sibert Cather but by Willa Cather. The seal of Houghton, Mifflin Company—"tout bien ou rien"—has been placed on the outside cover. Inside, one discovers that the new edition lists all the other books by Miss Cather, although at least five are published by another house. This generosity shows how far Boston is behind the times.

But what a fine excuse this new edition gives for rereading this splendid book! *My Antonia* has the great quality of an impeccable style. The theme is married to the method. The language is redolent of the soil, clean-cut American writing, and yet dignified. It pulsates with the life of the people it describes.

Such an examination of life makes all argument about method futile. In any book the mind of the author, as it filters through his medium, is the thing. Confronted with a book like this, what care we for arguments about impressionistic writing, coherence or incoherence, or literature as an olfactory art? Like the great prairies of the West, *My Antonia* is an ineradicable part of the American scene.

Checklist of Additional Reviews

Elia W. Peattie, "Miss Cather Writes Exceptional Novel in *My Antonia*," [Omaha *World-Herald*, 1918], clipping in Faulkner-Slote Collection, University of Nebraska Library, Lincoln.

YOUTH AND THE BRIGHT MEDUSA

YOUTH
AND THE BRIGHT MEDUSA

BY

WILLA CATHER

"We must not look at Goblin men,
We must not buy their fruits;
Who knows upon what soil they fed
Their hungry, thirsty roots?"

Goblin Market

NEW YORK

ALFRED · A · KNOPF

MCMXX

"Short Story Art and Artifice," *Nation*, 111 (25 September 1920), 352–3

Miss Willa Cather has worked at herself and her art. Today the product is finished and represents the triumph of mind over Nebraska. This is no jest. Consider even the sounder of our writers from the "great valley" and beyond—William Allen White, Vachel Lindsey. How gifted they are and how incurably provincial. Miss Cather started out, fortunately, not only with a burning sense of beauty, but with a really honest mind. She settled in Greenwich village and was able to separate its wheat from its tares. Her vision has come to be of an intense and naked clearness and she herself one of our few thoroughly serious artists.

The form no less than the substance of these stories bears witness to a fine self-discipline. It has neither the French nor the contemporary American short-story mechanism. The fable is driven neither toward a sting nor toward a burst of rose-color. The structural line is long and firm; it is never broken by a moral timidity in the guiding hand. As a result the stories have the radiance of perfect cleanliness, like the radiance of burnished glass. The style has not yet been burned quite clean. There are still patches of magazine English —unvisualized similes, pulpy adjectives. But Miss Cather knows exactly the effect she is after, spare yet imaginative, sensuous yet cool. And at times, as in the young painter's vision through the magic knot-hole in his wall, she achieves it completely.

The theme of her stories is the life of art, specifically of music. Or, rather, it is the life of art as contrast, criticism, symbol, refuge, as the one imaginable escape for an American from ugliness to beauty, from bondage to freedom. Among the earlier stories here gathered "Paul's Escape" strikes a key-note of the artistic soul's escape from Pittsburg into a brief light and then into death, since death is a nobler consummation than such a murder of a soul by a Nebraska village as is described in "A Wagner Matinee." In the later stories the protagonists have made their escape: fully and magnificently and with a fine pagan flourish and melancholy, too, in "Coming, Aphrodite"; partially in "The Diamond Mine," since Columbus does break down and corrupt the life of Cressida Garnet in the end; with a touch of conscious defiance through which the chain still clanks a little in "A Gold Slipper," with its superb embodiment of the adversary, the Philistine, the righteous man in the beefy soul and furtive dreams and final poverty of Marshal McKann. The debate between him and Kitty Ayrshire in the Pullman car is a triumphant statement of the book's central thought— an American debate between the body and the soul, in which the soul is not yet wholly liberated but still feels as though heavy earth were strewn upon its wings. Thus Miss Cather's book is more than a random collection of excellent tales. It constitutes as a whole one of the truest as well as, in a sober and earnest sense, one of the most poetical interpretations of American life that we possess.

Blanche Colton Williams, "A New Book of Stories," *Bookman* (New York), 52 (October 1920), 169–70

Discriminating readers find confirmation of their taste in the recent pronouncement of an English novelist, who places among three American writers highest in achievement the name of Willa Cather. Although Miss Cather reaches the public chiefly through her novels, her initial success was in the field of the short story. Just fifteen years ago appeared her slender volume, *The Troll Garden*. Now, under a title beguiling and provocative, are reprinted four stories from this early collection, with three from *McClure's*, *Harper's*, and *The Century*, and a single new one, "Coming, Aphrodite!"

Patently, the tales are the work of an artist sensitive to the rhythm of prose; significantly, with the exception of "The Sculptor's Funeral," they are about musicians. There is unmoral Eden Bower, of flawless physical beauty, "a vision out of Alexandria, out of the remote pagan past." There is her foil, generous hardworked Cressida Garnett, whose relatives regarded her as "a natural source of wealth; a copper vein, a diamond mine." There is Kitty Ayrshire, heroine of "A Gold Slipper" and "Scandal." So capitally conceived and portrayed are these prima donnas as to suggest the hand of the biographer and to set speculation alert for prototypes. "Scandal" is of particular merit in its apparently casual study of Siegmund Stein, clever in its manipulation of indirection as was that gentleman himself. His picture, formed through the superposition of two films, springs fully into life-likeness only with the final adjustment. When "Scandal," was first published (1919) one editor ranked it first of the year's short stories. But for a topheavy introduction, it would be well-nigh perfect, as a sketch.

For if these later tales, which compose two-thirds of the book, receive their meed of applause as literature, they will be judged not as short stories. Literature is greater than any of its forms, and of this entire volume there can be no question of the literary value. The author perceives life from many angles, all subsidiary to her comprehensive outlook; she has the faculty of getting under the skin of each character, or of speaking from his mouth; she is economical, therefore powerful, in her management of action, interaction and contrast; she succeeds remarkably in conveying the sense of detachment which the "different" from their kind experience. But these excellencies are of the novelist, the novelist of *O Pioneers!* and *My Antonia*. "The Diamond Mine" is a condensed novel; the other three numbers might be tentative studies for novels, or preliminary sketches, like the drawings of Leonardo. Character, not narrative, is the final residuum. Miss Cather's *Alexander's Bridge* spans the gap between her short stories and her novels; these new essays in fiction are on the hither side.

The cleavage between her earlier and later work is clearly marked. "Paul's Case," "A Death in the Desert," "A Wagner Matinee," and the incident of the sculptor's funeral (all from *The Troll Garden*) have the essentials of the short story as the later sketches have not. They are dear to some of us for their pathos, dealt out with Thackerayan reserve, in the behavior of the aunt at Grand Opera after a quarter century, in the comfort the dying singer found in the double of the man she loved, in the tragedy of Paul and his sacrifice to beauty. Paul breaks through language and escapes, a flesh and blood brother of Andreyev's "Little Angel." This story, bearing witness to the author's career as teacher, reveals her development out of the materials of life. In this development she has advanced a long way. And if in her new stories she chooses to run the gamut of emotion, it is doubtless because she has surrendered the easier appeal to feeling for the more difficult challenge to the intellectual and the æsthetic.

"Latest Works of Fiction: Miss Cather's Stories," *New York Times Book Review*, 3 October 1920, p. 24

If Willa Cather had written nothing except "Coming, Aphrodite!" the first of the eight stories in her *Youth and the Bright Medusa*, there could be no doubt of her right to rank beside the greatest creative artists of the day. This pagan paean to Beauty, symbolized in the love story of an artist and written with exquisite sympathy, is a veritable Koh-i-noor in the rhinestone and paste tiara of contemporary literature. All clamorers at the gates of art who have bitterly felt the sting of worldly success withheld will want to lay wreaths of gratitude at the author's feet for the artistry with which her story has given voice to that loneliness of spirit which is the ultimate tragedy of their lives.

The theme of this story—youths' adventure with the many-colored Medusa of art—runs like a golden thread through the entire collection, a thread so dazzling that delight in its gleam swept the reviewer away from sobriety of expres-

sion into a mood of molten appreciation that made him grab a sheet of notepaper and write to a friend, "Don't fail to read Willa Cather's latest book if you have to beg the price of it." And facile enthusiasms are not one of his weaknesses; out of the last hundred books of fiction he has reviewed for these columns not one has moved him to unreserved praise.

"Coming, Aphrodite!" is a gem so bright that it glitters even in the setting of its companions, every one of which has power to compel admiration from all readers who appreciate a writer's ability to bare the very veins of human emotion. "The Diamond Mine," the story of an opera singer's life, is equally rich in illuminating phrases and flashes of bold, imaginative insight. In it, Miss Cather gives us in a single adjective a flashlight picture of a great heart, presents in each sentence a page from a tragic career. The restless quality of her imagination and the uncompromising truthfulness of her analysis enable her so vividly to bottle up in a paragraph the essence of a character that her word portraits are unforgettably limned upon the reader's mind.

"A Gold Slipper" and "Scandal" also reconstruct chapters from the life of a prima donna, not the same singer who figures in "The Diamond Mine," but a woman the original of whom will be recognized by many American music lovers. The four remaining stories in the book, "Paul's Case," "A Wagner Matinee," "The Sculptor's Funeral," and "A Death in the Desert," are reprinted from the author's first book of stories, which appeared in 1905 under the title of *The Troll Garden*. With the possible exception of "The Sculptor's Funeral," they are not as fine as the first two stories in the present collection, but they are yet sketches of which any writer might well be proud.

Youth and the Bright Medusa is decidedly a literary event which no lover of the best fiction will want to miss.

Edmund Lester Pearson, "Old Books and New," *Weekly Review*, 3 (13 October 1920), 314

Sex is a great subject for fiction; murder is a great subject for fiction; war is a great subject for fiction. We all agree that books about murder and books about war may become tiresome; how is it that so many young writers do not understand that just at present books about sex have become a little tiresome?

As soon as the preceding sentence was written, my remark was in a sense confuted, and I was shown what a mistake it is ever to denounce any class of books, or to attempt to draw the line about the subjects. It is all a matter of the individual book, of the author's treatment of the subject. It is certain that there are many other readers besides myself who are fed up with stories about passionate love affairs in which the lovers have dispensed with the church's blessing, and even with a magistrate's sanction. There is probably no other type of story with which we are so actually gorged, in magazines, in novels, or on the stage, as those concerning "artists," actresses, and singers, living in the vicinity of Washington Square. And then—-along comes Miss Willa Cather, and in the first story in her new book, *Youth and the Bright Medusa*, writes a tale about all these hackneyed subjects, and does it with such firmness, delicacy, and appreciation of the beauty and warmth of passion that you resolve never to indulge again in generalizations.

"An Artist in the Short Story," *World Tomorrow*, 3 (November 1920), 351

The Bright Medusa is art; and each story in the collection deals with some phase of youth's many adventures with art—and life. Whether delicately and by implication or strongly and directly, the stories are all tragic. There is an undercurrent, too, of that disillusion which is inseparable from the tragedies of youth.

Miss Cather is one of a small group of American authors who are producing literature of a high type and adding to the literary laurels of America in Europe. She is an artist with a sure touch in moulding a plot and depicting a motive. The longer stories here—"Coming, Aphrodite" and "The Diamond Mine"—are consummate in both respects. The shorter stories are nicely polished examples of short-story art. Indeed, the book is meat for several pleasurable hours.

Henry Louis Mencken, "Chiefly Americans," *Smart Set*, 63 (December 1920), 139–40

... The book is made up of eight stories, and all of them deal with artists. It is Miss Cather's peculiar virtue that she represents the artist in terms of his own thinking—that she does not look *at* him through a peep-hole in the studio-door, but looks *with* him at the life that he is so important and yet so isolated and lonely a part of. One finds in every line of her writing a sure-footed and civilized culture; it gives her an odd air of foreignness, particularly when she discusses music, which is often. Six of her eight stories deal with musicians. One of them, "Coming, Aphrodite!" was published in this great moral periodical last August. Another, "Scandal," was printed in *The Century* during the Spring, to the envious rage of Dr. Nathan, who read it with vast admiration and cursed God that it had escaped these refined pages. Four others are reprinted from *The Troll Garden*, a volume first published fifteen years ago. These early stories are excellent, particularly "The Sculptor's Funeral," but Miss Cather has learned a great deal since she wrote them. Her grasp upon character is firmer than it was; she writes with much more ease and grace; above all, she has mastered the delicate and difficult art of evoking the feelings. A touch of the maudlin lingers in "Paul's Case" and in "A Death in the Desert." It is wholly absent from "Coming, Aphrodite!" and "Scandal," as it is from *My Antonia*. These last indeed, show utterly competent workmanship in every line. They are stories that lift themselves completely above the level of current American fiction, even of good fiction. They are the work of a woman who, after a long apprenticeship, has got herself into the front rank of American novelists, and is still young enough to have her best writing ahead of her. I call *My Antonia* to your attention once more. It is the finest thing of its sort ever done in America.

E. A. B., *Freeman*, 2 (1 December 1920), 286

The constant preoccupation of the alert minority which is making literature in this country is the relationship between America and the artist. The last few years have witnessed a remarkable crystallization of opinion in a definite consciousness of the conflict between what are known as "American ideals" and æsthetic values. More and more articulate becomes a generation of writers who declare that Americanism, as popularly understood, is absolutely incompatible with the development of the artist. One can not imagine a work of art whose creator could be described by that grotesque phrase, one hundred per cent American. The term might fully describe an eminent automobile builder, a wealthy purveyor of "glad fiction" or the prophet of some pseudophilosophy at ten cents a word, but never a creative genius in literature, music or painting. A whole literature is growing up which is nothing less than a prolonged narrative of the plight of the artist, of the individual, in a civilization which has never contemplated such phenomena and has so little use for them that it can actually destroy them out of pure kindness. In Miss Cather's new book this conflict is the theme, and it might just as well have been entitled *America and the Bright Medusa*, were it not for the exigencies of a work of fiction, which could not be handicapped with a title suitable for a volume of essays. The author illustrates in a series of stories the adventures of the Medusa of art in the wilderness of successful Americanism. There are eight chapters of which the last four are reprinted from Miss Cather's first book. Without this information it would not have been difficult to guess that an interval of the richest development separated the first and last halves of this volume. Miss Cather's strength has grown considerably since she left her early efforts so far behind as to write "Coming, Aphrodite!" Without a superfluous word or an ounce of sentimentality she tells here the story which has tempted a hundred others, the story of two young artists in a Washington Square garret, Don Hedger, the painter, and Eden Bower, the singer, who drift together, love for a passionate interlude, and then drift apart. The thing is told with the utmost skill, and the deftest effects of descriptive incident. The two contrasted personalities are projected as firmly in a few strokes as if a whole novel had been filled with the details of their careers. There runs all through the story the undercurrent of antagonism to the creative artist which is superbly described in "A Gold Slipper." Here Miss Cather analyses the reactions of a typical business man who attends a concert given by a prodigal daughter of America on her return to her own people from her European triumphs. The national soul as mirrored by Mr. E. W. Howe is again reflected in Miss Cather's vastly more subtle pages. Miss Willa Cather is, therefore, at one with the most distinguished of her contemporaries in her indictment of Americanism. It would be idle to deny the force of this general complaint, but is there not an element of illusion in the alleged superiority of older countries? The commercialized artist here has no keener competitor than the European visitor, whose desire for dollars enables him to dissimulate his unjustified contempt for his American patrons. In these stories of Miss Cather's, and elsewhere in fiction and essay, the desolating blight of small-town life, and the crass ignorance of the business bourgeoisie, are depicted. But what of Flaubert's Homais, of Bouvard and Pécuchet? Are they not also one

hundred percenters? Octave Mirbeau has exposed the horrors of middle-class French life, as Maupassant has described the brutal peasantry. There is a danger in overlooking the universality of the conditions against which literary America is in reaction. The bright Medusa is no less an object of suspicion amongst the mass of Europeans than in those communities which Miss Cather has so well described.

Orlo Williams, *Athenaeum* (London), no. 4731 (31 December 1920), 890

This book contains eight stories of different lengths by one who—as recorded in our "Literary Gossip" of the 10th inst.— is an American writer of considerable reputation. One of the stories, "Paul's Case," seems to be the clue to this reputation, and no wonder, as the delightful green wrapper tells us, it has been "studied, imitated and plagiarized" by young writers. Paul is the adolescent son of a respectable citizen who lives in Cordelia Street, Pittsburgh, where on Sunday afternoons the burghers in their shirt-sleeves and with waistcoats unbuttoned discuss the prices of things or the sagacity of their commercial chiefs. Church, Sabbath school picnics, petty economics, wholesome advice, how to succeed in life and the smell of cooking nauseate Paul. In music and surreptitious attendance on the performances of a stock company he finds the glamour which banishes the nausea of daily mechanical existence. Cut off from this and put into an office, he makes off one fine day with a thousand dollars, spends the money in one delicious week of luxurious, not depraved, life in a great New York hotel, and, at the end, goes out into the snow and jumps in front of a train. Paul, one feels, is a whole section of America, the largest section, perhaps, of which none of us in England has any conception. Paul stands for their men; and for their women stands Aunt Georgiana, who, brought in her old age to a Wagner concert, sobbed, " I don't want to go."

I understood. For her, just outside the concert hall, lay the black pond with the cattle-tracked bluffs; the tall, unpainted house, with weather-curled boards, naked as a tower; the crook-backed ash seedlings where the dish-cloths hung to dry; the gaunt, moulting turkeys picking up refuse about the kitchen door.

When she sees these things Miss Cather is strong; she has known the prison of the West and speaks of it with bitter indignation. From *her* lips comes Jim Laird's denunciation of his fellow-townsmen gathered round the coffin of the great sculptor who had broken away; hers is the regret of Katherine Gaylord dying in the sandy desert of Cheyenne. One can only gaze with pity and admiration at the vast commotion in America's bosom to which such stories as these and the early poignant chapters of Ella Wheeler Wilcox's autobiography bear witness. Here, in the vast wilderness, in the little townships, in the grimy cities, is growing a mighty protest against the sordidness of existence. Much that is comic, much that is cheap, comes of this protest; but more has come and will come. Already this is the public to which astute literary agents are looking: it is they who buy the multitudes of hasty translations of foreign books and from whom American professors of English can earn bread by books on literary process which would not sell a hundred copies in England. It is

all still vast, formless and pathetic, this yearning after the "bright Medusa," but there are a force and a power behind it for which we may look in vain in this old country.

The last four stories in this book have been mentioned: they are early ones, now reprinted: the first four are longer and more ambitious, but not so strong. Miss Cather has the "bright Medusa" by the hair now, but is not yet Perseus. She turns her gaze from the sordid, yearning West to the glamour of the successful artist, but often betrays her origin by such little things as writing of "Eaton" jackets and putting American-French phrases into the mouth of a Bohemian who is supposed to speak French well. But her real short-coming is that she is at present quite without a "style": placed beside any European model of imaginative prose she is dowdy and rough, wanting in rhythm and distinction. Her longest story, "The Diamond Mine," is a truly fine idea, but quite inadequately carried out. In the career of the great singer, who supported in turn four husbands, besides a Greek accompanist and a greedy, jealous family, there is as our green wrapper truthfully avers a whole novel. But oh, how far is Miss Cather from having written it!

Francis Hackett, "Miss Cather's Short Stories," *New Republic*, 25 (19 January 1921), 233–4

From Miss Cather's novels one receives a powerful impression of direct experience. In Nebraska, the Nebraska of the prairie, of Swedes and Bohemians and French and Russians, one feels she is thoroughly and deeply at home. She is not a restless analyst. Out of the strong women whom she delights to portray she seems above everything eager to write an epic, an epic of lonely struggle and staunch character, wistfulness of beauty and fidelity to dream. Her novels belong to the New World as it existed on the stubborn frontier, but the glamour in them is the glamour of the Old World reborn in the eye of the sunset, in the Old World with its music and its poesy, its passionate temperaments, its society, its color. It is as an insider she speaks of the quiet old European mothers who want only to grow a garden, the sensitive European father who was a handworker and does not understand the untamed nature of the plains. And it is as an insider she writes of youth in the sod-houses and log-houses, in the wet pastures, and on the lonely frost-ridged roads. The bleak cemeteries of those new communities are immemorial in her compassionate chronicles. She is one of the few American novelists who has really traced the cycle of the later non-English pioneers.

When it comes to this volume of short stories Miss Cather appears definitely to have moved East. She has come, in a sense, to an assuagement of the nostalgia which penetrates the Nebraskan stories—a nostalgia which the unity of beauty is supposed to end. All her main characters in *Youth and the Bright Medusa* are men and women, especially women, who suck the honey of beauty and build its honeycomb. The uncouth background from which they come to scuplture and music is no longer defined with tenderness. A fierce resentment is poured by Miss Cather into "The Sculptor's Funeral" and "A Gold Slipper" and "A Wagner Matinee." "Paul's Case" goes no farther back to the "raw, biting ugliness" of the frontier than Pittsburgh, but there too is "the yearning of a boy, cast ashore upon a desert of newness and ugliness and sordidness, for all that is chastened and old, and noble with traditions." This yearning, however, turns to criticism and didacticism only in two stories. It is not in Miss Cather's staid spirit to insist on her moral. And her moral, in most cases, is not an argument as to the frontier but an escape to lives preoccupied with something besides land.

Her real fellowship is with artists, successful and unsuccessful, genuine and meretricious. But what seems to interest Miss Cather about Eden Bower (Eden Bowers), Cressida Garnet, Kitty Ayrshire, Katharine Gaylord, is not so much their art as their career. Their art is, after all, a medium of self-expression. The character that is employed inside that medium is the thing on which Miss Cather unfailingly concentrates. Hence, though the fascination of sculptors and opera singers and artists is evidently the magnet of these stories, the essence of them is the interplay of character and happiness. It is Miss Cather's gift to make much of this interplay.

Cressida Garnet is "the diamond mine" exploited by her sour family, her four husbands, her profession, her spoiled son. "A beautiful soundness of body, a seemingly exhaustless vitality, and a certain 'squareness' of character as well as of mind, gave Cressida Garnet earning powers that were exceptional even in her lavishly rewarded profession." This type, which appeals to Miss Cather, does not preclude her amused understanding of the capable opportunist Eden Bower. "People like Eden Bower are inexplicable. Her father sold farming machinery in Huntington, Illinois, and she had grown up with no acquaintances or experiences outside of that prairie town. Yet from her earliest childhood she had not one conviction or opinion in common with the people about her,—the only people she

106

knew. Before she was out of short dresses she had made up her mind that she was going to be an actress, that she would live far away in great cities, that she would be much admired by men and would have everything she wanted." And she does. Her Chicago capitalist, "the most circumspect of bachelors," she manages perfectly. Her only aberration is the artist Don Hedger, whom she tries to make successful. That aberration, with Don Hedger's peep-hole courtship, is joyfully imagined by Miss Cather, even to Coney Island and Washington Square and the Brevoort and the flock of pigeons "from somewhere in the crowded Italian quarter to the south."

The ironies of the artistic temperament are scrutinized not only in Blasius Bouchelka, Cressida's wild-eyed husband who becomes tame and fat in prosperity, and in Paul, who commits suicide after one glorious week of escape to the Waldorf Astoria; but also in the drunken lawyer who perorates at the sculptor's funeral and in Siegmund Stein, the "deep, mysterious Jew" who invented an affair with an opera star and whose "business associates thought him a man of taste and culture, a patron of the arts, a credit to the garment trade."

Miss Cather's incisive description of this gentleman whose motto was substitution is worth quoting. "He is one of the most hideous men in New York, but it's not at all the common sort of ugliness that comes from over-eating and automobiles. He isn't one of the fat horrors. He has one of those rigid, horselike faces that never tell anything; a long nose, flattened as if it had been tied down; a scornful chin; long, white teeth; flat cheeks, yellow as a Mongolian's; tiny, black eyes, with puffy lids and no lashes; dingy, dead-looking hair— looks as if it were glued on." The sort of man who gives you nostalgia for Nebraska.

In making her stories interesting Miss Cather employs a definite technique. Her eight beginnings illustrate her remarkable magazine-craft, and account both for her effectiveness and for something else:

"Don Hedger had lived for four years on the top floor of an old house on the south side of Washington square, and nobody had ever disturbed him." ("Coming, Aphrodite!")

"I first became aware that Cressida Garnet was on board when I saw young men with cameras going up to the boat deck." ("The Diamond Mine")

"Marshall McKann followed his wife and her friend Mrs. Post down the aisle and up the steps to the stage of the Carnegie Music Hall with an ill-concealed feeling of grievance. ("A Gold Slipper")

"Kitty Airshire had a cold, a persistent inflammation of the vocal cords which defied the throat specialist." ("Scandal")

"It was Paul's afternoon to appear before the faculty of the Pittsburgh High School to account for his various misdemeanors." ("Paul's Case")

"I received one morning a letter, written in pale ink on glossy, blue-lined note-paper, and bearing the postmark of a little Nebraska village." ("A Wagner Matinee")

"A group of the townspeople stood on the station siding of a little Kansas town, awaiting the coming of the night train, which was already twenty minutes overdue." ("A Sculptor's Funeral")

"Everett Hilgarde was conscious that the man across the aisle was looking at him intently." ("A Death in the Desert")

The first-quoted beginnings are later and clearly more expert. They show how, in the management of her reader, Miss Cather has progressed. They also indicate her limitation. It is her admirable gift to discern certain excellent themes and to treat them with fastidiousness and sympathy. It is apparently the paucity of her gift that she does so deliberately, with her inspiration perfectly in hand. The most exciting kind of genius, after all, whether in poetry or prose, meets us "burning bright," like Blake's tiger. This is not the type of genius to expect from Miss Cather. She burns illuminating and steadily, but mainly because she is sane and capable. Feeling she has, and romantic glamour, but at no time does she seem easily irradiant. For this reason her very effectiveness, her shrewd impersonal security in the arrangement and despatch of her story, has a formality that takes away from the flowing line of real self-expression. Better than the familiar vast ineptitude, this formality. But Miss Cather is perhaps still withholding from her fiction something that is intimate, essential and ultimate. That, in creative art, is the Great Divide.

informed appraisal, cold, cut cameo-like against a blank background of experience. In itself almost a trick, this stark treatment of the most emblazoned persons of our world is at once intriguing and disturbing. Sifted by such scrupulous analysis the residue comes through too completely cerebral to be quite comprehended in a sentimental world. As studies of success, of the successful, of the victims of "big careers," as simply of ambition, above all of the quality of ambition in women, they probably are not surpassed; but a coldness, a minimizing of the emotional element, even in an emotional situation—perhaps essentially lacking in such people, it can be argued—will disappoint and baffle the public which greedily seeks the story—only the story.

F[lo] F[ield], *Double Dealer*, 1 (February 1921), 73–4

To one who has the inner understanding of that humor and sadness which go to make up life, style in literature becomes less a matter of outward grace, than of inward beauty. A conception of truth molds a form. The Greek vase-makers did not always get their sides to balance, but when this was done mechanically, it ceased to be art. In the recent volume of short stories, *Youth and the Bright Medusa*, by Willa Cather, truth has been attained with simplicity. The balance matters not so much to her as the thing she wishes to express and there is carried, even to the common-place appreciation, the freshness of feeling, the poignant realization of a new unsullied power.

Usually one feels the boundaries of a

Dial, 70 (February 1921) 230

Perhaps the striking interest, the catch charm of Miss Cather's stories lies in the fact that they take us behind scenes with the sort of person generally revealed to us only in Sunday supplement articles. The "bright Medusa" is art, and in six of these eight stories, including some of her earliest and of her most recent work, it is of the art of music and of its votaries she writes. Not romantic pictures of the great women of the opera, they seem an short story, partially concealed. Dots do quite a bit to create space and the snappy ending cuts contemplation short. But in this delighting volume, there are no tricks of trade, nor concession to any sort of dear Reader. Life flows beneath the eye, unhurried in telling, with every closeness of detail and vision of perspective. Atmosphere is captured with a living breath and color. One is scarcely surprised that her slender output—very slender as compared to our foremost and most joyous magazine contributors—is this result of a year or so to a book. Mr. Mencken rightly finds this the most encouraging hope for American letters in general.

Perhaps, in its larger truth, "Coming, Aphrodite!" seems the finest story of the group. It is that of two people, each with an art. The woman wins success with her hard ideal of it. Her very desires are utilized to an end—her name blazons in electric light. The man wins by being, as you would say—original. He advances with his art. He works always for truth, to make the way. He is heard of later, a word now and then, as a prophet for the young. And between the epoch of Washington Square studio and their divergent goals, these two have their moment of "the perfume and passion of youth." The marvel is how into the calyx of this episode, is drawn all the truth of these two alien factors in art; the one who understands his own soul and the other who has none to question.

Willa Cather's humor is that comprehensive one of a great heart. And after all, is it not great-heartedness that makes genius? "The Diamond Mine" and "The Sculptor's Funeral" are written with a perception that contents itself to find the irony of facts sufficiently droll. Both strike the note of the tragic humor in the Every Day. In "The Diamond Mine," the family "genius" is fed upon by family parasites.

They are the burden of courage and an art so driven to meet their demands, as to miss its own greatness. Cressida's family have "the Garnet Look," which "though based upon a strong family resemblance, was nothing more than the restless preoccupied expression of an inflamed sense of importance." Her very loves feed upon her profits to the hour of a death laid at the door of advertising.—Oh, my countrymen, what abstract truths in personal history!

"A Gold Slipper" is a delicious fling. Kitty Ayshire impales the tribe of Wingless Mind, they "who go deep, but never go high." "You don't give me any good reasons," she tells McKann. "Your morality seems to me the compromise of cowardice, apologetic and sneaking. When righteousness becomes alive, you hate it as much as you do beauty. You want a little of each in your life, perhaps, adulterated, sterilized with the sting taken out." ... "McKann hated tall talk."

There is a mission in all this, if the word is not too deadly. From her first writings Willa Cather has shown her belief that writing must be awakening as well as entertainment. Brief form is to her all the surer urge for conveying vision. "Paul's Case," one of her earliest stories, shows this very clearly. The tragic demand of a boy's nature through damnable surroundings is traced with merciful analysis. Such demands—and who shall plumb their cravings?—bring Youth to Death. In "A Wagner Matinee"—and this the sulphitic reader will relish as a Serialbine prelude—the same living idealism is at work to arouse the faint or misled spirit— "It never really died then, the soul which can suffer so excruciatingly and so interminably; it withers to the outward eye only, like that strange moss which can lie on a dusty shelf half a century and yet, if placed in water, grows green again."

Such a lyric touch as this rouses the "tears of divine despair." Here is a clearer ideal for the short story. Only a writer will know what lucid concentration that ideal demands.

To pass on the inner understanding that upholds the arts and does not overlook the gentleman in the lavender striped shirt sleeves (with the ladies' permission)—is indeed achievement in literature. To some *Youth and the Bright Medusa* will be a thorn in the side of a righteous man, even as Kitty Ayshire's slipper, but to others who know the heights and depths of life, a treasure akin to that which must be fed on in the heart with thankfulness.

D[orothy] C[anfield] Fisher, "Among New Books: Some Books of Short Stories," *Yale Review*, 10 (April 1921), 670–1

There is no writer living in whose excellence Americans feel a warmer, prouder pleasure than we all feel in the success of Willa Cather. I do not by "success" mean the wide recognition given her, although that is delightful to see. I mean what must give much more satisfaction to Miss Cather herself, her real inner success, her real excellence, her firm, steady, upward growth and expansion into tranquil and assured power. It is as heartening and inspiriting a spectacle as the rich, healthful growth and flowering into splendor of a plant in our gardens; for she is a plant of our own American garden, to her last fibre. Here is an American writer to whom European culture (and she has always had plenty of that) is but a food to be absorbed and transformed into a new product, quite different, unique, inimitable, with a harmonious perfection of its own. I cannot imagine any exercise which would be of more use to a young writer than to take the last story in her new volume *Youth and the Bright Medusa* (what an inspired title!) and compare it line by line with the original version which was published in the January number of *Scribner's* in 1903. The whole story of Miss Cather's development is there, and an unformed writer would learn more by pondering on the changes made by Miss Cather in her own story after eighteen years of growth and work, than by listening to many lectures from a professor of literature. So often writers, even very clever ones, spoil their earlier work when they try to alter it, have not the firm mastery of their craft to know how to smooth away crudeness without rooting out the life, are so startled by the changes in their own taste that they do not know where to begin. Miss Cather, conscious, firm-willed artist that she is, has known just where to lay her finger on the false passages and how to lift them out without disturbing the life of the story. To see her do it gives me the complete and rounded pleasure that only fine craftsmanship can give.

After "Coming Aphrodite," the story called "The Diamond Mine" is by far the best of the collection. This is a subject which Miss Cather has already treated with deep feeling in her other work—the sister, successful and prosperous who encounters in her family, instead of sympathy, a sour, suspicious envy and hatred. It is a subject rather new to fiction, since the woman successful and prosperous by her own efforts is rather new to the world. Henry James treated it thoroughly and finely in that one of his short stories which is said to have had George Sand as original; and an English novel of last autumn was built around the same theme, a woman writer this time, who made the money for her family and was looked down on by them. It is a subject full of pathos, and "The Diamond Mine" is deeply pathetic from the beginning to the end. This, too, is an achievement, successfully to present pathos to the modern world which thinks it has so little patience for it. The simple-hearted Ohio singer, who had nothing to make her way but a big voice which she did not know how to use, a handsome body, and any amount of driving power, who was exploited and cheated and deceived by everyone who knew her, is a touching figure, the presentation of which is warmed throughout by sympathy and pity and indignation, qualities which, quite as much as the finest craftsmanship, mark Miss Cather's big and generous art.

Carl Van Doren, "Contemporary American Novelists: Part VII. Willa Cather," *Nation* 113 (27 July 1921), 92–3

When Willa Cather dedicated her first novel, *O Pioneers!* to the memory of Sarah Orne Jewett, she pointed out a link of natural piety binding her to a literary ancestor now rarely credited with descendants so robust. The link holds even yet in respect to the clear outlines and fresh colors and simple devices of Miss Cather's art; in respect to the body and range of her work, it never really held. The thin, fine gentility which Miss Jewett celebrates is no further away from the rich vigor of Miss Cather's pioneers than is the kindly sentiment of the older woman from the native passion of the younger. Miss Jewett wrote of the shadows of memorable events. Once upon a time, her stories all remind us, there was an heroic cast to New England. In Miss Jewett's, time only the echoes of those Homeric days made any noise in the world—at least for her ears and the ears of most of her literary contemporaries. Unmindful of the roar of industrial New England, she kept to the milder regions of her section and wrote elegies upon the epigones. In Miss Cather's quarter of the country there were still heroes during the days she has written about, still pioneers. The sod and swamps of her Nebraska prairies defy the hands of labor almost as obstinately as did the stones and forests of old New England. Her Americans, like all the Agamemnons back of Miss Jewett's world, are fresh from Europe, locked in a mortal conflict with nature. If now and then the older among them grow faint at remembering Bohemia or France or Scandinavia, this is not the predominant mood of their communities. They ride powerfully forward on a wave of confident energy, as if human life had more dawns than sunsets in it. For the most part, her pioneers are unreflective creatures, driven by some inner force which they do not comprehend: they are, that is perhaps no more than to say, primitive and epic in their dispositions.

Is it by virtue of a literary descent from the New England school that Miss Cather depends so frequently upon women as protagonists? Alexandra Bergson in *O Pioneers!*, Thea Kronborg in *The Song of the Lark*, Antonia Shimerda in *My Antonia*—around these as girls and women the actions primarily revolve. It is not, however, as other Helens or Gudruns that they affect their universes; they are not the darlings of heroes but heroes themselves. Alexandra drags her dull brothers after her and establishes the family fortunes; Antonia, less positive and more pathetic, still holds the center of her retired stage by her rich, warm, deep goodness; Thea, a genius in her own right, outgrows her Colorado birthplace and becomes a famous singer with all the fierce energy of a pioneer who happens to be an instinctive artist rather than an instinctive manager, like Alexandra, or an instinctive mother, like Antonia. And is it because women are here protagonists that neither wars, as among the ancients, nor machines, as among the moderns, promote the principal activities of the characters? Less the actions than the moods of these novels have the epic air. Narrow as Miss Cather's scene may be, she fills it with a spaciousness and candor of personality that quite transcends the gnarled eccentricity and timid inhibitions of the local colorists. Passion blows through her chosen characters like a free, wholesome, if often devastating wind; it does not, as with Miss Jewett and her contemporaries, lurk in furtive corners or hide itself altogether. And as these passions are most commonly the passions of home-keeping women, they lie nearer to the core of human existence than if they arose out of the complexities of a wider region.

Something more than Miss Cather's own experience first upon the frontier and then among artists and musicians has held her almost entirely to those two worlds as the favored realms of her imagination. In them, rather than in bourgeois conditions, she finds the theme most congenial to her interest and to her powers. That theme is the struggle of some elect individual to outgrow the restrictions laid upon him— or more frequently her—by numbing circumstances. The early, somewhat inconsequential *Alexander's Bridge* touches this theme, though Bartley Alexander, like the bridge he is building, fails under the strain, largely by reason of a flawed simplicity and a divided energy. Pioneers and artists, in Miss Cather's understanding of their natures, are practically equals in single-mindedness; at least, they work much by themselves, contending with definite though ruthless obstacles, and looking forward, if they win, to a freedom which cannot be achieved in the routine of crowded communities. To become too much involved, for her characters, is to lose their quality. There is Marie Tovesky, in *O Pioneers!* whom nothing more preventable than her beauty and gaiety drags into a confused status and so on to catastrophe. Antonia, tricked into a false relation by her scoundrel lover, and Alexandra, nagged at by her stodgy family because her suitor is poor, suffer temporary eclipses from which only their superb health of character finally extricates them. Thea Kronborg, troubled by the swarming sensations of her first year in Chicago, has to find her true self again in that marvelous desert canyon in Arizona where hot sun and bright, cold water and dim memories of the cliff-dwelling Ancient People detach her from the stupid faces which have haunted and unnerved her.

Miss Cather would not belong to her generation if she did not resent the trespasses which the world regularly commits upon pioneers and artists. For all the superb vitality of her frontier, it faces— and she knows it faces —the degradation of its wild freedom and beauty by clumsy towns, obese vulgarity, the uniform of a monotonous standardization. Her heroic days endure but a brief period before extinction comes. Then her high-hearted pioneers survive half as curiosities in a new order; and their spirits, transmitted to the artists who are their legitimate successors, take up the old struggle in a new guise. In the short story called "The Sculptor's Funeral" she lifts her voice in swift anger, and in "The Golden Slipper" she lowers it to satirical contempt, against the dull souls who either misread distinction or crassly overlook it. At such moments she enlists in the crusade against dulness which has recently succeeded the hereditary crusade of American literature, against wickedness. But from too complete an absorption in that transient war she is saved by the same strength which has lifted her above the more trivial concerns of local color. The older school uncritically delighted in all the village singularities it could discover; the newer school no less uncritically condemns and ridicules all the village conventionalities. Miss Cather has seldom swung far either to the right or to the left in this controversy. She has, apparently, few revenges to take upon the communities in which she lived during her expanding youth. An eye bent too relentlessly upon dulness could have found it in Alexandra Bergson, with her slow, unimaginative thrift; or in Antonia Shimerda, who is a "hired girl" during the days of her tenderest beauty and the hard-worked mother of many children on a distant farm to the end of the story. Miss Cather, almost alone among her peers in this decade, understands that human character for its own sake has a claim upon human interest, surprisingly irrespective of the moral or intellectual qualities which of course condition and shape it.

"Her secret?" says Harsanyi of Thea Kronborg in *The Song of the Lark*. "It is every artist's secret . . . passion. It is an open secret, and perfectly safe. Like heroism, it is inimitable in cheap materials." In these words Miss Cather furnishes an admirable commentary upon the strong yet subtle art which she herself practices. Fiction habitually strives to reproduce passion and heroism and in all but chosen instances falls below the realities because it has not truly comprehended them or because it tries to copy them in cheap materials. It is not Miss Cather's lucid intelligence, alone, though that too is indispensable, which has kept her from these ordinary blunders of the novelist: she herself has the energy which enables her to feel passion and the honesty which enables her to reproduce it. Something of the large tolerance which she must have felt in Whitman before she borrowed from him the title of *O Pioneers!* breathes in all her work. Like him, she has tasted the savor of abounding health; like him, she has exulted in the sense of vast distances, the rapture of the green earth rolling through space, the consciousness of past and future striking hands in the radiant present; like him, she enjoys "powerful uneducated persons" both as the means to a higher type and something as ends honorable in themselves. At the same time, she does not let herself run on in the ungirt dithyrambs of Whitman or into his followers' glorification of sheer bulk and impetus. Taste and intelligence hold her passion in hand. It is her distinction that she combines the merits of those oddly matched progenitors, Miss Jewett and Walt Whitman: she has the delicate tact to paint what she sees with clean, quiet strokes; and she has the strength to look past casual surfaces to the passionate center of her characters.

The passion of the artist, the heroism of the pioneer—these are the human qualities Miss Cather knows best. Compared with her artists the artists of most of her contemporaries seem imitated in cheap materials. They suffer, they rebel, they gesticulate, they pose, they fail through success, they succeed through failure; but only now and then do they have the breathing, authentic reality of Miss Cather's painters and musicians. Musicians she knows best among artists—perhaps has been most interested in them and has associated most with them because of the heroic vitality which a virtuoso must have to achieve any real eminence. The poet may languish over verses in his garret, the painter or sculptor over work conceived and executed in a shy privacy; but the great singer must be an athlete and an actor, training for months and years for the sake of a few hours of triumph before a throbbing audience. It is, therefore, not upon the revolt of Thea Kronborg from her Colorado village that Miss Cather lays her chief stress, but upon the girl's hard, unspeculative, daemonic integrity. She lifts herself from alien conditions hardly knowing what she does, almost as a powerful animal shoulders its instinctive way through scratching underbrush to food and water. Thea may be checked and delayed by all sorts of human complications, but her deeper nature never loses the sense of its proper direction. Ambition with her is hardly more than the passion of self-preservation in a potent spirit. That Miss Cather no less truly understands the quieter attributes of heroism is made evident by the career of Antonia Shimerda—of Miss Cather's heroines the most appealing. Antonia exhibits the ordinary instincts of self-preservation hardly at all. She is gentle and confiding; service to others is the very breath of her being. Yet so deep and strong is the current of motherhood which runs in her that it extricates her from the level of mediocrity as passion itself might fail to do. Goodness, so often negative and annoying, amounts in her to an heroic effluence which imparts the glory of reality to all it touches. "She lent herself to immemorial human attitudes which we recognize as universal and true. . . . She had only to stand in the orchard, to put her hand on a little crab tree and look up at the apples, to make you feel the good-ness of planting and tending and harvesting at last. . . . She was a rich mine of life, like the founders of early races." It is not easy even to say things so illuminating about a human being; it is all but impossible to create one with such sympathetic art that words like these at the end confirm and interpret an impression already made.

My Antonia, following *O Pioneers!* and *The Song of the Lark*, holds out a promise for future development that the work of but two or three other established American novelists holds out. Miss Cather's recent volume of short stories, *Youth and the Bright Medusa*, striking though it is, represents, it may be hoped, but an interlude in her brilliant progress. Such passion as hers only rests itself in brief tales and satire; then it properly takes wing again to larger regions of the imagination. Vigorous as it is, its further course cannot easily be foreseen; it has not the kind of promise that can be discounted by confident expectations. Her art, however, to judge it by its past career, can be expected to move in the direction of firmer structure and clearer outline. After all, she has written but three novels, and it is not to be wondered at that they all have about them certain of the graceful angularities of an art not yet complete. *O Pioneers!* contains really two stories; *The Song of the Lark*, though Miss Cather cut away an entire section at the end, does not maintain itself throughout at the full pitch of interest; the introduction to *My Antonia* is largely superfluous. Having freed herself from the bondage of "plot" as she has freed herself from an inheritance of the softer sentiments, Miss Cather has learned that the ultimate interest of fiction inheres in character. She has still before her the task of putting flawlessly into effect the perception she must already have—that it is as important to find the precise form for the representation of a memorable character as it is to find the precise word for the expression of a memorable idea.

M. H. Doorly [undated clipping from an unidentified Nebraska newspaper in Willa Cather scrapbooks, Red Cloud, II-19]

Nebraska may justly feel proud of the achievements of one of her authors, as represented in this volume of striking and remarkable short stories. She has a brilliance of style and a sureness of touch that are more ordinarily found in the writings of men than of women, though there is no lack of subtlety and deftness of suggestion. There is a certain strain of tragedy in the tales, though not of a quality to depress the casual reader. Most of them deal with the eternal struggle of soul with circumstance, especially the struggle of the artistic soul to free itself from the ugly things of life, and find free and wide expression. This is not to be misconstrued as meaning in any way the commonplace appeal for mere Bohemianism. In one of the most artistic tales it is represented by the pathetic person of a western woman, a farmer's wife, once a music teacher, who visits New York, and after twenty years of "silence" hears a symphony orchestra render a Wagner program. Another tale with a simple, but strikingly developed theme is "The Sculptor's Funeral." The most picturesque

story in the volume is the first one, "Coming, Aphrodite!" but it lacks the high quality of appeal possessed by some of the other and less unusual tales.

Willa Cather has the gift of expressing the inexpressible. Feelings, longings, dreams, generally vaguely felt or at best suggested, she has contrived to put into words. Particularly is this noticeable in "Paul's Case," which shows remarkable insight into the feelings of youth. Some may consider this particular sketch morbid, but many will recognize in it the hatred of the young and undisciplined dreamer for the sordid and unbeautiful surroundings in which he is misplaced.

Some, quite naturally, are better than others, but one and all, the stories in *Youth and the Bright Medusa* are startlingly original, and prove their author to be one of finished skill.

To those who have read Willa Cather's *My Antonia* these new stories will require no further introduction and all Nebraskans, through pride in the growing fame of one who was formerly of this state and who is an alumnus of the University of Nebraska, should feel an especial interest in her latest book.

Checklist of Additional Reviews

Times Literary Supplement (London), 14 October 1920, 670.
Booklist, 17 (December 1920), 115.
"Willa Sibert Cather Author of New Volume," *Bladen* (Nebraska) *Enterprise*, 28 January 1921, p. 1.

ONE OF OURS

ONE OF OURS

WILLA CATHER

"Bidding the eagles of the West fly on . . . "
Vachel Lindsay

NEW YORK
ALFRED · A · KNOPF
MCMXXII

Dorothy Canfield Fisher, *New York Times Book Review*, 10 September 1922, p. 14

One of the most beautiful passages in Miss Cather's writing is her description (in *The Song of a Lark*) of the noble upward flight of an eagle, soaring to the sky through a flock of swallows chirping and fluttering and never rising higher than the dark walls of a canyon.

It is a passage which recurs to one's mind on reading her latest novel. We have all heard the twittering chatter which has filled the stagnant air since the end of the war. And we have all been heartsick over the pettiness and wrong-headedness of so many of the "attacks on American civilization" based as most of them seem to be on petty grounds, on uneasy self-consciousness, or wounded vanity, or a naive untraveled illusion about what life is elsewhere than in America. To read Miss Cather's novel is to see an eagle soar up through all this pettiness, on broad sure wings, carrying us in spirit with her to the heights.

Both sides of the quarrel about the war have been furiously overstating their case. And the same is true of both sides of the quarrel about the value of our American Middle-Western life. It is hard to keep a level head in the midst of all the exaggerated unfairness which has marked those discussions. Miss Cather writes as though she had never heard of their dispute, considers the case on its merits, with the calm dispassionate intelligence of an able mind and a deeply sympathetic heart. Unlike many American intellectuals, she has not lost her sense of reality in the intellectual reaction just now in fashion against the sentimental savagery of some would-be patriots or patrioteers. Unlike nearly every one else nowadays who has occasion to mention the war, she has no fear of the bitter tongues of the disillusioned, makes no attempt, as nearly all knowing writers do, to disarm them by giving occasional knowing hints that she is quite as smartly modern and skeptic as they. She does not, as a matter of fact, give them a thought, nor consider in the least what they will think of her. All her thoughts, all her great brain and heart are concentrated on the meaning of the human lives she depicts, on the wonder and pathos and delicacy and power and weakness and tragedy of human beings like Claude and his mother, and the old Mahailey.

It is an amazingly rich book, rich as no other living American could write, many-peopled, complicated as life itself is complicated, but composed with a harmony and unity which only art can have. All its rich complication of varying backgrounds (presented with a wonderful ability which almost passes unnoticed in the greatness of the book as a whole), all its characters, periods, events, have one unvarying purpose, to tell the story of Claude, Claude whom we know as we know one of our very own, for whom in his baffled fineness we feel the sore, indignant, loving, helpless sympathy we would have for a dear, much-loved younger brother caught in the same *impasse*.

This is the whole purpose of the novel, to make us see and feel and understand Claude and passionately long to open the doors to his living brothers all around us, imprisoned and baffled like Claude in a bare, neutral, machine-ridden world.

The part played by the war in Claude's life has nothing to do either with the defenders or opponents of the war. For Claude, as for hundreds of thousands of other fine-natured, idealistic, inarticulate American boys, the war came as a purpose high and great enough to satisfy their high and great souls. And Miss Cather has simply told the truth about it. The war tore Claude away, as nothing else in the world could have done, away from the world where he had been born but where he did not belong, and swept him off for one glimpse of the other unknown, guessed-at world for which his lonely life had been one long nostalgia. The book is no tragedy, although it ends with Claude's death on the battlefield. He died in the world he had longed to reach, and before he had time to learn the ugliness and malice and decay which tarnishes so much of the suave ripe harmony he saw about him at last.

Miss Cather has held the scales even with an honesty of which perhaps no other American writer is capable. She shows us Claude's rare personality starving, but she shows us also the plenty amid which he starved, rich plenty for other natures, not for his. Nowhere in any of her books has Miss Cather given us a more glowing portrayal of life on the fertile Western plains, of the very throb and pulse of life lived by the seasons and not by the clock. It is enough to make some full-blooded, adventurous French boy, shut up in the gray, rigid traditions of his caste, grow heartsick with envy to read. Miss Cather's triumph is to create so masterfully this vital, exuberant, sun-flooded, gloriously living scene, and at the same time to show a young soul finding nowhere in it the absorbing aim which is all that can reconcile a seeking nature like Claude's to the act of living. It is perhaps not without intention that Claude's ancestry is all New England. Those "Summer evenings when he used to sit dumb by the windmill, wondering what to do with his life," would not have been so bitterly empty to a nature with a larger share of sensuous, easy-going capacity for compromise. It is not enough for Claude to have money, and a fine car, and a pleasant home to live in, and good health and more money to be had for the making of it. He intensely desires to "do something with his life," something shapely and harmonious. His tragedy is that in all the prosperous, full-veined, material life about him, he finds no one who can set him on his way, not even his dear, dear mother, coming down from the beautiful, serene heights on which her soul lived, to agonize with Claude, terribly to long to help him, only to add one more fetter to his chains with the narrowness of her orthodox evangelical theories and prejudices. His exquisite mother's life was passed on another plane from Claude's, and, love him more than life, as she did, grope desperately to be one with him, she could never know what it was that Claude needed, what was the lack that drained his days dry of hope. The old Mahailey, miraculous in her scriptural simplicity of heart, was oftener nearer to comforting Claude than his mother; although never in any book that I ever read is the love of a son for his mother more poignantly, more deeply imagined and portrayed.

To present this noble and tragic theme Miss Cather has so lost her personality in that of her hero that again and again the reader thinks of the phenomena known as "reincarnations." How could anything short of a reincarnation enable a mature, sophisticated, traveled cosmopolitan like Miss Cather to sink herself so wholly in this simple-hearted, great-souled, untraveled, unfulfilled American farmer? One of the beauties of the book comes from this astonishing absorption in her theme; the entire lack of any merely clever or literary writing, the entire lack of any attempt to portray mere surfaces rather than what lies under them. The massive sincerity of her style makes the work of many of her able contemporaries seem like hard, bright, detailed photographs on high-gloss paper. And yet the book is full of the most enchanting detail, of secondary characters, drawn with the utmost racy zest and color. Sometimes this color is effortlessly and insidiously sardonic, as in the matter-of-fact description of the excellent cold supper which Claude's white-faced, cold-blooded horror of a wife leaves in the ice-box as an all-sufficient substitute for what a wife should be to her husband. That meal reeks with Enid's rancid self-righteousness!

Sometimes these characterizations of Miss Cather's are quietly humorous and good-natured, like the presentation of Claude's stubfingered, perfectly-satisfied-with-life brother Ralph, who on Sunday morning "rolled out of bed and callously put on his clean underwear without taking a bath. This cost him not one regret, though he took time to polish his new ox-blood shoes tenderly with his pocket handkerchief." That one passage tells you all you need to know about Ralph. That is Ralph.

The portrait of Claude's father is one of Miss Cather's best, as substantially painted as a Rembrandt. She draws to the life the vital, mocking, conscienceless, tolerant, thick-skinned, able Yankee, Ralph's father, not Claude's.

Of course, every one who reads the novel will love most of all the portrait of Claude's mother. Like everything else in this wonderful book, she is given to the reader at first hand, without the slightest formal literary description. You see her as you see a living person dear to you, by her expression, not by her physical characteristics. At the moment of Claude's death Miss Cather speaks of the disappearance of the "look that was Claude." Throughout the book she gives you "the look" that is the soul of things.

I must draw back for lack of space from any attempt at a mention of the savory gusto with which the secondary characters are drawn. Especially in the second part, Claude's great adventure in France, the canvas is filled with personages as living, with their bright liquid eyes and their frank, human look into your face, as portraits by Hals.

It is evidently Miss Cather's intention to have them all overshadowed by the figure of David, the fine, cultivated, disciplined man-of-the-world and artist, who symbolizes to Claude all that he has missed in life and might have made his own. For me, personally, the figure of David is not one of the most complete successes in the book. Compared to Claude whom by that time I deeply respect and love as one of my own, he seems rather thin, hardly worthy of all Claude's wistful, overestimating admiration. It is a little like trying to imagine Lincoln wistful and admiring before a smoothed, tea-drinking, cosmopolitan John Hay. I admit, however, that I am swept away out of this grudging feeling toward David in the beautiful and poignant passage where David plays his violin for the last time, where the music reveals to poor Claude a Promised Land of Beauty from which, quite casually, through nobody's malice, and yet irretrievably, he has been shut out. The climax of the book is there, in that cry of suffering in which hurt vanity has no part. It is an almost disinterested, impersonal anguish which Claude suffers there, such as wrings our own hearts throughout the novel, at the sight of splendid youth cheated out of its share of the glory of life, at the sight of noble human stuff wasted and warped and thrown away.

From the moment the now venerable S. S. McClure, alight with enthusiasm over a short story manuscript from an obscure school teacher from Nebraska, sent posthaste for her to come to New York that they might talk over the possibility of his taking her on as an editorial assistant, Willa Sibert Cather (who has now dropped the Sibert) was on the fair road of writing what her eyes had seen and her heart had felt in the broad waste spaces of the Western prairies. Incidentally, it was her first heft up in her climb to the peak of fictional achievement in America. She may look around her now with almost as complete a feeling of loneliness as that which first oppressed her when her pony pricked up his ears at the coyote's call in the murky dusk on the Nebraska grazing lands. No other woman writer shares her eminence in Darian—and, for the matter of that, few men may call her neighbor without impertinence.

It is no great secret, I should imagine (though I have never met Miss Cather) that the first hurt of the early loneliness has never been quite alleviated, not even by her writings, which are a sequence in beauty, wrung from her hurt; for its poignancy is something from which her central characters never quite escape. It has been the leaven of her philosophy as well as the lees in her cup of life, and from out of its persistence she has made a poetic preachment of revolt. She is forever on the side of the Shelleyan angels, whispering encouraging assurance that it were better to be an outcast with Lucifer than to dwell in the drear Miltonic paradise and sit meekly at the right hand of the Puritan God. One has but to remember the passionate bitterness behind her sympathetic portrayal of the young absconder in "Paul's Case"—concerning a weak and baffled dreamer who bought one glimpse of glittering beauty at a terrible price—to know where her heart lies.

There is a blood-brother to the pathetic Paul in *One of Ours*, and from the moment he enters the scene you know he is Miss Cather's pet and that she winks comfortingly at his weakness. He is swanky in an airman's costume, he has a cockney drawl and a cosmopolitan air, he is knowing about the ladies, and he hails from a clerk's highstool in a seedy bank in Crystal Lake, Iowa.

"Why, we thought you were an Englishman," ventures Claude on board the troop ship Anchises.

"Not quite. I've served in His Majesty's army two years, though."

Claude admires, because Victor tells the truth. Any one who escaped from Middle Western small town life by his own exertion won Claude's admiration—Claude, with an overwhelming desire to escape, had been pushed out of his hell: "Yes, things are pretty tame at home."

"Tame? My God, it's death in life! What's left of men if you take all the fire out of them? They are afraid of everything. I know them; Sunday school sneaks, prowling around those little towns after dark!"

And so the gallant Victor, playing the shabby little role he had created for himself as a man of the great world, pinning his faith on a blowsy Dulcinea of the flesh marts of London as a sympathetic and sophisticated woman who adores him, pitying with a genuine grief a brave German airwoman he had shot down in battle, and winged at last in high adventure above the German lines, he, too, has Miss Cather's heart and pity, for he, too, took his Icarus flight toward the sun, from the drab, materialistic, Puritanic regimen.

"Go ahead," says Victor to Claude, "drink to the Kaiser."

"Why to him in particular?"

"It's not in particular. Drink to Hindenburg, or the High Command or anything else that got you out of the cornfields."

There you have the ironic keynote to the poignantly beautiful drama Miss Cather has unfolded for us through the pages of this, the best sustained and most powerful novel she has written. To the contriver of carnage, whoever he was, Claude Wheeler owed, and had a perturbed inner knowledge that he owed, a sinister debt of gratitude for the one expanding thrill of adventure he had craved in his cramped existence on the Nebraska farm. The tale is further tinged with irony by the fact that fulfillment of the magnificent, repressed energies of this splendid, sensitive youth, who had no quarrel with any living human being, should be found in—"The blood dripped down his coat, but he felt no weakness. He felt only that he commanded wonderful men . . . Bert tore his shirt open; three clean bullet holes—one through his heart. By the time they looked at him again, the smile had gone. The look that was Claude had faded. Hicks wiped the sweat and smoke from his officer's face."

Claude Wheeler alone is not the hero of *One of Ours*. That hero is the American youth with fettered wings in the suffocating far inland towns, where no refreshing breath of adventure comes, where play is sinful and leisure is dedicated to a mournful preparation for death, where the pulse of life suffers a slow attrition from the incubus of a bleak tradition of duty, work, silent suffering, piety and death. The problem that Claude faced is the problem all aspiring youth face in the cramped, mean, unpleasant environment of the stagnant inland towns of America, towns where the pioneer spirit has died from the spread of modern industrialism and no spirit whatever has taken its place. That problem is concerned with the effective release of the creative energies of youth in satisfying experience, joy in work and happiness in play. As conditions obtain now, there is the alternative of severing all in precarious flight, submitting humbly with bowed and bloody head—or, by a frightful miracle, war.

But, let me insist, this is not a war novel. War occupies less than a third of the book. It is the *deus ex machina* which solves in ironic fashion the perplexities of Claude. It is war which offers him adventure, release for his pent-up energies. The body of the story is concerned with the frustrations of those energies, not through the specific fault of any one, but through the fault of things as they are. *Hinc illae lacrimae* Claude Wheeler is a finely organized, nobly knit youth, worshipped by his mother, intimidated but loved by his father. They are industrious, fairly prosperous, pious Nebraska farmers. "His mother was old-fashioned. She thought dancing and card playing dangerous pastimes—only rough people did such things when she was a girl in Vermont—and 'worldiness' only another word for wickedness. According to her conception of education one should learn, not think; and, above all, one must not inquire. The history of the human race, as it lay behind one, was already explained; and so was its destiny, which lay before. The mind should remain obediently within the theological concept of history. Nat Wheeler didn't care where his son went to school, but he, too, took it for granted that the religious institution was cheaper than the state university; and that because the students there looked shabbier they were less likely to become too knowing and offensively intelligent at home." There you have the spiritual milieu of Claude's home, lightened only by parental affection: obedience to narrow theological dicta and chinchery of the purse as well as of the spirit. The girl Claude falls in love with and marries is withered by the same blight. Love to her is a negligible and shameful thing. Claude's tortured dream for a great emotional experience fades; he is lonely, miserable, submissive, but bitter, with a wistful, hurt pride and a sense that life has cheated him. The coming of war did not interest him; he had no inclination to fight; his father had, in effect, to urge him into it. . . . But that is Miss Cather's story, and she has told it with an epical dignity, simplicity and impressiveness. It is the high-water mark of her achievements as a literary artist—not so well rounded a story as *My Antonia* perhaps, but a harder one to write, a more ambitious theme, handled with distinction and genius.

E[dwin] F[rancis] E[dgett], "Into the Path of Manhood," *Boston Evening Transcript*, 13 September 1922, part 3, p. 4

The chorus in exaltation of Miss Cather's greatness as a story-teller has recently become so vociferous and persistent that the reader who has been unfortunate enough to have passed by *Youth and the Bright Medusa, O Pioneers!* and *My Antonia* has eagerly awaited her next novel, her first in a four-year period. The reason why she has waited so long is not disclosed, although the advance praise of it is so sufficiently loud and unrestrained to keep our expectancy at something more than normal heat. It "shows her at the very fulness of her powers," we are told, and "nothing that Miss Cather has ever written has quite prepared one for this book," while to cap the climax we are informed that it is "an authentic masterpiece—a novel to rank with the finest of this or any age."

Only one word will express the true feeling about this sort of praise, and that word is "bosh." To print such exaggerative statements on the paper jacket of a novel is absolutely the most injudicious way to prepare a reader for something good. It discredits the author and the publisher, and it insults the intelligence of the reader. No novel can possibly live up to such extraordinary praise, and it reacts upon its maker and upon the person in whose interest it is made. If any novelist reaches such heights it will be for the future and not for the immediate present to determine.

What manner of novel, it may reasonably be asked, is the object of this adulation? Where are its scenes, what are its incidents and who are its characters? These questions may be briefly answered by the statement that during its first three-quarters it deals with the family and personal relations of a group of people in the farming region of western Nebraska, with an occasional journey farther westward to Denver, and that its remaining pages carry the reader through those wearisome episodes of the European battlefields that are now too frequently the last resources of the story teller who can devise no other expedient for the dispositon of a troublesome personage. It describes easily and with realistic skill of phrase and fact the life of a young man who is brought up on a prosperous farm, but whose efforts at making his way are thwarted again and again by temperamental inability to make the most of the life and the duties amid which he is placed by the combination of fate and the novelist.

When Claude Wheeler fell in love it was with the wrong woman, and when he married her he was made aware of that fact from her own lips within a few hours of the wedding ceremony. They took the train for the West after the usual festivities in the bride's home, and when after smoking his cigar Claude knocked at the door of his stateroom, "It opened a little way, and Enid stood there in a white silk dressing gown with many ruffles, her hair in two small braids over her shoulders. 'Claude,' she said in a low voice, 'would you mind getting a berth somewhere out in the car tonight? The porter says they are not all taken. I'm not feeling very well. I think the dressing on the chicken salad must have been too rich.'" Of course he complied with her request, and we are permitted to gather from the novelist's reticence during the further course of the story that the effects of the chicken salad were continuous. . . .

As a whole, the story is better than might be expected from its extravagant advance praise. It takes little pieces out of real life and makes of them a whole that, while it by no means reaches imaginative perfection, goes a considerable way towards that goal. It touches commonplaces with an ingenious hand that makes them something more than the conventionalities of the printed page, and it selects with no little skill the salient features of the passing years in the life of a young man. But it is not great, and is merely one of many excellent novels that traverse a well-worn pathway of fiction. If Miss Cather ever expects to achieve greatness, she should first pray to be delivered from the clutches of undiscriminating publicity experts.

Heywood Broun, "It Seems to Me," *World* (New York), 13 September 1922, p. 13

Miss Zoe Akins has promised to review Willa Cather's *One of Ours* for this column, and we are reliably informed that her copy will surely reach the office tomorrow. We are under the impression that Miss Akins likes the book and so we are going to state our case against the novel first. To us it is a bitter disappointment. *One of Ours* is the first long novel from Miss Cather since 1918. It is deliberately and carefully considered. The book is not an accident.

Already fervent praise has been bestowed upon Miss Cather's new book. Possibly it is a good book, but it is not our kind of a good book. We must wait another four years, or perhaps forever, to be blessed again by the glow which came to us from *My Antonia*. Our personal tragedy is not only that we do not like *One of Ours* as well as *My Antonia* but that we do not like it at all. We skipped nothing, but went ahead steadily through the entire book, and could not get away from the fact that to us the novel is deadly dull. There are not more than fifty pages out of the four hundred and fifty-nine which established any spell. This is a dogged book, and we read it doggedly.

To a certain extent the war came between this particular reader and the reviewer. Here our own particular prejudices might rise up sharply enough to get in the way of our taste, which we are fond of calling our "critical judgment." But the war theme is secondary in Miss Cather's story. We didn't like it even before we discovered to our horror that Miss Cather was going to take what seems to us a sentimental attitude toward the war.

Briefly and crudely restated, the theme of *One of Ours* is that life in America may be so fearfully circumscribed by national character and conditions that the only escape for the individual lies in a great war. It seems to Miss Cather that the war was not without purpose, since it gave a significance to the life of farm boys in Nebraska. The hero of the book loses his life and finds his soul. We happen to believe that there is such a thing as setting too high a price even upon souls, and war is too high a price.

But, aside from that, we do not feel that the reaction of Claude Wheeler to the conflict is as characteristically American as Miss Cather seems to believe. Obviously there were some—many, indeed—who found exaltation in the war, but, in our opinion, they remain exceptional: More than that, we do not understand their emotional processes. Miss Cather has not made us understand. We simply feel that she does not know enough of the situations concerning which she writes in the latter part of her book. For us *Three Soldiers*, in spite of exaggerations, is more nearly true than *One of Ours*. It is fair to say that Miss Cather does not let herself become lost in any early Coningsby Dawson attitude. The horrors of war are noted and in at least one episode gruesomely described. But above all that she finds grandeur. When Claude died his comrades [found] "three clean bullet holes—one through the heart."

Horror and heroism both are found in the war by Willa Cather. With that no one can quarrel, except, perhaps, concerning the exact proportions. But it seems to us that Miss Cather has lost sight entirely of the mood which was most prevalent and characteristic of the war. She has left out the boredom. It is our notion that war is a pursuit less romantic even than farm life in Nebraska. We can imagine no more ironic conception than the belief that in war the individual might find freedom from the chains of circumstance. Mankind has invented nothing in which routine rages more fiercely than in modern warfare.

Our own experience with war was made up of the more or less casual contacts of a correspondent, but we never visited a trench without finding that there was nothing poignant enough in the hearts of soldiers to withstand weariness. Even a newspaper reporter came under the head of welcome diversion. For days and months and years these men were waiting. During the greater part of that time there was no opportunity for their idealism to function. Sustaining things such as hope and hate died. And when the men died too it was hardly characteristic for the end to come as it did with Claude. He leaped upon a trench and stood there shouting encouragement to his men. It was a bullet through his heart which ended him.

Miss Cather has specified that it was a clean wound. It is our impression that this was a war in which even the wounds were not clean. And then people defending trenches didn't stand on top of them much: Willa Cather has moulded the war pretty much to suit her novel.

[Henry Seidel Canby],
"Editorial: Two
Americas," *New York
Evening Post, The
Literary Review*, 16
September 1922, p. 23
[reviewed with Sinclair
Lewis's *Babbitt*]

One of the best pieces of fiction about the war which we know was a short story which appeared in one of the weekly magazines. Of course we ought to know the name of the story and of the author, but we don't. Anyhow, it was a story of a young man confined to dull routine by his peace-time duties. He was a shoe clerk. To him the war seemed the opportunity for romance. Eagerly he enlisted and was accepted. During the course of his examination he was asked what occupation he had followed before entering the army. He told the examiners. Three days later he received an order to report at a certain base and join the Quartermaster's Department. He was assigned to the shoe department.

Among the arbitrary and unfair things which Miss Cather does is to take the meanest character in the book, a materialistic Uriah Heepish sort of person and make him the one pacifist of the novel. This is a little more than careless. If Miss Cather does not understand the essential motives of men who opposed war she is likely to go equally wrong in describing the mental processes of those who fought.

The trouble with the early part of the book, which concerns the life of Claude Wheeler on the farm, is that the novelist has been too ready to make her case by means of a mass of evidence rather than by using less and more telling testimony. Miss Cather has succeeded in making the farm not only dull for the farmer but for the reader as well. Only in her description of the snowstorm do we find anything that is animated by the same spirit which blazed in *My Antonia*.

Our passion for Prohibitionists is not great, but again it seems to us careless and slipshod for Miss Cather to explain the sexual frigidity of Enid, the wife of Claude, almost entirely on the grounds that she is opposed to alcoholic beverages. If there was any truth in such a notion about Prohibitionists the rest of us would hardly need to worry. By taking thought the unregenerate could raise up a new generation to bring back beer and light wines.

Sinclair Lewis, "A Hamlet of the Plains," *New York Evening Post, The Literary Review*, 16 September 1922, p. 23

Moments of beauty which reveal not an American West of obvious heroisms but the actual grain-brightened, wind-sharpened land of to-day; moments out of serene October afternoons and eager April mornings and cold-gasping winter nights; all of them as tenderly remembered as the hedges of "A Shropshire Lad."

A portrait of a farm boy, whom the publisher in his rather vociferous jacket note has reasonably called "a young Hamlet of the prairies."

A decidedly interesting chronicle of the boy's marriage to a determined young female who loved the souls of the missionized Chinese; but who disdained to love the splendid flesh of the Nebraska farmer.

A question as to the value of modernizing, of the motors, phonographs, cameras, farm machines for which the farmers trade their corn and wheat, their leisure and their contentment. A picture—scarce sketched before—of the new and mechanical type of farming which has been replacing the earlier isolated agriculture.

Half a dozen brilliant "minor characters": Mahailey, the mountaineer woman; Mrs. Wheeler's shy beauty; Wheeler, the pioneer farmer, curious about everything, extravagantly fond of a jest, viewing a joy in learning as absurd; a German family, which, in a diligent but dismal university town, retain the florid yet warm and comforting music love of its lost home.

The courage to be tender and perfectly simple, to let the reader suppose, if he so desire, that the author lacks all understanding of the hard, varnished, cosmopolitan cleverness which is the note of the hour.

These admirable discoveries are to be made in Miss Willa Cather's novel *One of Ours*, an addition to the ever distinguished fiction list of Mr. Knopf. Miss Cather ranks with Mrs. Wharton, Mr. Tarkington, Mr. Hergesheimer, and a few others as one of the American talents which are not merely agreeable but worth the most exact study, and a new book by her is an event to be reported intently.

Yet her name is, even after such novels, as *My Antonia* and *O Pioneers*, scarce known to the general [public]. Many a women's club which is fervent in its knowledge of all the novelists who seize attention by sneering, by describing frocks, or by fictionalizing handbooks of psychoanalysis has never heard of this quieter competence. Her style is so deftly a part of her theme that to the uncomprehending, to the seekers after verbal glass jewels, she is not perceivable as a "stylist" at all. But to the more discerning Miss Cather is a phenomenon to be examined excitedly, both as a pure artist and as an interpreter. Particularly is that true at present, during the discussions of a so-called "Middle Western group," whose grouping lies in the fact that they happened to be born within a couple of thousand miles of one another. Of the somewhat fabulous Middle West not even Mr. Hamlin Garland has given a more valid and beautiful expression than has Miss Cather.

Because of these tokens of significance all sophisticated readers have prayed that the new novel, *One of Ours*, might be the book which would at last bring to her the public acclamation which she has never courted, but without which, perhaps, she would never be quite content. Is *One of Ours* that book? Probably not. There is ground for fearing that, despite many excellences, it is inferior to others of her novels. It is indeed a book which, had it come from an experimenting youngster, would stir the most stimulating hope. And in any case it is one of the books of the year which one must recommend, which must be read. Yet from Miss Cather it is disappointing. The penalty of her talent is that she must be judged not by the tenderly paternal standards which one grants to clever children, but by the stern and demanding code befitting her caste.

The most important defect is that, having set the Enid problem, she evades it. Here is young Claude Wheeler, for all his undecisiveness a person of fine perceptions, valiant desires, and a thoroughly normal body, married to a bloodless, evangelical prig who very much knows what she doesn't want. The scene of Enid's casual cruelty on the wedding night is dramatic without affectation—a rare thing in domestic chronicles. And here are two possible and natural sources of complication: the young woman whom Claude should have chosen and the itinerant minister who fawns on Enid. In all of this, even without the conceivable external complications, there is infinitude of possible interest. But Miss Cather throws it away. With Claude's relations to Enid left all unresolved, the author sends Claude off to war. She might as well have pushed him down a well. Such things do happen; people with problems fairly explosive with vexatious interest do go off to war—and do fall down wells. In the war Claude is so heroic, so pure, so clever, so noble that no one can believe in him. Except for the arousing scenes on the army transport, with influenza stalking, her whole view of the war seems secondhand and—for her—second-rate.

It is a common belief that when the mountain portentously gives birth to a mouse the affair is ridiculous. In the arts the opposite is clearly true. It would be absurd for an active mouse to take time to produce a lumpish mountain. In Flaubert his provincial housewife is more significant than Salambo. The Dutch pictures of old women and cheeses are not less but more heroic and enduring than the eighteenth-century canvases massing a dozen gods, a hundred generals, and a plainful of bleeding soldiers.

In the world of the artist it is the little, immediate, comprehensible things—jack knives or kisses, bath sponges or children's wails—which illuminate and fix the human spectacle; and for the would-be painter of our Western world a Sears-Roebuck catalogue is (to one who knows how to choose and who has his inspiration from living life) a more valuable reference book than a library of economics, poetry, and the lives of the saints. This axiom Miss Cather knows; she has lived by it not only in her prairie novels but in

the sketches of that golden book *Youth and the Bright Medusa*, in which the artist's gas stove and the cabman's hat are paths to everlasting beauty. In *One of Ours* that truth does guide the first part of the book, but she disastrously loses it in a romance of violinists gallantly turned soldier, of self-sacrificing sergeants, sallies at midnight, and all the commonplaces of ordinary war novels. . . . Lieut. Claude Wheeler could not have been purer if he had been depicted by that sweet singer of lice and mud, Mr. Coningsby Dawson.

It may well be that Claude was suggested by some actual, some very fine person who was tragically lost in the war. It may be that because in this book Miss Cather's own emotion is the greater she rouses the less emotion in the reader. Certainly there is no intentional cheapening of her work to tickle the banal reader. But it is the hard duty of the artist to slay his own desire for his eternally selfish characters; to be most cool when his own emotion is most fiery; and in the death of Claude Wheeler there is far less beauty than in the small-town burial of the sculptor in *Youth and the Bright Medusa*.

As to the story of *One of Ours*, it is excellently natural. It concerns the unfolding of a youngster who, more by his own inability to explain himself to his father's coarse incomprehension than by any tricky complication of fate, is torn from his career and a chance to discover what he wants to do with life and sent back to farm work, which is—for him if not for his mates—a prison. The war gives him an escape which is closed by his death.

Miss Cather does not seem to be quite certain what does happen to him. At times she is as undecisive as her own hero. There might be, in his losing all in what seemed to be the freedom of the war, a noble irony like the irony of the brooding Hardy. Perhaps there is meant to be. But it does not came through to the reader.

One of Ours is a book which must be read. It is a book to which it would be an insult to give facile and unbalanced praise. It is a book for discussion. And one reviewer, at least, will rejoice if he be convinced by more competent discriminations that *One of Ours* is not only as good as he thinks but incomparably better. There are books which it is a joy to attack; lying books, mawkish books, pretentious dull books, the books which stir a regrettable but natural spirit of deviltry, a desire to torture the authors, and a desire to keep people from reading them. *One of Ours* is quite the opposite. It makes the reader, for a moment of modesty, hope more for its success than for the authority of his own judgment.

P. G., "Story of Nebraska Boy's Revolt Told in Willa Cather's New Novel," *Sunday Bee* (Omaha), 17 September 1922

In behalf of Nebraska it may be said that the books of Miss Willa Cather are quite as popular here as elsewhere in America. The mirror of her tolerant realism unfailingly is held up to the people of her native state, who regard their own reflections unflinchingly and with interest.

It is not a flattering picture of Nebraska life that she paints in her novel just out, *One of Ours*. Her hero, though a farm bred boy, never found his true place among us and was happy only when the call to war gave him escape from the dullness of the prairies and fealty to the anemic wife that he had found in the nearby town.

When, on an influenza stricken transport, the surgeon suddenly asked him, "What would you give to be out of it all, and safe back on the farm?" Lieut. Claude Wheeler flushed but did not answer. Men were dying all about him, and he was on his way to slaughter, but he could not find it in his heart to wish himself back here in his trim bungalow on the plains.

We are told, in the end, that it was for the sake of an ideal that he entered an officers' training camp, and yet at the time it seemed to him and to those reading of him, that it was mainly to get away and satisfy his long-suppressed desire to live more fully.

There was not much in his boyhood home to satisfy this craving. His father was a bonanza farmer, with two or three automobiles and numerous tenants. The profits from their land brought a rude sort of comfort represented by labor-saving devices in the kitchen as in the fields, but nothing of those mental and spiritual graces known as culture. The quiet heroism of his mother, a New England school teacher, was unable to do more than counterbalance the jovial crudeness of his father.

It was not until Claude had spent two years in college that he gained a glimpse of the life that his spirit sought. This came through acquaintance made on the football field with Julius Ehrlich. The home to which Julius took him was small; it had a mortgage on it, but for all that it was a haven where Claude caught the first insight into the world of art, music and literature. It was the little things that he noticed first. The jar of cigarets on the table—at home he had to go down to the barn to smoke—the cordial manner of the five brothers and their interesting conversation.

Miss Cather in all her work seems impressed with the superior art of living practiced by those of near European tradition. Readers of *My Antonia* can scarcely have forgotten the comparison made there between the human values of immigrant daughters and the children of native Americans. In that previous book she wrote what may be closely described as the epic of the hired girl. In this new one she tells the tragedy of a middle westerner's struggles for self-expression and self-realization.

Of Claude Wheeler in the home of Mrs. Ehrlich it is said: "He had grown up with the conviction that it was beneath his dignity to explain himself, just as it was to dress carefully, or to be caught taking pains about anything. Ernest was the only person he knew who tried to state clearly just why he believed this or that: people at home thought him very conceited and foreign. It wasn't American to explain yourself; you didn't have to! On the farm you said that you would or you wouldn't; that Roosevelt was all right, or that he was crazy. You weren't supposed to say more unless you were a stump speaker—if you tried to say more it was because you wanted to hear yourself talk. Since you never said anything, you didn't form the habit of thinking. If you got too much bored, you went to town and bought something new."

. . . [When] Claude returned [to the farm over] Christmas vacation, he sought this neighbor [Ernest] out for the exercise of his new fluency.

"What do we get out of it?" he asked. "Take a day like this: you waken up in the morning and you're glad to be alive; it's a good enough day for anything, and you feel sure that something will happen. Well, whether it's a workday or a holiday, it's all the same in the end. At night you go to bed—nothing has happened."

"But what do you expect?" the Bohemian replied. "What can happen to you except in your mind? . . . You Americans are always looking for something

outside yourselves to warm you up, and it is no way to do."

That lesson Claude was never to learn. We are asked to believe that it might have been different, somehow, if his parents had allowed him to attend the state university instead of the denominational college on the outskirts of Lincoln. Not for one instant is it to be believed that Miss Cather is seeking to revenge herself on her native state, or any part of it, and yet she bears down heavily on this educational institution.

And so it came about that Claude drank a toast to Hindenburg, or whoever it was that lifted him out of the cornfield and into the adventure of war. He never came back. But the tragedy of it is that he never intended to come back had he lived.

Neither at home, nor about the community, nor even in college, were the beauty and opportunity of life on the Great Plains interpreted to him. How many such restless seekers for broader living there are on these prairies not even Miss Cather could estimate. Some time, somehow, they will be brought together in understanding. A prairie culture will be born, taste for the fine arts will be both stimulated and satisfied. Then not even literary masters such as Miss Cather will feel the necessity for leaving Nebraska for New York and Paris.

One of Ours is a book that it is well to read, quite as much for its fine quality as for the local interest in its subject. Like all the novels that Miss Cather thus far has produced, it is in the main a study of character. The form of it is scattered; characters and incidents are brought up that have no vital connection with the plot, and yet, when the picture is viewed as a whole, each one contributes some small bit to the understanding of Claude Wheeler.

This is not a masterpiece: it would be

unfair to Miss Cather to say that she will not produce a greater work. For all that, it is one of the notable books of the year, and not to be missed by those who read for pleasure or profit.

Zoë Akins, "It Seems to Me," *World* (New York), 19 September 1922, p. 9

[Cather's interpretation of the war] will make clear in the ultimate courts of the world's opinion that there were beauty and goodness and glory and neither fear nor self-aggrandizement in the impulse that drew us overseas to fight in the cause of the Allies. . . . *One of Ours* would be a great novel even if it were only a study of a young man's temperament and drifted to an ending by simply stopping and leaving its hero in the fog of his future. But nothing has been written on this side of the Atlantic since we have been a nation that can approach in value, both as art and history, this version of America's performance in the great war. . . . It was this emotion, this passionate sympathy in behalf of France and her allies, this belief in the rightness of their cause that summoned us to her side. This—and only this. If all America had not felt as Claude felt, we could not have done what we did; we could not have drafted young men for that long journey which, in itself, represented to many concerned a separation little less final than death. And at this time any one— statesman or financier or clergyman or poet—who tries to give any other reason than this high and romantic one for our participation in the war lies, and lies abominably, against the spirit of America, against all citizens, men and women,

living or dead, to whom that event was a tragic reality.

Heywood Broun, "It Seems to Me," *World* (New York), 20 September 1922, p. 11

We have had a good many letters about Willa Cather's *One of Ours* and most of them deal with the picture of the war which is drawn in the novel. As a rule, *Three Soldiers* is mentioned. The letters are not numerous enough to make it fair to found any generalizations upon them, but it is just, perhaps, to state the fact that a large majority of the men who served write to say that Dos Passos has written more truthfully, according to their point of view, than Miss Cather. Here is a typical letter which comes from Lebanon, Pa., and is signed "Jacob":

"I've just finished Willa Cather's *One of Ours* as well as your criticism of it. I stick with you in your prejudices, but I don't think you gave the book a fair deal.

"I agree that war was a dreary, un-heroic business, that *Three Soldiers* is a recognizable picture, and that war is too high a price to pay for finding one's soul. I remember spending thirty-six hours in a shell-hole with a dozen other men on the ridge of a hill under fire. Under the leader-ship of a travelling salesman we spent practically all our waking time in tell-ing smutty stories—except once or twice when the shells came unusually close.

"And yet why should Miss Cather emphasize boredom, 'the mood most prevalent and characteristic of the war'? She is clearly dealing with a special case, who didn't fit in with the dominating mood of peace at home. Why should he fit in with the humdrum of war? After all, he was in it a very short time and his mood would correspond with Brooke's rather than Sassoon's.

"On some points both you and Miss Cather deserve criticism. Officers did leap up under fire—and they usually got shot. After about a month at the front all the officers in my company were killed or wounded—even a cowardly cuss who never leaped anywhere except into his dugout. Again, many men were shot in the heart. Miss Cather has plenty of other casualties of other sorts; furthermore, to kill her man she had to hit him in a vital spot. However, I agree with you that the adjective "clean" should not apply to bullet holes. I notice too that she uses "guide right" for "right guide" and speaks of the gold hat cord of a second looey. Her use of 'Hun' as a term applied by our soldiers offends my ear; it sounds like a Y.M.C.A. word popularized by headline writers.

"But what I want to know is why you are persistently silent about *Disenchantment*, by C. E. Montague, the best war book that England has produced? Must I lend you my copy, or will you promise to buy one?"

Well, as a rule, we don't buy books, but as a special favor to our correspondent we promise to get *Disenchantment* and read it and review it. As for the rest, it seemed to us that Miss Cather intended Claude to be not an exceptional type but a thoroughly representative American soldier. Certainly this has been the interpretation placed upon the novel by most of the reviewers who have praised it. Again and again we have heard that the characters in *Three Soldiers* were neurotic and exceptional and that Miss Cather had answered the Dos Passos book by showing through her hero what the average American was like.

Naturally, we did not intend to deny that men were shot through the heart or died by recklessly exposing themselves. We wish to note, however, that Claude is not leading an attack but is defending an intrenched position, and that therefore his leap upon the parapet seemed not the best of military strategy. The point is that with all the war from which to choose Miss Cather has selected for her hero a quick, clean and altogether romantic death. We doubt if that may stand as characteristic. . . .

One of the reasons why the story of the war was not altogether accurately told lay in the fact that all the early reports came from writing rather than fighting men. Unquestionably some of the correspondents took great chances. A few were killed and several were wounded, but even the bravest newspaper man had a privilege not accorded to the soldier. When he made up his mind that he didn't want to stay any longer he could get out. . . .

Nancy Barr Mavity, "One Soldier to Whom War Remained Bright Adventure," *San Francisco Chronicle*, 24 September 1922, p. 5D

Willa Cather is the least feminine of American women novelists—that doubtless is one reason why Hugh Walpole and the *Literary Digest*'s indefatigable vote gatherers are agreed in giving her a ticket to the reserved seats of the mighty. She faces her subject massively, objectively, impersonally, and there is no trace of perfume or silk or "delicacy" on her pages.

This is not to say that the first set of qualities is masculine and the second set feminine—there is plenty of perfume and silk about Hergesheimer and Cabell, who are also among those present for Walpole and the *Digest*—but that this *One of Ours*, Miss Cather's first novel in more than three years, seems less a personal creation, reflecting the author's own contenance, than a work of nature, like a boulder set firmly on a hillside.

Claude Wheeler's story is that of a Nebraska farm boy who yearns to make life splendid and only finds it dull. None of the people around him—prosperous farmers, the second generation reaping where the pioneers have sown—share in his dissatisfaction with a life through which there runs no crimson thread. Romantic dreams are not considered respectable in the vicinity of Frankfort.

Claude has glimpses of a larger world when he takes a course in European history at the State University and becomes acquainted with the family of a fellow student, Julius Erlich. But the farm claims him again, and so also does Enid Royce, whose frigidity he mistakes for delicacy until marriage punctures the delusion.

And then comes the war—and a new world. "You'll admit it's a costly way of providing adventure for the young," says one of Claude's comrades, and yet there is no denying that it is thus the war appeals to him, enlarging his experiences of scenes and peoples, transfusing his ideals with reality, giving his emotions a deeper channel. Here are things worth while, here is life shot through with splendor and meaning.

Another type of soldier who finds in the war a release from triviality is Victor Marsh of Clear Lake, Iowa, ace of the Royal Flying Corps, with his English accent and his delighted discovery of metropolitan vices—"a sort of debauched

baby he was, who went seeking his enemy in the clouds. What other age could have produced such a figure? That was one of the things about this war; it took a little fellow from a little town, gave him an air and a swagger, a life like a movie film—and then a death like the rebel angels."

One of Ours thus far reads like a book written during the war instead of after the shock of awakening. Can Miss Cather be so simple as all that? No, but Claude is, and the identification of the author with the character is so perfect that not a line of criticism, of ironical comment is allowed to seep through. Some felt like the *Three Soldiers*, but very many felt like *One of Ours*.

And then Claude is killed—killed in time. "For him the call was clear, the cause was glorious. Never a doubt stained his bright faith. He died believing his country better than it is, and France better than any country can ever be. And those were beautiful beliefs to die with. Perhaps it was as well to see that vision, and then to see no more." She (his mother) would have dreaded the awakening—she sometimes even doubts whether he could have borne at all that last, desolating disappointment.

"One by one the heroes of that war, the men of dazzling soldiership, leave prematurely the world they have come back to. Airmen whose deeds were tales of wonder, officers whose names made the blood of youth beat faster, survivors of incredible dangers—one by one they quietly die by their own hands.... They were the ones who had hoped extravagantly—who in order to do what they did had to hope extravagantly, and to believe passionately. And they found that they had hoped and believed too much." They are the ones who had to face not only horror but futility, and theirs, not Claude's, is the ultimate tragedy.

George L. Bryan, "On *One of Ours*," *New York Evening Post, The Literary Review*, 30 September 1922, p. 78

To the Editor of *The Literary Review*:
Sir: The following sentence in Sinclair Lewis's review of Miss Cather's *One of Ours* in a recent *Literary Review* caught my attention: "One reviewer at least will rejoice if he be convinced by more competent discriminations that *One of Ours* is not only as good as he thinks, but incomparably better." I dare not pretend to the "more competent discrimination," but I do feel so strongly about this book that I may be able to disclose an angle which Mr. Lewis neglected to reveal in his review.

When Claude went to war, he left behind him a life of unrealized, unformulated ideals. The farm had meant monotony and pettiness and finally the drab coldness of an indifferent marriage. His mother alone approached understanding, but even she failed to probe out the subtleties and fineness of Claude's ideals and ambitions. And so with every ideal straining towards materialization, he went to war and Romance held sway. The transport, the trenches, the deaths, the wounded, all this spelled Romance for Claude. That is why the picture which Miss Cather has drawn is not the picture we are accustomed to visualize from such literature as *Three Soldiers*, *Now It Can Be Told*, *Men in War*, and a host of others. The reader sees the war through the eyes of Claude, sees everything in a bright glow, everything exalted and sublimated. For Claude there is no such thing as pettiness and hardship and sordid reality—those are part of his former dissevered life. Sorrow, tragedy, sacrifice, heroism, these emotions he saw and exaggerated and worshipped for they were the emotions of a melodramatic scene which he was acting out. Mr. Lewis says, "her view of the war seems second hand and—for her—second rate." It is second hand—for Miss Cather has merged herself so completely into the character of Claude that we see the war not as Miss Cather may have seen it, but as her creation saw it—but it is never second rate. Miss Cather is the first novelist since the war who has had the courage to defy every standard set by the huge influx of war novels, to sniff at realism, and to create through the eyes of Claude a war suffused with Romance and glorious adventure.

Death came to Claude at the highest point in his life. If he had seen much more of the war, he too might have become hardened to its romantic elements and merely been one of the hundreds of thousands who fought mechanically and monotonously. He died in time, his ideals had found their consummation.

Time will hallow the unpleasant incidents of the war and give us a picture much as Miss Cather has drawn. The French Revolution, which was in reality a series of street brawls and unspeakable atrocities, is now idealized as a beautiful and romantic struggle for liberty. The Crusades, which was one of the greatest examples of oppression and intolerance, is now the romantic ideal of Christian militancy and devotion. And so our war too will become idealized. Only Miss Cather has had the genius to foreshadow events.

There is one other matter wherein I disagree with Mr. Lewis, namely the evading of the Enid problem. Miss Cather does not seek to make Enid the all-engrossing element in Claude's existence, but merely an episode in the dullness and disillusionment of his early life. Before their marriage Claude sees in Enid a possible fruition of his ideals. He sees refinement, a vague sympathy which proves to be misplaced, and a halo of self-sacrifice in her devotion to her mother, only to find upon closer inspection that each of these qualities bears a huge sign and the sign reads: "Hands Off." And so Enid passes out of his life, an episode, but an important one, making his reaction to his former life much more keen and violent.

If I have in any way brought you or Mr. Lewis to the realization of a new angle to Miss Cather's great novel, I will feel more than amply repaid. Mr. Lewis's review was so thoroughly tolerant and broadminded that I have taken the liberty of writing this reply. [Signed] George L. Bryan, New York.

Sidney Howard, "Miss Cather Goes to War," *Bookman* (New York) 56 (October 1922), 217–18

To treat the small facts and the microscopic phenomena of everyday as significant of the dominant energies and emotions of living, this is pretty generally the woman's method of novel writing. So clearly hers, as it seems to me, that when I find men following it, as Henry James was wont on occasion to do, I see in them not less of value but less of masculinity. And when women disregard it after the tall hat manner of Mrs. Wharton, they seem to withhold the best that they can give and to offer shoddy merchandise as substitute. The feminine mind may not bring forth stories of the Titanic stamp of *Tom Jones* or *War and Peace*, but it

presents a vital thing for the writing of novels as we of today like to read them. It sees life as twilight sees the face of nature, lacking the virulent contrasts of high noon, dealing in the delicate modulations of tone (superb or sinister as you please to take them), the violets and greys, the opalescences and cool lucidities. The best of our taste comes of our subtlety, the sophistication of our spiritual development, and the pleasure we take in a nicety of workmanship and an individuality of approach. Wherefore the best writing of women is perfectly and exquisitely attuned to our mood of things and of vision and is for us at once sympathetic and relentless, broad and deft.

Two novels, *My Antonia* and *O Pioneers!*, set Miss Cather easily at the head of our women writers. Two books they were of a beautiful clarity, of the true classic realism, as solid and as simple as though they had been engraved upon crystal as widely fresh as the prairies with whose folk they dealt. They were of the truest that women have done and no great way removed from the high company of the very great. And they were so completely and satisfactorily "legitimate"! Any book of Miss Cather's is long awaited and expectantly tasted in anticipation. It is a real grief that *One of Ours* should prove a disappointment.

While Claude—so the hero is named—sticks to his own western lands, the thing is above reproach. He nourishes ideas and faith and curiosity upon the meagre food of prairie normalcy. He defeats misunderstanding and bigotry and gets strength of the battle and walks serenely and rebelliously in turn beneath the sun and wind and the night sky. He is convinced and self doubting, a radical philosopher at heart, his mother's slave in act, defiantly fearless and shy to dumbness. He can marry wretchedly and lose his wife to the China missions and build upon the ruins. All of him, all of his family and associates and locale is perfect because Miss Cather has written them as only she can write of such matters. The washing of a car, the minister's elbows at table, a first dress suit, an electric separator, a train hands' restaurant—these are the elements for her uniquely sensitive authority.

Then, about the middle, she undertakes a large offensive, packs her hero in her wardrobe trunk, and carries him bodily to the war in France. The book is done for. Small things are significant in her hands: the tremendous insignificance of war bewilders her. Claude's enlistment and debarkation rise with the writing of his character. Miss Cather allows her tritely sentimental, wholly glorious doughboys one poignant moment of farewell, Liberty in New York Harbor, the troop ship steaming to sea, and the beauty of that moment is heartbreaking. The rest is a potpourri of soldier yarns and impressions of Rheims two years after, amalgamated into a *Saturday Evening Post* version of *Three Soldiers* and about as true to the actuality of warfare as propaganda for the bonus.

It seems to me a book to show what a woman can write supremely and what she cannot write at all. Scott on Jane Austen; that hit the nail once and forever. The pity is that Miss Cather did not know war for the big bowwow stuff that it is and stick to her own farms and farmer folk.

Gilbert Seldes, "Claude Bovary," *Dial*, 73 (October 1922), 438–40

We have been lately advised to confine ourselves, in dealing with our contemporaries, to book-reviewing and to leave criticism alone. It may do for criticism to be concerned with the past; and for the future to deal with our present. But for the present to react effectively on the present is, for some reason, considered superfluous and perhaps ill-bred.

Miss Cather's new work is an exceptionally good example of the kind of work to which mere reviewing is inadequate, the kind which must be criticized or let alone. The reviewer can guide the reader and buyer of books, but the critic, having his centre of interest in the art which is being practised, and the centre of influence in the public taste, with more than a slight concern for the creative process, looks to something a little more serious than the sign-post for his symbol. He has to think, when he considers a novel, of what the novel has been and can be; he has to remember how books are read as well as what books; he has to want, however presumptuously, to assist the creative power by giving it a wider appreciation as well as by indicating its present lapses and its possible achievements. No less than all of these things Miss Cather calls for, even by such a novel as *One of Ours* which has a fatal defect of dulness. Because she is a serious writer, and a meritorious one. Her merit lies in her exceptional honesty; she has not, in the novels of Nebraska, written a meretricious line. It lies in her having an intelligence above that of most practitioners of her art. It lies in a certain dignity.

Honesty, intelligence, and dignity are no mean equipment when they are joined to a special faculty which is the power to communicate (it is his personal vision of the world that the novelist seeks to communicate to us by reproducing it, according to Guy de Maupassant) which has been intensely apprehended (the novel, according to Henry James, is a personal, a direct impression of life; "that . . . constitutes its value, which is greater or less according to the intensity of its impression"). Let modern aesthetics persuade us that the two things coincide, that the impression conditions the expression (or communication); the reader of Miss Cather's novels cannot help feeling a small abyss between them; he cannot help feeling that the impression must have been a little more intense than it seems; that the lines of communication have somewhere broken down.

This is more remarkable in *One of Ours* than in *My Antonia* and it coincides with Miss Cather's increase of impersonality. She may well have become weary of those who treat rustic life with irony or contempt; in *My Antonia* she herself treated it with a remarkable degree of impartial sympathy. In *One of Ours* it seems that she has ceased to treat it, or anything, at all. Despairing, possibly, of the novel afflicted with too protrusive a point of view, she has managed to write one with none at all; she has recorded without creating; she has described without evocation. The second half of the book is a real *tour de faiblesse*: the war built up out of any number of immutable facts and probably incidents, brightly and brilliantly ineffective. It is in this portion of the book that Miss Cather has entirely given up the effort to communicate; she has almost stopped writing fiction altogether. For after noting the Doctor's report that "a scourge of influenza had broken out on board, of a peculiarly bloody and malignant type," she adds a foot-note, "the actual outbreak of influenza on transports carrying United States troops is here anticipated by several months."

It seems to me that such a foot-note, so thoroughly giving away Miss Cather's fictional case, could only have been added to prevent unfavourable criticism on the ground of historical inaccuracy: and this apprehension, dismal as it is for the author, illuminates by its justness the equally sad plight of the critics. It at once abdicates the sovereign throne of the creative artist and reproaches the pretenders. But it concedes everything, which is too much: and it gains nothing. The whole matter has been discussed in *The Poetics*.

But if our novelists will not study Aristotle, they surely will not object to reading Flaubert. The first half of *One of Ours* freely suggests *Madame Bovary*. Claude Wheeler ought to be even more interesting than Emma, since he is both emotionally and intellectually at odds with his circumstance. The narrowing of his radius, the cruel stoppage to his freedom, the trap which fate springs for him, are, fact for fact and movement for movement, as capable of interesting us as the sad events of the Bovarys. The influenza epidemic ought to be as good as the horrible amputation; the war, as background, offers more than Flaubert chose to use. And that this book fails to come to life is not to be set down to a lack of genius, for a fair talent can make a book live. It is due, I think, to the calculated pursuit of a purpose alien to fiction, the purpose to record, rather than to create.

When this purpose is forgotten Miss Cather's deliberate care in statement, her occasional utterance neither shrill nor weak of passion, lead her to veritable creation. Claude's mother emerges; better still a fine emotion is conveyed in a brief chapter in which Claude's prospective father-in-law tries to tell him what life is like, and knows that he cannot express it. In one half page the misery of the inarticulate is set down as in the whole book the emotions of Claude never are. The small successes are fine indeed and from them one gathers certainty that Miss Cather can do pretty nearly whatever she wants to do; one feels from them that the fields of ripe corn and the tides of human joy and suffering have with intensity been present in her mind's eye, that she has checked the buoyant power, the humour, the vitality which tried to get into her book. Possibly she found no place for them in a record of small and dispirited things and people. It is an error in conception, and the error in design (common in her work: the book breaks in half) illuminates. For the trouble is not that the war cuts off the solution of Claude's problem in marriage; it is that the second half of the book is about the war, and cuts off the solution of the aesthetic problem as well.

Hunter Stagg, *Reviewer*, 3 (October 1922), 710–11

Two women—one of them American and the other British—are responsible for the two best autumn novels up to this writing. Specifically, Willa Cather in *On of Ours*, and Rebecca West in *The Judge*, have produced in their several fashions works of the rarest distinction and power.

Miss Cather offers, indeed, in the first two thirds of her new book, the best work of her career—which is not to say that the last third is not good. It is good, and more than good—but it is not worthy of the major portion of the book, over which the wide quiet personality of this writer spreads like the clear light of her own prairies. *One of Ours* is the story of the late boyhood and early manhood of a prosperous Nebraskan farmer; of his childish, futile revolts against the inhibitions of his life, hardening too soon, into the dumb resentment of manhood, till at last the war comes to open to him the world. But *One of Ours* is not a war book—odd how we jump to assure possible readers of that. But it is the truth. Though Miss Cather follows her hero through the war, *One of Ours* is not a war book. In it Miss Cather merely uses the war to show that when freedom from humdrum existence does come to the average American it comes too late. Given the field of adventure, he cannot become an adventurer. He can only "do" adventure as he might "do" the Tower of London and the Louvre. In Miss Cather's vision, the only freedom he can look for after a certain point is freedom from life itself. And, similarly, *One of Ours* is, primarily no more a story of the Nebraskan prairies than it is of the war. Although the greater part of it unfolds in that spacious country, in its essentials it might have been placed anywhere in America. But the prairies serve to give it the setting of loneliness, the proper setting for a story of the loneliness of the human soul.

The story Miss Cather has to tell never flags in interest, and the men and women it involves are people not to be forgotten soon. Even so, however, the larger value of the book is in the opportunity it affords for communion with the large personality of Willa Cather. In all her writings that personality is one which, to borrow a word of Wilson Follett's upon Joseph Conrad, conveys "a kind of tempered melancholy, a sense of seeking and not finding—" and a fascination with "the immense indifference of things": which, to borrow, now, a word of H. L. Mencken's, defines "both the mood of the stories as works of art and their burden and direction as criticisms of life."

Burton Rascoe, "Mrs. Wharton and Some Others," *Shadowland* (October 1922), 35–6

The high place Mrs. Wharton's achievement occupies in the lay and critical opinion of America is, I think something of an accident. She was for a long time, by default, the best woman novelist we had. Her social position was secure, her intelligence unquestioned, her gifts considerable, and her novels distinguished by good taste, technical brilliance, assurance, shrewd observation and a certain wealth of information concerning the activities, manners, and interests of smart people which other novelists did not have. She was, in fine, a capable novelist of society who happened to be in it. She enjoyed the friendship of Henry James and he, in sincerity, bestowed upon her the accolade of Sir Hubert's praise. That fact, I suspect, had much to do with the case. Certainly now there are few critics who dare not show her the deference due an artist of the first rank. This, I risk the heresy of believing, she is not. She is not, I think, even the first among the women writers of America. That position, I contend, is held by Miss Willa Sibert Cather.

The difference between Mrs. Wharton and Miss Cather is largely a difference between the fine workmanship and genius, talent and passion, good taste and ecstasy. It is, essentially, that Miss Cather is a poet in her intensity and Mrs. Wharton is not. Miss Cather's work has that vital quality requisite to moving and enduring art which was designated by a profound critic when, viewing the canvas of a new painter, he said: "Yes, it is well drawn; it is correct in color, line, propor-tion. There is nothing wrong with it. But, it lacks that!" And he snapped his finger. Mrs. Wharton gives us correct pictures; Miss Cather gives us life and the poetry and beauty of its emotions.

Nearly four years have intervened between the publication of *My Antonia* and Miss Cather's new novel, *One of Ours*. She writes slowly; her work will probably never be voluminous. There is too fine and delicate a cadence, too much singing vibrancy in her sentences for her to write much. She is concerned in her new book with the presentation of a highly sensitized youth in relation to the national culture of America as it is evidenced in the prairie towns of our Middle-West. It is the story of a struggle with destiny, a struggle wherein man is inevitably defeated whatever his triumphs, and which alone among human efforts is always beautiful and tragic and pathetic in its ironic implications.

Claude Wheeler, the hero of *One of Ours*, is a youth with tremendous potential energies which are frustrated and inhibited on every side by a close and sterile environment. He is driven in upon himself by the covert hostility his individuality inspires, only to break out intermittently in stormy and futile protest. We follow him, a baffled, meditative, aspiring and tragic figure thru a dramatic career which, like Hamlet's, takes place largely within himself. In Claude Wheeler, Miss Cather has created a figure essentially indigenous to America, whose problems are the spiritual concerns of the race and whose aspirations are the highest aspirations of our native culture.

Miss Cather's style is rich in melodic overtones. It has a haunting and caressing beauty. It is a highly personal style, rhythmic, well wrought, delicately modulated, changing in key and tempo in accordance with subject matter of the moment. As her novel may be said to have symphonic form, so may her style be likened to the effect of an orchestra, the strings and wood-winds dominating. Were it not that she already has three novels and a volume of short stories to her credit which are full of beauty and distinction, it would be possible to say of *One of Ours* that this is the work of a prose artist at the full maturity of her powers. That might as well be said of Miss Cather's first published work. But certainly this is, and for that very reason, one of the outstanding books of the season.

H[enry] L[ouis] Mencken, "Portrait of an American Citizen," *Smart Set*, 69 (October 1922), 140–2

Miss Willa Cather's *One of Ours* divides itself very neatly into two halves, one of which deserves to rank almost with *My Antonia* and the other of which drops precipitately to the level of a serial in the *Ladies' Home Journal*. It is the first half that is the good one. Here Miss Cather sets herself a scene that she knows most intimately and addresses herself to the interpretation of characters that have both her sympathy and her understanding. The scene is the prairie-land of Nebraska; the characters are the emerging peasants of that region—no longer the pathetic clods that their fathers were, and yet but half rescued from mud, loneliness and Methodist demonology. Her protagonist is one who has gone a bit further along the upward path than most of the folks about him—young Claude Wheeler, son of old Nat, the land-hog. Claude's mother was a school-teacher, and if the

dour religion of the steppes had not paralyzed her faculties in youth, might have developed into a primeval Carol Kennicott. As it is, she can only hand on the somewhat smudgy torch to Claude himself—and it is his effort to find a way through the gloom by its light that makes the story. Defeat and disaster are inevitable. The folks of Frankfort are not stupid, but beyond a certain point their imaginations will not go. Claude, fired by a year at the State University, tries to pass that point, and finds all that he knows of human society in a conspiracy against him—his father, his brothers, the girl he falls in love with, even his poor old mother. He yields bit by bit. His father fastens him relentlessly to the soil; his wife binds him in the chains of Christian Endeavor; his mother can only look on and sigh for she knows not what.

Then comes the war, and deliverance. The minds of that remote farmland are easy victims of the prevailing propaganda. They see every event of the first two years of the struggle in the terms set by the Associated Press and the *Saturday Evening Post*. Comes 1917, and they begin flocking to the recruiting-offices, or falling cheerfully upon the patriotic business of badgering their German neighbors. Claude is one of the first to volunteer, and presently he finds himself on the way to France. Months of hope and squalor in the mud, and his regiment goes forward. A brush or two, and he is a veteran. Then, one morning, a German bullet fetches him in the heart. . . . He has found the solution to the riddle of his life in this soldier's death. A strange fish out of Frankfort, Neb., his world misunderstanding and by his world misunderstood, he has come to his heroic destiny in this far-flung trench. It was the brilliant end, no doubt, of many another such groping and uncomfortable man. War is the enemy of the fat and happy, but it is kind to the lonesome. It brings them into kinship with their kind, it fills them with a sense of high usefulness—and it obliterates the benign delusion at last in a swift, humane and workmanlike manner.

What spoils the story is simply that a year or so ago a young soldier named John Dos Passos printed a novel called *Three Soldiers*. Until *Three Soldiers* is forgotten and fancy achieves its inevitable victory over fact, no war story can be written in the United States without challenging comparison with it—and no story that is less meticulously true will stand up to it. At one blast it disposed of oceans of romance and blather. It changed the whole tone of American opinion about the war; it even changed the recollections of actual veterans of the war. They saw, no doubt, substantially what Dos Passos saw, but it took his bold realism to disentangle their recollection from the prevailing buncombe and sentimentality. Unluckily for Miss Cather, she seems to have read *Three Soldiers* inattentively, if at all. The war she depicts has its thrills and even its touches of plausibility, but at bottom it is fought out, not in France, but on a Hollywood movie-lot. Its American soldiers are idealists engaged upon a crusade to put down sin; its Germans are imbeciles who charge machine-guns six-deep, in the manner of the war dispatches of the New York *Tribune*. There is a lyrical nonsensicality in it that often grows half pathetic; it is precious near the war of the standard model of lady novelist.

Which Miss Cather surely is not. When she walks ground that she knows, her footstep is infinitely light and sure. Nothing could exceed the skill with which she washes in that lush and yet desolate Nebraska landscape—the fat farms with their wood-lots of cottonwood, the villages with their grain-elevators and church-spires, the long burning lines of straight railroad track. Nor is there any other American novelist who better comprehends the soul of the American farmer-folk—their slow, dogged battle with the soil that once threatened to make mere animals of them, their slavery to the forms and superstitions of a barbaric theology, their heroic struggle to educate and emancipate their children, their shy reaching out for beauty. To this profound knowledge Miss Cather adds a very great technical expertness. She knows how to manage a situation, how to present a character, how to get poetry into the commonplace. I give you an example from *One of Us* [sic]. In one chapter Claude visits a German family named Erlich, and one of the other guests is a remote cousin of the house, a celebrated opera-singer. She is there but a day or two and we see her for but a few moments, but when she passes on she remains almost as vivid as Claude himself. It is excellent writing, and there is a lot more of it in the first half of the book. But in the second half good writing is not sufficient to conceal the underlying unreality. It is a picture of the war, both as idea and as spectacle, that belongs to Coningsby Dawson and 1915, not to John Dos Passos and 1922.

Perhaps the war novel is intrinsically impossible in America, at least for the present. The best one could say of a good one was that it was as true as *Three Soldiers*. The fact is that the genuinely typical American story of the war would probably not deal with the fighting at all, but with the astounding and unparalleled phenomena that accompanied and supported that fighting at home. After all, very few Americans actually saw any slaughter in the grand manner. By the time the main army got into action the Germans were too exhausted to offer much resistance, even to rearguard attacks. Perhaps this fact explains the tin-soldier bombast and poltroonery of the

American Legion; it is run, not by soldiers who fought and endured in a real war, but by men whose actual service in the field was very brief and not at all arduous. There were probably chaplains and horse-doctors in the German, French and English armies who saw far more hard fighting than the average of them. Moreover, even these men constituted but a small percentage of the total American population. Among the Germans and the French, probably one adult male out of two was under rifle, machine-gun and shell fire during the war; among Americans not one in twenty had that experience. But practically every American, male and female, had some hand, either as actor or as victim, in the grotesque and inordinate monkey-shines that went on at home—the loan drives, the cadging for the Y.M.C.A. and the Red Cross, the looting of enemy nationals, the spy-hunt, all the other patriotic whoop-las of the period. In that period there is abundant material for a penetrating and ironical novel. It would be amusing as literature and valuable as history, and it would let some needed lights into the dark places of the American character. No other participating nation was so safe from all peril in the war, and yet none other was so horribly scared or so shameless about revealing it.

Edmund Wilson, "Mr. Bell, Miss Cather and Others," *Vanity Fair*, October 1922, pp. 26–7

Can Mr. Mencken have been mistaken when he decided that Miss Willa Cather was a great novelist? I have not read *My Antonia*—which I suppose is her best book—but I have not been able to find anything in her two last ones which seemed to bear out his description. Her new novel—*One of Ours*—seems to me a pretty flat failure. She has taken what might under happier circumstances have proved a very interesting theme—the career of an imaginative Nebraska boy who, though charged with the energy for great achievements, is balked and imprisoned first by the necessity of shouldering the responsibility for his father's farm and then by marriage with a cold, pious and prosaic Prohibition worker, but whose noble and romantic impulses are finally liberated by the war. But she has certainly never succeeded in making her hero a reality.

The publishers hint that Claude Wheeler is a sort of symbol of the national character—or rather, I suppose, of the more generous elements of the national character—and one can see that Miss Cather has taken pains to make her personages typical; the jocular, unintelligent money-making farmer father, the sympathetic religious mother, the son made miserable with fine passions for which he can find about him no fit objects, which are outlawed among his neighbors, and which he is finally obliged to extinguish in the dubious crusade of the war—these might have made the heroic materials of a tremendous national document. But I feel in the case of this book—as I did in that of *Youth and the Bright Medusa*—that it costs Miss Cather too much effort to summon her phantoms from the void and that when she has done so they are less like human beings or even the ghosts of human beings than like the pale silhouettes of men and women cut neatly out of neutral-colored paper and put through the paces of a skilful but slightly mechanical minuet. Even when the incidents are felicitously invented—as in the first night of Claude's wedding-trip, when his new bride coldly informs him that she is ill and requests him not to share her stateroom—the feelings of the hero are not created. We do not *experience* the frustration of Claude when his wife will not return his love and in the latter part of the book, where Miss Cather has imposed an extra handicap upon herself by attempting to present the development of the hero under the stimulus of the war we feel that she has told us with commendable accuracy almost everything about the engagements she describes except the thing which is really germane to the novel—what they did to the soul of her hero.

Admirers of Miss Cather will tell me that I do not understand her method—that she is not trying to depict emotions from the inside, like Dostoevsky, but is rather, like Turgenev merely telling you what people do and letting the inner blaze of their glory and grief shine through the simple recital. But, in this case, though the method is different, the effect should be the same: the people should come to life for us; but Miss Cather's never do. Flaubert by a single phrase—a description of some external object—could convey all the pathos and beauty of human desire and defeat; his statement of some prosaic matter will have the dying fall of great music. But Miss Cather has never found this phrase.

Let it be counted to her for righteousness, however, that she has devoted all her life to the search. She knows how fine work should be done even if the life with which she animates it is shadowy. She knows that in a decent novel every word should be in its place and every character in its right perspective and that every incident should be presented with its appropriate economy of detail. If her novel only had more vitality it might put the fear of God into all our hearts—as *Ulysses* has

done to those who have read it. It might bring the salutary blush of shame to many a complacent cheek. But, as it is, "the younger novelists" can evade the moral of Miss Cather's example by protesting that she is dull; and I am sorry that I should not be able to contradict them.

Ludwig Lewisohn, "A Broken Epic," *Nation*, 115 (11 October 1922), 388

The extravagant claims made for Miss Cather's new book cannot conceal its structural weakness. They cannot conceal the fact that this structural weakness points to an act of either artistic self-deception or conscious intellectual abdication on Miss Cather's part. This story of hers, so nobly epic in mood, so rich in life, so full of the tang of her native earth, so clear in its minor intellectual perceptions, yet shares the common fault of the quite vulgar story, novel, or play. It proposes and lets catastrophe dispose. It leads us along a road of life and at the road's end Miss Cather might have shown us either a wide prospect or a dismal swamp. Claude Wheeler might, in any one of a thousand senses, have saved or lost his soul. Instead a *deus ex machina*—it is, of course, the Great War—destroys the road and carries Claude to an alien earth and end where his fate could fulfill itself in no fashion. For that earth and end had no relation to his life and fate. We are still waiting, we shall always be waiting, for the end of his story which catastrophe cut short but could not complete.

We are not quarreling with Miss Cather's execution at any point. She has ripeness, sobriety with passion at its core, an unobtrusive love of perfection. The French scenes are almost as full of the savor of living as the Nebraskan ones; the fourth book of her narrative, The Voyage of The Anchises, is an extraordinarily rich and sustained piece of writing. The well-formed cup is full to the brim; not a drop is spilt. To re-read this account of the voyage of the pestilence-stricken troop-ship alone is, indeed, to gain a very high idea of Miss Cather as an artist. Perhaps briefer forms are more expressive of her native gift. The fact remains that the fable of *One of Ours* breaks in the middle and another tale and epic motivation intrudes.

It is a great pity. We have had the story of Lee Randon who found something warped at life's center; we have had the story of George F. Babbitt who felt that he was being dragged through existence by alien forces. Miss Cather began by beautifully and movingly telling us the story of this lad from the Nebraskan farm-lands who was troubled in essentially the same way as the Philadelphia millionaire and the Zenith "realtor." Claude Wheeler had "the conviction that there was something splendid about life, if he could but find it." He thought his German friends, the Ehrlichs, had hold of the secret; it seemed to elude him. He speaks to the chill-blooded fanatical girl on whom he wastes his youth and passion in terms that both Randon and Babbitt might have used and with them how many thousands of Americans! "I've never yet done anything that gave me any satisfaction. . . . I wonder whether my life has been happening to me or to somebody else. It doesn't seem to have much connection with me." And his friend Gladys echoes him when in her wistfulness she wonders whether life is "worth the chagrin it held for a passionate heart like hers." Yes, it is the passionate heart of

America's best that is speaking out, that is crying out against the cult of things and words and empty, oppressive forms and making articulate its yearning for freedom and for beauty. And Miss Cather's full epic testimony would have had a special freshness and preciousness because she is neither essentially an aesthete like Joseph Hergesheimer nor an intellectual satirist like Sinclair Lewis, but a woman with a brooding earnestness of mind, with reverence tempering her rebellion, and with patience softening her protest. Yet her testimony is the same. Or, rather, it would have been the same, had she told us to the end the story of Claude and Enid and the story of Gladys and had let us hear old Royce speak out his mind concerning the lies which had throttled his whole life. That she has not chosen to do so is both our loss and her own.

Robert Morse Lovett, "Americana," *New Republic*, 32 (11 October 1922), 177–8

These two novels are both extremely competent examples of that local realism which has been the chief characteristic of American fiction during the last thirty years. The scene of Mrs. [Kathleen] Norris's story [*Certain People of Importance*] is California; of Miss Cather's, Nebraska. In form and method, however, they are supremely different. Mrs. Norris's story belongs to the genre of the family novel. While the pattern most characteristic of the English novel is biographical, family and domestic relations have always figured largely as background; and it sometimes occurs that the family itself becomes the chief character in a novel, the family as a social fact speaking through its various members, no one of whom can be regarded as the hero. . . .

Miss Cather in *One of Ours* has followed the more usual plan of narrating the life of her hero. Claude Wheeler passes from boyhood on a Nebraska farm, through a short episode of college and an unsuccessful marriage, to enlistment in the army and death in action. The first half of the book consists of material with which Miss Cather is thoroughly familiar and which she uses admirably; the second half involves experience and characters which she controls less perfectly. While Mrs. Norris has carefully avoided the emphasis of decisive events and the testing of character by them, Miss Cather has deliberately sought these things. The criticism on *One of Ours* will be that she has sought them by means too obvious, and has invoked the great war to bring her story to a climax and to release her hero from his hesitations and uncertainties by an adventitious sacrifice. She has given, however, a true record and a typical one. The character of Claude Wheeler unifies the story. The war to him was not a conversion, or an escape, or a redemption. It was a fulfillment. He carried into it the personality which he had built up in his Nebraska home, with the difference that under the compulsion of a manifest duty his doubts vanished into singlemindedness, and under authority he gained freedom to be fully himself. It must have been so with many of that generation, to which there came the same voice without reply. His companions in the regiment were like him, American boys never more American than in foreign surroundings and in circumstances unforeseen, inexplicable and appalling. It may be that *One of Ours* will have only a temporary and an immediate appeal to those who knew those boys, but to us that appeal is beyond words. We are proud of them.

R. D. Townsend, "Among the New Novels," *Outlook*, 132 (11 October 1922), 253

. . . In quite a different way [than Sinclair Lewis's *Babbitt*] Miss Willa Cather's *One of Ours* is also centered on one person, Claude, the fine and lovable though not very articulate farm lad of Nebraska. As Dorothy Canfield puts it in a review of Miss Cather's admirable book, it "is the whole purpose of the novel to make us see and feel and understand Claude and passionately long to open the doors to his living brothers all around us, imprisoned and baffled like Claude in a bare, neutral, machine ridden world."

The tone of the story is sympathetic rather than sarcastic, and the subsidiary characters are carefully built up, not merely sketched in. Moreover, we have here, as always in Miss Cather's novels, the atmosphere and charm of outdoor life, realism touched with deep feeling for nature as well as man. Claude is unsatisfied rather than dissatisfied; his natural tendency toward expansion on the side of thoughtful idealism is hemmed in by his surroundings, by sordid necessities of heavy toil, by a facile and selfish brother, a jocose materialistic father, and finally a narrow, cold, and undomestic wife who insists on going to China to help the missionaries rather than care for home and husband.

The novel is, so to speak, broken apart in the middle by that which broke apart so many things—the World War. It is disappointing that Claude's problems; so well set forth, should not be worked out to any conclusion. The war scenes are vivid; Claude's experiences are in some respects singular and evidently based on authentic war knowledge, and the inevitable tragic end is moving. The two parts of the book are painfully disjoined; as Mr. Lewis has written of this book, Miss Cather might as well, so far as working out its theme is concerned, have pushed Claude down a well as have sent him to war.

There is a clear note of sincerity in all of Miss Cather's writing. *My Antonia* remains her best book, but *One of Ours* is in impressionistic effect far above the average novel.

Marion Ponsonby, "Across a Chasm," *New York Evening Post, The Literary Review*, 21 October 1922, p. 138

To the Editor of *The Literary Review*:
Sir: You have already published a letter about Mr. Sinclair Lewis's review of Miss Willa Cather's latest book, *One of Ours*. May I add my comment?

The interest of Mr. Lewis's criticism undoubtedly lies mainly in the uniquely different outlooks and temperaments of reviewer and reviewed. When tempers so different meet on grounds vital to both the reaction is apt to be oddly personal. In this case Mr. Lewis's reaction to Miss Cather sheds more light on himself than on Miss Cather. Perhaps this is because Mr. Lewis confessedly does not understand Miss Cather all the way; "for a moment of modesty" he admits himself to

be in the presence of a spirit that he may not understand. If this admission is more revealing to his readers than he himself knew, his candor softens the self portrait which his review paints with a surprising clarity. In spite of the excellence of Mr. Van Doren's survey of *Babbitt*—which shares the page with Mr. Lewis's of *One of Ours*—one could wish that editorial curiosity had here submitted Mr. Lewis's book to Miss Cather! One feels that her reaction would have been as personally revealing as his.

For Miss Cather's stock virtues, her honesty, the fresh reality of her observations, Mr. Lewis shows sincere appreciation. But even here is his comprehension of her accurate?

For instance, take the following paragraph:

[Cather has] the courage to be tender and perfectly simple, to let the reader suppose, if he so desires, that the author lacks all understanding of the hard varnished, cosmopolitan cleverness which is the note of the hour.

Now, "the courage to be tender and perfectly simple," though a fine phrase, does not seem entirely right for Miss Cather's deep-hearted interpretation of life's many complications. To be sure, to meet the mind and heart-breaking aspects of life with simplicity and directness is perhaps the endeavor most evident in everything Miss Cather has written. This in turn seems to spring from a desire for sincerity so intense that at its one extreme it blunts her sense for effect and stiffens her dialogue, at its other, lends her a perfect blend of outer detail and inner meaning, gives her a presentation entirely her own and unequalled for tender power in America. But an endeavor as basic as this comes from inside and automatically counts out any assumed role, however courageous. It is simply Miss Cather herself versus life, and Miss Cather would care so little for the reader's opinion of her own sophistication that to "brave" it would take little bravery in her. No, Miss Cather's special quality is not at all the sort of thing implied by Mr. Lewis's paragraph, the French mode of purity and simplicity in spite of sophistication, applied to America. Miss Cather, like Mr. Lewis himself, is America incarnate, stoutly forthright.

Indeed, contrasting as these two are, both are American to such a degree that inevitably they have gone to meet each other in their work—and to step on each other's toes! Neither could resist making a lifework of a country which so clearly expressed in the large the qualities of each. Both are busy writing from close observation of America, not as each might wish to see it, but as it actually appears to each. And, of course, the importance of Mr. Lewis's review lies in its unconscious exposition of the bewilderingly different Americas evolved by these two eagerly gazing realists.

Mr. Lewis's own world, from which of course his America springs, may be said to be defined in this review by the line at which his comprehension of Miss Cather stops. He appreciates her more obvious qualities. But there he halts, admittedly and unconsciously baffled by the strange things Miss Cather will do with her story. And rather weakly he falls back upon accusing her of bewilderment. Here the present correspondent must hasten to explain that it is only because of instinctively belonging in Miss Cather's world—and so instinctively understanding her—that a greater knowledge of Miss Cather than that possessed by "the foremost novelist of America" [Lewis, as described by the editors of *The Literary Review*] is about to be assumed.

"The whole introduction of the war is doubtful.... Having set the Enid problem, she evades it." Mr. Lewis knows how he would have handled Claude's cruelly cold marriage ... and he is horrified that Miss Cather should ship Claude off to war with every personal thread left dangling. Since neither sex nor a career is furthered, Mr. Lewis hazards a guess that Miss Cather sent him over for dramatic effect. Now, to a real Cather reader it seems obvious that Miss Cather was not plotting or planning either about Claude's life or her own dramatic effect. It seems true, if not obvious, that what she was doing was a thing so big and simple that it naturally cut hero and story adrift from ordinary moorings. The book cannot be judged by ordinary tests of plot or situation. It is surely the unassuming epic in colloquial form of Miss Cather's own salient passion, obvious again in every word she has written, and at the root even of that other passion of hers for sincerity—I mean the passion of *caring*. This book is her epic of caring versus calculation and self-interest. And in the great war, in the story of young men who went to war, she found her simplest, most perfect opportunity to write about her own deepest passion.... She knows in all her books that people everywhere care enough to die for caring, but here she builds her whole story on humanity's epic manifestation of that fact. In a sense the book must have written itself. She does not have to argue the fact of caring; the war illustrates it. She does not have to explain the sort of fact caring is; the war shows explicitly that caring is a hard fact that gets your life blood sooner or later. She does not have to deal in intricacies of development or in open symbols—a straightforward story without even a plot does the task. I imagine the writing of this book must have been a sort of "watchful waiting." Things take their course. Claude goes to war as the sparks fly upward. Cold Enid is forgotten by him and by Miss Cather as soon as coldness and indifference are lost on outgoing tides.

All this seems simple of explanation. But having reluctantly followed Claude overseas, Mr. Lewis becomes more seriously puzzled. Nothing intelligible or decisive happens to Claude through the rest of the book—what *is* Miss Cather doing with him now [that] she's got him here? The "war-stuff" to me appears simple and first hand, intimately belonging to *One of Ours*, but Mr. Lewis says it is journalism, and he should be able to speak with authority about that sort of reporting. But when he objects to Claude himself, to his remaining so pure and noble overseas "that no one can believe in him," one cannot help but suspect a defect in Mr. Lewis's experience. If Miss Cather set out to write an epic of caring, it seems that she did well to choose for her central figure a spirit that cares from birth, a boy essentially pure if not innocent, essentially indifferent to the baser elements. Mr. Lewis has apparently never met a youth like Claude! They do come. And usually they are just such faltering, high-minded, unassuming boys as Claude. But Mr. Lewis objects not only to Claude, but also strongly to his joy in the war, which he sets down as idealism. Clearly it is part the joy of novelty and rapid experience to a starved mind and heart, but the depths of it as clearly are not idealism. Ugliness is not dwelt upon, but it is not evaded. Indeed, it unexpectedly becomes the focal point of Claude's private life. For it was only because people could go through such killing ugliness as he had not dreamed before that at least, after a youth overshadowed by calculation and self-interest, he was sure they cared. However, this does not answer Mr. Lewis's anxiety as to what happened to Claude overseas. ... Well, Miss Cather's readers will have to admit that nothing whatever happened to Claude in a Main Street sense. ... Must it be left to this humble correspondent to point out to Mr. Lewis that sometimes in life things come along that sweep the most sizzling personal problems into nonexistence? (Temporarily, of course. If Mr. Lewis doubts Miss Cather's knowledge of frustration, of humanity's ability to slump, he has omitted reading the last page of *One of Ours*.) And must I add that at such moments of personal annihilation, the spirit's victory has a way of unexpectedly accomplishing itself? Nothing whatever happened to Claude overseas but a hard and simple spiritual and mental fulfillment through caring justified, and death which crystallized his moment of inner victory, *his* caring. Finally Mr. Lewis objects to the claptrap heroics of Claude's death. It seems that there were enough of "Ours" who died bravely at the top of the trench to warrant Miss Cather's choice of a heroic death as her final symbol of caring.

If Mr. Lewis were not puzzled, he might not object to so many things. Just why is he puzzled? To one reader's mind, at least, the root difference between Miss Cather and Mr. Lewis is not in method of realism, though here is a technical study for those interested. Nor is it a difference in values, in things valuable to either writer, things cared *about*. Though here again Miss Cather would choose *these* facts about something, Mr. Lewis *those*, so that the identity of their two subjects could scarcely be guessed. Each set of facts and values are generally actual, and so are valuable for the files of our country. But Miss Cather writes and chooses *this* way, Mr. Lewis writes and chooses *that* way because of a root difference between passion and criticism. Miss Cather's people are shown up on a basis of passionate caring or not caring; caring makes the focal point and interest of her books. In Mr. Lewis's works, the passion of caring has turned into an almost kiddish joy in seeing, not into, as Miss Cather does, but through his characters. There is little passion of any sort. He is the clever younger brother of America who can at once mimic and take off his more serious older family. I realize that this description is not adequate for as serious and honest a writer as Mr. Lewis, one who cares tremendously about his books and about liberty of thought. But on the whole Mr. Lewis's work is lined up on the basis of a shrewd and valuable observation, largely mental and critical. Now when one cares, one immediately begins to feel, and feeling brings intuition; when intuition is interpreted by a steady mind, one gets things that the cleverest mind unaided by intuition cannot analyze. And here, closely connected with the root difference in intensity, one catches at a glance the reason why Sinclair Lewis must be puzzled by Miss Cather . . . Miss Cather's America is a closed book always to Main Street, and certainly it is one with leaves scarcely cut to the writer who has made himself famous by seeing through Main Street. Mr. Lewis simply has not got the intuitional equipment for understanding Miss Cather, although he has an uncanny intuition for public psychology! Their worlds, their Americas, overlap only part way. And I doubt if Miss Cather could really comprehend Mr. Lewis. She could not take him objectively enough to be fair to him. And yet—Mr. Lewis has just published a fine book about Babbitt, a man who is emerging like his city from the Main Street sort of thing. This man does care in his fashion, and when caring begins the Main Street sort of thing begins to shift and merge into Miss Cather's sort of thing. . . . Well, we need badly enough both the self-consciousness of criticism and better intuition. Perhaps the America of the future will know how to use and blend the two.

"Hero and Dreamer from Middle West," *Springfield* (Massachusetts) *Republican,* 29 October 1922, p. 7A

Miss Willa Cather's *One of Ours* again demonstrates the author's power of employing the novel realistically for vitally imaginative purposes. She makes a homely setting, plausibly and truthfully sketched, and with it surrounds an equally plausible, though unusual, personal tragedy. Moreover, she uses the background and the narrative as an analysis of national culture. Here, surely —granted the gift of incisive character-drawing—is the scheme of as significant fiction as our modern realistic taste can expect. One cannot say that Miss Cather has entirely realized the possibilities of the scheme; but her new work, though without marked individuality of style, represents a high degree of artistic creation, as well as a strong achievement of emotional story-telling.

The book fails in design just because the war is used to solve its basic problems. We know now that the war solved no spiritual questions for America, to whatever degree it may have resolved the spiritual perplexities of individuals. The 200 pages devoted to the war are a tour de force of descriptive writing, and they do reveal to some extent what the "discovery" of Europe meant to the boy from the farms of the Middle West. But, in reality, it must be believed that the ultimate and collective response of the middle western farm boy to his war-time European adventures was not a desire to assimilate what is

150

abidingly beautiful in Europe, but a desire to get back home. Consequently, the war chapters of the book, filled with incidents that are vivid perhaps but not eloquent of character, seem almost as alien to Claude's development as the war itself to America's Middle West. And this despite the fact that one of the purposes of the novel was to portray the effect of the war upon the middle western mind.

The strong imaginative power of the author is illustrated in her portrayal of the hero and of the persons and scenes surrounding his early life. Claude Wheeler, son of a practical-minded but whimsical Maine man and an earnest, gentle, religious Vermont woman, is gifted with a kind of sensibility that reveals the cultural limitations of his environment. Circumstances are not kind to him. He is obliged to give up his education at just the point when he is most likely to profit by it, and perhaps find opportunity for the development of such intellectual powers as he possesses. He marries—though warned by her father—an unlovable woman—one whose idealistic vein, such as it is, is solely occupied with religion, which intensifies her lack of sympathy with human affections and aspirations.

Claude's principal early joy arises in his friendship with a family of Germans. "He had supposed the Ehrlichs were rich people but he found out afterward that they were poor. The father was dead, and all the boys had to work, even those who were still in school. They merely knew how to live, he discovered, and spent their money on themselves, instead of on machines to do the work and machines to entertain people." Claude is too practical to be an idle dreamer, but his sympathy is with the people "whose wish is so beautiful that there are no experiences in this world to satisfy it." Fleeing even more from his divine dissatisfaction than from a loveless marriage, he enlists for service,

makes a kindly and sensible officer, and is killed.

Miss Cather's characters divide between those who have this sense of the beauty and mystery of the world, and in whose lives runs this vein of aspiration, and those who are satisfied with prosaic realities—more prosaic, no doubt, on the Nebraska farm than in the cities and villages of the East, all with their organized sociability and their commercial amusements. In the former group besides Claude, are enrolled his mother, whom religion ennobles, the old Negro servant Mahailey and a girl Gladys, whom he should have married, but who is courted by his mean-spirited avaricious brother, Bayliss, advocate of Pacifism from narrow and sordid motives and devoted to Prohibition. Miss Cather is not biased or one-sided in her portraiture, though it seems to be a tendency of hers to make her aspiring, artistic people musicians or devotees of music. Possibly the author has more sympathy with the German than the Anglo-Saxon strain in the Middle West, considered in its whole contribution to the composite culture of that region.

Gamaliel Bradford, "The Atlantic's Bookshelf," *Atlantic Monthly*, 130 (November 1922), n.p.

Miss Cather's new story is a profound and powerful epic of the great war.

The foundation is laid in the Middle West, which Miss Cather knows so well and always depicts with such a loving touch. We see the strangely mixed and blended races, typified in vividly natural and contrasted human figures, tilling together the huge, rich, dumb, responsive earth. Life creeps onward from day to day, repeating its old, common, monotonous comedies and tragedies, poignant to those who play in them, tame to superficial observers and meaningless.

The hero of the book is a plain American, Claude Wheeler, who does his work, ploughs and harrows, earns and spends, eats, drinks, and sleeps, with the rest. Yet he differs from the more stolid souls about him in that life puzzles and perplexes him, seems to mean nothing and to lead nowhere, yet somehow suggests vast possibilities which leave his eager, restless spirit forever unsatisfied. What does it all mean? What is it all tending to? What is the eternal use, the purpose, the profit of this great, rich, sensual, industrious, middle-western America? To what end are the powers and sensibilities that he feels stirring in himself—only to die?

He asks these questions obscurely, half consciously, while his earnest muscles go about their daily labor and the months and years slip away. He asks—and no one answers. His stalwart, prosperous, cynical father does not answer him. His mother's remote, hidden God does not answer him. His cold, mild, persistent, unresponsive wife does not answer him.

Then the great war comes. Claude is swept into it, with a million others, is swept over the vast, strange ocean, with deaths crowding about him even there, is swept over the sunny fields of France, and dies, like so many others, the death of a hero, still with the puzzle in his heart, and in Miss Cather's heart, and in the reader's heart. But the solution suggested is in the sanctification of glory over duty done.

The sense of mystery and the sense of beauty make the charm of this latest book of Miss Cather's, as they made the charm of the lovely *April Twilights* twenty years ago. But the mystery has perhaps deepened and darkened under the strain of life;

and the feeling of beauty, if no less intense, is somewhat less permeating. And I like to turn back from Claude's heroic sacrifice to the verses which have sung so long in my memory and which make so touching an epilogue to the later book:

So blind is life, so long at last is
    sleep,
And none but Love to bid us laugh
    or weep,
    And none but Love,
    And none but Love. ["Evening
    Song"]

Florence Fleisher, "Prophets in Their Own Country," *Survey*, 49 (1 November 1922), 192, 201

... Whatever their artistic defects, *Children of the Marketplace* by Mr. Masters, *One of Ours* by Miss Cather and *Babbitt* by Mr. Lewis are the books among the latest American fiction most worth reading. They are all concerned with the immediate moment in this country.

Only apparently is *Children of the Marketplace* a historical novel centering about the political career of Stephen A. Douglas and showing the economic forces directing the expansionist stage of our national development. In effect it is an analysis of the present in the light of that period. The first-person narrator of the story can be taken as a symbolic figure of America as was the central character in Mr. Master's previous *Domesday Book*. But this comparison adds little to the point. In revivifying a past of which we are the uncomprehending heirs, Mr.

Masters has done an admirable piece of work. The story itself is of little consequence.

With all respect to Edith Wharton, Willa Cather is nevertheless our most considerable woman novelist. Her people are the stuff of our life as she knows it from her own state of Nebraska: Bohemians, Germans, Norwegians, Swedes, French—all pioneer Americans. She recognizes the caliber of material it takes to understand the "little joke" of the land which "pretended to be poor because nobody knew how to work it right; and then, all at once, it worked itself." In *One of Ours* she leans back to ponder what the land has to give the descendants of those men and women who have won it. She shows the son of a homesteader in his attempt to get satisfaction in his small environment, his small college, his small marriage (the small life in a large country, as one of our university presidents has recently put it). Every day passes, half played. The war comes to him as it came to thousands of other boys and adult men, a release. Not from the misadventures of youth; a release for the extravagant pouring forth of faith and service. "He died," says Miss Cather, "believing his own country better than it is, and France better than any country can ever be. And those were beautiful beliefs to die with. Perhaps it was as well to see that vision, and then to see no more." What is the matter with our land, is her message, that it has beautiful beliefs only for death? This boy was no exceptional boy, no particular hero—merely one of ours.

H[enry] W[alcott] Boynton, "Sweeping the Sky," *Independent*, 109 (11 November 1922), 278–81

Among the select lists of our most eminent no names have been more secure of late than Cather and Hergesheimer. However we may be partitioned from each other by differences of generation and temperament and opinion, we seem to come together on a common zone of respect for these two among contemporary American novelists. And this is a good sign, since our respect is given for the purity and single-mindedness of their art. Ever since *The Song of the Lark*, ever since *The Three Black Pennys*, we have felt securely that with all the reporting and the propaganda and the lively irresponsible commentary in the recent fiction, nevertheless the art of story-telling, the art of responsible and imaginative interpretation, is by no means lost. . . .

Miss Cather's *One of Ours* is on the surface a story of now familiar type. Her Claude Wheeler is the sensitive, blundering young American who finds himself, or his reason for being, through the war. He is "one of ours" in both the national and the military sense; in the local sense, too, as a "son of the middle border." Wheeler the father, however, is not of the heroic, unrewarded pioneer type. He has homesteaded in Nebraska in the early days, and remained to grow rich in land-trading. Nominally a farmer at the time of the story, he leases most of his land and lives in jovial ease, a well-liked and on the whole beneficent citizen. His wife has brought from Vermont the New England piety and primness. Their three sons differ as resultants from such an union. The oldest, Bayliss, is a prig and a money-grubber. The youngest, Ralph, has much of his father's careless geniality and interest in the world in general. It is with the second boy, Claude, that we have to do.

Claude Wheeler is, in type, a pathetic commonplace. He is a misfit; a good, intelligent lad with a yearning but without a star. He is too sensitive to be satisfied with his father's good-humored cynicism, too intelligent to accept his mother's old-fashioned reliance upon an orthodox God. He has vague aesthetic and intellectual possibilities, but not the will to develop them despite an unfavorable environment. He murmurs ineffectually against conditions which a determined rebellion would change for him. And, with the right woman in plain sight, he lets himself be married by the wrong woman. This is fatal for him, since he is the sort of man who must be properly mated or be naught. Enid, indeed, is one of those unendurable wives who are being revealed, or travestied, in so many recent novels—If Winter Comes, for example. She is prude and bigot and egotist; we sigh with relief when she makes off to China, and we and Claude are done with her. Claude is left to close the shell of a home he has built with so pathetic hopes. There remain his mother, who yearns over him but cannot give him happiness, and his work upon the homestead farm, which he performs with a sort of dogged fidelity. He is a failure in his own eyes; his life, it appears, is over.

But it is now 1917. For three years the war has been coming closer to America, even the sheltered America of the Middle West. For Claude Wheeler our entrance into the war that is to unmake war, is a life-boat upon the dark welter of existence. He goes to training camp "burning with the first ardor of the enlisted man.

He believed that he was going abroad with an expeditionary force that would make war without rage, with uncompromising generosity and chivalry." Thus, at the end of the Book Three, we see him setting forth for the embarkation, with the blessing of his patriotic parents, and of the woman he ought to have married. So far we have been hearing the story-teller at her best. The scene and persons of the tale are as vivid and indigenous, as full of homely truth, as the scene and persons of Rose of Dutcher's Coolly, or Silas Lapham or My Antonia. And with Claude's departure for France the action is complete.

Therefore I am doubtful, I own with reluctance, about the artistic value of Books Four and Five—some two-fifths of the whole narrative. All they amount to so far as Claude is concerned, is that he passes through the agonies and squalors of modern warfare without losing his high satisfaction in service to a worthy cause; and dies, with exultation, a soldier's death, instead of having to face the disillusion and enervation of the after-war years. For the rest, these two parts strike me as a remarkable tour de force, a study of actual conditions at the front fit to be compared with a dozen others, from Ordeal By Fire to The Test of Scarlet, which have realistically projected an experience most of us by now (weakly, no doubt) are fain to forget. There are moments when Miss Cather employs a naturalism merely revolting. The upshot of it all is that the war is a nearly meaningless and fruitless enormity, and that Claude is lucky to die in the full glow of his romantic dream. "For him the call was clear, the cause was glorious. Never a doubt stained his bright faith. . . . He died believing his own country better than it is, and France better than any country can ever be." And his mother, understanding that he has always been of those who "in order to do what they did had to hope extravagantly, and to believe passionately," thanks Fate for "one she knew who could ill bear disillusion . . . safe, safe."

Lorna R. F. Birtwell, "*One of Ours* Again," *New York Evening Post, The Literary Review,* 25 November 1922, p. 254

To the Editor of *The Literary Review*:
Sir: The letter on Willa Cather's *One of Ours* by Marion Ponsonby in a recent *Review* was deeply reassuring to some of your readers. Here, at last, was a finely sensitive response to one of our most significant books, in place of an attempt to superimpose the preconceived and rather trite notions of the critics on a work whose distinction it is that it escapes from just such grooves as they would mark out for it.

Because Miss Cather's art more than any other today troubles the heart with truth and beauty, I have watched the bewildered response of the professional critics to *One of Ours* with painful attention. Was ever such an exhibition of spiritual and emotional dullness? It is as if the need to say something, to fix the status of the book once and for all, to classify and pigeon-hole, had paralyzed the power to read, understand, and enjoy, which is the privilege of those not called upon to mould the public taste.

The various groups of critics are magnificently disagreed in their diagnosis, many of them loving what others hate.

Heywood Broun, who had almost persuaded us that art should not be propaganda, quarrels with *One of Ours, a priori,* because it is not sufficiently good anti-war propaganda. How it can be regarded as propaganda of any sort is difficult to see. Yet Broun is not alone in attacking it on this ground.

Still another group, headed by Sinclair Lewis, see only one solution for Claude Wheeler's demand for a richer life— namely an illicit adventure in sex. But if we read Claude aright, his unfortunate marriage was only one of many ways in which he felt himself defrauded; and a happy union would have been only one of many ways in which he might have obtained some measure of fulfillment. Moreover, if Gladys Farmer be the one selected by Mr. Lewis and the rest to round out Claude's experience in this respect, it is obvious that, passionate and generous as she is, she would not, for a hundred little considerations not recognized in machine-made fiction, have played the role, nor would Claude have proposed it.

Then there is the esoteric school of critics, represented perhaps by Gilbert Seldes. We fancy that he believes or rather hopes, that he may have said something in his review in the October *Dial*. He speaks in a vaguely oracular way of the difference between "recording" and "creating." We know of no real creation, however, other than a finely selective recording with the creative imagination as arbiter. How beautifully selected, how delicately stressed, how vitally fused are the "recordings" in *One of Ours*. Not once is a rare detail insisted on for its own sake. It is touched lightly, surely, and then let go.

There are those who find *One of Ours* dull! Upon what neurotic stuff have they fed that its sustained noble movement, its vibrant overtones leave them unsatisfied?

With what fireworks have their eyes been dazzled that they cannot see the quiet, steady shining of stars?

Of all of these Lewisohn alone in the *Nation* writes with depth and understanding. He says of Miss Cather, "she has ripeness, sobriety with passion at its core."

Yet even he wants to "do something" with the book in accordance with a preconceived idea. It might seem that an author capable of the above excellences could be trusted to preserve the organic unity of her work and to know its climax. But Mr. Lewisohn has discovered that death, formerly too often invoked as a solution, must *never under any circumstances* be the end, that it is a mere evasion. Rightly discarding the pistol shot or dagger thrust that brought the old fashioned tragedy to a close, he, nevertheless, is in a fair way to found a dogmatism as rigid. He finds *One of Ours* "a broken epic," and adds: "We are still waiting, we shall always be waiting for the end of the story which catastrophe cut short but could not complete." Yet, surely, the will to look at death steadfastly, to be tasked and strained to the utmost, "to render all, no less," is one of the major adventures of life, and one that would be ardently embraced by a passionate heart like Claude's. William James has commented on the universal desire of humanity "to be stretched to its capacity." Rupert Brooke, snatched from the midst of all that Miss Cather's hero had lacked, sang his great song on this theme and found, with thousands of others, this particular end to the high endeavor. Almost, one might believe, there is no other solution, in war or in peace, than this, no other way of finding life worth living. Like Rupert Brooke, Claude Wheeler leaves with us,

. . . a white
Unbroken glory, a gathered radiance,

A width, a shining peace, under the night.

As for the critics, kindly but blundering, again in the words of Rupert Brooke, one might say:

You came and quacked beside me . . .
By God, I wish, I wish that you were dead!

[signed] Lorna R. F. Birtwell. Maplewood, N.J.

Donald R. Murphy, Des Moines *Register* [Autumn 1922]

The more guileless of the tender-minded novel readers who think that Coningsby Dawson is a great writer and that *Three Soldiers* is an insult to the American army, are likely to rejoice greatly at first over Willa Cather's *One of Ours*. Indeed, Miss Cather stands in great danger of getting the same sort of chautauqua salute that was tendered to Dorothy Canfield when she wrote *The Brimming Cup*. *The Brimming Cup*, you see, was an answer to *Main Street*. And *One of Ours*, in some circles and for a few days, may be considered as being an answer to *Three Soldiers*.

Yet, as the legion of the simpleminded reads the book over, doubts may arise. Given a small degree of intelligence on the part of the readers, these doubts will become certainties. Eventually they may see, and with horror, that what Miss Cather is saying is that the only justification for the war was that it got the middle western boy away from the small town and the farm, and that the only real tragedy of the war was that he had to go back to Nebraska after it was over.

What will fool some readers for a time is that Claude Wheeler likes the army; he likes France; he even is permitted a few final thrills in the moment of his death. But Miss Cather makes it devastatingly plain just why Claude finds delight in a life that drove Andrews in *Three Soldiers* to rebellion and a tragic end.

Wheeler is a farm boy from Nebraska. His is the limiting small town and farm environment that Miss Cather has shown so well in *My Antonia*, in the short stories in *Youth and the Bright Medusa* and in *The Song of the Lark*. A boy with an instinct for living, with a living for beauty and for adventure, he is beaten at every hand by the town, by his father, by his wife. At twenty-five he is getting to be like his father-in-law, just "a big machine with the springs broken inside."

The war lifts him out of all this. He gets the romance of the idea of America as the Galahad of the nations. His illusion is one with that of millions of other boys in 1917 and its presentation is so adequate that Miss Cather runs some risk of being made an honorary member of the American Legion on the strength of it.

Gerhardt, Claude's friend is a soldier of much the same temperament as that of Andrews in *Three Soldiers*. He escapes the tragedy of Andrews largely because his lines have fallen in pleasanter places. Gerhardt and Wheeler both hold commissions and so do not suffer the brutality which the army metes out to enlisted men in the name of discipline. They are attached to a regiment, which in the immortal words of Major Peck, "shows all the earmarks of a national guard outfit," and so escapes some of the Prussianistic traits of which the regular and the national army were so proud. Yet, even at that, Gerhardt looks upon the war as nothing but so much purposeless floundering in the muck. His profession and his mode of life have given him adventures of the spirit and the intellect that make the war seem a pale and badly acted melodrama. Wheeler, just paroled from Nebraska, finds it the great adventure of the age.

Wheeler's is a sad enough existence, bounded on one side by an unsympathetic environment and on the other by an untimely death in action. Yet, in the space between, he had a few months to rejoice in the company of men like Gerhardt, or like Morse of Crystal Lake, i.e., liberated from the middle west for a few years of folly, and of heroism. Wheeler had a little time to love a people and a civilization that accounted art and music and letters worth thinking about. The war, for him, is a moment of beauty between two horrors.

Wheeler is killed in the Argonne. He has the tremendous good fortune of not being forced to face a future which was to show that the war was really a rather scurvy joke on the idealists who took part in it. As to those who survived, Miss Cather has this to say in a page that will make the people who dislike Dos Passos add Willa Cather to their index expurgatorious:

"He died believing his own country better than it is and France better than any country can ever be. And those were beautiful beliefs to die with. Perhaps it was as well to see that vision and then to see no more. She (these are the thoughts of Claude's mother) would have dreaded the awakening— she sometimes even doubts whether he could have borne at all that last, desolating disappointment. One by one the heroes of that war, the men of dazzling soldiership, leave prematurely the world they have come back to. Airmen whose deeds were tales of wonder, officers whose names made the blood of youth beat faster, survivors of incredible dangers—one by one they quietly died by their own hand. Some do it in obscure lodging houses, some in their office, where they seemed to be carrying on their business like other men. Some slip over a vessel's side and disappear into the sea. When Claude's mother hears of these things, she shudders and presses her hands tight over her breast, as if God had saved him from some horrible suffering, some horrible end. For, as she reads, she thinks those slayers of themselves were all so like him; they were the ones who had hoped extravagantly—who in order to do what they did had to hope extravagantly, and to believe passionately. And they found they had hoped and believed too much."

"Mrs. Sheldon Reviews Willa Cather's Novel" [clipping from unidentified Lincoln newspaper, Autumn 1922, in Willa Cather scrapbooks, Red Cloud, II-29], p. 4B

A review by Mrs. Addison E. Sheldon of Willa Cather's latest novel, *One of Ours*, followed by an open discussion of the book, was the principal feature of the program of the A.A.U.W., which met at the Woodburn Saturday for luncheon....

Widely varying opinions of the truthfulness and excellence of *One of Ours* were expressed after Mrs. Sheldon's resumé of the plot. Mrs. Ellery Davis declared that she felt while reading it that

she was taking a post-graduate course on middle western life that followed a very unpleasant undergraduate course with Sinclair Lewis. She considers it, however, the most interesting thing she has read on the war, representing the hero as a prisoner escaped from narrowness and meeting his experience with bright and keen enthusiasm.

Mrs. C. A. Sorenson declared that she, on the other hand, likes Willa Cather principally for the challenges her writing offers, and quoted brief passages from the book in which the author attacks various narrow-minded prejudices.

Miss Stella Kirker commented on what she considers the superb description of the Westermann library and other scenes familiar to Lincoln and Nebraska people.

Both Miss Ida Robbins and Mrs. Maurice Deutsch felt that the novel was not fair to the small communities of Nebraska or to the university, that the conditions it describes were more typical of the early nineties than they are of the present. Mrs. Deutsch declared that to her the most striking feature of the book was the suggestion it must give to Lincoln people of the possibilities there are for them in influencing the lives of students here in university.

The restlessness of the hero, Mrs. E. L. Hinman considers the inseparable characteristic of youth, and she likes the hero, Claude, but resents Enid, his wife. In her opinion the ending is not tragic, for Claude is saved from the tragic disillusionment that many soldiers met in finding that their sacrifice in the war had not brought the new day.

The discussion was closed by Mrs. Sheldon, who stated that in preparation for her review of *One of Ours*, she had read everything she could that has been published in recent years about the middle west and that she thinks Willa Cather's representations of it are better than any others, in landscape, in understanding of the life of farmers, and in nature setting.

She praised the marvellous simplicity of Miss Cather's plot and her ability to make her characters stand forth distinct and dissimilar. Her great interest, Mrs. Sheldon believes, is in the intellectual and she is not so understanding when she portrays reformers, church people, or church colleges.

Commenting on the motive of the book, Miss Sheldon took exception to Dorothy Canfield Fisher's review which declared that Miss Cather's purpose was to arouse sympathy for the ex-service man. Altho this may have had some part in Miss Cather's purpose, Mrs. Sheldon believes that the author was there absorbed in another problem, which she could not solve because it has never been answered in life, that of the meaning of existence. . . .

me sentimental and unreal. I have just reread the book and have considerably revised my opinion. There has been so much grim realism about the war that Miss Cather's views are surprising; and then one reflects that she is a woman who was not, so far as one knows, in the war, and that, therefore, her pictures are at second hand. But on second reading one is expecting her point of view, and one sees how subtly and carefully it is approached throughout the book. More and more symbolism stands out from the latter pages of the book, and altho there is still something of a borrowed vision about Miss Cather's war pictures, they have seemed to me more justified by far than I had first supposed. About the first half of the book there can be no question. It is magnificent in its pictures of nature; its creation of individuals; its humor and its type of American soul. The old farm servant is an unforgettable creation of genius.

Hugh Walpole, "The Year's Harvest in Fiction: An English Critic's View of the Six Best American Novels," *Literary Digest International Book Review*, 1 (January 1923), 7, 70

About Miss Cather's *One of Ours* there has been a storm of controversy. The reviewers have almost without exception attacked the second half of her book—the war episodes. I must make a confession here. I first read the book some two months ago and was deeply disappointed in the last hundred pages. They seemed to

Louise Maunsell Field, *Literary Digest International Book Review*, 1 (January 1923), 58–9

Exceptionally well written, yet by no means a great novel, Miss Cather's *One of Ours* tells acceptably the story of one of those gallant young doughboys of whom all true Americans are proud. In the beginning, the long descriptions of farm life are tedious, and the sharp break between the book's two sections, which comes when Claude Wheeler goes to the war, injures its continuity. Its point of view is extremely pessimistic; Claude's mother, who is obviously the author's mouthpiece at the end, feels that to die was the happiest fate which could have befallen the son she dearly loved. For those who, like Claude, were idealists could not endure their disappointment. "One by one, the heroes of that war, the men of dazzling soldiership, leave prematurely the world they have come back to. ... One by one they quietly die by their own hands. ... They were the ones who had hoped extravagantly—who, in order to do what they did, had to hope extravagantly and to believe passionately. And they found they had hoped and believed too much."

Nor is it only in its conclusion that the novel is pessimistic; its view of the farmers and of the general life of the Middle West is almost as unflattering as that of *Main Street*. Claude Wheeler was an alien among his own people because he could not share their passion for "things"—for new reapers and new automobiles and talking-machines and cream-separators which were more trouble than anything else, nor believe as they did in the supreme importance of making and spending money. There is little of nobility, little of beauty, much of the materialistic in this Middle Western life as Miss Cather presents it, a life in which flesh is all, and spirit little or nothing. When there is religion, it is a religion like that of Claude's mother, who firmly believed that "the mind should remain obediently within the theological conception of history." Yet Mrs. Wheeler, for all her narrowness, had something of fineness too, and tho the daily existence here depicted scenes nearly as dreary to the reader as it did to Claude, most of the characters have at least a few good qualities of their own. Claude himself has been carefully drawn, and he wins a certain amount of sympathy, while many of the minor characters are flesh-and-blood people—Enid, the exceedingly

unpleasant female Claude married, her dissatisfied father, the delightful Sergeant Hicks, and others.

The overseas part of the novel is very much the more interesting. It has incident and color, and tho Claude's friend Victor Morse is not entirely convincing, several of the other people he meets are very well done. The book snows understanding and sympathy, and its descriptions are often vivid. It is an essentially tragic novel; tragic, not because Claude is killed, but because its point of view is that in this world there is no place for the idealist, that just because Claude was fine and sensitive, cleansouled and aspiring, the best that could possibly be wished for him was death.

Christopher Ward, "The New Curiosity Shop: *One of Ours*," *New York Evening Post, The Literary Review*, 3 February 1923, p. 435; reprinted as "One of Hers: Long After Willa Cather," in *The Triumph of the Nut . . .* (New York: Holt, 1923)

(*This chapter does not appear in Willa Cather's book.*)

Claude and his men, B Company, were holding the Boar's Head trench. He knew that the German attack might be expected about dawn. The smoke and darkness had begun to take on the livid color that announced the coming of daybreak, when a corporal hurried to him, saluted and announced that the linemen had completed the connection and that Claude was called on the telephone.

He went to the dugout, took down the receiver, and David, who was just outside, heard the following conversation:

"Lieutenant Wheeler, in command of B Company in H-2, speaking.

"What? Miss Willa? For the land's sake, what're *you* doing away out here?

"Course you are, Miss Willa. I know that, but you hadn't ought of come out in such a dangerous place just to look out for me. Really, ma'am, I'm getting along all right. You don't have to tell me every little thing.

"You want me to *what*?

"On the *parapet* when the *attack* comes?

"Why, good Lord, Miss Willa, I wouldn't do that for a farm.

"I *got* to do it? How's that? I don't see why.

"Yes'm. I know that. I know you are. I read it in a piece in a magazine. Said you were one of America's serious novelists. Yes'm, called you a serious artist of high purpose, the piece did.

"But, say, you know that's awful dangerous. I might easy get killed.

"You *expect* me to? Look here, lady, I don't know what you're driving at.

"Oh, yes, o' course, I know that. I know I got to do what you say after I signed up with you.

"No'm, I might not be. I know that. I might be in the draft at a trainin' camp or somewhere back there or prob'ly I'd got exempted on account of bein' the only one on the farm—if it wasn't for you.

"Well, if you was right out in this trench now I don't think you'd think there was any special thanks due for you gettin' me here.

"No, *ma'am*! I *don't*! I ain't hungry for just that kind o' glory. *You bet not.* I'll be satisfied to go home alive.

"Oh, Lord, yes! I got plenty to do when I get home.

"How's that? Spoiled? Oh, no, Miss Willa, my life ain't spoiled yet, but I've got a hunch it would be if I got up on that parapet. Oh, no, I've got a lot o' plans. Don't you worry about that. Ain't many young fellows get their life spoiled at twenty-three.

"My wife? Sure, she's left me all right. An', Miss Willa, I hope you won't get mad if I say I think that was really your fault. I'm pretty sure Enid wouldn't have gone to China 'f you hadn't kind of mesmerized her and made her go. I think 'f you'd a let her alone she'd be on the farm now.

"Yes'm, she did. She went all right and I'm not sure she's comin' back; but if she don't, why there's plenty more. Gladys, f'r instance. And that's another thing I kind of got against you, Miss Willa. If you'd left the three of us alone, I think me and Gladys might of——

"Oh, yes, course I know that there wouldn't of been much of a book 'f you hadn't mixed in some. Still, 'f I get home I think I can straighten things out. After I get a good rest on the farm I'm thinkin' some of goin' to look up the Erlich boys out at Lincoln an' maybe go in business with them.

"No'm, I ain't tryin' to get off the point."

"Go out on that parapet when the attack begins an' get killed? No, ma'am, I most certainly an' absolutely *will not*.

"Yes'm, I know it. I told you I know you're a serious novelist an' I suppose you got to do those kind o' things to make it tragic and important an' all that, so's not to have a happy endin'.

"No'm, I don't think it is natural, if that's what you want. There ain't only about six killed in action out of a

161

thousand Americans in this war an' I don't see why you pick on me. How'd I get elected?

"Yes, *ma'am*, I said three times already I know you're serious. Good land! Miss Willa, I ought to know. Why, I haven't had a real good laugh hardly once since I began working for you. But you don't seem to understand I'm serious, too, an' this whole business you're proposin' is more serious to me than it's got any chance of bein' to you. I've got a *lot* of things to do in the next fifty years.

"No, lady, I will *not*.

"Well, first place, that's no place for an officer in command. Officers are supposed to take care of their selves an' not expose their selves unnecessarily. They got to look out for their men, not try to be heroes or anything.

"Well, I s'pose it will. But see here, if I've got to choose between spoilin' the book an' gettin' spoiled myself—forever, it's only natural, ain't it?—*Say, listen!* D'you ever go to the *movies*?

"Oh, excuse me. I thought maybe you might of once or twice.

"No, nothin'. Never mind. But, say, have I really got to get shot on the parapet? Won't anything else do?

"A-a-all *right*, then. I s'pose I *got* to. I'll manage it somehow. You leave it to me. Don't you worry.

"Don't mention it. That's all right. Anything to oblige a serious lady novelist. Good-by, Miss Willa."

Claude was very busy for the next fifteen minutes. Just as he again took his position on the firing-step there was an explosion that split the earth and went up in a volcano of smoke and flame. He was thrown on his face, and when he arose the Hun advance had begun.

Here they were, coming on the run. The men were on their feet again. The rifles began firing. Then something extraordinary happened. There was their commanding officer on the parapet, outlined against the eastern sky! Stiffly erect he stood, one arm upraised, facing the oncoming foe. They heard his voice. "Steady men! Steady! It's up to you!"

They were amazed, astounded, but they responded. A withering fire swept the Hun lines; men were stumbling and falling. Then the solitary figure on the parapet was discovered by the enemy. A bullet rattled on the tin hat, one struck it in the shoulder. It swayed, lost its balance, plunged, face down, outside the parapet. Hicks caught a projecting foot, pulled— and it came off in his hand.

At the same moment the Missourians ran yelling up the communication trench, threw their machine guns up on the sand bags and went into action.

Hicks stood petrified staring at the foot in his hand, when Claude, clad in his Jaegers only, appeared, reached out and dragged the limp figure in by both legs.

"Here, Sergeant, help me with this to the dugout, so I can get my clothes on before it gets too public."

"My God, Lieutenant, I thought you was killed. What's this for? To fool the Heinies?"

"No—that was for the home folks who read serious novels."

"Criticizes Willa Cather: Rev. W[ilbur] T[heodore] Elmore Dislikes Her View of Ministers," *Nebraska State Journal,* 19 February 1923, p. 6

Rev. W. T. Elmore took Willa Cather, the noted author, to task in a sermon preached Sunday evening at the First Baptist Church on the subject of her book, *One of Ours* in which he says she belittled the ministers. Doctor Elmore takes a different view of the subject and presents some men who were of heroic type in the ministry.

"I hesitate somewhat to take this subject because Willa Cather is really herself, one of ours. Not only is she a Nebraska girl with all the flavor of the prairies in her writings. She is a graduate of our state university, class of '95. My class was '96. In her freshman days she was a regular attendant in this church. She is very much one of ours.

"While at times the detail in this work seems tiresome, and there is almost nothing of plot, and but little to appeal to the imagination, yet for Nebraskans there is certainly a great charm and interest in the accuracy of her picturing of the life of the prairies. We are glad to have easterners know that our farm people, some of them, drive Cadillacs, as well as Fords, and one farmer's wife drives an electric. She makes no mistakes as to any detail. She knows farm life even to the psychology of the horses. Her frankness in detail sometimes goes beyond conventionality.

"But it is of the views of religion expressed in this work that I speak. First, her attitude toward ministers and ministerial students. With one possible exception in a reference to a retired minister of New York City, her references invariably belittle the minister. I can scarcely understand this. When she attended this church it was under the ministry of Dr. O. A. Williams, a man once my pastor, whose successor I now am. A man of the highest possible type, whose name will always be revered in Lincoln. No doubt she met pathetic preachers in the early days, but she must have met some of the heroes, too. Some men of the highest culture

helped to found our work. I think of Newell, Keeler, Powell, Bedell, Scott, Lawlor and others, and I believe there were giants in those days.

"Perhaps it was we ministerial students who gave this impression, for I was one of them! She says, 'Young men went into the ministry because they were timid or lazy, and wanted society to take care of them; because they wanted to be pampered by kind, trusting women, like his mother.' And I was one of them!

"This leads me to ask who these ministerial students were. They were located at 'Temple,' which is Wesleyan University, but we were the ones Miss Cather knew.

"I think of Dave Forsyth, giant from the plains. Certainly neither timid nor lazy, now at the head of all the home mission work of the Methodist church. I think of Norman Barr, the first man to grasp my hand when I entered the old main building for the first time. Barr was from Holdrege, a man of magnificent physique, who made money whenever he needed it and had great business prospects. For twenty-five years he has been in Chicago. His mission in 'Little Hell' has grown to one of the greatest institutional works in the city with a summer camp at Lake Geneva. Fifty people at least work with him.

"I think of Francis Tucker, not robust, but a leader, now at the head of one of China's greatest hospitals. A man so trusted that he was in charge of all the great famine relief work for northern China during the last famine. I think of William Axling, surely *One of Ours*, member of our own church, who was called the 'Moody of the Platte,' and perhaps because of his youth, his ruddy cheeks, and his great popularity wherever he went to preach, might have been a subject for a little satire. But Axling now has the Japanese language the best of any American in Japan, and his influence there is so great that we all recognize him as our own, an ambassador, with influence in all good things exceeding that of many an accredited government diplomat.

"I think of Steve Corey: 'timid?' He certainly was not the day of the cane rush. At least some boys with broken heads would not so testify. He certainly was not the day he kept his place in the football line until he was finally carried fainting from the field with an injured leg. Steve is now the foreign mission secretary of the Christian board.

"I think of Zeke Moore, great bicycle rider, now a district superintendent in Iowa; of John Marshall, daily seen on our streets, still refusing a salary, the devil's worst enemy, and ready at any time to take a place at the stake with Savanorola or John Huss; or Lewis Thayer, prevented from carrying out his plans, physician and land owner in the west.

"The book mentions one name. The description we would scarcely recognize; 'His top-shaped head hung a little to one side. The thin hair was parted precisely over his high forehead and hung in little ripples.' He appeared regularly at meal-times to ask a blessing upon the food and to sit with devout downcast eyes while the chicken was being dismembered. He is located as coming from 'Temple,' but the man whom she names was a classmate of Miss Cather, and later was pastor at Hastings, as represented in the book.

"We know him: He was 'One of Ours,' a member of our church, quiet and dignified, gentle, perhaps too gentle in his ways. But he was most popular and influential, president of the Y.M.C.A. and plenty of other things. He held pastorates at Wayne, Peru and Hastings, and then because of a nervous breakdown, went into business, and now if you wish to reach him by name at Hollywood, and if you wish to see him you had better make an appointment, for he is an outstanding business man in that growing city, and bids fair to be able to buy out half his class some day. So much for one 'timid or lazy.'

"The missionary of the enterprise suffers in this book. The hero marries a precise Christian girl with many good qualities, but with no marital affection. Her mother was odd. Her older sister was peculiar and went as a missionary to China. And finally this sister leaves her husband and goes to take care of her missionary sister for a year or more. She disappears then from the story.

"For fifteen years I had most intimate relations with missionaries. I have seen them in the making. I have sailed the seven seas with them. I have been their guest and have been host to large numbers. I have worked with them, played with them, disagreed with them, and associated them in every normal sphere. And I have not met this type.

"As to the missionaries themselves, the most vital, virile people I have ever met are these people. It seems to take a certain emotional fervor to make a good missionary. A bloodless, loveless individual usually doesn't have any such interest, and if one such should go abroad his or her career would be short.

"I have heard of wives leaving their husbands. I have even heard of ministers' wives leaving their husbands. But it was not to go as a missionary. It was more likely to elope with the choir master. Fortunately my illustrations of this are limited to one. The presentation is not according to the facts. It is not a fair representation.

"If the author can find such an illustration in real life, I am prepared to find illustrations, a hundred or more for each one, where women have left their husbands, not because of missionary leanings, but because of the dance hall and the unChristian conditions of modern society. For domestic felicity, for the truest devotion to their families, for real comradeship, and for the great loving, sympathetic heart which will go thru fire and flood with the object of one's love, and never deserts, give me the women touched with the missionary devotion. I know them.

"The book makes much in its earlier chapters of a certain denominational school, 'Temple,' on the borders of Lincoln. This is of course University Place and Wesleyan. The school is pictured as an uninteresting place, with the most of the students impecunious ministerial acolytes. The main object of the school appears to be to teach a 'faith which was a substitute for most of the manly qualities he admired.' The faculty were mostly ministers who were a failure.

"At the present time there are about fifty on the Wesleyan faculty, and only three of these besides the president can classify as ministers. I believe the era of the denominational school is coming, not waning. The state schools are getting to be so large that the students in the first two years at least are lost in the throng. There is but little personal attention. The leading men on the state faculties wish that large numbers of these students could take at least their first two years in smaller schools.

"When it comes to showing men turned out, and women too, our smaller schools have no reason for fear. It can probably be shown that in proportion to numbers graduated, the smaller schools can show the largest percentages of the great and near great.

"The book represents a young man, out of touch with his environment, looking for the larger life. Religion is definitely closed to him. Not one strong Christian character appears. His mother is good, a Christian, but weak, and dwarfed by her faith. She is a hindrance to him.

His wife leaves him because of her religion. His brother is a Christian, but a prig and a bigot. Not one Christian home is shown.

"Is this true to life? Are our Christian mothers dwarfed by their faith? Have we no almost ideal Christian homes? Is every religious young man or woman a prig, a bigot, or cold blooded and unloving?

"I think again of those in my day who were seeking the larger life, and who came to our university. I maintain that none have more found it than the men whom I have named above who were ministerial students in those days. I find other Christian men, products of the same generation and the same environment. They have found life where others have found a wilderness. The hero, Claude, what a Paul Harrison or a William Axling, a John Mott or Robert Speer, a Fosdick or a Charles Gilkey he might have made!

"The war is over. It is easy to have a hero find his soul in that great sacrifice, but we cannot provide a war and a sacrificial death for all. We must live, and find life in more commonplace ways. There was one who found life. It took him to Calvary. And he said, 'This is life indeed, to know thee . . . and Jesus Christ whom thou hast sent.'"

J. Middleton Murry, "Miss Willa Cather," *Nation and Athenaeum* (London), 33 (14 April 1923), 54, 56 [reviewed with *Youth and the Bright Medusa*]

Unless all my information is misleading—it is admittedly partial, and therefore may be—the publisher of these two books by Miss Willa Cather is not far wide of the mark when he says that "more and more have we"—that is, the section of the American public whose affair it is to know what's what—"come to recognize in Willa Cather our greatest living woman novelist." At any rate, during the last few years, in my reading of American periodicals, I have continually been tripped up by the name of Miss Willa Cather, in contexts of this kind: "No," says the American critic, "we haven't much in the way of women-authors to put up against England—but there is Willa Cather." Or it would be just a brief little phrase: "Our few real literary artists, such as Willa Cather."

Quite enough, in fact, to make one determined to read any of her books if they happened to fall in one's way: not quite enough, or perhaps not quite the kind of thing, to set one hunting for her works. And now that I have read two of them, and read them with enjoyment, I feel very much the same as I did before. If another comes my way, I shall read it; but I shall not exert myself to make the encounter inevitable. Miss Willa Cather does not move me enough for that. I know that, whatever I should read of hers, she will never let me down. She will never write a slovenly page, and it is pretty certain she never has written one. She will never "fake," never scamp, never leave her reader in the least doubt of what she means, never willingly deviate by a hair's breadth from the record of the truth as she sees it. She is one of the most obviously honest and honorable writers of the English tongue to-day. It is no small thing to be able to produce such an impression. Miss Willa Cather produces it.

But, though she will never let me down, I doubt very much whether she will ever carry me away. Of these two books, which I have spent many hours in reading

as carefully as a writer of her quality deserves, very little remains with me. It is an effort to recollect them at all. When the effort is made, what is there? First and chief, a sense that she has been dealing, with her own patient and candid honesty, with the perennial problem of the educated and sensitive American—the gulf between the materialistic values of the American nation at large and the spiritual values we vaguely associate with the European tradition. Every one of the short stories in *Youth and the Bright Medusa* has an artist of some sort for its chief character: and the issue involved is either the conflict between what he stands for and the blank incomprehension of his neighbors, or the unresolved disturbance caused by him to men and women who have a glimmering sense of the value of his idiosyncrasy; people who do not understand, but are fascinated; who would like to deny, but cannot, the reality of this phenomenon for which there is no place in their scheme of things. Art, we suppose, is the bright Medusa, and Youth the American nation; or it may be that Miss Cather is cynical enough to believe that any young American who succumbs to the fascinations of art and the consciousness which allows for it is as good as turned to stone, for all the active part he can bear in shaping the life of his own people.

One of Ours is a novel with the same essential theme. A young farmer of the Middle West, with vague aspirations towards he knows not what, and a dim, inarticulate sense that life could be a different thing from the life he knows, sinks back on the farm after a glimpse of university life, marries a frigidly puritanical girl in a mist of romantic idealism, and finds release only in service as an American soldier in France. He touches civilization there, and he dies, willingly, for what he discovers. And here, for once, Miss

Cather seems to evade her own problem. That Claude Wheeler should have died for the unknown thing he longed for at the moment he touched it, was, as old Burton says of a like enterprise, "heroically done: and I admire him for it." Nevertheless, what we desire to learn is how the young man would have adjusted himself to his new-found knowledge. Would he have sunk back once again on to the farm? Would he have settled the question of his hopeless relation to his wife? Would he have joined that ever-growing army of young Americans who spend their days glued to the café tables in Paris, thinking of what they might have done if they had been born in a real country?

For Claude Wheeler dies a romantic idealist as he lived one. The only thing, indeed, for a romantic idealist to do is to die. But the death need not be violent, nor in the least heroic. A bullet in the heart in October, 1918, is, for the problems of a young American, nothing less than a *deus ex machina*. The interest would have been to follow the process of his slow death by starvation in Nebraska, or his quicker death by surfeit in Paris, or perhaps—and this would have been best of all—to learn how he managed to keep his newborn soul alive. Instead, he departs in a cloud of glory with none of his pressing accounts settled—neither the domestic account with his wife, nor the larger account with American society.

And here, perhaps, we stumble on the cause why so little remains when we have read Miss Cather's books. She does not really dig deep enough into the problem she raises. Tchehov says, indeed, that the business of the artist is to suggest problems, not to solve them. Unfortunately that good advice is meant for the genius alone, for he alone can make his representation of life so enchanting that we feel it's not worth while to bother about answering the questions. Life is, and it is

good enough to go on with. But to convince us of that you have to be something of a Tchehov yourself. Failing that gift of discerning and communicating the eternal freshness of the things that simply are, you have to settle down as a humble follower of men who were great in other ways, and look for an answer to the problems that preoccupy you.

To this Miss Cather may reply that she is content to present life as she sees it. But the trouble is that we are not quite content with what she presents. She does not see quite vividly enough or quite deep enough to make a permanent impression. Even the landscape of her Middle West in *One of Ours*, on which she has so evidently lavished her pains, is indistinct. And what do we (or what does she) really know of the crucial encounter between her hero and his wife? At the moment of crisis the vital thread of her story slips through her fingers. In her short stories the weakness is less apparent. "Coming, Aphrodite!" has moments of brilliance, and it must surely be one of the best short stories written in America in the last few years. "A Gold Slipper" is more than efficient, though the brilliance which was warm and living in parts of "Coming, Aphrodite!" seems almost mechanical.

But our final feeling is that it will not do to be grudging about Miss Cather. She writes as few Americans and few Englishmen write, with the conscience of an artist. What she does not do, she cannot do. She invites judgment by the finest standards, and if she seems to fail by them—well, it does not vastly matter. There is substance enough in her failure to make a dozen more apparently successful writers. There are not ten lines of shoddy in these two books, but there are pages of writing with the unassuming excellence of this (it is the scene of Claude's parting from his mother):—

"She recognized a heavy, hob-nailed boot on the stairs, mounting quickly. When Claude entered, carrying his hat in his hand, she saw by his walk, his shoulders, and the way he held his head, that the moment had come, and that he meant to make it short. She rose, reaching toward him as he came up to her and caught her in his arms. She was smiling, her little, curious intimate smile, with half-closed eyes.

" 'Well, is it good-bye?' she murmured. She passed her hands over his shoulders, down his strong back and the close-fitting sides of his coat, as if she were taking the mould and measure of his mortal frame. Her chin came just to his breast pocket, and she rubbed it against the heavy cloth. Claude stood looking down at her without speaking a word. Suddenly his arms tightened and he almost crushed her.

" 'Mother!' he whispered, as he kissed her. He ran downstairs and out of the house without looking back."

To be better, that would have to reveal a quality which Miss Cather has not. Few people have it, for its name is genius. But Miss Cather certainly has the next best thing. It is right that her country should be proud of her; it ought to be.

Mary M. Colum, "Three Women Novelists," *Freeman*, 7 (18 April 1923), 138–40

In the whole range of literary history there have been but few women writers; and, of these few, still fewer have given expression to that something which differentiates a woman's mind, emotion, and temperament from a man's. Now of all the novels recently written by women, Rebecca West's *The Judge* is the only one which is really a woman's book. The others, laying aside certain femininities, or certain feminine mannerisms or puerilities, might just as well have been written by men. In nearly every one of its essentials, Rebecca West's book could never have been the work of a man; and this amazingly distinguished quality it shares with the books of the half-dozen women writers whose work, no matter how long ago it was produced, perpetually gives a new thrill to readers. Women writers commonly write in one of three manners: they either write exactly like men, as George Eliot has done, in which case they are frequently dull and stodgy; or they write as men expect them to write, which accounts for a great deal of the mushy love-poetry and mother-poetry; or, rarest of all—like Emily Brontë, George Sand, Jane Austen, Madame de Staël, Sappho, and the unknown women singers of "The Love Songs of Connacht," whose influence no modern Irish writer has escaped—they give a genuine expression of themselves. The quality which is their own is one that can make them the peer of the greatest men artists without being at all like them. We know that Sappho was the peer of Catullus—probably the only poet whom Catullus himself would have regarded as his equal—yet unnumbered atoms separate them in kind. Emily Brontë is the peer of the Abbé Prevost, and the passion of Catherine and Heathcliff is, in its intensity, equal to that of Manon and des Grieux, though it is completely different in kind. Yet the quality which differentiates *Manon Lescaut* from *Wuthering Heights* has nothing whatever to do with what is commonly called virility or femininity; as a matter of fact, Emily

Brontë's book is by far the more virile in the common understanding of that word. But think of any scene in Prevost's book in which is expressed des Grieux's love for Manon, think of any expression of love in the whole range of literature, and compare it with Catherine's expression of her love for Heathcliff in *Wuthering Heights*, and that single comparison will be more illuminating than a hundred treatises in sex psychology.

[. . .]

Now to take as exhibits the books of three of the most important women writers who have published novels within the last few months: Miss Willa Cather in *One of Ours* writes like a man and succeeds in being dull; Miss May Sinclair in *Anne Severn and the Fieldings* is feminine and charming, and a little puerile, not to say infantile; and Miss Rebecca West in *The Judge* gives a genuine expression of a woman's mind, and this although the book is not a very successful book.

[. . .]

With all its faults—and these are almost incredible—*The Judge* is a distinguished book, and the profundity of the life it reveals is in strong contrast to the slight texture of life that May Sinclair gives us in *Anne Severn and the Fieldings*.

[. . .]

After reading *One of Ours*, with its slow recording of life on a Western farm, one feels inclined to say with Victor Morse the ace, who occupies a few pages in the portion of the book that deals with the war, "I'd rather be a stevedore in the London docks than a banker-king in one of your prairie States. . . . My God, it's death in life! What's left of men if you take all the fire out of them? They're afraid of everything." In this book Miss Cather chronicles the life of a commonplace young farmer called Claude Wheeler, who rather conventionally finds his soul in the war. No doubt it is all a very accurate account of life in the Northwestern States, but an accurate account of any life is rarely of interest. The mere chronicle of the life of Hamlet, Prince of Denmark, might not be of any more interest than the memoirs of the Crown Prince of Germany; Shakespeare made his prince a figure of immortal romance and tragedy by endowing him with a life out of his own spirit. If Miss Cather can not give the Western farmers some strong life and emotion out of herself, writing about them in this ardourless way will add little to life or literature. How poor in emotion, in experience, in love of living her farmers are may be seen if one compares this book with Selma Lagerlöf's stories of farmlife in Sweden. The war removed Claude Wheeler from his dull life and gave him the opportunity to die for a cause; pitifully enough, the war gave to many people their one great emotion, and in many cases this was hate. Miss Cather seems to see the war through some one else's mind, and her attitude towards that colossal calamity is a cross between that of a radical humanitarian clergyman and a red-blooded columnist. Calling the Germans "Huns," and referring to the hand of a dead German as a "huge paw" is no occupation for a writer of Miss Cather's distinguished gifts. The author is perhaps far more familiar with the farmlife she writes of here than with the life she wrote of in her magical book *Youth and the Bright Medusa*; but familiarity with a life is often a handicap to a writer, for great is the temptation merely to recollect and chronicle that life. Familiarity with what one writes about is of far less importance than the moralistic critics would have us believe. "The vision of the artist," said Oscar Wilde, "is far more important to us than what he looks at." After all, is not one of the most real of American plays, *The Shewing-up of Blanco Posnet*, by a man [George Bernard

169

Shaw] who never saw an inch of American soil?

"She Sees More in War Than 'Horrors,'" *New York Times*, 15 May 1923, p. 18

Of all the many novels produced last year by American writers, the [Pulitzer Prize] judges picked out Willa Cather's *One of Ours* as the best. That, it must be confessed, was to risk many protests, some of which will be well supported as well as vehemently urged. The makers of the choice will be able to maintain their position, however, for, while they cannot prove the book better than the best of its rivals, they will have no trouble at all in proving that it has a double merit which not a few of the others, especially those in its own class—that of "war stories"—very obviously lack.

In the first place, *One of Ours* is admirably written, in English always lucid, and that is refreshing in its contrast with only too many books of the day. In the next place, Willa Cather, unlike something close to a majority of her competitors in this field, realizes that the World War had an object, a fact which is not even hinted in several well-read and well-advertised productions.

She knows as well as any of them that war has "horrors," and doubtless she hates it as much as any of them; certainly she does not laud it as among the more commendable of human activities. But she is as little of a pacifist as of a militarist; she is a sane woman who understands that there are worse things than war.

Hence is it, presumably, that, though her young hero suffers much in the war and finally dies in it, she does not ask pity for him as the victim of a malignant conspiracy on the part of "old men," and she does not picture his proud heart as breaking under the cruel compulsion to salute soldiers of higher rank than himself. He was not that sort of soldier, nor is Willa Cather that sort of writer.

Herbert S. Gorman, "Willa Cather, Novelist of the Middle Western Farm," *New York Times Book Review*, 24 June 1923, p. 5

Willa Cather is a regional novelist, first of all, and because she is such a clearly defined representative of this genre, she may serve as an example of the chief modern tendency in modern American fiction. It is a tendency that is not at all a new thing. Practically all of our finest novelists and short-story writers have sought certain specific sections of the country for their inspiration. In so doing they managed to escape the English influence, an influence that has diminished of late years, but which at one time threatened to engulf any authentic American note in world letters. The American scene brought more to our novelists than a shift of scenic locale: together with the exposition goes a new technique, a new method of approach. This is to be expected, for a new life carries a new ethical conception, a new urge toward existence, an individual way of looking at things in general. The old New England could be looked at through English eyes and set down in

English terms. There was a similarity there. The life was but transplanted. It was not implicit in the roll. But it is impossible to do this today. We cannot look at the Middle West, Nebraska or even the renewed vigor of new England through English eyes and find the scene fitting in with English conceptions. The old influences have worn away or been absorbed into a system of things that has so intensely transmogrified them as to render them essentially native.

This process, of course, took longer in the East than it did in the Middle West or Far West. New England, New York, Virginia, here was a sturdily planted English cultural stock in whose very bones were bred the sensations and intuitions of England. Only time could wear these things away. But the West received an influx of pioneers, the children already of native Americans. It is true that they paid but little attention to letters, for they were far otherwise employed subduing the country, making it habitable, tearing a hard livelihood from the soil. When national consciousness did come it flowered from a rough-and-ready stock. An English heritage might be there (it is never wise to wholly ignore it), but it was weak in comparison with New England. It was not even strong enough to arouse any particular literary ambitions, if we except the school of writers who made San Francisco their headquarters. Now, however, pioneering is a story of the past. There is ample time to gaze about, to take in the spiritual vista, as it were, and to comment on this life that is so strangely dissimilar in various portions of the country. The New England group came and passed away, leaving but a weak shadow of itself in the prose writers who represent New England today. The Middle West, rearing like a young giant, is occupying the centre of the stage. Sherwood Anderson, Edgar Lee Masters and, in a polite way, Booth Tarkington are men of the moment. To this group, in a sense, belongs Willa Cather. Her especial territory, Nebraska, lies out of the general run of our modern novelists, but she has pictured it in such a way that it has become an integral part of our American literary heritage.

In those novels by her which are particularly concerned with the life of Nebraska, *One of Ours* and *My Antonia*, for instance, she displays a powerful naturalism that takes precedence over any art she may exhibit as a technical master of plot. The plot does not matter in these books; it is the life that grasps the reader. In her other tales, such as the stories of New York artistic life in *Youth and the Bright Medusa*, she is clever, but her psychology is superficial. But when she is describing a Nebraskan blizzard which is engulfing some pitiful farm set down on the plains far from a city, then Miss Cather becomes an authentic artist, a craftsman of the first rank who is to be reckoned with in any summing up of contemporary American letters. For instance, there is no particular rounded plot in *My Antonia*. Here we have the story of a Bohemian girl, first of all, and her immigrant family secondarily set down penniless, confused and helpless in Nebraska. Antonia is traced through the sympathetic eyes of the narrator, supposedly a man who grew up with her, from the time she first learns English as a child of 14 to that period of her life when her ten or eleven children cluster about her, and she can look back on her life discovering much that was good and other things that were not so good. There is a high naturalism in this narrative; an intense reality that pervades the book. Antonia gradually unfolds before the reader until her life story may be taken as symbol of the life story of youth in Nebraska. Threading the book, almost as important as the tale, is the land. It influences character; it molds human beings. We cannot doubt in the last analysis that it is Nebraska that makes Antonia what she is, gives her the superb poise and courage which is her portion, makes life hard but endurable.

So few American writers have this faculty of bringing the very soil to life and converting it into the protagonists of their tales that it may be wise to linger on this point for a little. There is, of course, the novel of the soil and there is the novel of character. Miss Cather in her best books has arranged a happy marriage between the two genres. *My Antonia*, for instance, is as much a novel of character as it is of Nebraska. Yet we experience the prime importance of both. The reason for this is not far to seek. In Miss Cather's work the environment becomes an essential part of the character. It is impossible to understand the Claude Wheeler of *One of Ours* unless we also understand the hard farm life that made him what he was. His heroism thus stands out the better, and we know him as a mute, unheralded Hamlet of the difficult farmlands, living his life with distaste because he is always conscious of that far-away call and the inexorable state of affairs that makes him what he is and no other being. Indeed, in Claude Wheeler and Antonia we have two figures which may be set in juxtaposition, figures that show what the soil can do and what it can undo. Claude is the nervous, introspective intelligence that sees beyond its status and understands only too bitterly how helpless it is. Here is a subtle, highly intellectualized system given to brooding and yet with enough spiritual fortitude to see the thing through. Antonia is the direct opposite. All that she is becomes of value because of the soil. When she leaves the hard farm life for Black Hawk we find that it is not for her good; that her development is essentially in the power of the long, swaying fields of wheat, in the hard days of plowing when she follows the share, hard-muscled and cheerful. It is not that she lacks intelligence so much as the fact that she lacks intellectuality. She is not a rarefied personage, but a healthy, matter-of-fact Bohunk, a Bohemian laborer filled with that deep peasant spirit that makes the ground upon which she works heaven enough for her. Her stay in the city, on second thought, does aid her in a certain way, for it impresses upon her mind the hard serenity of the farmland. Claude Wheeler could never be satisfied in this way, and when, after his bitter, unsatisfactory marriage, he dies at the head of his company in France the reader feels that he could have made no other end. He was born the leader of a forlorn hope, the man who is destined to move through life altogether too conscious of its spiritual tribulations and uncouthness.

Yet in spite of his apparent disregard for the farm, for the meagre Nebraskan existence, the long Winters shut in by high snowdrifts, and the hot Summers with the sun ruddily staring down on blond wheat, we feel that Claude is certainly the child of his environment. He could have developed nowhere else. His very nature was quickened by the labor and loneliness that were his portion. It is true that he was an exotic, as exotic to Nebraska as his name is with its romantic twist, but in all the peregrinations of his spirit the tense consciousness that has been stimulated by laborious days is eternally manifest.

It is this revelation of the impingement of spirit and environment that would seem to be the high watermark of Miss Cather's art. Her best novels are compact with it and because they are so they must be regarded as among the best of our contemporary novels. It is easy enough to tell a story. It is easy enough to develop an entertaining character. The difficulty starts when the author molds his character into his environment and so makes the tale an actual footnote to life. The strength of Mrs. Wharton's *Ethan Frome* is added to immeasurably by the cold, dreary New England atmosphere that hovers mournfully about it. The tragic tale could in nowise have attained the dignity that it does if it were laid in Florida. The land has been used. And whenever the land is wisely used, whenever our writers build up their achievements out of the actualities upon which they have gazed we may rest assured that the result will be distinguished. One needs only to point at the lonely figure of Thomas Hardy and to consider such books as *The Mayor of Casterbridge* and *The Return of the Native* to witness what high accomplishments may be consummated in this genre. Of course, it required genius. Nobody but a genius can do this sort of writing in such a way as to carry conviction to the reader.

Because this fictional form may be made so distinguished and because its potentialities in America are so vast one cannot but be gratified in noting that so many of our novelists are employed in this form. The Great American Novel is not spoken of today, possibly, because most of us have realized that there are several Americas. There is New England and there is the South, and there is the West. In every locality life has its own individual aspects. Which is America? It is all America, of course, but it would take more than a lifetime for a single person to imbibe it all, to drink in its characteristics with that meticulousness that should be the foundation of every true novelist. The underlying spirit may be the same and the complete exposition of their underlying spirit may eventually become our nearest approach to the Great American Novel, but the crusts are vastly different. Therefore, it is of major importance to have all these portions of the country properly

exploited in fiction, their differing traits wisely pictured and set forth, and the spiritual content of each region expressed in authentic art. The old New England has been set before us. So, too, has the Middle West. We may rather suspect the spiritual sullenness of Winesburg, Ohio, and imagine that there is another side to that lugubrious town, but at the same time we cannot doubt the sincerity of Sherwood Anderson. It is when he turns from the development of the battle between environment and personality, as in *Many Marriages*, to a psychological change that we wonder whether his art is to be entirely trusted or not.

The same is true of Miss Cather. It is when she forsakes her Nebraskan farms and cities and travels to artistic New York (if there is an artistic New York) or to the battlefields of France that we wonder whether or not she is quite within the radius which has been ordained as her particular province in letters. A deal of praise has been bestowed upon the stories in *Youth and the Bright Medusa*, for superficially considered they are brilliant enough. But the dogged soundness of great art is not to be found there any more than it is to be found in *The Troll Garden*. There is fine writing, to be sure, fine writing in abundance and short stories that are brilliant in so far as they are beyond the capabilities of most of our short-story writers. But the foundations are shaky. The psychology is in doubt. Indeed, Miss Cather is not primarily a psychologue: Her gift is a vivid expositional narrative form that reveals the soul through remarkable characterization. Her psychology never goes deeper than it does when her characters are working endlessly on their farms or battling their way through the terrible Nebraska blizzards. Then a rich magic creeps into her pages. She is setting there a life that is indubitably near and dear to her, that she knows with almost the intimacy with which a mother knows her child. There is no American author living who can better exploit her own region than Miss Cather, not even Mr. Anderson. And this is because she is objective for the most part and rather wary about indulging in subjective analysis. She is picturing a life and revealing a personality through that life. And because this is true the first part of *One of Ours* is so much better than the rest of it. Claude in France is no more distinguished than John Dos Passos's much criticized *Three Soldiers*. But Claude in Nebraska is an essential part of that high art of which Miss Cather is so capable and because of which she may receive the Pulitzer award with well-grounded justification.

Times Literary Supplement (London), 28 October 1923, p. 688

It is perhaps not an unfair comment that as the Americans were a little slow about getting into the war, so they are a little slow in leaving it. Their war novels seem to be just beginning. A few weeks ago Mrs. Wharton published hers; and now we have *One of Ours*, by Willa Cather, which spares us nothing, not even influenza and roses in Picardy, but which is true and graphic, written obviously because an irresistible driving force impels a distinguished pen to pay its tribute to the "Doughboys." The story of Claude Wheeler, the Nebraska farm boy with the "sissy" name, from early childhood until his death in action at twenty-five, is told with a faithfulness of detail that obliges the reader to endure with him the half-

articulate pains and pleasures and bewilderments of his youth, and to live through the change of seasons on the farm. The book called "Lovely Creek" presents the Wheeler family in the unshaded briliance of their own skies; the facetious father, the religious, withdrawn sweetness of the mother, with her delicate hands that become a symbol for her son; the three boys, the farm hands; the old servant Mahailey with her woolly wits and her profound perceptions of life and character, expressed only by her actions, since she has no words. The narrowness of the life, the arid minds, would be depressing but for the faculty within us that makes us accept the fate of other people without complaint. The energy and beauty that one looks for in the work of the writer of *My Antonia* are in every line.

Claude, whose instincts are sharper and deeper than those of his brothers, muddles through mistake after mistake, always an unconscious idealist, defeated and baffled by the barrenness of experience, and because life at no point opens gloriously like a flower for his joy and comprehension. The second book, "Enid," records his mistaken marriage, again with a reality, an exaggerated deadliness, that lets the reader into the heart of the house that Claude built. "Sunrise on the Prairie" is the beginning of hope. "The Voyage of the Anchises" sees Claude on board a troop-ship (of the worse variety) satisfied at last. The scenes in France seem stale in a way that perhaps reflects on our capacity to retain the emotions of pity and fear; but nothing is omitted to make a complete picture, as seen by a non-combatant, a writer, a woman. It is imagined, reported experience, and as an arrangement is as good as it can be. Claude lives his crowded hour, finds a brief friendship with another man, dies content. The last scene, brief and moving, is of the two proud, grieving women in the farm kitchen, the mother and Mahailey the servant, resigned under God's hand, comforting each other.

Gerald Bullett, "America's War Novel," *Spectator* (London), 131 (3 November 1923), 661

It is not difficult to believe that this novel has taken America by storm; but, without wishing to anticipate the jury's verdict, one may safely predict that the British public will not be so easily won. This implies no very serious criticism of the book's literary qualities, which, indeed, are far from despicable. Miss Cather is mistress of a clear and forceful style; she is quick to see the broad general features of a situation, and to present them acceptably to the eye of the reader; and she succeeds in expressing popular emotion. These are talents that make for commercial success, and no one need grudge her that success. She is, moreover, a sensitive and a restrained writer, with a genuine feeling for words, and not only for words. Mr. Hugh Walpole calls her "an artist of the very first and finest order." The qualifying phrase is merely absurd; but that Miss Cather is an artist may be readily conceded. As a piece of good journalism, as a faithful and sympathetic record of the times of which it treats, it may be remembered for some little while in America; but, lacking as it does the quality that makes for permanence in literature, it cannot fail, sooner or later, to go the way of all topical fiction. It cannot hope for so long a life as that hasty and hysterical yet more entertaining book *Mr. Britling Sees It Through* [by H. G. Wells]. And its appearance in England is inopportune, to say the least. American hearts may still be vibrating to the emotional appeal of the Great War; for their part in it was as brief as it was admirable. Ours, on the other hand, was a slow and monotonous agony; and we must be pardoned if we seem reluctant to renew it, even in imagination. The War we have always with us, and as a subject for art it is altogether too near and personal a matter. To read of it, even five years after the event, is either a torment or a bore.

One of Ours is the history of America's average "nice boy," his eagerness to fight for civilization, his ardent soldiering, and his death in France.

[...]

During her [Enid's] absence America declares war on Germany, and Claude exultantly volunteers for service. Whereupon the novel promptly goes to pieces. The interest becomes disconcertingly general. We are treated to an account of the voyage to France in a troopship. A virulent form of influenza breaks out. There are sketches of Claude's brother-officers, non-commissioned officers, and men; scraps of realistic dialogue, more or less amusing and characteristic; a description of life in French billets behind the line; and finally, a battle, exceedingly well written. But the reader, I venture to suggest, will have none of this. He is interested in the psychological growth of Claude Wheeler, and in his various social relationships—that is, he is interested in the first half of this book. But with this war-correspondent stuff he is impatient. No doubt it is fitting, relentlessly true to history, that Claude's story should be cut short by the War. But the War having spoiled so many lives, it seems a pity to let it spoil our novels as well.

Nation and Athenaeum (London), 34 (10 November 1923), supplement, 258

Claude Wheeler, the hero of this book, might well have said:—

"When shall this slough of sense be cast,
This dust of thoughts be laid at last,
The man of flesh and soul be slain
And the man of bone remain?"

Shy, suppressed, and self-conscious—"to begin with, Claude is a 'sissy' name"—he "finds himself," as the saying is, in the Great War. The book does not find itself: it is smooth, well-fed, healthy, adult; but it lacks what Professor Housman calls the Immortal Part. It does not, like Claude, "travail with a skeleton." And so we miss that balance and poise in the construction of the book which the Elizabethan dramatists mastered, and which made Walter Pater think of a supreme work of art as an athlete in repose. Claude, on his flourishing South American farm, reminds one strongly of Levin in *Anna Karenin*, scything with the peasants on his estate. But Tolstoi weaves a double strand, keeping Levin and Kitty as a foil to Vronsky and Anna, with enormous advantage; here we have no contrast, no combination, no conflict, but only the change after two hundred pages from peace to war. Claude's struggle with prosperity should be more emphasized to hold the book together. The style is admirable, and the feeling for nature, as Mr. Walpole says, exquisite, but not, we think, intense. In Miss Willa Cather's next novel we ask for one thing—"steadfast and enduring bone."

"Minor Characters Well Done in *One of Ours*" [unidentified Midwestern review in Willa Cather Red Cloud scrapbooks, II-22]

It seems to us that the minor characters in *One of Ours* are all of them better depicted than is the major character. We can see and delight in the vividness of Nat Wheeler and Mahailey and Mrs. Wheeler and Bayliss, but we can't quite realize Claude. Willa Cather knows her Nebraska folks and on the canvas of her novel she can reproduce them in all seeming verity, but when she abandons the soil of the prairie, when she leaves behind her the earthy touch and soars into the exotic realm of dreaming, utopian-minded humanity, she loses her sureness of contact and the result is likely to be a picture with aberrant lines.

In Claude Wheeler Miss Cather has attempted to portray a character dissatisfied with and in revolt against the narrow manmade customs that cramp rural life in the Middle West, who at last finds his escape in the world war. But in the building up of his character, in the attempt to make him convincing, Miss Cather shows instances of conduct that strain the reader's credulity. For example, there is the incident of the cherry tree. One spring day when Claude was 5 years old he heard his mother entreating his father to go to the orchard and pick the cherries from a tree that hung loaded. She said she could not reach them herself. Nat Wheeler, a rather thick-hided farmer with quite unsensitive ideas concerning jokes, went out and sawed the cherry tree down.

Then he returned to say that it would now be an easy matter for Mrs. Wheeler and Claude to pick the fruit. Confidently the two went to the orchard with pails. But when little Claude beheld the sight of the cut down tree, with a scream he became a little demon. "He threw away his tin pail," writes Miss Cather, "jumped about howling and kicking the loose earth with his copper toed shoes until his mother was much more concerned for him than for the tree.

" 'Son, son,' she cried. "It's your father's tree. He has a perfect right to cut it down if he wants to. He's often said the trees were too thick in here. Maybe it will be better for the others.' "

" 'Tain't so! He's a damn fool, damn fool!' Claude bellowed, still hopping and kicking, almost choking with rage and hate."

Who ever saw a 5-year-old boy with such grown up faculties of perception? Wouldn't it be more likely that a child would clap his hands in delight at the vision of the red fruit all within easy reach for his little hands to pluck? Incidents like this make for unreality in the character of Claude.

When the war came and Claude went overseas, he still seemed unreal. Although he spent months over there, he retained to the very last that same exalted view of France which inspired the American purchaser of Liberty bonds three or four thousand miles away. Miss Cather didn't know the American soldier if she believes the lofty vision of French life which many held on this side [of] the water did not fall away like the illusion it was when such soldiers came into intimate contact with French life. Not that the French people were less noble than the American; but the doughboy on French soil was bound to realize the mere humanity of the *poilu* [World War I French soldier]. Yet Miss Cather tells us that Claude Wheeler "died believing France better than any country can ever be." We cannot imagine an American lieutenant like that. But the title, *One of Ours*, indicates the author intended him to be typical of thousands from the corn belt.

So this is why we think the hero of Miss Cather's latest novel is not drawn true to life.

Nevertheless, *One of Ours* is an extraordinarily good book of the day. As noted before, the minor characters are truly limned. They move and talk close to the dark, rich soil of this great farm land. And as one derives pleasure from watching simple folk in their routine, daily business of living, one will derive pleasure from the reading of Miss Cather's book.

Perhaps the most remarkable thing about Miss Cather's work is her style. It is a styleless style. Stripped of practically all inessentials it stands out in its simple, direct beauty, unaffected, wholly pleasing and convincing.

But the demand for the grand, balanced American novel on the late war remains unsupplied. *Three Soldiers* stands at one extreme—*One of Ours* at the other extreme. The former gives us the wholly sordid and pessimistic view; the latter gives us the wholly exalted and idealistic view. The novel we are still awaiting will give us both of these, and it will give us at the same time, and in greater measure, the vast middle ground, which is nearer the truth when taken alone than either of the other two when they are taken alone.

Checklist of Additional Reviews

Zoe Akins, "It Seems to Me," New York *World*, 14 September 1922, p. 11.

Wisconsin Library Bulletin, 18 (October 1922), 217.

"Bidding the Eagles of the West Fly On," Greensboro (North Carolina) *Daily News*, 8 October 1922, section 2, p. 8.

Hildegarde Hawthorne, "The Season's Books as Christmas Gifts," *Literary Digest International Book Review*, 1 (December 1922), 70.

Booklist, 19 (November 1922), 52.

Open Shelf (Cleveland), November 1922, p. 84.

Pertinax, "Fine Work: But Willa Cather is Lacking in Architectural Sense," Minneapolis *Sun*, 5 November 1922, p. 3.

Pittsburgh Monthly Bulletin, 27 (December 1922), 532.

New York Times, 15 May 1923, p. 18.

Henry Walcott Boynton, "The Pulitzer Prize Novel, *One of Ours*," Providence Sunday *Journal*, 20 May 1923, p. 13V.

A LOST LADY

A LOST LADY

BY

WILLA CATHER

" . . . . *Come, my coach!*
Good night, ladies; good night, sweet ladies,
Good night, good night."

MCMXXIII

ALFRED · A · KNOPF

New York

John Farrar, "Willa Cather: Long an Apprentice, She Is Now a Brilliant Technician," *Time*, 2 (10 September 1923), 15

The personality of Willa Cather is characterized chiefly by firmness. She is positive, determined, a trifle withdrawn. Her charm is undeniable, yet it has the air of being at times carefully reserved for a greater occasion. She has no great interest in the small affairs of the world, yet she is gracious and her opinions, when vouchsafed, are well considered and delivered with positiveness. She would find folly a difficult companion. This precision of thought and character illuminates her writing. It is, perhaps, what makes *My Ántonia* and *A Lost Lady* the works of art which they are. . . .

I saw her last Summer in the Vermont mountains. She was to deliver a series of addresses on the craft of writing. She spent days in careful thought and preparation. She walked alone in the woods and fields. Her talks are said to have been superb. The students literally worshipped her. It was this tremendous force of hers, breaking through an equally tremendous reserve, that made her lectures so inspiring.

My enthusiasm for her latest book is unqualified. *One of Ours*, her story of the War, which was awarded one of the Pulitzer Prizes last year, I did not care for. It is not nearly so wise a book as Edith Wharton's poignant *A Son at the Front* or Thomas Boyd's *Through the Wheat*. *A Lost Lady*, however, is a character study of strength and beauty. The story of a highstrung, attractive, weak woman, told as she is reflected in the lives of her various lovers, is superbly wrought. I can think of no other picture of broken idealism so striking as that of young Neil confronted with the truth about his idol, Marian Forrester. The background of the Middle West of the last century seems thoroughly inconsequential. The story is that of Marian Forrester. Here, surely, is writing one of the most brilliant technicians in American letters!

Fanny Butcher, "Willa Cather's Story of A Lost Lady Is Lovely, Fragile Work," *Chicago Daily Tribune*, 15 September 1923, p. 9

Willa Cather's new novel—little more than a novelette, but exactly the proper and perfect length for the story it tells—is, in a strange way, reminiscent of everything that she has done before. It is not like anything else, any one thing, but in it there are undeniable but delicate dashes of all the masterful strokes which have made her novels American literature. And that, I feel, is the unmistakable test of genius—to grow so logically in each way that every succeeding piece of work reflects the finest technique of the finest things one has done before.

To do the same thing over and over, as many American writers are wont to do, shows no mastery of one's art. It shows merely a technical laziness. To undertake another type of work and to give to that the fullest fruition of one's art; to be guided from one's past efforts into a surer power, is art, indeed. That that process is perhaps unconscious is the work of genius.

A Lost Lady is a delicate, lovely, fragile piece of literature—a character etching, with the lines cleanly eaten by the powerful acid of truth, a work of art exquisite in its delicacy. To many it will be merely a very "nice" story of a lady who wasn't "nice." It will go into the class of the stories of those who, from Madame Bovary down through literature, have not obeyed their marriage vows. Probably many will read it for that reason (one can't help being cynical about public taste these days), and I, for one, hope that they will, even under a misapprehension that it will be "naughty," for they will find in it as fine writing and as artful a technique as anywhere in American letters today and it may, unwittingly, tempt them to finer things. It isn't by any means the greatest of Willa Cather's novels. It is rather a sampler of them all, a beautiful, delicately wrought thing.

A Lost Lady is the story of a woman so exquisite in her beauty and her allure as to be wholly apart from the small town in which she lived, a creature exotic in her charms only because the Iowa village which was her background was so commonplace, a being of the utmost delicacies and sensibilities, a devotee of beauty. The story opens while she and her husband—older than she is—are making one of their occasional visits to the town which is destined to be her home. It closes with the news of her death, again a wife, in South America. The years between, when her spirit was drooping its wings—almost imperceptibly, are the largest part of the book. It is sheer mastery the way Miss Cather shows how every one thought that she was the sparkle of life, the flicker of light in the household, the creature almost too bright and good for human nature's daily food, how she accepted her part as master of life, and how, when her seemingly negligible husband was no longer able to direct their lives, she became in truth a lost lady. She is the type who must have a strong man to lean upon, who demands the background of adoring respect. When that was removed from her, she mistook desire for what she really wanted, and became, in spirit, a lost lady. Her lostness is not the tragedy of a violet tramped down by an unheeding boot. There is nothing violent or harsh about it. It is rather the tragedy of the flowering vine, once supported by a hidden and ugly stick, hopelessly trying to go on climbing when the stick has crumbled. It is never a crushed or ugly thing, merely a futile one. And by its side there grows as sturdy and beautiful a flower of love as one can find nowadays in books, love of a boy, passionate but too worshipful for utterance.

With a theme quite unlike any that Willa Cather has chosen before she has made a novel with, as I suggested, reminiscences of the beauties of her other work. There is the same calm and peace in it that makes *My Ántonia* one of the really great books of the last decade. There is a sophistication about it that made the stories in *Youth and the Bright Medusa* such a joy to many. There is the same sparseness of detail, the same absoluteness of phrase that made *One of Ours* seem so bare and sturdy an outline. It is written in the unadorned manner of *One of Ours*. (When Willa Cather uses an adjective nowadays it glows like a light—she has stripped her style of every nonessential. Even *O Pioneers!* and *The Song of the Lark* have given of themselves to *A Lost Lady*. And yet *A Lost Lady* is not a great and powerful book. It is that very rare thing, a perfect thing in parvo. It is a delicate miniature as compared to the almost heroic portraits which Willa Cather has made, but it proves her the greater artist for being so the master of her technique as to be able to scale all of her art down to *A Lost Lady*.

C. R. W., "Miss Cather's Latest Novel," *Christian Science Monitor*, 19 September 1923, p. 14

What is it about the writing of Willa Cather that makes the reading of her books pure delight, that commands admiration and interest even though the turn of the plot may not always be to our liking? Is it not her deep sincerity, her honesty, her simplicity? She has lived and worked with her characters for a long time, perhaps for years as was the case with *One of Ours*. They grow and develop as if from long companionship with her, their friend. The proof of this living quality is in the fact that they dwell in the memory as distinct personalities long after putting down the book.

Miss Cather's background is always as skillfully created as are her characters and is quite vivid. In *A Lost Lady* it is an atmosphere full of the color and feeling of a past epoch. Here is a story, not of the prairies, but of a little town which dreamed of being great with the coming of the Burlington Railroad to its door. Circumstances denied this rosy future to Sweet Water, but Capt. Daniel Forrester, who had built many hundreds of miles of that railroad across the plains, lived on at his place a mile out of town. So, too, did his beautiful wife, Marian Forrester. This is her story—the story of woman of irresistible charm, at once weak and incredibly strong, subtle and yet simple. When the last page has been read, one is almost more inclined to call it the Captain's story.

For dominate the scene as Mrs. Forrester certainly does in her beauty and her fascination, her husband, quiet, formal, old-fashioned, scrupulously honorable, is her balance wheel. In later years, without him, she is not her whole self.

"... On a low, round hill," in their "white house with a wing, and sharp sloping roofs to shed the snow," lived these two. All about was a cottonwood grove, but the house stood high enough to be "the first thing one saw on coming into Sweet Water by rail, and the last thing one saw on departing." And the Forrester place was famous for its hospitality. Railroad presidents and bankers, old friends of the captain, liked to stop off there. They found the lavish generosity which was a part of the age—and, above all they found Marian Forrester.

To tell more of the characters and the setting would be to rob the reader of much pleasure. It is not a brilliant story— and yet the telling of it is brilliant. But the best thing about it is its reality, the simplicity of its unfoldment. Miss Cather has a clear vision and an intense sense of beauty. Every page bears witness to this, and one turns each with regret for what is past and eagerness for what lies ahead.

E[dwin] F[rancis] E[dgett], "*A Lost Lady*: Another Willa Cather Story of Mid-Western Scenes," *Boston Transcript*, 22 September 1923, book section, p. 4

A year ago *One of Ours* was published and acclaimed. It was called "a rich book," "one of the best pieces of fiction writing that has been done in America," "a poignantly beautiful drama," and "a big, wholesome American novel," and much else that was positive, comparative and superlative. A little later it was awarded the Pulitzer Prize for the American novel of that year which "best presents the wholesome atmosphere of American manners and manhood." There were dissenting voices, of course, but they were heard but faintly above the vociferous clamor of approval.

Within a year or thereabouts, Miss Cather follows *One of Ours* with *A Lost Lady*. It is not a full length novel in the sense that it fills some three hundred pages, but in about half that length it tells a complete story of certain episodes in the life of a woman who was with more than one man unfaithful to her marriage vows. That is the sum and substance of *A Lost Lady* discreetly expressed; but it might be more directly characterized as the story of an adulteress. It is, therefore, not venturesome to say that its author will not receive another prize for a story which "best presents the wholesome atmosphere of American manners and manhood," if the word "manhood" has a bi-sexual meaning which makes it inclusive of "womanhood." Well written in a somewhat highly colored style with occasional exaggerative infelicities—for example, "as she turned quickly away, the train of her velvet dress caught the leg of his broadcloth trousers and dragged with a friction that crackled and drew sparks," the story covers a long period of years, taking us hither and thither, forward and backward from Marian Forrester's first meeting with her husband in California to her death, after various extra marital experiences and a second marriage in South America. It may be, however, that the passage just quoted is meant to be symbolic, for the gentleman who drew sparks happened to be one of the heroine's paramours.

Excellent word pictures of Middle Western life, scenes, and character enter into the story, and while they are in a measure realistic and accurate, there is nothing extraordinary in them. Miss Cather's is not the first story to utilize this picturesque life in fiction, nor is her rural Nebraska any more exact than the rural Kansas, the rural Illinois, the rural Missouri, of many another story-teller. She is simply following a well-blazed trail, but in doing so is it necessary to bring to life a time-honored plot that has done duty many thousand times, and that cannot be bettered as it is told by those French specialists whose work has become classic.

Miss Cather may of course argue that man and woman and life wear much the same aspect of sex in Nebraska as in Paris, and that it is her duty as a story-teller and artist to depict it. Possibly, and possibly she may be the great American novelist that she is claimed to be by certain ecstatic authorities. Time alone will tell, and for the present a few people will keep their heads, await further developments, and decide that *A Lost Lady* is simply a very well-told episodic story dealing in a conventional way with a very ancient and commonplace theme. That the publisher has confidence in it from a commercial standpoint is revealed by his statement, on the back of its titlepage, that he has printed twenty thousand two hundred and twenty copies of its first edition, two hundred and twenty being numbered, and bearing the signature of the author.

184

Henry Seidel Canby, "Cytherea," *New York Evening Post, The Literary Review*, 22 September 1923, p. 59

Books with substance to them or endowed with haunting beauty set you thinking of other attempts to grasp the elusive mysteries of living, those dooms and perplexities and surprises which sink deeper and deeper into the consciousness as one grows older. *A Lost Lady*, for all its simplicity, has this power. Its story means more on each recall. It is to the eye and perhaps to the first impression the slenderest of Miss Cather's novels; it is also, I think, the most perfect.

A boy tells the story, or at least this history of a Nebraska family which begins in the sunset of pioneer days and continues into the chill dawn of mediocre modernism as seen through his eyes. He is a healthy, sensitive boy, like the hero of *One of Ours*, and it is for him that the lady is lost; it is for him that her infinite feminine charm is sullied because it moves like will-o'-the-wisp into regions which disgust him. He cannot reconcile the alliance of loveliness with desire.

The Forrester home was famous in the railroad days of Nebraska. Mr. Forrester, the fine old incorruptible, had been a road builder, a handler of men. Much older than she, lame and retired, he lives on his hill, where old friends come. She welcomes them. The house has atmosphere, a moral dignity, a Cytherean charm. For the boy, Neil, it is civilization and idealism. Mrs. Forrester loves pleasure, loves beauty around her, of which she is a part. She loves men, irresistibly, that is the secret of her charm, and old Forrester

knows it. When she is with him she is lovely and loyal. When he is called away she is still lovely, but quickly, ruthlessly, takes a lover. The boy is shattered. Unlike the old man, he cannot understand.

For Mrs. Forrester is Cytherea, inexplicable by moral laws, yet herself a virtue most precious to men. "There could be no negative encounter, however slight, with Mrs. Forrester. If she merely bowed to you, merely looked at you, it contributed to a personal relation. Something about her took hold of one in a flash; one became acutely conscious of her, of her fragility and grace, of her mouth which could say so much without words; of her eyes, lively, laughing, intimate, nearly always a little mocking."

Then comes poverty, then the old man's death. Loyalty no longer held her, even a little. The detestable Ivy Peters comes closer; her own kind being gone, she pursues its crude substitutes in the town, now passed out of its generous pioneering age—"only the stage hands were left to listen to her. All those who had shared in fine undertakings and bright occasions were gone." And for Neil she is a lost lady. "Beautiful women," he wonders, "whose beauty meant more than it said . . . was their brilliancy always fed by something coarse and concealed? Was that their secret?"

What I am trying to show is that this brief novel is like a piece of fine Oriental fabric, with a color and texture that catches the interest at once, and then, for reflection, a significance of things deeply and perplexingly human. The story is so firmly and so quietly told that only gradually does it become a plot whose intensity depends not upon the history of a family, but rather upon a mystery of character which is, as with Hawthorne at his best, never quite revealed—the mystery of evil in good, of life fed by corruption, of that quality of beauty which flowers from the senses and can live only when they are fed.

The lady is not lost. From a debased home with a hard lover who casts her aside she escapes to scenes of earlier happiness, and years afterwards Neil comes upon her traces. She had married a kind husband; wealth had given her opportunities for pleasure; she was charming to the end. The story is not tragedy—she had no tragedy; the story is of her, a personality, feminine charm so transcendent that it had to be fed. If the fine could not keep her, then it would be the base. She preferred the fine.

Irene in Galsworthy's *Forsyte Saga* is such an embodiment of Cytherea, but her own inner nature supplies the aliment her qualities need. Her fire is self-fed. Marian Forrester is a subtler study. In her all transmutes to beauty, but charm, no matter how exquisite, has sensousness as its base. She will be good if she can, but first she must live, and to live for her is to love and be lovely. Even more striking is the parallel with "The Lost Girl" of D. H. Lawrence, who follows her brutish Italian to the harsh Italian country, where she is satisfied, if not happy, for she required most of all things love. The old incorruptible Forrester, he whose sense of duty was his life, knew that women could be like that, knew that "Maidy" was like that and yet was lovely, and he held her and protected her because he understood. Miss Cather is no more subtle than Lawrence, but she is perhaps wiser in her version of Cytherea.

In sheer art I think that this book is Miss Cather's masterpiece. She has painted broader canvases elsewhere, given greater substance, created a community instead of a character. Here she has been content with a woman's personality, and it is enough.

World-Herald (Omaha), 26 September 1923, p. 10

For those who know and love good books it has come to be a notable event when a novel appears from the hand of Willa Cather. And for Nebraskans there is the added interest that it is so often of this state and its people that Miss Cather writes, and as one intimately familiar no less with the spirit than with the color, form, and texture of her subject matter. While her appeal, as that of all writing deserving to rank as literature, is universal, in that it lays bare naked and quivering soul to curious soul, so steeped is Miss Cather's pen in local color that she promises yet to do for the great plains region, extending from the Missouri to the Rockies, much that Thomas Hardy has done for Sussex. If sometimes with her firm and searching probe she causes us who are habitants to squirm uncomfortably, the writhing is doubtless good for us. The fact that we do writhe, when the soul is exposed and the pitiless mirror of the spirit is held before us, is indicative that there is hope, with a little prodding, of our rising to better estates.

Miss Cather's latest book tells the story of *A Lost Lady*—of a lady very much not to say totally lost. Lost not so much or so poignantly, perhaps, with respect to hell fire and damnation, as in her helpless inability to orientate herself. A lovely lady, a charming lady, friendly, kind, yet in a sense exquisite and aloof, who slides down the descent to Avernus with painful rapidity and lack of struggle and with companions distressingly coarse—companions in no sense but the grossly physical at all worthy of her. It is a most delicate study of what we may hope is an unusual personality—a lily gone rank—that Miss Cather undertakes. And if one is not very careful to follow the exposition with open and sympathetic mind, to view it subjectively as well as objectively, in the spirit of the good Bishop of London watching the tumbril bearing the culprit to the gallows, there is danger of the reader being lost together with the lady.

This lady is transplanted from her sunny California to the plains during the state's first transition period. The heroic age of pioneers and builders was nearing an end; it was the twilight of the gods. The second generation was coming on apace, and Miss Cather does not find the second generation at all god-like. . . . There are clods and boors, one hundred per cent pure. There are other clods and boors lightly veneered. There are money grabbers and gossips and dumb-bells. Such lights as there are burn dimly. There is precious little leavening to leaven the lump. The gay and spritely Marian Forrester, with the air of culture and refinement she has brought with her to the provinces, is wedded to one of the gods, an adoring god, twenty-five years her senior, one of the great characters limned in contemporary fiction. For, despite his companionship, for want of her joy of being, she is dependent on his old associates, railroad men and bankers, from Denver and Omaha. And these, with the advent of crop failures and hard times, gradually stop coming. One of them in particular, a magnificent beast of a man, does not stop nearly soon enough. The aged husband, broken in body and purse and spirit, fades out, and the lovely lady is left to the drab and sordid life of the prairie small town, with such poor consolation as French brandy and a mucky lover can afford. This latter, beady-eyed and pig-minded, Ivy Peters by name, seems somehow meant to symbolize the Nebraska of the decadence, sunk deep in the swamp from its glorious morn.

The charming Marian disappears at length from the Nebraska milieu, as a brand snatched from the burning. She reappears in far South America, with a new husband, older than the first, and with the furs, jewels and limousine appertaining thereto. And the young dreamer of the tale, through whose clean eyes we see its soiled convolutions unfold, though she has made nightmares of his dreams, is chivalrous enough to be heartily glad to learn of her good luck. And then, too, despite her weakness, and for all her appalling misfortune in not having found her proper place in life wherein she might have shone with an exceeding glory of goodness as well as light, Marian Forrester was a woman of wonderful charm. Ivy Peters, the swinish, unprincipled, ruthless, takes over the Forrester home, the crown and pride of the old day, and, successful lawyer, farmer and entrepreneur, promises to become the new god of the new.

We trust we do injustices neither to Miss Cather nor to Nebraska, when we seem to see in Ivy Peters her symbol of the post-pioneer Nebraska. Perhaps, and more truly, he was meant rather for a symbol of a wider, a universal, application. Nebraska may be lousy with Ivy Peterses. But so, too, is America. So is civilization. But after all they are only lice on the body of the social order. They are not the body itself. They are representative of themselves, of the disease of greedy and carnal materialism they carry, but they are not representative of Nebraska nor of this union of states. It is true that idealism may seem to be in eclipse. But it is still alive, vigorous and vital, and when the test comes, as it came only six years ago, it rises triumphant and sun-kissed to meet the great occasion.

Mankind cannot be judged by samples from the mill run. In all the ages, luminous or dark, the lamp has been carried in the hands of minorities. The voice of the people has spoken as the voice of God, but not in chorus. Though it has come from the tongues of the few, the despised and rejected, it has prevailed, and has swept humankind along with it. The Ivy Peterses are never our prophets. Therefore they are never ourselves. Nebraska knows them, in its every community. But it does not love them. It does not respect them. It does not follow them. We have no doubt that even among the rudest and lowliest of "Sweet Water," the Nebraska town that is the scene of Miss Cather's story, Ivy Peters was about as unpopular as he is with Miss Cather herself.

Heywood Broun, "It Seems to Me," *World* (New York), 28 September 1923, p. 9

Willa Cather is back from the war safe and sound. She has never done a better novel than *A Lost Lady* nor is she likely to. But then neither is any other writer of our day. This seems to us truly a great book.

To us *One of Ours* was a most indifferent piece of work. The gap between the books is so great that we are inclined to seek causes. There may be an explanation in something as simple as the physical dimensions of the two books. *A Lost Lady* can scarcely be above 40,000 words, and Miss Cather is not burdened as she was in her prize winning novel by the task of sustaining her story. For her gift is not a narrative one. Or at any rate

not primarily. She is at her best in picturing for the reader people and places. And picture is an insufficient word. Here at any rate one gets the look, the sound, the essential spirit of the Forrester home. Miss Cather has caught the important relationship which may exist between a person and a room. Human action is motivated as in this story, by glass and wood and linen.

The story is centralized upon a single house and a small group of people, but no set frame can be placed around a perfect miniature. The particular, when firmly drawn, casts its shadow widely. To know Capt. Forrester and Marian Forrester is to have an understanding of an age and a class in America. This is a novel of the early days of America's railroad aristocracy. Capt. Forrester is one of those who laid a railroad across the plains. Hardly a hundred words of speech are assigned to him in the whole book and yet the character stands out clear and complete.

But it is not the freedom from the burden of length which has animated Miss Cather's new book into magnificence. A more grievous weight has been removed from the shoulders of the novelist. In *One of Ours* Miss Cather set herself the task of sustaining a moral. Now there are no interfering external judgments. The finest figure in the book is Marian Forrester, and there is ample opportunity in this story of a passionate woman for her friend, the author, to moralize and deplore. Such temptations are rigorously resisted. At no point are we asked to applaud or denounce. The reader is reduced to his proper function of being allowed to watch and observe and keep his mouth shut.

And yet Miss Cather does not play the rather chilling role of the perfect neutral who coldly creates characters in some way flawed and marred and then remains indifferent to what may be thought of them once they have moved beyond her fingertips. Marian Forrester is insulated against the potential harshness of the reader by sympathy, a sympathy practically never directly expressed but implied and indicated by the care and understanding with which the figure is drawn.

And there is a shrewd device in the telling. Often Miss Cather allows us to see Marian Forrester through the eyes of a young man to whom she remains glamourous to the end, even though she crumples again and again his idealistic conception. . . .

"He came to be," writes Miss Cather, "very glad that he had known her and that she had a hand in breaking him in to life. He has known pretty women and clever ones since then—but never one like her as she was in her best days. Her eyes, when they laughed for a moment into one's own, seemed to promise a wild delight that he has not found in life. 'I know where it is,' they seemed to say, 'I could show you!' He would like to call up the shade of the young Mrs. Forrester, as the Witch of Endor called up Samuel's, and challenge it, demand the secret of that ardor; ask her whether she had really, found some ever-blooming, ever-burning, ever-piercing joy, or whether it was all fine play-acting. Probably, she had found no more than another; but she had always the power of suggesting things much lovelier than herself, as the perfume of a single flower may call up the whole sweetness of spring."

Certainly nobody has ever succeeded so admirably in establishing a character with a single stroke as has Miss Cather in presenting us to Frank Ellinger, "a man who good humoredly bowed to the inevitable or to the almost inevitable."

It might be a good rule which would allow the writing of romances only to realists. Miss Cather is realistic in her methods, and probably neither *My Antonia* nor *One of Ours* would be classed as romantic. And so when Miss Cather brings out *A Lost Lady*, undeniably a romance, it seems more persuasive than any book by an author confirmed in the task of tinting life. Your veteran romanticist hardly ever escapes floridity. In fact, once the consciousness of romanticism descends upon an author he is lost. He overplays his hand and poses and struts and listens. Very possibly Miss Cather was not conscious of her mood. She is painstaking in establishing glamour. Romance it may be, but she will not be content unless she makes it real.

One excellent test of the true quality of a novelist is to require him to set a fine dinner before his characters. We have Joseph Hergesheimer in mind, for it is his particular test which always establishes him in our mind as a writer heavily streaked with the spurious. Just let the wines appear and Mr. Hergesheimer becomes the least warmly invited guest at the party. He rushes about and reads the dates and the labels in a vain effort to prove himself a familiar at the feast.

These dinners in a Hergesheimer book are never really eaten. Instead the food is whisked about like the unconvincing properties provided for a stage banquet in a stock company. The glasses raised to the lips of the characters are empty. They may pretend to eat, but they will not be nourished.

When Capt. Forrester gives a dinner in *A Lost Lady* there is an undeniable, pungent odor. These ducks might almost grease the page. Even the cocktails, mixed of paper and printer's ink, seem to cool the throat and warm the belly.

Miss Cather has put the proper ingredients into her novel and has shaken them until they foam and bubble.

There is a romantic ballad somewhere in German literature about a race of giants who dwelt in Alsace. Their castle was Niedeck and their cites lay high up surrounded by a rich champaign. The refrain of the ballad is touchingly melancholic. It tells us that Castle Niedeck is now a ruin, that the cities are waste and desolate.

Du fragest nach die Riesen,
Du findest sie nicht mehr.

"You ask after the giants, you find them there no more."

A dim memory this of schooldays and schoolboy German, yet it rose sharply into the reviewer's consciousness upon reading Miss Cather's brief but charming little opus. It is hardly a novel and yet it is too full and good for a short story. It is simply a little work of art.

Miss Cather is a realist. Who would dare to call her otherwise? Not this reviewer, at any rate, who has just been classifying her elsewhere as one of America's most promising realistic writers. But the memory of that German ballad emerging so insistently upon reading *A Lost Lady*, gives the show away. The truth is, Miss Cather's romanticism, long repressed, bursts forth almost in spite of her and she has painted a vivid, brilliant little picture of an age that is gone not to return. One feels almost that one ought to keep Miss Cather's confidence.

"I know this is a romance," she seems to be saying, "but please don't tell a soul."

Men like Captain Forrester—a Civil War Captain this—who helped to build the Burlington, or, say, the Union Pacific, are as extinct as the Prince Alberts they used to wear. Honest, well-to-do, incorruptible, patriotic, generous to a fault—as the phrase is—old-fashioned Americans like that are not often to be found now even in the West. Modern Americans, even with many of Captain Forrester's virtues, are too businesslike to be either so chivalrous or so generous.

And Marian Forrester—gay, handsome, very feminine, very courageous, reckless, even, somewhat weak and immoral, but as generous as her husband, the kind of woman who would be popularly described as "such a lady!"—Are there any like her remaining? No. Miss Cather very fittingly describes her as a lost lady.

"You ask after the giants, you find them there no more."

"Thirty or forty years ago, in one of those gray towns along the Burlington Railroad which are so much grayer today than they were then, there was a house well known from Omaha to Denver for its hospitality and for a certain charm of atmosphere. Well known, that is to say, to the railroad aristocracy of that time...."

"When the Burlington men were traveling back and forth on business not very urgent, they found it agreeable to drop off the express and spend a night in a pleasant house where their importance was delicately recognized."

Except for the American names, might not this have been the opening of a long short story by Turgenief, say, out of "The Annals of a Sportsman?"

In telling the story of Captain Daniel Forrester, and particularly of his young wife, Marian Forrester, Miss Cather keeps this note of worldly wise, yet benevolently philosophic, interest throughout. It is the note of the spacious realist, of the unhurried ones, like the Russians, it has nothing of the hot, fetid realism of some of the Frenchmen. This spaciousness and the leisured, lingering charm make the story more romantic than romance itself.

What is the story? Well, that is nothing marvelous in itself. It is the story of Captain Daniel Forrester's decline from wealth to virtual poverty because depositors in a certain bank in Denver trusted in his name. He could not let them down, so he simply turned his wealth over to them.

As to Marian, whom he married under romantic circumstances, he simply worshipped her. And she was adorable—with that mysterious gift of Venus that at times makes a woman irresistible. She was as courageous in adversity as she was generous to what she regarded as her inferiors—and as frail in her morals as she was both. Even while the Captain was yet living she had a lover. After his death, well—but somehow she never lost her charm. Her vagaries in no way impaired her other qualities. To the end she was charming. Men loved her. They knew her faults as surely as Captain Forrester himself had known them, but they were fond of her. She died the wife of a rich Englishman in South America. One of the boys of her small town, subsequently a prospering engineer, saw her as an old lady in that foreign land. And still she was charming.

Captain Forrester, railroad magnate in the days of western railroad building, is a terrifying figure. Thoroughly lovable, vain, capricious, daring—Miss Cather has used her as a pivotal point around which to swing the characters of several types of men. They are brutal portraits in a way, quick, incisive, arresting. Miss Cather does not pause for morbid detail. Her sadistic Ivy Peters is a masterpiece of quick characterization. Captain Forrester, bluff, good humored, tolerant, sad; in all the true meaning of chivalric codes, a gentleman. Neil, the young dreamer, to whom Marian is a symbol of womanly love, whose disillusion is heartrending but who works through to a real admiration of the brilliant Mrs. Forrester. Francis Ellinger, the Don Juan, arrogant, thoughtless, bold. Quite simply, without elaborate machinery, Miss Cather has drawn her allegorical presentation of love in its various phases. It is portrayed from the masculine point of view, yet by a woman who has seen her men characters and understands them. The method, while it will remind you of Henry James, is more lucid. This is a fine piece of psychological writing. I can think of nothing of its kind so good in recent American fiction, with the possible exception of *Ethan Frome*.

John Farrar, "A Triumphant Character," *Bookman* (New York), 58 (October 1923), 200

This portrait of a lady by Willa Cather is as brilliant as a summer dawn, as clear, as beautiful. I suppose *A Lost Lady* can hardly be called a novel, yet it is more than a novelette—we might let it go at, a short novel. Marian Forrester, wife of

John B. Edwards, *Sewanee Review*, 31 (October–December 1923), 510–11

Literature seems full of lost ladies, so that one more will make possibly no great difference; no doubt, "cherchez la femme" was originally devised to assist in the search for some lost lady. I venture to say, however, that in proportion to the total feminine population of all the novels and romances the quota of the lost is extraordinarily high if compared with the greater realism of the actual world. Consequently, a study by a feminine consciousness of an imaginary lost woman, no matter how pretty the style may be, is apt to partake more of the nature of malicious gossip than of the quality of literature. Still, as Thackeray has it, "What would we do for conversation if it were not for the lady who has just left the room?" Now to make the room the imagination of a nice young man and describe the exit of the lady as he realizes more and more surely that she really was "lost"—one can almost subscribe to such "technique", for it would seem that writers are especially appreciative of heroes or heroines of the sex complementing their own. The author seems to regard morality as a matter of taste; but this is not realism, for taste is rather a matter of morality. A character can be revealed as evil, for instance, without dragging in the disgusting horror of Ivy Peter's treatment of the woodpecker. True, the Lost Lady is as cruelly blinded herself, and her flight through the book is even more heart-rending. I should object to this book on both scores, that of taste as well as essential morality. The author's talent is of high order and might well be employed in exploiting higher themes.

E. W. Osborn, "The Artistry of A *Lost Lady*," *World* (New York), 7 October 1923, p. 10E

By a curious fall of circumstances there is left for the very end of this running review mention of the finest piece of literary artistry that came our way while the strike was on and our book pages were not. We refer to A *Lost Lady*, a novel of few pages and many charms, which is the latest offering of Willa Cather. This is the story of that lovely lady who, in faraway Sweet Water, on the Burlington line, keeps the home fires burning for Capt. Daniel Forrester and at the same time manages to keep alive and breathing in the community a warmth of interest largely fed by tales of a past life in which gay young men of California and Colorado figure mysteriously. Not that she is a lady full of years even as our book begins. She is twenty-five years younger than the Captain and is so altogether attractive to the eye that dishabille cannot stale nor the marks of kitchen work take the edge from her fascinations.

The story of Mrs. Forrester is one that calls for delicate telling. In particular, it is well to write softly, so to speak, of the place in the lady's calculations held by one Frank Ellinger, a frequent and assuming visitor, a fellow of masterful ways and an amazing fur overcoat. And yet, before all is told, the Ellinger person has spoken out quite audibly on his own motion. Mrs. Forrester lingers and illuminates in Sweet Water all the while young Niel Herbert is growing up and becoming wiser to the lady and wondering just how much it is that the rare old Captain knows and holds to himself. After Forrester has failed and died, and after Niel Herbert has found his sphere away from the Burlington line, the lady herself moves from Sweet Water. From being a very present wonder, she comes to be a memory. Later on it is but echoes from this place and that which deal with her. Finally even the echoes cease. The story is told.

Only as we close the pages of A *Lost Lady* do we become aware how faithfully and unforgettably the very self of its fair and frail heroine has been stamped upon our mind. She stays with us just as, in the book, she is shown to live to the appreciative gaze of Cyrus Daizell and the other great ones of the Burlington line who are welcomed by her as they drop in to enjoy the hospitalities of the Forrester home. (The lady's temperament may get out of control but she can keep house and she does it faithfully, as we have said.) As she fills the book before us she is further created proof of the rarity and completeness of her author's great gift in writing.

Russell Gore, *Detroit News*, 14 October 1923, metropolitan section, p. 12

Marian Forrester's eyes seemed to promise a wild delight not to be found in life. "I know what it is," they seemed to say, "I could show you!" Niel Herbert felt that he would like to call up the shade of the young Mrs. Forrester, as the witch of Endor called up Samuel's, and challenge it, demand the secret of that ardor: ask her whether she had really found some everblooming, ever-burning, ever-piercing joy, or whether it was all fine play acting.

With a woman like this dominating the pages of Willa Cather's *A Lost Lady* we have some such effect as that conveyed in Joseph Conrad's *The Arrow of Gold*. We leave Marian Forrester as we leave Dona Rita—puzzled as to the exact source of her charm, wondering just why she maintains so strong a hold on men's faculty for adoration. Men are easily attracted, but not so easily held. How did Marian Forrester manage it? And with so many? For it was the same with Daniel Forrester,

the husband to whom she was unfaithful; with Niel Herbert, the clean, lofty boy through whose eyes we see the panorama of the story; with the detestable Ivy Peters.

Perhaps the secret lies in her vitality. When the husband she deceived but to whom she gave a generous devotion in the long illness following his financial ruin was a helpless invalid on her hands she said to Herbert, "I feel such a power in me to live, Niel." Before the crash that carried her sturdy mate down Mrs. Forrester had been to the little town of Sweetwater "an excitement that came and went with summer." Her winters were danced away in Denver. Always she was that—an excitement, perhaps also an incitement. "Mrs. Forrester looked at one, and one knew that she was bewitching. It was instantaneous and it pierced the thickest hide. . . . Where Mrs. Forrester was dullness was impossible."

And yet a rather shocking lady—a "lost lady," indeed. No wonder Niel Herbert, the boy who adored her, wondered where she kept all her exquisiteness when she invited men like Frank Ellinger to her home during her husband's absence. Where was her exquisiteness when, the play over, she gave a second performance for the benefit of the stage hands—common fellows who "knew a common woman when they saw her?" And yet, from South America, married again to the rich Englishman who had succumbed to her charms, she sent every year a check for the grave of Capt. Forrester—the husband whom perhaps she never fooled.

This husband, by the way, stands out in the book—massive, Biblical. "His clumsy dignity covered a deep nature, and a conscience that had never been trifled with. . . . His sanity asked nothing, claimed nothing; it was so simple that it brought a hush over distracted creatures." Fit milestone to mark the end of the era

193

which is the background of the story—the era of the railroad building west. A huge figure, pitiable and tragic in his simplicity, silhouetted against "the sunset of the pioneer."

It has been said that this book is unlike Miss Cather's other stories. It is not. It is the flowering, in a slender volume of 174 pages, of her power, superbly demonstrated by six preceding prose works, to give a sincere and unhurried transcript of life—especially of the life of our American west. The calmness and dignity of what she wrote of Nebraska for the *Nation*'s series on "These United States" is in this book of the country near Denver. The cottonwoods of *The Song of the Lark* are here; and here, too, are the lagoon flowers—which one reading the magazine article knows are coreopsis—growing in what were once the buffalo "wallows," depressions which the trekking herds made into firm cups of earth.

As always, one finds in Miss Cather largeness of vision, poignancy, power, beauty. No pausing in this volume over the sins of a sinning woman; instead an acceptance of her as she is, a courtesan modified by environment, and a movement onward to catch the phases of her charm which lay behind the base and the ephemeral.

Miss Cather does not preach. Perhaps that is why in the end the reader pauses over the "lost lady" of her story with pity, with the sorrowful sense of something beautiful drawing strength and vitality from rotten soil.

"Lillies that fester," said the boy when he found her out, "smell worse than weeds." And yet when the grave covers the lovely, vicious, sparkling atom of dust known as Marian Forrester one wishes the gay, false spirit well.

Nancy Barr Mavity, "Old Railroad Aristocracy Depicted in *A Lost Lady*," *San Francisco Chronicle*, 21 October 1923, p. 5D

Willa Cather, in a very short novel of only about 40,000 words, yet contrives to give an effect of breadth and sweep, the epical quality that makes individual fate and fortune fall into place among the wider, slower movements of which they are a part. *A Lost Lady* depicts "the end of an era, the sunset of the pioneer. This was the very end of the road-making West."

"The old West had been settled by dreamers, great-hearted adventurers, who were unpractical to the point of magnificance; a courteous brotherhood, strong in attack, but weak in defense, who could conquer but could not hold. Now all the vast territory they had won was at the mercy of men who had never dared anything, never risked anything. The space, the color, the princely carelessness of the pioneer they would destroy and cut up into profitable bits, as the match factory splinters the primeval forest."

The passing of the old railroad builders is the background against which flits Marian Forrester, gay, brilliant, avid of life, upheld more than she knew by the substantial dignity of her elderly husband. Captain Forrester, a creature frail and yet gallant, needing always to be guarded by a stronger personality than her own, falling from aristocratic graciousness to common hugger for joy and admiration—any one's admiration—and yet, somehow, brave and lovely, even when most lost.

Externally, there is no point of comparison between Willa Cather and Joseph Conrad in manner or theme, yet in underlying philosophy they are akin; for Miss Cather also takes that view of the universe as a spectacle, so magnificently expounded in Conrad's *Notes on Life and Letters*. Her objectivity is so perfect that it sometimes leads the reader astray, as when critics with varying degrees of enthusiasm pounced on the naive attitude towards the war of the country boy in *One of Ours*, as if it were the author's own attitude—even though, in that particular book, she guards against this very assumption by stepping out of the picture frame and speaking in propria persona for three pages at the end.

It would be natural enough to call Miss Cather an "author's author," though her sales demonstrate that she is not just that. But her rigorous simplicity, a quarried quality in her prose, as if it were hewn out of hard rock with utmost precision and economy, may well fill the writer who knows how fuzzy and recalcitrant words may be, with a despairing admiration.

She has her "eye on the object," whether that object is a face or an attitude or a state of mind or an historical epoch. Her descriptions do not seem to be personal felicities of phrase, but a direct translation from the medium of sight to the medium of words. . . .

The description of Ivy Peters, and of the old captain, sitting "with the soles of his boots together, his legs bowed out," are the visualizations of one who watches life. Perhaps the best motto for the writer is the phrase of the railroad crossing: "Stop! Look! Listen!"

H[enry] W[alcott] Boynton, *Independent*, 111 (27 October 1923), 198–9

Miss Cather has made a remarkable addition to her gallery of feminine portraits, Thea Kronborg, Antonia, Enid Royce, Gladys Farmer. Mrs. Forrester, her "lost lady," sublimates still another type of womanhood. In scale and method the story somewhat resembles *My Antonia*. It is neither "novelette" nor full-length novel. It is a complete and significant action distilled so that the whole of its sparkling potency may brim without overflowing the small crystal vessel of its form. Another point of similarity is that here, as in *My Antonia*, the central figure is seen through the eyes of a male who stands rather wistfully outside the sphere of her most intimate and intense experience. And, not to carry the analogy too far, we may note that Mrs. Forrester and Antonia represent opposite or complementary types, the woman who excites and delights, and the one who warms and sustains.

"Thirty or forty years ago, in one of those grey towns along the Burlington railroad, which are so much greyer today than they were then, there was a house well known for its hospitality and for a certain charm of atmosphere." So, in the opening sentence, the tale is timed and placed. In making a rough classification of recent American novels, I have just found myself hesitating whether to put *A Lost Lady* among the studies of character or among the studies of place and time. There would be the same difficulty in pigeonholing *The Song of the Lark* or *O Pioneers!* or *My Antonia*. They are equally valuable and impressive as records of what may be called the transition period in the Middle West, and as interpretations of typical figures of the period. In one aspect *A Lost Lady* is priceless for the clarity and richness of its scene and atmosphere, conveyed as they are by so few and firm (though at a glance almost casual) touches of Miss Cather's brush. We have here, in these few pages, a picture of the second or after-pioneer generation possessing and exploiting the land. The marshy acres which Mr. Forrester has gallantly neglected so that their beauty might be preserved, and which are promptly drained and used as soon as they fall into the hands of ruthless and vulgar Ivy Forrester, are symbolic of a larger change. . . .

It is the period of Miss Cather's own youth which this story, like all her best novels, warmly and a little wistfully records. "Vidi tantum"; she also, like her young Niel Herbert, was born soon enough to catch a gilmpse of the departing glory of the heroic West. "He had seen the end of an era, the sunset of the pioneer. He had come upon it when already its glory was nearly spent. . . . This was the very end of the road-making West; the men who had put plains and mountains under the iron harness were old; some were poor, and even the successful ones were hunting for rest or a brief reprieve from death. It was already gone, that age; nothing could ever bring it back. The taste and smell and song of it, the visions those men had seen in the air and followed—these he had caught in a kind of afterglow in their own faces—and this would always be his."

This note of elegiac melancholy, of mild lament for the passing of a heroic race and time, delicately as it is sounded here, has been frequently heard from the more sensitive writers who belong to that period of afterglow—Hamlin Garland,

Herbert Quick, and the rest. After all, *A Lost Lady* is primarily the story of a woman. Moreover, though she is a woman outwardly fashioned and adorned by her time, we recognize her as a being of all time. She happens to belong to the era of ladyhood, when pretty manners and modest attire were valued highly by the male world, in its domestic womankind, at least. To her, the soft enchantress, this convention, with its emphasis upon sex difference, is recognized as an asset. Mrs. Forrester, pagan, tippler, lover of men, possesses many of the virtues and principles of her time. As a young girl she has married, in a moment of emotional crisis, a widower twenty-five years older than she. She is still lovely, still full of ardor, when he has become an old man. She takes the best of care of him, endures a sort of banishment for his sake, gives him to the end her genuine affection. She can even hold herself to a code of technical fidelity so long as they are under the same roof. So she "saves her face," being freed by her husband's absence to take the earthy lover who renews her sense of youth. So runs the hidden Victorian code: Mrs. Forrester esteems it, and resents accordingly, the incursions of a new fashion of woman. It is long after young Niel has discovered the fallibility of his goddess, that she asks him about this disconcerting change in the feminine code:

"And tell me, Niel, do women really smoke after dinner now with the men, nice women? I shouldn't like it. It's all very well for actresses, but women can't be attractive if they do everything that men do."

"I think just now it's the fashion for women to make themselves comfortable, before anything else."

Mrs. Forrester glanced at him as if he had said something shocking. "Ah, that's just it! The two things don't go together. Athletics and going to college and smoking after dinner. Do you like it? Don't men like women to be different from themselves? They used to."

In short, she is jealous for the power of sheer feminine loveliness, that may innocently, or not so innocently, seduce the muscular and forthright male. It is the magic of the sea-born one, of her who burnt the topless towers of Ilium, that she so earnestly defends.

For her, certainly, that magic suffices. Nor is it a vulgar or a shallow magic. There is real tenderness in her feeling for "Mr. Forrester," to the end, and real dependence on the love of her friends. Old Cyrus Dalzell has only to tell her how her old companions miss her: "Tears flashed into her eyes. 'That's very dear of you. It's sweet to be remembered when one is away.' In her voice there was the heart-breaking sweetness one sometimes hears in lovely, gentle old songs." It is not a vicious woman upon whose presence old Forrester depends in his failing days: "Often when Mrs. Forrester was about her work, the Captain would call to her, 'Maidy, Maidy,' and she would reply, 'Yes, Mr. Forrester,' from wherever she happened to be, but without coming to him, as if she knew that when he called to her in that tone he was not asking for anything. He wanted to know if she were near, perhaps; or, perhaps, he merely liked to call her name and to hear her answer. The longer Niel was with Captain Forrester in those peaceful closing days of his life, the more he felt that the Captain knew his wife better even than she knew herself; and that, knowing her, he—to use one of his own expressions—valued her."

For us, as for young Neil, there remains the eternal paradox of such a woman's poise and such a woman's abandon: "He burned to ask her one question, to get the truth out of her and to set his mind at rest: What did she do with her exquisiteness when she was with a man like Ellinger? Where did she put it away? And having put it away, how could she recover herself, and give one—give even him—the sense of tempered steel, a blade that could fence with anyone and never break?"

And after all, she never does quite break, since she is never conscious of defeat, never false to the Cytherean code. It is true that after the Captain's death her poise leaves her; and when young Neil becomes convinced that she is become mistress of the Philistine Ivy Peters, he turns from her in disgust, never to see her again. But force remains in her yet, some residue of the vitality and will to enjoy which have always lain beneath her charm. Many years later Neil hears that she has made a comfortable marriage, and has been cherished till her death: "So we may feel sure that she was well cared for, to the very end," said Neil. "Thank God for that."

Long before this Neil has outgrown his youthful intolerant disgust. He has lost his lady, his boyish ideal of feminine perfection; but she has given him something priceless, after all. "He came to be very glad that he had known her, and that she had had a hand in breaking him in to life. He has known pretty women, and clever ones since then, but never one like her, as she was in her best days. Her eyes, when they laughed for a moment into one's own, seemed to promise a wild delight that he has not found in life. 'I know where it is,' they seemed to say, 'I could show you!' He would like to call up the young Mrs. Forrester, as the witch of Endor called up Samuel's spirit, and challenge it, demand the secret of that ardor; ask her whether she had really found some ever-blooming, ever-burning, ever-piercing joy, or whether it was all fine play-acting. Probably she had found no more than another; but she had always the power of suggesting things much love-

197

lier than herself, as the perfume of a single flower may call up the whole sweetness of spring."

Burton Rascoe, "The Lost Lady," *New York Tribune*, 28 October 1923, section 9, pp. 17–18

Miss Cather has written (as in time she would) her story of the modern Cytherean, and she has written it more beautifully than any one before her. For all the light, fine gallantry of Mr. Arnold Bennet's touch, his *Pretty Lady* becomes in retrospect something like a challenging defense, briefed by an industrious notetaker who preens himself on his understanding of women. Mr. W. L. George's *Bed of Roses*, too, is an elaborate bow of homage which has something of a stiffness and a condescension in it. The lovely Dona Rita in Mr. Joseph Conrad's *Arrow of Gold* hangs upon the cheek of night in such radiant and inscrutable splendor as to reduce her youthful worshiper to inarticulate praises; she remains a symbol, not a thing of flesh and blood. There is a bit too much of the work of what Mr. D. H. Lawrence calls the dark gods in Mr. Joseph Hergesheimer's *Cytherea*. And Mr. James Branch Cabell's Melicent in *Domnei* and his light-hearted Margaret Hugonin in *The Eagle's Shadow* are the same visions of the lost lady glimpsed by Miss Cather through the eyes of the boy, Niel Herbert.

This is the finest novel Miss Cather has written—which is to say that it is one of the best novels in contemporary English and American fiction. Omitting one excruciating detail of characterization on page 24—an unnecessary incident which wrenched my nerves and afflicted me for a moment with a violent nausea—everything in this novel, I should say, is perfect, beautifully real, poignantly true to life. *My Antonia* contains more moving pathos and more comforting charm; some of the short stories in *Youth and the Bright Modusa* are tinctured with a deeper stain of irony and are more unusual in theme; but none of her work has the serenity, the clear, unruffled insight, the magical art of this novel.

With *A Lost Lady* Miss Cather has, I believe, entered into a new period in her career. She has got rid of her old resentments; she has given up beating her wings against the void; she has begun to accept life as something precious, fine and beautiful even in (or perhaps because of) its trivial tragedies, its disillusions and disappointments. Hitherto she has set most of her characters in vague, persistent revolt against the limitations of life, against surroundings, against material circumstance. In *A Lost Lady* there is none of that. There is a brief, sharp protest against the vulgarity consequent upon the social changes brought about by the passing away of the pioneer and empire-building generations of the Middle West and the rise of a generation of coarser-grained money grubbers and exploiters, but even in this protest, there is understanding and even a certain pitying sympathy.

Miss Cather has wrought her style to exquisite perfection. All the slight defects of manner, all the tendencies to over-emphasis, all the patches of "fine writing" in the earlier books are gone. She has learned concision, economy. The brief passage wherein she betrays Mrs. Forrester's dereliction, the sentence whereby she discovers to the reader the nature of the humble loyalty Mrs. Forrester had inspired in a butcher's boy, the amazingly revelatory flash which establishes the nobility of Captain Forrester—such triumphs of artistry are matters to which we must show the deference due to genius.

Mrs. Forrester is at once a type and an individual. She is a very light-hearted, vital, generous natured, shallow, attractive woman whose personality is a changing thing conditioned upon the feminine ideals of the men with whom she is thrown into contact—a woman who is all things to all men—who is without any definite character except such externals of it as men are pleased to find in her. And yet she is as fully realized as any individual may be realized in fiction.

Mrs. Forrester is the feminine magnet of the story, drawing to her new blades of finely tempered steel, heavy serviceable nails, pine and rusty filings. She is, when the story opens, married to one of the pioneer construction engineers who built the great railroads through the fertile lands of the Middle West—a man of force and integrity, with an expansive and noble code built upon a generous sympathy and understanding of people. She is twenty years his junior and, so long as Captain Forrester is alive, her personality is kept radiant by the protective influence of her husband. Moving gay and fresh in a world of wealth, power and assurance, "she had always the power of suggesting things much lovlier than herself, as the perfume of a single flower may call up the whole sweetness of spring. . . . Her eyes when they laughed for a moment into one's own seemed to promise a wild delight that he had not found in life. 'I know where it is,' they seemed to say, 'I could show you!' "

Niel Herbert is one of the youths to whom Mrs. Forrester existed as a flaming ideal, fashioned in the gossamer of his poetic fancy about beauty, purity and innocence; and so long as she could play up to that ideal, she held his devotion. But when events forced him to see her in relation with others whose view of her differed from his own, he hated her for it. This device of presenting Mrs. Forrester as she existed in the minds of other people, and especially in the eyes of Niel Herbert, is an extremely difficult technical feat which she has managed by superb adroitness; and it has been the means of heightening the drama of the story. For Niel Herbert's sudden revelation that Mrs. Forrester was not merely a blessed damosel hanging out from the gold bar of heaven, but a tigerishly real woman of passionate flesh and blood, turned shrewish and coarse with hate and desperation when she discovers that her lover has married—this revelation was to him heart-breakingly tragic; it brought him to earth with a thud from which he was long recovering; and Miss Cather has realized the full force of the pathos and irony of it.

The conclusion of the story is courageously conceived and is beautifully executed. In current literature there is far too little of such art as Miss Cather has shown in this book for us not to make the proper obeisance before it.

"Big Theme under Common Story in New Cather Book" [Autumn 1923 clipping from unidentified newspaper in Willa Cather scrapbooks, Red Cloud, II-7], p. 6

Whatever differences of opinion may have existed when the 1923 Pulitzer novel prize was awarded to Willa Cather for her book *One of Ours*, there will be no doubt in the case of her latest story *A Lost Lady*. No one will choose it as a portrayal of "the wholesome atmosphere of American manners and manhood." For it is rather a sad picture of certain aspects of unwholesomeness in the American atmosphere.

Miss Cather's style in her new book is as excellent as it was in *One of Ours*. As an artistic piece of work, this briefer story is hardly inferior to *One of Ours*. But just as the hero in that book did not seem altogether convincing to us, so the heroine in *A Lost Lady* seems even less true to life. Marian Forrester is pictured as a highly sensitive character, a devotee of beauty, and at the same time she is shown as deriving pleasure and satisfaction from the gross advances of ugly Frank Ellinger and repulsive Ivy Peters. We cannot conceive of such a woman character, unless it be frankly a case of double personality.

We should say, then, that Willa Cather is erratic in characterization, but excellent in her style of expression. Even the honorable and admirable characters of Niel and Mr. Forrester are not altogether vividly drawn; there is about them always a somewhat haziness of outline that makes one a bit uncertain how to pigeon-hole them. She seems most successful in the portrayal of her meanest character; Ivy Peters sinks into the reader's brain.

In the art of writing English, however, Miss Cather undeniably stands at the top with two or three other American women. We so not think she is quite equal to Edith Wharton, but she can touch her with her finger tips. Stripped of all inessentials, her sentences stand forth sharp and clear, like bare branches against snow. When she uses one of her sparing adjectives it colors the whole page. The strength of Willa Cather lies in the simplicity and precision of her diction. . . .

The story Miss Cather has in mind in *A Lost Lady* is of the passing of the generous and nobleminded pioneers who dreamed grandly and built largely—the passing of these men from the West and the filling of their places by little minded, stingy, materialistic, bone picking money grubbers. Captain Forrester, the railroad builder who helped "dream the railroads across the mountains," was the exemplification of the first. Ivy Peters, the shyster, the cheater of Indians, personified the second. . . .

But this fine, big story is made the background for the common, rather disgusting story of an unfaithful wife. Captain Forrester's second wife was 25 years younger than he, and when the captain's infirmities of body and the loss of his fortune compelled them to spend years in a little gray town on the Burlington railroad, between Omaha and Denver, Mrs. Forrester sought diversion in an "affair" with Frank Ellinger. Over against this Miss Cather sketches the noble character of the captain who, although he knew Mrs. Forrester better than she knew herself, never uttered a word in censure; and the career of Niel Herbert, the model young man who loved Mrs. Forrester with a beautiful, disinterested love, and was not disgusted by the object of his affection until he had been repeatedly convinced of her defection.

A Lost Lady is disappointing. In the background is a great theme, but it is covered over with that anciently common plot of uxorial adultery. We admire greatly the polished technique of expression, but the story leaves us a bad taste in the mouth.

Edward Williamson, "Willa Cather's Latest Book Is Another Triumph" [Autumn 1923 clipping from an unidentified Nebraska newspaper, Willa Cather scrapbooks, Red Cloud, II-5]

Willa Cather, Nebraska novelist, whose novel, *One of Ours*, won the 1922 Pulitzer prize, has added a new triumph to her already rather imposing list with *A Lost Lady*, published in book form by Alfred A. Knopf.

Like her other major works, it is a tale of the western prairie. In it lives once more the spirit of the Nebraska plains which Miss Cather, better than any other, knows how to portray.

Not the west of the pioneer this time, but of the railroad aristocracy that grew up when the great transcontinental lines were being pushed across the plains. Hard times had not yet come to mar the faith of these builders of empire, these conquerors of the wilderness.

Such a one was Captain Forrester, and about his young and pretty wife, Marian Forrester, marooned in the captain's mansion in a little Nebraska town, the tale is built.

Men were necessary to Marian Forrester. On this hypothesis Miss Cather has constructed her plot. It is ordinary. The book is nothing of the sort. Miss Cather has built it into a narrative which, if it is not art, is at least first rate literature.

She knows the implements of her trade, does Willa Cather. She employs them with an expertness which conceals all scaffolding of technique. Her tales appear hewn in the rough, as though by swift, telling strokes of a woodman's ax. The result leaves an impression of utter simplicity.

The edges, of course, a trifle rough, and here and there a projecting knot which might well have been trimmed down, perhaps.

Rough? Examine that knot. It was fashioned with a jeweler's chisel. That is the gift of concealment of literary effort which is Willa Cather's.

Of Marian Forrester, Miss Cather says: "If she merely bowed to you, merely looked at you, it constituted a personal relation. Something about her took hold of one in a flash; one became acutely conscious of her, of her fragility and grace, of her mouth, which could say much without words; of her eyes, lively, laughing, intimate, nearly always a little mocking."

Banal? Adjective besprinkled?

Find me a better paragraph of its sort, and I will go with you to sing anthems under the author's window.

From a plainsman, driver for a freighting company that carried supplies across the prairies from Nebraska City to Cherry Creek, as Denver was then known, Captain Forrester had forged upward to become a builder of railroads. An inherent dignity and poise permitted him, in affluence, to occupy the place customarily reserved in fiction for Kentucky colonels.

A staunch man, and a kindly man, withal, was the captain, whose reputation of absolute integrity was known to railroad men from Chicago to the coast, and whose name for open handed hospitality brought a constant stream of visitors to his comfortable estate at Sweet Water.

They were directors, general managers, vice presidents, superintendents, auditors, freight agents and departmental assistants. The fact that they were "connected" with the railroad gained them entree like a badge of knighthood. These were the aristocracy of the middle west of the period.

And men were necessary to Marian Forrester.

For the rest, the book moves swiftly, but with meticulous care. Robbed by death of her husband, from whom, although she was unfaithful to him, she appeared to draw that insouciant vigor which was the charm of her personality, she fell and disintegrated like the steel of a rapier turning to tin.

Her former position as queen of the village had left her but few friends in the place; and those who were her friends, she drove away by the baseness of her descent.

She had never, perhaps, been wholly virtuous, but she had had strength of character, she had inspired virtue, and she had been charming. Now she was no longer charming.

The response of the village to this change in her is used with telling effect. Marian herself remains inscrutable in her weakness and in her reckless courage.

The first edition of the book contains 20,220 copies. Nebraska might do worse than to absorb them.

Joseph Wood Krutch, "The Lady as Artist," *Nation*, 117 (28 November 1923), 610

Since American criticism is as tolerant as it is, only her own artistic conscience can explain the fact that Miss Cather has slowly and surely perfected herself in her craft. Easily pleased in general we are; we praise one writer for his interesting story, another for his satirical keenness, another for his philosophy, and still another for his realistic detail, without crying out much in protest when the defects are as glaring as the virtues. Obviously, Miss Cather has had her own counsel of perfection which has made her not so easily pleased. She has not been content to be praised justly for the vividness and freshness of the sketches which made up *My Antonia* nor for the adroitness in the handling of plot which she exhibited in the stories composing *Youth and the Bright Medusa*. Instead, she has constantly struggled to achieve that synthesis of qualities which alone can make a novel really fine, and in *A Lost Lady*, short and slight as it is, she has achieved it. There would be no excuse for calling it a great novel—it is not that; but there would be equally little excuse for not recognizing the fact that it is that very rare thing in contemporary literature, a nearly perfect one. Miss Cather has come to the point where she can do the two or three things at once which a novelist must do. She can evoke by a few characteristic touches and by subtle suggestion a scene and a society without producing merely a "document"; she can present a character without writing a psychological treatise; she can point a moral without writing a sermon; and hence she is a novelist.

Memory is in a very true sense the mother of her muse, for in her youth she gathered a remarkable wealth of impressions, but instead of "pouring forth" this material in the approved contemporary fashion she has brooded upon it and formed it until her picture has both composition and meaning. Thus in the new book she has evoked again an epoch of the West, the epoch which she loves, when the land had been settled by "great-hearted adventurers who were unpractical to the point of magnificence" but had not yet passed from the hands of the pioneers into the hands of the swarm of exploiters and business men who came to "develop the country" with railroad, with factory, and with the hosts of thrifty hard-headed farmers who destroyed the "princely carelessness of the pioneer" and made the land populous and hence competitive and hence mean. But at the same time she has given us an original character completely integrated with the scene and a subtle problem in morals or aesthetics.

Miss Cather has been praised, and adequately praised, so many times during the last few years for her pictures of a civilization just past that in the case of the present book a fresher task will offer itself if the critic will turn from that aspect of her work and ask himself what she means by her story and what it reveals of the things to which her soul is most loyal. This lady, lost not upon the plains but lost to "ladyhood," who seemed in her big and gracious house an embodiment of the delicacies and refinements of a civilization which, save in her, had not yet reached the plains, but who was spotted within by a secret and unworthy passion —what does she mean to Miss Cather and what is the nature of her guilt? To the romantic boy through whose eyes we see her she is simply the problem as old as the time when women first were fair and false, but to Miss Cather, I think, the guilt is not moral but aesthetic, and aesthetic in a very particular way. The lady, though she did not write nor paint nor act nor sing, was essentially an artist. She was consciously a lady, and she had devoted her vitality to the creation of a person who was more than a person, who was The Lady as a type and as a work of art, so that when she failed she failed as an artist. In a completer civilization she might have found lovers worthy of her who would not have spoiled her creation but she failed because she was not artist enough

to refuse to do at all what she could not do worthily. Her life on the frontier with her aging husband would have been dreary enough, and any mere private person might have been forgiven for seeking diversion wherever he could find it, but the artist must sacrifice himself for his work. The lost lady was guilty and lost because she put her own happiness before her art and betrayed her ideal to snatch at the joy of life.

When *One of Ours* was published many critics went into sackcloth and wept for a talented writer who seemed to have given her allegiance to a vulgar ideal, but *A Lost Lady* will serve to set fears at rest. It makes clearer than any of her previous books has done the essentially aristocratic character of Miss Cather's sympathies and explains her choice of subjects. The artists and the pioneers whom she has always written about are united in their spirit of high adventure, in the romantic impracticability of their aims, and in their success in the creation of comely and rounded types—hence her interest. It is obvious that Miss Cather looks not only at her own craft but at life as well from the standpoint of one to whom fitness is all.

George Gordon, *Literary Digest International Book Review*, 2 (December 1923), 70

Having been awarded the Pulitzer Prize for *One of Ours*, a novel not much above the average, Miss Cather proceeds to write in *A Lost Lady*, one of the fine novels of all time. Here, beyond any question is literature. Here is life, truth, beauty and romance. Here is an infinite pathos and a gentle irony.

"We rot and rot," the fool said in the forest. We rot, and thereby hangs a tale; many tales, all tales perhaps, this one certainly, for here Miss Cather tells of how beauty fades, how time deals with the weak, how fragile toys are broken. An old story, of course. It has been told by Miss Akins in *Déclassée*, and by Pinero and F. Scott Fitzgerald, but never so wisely told as now. Miss Cather quotes from one of Shakespeare's sonnets:

Lilies that fester smell far worse than weeds.

She takes us to Nebraska and shows us there the open house kept by Captain Forrester, one of the builders of the Burlington road. She shows us his second wife, the gracious and lovely Marion, some twenty years his junior; and then, as it imprest itself upon Neil Herbert, a boy still some twenty years younger, she recounts the gradual decline of the fortunes of that house. At first a meeting-place, a stopping-off place, between St. Paul and Denver, for the men of the Burlington, the men who had made, developed, colonized the West; and in the end almost deserted—quite deserted, in fact, except for Marion!

We begin with a dinner and much fine talk, fine food, wine and sweetmeats. We close with the disappearance, after the Captain's death, of Marion, the Marion who had been hostess to so many of the great and had become the prey of every petty sharper. She had compromised with life. Slowly, scene by scene, we watch while she grows sloven, careless, no longer the hopeful, high-spirited girl whom the Captain had met and married in California.

Some time before the book begins, the Captain had retired from active interest in his various business enterprises, but he had made a name and he was still a power—a man of the highest integrity, of rugged strength, great generosity. And, because he knew that she too was fine, he trusted Marion. But she had watched their wealth grow ever less under the Captain's management, and she came to distrust his strict and narrow code of honor. She thought herself wiser than he. She was of the younger generation; and she saw that it was the shrewd and cunning who succeeded. She decided to be shrewd. Why not? She wanted to succeed: to get something, almost anything, out of life. *A Lost Lady* is the story of her pitiful search for understanding, for sympathy, for love. She was lonely there in the big house on the Nebraska plains. She was restless. But she was brave: and she would make the best of things; she would take what offered. And if she could not have a prince for her lover—well, some Denver clubman would have to do. Slowly her life became a thing of makeshifts, of cheap substitutes. It is a tragic story, and it is beautifully, wonderfully well told.

T. K. Whipple. "Willa Cather," *New York Evening Post, The Literary Review*, 8 December 1923, pp. 331–2

In *This Simian World* Clarence Day comments shrewdly on the monkey-like curiosity of human beings—"their swollen desire for investigating everything"—which he plausibly takes to be their dominating trait. Nothing is indifferent to all men, from the chemical composition of the remotest star and the Tibetan shoe trade in the eleventh century to the rules of Mah Jongg and the fourth dimension. Therefore, it seems, no book which conveys information of any nature can fail to find readers; there are men and women who long to know about life in Paphlagonia under Nicephorus III and there are those whose curiosity attaches to life in Nebraska under President Cleveland. These latter, as is but natural, have an unbounded enthusiasm for the novels of Miss Willa Cather.

No disrespect is intended either to Miss Cather or to Nebraska. A really good account of Nebraska would possess immense value and interest; and it may be that Miss Cather's writings possess that value and interest. No one wishes to contradict the statement that *My Ántonia* has "historical value for its minute and colorful depiction of life on the Nebraska prairies and in the Nebraska towns about 1885." The point is merely that after all Miss Cather is only secondarily a historian and an anthropologist; that (in spite of the reviews) she has not done single-handed for Nebraska what Guizot and M. Joanne between them have done for France; that her novels may interest people who have no special cult for Nebraska. In short, she writes fiction; she is a creator primarily, a recorder incidentally, if at all.

Yet those who think of her chiefly as a recorder have this justification, that she has at times so seemed to regard herself. She has not been altogether innocent of the modern novelist's favorite motto: "Kodak as you go." Her interest in the peculiarities of Nebraskan life is obviously intense, and she has sometimes dwelt on them for their own sake. It is said that she "evidently studied this life close at hand," and so she did: for ten years, from the age of nine to nineteen, she "studied" it constantly, much as blotting paper "studies" ink—that is, she absorbed it. And that she is well endowed

with that fundamental trait, not only of the writer but of all artists, capacity for absorbing experience, is obvious. This trait is much more than a mere knack for observation, more even than keenness of the senses; it is an assimilative power which is essentially emotional, a power to identify oneself with one's environment, to be absorbed by experience perhaps even more than to be receptive to it.

Furthermore, like most novelists and like nearly all American writers of the least consequence, Miss Cather has seen fit not to transmute this experience into entirely new forms; she is content to work with it as she finds it; she has the type of imagination which is assisted by definite limits of time and place; this is to say, she is to a considerable degree what is called a "realist." That this need of relying on the actual is to some extent a confession of comparative weakness I am convinced; but at least it is a weakness which only the greatest are without and which has been compatible with the most excellent writing, from the *Canterbury Tales* to *Tess of the D'Urbervilles*. We may think that our novelists and dramatists and poets ought to be able to imagine a life more satisfying than any they have known; but the fact remains that very few of them can or apparently wish to. So Miss Cather, in her clinging to the actual, is in excellent company.

In any case, it is not right to treat her work as if it were all of one piece. On the contrary, it shows a marked development. Her purpose in writing, her whole conception of her art, has altered almost from volume to volume. As time has gone on she has become less and less of a realist. Her own account of these changes is interesting. During her first three years at the University of Nebraska she wrote stories of immigrants, but it was only towards her senior year, she has said, that she became interested in the art of writing for its own sake: "In those days no one seemed so wonderful as Henry James; for me, he was the perfect writer." The reader of *Alexander's Bridge* is prepared to learn of this early enthusiasm. According to Miss Cather herself:

"In *Alexander's Bridge* I was still more preoccupied with trying to write well than with anything else. It takes a great deal of experience to become natural. A painter or writer must learn to distinguish what is his own from that which he admires. ... What I always want to do is to make the writing count for less and less and the people for more. I am trying to cut out all analysis, observation, description, even the picture-making quality, in order to make things and people tell their own story simply by juxtaposition, without any persuasion or explanation on my part. ... Mere cleverness must go. I'd like the writing to be so lost in the object that it doesn't exist for the reader."

Surely, in spite of all that Miss Cather says as to being natural, it is plain that so far from abandoning art in favor of a return to nature, she has simply altered her conception of art. From start to finish she is the conscious artist, most of all in her efforts to conceal her art. And together with this shift in her views on writing has gone a parallel change of emphasis in her treatment of her material. A glance at three of her novels will make this development clearer.

In *O Pioneers!* Miss Cather's aim is divided, even scattering; she has gone hunting with a double-barrelled shotgun, not with a rifle—as we might expect of a novel which takes its title from Whitman and which is dedicated to the memory of Sarah Orne Jewett, "in whose beautiful and delicate work there is the perfection that endures." Did Miss Cather hope to do for Nebraska what Miss Jewett had done for Maine? Perhaps; the book has much "local color"; it's full of description,

of *genre* pictures remarkable for minute detail and close observation. On the other hand, it verges on the psychological novel; it contains much analysis and explanation of character. In writing it Miss Cather seems to have had in mind several purposes and several themes which she has not brought to a focus. And the various interests clash in the reader's mind; we are divided between the purely local aspects and the universally human themes of Alexandra herself and Emil's tragic love. At any rate, the novel is interesting chiefly because it contains something far finer and rarer than local color or psychological analysis—a sense, namely, of essential human nature and, above all, tragic passion. Alexandra might have been—is, almost—a classic heroine. It is this phase of *O Pioneers!* which makes one unwilling to have it dismissed as "a study of pioneer life in Nebraska," though it is that; its appeal is not merely to the curiosity which likes to see how people live in strange places, but to universal emotions. It lacks Miss Jewett's "perfection that endures," but it draws from wells of feeling at which Miss Jewett never dipped.

My Ántonia shows distinct improvement over *O Pioneers!* It is no less lavish of detail and minute in observation; it, too, contains many idyllic *genre* pictures; but the people are scarcely analyzed or explained for us at all. They are so clearly set before us that explanation is unnecessary. And while one cannot say that all the detail and all the realistic scenes are germane to the theme, the irrelevancies have been enormously reduced. The background is almost all required for the presentation of the subject, the portrait of Antonia. And the all-important thing, Antonia's character, so far from being peculiar to time and place, has the quality of the immemorial.

A Lost Lady has attained classic economy; the development away from realism, from profuse detail, from snapshot photography, and from psychological analysis is complete. Miss Cather has forgotten that she is supposed to portray Nebraska, has concentrated on the human as distinct from the local interest. The non-essentials, the setting, the historical and geographical background, have become subservient, ancillary. True, they play their part in the story; Mrs. Forrester's career would have been different anywhere else, at any other time. But will any one assert that she is of interest primarily as "a Nebraskan type"?

Yet is not Miss Cather, to repeat her own expression, "still more preoccupied with trying to write well than with anything else"? Her notion of what constitutes good writing has altered, to be sure, has become simpler and more severe, as her interest has shifted from the local and accidental to the essential elements in her stories; but her primary concern surely is still with telling these stories as well as she can, with producing the effects she wishes to produce. As her conception of her art has deepened her artistic power has correspondingly grown. Especially she has strengthened that particular power which is all-important to the novelist, the creative power, power by virtue of her words to make people live in her pages. The change, in a word, is that she has become increasingly objective. Perhaps it is because our own knowledge of actual people is derived solely from the outside, from seeing and hearing them, that the objective treatment is so superior to the analytical, that in novels the characters are dissipated, vaporized, by explanation and dissection; however that may be, it is certain that as Miss Cather has restricted herself to showing us her people they have taken on a more solid reality.

Her characterization, even so, inclines towards biography and portraiture rather than towards drama or epic. Of this the early chapters of *One of Ours* afford an excellent illustration—work to which justice has not been done because the second half of the book is disappointing. She brings Claude himself, his family, and his associates visibly before us and gives us an intimate knowledge of their personalities by infinitesimal but graphic detail. This cannot be illustrated by quotation; without the context, the fact that "Claude muttered something to himself, twisting his chin about over his collar as if he had a bridle-bit in his mouth," looks insignificant; yet in its place that sentence contains all of Claude Wheeler. It is subtle, strong, and penetrating. Such portraiture is the result of insight and understanding, as well as of observation.

On the other hand, Miss Cather is comparatively indifferent to action; she is sparing of those scenes and deeds in which character is elicited and crystallized, made permanently memorable. True, as Stevenson says, "this is the highest and hardest thing to do in words; the thing which, once accomplished, equally delights the schoolboy and the sage"; yet the novelist who foregoes this appeal, the appeal of the scene in which character and emotion at their utmost come to a crisis in physical action, is foregoing the strongest appeal which literature commands. It is the height of narrative, and I doubt whether any story-teller who lacks it can attain greatness. It is not altogether absent from Miss Cather's books—witness the snowstorm in *One of Ours* and the scene with the long-distance telephone in *A Lost Lady*—but her scenes tend rather to idyllic picture than to dramatic crisis or stirring action.

Sidney Howard has well said of her, "To treat the small facts and the microscopic phenomena of everyday as significant of the dominant energies and emotions of living, this pretty generally is the woman's method of novel writing." It is commonly by such means that Miss Cather gives us our thrills, by the subtly significant. In *A Lost Lady* Neil overhears the murmur of two voices, a man's and a woman's, or Capt. Forrester picks up a letter written by his wife and comments on the handwriting—such are the exciting crises of the story.

Perhaps Miss Cather's avoidance of big scenes, her preference for significant detail, is a sign of literary tact in her. One comes to doubt whether her ability to write is equal to the strain of the big scene. Signs are not lacking that her art is extraordinarily conscious, chiefly conscious exclusion. Observe the difficulty with which, in the beginning, she focussed her subject; observe the slackness of her style—the infrequency, that is, of any emotional tension or lift in the writing itself; observe the occasional false notes of sentiment in the early work; the wild roses, for example, which at the climax of *O Pioneers!* "open their pink hearts to die." Are not all these signs of the same single inner deficiency? A deficiency, I hazard, in high temperature and sustained pressure of imagination. Surely a writer who is sufficiently possessed by his theme does not have to lop off irrelevancies, to be always on his guard. He finds appropriate expression, with difficulty, perhaps, but instinctively; his expression may sometimes be inadequate, but it cannot be false. Such intensity of conception I suggest that Miss Cather lacks. The completed work is not the crystallization of the conception; if it were, she would not be tempted to digress or to strike false notes. Her unity is attained, if at all, not under compulsion of an inner force, but by careful pruning off of excrescences. Her earlier novels expecially seem not to have grown from a germ but to have been put together, built up—even to owe much to a notebook.

This flaw (if my analysis is not in error)

is all the stranger because Miss Cather obviously has passion. Intensity of feeling, especially a keen sympathy, is manifest in all her work. The trouble is that it is seldom communicated to the reader; we perceive its presence, but we do not ourselves fully experience it, at least not more than two or three times in a novel. Her emotion should fire her imagination, and so, in turn, her writing; but there is a break somewhere in the chain. All this, however, is but to suggest that Miss Cather does not attain perfection; it is not to deny the high merit of her writing. The flaw I mention, if it exists, is somewhat offset by other admirable qualities of her work. In attempting to answer that question which it is the critic's business to set himself, "What is the nature and value of the experience afforded by these books, of what sort is the world the author has created and what do we get from our imaginative sojourn there?"—in seeking the answer, we find that if Miss Cather's world is sometimes a little blurred, if it is a little less thrilling than one might wish, if it does not altogether satisfy the imagination, it is, nevertheless, a country which well repays the visitor.

Nothing is more striking about the Cather country than the vein of hardness, as of iron or flint, that runs all through it. Sometimes it is harsh, even brutal. No other quality of Miss Cather's is more impressive than her sense of fact, than her clearness of eyesight and honesty of mind. If she may properly be called refined and fastidious, these traits come not from squeamishness, not from the shrinking, timorous *noli me tangere* which vitiates so much American writing. In *A Lost Lady* particularly she has achieved an exquisite delicacy without fragility; hers is the delicacy, the refinement, of mastery, not of weakness. The Americans who confound crudity and strength will get no comfort from her. She is at once fine and strong, and this uncommon union more than anything else distinguishes her from her contemporaries. She has poise and balance.

A similar distinction from other writers of the day lies in the fact that her world is tragic (otherwise she would not be a modern) but not futile. Whether her protagonists succeed or fail, the tragic aspect is there; if, like Alexandra and Thea, they succeed, it is at great cost in suffering and in a sort of hardening of the spiritual arteries. If they fail, the waste is still more obvious—for the essence of her tragedy, as perhaps of all tragedy, is the waste of human possibilities. Yet, with all its waste, life in her rendering is not futile. In her favorite theme, the struggle of a superior individual with an unworthy society, there is compensation in the very fineness which separates her protagonists from their neighbors. Passion is its own reward; to have cared intensely about anything, even if one has not gained it, is not to have lived in vain.

The natural setting of her world, the vast plains, lends itself to tragedy. Against this setting of the boundless prairies her social background stands out in contrast. The community, whether family or town or neighborhood, is the villain of the piece. It is the foe of life; it is worse than sterile—deadly, poisonous, hostile to every humane quality. She shows us communities of people who are little and petty but withal complacent and self-satisfied, who are intolerant and contemptuous of what differs from themselves, who are tightly bound by conventionality—not the sort that springs from free, deliberate approval of conventions, but the sort that has its source in cowardice, stupidity, or indolence—of people who hate whatever does not jibe with their two-penny ha'penny aims, who hate everything genuine and human—genuine thought, or religion, or righteousness, or beauty— everything that means being genuinely alive, everything that shows true mind or feeling or imagination.

We must not forget that this is her version of the world from which she herself came. Perhaps the shrewdest criticism yet made of Miss Cather is that she represents the "triumph of mind over Nebraska." The victory was not bloodless; it has left its scars. Among her many difficulties, much the most serious has been that in her youth her imagination was undernourished. A desiccated and sterilized life affords little sustenance to poet, dramatist, or novelist. The marvel is that she has been able to achieve so much, to discover so much humanity in that flat and vacant land, with its rich soil and human poverty. If her books suffer in comparison with those of writers who have grown in a more fertile society, they are yet opulence itself compared, say, with those of Sinclair Lewis. If the world of her creation does not abound in variety and intrinsic interest, it is because the material on which her imagination fed was lacking in those elements. She has extracted from it all the meagre juices it afforded.

Yet Miss Cather has triumphed. She has not sought refuge in Europe or in romantic fancies. She has had the strength to give herself to her natural environment, and in A Lost Lady she has actually succeeded in transforming her material into the universal forms of art—no easy conquest. Literary pioneering—the first subjugation of any life to the purposes of literature—is as difficult a kind of pioneering as any other. It is that first breaking of the tough sod that is arduous; after that, any one can grow crops in the field. Herein, in this subjugation of a continent, lies the great achievement of Miss Cather and her contemporaries, rather than in their absolute artistic performances. And Miss Cather has a high place in this band

209

who are fulfilling Whitman's prophecies of American literature, who are occupying the Promised Land which he saw in the distance from Pisgah.

If, as is the case, American books are more often discussed as social documents than as pure literature, there is good reason. They are commonly more interesting as social documents. I do not mean that the chief value of Miss Cather and the other moderns is as recorders of local and temporal conditions; I mean that their chief value is that they have been able to adopt the artist's attitude towards American life, and that in doing so they have made it easier for those who are not artists, who have weaker perception and less emotion, to adopt a similar attitude. This heightening of awareness, this intensification of consciousness, is always one of the services of art; but in the United States at the present moment it has a quite special and extraordinary value. Americans, I suppose no one will deny, have always, since the days of Franklin, been predominantly practical; few of them have cared for experience, for living, for its own sake; they have cultivated the practical, active, acquisitive life to the exclusion of the theoretic or speculative, the contemplative, creative life; they have been too preoccupied with getting on to care much for the life of realization. To this characteristic must be attributed the comparative human dearth of the American scene. The main importance—one hopes—of current American literature is as a sign that a change approaches, that the tyranny of the practical is becoming mitigated. One of the most cheering omens in this respect is the fact that such a writer as Miss Cather has been produced ("produced" here, to quote Sir Leslie Stephen, means "not extinguished") has been able to survive, has encountered something like adequate recognition and support in her effort to do the best of which she is capable.

Robert Littell, "Rich and Strange," *New Republic*, 37 (19 December 1923), 99–100 [reviewed with Sherwood Anderson's *Horses and Men* and Fannie Hurst's *Lummox*]

Here is one "regular" novel, and two experiments. Mr. Anderson is always experimenting, groping his way toward a distant and extraordinary truth, and Miss Hurst is trying something which for her is quite new. Alone of the three Miss Cather is not experimenting. She has arrived; she is no longer in the laboratory, nor, if we look back at *My Antonia*, does she seem ever to have been there. Miss Hurst has just begun, and Mr. Anderson will perhaps always be on the way.

By contrast with these others, which are distinctly the product of a puzzled, seeking age, which are incomplete, which are attempts, not always successful, to break down the fortifications guarding the citadel of truth, *A Lost Lady* is indeed "regular." It is in the line of an old and substantial tradition of fiction. Its method is the familiar one of revealing a character by telling only what happened and what the character said. The character occupies the foreground; the author's preoccupations, if any are happily concealed. Miss Cather does not pretend to know any more about her Lost Lady than she can make a reader understand. She accomplishes exactly what she sets out to do, and no more. Such purpose and self-restraint go far to explain the singular reality and solidity of the heroine, who remains in our minds as one of the most vivid inhabitants of any American novel of recent years, but they do not explain her charm.

Mrs. Forrester—the Lost Lady—lives in one of the small western towns which sprouted up along the railroad. Her husband, a man much older than herself, helped build the railroad, and belongs to that more adventurous, generous, free period of the railroad pioneers. The heyday of those men is well past; the prairies have been crossed and settled, and all along the railroad are growing mean, gray little towns, the spawn of narrower times and narrower hearts. In Miss Cather's phrase, we are watching "the sunset of the pioneer," when "the men who had put plains and mountains under iron harness were growing old; some were poor, and even the successful ones were hunting for rest and a brief reprieve from death. It was already gone, that age, and nothing could bring it back."

But The Lost Lady "was not willing to immolate herself, like the widow of all these great men, and die with the pioneer period to which she belonged. She preferred life on any terms." Gifted with too much life, she spent its gold freely— which was her charm, and when the gold was gone, she spent desperately the small change of it, penny by penny—which was her tragedy.

The tragedy and the charm are inextricable in Miss Cather's quiet, uninsistent account. They are impressions all the more durable because she assumes the rôle of witness rather than that of interpreter, just as in *My Antonia*. Mr. Sherwood Anderson, on the other hand, is an incurable interpreter, whose own explorations and questionings, often unrewarded by either discovery or answer, hang so opaquely between his characters and the reader. Mr. Anderson usually begins by insisting how remarkable or significant or wonderful is such and such a character or story he is going to explain to us. What would he have done to Mrs. Forrester, who remains remarkable in great part because Miss Cather never interrupts to recall to us how remarkable she is?

[. . .]

While Miss Cather lets words flow from her characters, and Mr. Anderson pours his words into their lives, Fannie Hurst leaves her Bertha, the Lummox, pretty much alone, a silent Sphinx of inarticulate flesh, about whose splay-footed pedestal swirl and dash the torrential breakers of her creator's language. What a queer wild language it is, chaotic and incisive, staccato and ecstatic, parenthetical and explicit, all at once. A less solid figure than Bertha would be drowned in it or eroded away. But Miss Hurst keeps, artistically, at a distance. By entirely different means she achieves some of Miss Cather's success in not invading the secrets of a character. She never enters too inquisitively Bertha's soul, and by this act of self-restraint, almost the only kind of restraint in the book, Bertha survives. How long will she survive in readers' minds? Not as long perhaps as Mrs. Forrester, but longer than most of the characters of Mr. Anderson, who is too puzzled by them to see them clearly, and who sees in them so much more than he is able to express.

Such questions of longevity are idle. The encouraging fact is that three such very different, and each in its own way extremely interesting books, can come from these United States in one year. Furthermore, it is encouraging that they are all chiefly concerned with people and not with some small town which suppresses or entombs the chief actors of the story. Miss Cather only faintly suggests Sweet Water, leaving it to our imagination.

211

Miss Hurst gives us a great deal of New York, but it remains a background. For Mr. Anderson, too, the small towns in which his characters puzzle out their lives are dimly visible backdrops. And yet somehow his obscure side streets and Miss Cather's inconspicuous Sweet Water are more living, threatening and mysterious than Main Street, because their people are so much more real than the majority of Mr. Sinclair Lewis's bromidic mouthpieces. This marks the difference between the superficial and what goes beneath the surface of small towns all alike to the lives of people in them, who are all, at bottom, quite unlike one another. The portraits of individuals can be literature, as is the case with the Lost Lady, Lummox and Horses and Men; the blurring of them by making them so many numbers on a street, is something more like propaganda.

"Californians Are Like That," *World-Herald* (Omaha) [winter 1923–24]

The mystery is cleared. We understand it clearly now and so can everybody else.

A writer in the *[New York Evening Post, The] Literary Review* recently undertook to explain Willa Cather's "undernourished imagination" on the ground that she spent her youth amid the "dessicated and sterilized life" of Nebraska. "The marvel," he wrote," is that she has been able to achieve so much, to discover so much humanity in that flat and vacant land, with its rich soil and human poverty."

The *World-Herald*, having indulged a few remarks appertaining to this curious

hypothesis, is now in receipt of a letter from Henry S. Canby, editor of the *Literary Review*, in which he says:

"I think that you should know that Mr. Whipple far from being a denizen of Greenwich Village is a Californian, a scholar and critic of some distinction, who, so far as I know, has never spent more than a night at a time in New York. I hold no brief for Greenwich Village, but after all Miss Cather lives there and Mr. Whipple does not, which is not what your editorial would imply."

No farther [sic] apologies are required.

Californians are like that. There is no god but Allah for them and California is his permanent address. It is likewise the permanent address of everybody else worth while. Beyond their Sierras there are yet people, it is true, but they are more to be pitied than blamed. And as for other skies than theirs, other configurations of the earth's surface, other flora and fauna, other social organizations, they have not the entree. They disturb Californians' golden dreams no more than mosquitoes buzzing in the night, and there are no mosquitoes in California—only fleas. And no flea has yet been evolved that could get under a native California hide.

We withdraw, therefore, our cutting retort, emitted in the mistaken notion that the libel on Nebraska came from a mere human being, and consider the incident closed.

Edmund Wilson, "A Lost Lady," *Dial*, 76 (January 1924), 79–80

Miss Cather's new novel does something to atone for *One of Ours*. Miss Cather seems to suffer from a disability like that of Henry James: it is almost impossible for her to describe emotion or action except at second hand. When James wanted to present Milly Theale, who was dying for lack of love, he abandoned the direct record of her emotions as soon as the situation became acute and allowed the reader to watch her only through the eyes of Merton Densher, and when the relation between her and Densher commenced to become really dramatic he evaded it altogether and left the culmination of the tragedy to the divination of a second observer who talked with Densher after Milly Theale's death. I am aware of the aesthetic advantages which James urged in favour of this reflective method, but I am inclined to believe that in his case it was arrived at through a limitation of imaginative scope. His tendency was always to present only so much of the drama of his daring and sophisticated protagonists as might have been observed or guessed by some rather timid and inexperienced person who happened to be looking on; *What Maisie Knew* is perhaps the most satisfactory of all his novels because in this case the person who is looking on and whose consciousness has to be laid before us is not even a grownup person, but merely a little girl, who consequently makes a minimum demand for experience or adult emotion on the part of the author. For a converse reason, *One of Ours* was one of Miss Cather's least satisfactory performances because in it she was confronted with the problem of rendering directly not only the frustrated passions and aspirations of a young Middle Westerner on the farm, but also his final self-realization as a soldier in the war.

But in *A Lost Lady* Miss Cather falls back on the indirect method of James (who was a great artist, as novelists go, for all his not infrequent incapacity to fill in with colour the beautiful line and composition of his pictures); and she achieves something of James' success. Here her problem is to present the vicissitudes of a young and attractive woman with a vivid capacity for life married to an elderly Western contractor of the "railroad aristocracy." For this purpose she invents another of those limpid and sensitive young men to whom she has always been rather addicted and makes him the glass through which we see her heroine. It is interesting to note that on the only two important occasions when she tries to show us something which was not directly witnessed by young Niel Herbert, in the first case—the brief scene between the lady and her lover in the house at night— she strikes perhaps the only false melodramatic note to be found in the whole story (" 'Be careful,' she murmured as she approached him, 'I have a distinct impression that there is some one on the enclosed stairway. . . . Ah, but kittens have claws, these days!' ") and in the second—the expedition in the sleigh—she is able to save the situation only by introducing a second limpid young man to be a witness to phenomena unmanageable for the first.

In any case, *A Lost Lady* is a charming sketch performed with exceptional distinction and skill. In fact, Miss Cather is one of the only writers who has brought genuine distinction to the description of the West. Other writers have more enthusiasm or colour or vitality—in which last quality Miss Cather is a little lacking— but Miss Cather is almost the only one who has been able to overlay any sort of fine artistic patina upon the meager and sprawling rural life of the Middle West. There are exquisite pages of landscape in *A Lost Lady* and the portrait of the veteran railroad pioneer is surely one of the most sensitive and accurate we have of the American of the post-Civil-War period—a type greatly preferable, I grant Miss Cather, in its simplicity and honour and for all its cultural and intellectual limitations, to the commercial sharpers who succeeded it.—Not, however, that Miss Cather sentimentalizes the Middle West or booms it as spiritually richer than it is—like Mr. Vachel Lindsay, for instance: through all her work there run two currents of profound feeling—one for the beauty of those lives lived out between the prairie and the sky, but the other—most poignantly in "A Wagner Concert," [sic] my favourite among her short stories, and now in certain scenes of *A Lost Lady*—for the pathos of the human spirit trying to flower in that barren soil.

Niel Herbert. How is that business achieved? It is achieved, it seems to me, very beautifully. The story has an arch and lyrical air; there is more genuine romance in it than in half a dozen romances in the grand manner. One gets the effect of a scarlet tanager invading a nest of sparrows—an effect not incomparable to that managed by Hergesheimer in *Java Head*. But to say that *A Lost Lady* is as sound and important a work as *My Antonia*—as has been done, in fact, more than once in the public prints—is to say something quite absurd. It is excellent stuff, but it remains a bit light. It presents a situation, not a history.

H[enry] L[ouis] M[encken], "Three Volumes of Fiction," *American Mercury*, 1 (February 1924), 252–3 [reviewed with Sherwood Anderson's *Horses and Men* and Joseph Conrad's *The Rover*]

Miss Cather's *A Lost Lady* has the air of a first sketch for a longer story. There are episodes that are described without being accounted for; there is at least one place where a salient character is depicted in the simple outlines of a melodrama villain. But this vagueness, I suspect, is mainly deliberate. Miss Cather is not trying to explain her cryptic and sensational Mrs. Forrester in the customary omniscient way of a novelist; she is trying, rather, to show us the effects of the Forrester apparition upon a group of simple folk, and particularly upon the romantic boy,

Lloyd Morris, "Willa Cather," *North American Review*, 219 (May 1924), 641–52

It is not surprising that the novels of Willa Cather have been widely admired. She writes of the West; and to all Americans who do not inhabit it, the West is more truly a mood of the imagination and a romantic nostalgia than a geographical fact. Although Miss Cather's West is without defence against the incursions of drab reality, it compensates our traditional expectations by being favourable to those virtues of character which a long literary discipline has taught us to believe most desirable. Writing in an age marked by the disappearance of the pioneer from the American scene, Miss Cather celebrates his legend and seeks his successor.

Her preoccupation with the pioneer brings Miss Cather's work within the main trend of American literature during the past century. At its best, as in the work of Emerson and Whitman, the literature of this main trend gave philosophical as well as emotional direction to the national life. It established the cult of the individual; it distinguished between individualism and egotism by formulating the democratic ideal; it taught the pioneer virtues of independence, self-reliance and perseverance; it substituted for the repudiated discipline of the past an epic vision of the national future. In these ways the literature of our main trend spoke with authority for its time. It responded to the immediate situation confronting us by furnishing an ideal compatible with the task of subduing a continent to the future needs of the race. For nearly a century the pioneer ideal expressed a vital necessity in our national life, and the energies of the country were largely absorbed by the enterprise of extending human control over the conditions of material existence. The impulse to that enterprise is reflected in the literature of the time. Reading it, we may learn that the frontier was to be conquered that a national destiny might be inaugurated; the task of subduing a continent was undertaken that, once subdued, it might yield a richer harvest of life and greater freedom for nobler uses.

Such was the account given by our earlier writers of the national spirit and the national life. Their account was remarkable for its vision of the future, for its confident attitude toward what that future might hold forth, for its emphasis upon the prospect of a national destiny. The epic attitude to them was congenial and natural; it was, so to speak, the only adequate standardization and mechanism which engages Mr. Sinclair Lewis, Mr. Sherwood Anderson and Mr. Dreiser, to name but a few. She does not, like Mr. Hergesheimer, retire to the worship of a merely decorative loveliness, or like Mr. Cabell, blend beauty with irony in purely imaginative forms. Her dissatisfaction with contemporary America is chiefly expressed in a revival of more heroic days when the competitive attitude, the instinct of self-preservation and the traits of the pioneer were consecrated to the necessary ideals of the race. "Whatever we had missed, we possessed together the precious, the incommunicable past." These words, which conclude *My Antonia*, supply an epigraph to Miss Cather's work to date. It is our past, rather than our present or our future, that she invites us to contemplate. . . .

But Miss Cather, writing of the close of an epoch in our national history and the beginning of a new one, discerns no fresh direction given to American life and therefore asserts no convinced vision of its future. When she reflects upon the immediate present, as she did in the first half of *One of Ours*, she conceives it to be chiefly engaged in securing the perpetuation of the mechanical organization of material existence which it inherited from the conquests of the pioneers. Her farmers of today continue a struggle for mere existence which has largely been made unnecessary by their comprehensive mechanical control of environment. They continue to struggle in spite of vast success, apparently because they perceive no other significance or purpose in life. Miss Cather's artists—a second favourite type—transfer this competitive attitude, knowing no other, to the channels of creative expression. They are pioneers who happen to be instinctive artists rather than artists who happen to be instinctive pioneers. This distinction, obvious to Miss Cather's readers, suggests why she celebrates the traditional pioneer virtues of character when, to judge from her own account of it, our contemporary life offers so few objectives which can appropriately enlist them, instead of interpreting our contemporary life as perhaps demanding other virtues. . . .

Critics were rightly troubled that Miss Cather solved Claude's problems and brought her novel to a conclusion by the simple expedient of having him killed in the war. Yet none of them, apparently, remarked the irony of this conclusion. It is only when Claude arrives in France that his capacities for loyalty find an appropriate object. He perceives that the French have cultivated the spirit as intensively as they have cultivated the soil, that to them intelligence and beauty and the opportunity to lead a humane life are immediately important. He discovers that they have subdued not only the soil, but the material organization of life also, to the needs of the spirit. And he dies not for the life that he knew in America, but for the life that he has discovered in France. The total absence from Miss Cather's work of an epic outlook upon American life is nowhere more strikingly revealed than in the concluding section of *One of Ours*. It is perhaps not without significance that Miss Cather, who is among the most thoughtful of our contemporary novelists, has failed to isolate in our national life any ideal faith or noble purpose deserving the allegiance that awaits its discovery. So remote is she from that discovery that she intimates the futility of the quest.

In reflecting upon Miss Cather's novels, we are apt to find that our abiding impressions derive from character rather than from story or from theme. It is notable that, on the whole, she has been conspicuously successful in the portraiture of women and considerably less successful in the portraiture of men. Had she not written *A Lost Lady*, it might have been possible to assume a deliberate restriction of her interest, even in women, to the pioneer-type of which she fixed three aspects in Alexandra Bergson, Thea Kronborg and Antonia Shimerda. But the bright radiance of Marian Forrester makes this assumption wholly inadequate. It is not, however, difficult to perceive a tangible relationship between Marian and her predecessors, though this relationship is grounded in the essential conditions of character rather than in the circumstances that elicit it. Character, as it finds expression in Miss Cather's heroines, is a product of delicately adjusted and unconscious instincts developed by the long past experience of the race. This conception, excluding so much that is casual and transient and accidental, indicates why it is that Miss Cather's heroines lend themselves, as she says of Antonia Shimerda, to "immemorial human attitudes which we recognize as universal and true." It likewise explains why her heroines, although firmly rooted in their immediate environment and time, seem like legendary figures to have accumulated within themselves a large wisdom and permanent significance.

The instincts which mould the characters of Alexandra and Thea and Antonia and Marian are, like many simple and primitive things, profound and enduring. Alexandra Bergson, unimaginative, prosaic and somewhat dull, struggles to establish a family and home, and her insistent thrift seems only that unconscious acquisitiveness which establishes a solid foundation for life without ever suspecting that life may offer other goals than its own perpetuation. Thea Kronborg, equally simple and unintelligent, exercises an instinctive impulse to self-preservation that she may resist the claims of an uncongenial environment. At first unconscious of her genius and never completely dominating it, she is urged on to revolt by an ambition which she never fully comprehends. So incapable is she of intellectual processes that only the rich fund of her feelings preserves her integrity uncorrupted. This same fund of feeling ultimately makes her a great singer and enables her to solve the problems of her art by means of sheer emotional energy rather than by the exercise of intelligence. With Antonia, perhaps the loveliest and most memorable of Miss Cather's heroines, instinctive passion assumes its noblest form. "A rich mine of life, like the founders of early races," Antonia is predestined to motherhood. The springs of action in her flow through deep channels of goodness. She spends herself in the service of others, wearing out the April of her beauty in labour, and rounding out her career as the overburdened mother of a dozen children. Yet there is in Antonia, as there is not in Miss Cather's other heroines, a consciousness of fulfillment and of destiny accomplished, and an heroic quality which lifts the common experience of her days above the humble, quiet level of its actual occurrence.

If Antonia is the loveliest of Miss Cather's heroines, Marian Forrester is the most provocative, and they are subtly alike though superficially different. Despite her sophistication and the strange nurture upon which her brightness thrives, Marian is formed by identically the instinct that dominates Antonia. Passion in Antonia is exclusively instrumental; it serves the purposes of an instinctive maternity. Passion, in Marian, serves no end but its own; it is immediate and gratuitous, an unquenchable force which, when threatened with frustration by lack of a stimulating object, spends itself recklessly upon any available recipient. Generosity, courage and comprehension are qualities not lacking to Marian, who is of all Miss Cather's heroines the most intelligent. But it is not impossible to perceive that her weakness is ultimately her strength, an incorruptible probity of instinct which submits to neither the denial of circumstance nor the restrictions of a discriminating taste. In Antonia Miss Cather has illustrated the workings of passion in the eternal Penelope; in Marian she has revealed the flowering of passion in the eternal Helen.

Having given us two characters as finely conceived, and in a measure as unique in our fiction as Antonia and Marian, it is perhaps ungracious to wonder why Miss Cather has only once achieved the creation of a masculine character in any sense comparable to them. The single exception among the men who people her stories is Captain Forrester, in whom she has drawn a sensitive and illuminating portrait made memorable by the old Captain's rugged honesty, unfailing courtesy and superb faith. But the other men in Miss Cather's stories are achievements on a distinctly inferior level. The artists of her stories are occasionally authentic and vital, but scarcely memorable. At her best, when dealing with artists, she achieves the reality of a Harsanyi. At her worst she descends to the flaccid jelly of a Frederick Ottenburg, a Missouri millionaire masquerading as Lohengrin. But she has wrought more adequately in the creation of artists than in that of a second group of characters which, individually considered, are modifications of a single type. That type is the impressionable and sentimental youth who, in various guises, enters many of Miss Cather's stories as a contributor to the action or as its narrator, and whose principal characteristics are chivalrous aspirations and impregnable romantic illusions. Such a young man is Alexandra's boy companion in O Pioneers! He reappears as Claude Wheeler in One of Ours; as Neil Herbert in A Lost Lady; as Jim Burden, the narrator of My Antonia; and in mature middle age as Dr. Howard Archie in The Song of the Lark. He is most serviceable to Miss Cather and least disturbing to her readers when he is the lens through which we see the characters actually involved in the action. When he enters the action directly or becomes its protagonist, his troubled sensibilities and incipient priggishness usually prove a source of irritation to the reader. At such times he is as thin to the imagination as a village Sir Galahad conceived in terms of [Thomas Day's eighteenth-century children's classic *The History of*] *Sandford and Merton*. In Captain Forrester Miss Cather has demonstrated her ability to create a masculine character whose essential nobility wins our admiration. The difficulty with her sentimental youths is that they are incapable of maturing into men like the old Captain. They are impressionable, but not impressive.

It is only in *A Lost Lady*, however, that Miss Cather seems to have achieved a balanced control over both content and structure. That book stands, from the point of view of art, as her most notable performance up to the present. It is all but faultless in structure; it possesses evident beauty of design and proportion, and the form of the story seems only an inevitable expression of its content. Miss Cather's use of the indirect method of presentation, perhaps the last vestige of the influence once exercised upon her by Henry James, has sometimes been challenged. It has been asserted that she suffers from a disability akin to that of James, a limitation of imaginative scope which prevents her from recording action and emotion except at second hand. But her use of the indirect method is amply justified by *A Lost Lady*, in which the channel of presentation is inextricably implicated in the action presented. . . .

At a time when many American writers of fiction seem content to record a merely faithful transcription of what they see before them, Miss Cather is reasserting the ancient distinction between nature and art and expressing the artist's old confidence that art is artistic precisely because it is not natural. Not content with mere naturalism, she has begun to subject what she has seen in the world around her to an imaginative reconstruction that is gradually gaining in depth of conception, beauty of design and emotional power. At her best she has created characters of distinction and significance and represented experience in some of its permanent aspects. At her best, therefore, she has achieved art by interpreting comprehensively what her somewhat narrow world has offered for her contemplation. It still remains to be seen whether Miss Cather can recover from the American past which she has celebrated, its own generous attitude. If she succeeds in doing so, she may yet dedicate the complicated organization of our contemporary life to some great ends. She will then take her place among the few contemporary American writers who are using contemporary American life to talk with to some significant purpose.

Percy H. Boynton, "Willa Cather," *English Journal*, 13 (June 1924), 373–80

If one were to speculate on what might be the literary output of a woman born in Virginia, diploma'd from a western state university in the nineties, schooled in an eastern newspaper office, and graduated from the staff of a popular monthly with metropolitan headquarters and a national circulation, it would be safe to look for some copiousness of material and some breadth of sympathy. And these are the characteristics of Miss Cather's work. Probably they are accounted for by her experience; at any rate they are true of her. The temptation is strong to pursue the theory that Miss Cather is the product of her changing backgrounds because her "Life and Works" are so typically related. More often than not maturing artistry comes into its own by slow degrees, starting with conventional form and conventional subject-matter, and only tardily arriving at individual style and substance. That is what accounts for Fielding's imposing array of early comedies, Scott's excursions into poetic romance, Poe's Byronic "Tamerlane" and "Politian," and Hawthorne's contributions to the sentimental annuals. Maturity and achievement lead genuine creative ability (as it led all these men) back toward fundamentals and into the literary form in which it can best express itself.

Miss Cather's first book was a typical "slender volume" of poems, published in 1903 when poetry in America was a pleasant parlor accomplishment. The reprint of twenty years later, even with its additions, is still slender in both size and content. There are verses of homely sentiment; classical echoes; Shakesperian, Arthurian, Italian, and Provençal verses of allusion; reminiscences of travel; laments for lost loves and lost youth; and, among them all, three or four bits that are unbookish, with the breath of the prairies in them. Next, two years later, came *The Troll Garden*, seven stories—artists' colony stories; painters, musicians, and music-lovers in New York, Boston, and London; and, among them, three with allusions to western life, with one grim picture of a little Kansas town to which a sculptor is brought for burial, contemned in life as in death by the sordid villagers. Then, in Miss Cather's roster, after a seven-year interval which seems to have been largely absorbed by editorial routine, came two volumes, international or transatlantic, apparently pointing her way down the paths often traversed by Henry James and Mrs. Wharton. All the books so far were the work of a lover of beauty who had grown up among spiritually arid rural surroundings, who was thrilled by all the possibilities for beauty in studio and concert hall, and somewhat allured by the engaging artificialities of polite metropolitan life. The only life that occupied Miss Cather thus far was a life of aesthetic self-realization.

With a difference, as much may be said of her work as a whole; the difference being that with her mature novels the focus of her work shifted from the happy enjoyment of self-realization to the harrowing struggle toward that end. *O Pioneers!* (1913) and *The Song of the Lark* (1915) marked Miss Cather's indubitable "arrival," although it was not until *My Ántonia* (1918) that this important event was generally recognized. With these books, as with the greater part of *One of Ours* (1922), she turned back to the richest of her sources—the pioneer figures of the prairie town—and in her employment of this material applied the principle which she ascribed to the lark who sang so divinely that "art is only a way of remembering youth." And so one comes to that trio of heroic women: Alexandra Bergson, Thea Kronburg, and Ántonia Shimerda.

Of the stories centering around these three *The Song of the Lark*, the chronicle of Thea Kronburg, is perhaps the least effective for the very reason that it is most explicitly given over to the struggle for artistic self-fulfilment. Thea Kronburg, daughter of a smugly complacent country parson and of a prolific and instinctively wise mother, grows up a solitary in the midst of a crowded household in a gossipy town. By natural gravitation she finds her happiest companionship with a broken-down, half-ostracized German music master and with a song-loving colony of Mexican outcasts. To please her father, whom she has no wish to offend or

219

estrange, she plays the hymns at the mid-week prayer meetings, though she finds no relief there from the muffling and numbing daily clamor about her, and always reads late after the recital of prayers and "experiences," yearning more avidly than usual to live with zest and to achieve some real happiness.

Under the old music master's monitions she toils doggedly. An instinct in her responds natively to his precept that "nothing is far and nothing is near if one desires. The world is little, people are little, human life is little. There is only one big thing—desire. And before it, when it is big, all is little." She needs only look within herself to know all of what he means when he declares, "The secret— what make the rose to red, the sky to blue, the man to love—in der Brust, in der Brust it is, *und ohne dieses giebt es keine Kunst, keine Kunst!*" (and without it there is no art!). Toward this Parnassian art, then, she aspires. Leaving home, eking out a livelihood in the big cities, accepting discouragement and rebuff, undeterred by lovers, or even by love itself, she comes through at last to a success whose chief reward is less in gold or plaudits than in the sense of fidelity to her own high purpose.

In the end she has learned of "the inevitable hardness of human life," but also of the richness of reward that comes with real creation. And in the end, too, she realizes once more the lesson of the old German that nothing is far and nothing is near; for with the world at her feet she discovers that is was potentially hers when she first set out from her home town with her little legacy. "I shall always measure things by that six hundred dollars, just as I measure high buildings by the Moonstone standpipe." "There is no work of art so big that is was not once all contained in some youthful body."

"Art is only a way of remembering youth."

In *My Ántonia* (An-ton-ee-ah) Miss Cather is not so kind to her heroine, at least in terms of material reward. Ántonia Shimerda is a Bohemian immigrant child of less than mediocre parentage, whose sole inheritance is a wholesome, hearty, clear-eyed courage. Brought up in the uses of adversity, she finds but one thing to which she can give a natural response; and that is, among the people of her own sort, "a kind of hearty joviality, a relish of life, not over-delicate, but very invigorating." This flourishes only among the folk who are held in despite by the respectables of the community. The dominant element are spiritually akin to the dominants of Spoon River and Gopher Prairie and Winesburg, Ohio, and to the selectmen of Friendship Village.

The life that went on in them seemed to me made up of evasions and negations; shifts to save washing and cleaning, devices to propitiate the tongue of gossip. This guarded mode of existence was like living under a tyranny. People's speech, their voices, their very glances, became furtive and repressed. Every individual taste, every natural appetite, was bridled by caution. The people asleep in their houses, I thought, tried to live like the mice in their own kitchens: to make no noise, to leave no trace, to slip over the surface of things in the dark. The growing piles of ashes and cinders in the backyards were the only evidence that the wasteful, consuming process of life went on at all.

Ántonia has no spark of creative artistry; yet she feels the artist's desire to live a full, free life. She falls in love with a cheap seducer, and is abandoned, on what she thinks is to be her honeymoon, to become a mother without benefit of clergy. Later she marries a good, dull man, brings up a big family, and in the play of her native courage finds a very homely and very old-fashioned fulfilment of life. "That is happiness—to be dissolved in something complete and great." The greatness of Ántonia's achievement lies in the completeness of her dedication to her task—no less complete than that of Thea Kronburg. In Ántonia's contented domesticity Miss Cather offers a modern variation on an old theme. In the pages of Mrs. Stowe the latter stages of Ántonia's career would have been treated as steps of abnegation, the surrender to a sense of duty in a home on earth which would be rewarded by a mansion prepared on high. By most contemporary novelists it would be treated as a complete defeat, with no compensation either here or hereafter. But Miss Cather, with all her zest for studio life, has retained an imaginative regard for four walls and a hearthstone, and the vital experience of mothering a family.

After *My Ántonia* came a pause in Miss Cather's own story. *Youth and the Bright Medusa* is a kind of intermezzo of hesitancy between prairie land and Bohemia. Four of the short stories are reprinted from *The Troll Garden* of eight years earlier; a study in the temperament of a city-bred boy whose appetite for beauty and luxury lead him to theft, a week of nectar and ambrosia, and suicide; the overwhelming experience of a concert lover's first taste of music after a quarter-century of exile on the plains; the death in the far West of a consumptive singer who yearns to the end for the thrill and the glamor of her finest years; and the already mentioned sculptor's funeral. The three purely exotic stories of *The Troll Garden* were not reprinted. It was the touch of the frontier that Miss Cather chose to save. Yet, oddly enough, the four new stories in

the later volume have none of this; all but one are wholly devoted to the songstress in prosperity, and except for that one they contribute but little to the achievement of the author.

Evidently Miss Cather was not even yet firmly established in the home of her imagination. As an artist she was attached to the prairie stretches and the pioneer types, but only in the half-sentimental fashion of Ántonia's successful friend, James Burden, who had gone out from obscurity into the world of men and affairs, and in his strivings and thrivings looked back with an affectionate sympathy which expressed itself in an occasional hurried visit to the old neighborhood. He had outgrown it, like his youth; and, like his youth, it symbolized to him "the precious, the incommunicable past." In this short-story intermezzo Miss Cather, sitting in a New York apartment hotel, after a turn around Washington Square, deals with the past tenderly and sympathetically, but she is evidently looking back toward it. She does not actually reawaken it as she had done before.

And so it is not surprising that in *One of Ours*, an aftermath of the war, Miss Cather allowed herself to be warped out of her own orbit, and that as she swung through space in this flight, she vacillated between a life that she knew to the heart's core and a life of which she had only a remote and idealized conception. The boy who was "one of ours" belongs to the same countryside as to Alexandra and Thea and Ántonia. He is made restless by the same dwellings and outreachings of spirit, and like his fellow-pioneers is vaguely uncomfortable in the narrowness of the bed that he has not made for himself. A brutal accident and gratitude to the woman who nurses him in his duress horribly mismate him. The woman who is flung into his arms has shown her one pale gleam of warmth while he is prostrate and helpless. There is nothing in her to respond to ardor or even to affection. She is absorbed in her own chill righteousness, which has been excelled in literature only by that most obnoxiously virtuous woman, the Lady, in "Comus." Her final repudiation, in the name of the Lord, of every wifely obligation sets him adrift just as America enters the war. Enlistment seems to offer him a hope of salvation. Fired with the fine zeal that inflamed the first thousands who responded to the call, he sets out on the crusade to save the world for democracy. Stupidity, sordidness, and chicane cannot overcome him. Reminders of the hollowness of his own lot cannot embitter him. In a final white heat of fervor he meets a glorious death on the battle field.

It is a fine conception and it is rather thrillingly executed. It is doubtless true to what happened in the experience of some of the fallen; and in its heroic consummation it is certainly what those left to mourn would like to believe of every man who fell. Yet, on the whole, the romantic conception of war as a purifying fire belongs to the hopes of the new recruit and to the cherished recollections of the mourner. Now that the story of the war has been told, Philip Gibbs seems to be nearer the truth than Miss Cather. I have yet to find a soldier returned from overseas who has read the book without being stirred to protest at the concluding chapters of *One of Ours*. Barbusse and Dos Passos are more likely to be to their taste. They have been so far disillusioned that the death of the hero has seemed to them the snuffing of a candle rather than the apotheosis of a lover of democracy.

However far Miss Cather may have strayed from the paths in which she treats with a sure foot when she rambled into the latter part of *One of Ours*, she was at any rate not abandoning the theme of all her best work—the strife for self-fulfilment. Her soldier-boy-to-be begins his career in the frontier region of her three heroines. He encounters there the jealous, leveling standards that would reduce all pioneers to jack-of-all-tradeship and general undistinction. And in his army career his restless spirit confronts conditions analogous to those that confront an artist in a philistine world. But in *A Lost Lady* Miss Cather loses her bearings altogether. The lost lady lives in the open west, and that is the only resemblance between her and the other major characters. Yet the distinction of the other characters is not that they live and work where pioneers or artists do, but that they have in them stuff of which pioneers and artists are made: health, courage, a desire for freedom, a will to achieve. If they come through the conflict their victories are worth winning; if they fail their failures are tragic because they have the possibilities of victory in them. But the lost lady is a weakling and a ne'er-do-well. She is a tarnished creature whose immorality lies not so much in the infraction of laws and precepts as in the fact that such a life as hers is inherently self-defeating. She is not even brilliantly alluring. The Elizabethans, with their sure-word usage, did well to call such a woman "a drab." Miss Cather's real creative work has been with really creative and colorful people.

These latter years have been disruptive and disconcerting. Miss Cather is one of many authors who seem to have been carried off their true courses by crosswinds and chop seas. Few of the men who have suffered this experience have even started back to port; most of those who have not foundered are hopelessly adrift. Yet one still hopes that this woman of clear observation and firm touch will find her way back to the elemental people whom she really knows. She was at her best when she was not distracted by the consciousness of current events or current problems. There are plenty of writers of less distinction to dabble with these. She may well return to her old ambition and say once more of the prairie lands. "*Primum ego in patriam mecum deducam Musam.*"

Times Literary Supplement (London), 4 September 1924, p. 538

There is so sensitive a feeling for words in Miss Willa Cather's manner of writing that her very artistry is deceptive; one is apt to lose sight of the peculiar clarity of mind which evokes it. She suggests far more than she says, but the delicacy of her suggestion is made possible only by a certain vigour of thought. In *A Lost Lady*, the blending of intuition and analysis is extremely subtle. Miss Cather attempts hardly a single direct observation on the mentality or temperament of her characters, but yet reveals with the most unfailing exactness their individual characteristics and motives.

The setting is Western America in the pioneer period of thirty or forty years ago, when railroads were being built over the sage brush and cattle country. . . .

The story is told with remarkable economy. Miss Cather seldom makes the mistake of explaining too much. Her restraint in describing or commenting upon human relationships is unusually effective: her apparent detachment from the aims and passions of her characters exables her to withhold obtrusive judgments, and, more particularly, to win sympathy for her heroine. With all her

strange imperfection and occasional artifice, the lost lady is an extraordinarily appealing figure.

C. A. Dawson Scott, Bookman (London), 67 (October 1924), 50

American novels representing a bad tradition are often published in this country immediately after or even simultaneously with their appearance in the States, while books of real value, such as Miss Willa Cather's *A Lost Lady*, do not appear here until some time after their original publication. When in New York last autumn I read *A Lost Lady*, and realised at once its quality. It is a very fine and delicate piece of work. It is literature. Yet, only now has it found a publisher here. Is it any wonder that being deluged with the cheap and obvious we fail to realise the richness of America's contribution to art?

A Lost Lady is a short story—they are the vogue—and is written with subtlety. Miss Cather suggests delicately, she neither narrates nor asserts. Her Lost Lady—Marian Forrester—is weak and passion-driven, an unforgettable figure, "who preferred life on any terms." Entranced, you watch her slipping from her high place, stumbling through oozy mud, but at the end caught into safety. Not the last safety of death but marriage with a man who loved and would care for her.

At one time or another most writers attempt to portray the deathless charm of the Golden Helen. Very few succeed, but Miss Cather is one of the few.

"Her eyes, when they laughed for a moment into one's own, seemed to promise a wild delight that he has not found in life. 'I know where it is,' they seemed to say. 'I could show you!' He would like to call up the shade of the young Mrs. Forrester, as the Witch of Endor called up Samuel's, and challenge it, demand the secret of that ardour; ask her whether she had really found some ever-blooming, ever-burning, ever-piercing joy, or whether it was all fine play-acting. Probably she had found no more than another; but she had always the power of suggesting things much lovelier than herself, as the perfume of a single flower may call up the whole sweetness of spring."

The other novels in this group of five belong to their convention. They are the commercial story, the shapeless real-life tale, the modern emotional study, the long, carefully woven novel, but in *A Lost Lady* we have a creation, a book that will stand for America by the side of Edith Wharton's *House of Mirth*.

John Boynton Priestly, *London Mercury*, 10 (October 1924), 658–9

Miss Cather succeeds just where Miss Sinclair [in *Arnold Waterlow*] fails, that is, not as a philosopher or a psycho-analyst or a metaphysician or a social historian but as a narrator. Her story is very slight (it cannot be more than a quarter of the length of Miss Sinclair's), in substance hardly more than a sketch, but it comes to life, it has artistic verisimilitude, it makes its points, and it lingers in the memory, an accomplishment. Miss Cather has the great gift of fusing her materials into one economic, single-minded narrative; and she has too the gift of an exquisite frugality. Her story, conceived in an atmosphere of gentle reminiscence, is of the Middle West of the United States some forty years ago, during the era of railway building, when a kind of railway aristocracy, composed of directors, general managers, superintendents, engineers, formed a separate social strata in the prairies states. Hospitality, in the old free-handed manner, was the order of the day. One of the best-known hostesses along the line of the Burlington railway was a certain charming Mrs. Forrester, wife of Captain Forrester, an elderly contractor. We watch this charming lady, and the hospitable household she manages and graces, through the eyes of an admiring boy; Mrs. Forrester, the Captain and their friends all stand out in exquisite relief; and then we see, as the Captain, a strong man on whom his wife really depends, ages and weakens and finally dies, the gradual coarsening of this lady and the gradual disintegration of the life she built about her, until at last her lovely legend crumbles, she disappears, and the boy, now a young man, and we with him, hears only rumours of her last years. It is neither a story to describe nor to quote from, but to read, in all its charm, atmosphere and almost disturbing reality. It has all the illusion of life, and like all things in art that have the illusion of life, it gives us the impression of symbolising, however vaguely, something vast, unwieldy and difficult that could not itself be treated directly. The little tale flows on easily like an hour's reminiscence, and yet when it is finished, we have a momentary impression of having witnessed, through a cloud, the Titans storming Olympus; and the Burlington and the Colorado and Utah railway tracks have somehow stretched out until they have brought us near to the twilight of the gods.

Mordaunt Hall, "The Screen: An Indiscreet Woman," *New York Times*, 19 January 1925, Amusements section, p. 14

The first few chapters of the film version of Willa Cather's novel *A Lost Lady*, which is the principal attraction at the Piccadilly this week, pass along fairly smoothly, except for occasional superfluous scenes and flashbacks. Afterward, Harry Beaumont, the director, sacrifices much of the interest in the story by overemphasizing some of the incidents and situations; he also commits the fault of leaving little or nothing to the imagination. There are too many close-ups in this production, and one would hardly think that it was necessary to devote time to scenes of trains to bring out the fact that they get on the nerves of the railroad magnate's young wife, especially when this is referred to in the subtitles.

Mr. Beaumont appears to be fond of seesawing back and forth in his scenes, in which the characters tell nothing more by the repetition. In quite a number of stretches the lighting with night effects is very artificial. The idea of having the inevitable electrical storm, with the young wife beating her way to a railroad station, then falling into a stream, and finally reaching her destination as the train is leaving, may be harrowing for a part of the footage, but it soon becomes ridiculous, especially when Marian Forrester runs along the tracks after the train and looks as if she could easily overtake it.

The faces of some of the characters, particularly during one period, do not show much signs of passing years, and Mr. Beaumont is also decidedly abrupt in depicting the outburst of affection Marian shows when Neil Herbert has been hurt.

All in all Marian appears to be a dolt, who does not know on which side her bread is buttered. She has a "home with a certain charm," and an elderly but nevertheless affectionate husband who has amassed great wealth. She yearns for a youthful mate, and is hopelessly indiscreet in her actions the minute her eyes alight upon an unwrinkled male countenance. At one period she is unusually demonstrative in her affection for Neil and the next she fawns upon a despicable lounger. Toward the end one loses all sympathy with her and feels somewhat gratified that Neil escaped her tentacles.

Mr. Beaumont shows Marian scrubbing the floor. She has a lock of black hair over one eye, which has obviously been combed differently when a close-up is made. Marian attempts to be coy as she looks through the stray strand of hair. Irene Rich, who impersonates Marian, goes a bit too far in her make-up toward the end, as then she presents an appearance that would hardly attract any young man. She is woefully subjective in her pleading to another man over the telephone, when she ought to have been the woman scorned and therefore storming.

The outstanding histrionic effort in this film is the sympathetic manner in which Matt Moore handles the delicate role of Neil Herbert. He is simple, but ingratiating, clumsy but courageous, gentle and sweet to the ever-dissatisfied Marian. George Fawcett delivers a sound performance as the elderly husband, but his mustache in the flashbacks to make him look younger is rather absurd. Some of the comedy touches are amusing, especially one in which one woman listens in on a telephone conversation between two others. Cutting here and there would add considerably to the entertainment value of this production.

Charles S. Sewell, "Irene Rich Does Remarkable Work in Warner's Dramatic Adaptation of Willa Cather's Novel," *Moving Picture World*, 72 (7 February 1925), p. 556

Willa Cather's celebrated novel of modern life, A Lost Lady, has reached the screen under the able direction of Harry Beaumont as a Warner Brothers production, serving as the second starring vehicle for Irene Rich.

The book was a literary sensation, not only because of its wonderfully accurate and human analysis of a certain type of woman but because of the deftness of its handling and the restraint with which the author coped with situations that could easily have been built up from the sensational side; making it stand out as radically different from the majority of stories dealing with social problems today.

Willa Cather in fashioning her story sacrificed appeal to the sympathies and a happy ending in order to make her portrait a realistic one. Her heroine is a woman who, married to an old man, even though surrounded with wealth, finds her lot irksome and longs to know love and life. How a combination of circumstances restrain her, how though she sticks by her husband when he loses his money though

her lot became continually more unbearable from her viewpoint, and how after his death she lets herself go until she disgusts an admirer who has looked up to her, and how she eventually marries another old man, furnishes the story.

The author's story has been faithfully transferred to the screen. Director Beaumont has made no attempt to gloss over the unpleasant angles and has refrained from providing a conventional, happy ending. As a consequence, while the picture differs from the usual screen story and is lacking in many familiar picture elements, it is intensely dramatic, a searching character study that will hold the attention of the intelligent patron.

We doubt if a more powerful characterization has ever reached the screen; and, without discrediting Mr. Beaumont's excellent direction, credit for this must go principally to Irene Rich for her superb work. Never really in sympathy with her, and though she finally excites even your disgust, so fine is her work, so human and convincing, that it rivets your attention, and even though your reaction toward the story may not be favorable, Miss Rich's work excites your admiration. The remainder of the cast, with Matt Moore in the lead, gives her support in keeping with her performance, and George Fawcett as the elderly husband gains new laurels as a kindly old man, really the only character that excites your full sympathy.

A Lost Lady is a picture that should exert a very favourable reaction with the highest class of audiences. So far as the average run of patrons is concerned, even though it is intensely dramatic and interesting, the fact that it gets away from many familiar angles of appeal, that the story is sad, the character of the heroine unsympathetic, and the conventional happy ending missing, may militate against it.

CAST

Marian Forrester	Irene Rich
Neil Herbert	Matt Moore
Constance Ogden	June Marlowe
Frank Ellinger	John Roche
Ivy Peters	Victor Potel
Capt. Forrester	George Fawcett

STORY

Married to an elderly railroad builder of great wealth, Marian Forrester feels the call of youth and love and begins to long to get away. Her chance comes when Frank Ellinger becomes interested in her and finally persuades her to elope. Just as they start out she learns that her husband has beggared himself by giving his fortune to save a workingman's bank and she returns. Later, when it seems she can stand no more, she finds out that Ellinger, whom she thought would return to her, is to marry someone else. She tries to go to him but misses the train and goes to Neil, who has always admired her. She phones Ellinger, who turns her down but says they can still see each other. Enraged, she starts to rebuke him but Neil cuts the wire. Neil takes her back to her husband who dies, and utterly dejected, she gives way to despair, taking to drink and becoming slovenly in appearance. Neil sticks to her tries to help her to fight back, until he finds her affectionate with a low country fellow. Disgusted, he tells her that lilies that decay are worse than weeds and leaves her. Years later when his views have been softened with age, he meets a friend who tells him he met her in South America, that she was apparently happy and prosperous, the wife of a wealthy old man.

Alva Taylor, "*A Lost Lady*: A Motion Picture Review," *Liberty*, 14 February 1925, p. 36

If moving picture producers don't take care they will soon be giving the public the bigger and better things in moving pictures that have been their slogan for some time. There have been released during the past months a number of first-class pictures which have shown signs of getting away from the commonplace. A putting of life and not of fairy tales upon the screen is getting more and more to be the style.

Recent and notable examples of this have been the films mentioned in last week's review: *Greed*, directed by Von Stroheim, and Griffith's *Isn't Life Wonderful*. Now, Warner Brothers are offering *A Lost Lady*, from the novel by Willa Cather.

The picture inherits a spirit of realism from the novel. *A Lost Lady*, as written by Willa Cather, is a tremendously vivid picture of the decline and fall of a lovely woman in a small town in the West. It is one of the best novels of the last few seasons.

The moving picture is so good a filming of the book itself and so well directed that it automatically takes on much of the excellence of the novel. Compact like the novel, the film wastes no time jumping from episode to episode, but moves along smoothly and logically, making one believe as it goes.

Perhaps I am unusually averse to excessive use of the subtitle in a picture. But many of them breaking up the action of the film takes away some of the authority from a movie. A moving picture should as far as possible tell its own story by movement.

This is one of the noticeably good points about *A Lost Lady* as directed by Harry Beaumont. The subtitles are few. They are inserted only for occasional necessary explanations, and to add to dramatic suspense. By the subtlety of the acting and the direction one is allowed to read the minds of the characters, instead of being told about them. This is true of all good pictures.

Irene Rich as Marian Forrester, the lost lady, does one of the best pieces of work in her career. It's not an easy part that she portrays. She is the young and beautiful wife of an elderly railroad magnate, who sought an ideal wife and found her too late in life.

Hungrily and unconsciously seeking the romance and emotion denied her in her marriage, she gives her beauty and loveliness to Frank Ellinger, young and more attractive than faithful to women. Loving him, she starts to go away with him, but is turned back by a news item that her husband has sacrificed his entire fortune to the workmen ruined by the failure of his bank.

She is then forced to mix a little poverty with her love. The longing for Ellinger, monotony of life with her husband, who now is afflicted with paralysis, causes Marian's beauty to fade and her spirit to droop. One night Marian reads of Ellinger's forthcoming marriage to a young heiress. At once she is the maddened, harassed woman, love gone, hope lost. Her husband dies. She sinks lower and lower. She takes to drink, and her faded beauty turns to haggard ugliness. She leaves town.

Years afterward Neil Herbert learns from a mutual friend that Marian is once more secure and content and beautiful. Married to an unromantic Englishman she is at least not lost. Neil Herbert, played by Matt Moore, is the young country boy who worships Marian from afar when she is young and beautiful and above him, who loves her and asks her to marry him when she is alone and less beautiful, and who turns from her in disillusionment when he sees her in the arms of Ivy Peters, but who is always haunted by her former loveliness.

The unconventionlity of the plot of *A Lost Lady*, the absence of a regulation heroine, who is sweet and perfect from beginning to end, the lack of a cut and dried happy ending is, of course, due to Willa Cather's story. But the producers of the picture are to be congratulated for not attempting to change this for the sake of sentiment.

Andre Sennwald, "The Screen: A Screen Version of Willa Cather's *A Lost Lady*," *New York Times*, 4 October 1934, Amusements section, p. 191

Since Willa Cather's novel happens to be a genuine American masterpiece, perhaps the screen edition of *A Lost Lady*, which opened at the Strand last evening, is mediocre only by comparison. Irene Rich participated in a silent film version back in 1925. The present variation, to one who cannot forget the haunting beauty of the book, is like a stranger in the house. For the particular charm of Miss Cather's work was her method, and that has been rather definitely lost in the process of transition to the screen. The original lost lady was presented through the eyes of a sensitive boy. Now she walks the screen in plain sight, a woman married to a man she does not love, tormented by her need of a man she cannot have. It simmers down to that, finally, with Barbara Stanwyck, Frank Morgan and Ricardo Cortez to make a competent, unexciting and familiar movie of it.

How far the film has strayed from the novel to which it traces its paternity cannot be described more soberly than by a quotation from the synopsis of Gene Markey and Kathryn Scola's screen play. "Here is a story," says the candid synopsis, "of love, of disillusion, of hopes buried and ideals crushed; a story, too, of sacrifice, of devotion, of unselfishness. It is a story of three men, and a woman who loved them all, each in a different way, each in his turn, but only one of them loved her." So now Marian's career, which Miss Cather described by the subtlest of indirection, is out in solid black and white for all to see. The magic has somehow gone out of it. You may watch the steps in her downfall; see her lose her interest in life when her fiancé is shot dead for philandering; see her marry the elderly, kind and admirable Dan Forrester; see her fall in love with Ellinger, and see her settle down at last to a life of gentle resignation with her husband.

Of the actors, Frank Morgan is the most successful in establishing a mood of bewilderment and helplessness in the face of a myopic destiny. As the generous husband, deeply in love with a fine woman who has only respect and friendship to give him, Mr. Morgan creates a vast sum of good feeling for the man. Miss Stanwyck gives the general impression of a very capable actress who can play almost anything, which is much the same impression as that conveyed by the photoplay itself. Change the title, remove Miss Cather's name from the credit line, and you have a made-to-order program film.

Credits: *A Lost Lady* adapted from Willa Cather's novel, directed by Alfred E. Green, a First National production, at the Strand.

Marian Ormsby. . . Barbara Stanwyck
Daniel Forrester. . . . . . Frank Morgan
Ellinger . . . . Ricardo Cortez
Niel . . . . Lyle Talbot
Ned Montgomery. . . . . . . Phillip Reed
Robert . . . . Hobart Cavanaugh
John Ormsby. . . . . Henry Kolker
Rosa. . . . . Rafaela Ottiano
Simpson. . . . . Edward McWade
Judge Hardy. . . . . Walter Walker
Singer. . . . . Samuel Hinds
Chinese Cook. . . . . Willie Fung
Lord Verrington. . . . Jameson Thomas

Checklist of Additional Reviews

"*A Lost Lady*: Miss Cather Reconstructs the West of the Railroad Kings," *Time*, 2 (1 October 1923), 14.

Wilson Follett, "The Atlantic's Bookshelf," *Atlantic Monthly*, 132 (November 1923), n.p.

Booklist, 20 (November 1923), p. 55.

Mary Pugh, *Present-Day American Literature*, 4 (May 1931), 206–7.

THE PROFESSOR'S HOUSE

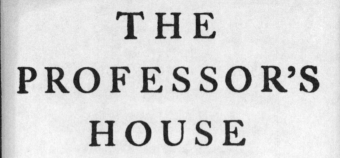

THE
PROFESSOR'S
HOUSE

by

WILLA CATHER

"A turquoise set in silver,
wasn't it? . . Yes, a turquoise
set in dull silver."

—LOUIE MARSELLUS

ALFRED·A·KNOPF

New York   *mcmxxv*

A. Hamilton Gibbs, "Contamination of Rewards: Willa Cather's Portrait of a Professor to Whom Success Was Extinction," *New York Evening Post, The Literary Review*, 5 September 1925, p. 1

Presumably one should expect a queer, unusual book from Willa Cather. Here it is—a study of a professor who, having achieved his life's masterpiece in the form of a history in eight volumes, suddenly realizes that he has no further use for life and who takes no steps to save himself when confronted with "accidental extinction."

But that isn't by any means all the story. The Professor has a wife who is rather beautiful and who from time to time drops a remark which one instantly picks up with the exclamation: "She's got a good mind!" The Professor was fooled like that when he married her. Hence his having to watch her dressing for her sons-in-law, one of whom calls her "Dearest," apparently to her great joy.

The two girls have both made mysterious marriages, one to a Jew, the other to a journalist, and although both the husbands are successful at their jobs and crazy about them, somewhere, somehow, there is a worm i' the bud.

From time to time the Professor brings a chapter to a conclusion—one to Miss Cather's, not to his own—by gazing out of his window and wondering dimly what it all means. I must confess to sharing the wonder with him.

Such, then, is the family. But they have their ghost in the person, the deceased person, of a certain Tom Outland. Outland was engaged to the older daughter, but when the war interfered he made a will in her favor and proceeded to get killed in the Foreign Legion. Besides leaving the girl and the will behind him, he also left an invention.

Now Outland is dead at the opening of the book and one learns all these things about him from the Jewish husband, who has exploited the invention, made fabulous sums of money out of it, built himself a mansion with some of the proceeds and named it "Outlands."

Hence a mysterious and enduring antagonism between the two sisters. At first one inclines to the belief that this antagonism is over the money. The Professor thinks this, too. But again he is wrong. It isn't anything to do with the money. It is something to do with the dead Outland.

In addition to the family there is an old German sewing woman named Augusta, a useful body in more senses than one, for it is with her that the Professor unbends from time to time, finding in her a health that his family lacks; and it is she, of course, who saves him from the accidental extinction.

These are the materials that Miss Cather has created for herself to work with and she has placed them in the town of Hamilton on the shore of Lake Michigan. The action of the story is entirely spiritual, and entirely concerned with the reactions of the Professor to his environment.

At the opening of the story success has just crowned him and he is in the act of moving from the old house of the days of his work and insignificance to the new one of fame and decline. But although his family moves, the Professor does not. He has to keep the shabby attic, so richly

233

furnished with memories—and with the rather obvious gas stove that everybody says is dangerous and which eventually nearly does the trick.

The change of houses, described in vivid detail, is important because it symbolizes the change in the Professor's grip on life; and the keynote of his character, of the whole philosophy of the book indeed, is struck at the end of the first chapter, when, in reply to his wife's asking him if he would rather have spent the money on something else than the new house, the Professor replies:

"Nothing, my dear, nothing. If with that check I could have bought back the fun I had writing my history, you'd never have got your house. But one couldn't get that for twenty thousand dollars. The great pleasures don't come so cheap. . . ."

And from that moment of self-realization the Professor gradually declines into an amiable old gentleman with nothing to do, a rather cynical old gentleman with the unpleasant habit of criticizing his wife—to himself; a rather doddering old gentleman who, having really had a full and good life, is so ungrateful as to look back all the time and ask himself where it was that he made his mistake.

He becomes at last so disgusted with his wife, his family and himself that when the gas stove, which has threatened so often, really does begin to asphyxiate him, he merely thinks to himself, "Suppose I don't get up? . . ."—and he doesn't.

In the depiction of this withering of the soul with the cessation of interest Miss Cather has employed subtle and delicate art. At times, perhaps, it is over-subtle—the meaning being too hidden; for if Tom Outland, having made his contribution to the welfare of mankind, is better dead before suffering the contamination of "rewards," the tragedy of the Professor is that he goes on living. Can Miss Cather be as cynical as that? Does she really feel that the only way out of this materialistic age is death, that even a man like the Professor, a man of courage, of culture, of philosophic background, of humor, of ideas, must sooner or later yield to the all-pervading taint of materialism and go on in a form of living death?

At least Miss Cather has not spared anything to drive home this momentarily (let us hope) morbid point of view. Every member of the Professor's household, to say nothing of the college for which he works, has been defiled by it—the materialism—in one way and another before she brings her argument to a conclusion.

The queerness of this book is due to the method of its development. The references to Tom Outland are made with a sort of dark hinting, as though it were going to work out into a mystery story and, as far at least as I am concerned, the tangled relationships between him and the two girls are never cleared up.

That he was engaged to Rosamond is stated as a fact; but whether he was in love with Kathleen, or she with him, I haven't the faintest idea. Nor am I able to grasp the reason why Miss Cather deliberately stops the narrative and devotes part two to the telling of Tom Outland's story. Is part two the "turquoise" set in the "dull silver" of the other lives?

That is the only possible theory I am able to form; and if it be a true one or not, it is an extraordinary thing to do in point of technique, because to all intents and purposes, it has nothing to do with the story. The facts about that character are already so developed that he has fitted into the general scheme.

He is sufficiently established without a whole part being given to him—especially as at the end of it one is left to draw one's own conclusions. Admirably though that part is done, it destroys the balance of the book, switching one away from the Pro-

234

fessor and his development, and plunging one into an atmosphere so absorbing and so utterly different that one only comes back to the Professor with a sense of disappointment and a sense of having to try and remember where he was when one left him.

Indeed it is hardly too much to say that the secondary story—Tom Outland's—is a great deal better done than the primary story of the Professor. It is so much more simple and dramatic, so much more real.

The reason of this is that while Tom Outland's story flows right along, Miss Cather leaves it to her readers to fit together the various clues in the Professor's. For while at first her main point in his degeneration is the cessation of interest in work, in life, at the conclusion of his history, the materialistic debasement is only inferred, and is, fundamentally, quite extraneous to his devolution.

Spiritually speaking, the Professor had passed out before the materialistic theme begins to be developed. Manifestly Miss Cather intended that; but, all the same, it is a little confusing.

"Willa Cather's *The Professor's House* among New Novels," *New York Times Book Review*, 6 September 1925, p. 8

Here in one volume—and one novel—are three books. Book the first is ingeniously invented and admirably carried along as far as it goes. It stops in mid-channel. Book the second is an amateurish essay in archeological adventure. It is flat, stale and unprofitable. Book the third finds Miss Cather far beyond her philosophic depth without adequate equipment of water-wings for keeping afloat what is left of the story so inconsiderately abandoned at the end of book one.

The catastrophe might not matter if the first book had not accomplished the creation of a group of human beings and captured for them both interest and sympathy—sympathy not less sensible because it is sharpened with repulsions and antagonisms, as in life itself. The group of human beings is set going in a family circle so that the friction of contact produces the sort of tense electrical condition often generated by family relations. Thus each individual is a highly charged personality. In the centre is the professor, whimsically composed, but in the right human image and convincingly alive. The other characters in the circle—the only ones that matter—are the Professor's wife, his two daughters, and his two sons-in-law. These also are alive.

Outside the family are others. But these are shadows and of little account—except a sewing woman, who for the purpose of the story, does not sew. She, if you choose, is symbolic—like the One Woman in *What Price Glory*—the girl Charmaine, who is so simply what she is. Just as simple is the sewing woman, though she is comfortress in quite another fashion than the tavern wench of the play. It is a long way from billets just behind the lines in France to the professor's college town in the Northwest of America. But the essential difference is that Mr. Stallings's misconducted marines were weary of their own war while Miss Cather's innocent Professor is weary of his own women. The instinctive want is the same. The blameless sewing woman (begging her pardon) also means rest from what has grown to be intolerable.

This is the heavy stuff which has sunk the story. It is more considerate to the author to speak of her living characters before her philosophy drowned them. First, the professor is presented in his attic, where he works at his books above all the hum of domestic existence, and where the sewing woman also works—but only when he is not working there. Then the Professor and his wife are seen entertaining at dinner their daughters and sons-in-law, getting on each other's nerves, and in that state revealing themselves each and severally to the curiosity of the reader.

The ingredients include first, the original professorial family mixture of French-Canadian and rural Methodist American, and, second, the added elements supplied by the sons-in-law, one of whom is a Scot and the other a Jew. The author's method is to make the pot boil not too furiously and to keep your attention on the boiling process so that you may see your prejudices—if you have such things—boiled down and evaporated and distilled into conclusions which need not entirely confirm those prejudices. The professor had prejudices, for instance, as well as daughters.

The point is, however, not the validity of any prejudice, but the revelation of character and the testing of human nature under the action of prejudice assisted by envy. One of the sons-in-law is poor, the other is rich: one daughter wears frocks from Paris and the other has hers made by the local dressmaker—or perhaps the symbolical sewing woman. One husband is expansive and demonstrative, the other is the opposite. These differences exasperate, and want of tact on both sides makes things worse.

It does not suggest a pretty picture—and it is not precisely a pretty picture which is drawn. But Lillian, the mother, practicing her arts of charm by turns on each son-in-law; Rosamond, the sumptuous daughter, and Kathleen, the intense daughter, and MacGregor and Louie, the two young husbands, are vividly presented to the reader's consciousness as sentient and active creatures—especially Louie, with whom his creator obviously has taken not contemptible pains. Miss Cather has not contemptible powers of characterization and gifts of projection based upon a real flair for personality and feeling for human values—as her earlier work has proved. These powers and gifts have not deserted her here, though she has let the gentle art of story telling so utterly escape her in snatching for something else out of her range and reach.

In the professor she has hit upon a very happy and human note. He has strength, humor, charm and that ironic twist which may in the end have to rely on itself to keep the world even tolerable as a place of residence. But she had no business hanging the professor's drama on a smoky gas stove in the attic as the alternative to living any longer with his women folk. No philosopher who pretends to the name takes the hemlock by mere accident. Deliberately or in due process of law he puts the cup to his lips and keeps it there till the last drop is drained. And even at the last, it is not because of Xanthippe that he drinks the bitter draught.

It is at least a comfort to think that death does not come this way to Miss Cather's picturesque and engaging professor who writes about Spanish adventurers when he is not shocking the Fundamentalists in his class-room lectures. The sewing woman intervenes. But snuffing out an amiable character with the aid of a defective gas stove is no trick for a novelist of proper feeling even to attempt. It is no sufficient excuse that her middle-aged hero has suffered the misfortune of falling out of love with the wife who delighted his youth in Paris and brought him daughters—and sons-in-law. Perhaps it is better for middle age to fall out of love than to fall in again. It can be done more gracefully.

But we wander. It is really not possible to take this work seriously as a whole. As you look back over the first book you have a recurring sense of gaps and vacancies, incompletenesses in the story—as if parts had been hastily cut out of the manuscript and the ends not joined up. Then there is that long parenthesis inserted in the middle of a story of psychological analysis of character. The only valid excuse for it would be to make the narrative of the discovery of the cliff-dwellers' city on the Blue Mesa a thing of magic in itself. And here is no magic.

Doubtless there is a purpose. But no need exists of so much digression to stage the contrast between the ideal ambition of a discoverer and the material ambition of a trader. For this part is the story of the young man who did not become the professor's son-in-law, who might have married the sumptuous daughter. He died in the great war, instead. It was the actual son-in-law who reaped where the other had sown—realized on an invention which he had left as a legacy to the girl.

As written, the story leaves this young man—the ideal son-in-law—also among the shadows for the reader, though to the writer he seems to mean much. The miracle of creation is not performed in his case. What is worse, perhaps, the author's quality as a writer, which is so refreshingly present in the first part of the novel, escapes her as she struggles with the mere narrative material of the western adventure. The adventure is not adventurous, the discoveries are not exciting. Perhaps the writer is not naive enough for that sort of thing. At least it is a trick which very naive writers have been able to turn over and over again.

Fanny Butcher, "Willa Cather Tells Purpose of New Novel," *Chicago Tribune*, 12 September 1925, p. 9

Willa Cather, whose latest book *The Professor's House* bids fair to be the big novel of the fall, was in town for a few hours between trains the other day, a vivid personality—the sort of person who seems, like Anteus, to gain sevenfold strength every time she touches her parent earth.

She has been for two months or so in New Mexico and stopped off at her home in Nebraska and she simply glows with the out-of-doors. She told me what she had tried to do in *The Professor's House*. "I wanted to make a design. I'll never again write a book which is just a story of a triangle or a tale for lazy people to read. If I can't do something different from that I'll never write another line and I'll go and be a cashier in my brother's bank. There is design in the life that flows by a cashier's window, and it's the design of life that I tried to get into *The Professor's House*.

"All of the arts have design, but it's more obvious in painting and in music than in literature. This story is built like a piece of music, the theme of St. Peter, then the theme of Tom Outland, and the last part of the book the mingling of the two themes. Incidentally, this is the first book I've ever written with any irony in it. Irony is something you don't feel when you are young. You're much too sentimental about life, or too thrilled by it to see the irony of it. I've always been much too interested in the way characters conquered fate to realize that, after all, fate conquers them in the end. And in this book I have tried to show how out of the boyish enthusiasm, the almost cinematographic quality of Tom Outland, who was so quixotic about never allowing his friendships or his enthusiasms to bring him any gain, there should have come involuntarily to St. Peter and his whole family wealth which brought little happiness.

"I also wanted to show that most of the really important events in our lives come to us through some entirely accidental contact. St. Peter, by the mere chance of Tom Outland's arrival, had in his life a series of circumstances started which inevitably eventuated in his realization—after his own youthful fevers had burned themselves out in his early love and his creative work, that he simply was not the same man, and in a sense, a very deep sense, he was more Tom Outland than he was himself. The book might have been called "A Man of Fifty Looks at the World," but he could never have looked at it just as he did without the presence of Tom Outland in his life.

"Another thing that I wanted to put into the book was what I call the cliff dweller thrill. When I was a little girl nothing in the world gave me such a moment as the idea of the cliff dwellers, of whole civilizations before ours linking me to the soil. The boys in Nebraska used to dig up arrow heads on the farms and those relics of former people gave them a thrill which nothing else could do. It's a perfectly natural passion, a youthful enthusiasm at the contact with the making of [t]his country. It was that thrill, that enthusiasm that I wanted to put into the story.

"When I was coming back from the west the conductor noticed my name on my ticket and told me that the railroad boys were saying that the book was the best picture of old railroad days that they'd ever read. As you know there isn't much about railroad life in it, but if that little bit has made it the kind of book that railroad men will read and like I am more excited than ever about having done it. That's what I want to do—the kind of thing that gets the design of life, not just the picture. I could have written the story of these two boys out on the mesa like a Zane Grey novel, but I would have died of boredom doing it. The fascinating thing to me is how that incident, that thrilling, exciting enthusiasm reacted on a group of rather middle-class unenthusiastic people."

We talked about other things for a while and then she suddenly said, "You made one terrible error in your review of the book. You spoke of me as a woman novelist. Woman novelist is as out of date as [such] a phrase as woman musician or woman painter, or woman anything else that women do as professionally as men. There are so many women writing novels nowadays that very soon the critics will have to begin talking about prominent male novelists."

Stuart P. Sherman, "Willa Cather," *The New York Herald Tribune Books,* 13 September 1925, pp. 1–3

Willa Cather has published a new novel, *The Professor's House.* If I should say no more than that, I should have said enough to send all discerning readers out for a copy. Miss Cather is not merely one of those rare writers who have taken a vow never to disappoint us. She is also indubitably one of the true classics of our generation. She is not merely entertaining. She is also important. Her work has a vital center, and its contours become steadily more distinct. It will become increasingly clear to us, I believe, that she has been expressing the new sense of values which we are all gradually and often unconsciously beginning to accept. She has been clarifying for us our sense of what we have in common with the generations before 1900, and our sense of the points at which we have departed from their ways.

Each of her novels—I am happy to possess and to reread them all—has been a desired event of which one could safely predict nothing but a style with the translucency of sky; a beauty, cool, grave, pervasive; deep feeling under perfect control; and a criticism of life both profound and acute—a criticism which deals as nobly with the simple elements as with the fine complexities of human experience.

The Professor's House is a disturbingly beautiful book, full of meanings, full of intentions—I am sure that I have not caught them all. Everything in it has its own bright surface meaning. And the somewhat bewildering jacket description suggests that Miss Cather is actually describing academic life. She is here addressing herself, we are informed, "to those who do not know or who doubt the American youth, to those who may be interested in the environment which their sons and daughters find in college."

The novel does, to be sure, present Godfrey St. Peter—a man of mixed French and American ancestry—professor of European history in a state university near Lake Michigan; his wife, Lillian—a woman of some elegance and beauty, with whom he seems to have almost nothing to do; the two married daughters and their

husbands; the seamstress, Augusta; the professor's favorite pupil, Tom Outland, explorer of cliff-dwellings and inventor, killed in the war, and a colleague or two. The professor has completed his life work, an eight-volume history of the Spanish Adventurers in North America. He has received a big money prize from Oxford. And the family is moving into the new house which he, or perhaps rather his wife, has built with the reward of his labors.

What happens after that point would strike me as inconclusive, slightly incoherent, and without vital thesis, if I did not regard *The Professor's House* as an Ibsenish title—as Ibsenish as *The Doll's House*. There is more in this house than meets the eye. The professor's former house was a poor old place, lacking many modern improvements, inconvenient and as ugly as a house could be. It had a tin bathtub which the professor tried to renovate with porcelain paint. It had a garret study. The professor wrote his Spanish Adventurers in a wretchedly bare little room under the mansard roof, without filing apparatus, and heated by a most dubious old stove. The room was further encumbered by a number of ancient dress forms, and he had to share it at times with Augusta, the sewing woman.

When money comes to the family from the professor's prize and from the marriage of a daughter to a Jewish engineer, who grows wealthy by exploiting a patent of Tom Outland's, all sorts of comforts and luxuries become available—cars, imported Spanish furniture, furs, jewels, wine, country houses, travel. The professor's wife and his children take with alacrity to the new standard of living; they blossom out, she renews her youth. But the professor is a tree of which the trunk has been hollowed out by fire. He is nearly burned out. He haunts the old home. He clings whimsically to the fleshless companions of his scholarly solitude—those old dress forms. He finds comfort in chatting with the antique sewing woman; and she saves his life when he is on the point of asphyxiation from the fumes of the old stove, the fire of which has been extinguished by the wind.

Out of a large acquaintance with professors, I can testify that Professor St. Peter is not an ordinary professor. Ordinary professors do not reluct against exchanging a ramshackle old house for a luxurious new one. Professor St. Peter is rather a spirit than a man. He is a spirit saying goodby to something much larger than the ugly old square domicile in which his life work was accomplished. He is a spirit reluctantly bidding farewell to a generation of American life, to a vanishing order of civilization. I find *The Professor's House* echoing and vibrating with the cumulative meaning of all the books in which Miss Cather has sought to record the quest of her generation for true romance, for the real thing, for that which enables one to forget everything else, for that which uses and consumes one adequately.

Miss Cather came out of a Western small town by way of the University of Nebraska some twenty or twenty-five years ago. From that statement alone one can infer, with small probability of error, that she had a good intelligent mother of "Puritan" upbringing; that her father was something of a pioneer, and that Miss Cather's early education was of what we call a New Englandish cast, qualified by a Western environment and contacts with German, Swedish and Bohemian settlers on the prairies.

When the University of Nebraska had done its best to kindle her curiosity and to open her mind, I infer that she came East with literature and music in her heart, and eagerly continued her education in Greenwich Village, in Paris, in London, and in many other places at home and abroad.

For nearly twenty years I have fondly preserved a second-hand impression of her before she was a famous novelist, as sitting every morning on a bench in Washington Square, reading Whitman's *Leaves of Grass*. I believe Miss Cather repudiates this reminiscence as imaginary. I am sure she has sat in Washington Square and that she has read *Leaves of Grass*, and I cling to the reminiscence for its symbolic truth. Looking back through the seven novels to discover the newcomer from the West, I see a young Nebraskan, hungry from the austerities and rectitudes of a prairie home, reading the *Leaves of Grass* in the morning sunshine on a bench in Washington Square and dreaming of the pioneers and of Paris. With that much by way of biography, one can in some fashion "account" for everything she has written.

Her first book, *Alexander's Bridge*, 1912, is rather more significantly hers that she admits. It is a short novel presenting a "critical moment" in the career of Bartley Alexander. He was by the gift of the gods a tremendous natural force, a great man of action. He came out of the West and distinguished himself as a bridge builder. He married a fine woman of talent and fortune and settled more and more firmly into the imposing structure of established society in Boston. But in his dangerous middle age his unexhausted youth fermented within him. He renewed a liaison of his student days with an Irish actress in London. When he returned to inspect his biggest bridge, then building, it collapsed and he was drowned in its ruin.

In 1922, eleven years after the composition of this tale, Miss Cather wrote an apologetic but extremely interesting preface for a new edition of the book. She said that the "subject matter" had originally interested her intensely, but that she now recognized it as not her "own material," not the field in which she was master. So far as the "subject matter" is concerned, I can't follow this explanation: she appears to possess the subject matter quite adequately for her purposes. But so far as the treatment is concerned, I see a point in the apologetic preface. She has tried to treat her theme in accordance with the New England tradition, established by Hawthorne and more or less perpetuated by Mrs. Wharton. She has moralized the story as Hawthorne would have moralized it: the collapse of the bridge is an obvious symbolical device for emphasizing the "collapse" of that pillar of society, Bartley Alexander. In its form and outline the tale looks like a tribute to that rigorously established order to which Mrs. Wharton used to offer sacrifices.

Now, nowhere else in Miss Cather's work, I think, is there any such tribute to "established society" as is implied in the title and the dominating symbolism of *Alexander's Bridge*. All her deepest sympathies, as her subsequent novels prove, were with, not against Bartley in his revolt against the prison-house of respectability, in which he felt that the primal energies of his nature were being progressively fettered and wasted. But in this first book she actually logs in a professor of moral philosophy, a Professor Wilson, to serve as spokesman for the ethical sense of his generation; and he—lightly, yet ominously—speaks of a flaw in Bartley's nature which he once feared might lead to disaster. In so far as the book is moralized in this manner, it is out of line with Miss Cather's practices and her convictions.

But in *Alexander's Bridge* itself, Miss Cather does strike into her own theme and material. She begins her own characteristic comment on life in these "mutterings" of Bartley to the professor of moral philosophy:

"After all, life doesn't offer a man much. You work like the devil and think you are getting on, and suddenly you discover that you've only been getting yourself tied up. A million details drink you dry. Your life keeps going for things you don't want, and all the while you are being built alive into a social structure you don't care a rap about. I sometimes wonder what sort of chap I'd have been if I hadn't been this sort; I want to go out and live out his potentialities too."

To live out one's potentialities: there is the clew to all Miss Cather's sympathies. There is her primary intuition of the "real thing," in harmony with which she has readjusted her entire scale of values. She sympathizes profoundly and intelligently with that aspiration. It is a major distinction of her work and of her literary generation. Her criticism of life, in both its negative and its positive aspects, springs from her sympathy with that aspiration, and from her intelligent repudiation of the repressive philosophy upon which Mrs. Wharton's established polite society, as well as the village society of New England, was based.

From polite society, Miss Cather turned abruptly in 1913 to one large division of her "own material" in *O Pioneers!* with which, for our purposes, we may immediately associate *My Antonia*, 1918. In these books, she tells us that she did not "build" her story; the story shaped itself inevitably in a loose, anecdotal, yet intensely vivid and poignant memoir. Here she is dealing not with the domain of convention, but with the domain of necessity. She is presenting the Bohemian, German, Swedish and native American farmers of Nebraska battling with the soil and the elements, against heavy odds. This is her account of what life is, and must be, at bottom. This is her picture of "romance" in its most elementary form.

241

For pioneers, these books tell us, there is naught but this: food, shelter, clothing and reproduction of their species; just not to perish; just to hold one's own on the hard bedrock of existence. In these conditions, the primitive struggle suffices to call forth one's best and one's utmost, and to make one oblivious of everything else—of all the graces and refinements and the large awareness of the world in which later generations endeavor to slake the thirsts of the soul.

Miss Cather has taken the pioneer into her brooding heart. She extenuates nothing, but she sets down naught in malice. She cannot, like so may of our jolly young novelists, write satirically or even bitterly of the long, lonely roads that lead to Main Street or of "the big, lonely country where people worked hard with their backs and got tired like the horses, and were too sleepy at night to think of anything to say." In her, this elementary struggle, whether she contemplates its symbol in the plow standing in the black furrows against the Nebraska sunset or in the shards and flints of the vanished cliff-dwellers who left their mournful vestiges under the turquoise heavens of New Mexico and Colorado, evokes a mood of luminous Virgilian sadness. No other American novelist, I think, has treated this theme with a beauty so grave, so wistful.

The heroine of O Pioneers! demands special mention as one of Miss Cather's important contributions to contemporary "feminism." Dux femina facti: the chief pioneer is a woman. Alexandra is one of several children on a poor Nebraska farm. On the death of her father she alone of the brood reacts positively and creatively to the new demands of the circumstances. Her brothers plod in the old ruts. She strikes out. She has enough vital energy to shape a little the terms of her struggle for survival, to make of it a big thing, an inspiring and rewarding activity. She finds what "romance" life has for her in buying up unvalued and forsaken farms, adding quarter-section to quarter-section, and competing with men in all the details from farm management. In this she is a notable predecessor of Ellen Glasgow's heroine in *Barren Ground*.

Alexandra is not inhuman, not emotionally stolid. She feels the normal woman's desires and needs. In the end she takes a husband. But in the end the husband's place in her life is perforce incidental. Before the time comes when he seems to fit in, she herself has already done, fully accomplished, what we used to call "a man's work in the world." Marriage for her is a side enterprise—as it is for a man. It cannot now fill her life to the exclusion of everything else. Her life is already full—all but full. She will live out her personal and domestic potentialities without interrupting the big constructive "romance," which for many years has occupied her mind and her imagination.

From the pioneers, Miss Cather turns to her second major theme in *The Song of the Lark*, 1915, and in her collection of short stories, *Youth and the Bright Medusa*, 1920. One theme develops, when it develops vitally, out of the other, as the pattern comes out on the waterpots of the cliff-dwellers. For Miss Cather there are two great things in the world: the struggle for existence, and the art which expands our measured interval with beauty or high passion till we forget that we must live and must die.

I am astonished to learn that there are still some intelligent persons who have not yet read *The Song of the Lark*. It is absurd. *The Song of the Lark* is certainly very near the top notch of American fiction. It seems to me one of the truest and profoundest studies of the mind and heart of a great artist ever written anywhere. It is a magnificent piece of imaginative realism. It is also, I believe, Miss Cather's most intimate book—the book which she has most enriched with the poetry and wisdom and the passion of her experience, and made spacious with the height and the depth of her desire.

It is the story of a Swedish pastor's daughter in Colorado, in whom there is gradually discovered a singing voice of the first quality. Gradually the voice is born in her. "Every artist," says her old German singing master, "makes himself born." Gradually she escapes from everything else till she is living to fulfill the possibilities of her talent—for that and for naught else. Then, as one of her lovers says, with a note of pity for himself, "she drifts like a rifle ball" to her object. All her childhood, all her labor, all her love, all her acquaintance with the wide world, her struggles, her frustrations, her triumphs—all are converted into music, into beauty. Everything else is incidental—as it is, as it must be—to every absolutely first rate artist. As for those who play with art, art plays with them. Then does not play.

Nothing in contemporary fiction has stirred me, I think, quite so profoundly as the deep rich harmonies Miss Cather makes in this story by the interweaving of her life-preservative with her life-expansive themes in those marvelous chapters where she shows Thea musically assimilating the history of humanity's struggle for survival among the ruins of the cliff-dwellers.

In all the stories of *Youth and the Bright Medusa* you will find variations on the central theme in *The Song of the Lark*. These are poignant tales of painters, sculptors, singers seeking their "real thing" as interpreted by polite society or the New England village or the Western Main Street. Their romance is the expansion of the allotted interval. Their motto, like that of the old play, is "all for love." The artist who will not give all, is no true

lover of his art, and in the end his mistress will forsake him.

The war tried in vain to divert Miss Cather from the development of her thesis. In *One of Ours*, 1922, she did indeed write one of the stories of the World War. As a reward for this work she received the Pulitzer Prize for the novel which "best presents the wholesome atmosphere of American manners and manhood." I am moved by the patriotic and military interest of the book. It is a sufficiently good war story. But war is not Miss Cather's "own material."

And, as a curious and ironic matter of fact, Miss Cather is much occupied in *One of Ours* with an implicit satire on "the wholesome atmosphere of American manners and manhood," and with exhibiting the superior literacy, intellectuality, and geniality of German men and women in the Ehrlich family at the University of Nebraska. The young hero who goes to fight the Germans has learned pretty much all that he knows of the amenities of life from his German friends and neighbors.

Miss Cather's hero is a Western boy from the farm whose deepest impulses and aspirations have been frustrated by precisely what I suppose the founder of the Pulitzer Prize imagined were essential constitutents of "the wholesome atmosphere of American manners and manhood." They have been frustrated by the hard frugality and thrift of prosperous American farmers; by the influence of a narrow denominational religion; by the average American man's contempt for gracious manners, art and the things of the mind; by the narrow mother and the narrower parson piously assuring a warm-blooded hungry boy that he will find his happiness "when he finds his Saviour"; by a chaste and frigid wife who abandons her young husband in order to nurse a missionary sister in China, etc.

Miss Cather has never been valuable to us as a flatterer of "the wholesome atmosphere of American manners and manhood." She has conspicuously served us by showing just how and where this "wholesome atmosphere" has corroded and wasted some of the precious resources of life. She has served us by showing again and again how the "alien" elements in our population—German, Swedish, Bohemian, Spanish, Mexican, French— have utilized what "we Anglo-Saxons" have suppressed and rejected.

Her next novel, *A Lost Lady*, is a remarkable case in point. Like *The Song of the Lark*, this is a story on her great theme of living out one's potentialities. But in this case the potentiality to which the heroine gives all is not artistic, but personal and specifically erotic, and to a certain extent illicit. Mrs. Forrester is a woman who, as we vulgarly put it, "trades" on her charm, though what she gets in barter is only adoration. She is animated and consumed by the passion for giving and receiving pleasure, which she uses incidentally as a means of refining the manners of those to whom she gives it. Her perfume, her rings, her furs, her voice, her eyes, her kindness, the touch of her fine hand upon one's arm are all bewitching, penetratively seductive. She cannot bow or give one a passing glance without establishing a personal relation of an indescribable sweetness.

Mrs. Forrester is the radiant Venus Anadyomene united in the holy bonds of matrimony to an honorable, crippled, corpulent, big-jowled railway man who looks and acts like Grover Cleveland. She is, in her own sense, unflinchingly loyal to this fine old wreck. But that is not enough. She is loyal to all men. She gives the best of herself to them all; and so she fascinates all men, and all boys, who come within reach of her voice and eyes. Personal charm is her one talent. In all circum-

stances, worthy and unworthy, she lives out its potentialities. She uses it as the musician uses music, to expand the allotted interval; and, like a public performer of music, she wishes to please all.

At the first reading of this book I did not lose my heart to Mrs. Forrester. I happen to have a deeply seated, perhaps ineradicable, prejudice against persons who desire to please everybody. Mrs. Forrester's passion for pleasing everybody left her, I thought, without that trait which is essential to pleasing people who are at all particular: it left her without discrimination. It seemed to me to betray her as estrangingly devoid of taste in personal relations. And when she submitted quietly to the embrace of the hard-eyed, carbuncled shyster Ivy Peters, I revolted from her charm as young Neil revolted.

But Mr. Heywood Broun, winking with the indulgence of the Almighty at Mrs. Forrester's unconcern about preserving "the wholesome atmosphere of American manners and manhood," assured me in print that in Mrs. Forrester I should find the genuine "portrait of a lady," which I had somewhere said was missing from current fiction. And not Mr. Broun alone, but all my acquaintances, academic persons, old maids, hardened old New England bachelors of the austerest virtue—all unite with Mr. Broun in surrendering to her charm and admitting— the austere old bachelors—that if they could have met anywhere in their generation a lady like Mrs. Forrester— well, their lives might have been very different.

On a third reading I see how *A Lost Lady* fits in with the main thesis of Miss Cather's work. Mrs. Forrester is a symbolic figure. Her story is Miss Cather's poem of personality and its values—its powers, its too-little regarded powers. In her calling she is as admirable at Thea is admirable in hers. She used the rare talent intrusted to her. She gave all for love. She consumed herself adequately in making personal relations charming. She illustrates, and her innumerable adorers illustrate, the coming around of our generation to Browning's position in the much quoted poem:

> The sin I impute to each frustrate ghost
>
> Is—the unlit lamp and the ungirt loin.

And now I think we are in a position to see a little more deeply into Miss Cather's extraordinary Professor and his extraordinary House. The Professor—he is the intellectual spirit of our American "Victorian Era." The old house, which he cannot persuade himself to leave—that is what our famous Young People call Professorial American. His wife and daughters and sons-in-law—they are the celebrated Younger Generation, building themselves new homes, enriched with all sorts of new devices which the professor values little. His mind and imagination have been occupied, splendidly occupied, in a long historical retrospect; his dream has always drifted backward to former glories, Spanish adventurers, Cliff-Dwellers, the storied past. And now the word is Forward. But he has consumed himself. His fire is out. He is a superannuated figure in his times. He clings to the old dress forms. He chats with Augusta.

"Miss Cather's Professor," *Springfield* (Massachusetts) *Sunday Republican*, 13 September 1925, p. 5A

Miss Willa Cather's new novel, *The Professor's House*, is inscribed to Jan "because he likes narrative." Either Miss Cather is ironical or Jan will be disappointed. *The Professor's House* not only lacks narrative (apart from an irrelevant story inserted in the book), but it deals with individuals in a manner that makes even their group relations seem lacking in significance. The professor's family are but a dim halo around the professor. The old house somehow symbolizes the professor's mind, yet it is not quite apparent how the new house causes a disruption of his habits. The professor himself has individuality: of that Miss Cather endeavors to give us a full and frank transcription; yet, his character is not firmly woven. A novel which challenges us by its lack of form finally fails to persuade us that it has offered us a valid pretext for formlessness.

Yet the professor mildly engages our interest, as Miss Cather herself mildly piques our curiosity by making it always seem probable that something is going to develop—some domestic strain, some conflict between souls, some emotional or intellectual revelation. The professor is, in conventional language, interesting; but he is never quite so engrossing as we constantly feel that he should be. Moreover, he betokens no large aspect of life. He is not wholly the self-contained intellectual indifferent to material prosperity; nor is he the worldly professor eager to get on and, perhaps, owing his preferment to

245

political connections, like one of his colleagues in the state university. Possibly the man is so real to Miss Cather that she has not made him real to us.

The professor is half of French Canadian and half of American farmer stock. He had a "practical, strong-willed Methodist mother" and a "gentle, weaned-away Catholic father." He was brought up in sight of Lake Michigan, which was "the great fact in life." Studying in France as a young man, he remained loyal to his lake and insisted that its blue was not that of the English Channel or of the Mediterranean. Yet he is not wholly a poet, and we are not convinced that his more dashing, more worldly wife thwarted any poetic or intellectually creative impulses of his nature. In fact, his great work of research proves an achievement of marked originality and wins him fame and a money prize.

Nor are we convinced that his self-satisfied daughters cause him any spiritual distress. "The professor had expected a better match for Kitty. He was no snob; . . . but he knew that Scott had a usual sort of mind, and Kitty had flashes of something quite different." Perhaps the same thing can be said of the professor; he has flashes of genius, but the flashes are intermittent. Within the space of a few pages he is astute and practical in giving advice, innocently neglectful of his overcoat on a cold day and humorously or caustically sapient in conversation. Miss Cather seems to have been overanxious to avoid extravagant contrasts and by subduing every trace of the unnatural to have left her canvas without lights and shades.

In structure the novel is highly deficient. It reaches normal dimensions only by the introduction of Tom Outland's story—which lacks connection with the rest. Moreover, this is introduced twice—first briefly and then at the length of several chapters. Tom Outland's story

does not pleasantly portray the reception accorded by officers of the Smithsonian Institution to enthusiastic amateur archeologists from the Southwest; but apart from this, one finds it rather anemic.

Dorothea L[awrance] Mann, "Willa Cather's Professor," *Boston Evening Transcript*, 16 September 1925, section 2, p. 6

It would be interesting to know how many persons there are who really choose their professions. One hears a good deal of talk on the subject from time to time, and of late years it has become the thing to take vocational advice just as one would take medical or legal advice—or as people used to take spiritual advice. Probably, however, no profession has ever benefited so much as the teaching profession by the fact that Nature—or the Life-force as some people call it—perpetually wars against the vocational guidance people. All along the line we find instances of how the Life-force obtains control of a man, and he falls in love and immediately he must have some position in which he can support a wife. He has a college degree, and it may be a little professional training as well, but if he wants money quickly he rushes for a position as teacher or professor.

Sometimes he fits naturally into the position, but very often he discovers afterward that he had been tricked by this same Life-force. Here he is with a family and the need for earning money, and he is not doing at all the thing he intended to do with his life. One fact few authors have

246

laid sufficiently to the credit of the male sex—and that is the patience and the philosophy with which they accept what has happened to them. Occasionally, when a good number of years have passed, the physician or the lawyer, or an unusually keen friend discovers that some of the tendency which the man's character—or even his health—has taken is caused by the fact that he has been forcing himself all through the years into the groove he was never intended to fill.

Professor St. Peter was one of those caught by the Life-force. He fell in love with a pretty and intelligent girl, and he rushed about to find a position which would support two people. He found it naturally enough in a Middle Western college, not too far from the shores of Lake Michigan. This one act determined all the rest of his life. Though he has led so exemplary a life, Professor St. Peter is not at heart a domestic person at all. As it is, he has found all sorts of small outlets for his restlessness. There have been the long summers when his wife and daughters were vacationing, and the professor remained at home, taking his work table down into the garden. The garden itself is another outlet. We know something of the desires which were consuming him when we realize that for all these years he had worked to make a French garden in his little American town. There is the strip of beach twelve miles away to which he repairs when he is too restless and spends happy hours swimming. Coming closer still there is the little wild strain in his conversation. Some of the love adventure in his blood works itself out in those sly quips, those answers which border almost on the risqué.

Professor St. Peter's wife, being an eminent[ly] practical person—like hundreds of other American women—ignores all these subtle danger signals. Like hundreds of other American women, she treats her husband very much as she treats her children. She humors him a little, she does not pay too much attention to his small misdemeanors, and she expects him to behave well in public. Outwardly this treatment works well enough. To the world Professor St. Peter shows an exemplary front. He grows in the course of years fond of his daughters. It is not until they are married and his life is complicated with sons-in-law, that the St. Peter's matrimonial craft shows signs of being in difficulty. One feels the absolutely typical quality of the story here.

Only once in the course of the years has the professor's wife shown evidence of jealousy or of a suspicion that the professor's life was not meaning all it might mean. She is palpably jealous of his one student who seems to him to justify the effort of his teaching career. Complacent as she seems she recognizes that there is something he gets from Tom Outland which she has never been able to give him. As it happens Tom Outland is inextricably interwoven with the family fortunes, so that mere prudence forbids her making this jealousy very keenly felt.

Miss Cather likes to found a story upon a symbol. In this case the symbol is the professor's old house. From the first we realize that it is as inconvenient and unattractive as a house could well be. There is no normal reason why Professor St. Peter should object to leaving his old house and moving to the comfortable new study which sudden good fortune has given him. His family humor father, though none of them can fathom why the professor keeps this strange attachment to the uncomfortable study in which for years he worked with poor light, uncomfortable furniture, no heat in winter, and being obliged to share it at certain seasons with a sewing woman. This is where we come face to face with the psychological twists which have become the most important thing in Professor St. Peter's life. Miss Cather further stresses the importance of the symbol by having the professor cling to the ugly disfiguring busts and forms which the sewing woman had kept in a corner of his study. He would be lonely, he tells her, "without his women." She is a little shocked. She probably does not know whether or not she should administer a deserved rebuke for his language. She understands what lies behind it as little as his wife does.

Something, however, we are given to understand of what this room stands for. The professor hires the entire house in order to keep the study, ostensibly because he can work better in the conditions to which he has been accustomed. Actually we realize that there are two reasons—which bound the whole of Professor St. Peter's life. The very uncomfortable quality of that study has stood for the justification of the sacrifice as he comes to feel it of his life. That meager little attic room stands for the fact that all the money he earns is necessary for the welfare of his wife and children. His life may be far from what he felt it could have been, but at least he has cared for three other people dependent on him. So long as they are materially and spiritually dependent on him, all that he sacrifices has a meaning. The true difficulty of the professor's life comes when he realizes that it is only custom, habit, the fear of public opinion—whatever you want to call the force which keeps the majority of persons from ever stepping from the path they are expected to tread—that holds him in the town and in his position. The other things for which the room stands is for the one glorious adventure which has made the great happiness of his life, the publication of his great historical work on the Spanish adventurers in America. The whole romance of his life is bound up in that work. The work is finished but to

leave the study where it was done means shutting the door more definitely on what has been the glory of his existence.

Psychologically Miss Cather finds the frustrated human being the most interesting. The man or woman with all his energy dammed up is like a butterfly on a pin. It is cruel to watch his struggles but some people find them fascinating. Professor St. Peter has his counterpart everywhere in the country, in colleges and out of them. They are men who were tricked and caught and have spent their existence fastened on a pin, specimens to be studied as they struggle. There is something almost unendurably painful about the professor's final struggle. The very humanity of the man, the naturalness of his crisis, makes his frustration almost beyond bearing.

Moses Harper, "Americans All," *New Republic*, 44 (September 16, 1925), 105–6

The Professor's House is a story within a story. Each half is in a way separate, and thoroughly unlike the other, yet each half sheds light on the other and mysteriously belongs to it. As much a part of the Professor's life and his family's life as if he still existed, the life of a dead man, Tom Outland, overshadows them. Tom Outland came, a greenhorn, as student to the university, bringing with him strange Indian earthenware and an inscrutable past. He did well, he invented something commercially valuable, which was only exploited after his death in France. The invention meant millions to the Professor's daughter, who was engaged to Tom, and married after his death. But the daughters and the sons-in-law and the

248

Professor and all this little family inherit a memory more substantial than money—loyalties and recollections which entangle them. The Professor's life drifts, seems to stop, regains a mellow tired fortitude from thinking of this other life that stopped.

The Professor has won a prize by his history, builds a new house; he does not need to go on renting the old one that he may work where he always has, but he does so. It is a symbol of his character, on the one side successful in a moderate way, and comfortable, on the other clinging to the charming discomforts and solitudes that were never separate from his work. Like most of Miss Cather's characters, he is drawn in the round, with calm, warm, generous strokes, a figure never in the same place, ever turning slowly a new side to us, changing, growing, even when the growth points a little sadly to a kind of death before death, a premonitory halt before the last stop. The Professor is one of her best, though not the best of all—he is a little more under her watchful eye than was Mrs. Forrester, and is not allowed to grow quite so much by himself. Something about him here and there seems a little too forcibly put together out of attractive pieces: his foreign name, his history, his family, his talk—the little things which should be revelatory, should pull him together into a whole, occasionally pull him apart.

Tom Outland never actually appears in the book. We see him through the eyes of recollection, and in the words of his own story as he told it to the Professor. A strange story, sharing that quality of distinctness from most other stories which belongs to Miss Cather. But Miss Cather runs away with him. She leaves us the most attractive of pictures, but he himself is not as sharp as the outlines of his story. This is chiefly because she tells his story for him. How could Miss Cather avoid

this? The story of the discovery of the ancient Indian city is not one she would be likely to trust to any other hands, and the description of the solitary Mesa, entirely her own, one feels to be not only one of the best bits of description she has done, but that any American writer has done. She had to take the words out of Outland's mouth: to have left them there would have blurred the Mesa.

Here, as in all her work, is a fine ringing clarity, a serene breadth and sureness, a slow solid sanity. She is one of the sanest of our writers, in a good sense. She does not strain, or hurry, or attempt anything which cannot clearly be carried out, and one feels constantly the steadiness of her own eye as she looks across the broad land of her work. But does one want her to be always so sane, so conscious? What do these solid things, these believable people, these confident words need? Surely a dash of something, a suspicion of madness, the small seed of irresponsibility, a sense that she may allow her creatures to run away with her a little now and then.

Fanny Butcher, "Willa Cather's Novel Wins Highest Praise," *Chicago Tribune*, 19 September 1925, p. 9

Twice I have read *The Professor's House*, by Willa Cather—once early in the summer in proof sheets and again just now to make sure that the impression it gave me at the first reading was a permanent one. The second reading has convinced me that I am not wrong in thinking it to be made with no pattern, and yet, that the complete achievement of it is of the noblest and truest pattern.

There has much been written about Willa Cather and her place in American literature. To many of us she is the most important woman writer in our country today. She has a genius for doing the almost perfect thing with the casual beauty of a quivering treetop against a city sky. There is nothing obvious about her writing. It has not the grandeurs of the spots thick with tourists. There is a subtle and unexpected reality about it. There is not one of us so blind to loveliness that he has not seen a flash of blue-black sky behind a city apartment building, and trembling against it a timid treetop touching a star that flutters through its branches. We see it every evening if our eyes are eyes at all.

That common loveliness is the quality which makes Willa Cather a writer who will not be forgotton. There is nothing oversentimental about her work, nothing forced. Everything is perfectly and beautifully, inevitably natural and ordinary. But it attains a high nobility. It is a quality of the spirit of literature rather than the flesh. It is mixed up with the soul of writing in a true sense, rather than with the fact of novel making. It is as it is because there is such a thing as nobility in art besides mere technique.

To me *My Ántonia* is one of the greatest books ever written by an American, and certainly the greatest written by an American woman for some time. Its greatness is easily understandable to the average reader, for it depicts character of the utmost beauty and simplicity. The greatness of *The Professor's House* is not so easily understandable. It is not—I believe—as fine a book as *My Ántonia*, but it is, in one way, a greater piece of work, for it is not an easily accepted story.

It is about a dead boy and the effect which his youth and exuberance and decency and brilliance had upon a group of middle western college people. It is not in any sense a tragedy—for the boy found his dream and was perfectly happy, and it is not in any sense a depressing book, and until you have finished it you do not realize that it is really the story of the boy all of the time, and not, as it seems on the surface, the story of the college professor who found in the boy a rejuvenating happiness of helpfulness. But of that strange, orphaned genius and his ideals is the story made. He invented a gas which brought a fortune to the professor's daughter, who had been the boy's fiancée, and the story of the corroding quality of wealth on the professor's daughter is merely a part of the simple but beautiful pattern of the book. It is in much the same sense that *My Ántonia* was a study of character, a map of a really fine nature, and of its effect upon other really fine and not so fine natures, but it is a much subtler relationship than that in *My Ántonia*, for it is an influence felt much more strongly after the death of the boy than during his life.

When I read the book the first time I felt a certain abruptness about the way in which Miss Cather told the story of the boy and his years among them. When I read it a second time, that abruptness seemed merely the utmost simplification of the narrative.

The Professor's House is certainly as important a novel as has yet been published this fall, or as probably will be published, and it certainly is a grippingly real one.

Miss Cather has written of the diary of Tom Outland in *The Professor's House* a paragraph of criticism which I envy her, for it is exactly what I would like to say about her writing if I had her gift of words. She says of the diary: "This plain account was almost beautiful, because of the stupidities it avoided and the things it did not say. If words had cost money Tom couldn't have used them more sparingly. The adjectives were purely descriptive, relating to form and color, and were used to present the objects under consideration, not the young explorer's emotion. Yet through this austerity one felt the kindling imagination, the ardor and excitement of the boy, like the vibration in a voice when the speaker strives to conceal his emotion by using only conventional phrases." Such words no critic could rival.

Joseph Wood Krutch, "Second Best," *Nation*, 121 (23 September 1925), 336

There is nothing which reveals more clearly the most characteristic defect of modern fiction than the fact that the theme—even the chief substance—of most contemporary novels is easily reduced to abstract intellectual terms; and there is nothing that indicates more clearly the nature of Miss Willa Cather's peculiar excellence than the fact that the intention of her works generally defies any such attempt at restatement. It is not merely that one would find it difficult to say what *My Antonía* proves, but that it would be almost equally difficult either to define the author's attitude or to describe the effect produced; and even when, as in *A Lost Lady*, there is unmistakably a theme, it remains as in solution, never crystallizing into an entity separate from the story which embodies it. The quality of the emotion aroused is perfectly distinct; toward the lady in question we have an attitude different from that inspired by any other person; but from the author we get no hint how we may analyze the subtle

guilt of her heroine or how we may formulate our charge against her.

Miss Cather begins, one is led to suspect, not with an intellectual conviction which is to be translated into characters and incidents but with an emotional reaction which she endeavors to recapture in her works; and she completes the whole creative process without ever having, herself, imperiled the fresh richness of the emotion by subjecting it to analysis. Some incident observed in life or recalled to memory appears in her imagination surrounded by an aura of feeling. It reverberates through her mind, awaking complicated echoes and making many strings vibrate with sympathetic overtones from which a haunting chord of music, soft but intricate and new, is born. As an artist her task is not to resolve this chord into its constituents nor to describe the strings from which it comes, but so to reproduce the various elements of her apperception as to transfer it bodily to the mind of her reader. She is not one of those who, knowing our stops, plays what melody she will upon them, but one whose skill consists in her ability to reconstruct a situation by which she herself has been moved.

Being essentially an intuitive artist she is at some times markedly more successful than at others, and her new novel is not among her best. Its method is characteristically hers, for though the theme is fairly distinct it never degenerates into a thesis; her story of a scholar whose faith in life fails him when he sees how fortuitous wealth destroys the spiritual integrity of his family is never made, as most contemporary writers would have made it, "an indictment of commercialism"; and, being always rather elegiac than argumentative or bitter in tone, its effects are purely artistic one. Yet in spite of many fine touches it does not live up to the promise of the earlier pages. Fragmentary and inconclusive, it starts off in several different directions but never quite arrives at any of the proposed destinations.

The initial mistake was, I think, the elaboration of the character whose story constitutes the second of the three parts into which the novel is divided. Miss Cather has wished to multiply the incidents which produce in the professor his dominant mood—the result of a conviction that while achievement is good its rewards, whether reaped by those to whom they are due or by others, are invariably evil. For this purpose she invents a young student who turns up at the university and carelessly presents the professor with some priceless Indian pottery which he had discovered in the West. Later he invents a vague but wonderful gas, rushes away to be killed in the war, and leaves it to the professor's bright son-in-law to commercialize the invention. In a fashion this young hero runs away with the story. He is glamorous, he has adventures, and he furnishes the reflection about which the whole book turns: "Fellows like Outland don't carry much luggage, yet one of the things you know them by is their sumptuous generosity—and when they are gone, all you can say of them is that they departed leaving princely gifts." Yet he has no business to dwarf as he does the professor, for he is not made one-tenth so interesting nor is he by any means so richly conceived. The professor's household was, I would be willing to wager, the observed or remembered situation with which the book started. It is the fact which appeared to the author with that aura of feeling of which I have spoken, and Outland is largely an invention. He is merely a hero, almost an abstraction; he has attributes but he has no character, and he is only very superficially convincing. Put beside Outland even the casually indicated Marcellus, the active son-in-law, and the former pales to a shadow.

In *The Professor's House* there is much that is very beautiful—passages which only Miss Cather could have written. Taken as a whole, however, the book is a disappointment to those who know how good her best work can be.

Henry Seidel Canby, "A Novel of the Soul," *Saturday Review of Literature*, 2 (26 September 1925), 151

This is the age of experiment in the American novel. No sooner had the seers of the academies decided that American life was too thin and too unsophisticated for mature fiction than a flood of novels began (and this new book is one of them) in which new methods of story telling, new angles of approach, new styles were exploited in order to catch the manifold facets of an American social history that suddenly began to seem the most important, the most auspicious, and, paradoxically, the most menacing phenomenon of the century. In ten years the American novel has become, if not deep, rich. Such an outburst of technical experiment is almost irresistible to the professional reviewer. He must take the new American watch apart to see how it works, and whether its parts are certified by experience. Yet technique is not important except when it fails, and if the new technique of *The Professor's House* creaks a little, a method is only machinery after all, and we may turn to the more interesting question of what Miss Cather has got into her book.

Miss Cather, I suspect, is wearying of broad pioneer movements and sharp contrasts between flaming emotion and commonplace environment. She is going deeper, and is prepared to defend the thesis that a new country may have old souls in it. An old soul is by no means a Main Street high brow dissatisfied with crudity. He is much too civilized to be upset by a difference of opinion over the value of culture. An old soul, as the philosophers say, is driven toward recognition. Life, for him, instead of consisting of so many successes, so many quarrels, so many events that can be ticketed for a biography, is a progress in self-realization, a series of discoveries as to what experience means for *him* when stripped of illusion and in its ultimate reality. Such a soul is most likely to fall away from his closest associates; success may be a burden, an admired wife a growing problem, children who become the hard worldlings that most of us are in our thirties, a depression rather than a comfort. Put such an old soul in a small western university, give him a charming wife who chooses the children's part, afflict him with two sons-in-law, one unctuous and one soured, and two daughters, one mean and one envious—and drama follows.

The Professor's House might readily have been written as a mirror of small town bickerings meticulously preserved in Miss Cather's cool, firm style. Professor St. Peter is too good for his job, and too civilized for his community; also he is a personality, with force, humor, distinction, charm. There have been two major experiences in his life, the writing of his great history of the Spanish adventurers, and his friendship with Tom Outland, the only first-rate mind that ever came into his classes. The history is written and has made him famous and financially independent. The boy is dead, killed in the war, but the patent he willed to his fiancée, the professor's daughter, has been exploited by the skilful Jew she married afterwards and has made the two of them rich and envied. Outland's fortunes, like Antony's, have corrupted better men, and brought pettiness to a family that was not necessarily committed to such a fate.

This is what happens on the smooth flowing surface of *The Professor's House,* but it is not the story; the story is beneath. The story is slow discovery by Professor St. Peter—of himself. His family have moved with prosperity to a new house, but he clings, hardly knowing why, to his attic in the old house, beside the dress forms where Augusta, the sewing woman used to drape the young girls' dresses. Why is he happier there than in the new house? Why does his family begin to weigh upon his nerves? Why does the memory of Tom Outland grow brighter until he sits down to write his story? It is a fourth of the novel, this story, antecedent to the main action, superficially irrelevant to it—the story of an orphan adrift in the Southwest who finds with his pal a cliff dweller's city on an unclimbed mesa, spends the best year of his life interpreting the experience of dead men, until from it he gets a perception of a life lived for ideas, a self-realization that this is how he wishes to live. Why does the professor, his work done, refuse to enjoy its fruits in travel, but rather cling to his loneliness, until, rather than face his returning family, he would, except for Augusta and the solid human nature she represents, have let the old gas stove, blown out by the wind, blow him out too?

These are the questions *The Professor's House* answers, not as a metaphysician would answer them, by analyzing the results of a self-realization which leads to new values that make the man different, but in rich and vigorous narrative. It is the difference between William James's study of religious experience and the narrative of a consignificance elsewhere always preserved. Yet I am more interested in this story than in other books of hers which are more perfectly achieved. The soul, after all, is the greatest subject for art. We have swung in our American writing from sophisticated studies of sophisticated personalities through unsophisticated romances of simple folk to satiric narratives of commonplace people who are interesting only because they are pawns in a national society. Yet the rich, subtle natures, whose problems have no relation to success or failure as our world sees it, and who are not types of social classes or particular environments, seem always to escape the novelist, although they are probably more numerous though less self-conscious in America than in older countries where conformity is not regarded as a prime virtue. Miss Cather, one of the ablest novelists now writing in English, believes, what no Englishman or no Frenchman can be convinced of, and no native novelist since Hawthorne has practised, that there is profundity in American life. A profundity not merely instinctive such as Sherwood Anderson is revealing, but a conscious spiritual profundity which poets like Robert Frost and Edwin Arlington Robinson have long seen. This, more than O *Pioneers!* is a pioneering book.

Schuyler Ashley, "Willa Cather's Professor Is a Living Character," *Kansas City Star*, 3 October 1925

Although he possessed a show study downstairs, Professor St. Peter, sensitive, handsome and thoroughly likable, preferred to compose his *magnum opus*, his "Spanish Adventures in North America," in a forlorn attic den. Like Anatole France's immortal M. Bergeret, he shared his workroom with "dress forms," spectral figures of his wife and daughters on which clothes were tried, symbols, perhaps, for Miss Cather of indomitable and ubiquitous femininity. The professor, though decorously devoted to the women of his family, found their society disquieting and far from stimulating. Primarily, they lacked any power of detachment from their own immediate interests. Recently he had acquired two sons-in-law, but, with the best will in the world, he could not find even their company exhilarating. He lived largely in the memory and inspiration of one friend, Tom Outland, a former pupil, who, had he lived, would have married his elder daughter. In a cheerful, unself-conscious fashion, Professor St. Peter was a very lonely man.

His character is indubitably the most valuable attainment of Willa Cather's new novel. To create such a man, talented, whimsical without eccentricity, and innately attractive; to make him credible and complete is a substantial accomplishment. As always, Miss Cather effects her portraiture through honest, simple craftsmanship. Her technique is all in the accepted tradition. Experiments of the moment—subjective analysis or psychological pointillism—have no place in her philosophy.

Professor St. Peter, with his vigorous masculine color and enthusiasm, is deftly centered within a revolving system of feminine selfishness. In this book Miss Cather is very hard on her own sex. There is something painfully convincing in the spectacle of Rosamond St. Peter and her florid, exuberant husband patronizing and condescending to all the little university town by reason of the wealth that her dead fiancé's invention had created. The women of St. Peter's family lacked that superfastidious sense of fitness which might have guided their conduct through situations just on the border line between manners and ethics.

Once only, when the professor had returned from Chicago after what he called "an orgy of acquisition" with Rosamond, did he give way to bitterness. After dinner his wife, "studying his dark profile, noticed that the corners of his funny eyebrows rose, as if he were amused by something.

" 'What are you thinking about, Godfrey?' she said presently. 'Just then you were smiling—quite agreeably!'

" 'I was thinking,' he answered absently, 'about Euripides; how, when he was an old man, he went and lived in a cave by the sea, and it was thought queer, at the time. It seems that houses had become insupportable to him. I wonder whether it was because he had observed women so closely all his life?' "

Now, the very essence and subtlety of Miss Cather's book lies in the fact that none of the women in St. Peter's household ever does anything that violates in deed the least of the canons of good society. Their jealousy, their spitefulness, their snobbery, are all nuances, shadows that are given depth by contrast with the generous, delicate-souled father. And, somehow, it is the very evanescence of their faults that makes them abominable.

The book closes on a note of tired resignation. But it is not only Professor St. Peter; one feels that Willa Cather, too, has grown a little weary of this household. The novel is marred somewhat by its ten-dency to wither at the conclusion. Such a fault is far from characteristic of the author; the endings of *One of Ours* and of *A Lost Lady* were marvelous bits of artistry; each book was sublimated and intensified by the last few pages.

Mention of *A Lost Lady* brings up the question of form. Probably no American fiction of recent years showed more perfection and economy of structure than that short, poignant epic of a prairie gentlewoman. In *The Professor's House* Miss Cather has discarded, quite deliberately, no doubt, this compactness and tensity of architecture. She inserts into the middle of her book a long and almost unconnected discussion, a story within a story, Tom Outland's account of his archaeological adventuring in New Mexico. It gives Miss Cather opportunity for some of her best descriptive prose, and, in tone, the incident concords finely with the rest of the book, revealing as it does the helplessness of the detached, scientific spirit before the entrenched and practical workaday world.

Nevertheless its inclusion is an experiment, and a daring one. So considerable is Miss Cather's record of accomplishment that all she does is significant. In *The Professor's House* she has revealed once more the richness and inexhaustible variety of what Henry James used to call, with the faintest intimation of distaste, "the American scene." But it would be the acme of injustice to this author to rubber stamp her novel with catch-phrases, such as "a study of the mid-western college town" or "story of the professional classes." That her creations are always individuals and never types is the epitome of Willa Cather's distinction.

James Weber Linn, "Miss Cather's New Novel," *San Francisco Examiner*, 3 October 1925, classified advertising section, p. 7

Ascribing "influences" in literature is both dangerous and unfair, unless the critic is absolutely certain of his facts, so I will not say that Miss Willa Cather, in writing her new book, *The Professor's House*, shows the influence of Miss May Sinclair.

Miss Cather's novel is certainly, however, a study in the psychology of relations, of the subtle effect of individuals on individuals. Part of it is good narrative (and of this fact Miss Cather is obviously proudly conscious), but most of it is a series of sketches of people, of family life, beginning nowhere in particular and proceeding to no conclusion.

Compared with *One of Ours* or *A Lost Lady*, the book will prove to most people, therefore, a disappointment. It will be thought to lack substance and to be at once over-conscious and unsatisfactory in organization. At least I hope it will, for that is what it proved to me.

If she is experimenting, she has surely earned the privilege of experiment. In *The Professor's House*, nevertheless, her experiment seems to me more than a trifle feeble. Her laboratory technique is as perfect as ever, but her compound is neither particularly explosive nor particularly fragrant.

The elements which constitute Professor Godfrey St. Peter (Phoebus, what a name!) are so extraordinary that they do not harmonize convincingly.

A romantic dreamer who is systematically industrious, a genius of the spirit finely competent with his hands, a beloved teacher, internationally famous for his historical research, who never gets a call to a better position—my dear Miss Cather, it really won't do!

As the farmer remarked on seeing the hippopotamus, there ain't no such animal.

To cap the climax, St. Peter is a gentleman of highly polished manners and a loving heart, who after thirty years is still on bad terms with his colleagues.

As for minor characters, is it possible Miss Cather does not see that Rosamond is a conscienceless snob, that Louie Marcellus is a smeary bore, that Scott and Kathleen and Augusta the sewing woman are all out of drawing, and that Mrs. St. Peter is a phantom-like product of a phantom misalliance between Henry James and Laura Jean Libbey?

But you may say that this is really the story of Tom Outland; that the professor and his family, whose affairs occupy much more than two-thirds of the 283 pages, are only accessory to Tom.

Accepting this view, though it is at best a lover's excuse, one has still to admit that Tom is as fantastic, as unreal, as the professor himself.

No shots ring out from the hillside in his story, but aside from this detail he is a spinster school teacher's dream of a Zane Grey cowboy.

Tom, from the moment of his rescue of Rodney Blake from the poker game to the moment of incredible callous carelessness by which, by his will, he excludes Professor Crane from all share in the profits of the gas which Tom discovered and which turned out to be so profitable after Tom's death, Tom is, in one word, preposterous.

Yes, the characters are absurd. Yet the book is not. It has, as I say, technique; and granting the Outland premise, the story of the mess is good narrative.

I feel, nevertheless, after perusing *The Professor's House*, rather as if I had come across a copy of Mackenzie's *Man of Feeling*, brought up to date, with a nickel novel bound in.

"Empty House: Miss Cather's Clear Native Metaphor for Middle-Age," *Time*, 6 (12 October 1925), 18

... The significance of any new work of Miss Cather's is that it is likely to be a permanent addition to the national library. She is one of the major artists of our time, austere, subtle, yet warmblooded. A great lover of shapes and surfaces, she permits herself to handle only a few significant ones and those thoughtfully, accurately. A facile psychologist, she ferrets out the secrets of human action in near-at-home areas of the spiritual plane rather than in those physiological resorts whose vogue seems to increase with their distance from normal life. *The Professor's House* has been declared "unsubstantial" beside *One of Ours* and *A Lost Lady*. Perhaps, but as a metaphor for that imperceptible reversal of adolescence that comes over all men, which they call middle-age and which is tragic or not, according as their lives have been spent with or without spirit, it is crystal clear, thoroughly native, unforgettable.

H[enry] L[ouis] Mencken, "Fiction Good and Bad," *American Mercury*, 6 (November 1925), 379–81

Miss Cather, in *The Professor's House*, shows all the qualities that one has learned to expect of her. Her observation is sharp and exact; she is alert to the tragedy of every-day life; she sees her people, not in vacuums, but against a definite background; above all, she writes in clear, glowing and charming English. I know of no other American novelist, indeed, whose writing is so certain of its effects, and yet so free from artifice. She avoids both the elaborate preciosities of Cabell and Hergesheimer and the harsh uncouthness of Dreiser and Anderson. She has, obviously, a good ear, and apprehends the world as symphony more than as spectacle. Her defect is a somewhat uncertain grasp of form; her stories often seem to run away with her. It is apparent even in *My Antonía*; in *The Professor's House* it comes dangerously near being fatal. Tom Outland's story, 75 pages long, almost breaks the back of the story of Professor St. Peter. It is, in itself, a story of singular power, and it is essential to what goes before it and yet more essential to what follows after; nevertheless, the feeling persists that throwing it in so boldly and baldly is bad workmanship —that the business might have been managed with far more nicety. One submits to the shock only because the book as a whole is so beautifully written—because the surface is so fine and velvety in texture that one half forgets the ungraceful structure beneath.

In brief, *The Professor's House* is a study of the effects of a purple episode upon a dull life—perhaps more accurately, of the effects of a purple episode upon a life that is dull only superficially, with purple glows of its own deep down. Professor St. Peter is a teacher of history, and spends half his life at work upon one monumental monograph. His subject is the early Spanish adventurers; he writes about them in the attic room of a colorless house in an inland college town, with the neighborhood seamstress for company. Into his quiet circle there pops suddenly a romantic youth from the very land of the ancient conquistadors—a fellow curious and mysterious, half hind and half genius. A few years, and he is gone again. But not from the professor's memory—not from his heart. Tom Outland lives on there, though his bones lie somewhere in France. (Once more, alas, Miss Cather hears the bugles of 1917!) ... Not, perhaps, much of a story. Rather obvious. But how skillfully written! How excellent in its details! What an ingratiating piece of work!

Herschell Brickell, "An Armful of Fiction," *Bookman* (New York) 62 (November 1925), 339

Willa Cather's *The Professor's House* will trouble some readers—it has already severely troubled some critics—because its meaning is not so unmistakable as the dénouement of a detective story, where everything is nicely and tidily explained. Like life, it has its overtones, its shadowy outlines, its symbolism, from which one may get much or little.

It *is* like life, this book. That is its outstanding quality, a quality arising from the wholly admirable character drawing, although "drawing" is hardly the word to be applied to people done so in the round; live people. The Professor is an unforgetable figure. Tom Outland, dead in France long before the story begins, and still playing a part secondary, if that, to the Professor's own, is equally well known to us. The Professor's handsome wife, and his daughters and their husbands, are presented with telling deftness and success.

Miss Cather has done a bold thing in breaking off the story of the Professor and his House to tell of Tom Outland's explorations on a New Mexican mesa. The interpolated story has a direct and vital symbolic bearing upon her theme, but there is a change of style and method that may trouble hasty readers. Her experiment succeeds; Tom Outland's story is not only hauntingly beautiful for itself but invaluable, as well, for the light it throws upon the Professor's problems.

It is difficult to put into a few words what Miss Cather means to say in this fine book, even if one were able to accomplish it, and it is fairer, perhaps, to leave the reader to work out his own theories. But it is easy to say that here again we have a translucent style, splendid character presentation, and deeply thoughtful criticism of life, embodied in the work of a novelist who has added several first rate books to American literature, but none more provocative and more genuinely interesting than this.

James L. Ford, "Willa Cather Visits the Cliff-Dwellers," *Literary Digest International Book Review*, 3 (November 1925), 775

From the moment when I first read "The Story of Paul," [sic] I have been interested in the writings of Miss Willa Cather, and that interest was materially increased a year or two later when I came upon "The Sculptor's Funeral," to my mind the best of her short stories. More than that, it is one of the very best short stories that America of the present century has given to the world. Since then I have read Miss Cather's novels, one or two of which, *My Antonia* and *A Lost Lady*, have pleased me greatly, not merely because of their intrinsic worth as fiction but also because it tickled my vanity to find that my early belief in her talent was fully confirmed.

While I regard Miss Cather's new novel, *The Professor's House*, as by far the best work of literature—I use the term advisedly—that has yet come from her pen, I find it lacking in so many of the ear-marks by which publishers are prone to note bestselling possibilities, that I hesitate to describe it for fear of killing the department-store sale. Here are some of those earmarks: I finished the book with the feeling that the author had not given full value for the money, so many were the things that should have been said, so much remained to be elucidated. It was as if I had turned away from the circus ticket-wagon to discover that I had been short-changed by the expert artist in that line. In other words, I was still hungry for more when I reached the final page, and a genuine best seller of the highest type seldom leaves me in that frame of mind.

I am still wondering how a novel devoid of that publishers' delight, love interest, ever ran the gauntlet of professional readers. I read on from chapter to chapter, confidently awaiting the appearance of the two young lovers, and expecting to follow them along the course that never does run smooth, up to the moment when "and so, under the silent trees with the moonlight touching the leaves with silver splendor, the old story, ever old yet ever new, was breathed to ears that listened while the stars glimmered in the skies above." But the lovers never appeared, for the principal characters had been married and settled before the novel began, and their love, so far as I could learn, had become rather luke-warm. But, altho there is not love interest in Miss Cather's pages, it grows warm in the hearts of her readers as they gradually comprehend the character of the Professor and are touched by the loneliness of his life, filled as it is with yearnings never satisfied. Such to me was the pathos of the man, that I was glad to find the book devoid of the usual happy ending.

In her method of construction we are reminded of "The Sculptor's Funeral," to which interest is imparted by what the sculptor did before his death. In *The Professor's House* the dominant character is a young man long since dead but to whom we owe the most interesting passages in the book. We learn that this young man of unknown antecedents had appeared in the Professor's garden many years previous to the beginning of the story, had become a student in the college, and had developed a valuable invention, which he bequeathed by will to the Professor's daughter, to whom he had become engaged; then he had gone to the war and been killed. But little was known of his previous history by his new friends, and not until we have read two-thirds of the novel does the Professor tell the story as he heard it from his pupil's lips. When I read that story I felt as a prospector might feel on coming upon a very rich vein of the precious metal.

The young man's narrative deals with his adventures in the Southwest in the employ of a railroad, and later as a cattle herder, and it was then that he and his companion, going forth on an exploring expedition among the canyons, came upon the remnants of an ancient civilization and saw the homes of the cliff-dwellers hanging like swallows' nests from the faces of the tall cliffs. The description of these dwellings and of what remained in them after hundreds of years is so interesting that one forgets for a time the Professor, his wife, his married daughters, his sons-in-law and the fortune acquired from the dead man's invention. The author has evidently made a close study of the region she describes, and of as much of its history as has been obtained by scientific investigation. Never have I read such a thrilling account of a dead-and-gone civilization as I find in her pages. Of course, one might say that it has nothing to do with the Professor's House—that it is not a part of the story—but in this case one would be wrong, for it is in reality the story, the one that will remain indelibly graven on the memory after the volume is finished.

I may add that altho the scene of the story is laid in the Mid-West, it is not of the prairie-sod school: nor does caked mud cling to the boots of the characters. It deals with the people of a college town in Michigan, where the air is cooled by the breeze that sweeps in through the forest from the great lake. As a scholarly contribution to literature *The Professor's House* is by far the best of Miss Cather's novels, nor do I recall any other recent novel of American life that equals it in interest, purpose and philosophy.

Open Shelf (Cleveland), November 1925, p. 107

A character study of Godfrey St. Peter, professor of history in a state university near Lake Michigan, the title referring to his inability, when the family moved to a beautiful new house, to detach himself from the inconvenient old study which he had shared with Augusta, the family sewing woman, and where he had accomplished his life work, a history in eight volumes of the Spanish adventurers in America. The tragedy of the story is St. Peter's discovery that he does not wish to follow the family expansion into modern luxurious habits and standards. In spirit he belongs to another generation and can not walk in the ways or think the thoughts of the new. The old study and the old house are merely the symbol of all for which his spirit feels a nostalgia depriving life of its meaning. The study is richly wrought but impresses the reader as a fragment of some larger work.

"New Novels," *Times Literary Supplement* (London), 19 November 1925, p. 770

"I haven't the pleasure of knowing Anatole France," said Professor St. Peter, of Hamilton, Kansas, [sic] when his son-in-law was inquiring about his friends in

Paris; but he had a certain affinity with M. Bergeret none the less. Miss Willa Cather, in *The Professor's House*, has quite consciously, and with reference to the original story, reproduced for her Professor the very conditions under which M. Bergeret used to work. True, the workroom in Kansas is a corner under the roof and M. Bergeret was forced to make the best he could of a cupboard under the stairs; but the inconveniences are the same, and, in place of the Wickerwork Woman, St. Peter had both a headless armless female torso covered with black cotton, and "a full-length figure in a smart wire skirt with a trim metal waistline . . . its bosom resembled a strong wire bird-cage." The American professor, in fact, occupied the sewing-room, sharing it with Augusta the plain and level-headed sewing-woman, with whom he had many jokes about his "ladies." When he made money and built a fine new house across the way for his wife, and even Augusta moved her belongings away, he refused to be parted from his ladies and bade her go out and buy herself some new ones. The entire house was dismantled save his room beneath the eaves, and there he continued to work and to spend as much time as he dared.

Godfrey St. Peter—his name a translation of the French-Canadian one borne by his grandfather—mounting towards the sixties, his daughters married, his wife no longer of any great consequence to him, his reputation made by his eight volumes on the "Spanish Adventurers," his scholar's pride satisfied because he has had one pupil who has made a great name for himself, is a simple and very appealing figure. The book is as a whole unsatisfactory; there are far too many loose ends; but as the presentation of a quiet group of university people, with their secret ambitions and weaknesses laid bare, it is admirably alive. The interpo-

lated story of Tom Outland's discovery of a stone city in the wilderness, the home of an extinct Indian nation of evidently superior attainments, is vivid and interesting, although it is thrust rather awkwardly into the body of the book. It has its value, of course, in illuminating the Professor's mind and explaining the apathetic condition into which he fell, with nearly fatal results; but it might have been managed more artfully. The book is so interesting and so fresh in its way that one resents a suggestion of haste in the workmanship. Like M. Bergeret, the American Professor wants acutely, in the end, never to see his wife again, although he has no good or even definite reason for his feeling that to live under the same roof with her will be unendurable. There is no M. Roux. Lillian has grown younger and gayer with prosperity, but she is a faithful wife. Unsatisfactory and provocative is Miss Cather's conclusion of the whole matter; she leaves the Professor where we found him, in the sewing-room, talking to the sensible Augusta, in the shadow of his two wire ladies.

Ethel Wallace Hawkins, "The Atlantic's Bookshelf," *Atlantic Monthly*, 136 (December 1925), n.p.

The *Professor's House* is a thoughtful and penetrating study of a middle-aged idealist's inner rebellion before he lays down aspiration and takes up fortitude instead. The Professor, Godfrey St. Peter,—lover of beauty, sensitive, high-minded, wholly unworldly, though no fool,—finds his life in a sort of backwater. The three women who form his family are more or less pre-occupied, in their different ways, with the material things that to him mean so little. To none of the three is he spiritually necessary. His wife is less interested in him than in the rejuvenating flattery of her delicately flirtatious relations with her admiring sons-in-law. His older daughter, never wholly sympathetic, is complacently absorbed in her husband, the young Jew, Louie Marsellus, and in her rather greedy enjoyment of the fortune left to her by her former fiancé, Tom Outland. And his younger daughter, once his darling and close ally, seldom turns to him except to pour out, now and then, her ugly envy of her sister's greater prosperity. Not only in his personal relations, but in his work, is the Professor in a backwater. He has taught for many years, indifferent to advancement, but always with the humble and eager hope of being helpful to the occasional student willing and able to receive what he has to give. Such students, however, have not been numerous. The last volumes of his Spanish Adventurers, the thrilling work of fifteen years, have been published, and the creative impulse seems dead. And young Tom Outland is dead—his ideal pupil, his closest friend, for all the difference in their ages, and his strongest stimulus. In short, the Professor's "golden years" are over.

To a reader inclined to carp, it may seem a little arbitrary that the incident which arms the Professor with a new philosophy and restores his grip upon life should have precisely that effect; but of the reality with which he and his household are presented there is no question. Louie Marsellus, the kind-hearted and florid young Jew, is drawn with particular skill and with a grave, implicit humor. In Miss Cather's work one does not look for humor as a major element: nor does *The Professor's House* take one by surprise

in this respect. It is suggested that the Professor himself is endowed with humor, but this is hardly demonstrated; his jocose passages with Augusta the sewing-woman, notably, are not altogether light-footed.

If one were a draughtsman it would be an interesting and an active exercise to make a design which should depict the very curious course of the narrative. Surely many filaments representing unfinished trails must go spraying off at the edges. And surely at the heart of the design must stand the crystalline chapters called "Tom Outland's Story," the story of the little city of stone, asleep on the blue mesa—symbol of an ideal beauty not to be realized.

Milton Waldman, *London Mercury*, 13 (December 1925), 211–12

Miss Cather's new book must be considered as the study of a man passing through the critical interval between middle and old age, else it is difficult to discover its *raison d'être*. It is the story of Professor St. Peter, a gentleman and a scholar, during a short period in his middle fifties; he begins as a family man, secure in his affectionate relations with his wife and daughters, ripe in intellectual powers and attainments, and passes through a spiritual crisis, which leaves him sapped and worn, but reconciled:

> ...He had never learned to live without delight. And he would have to learn to, just as, in a Prohibition

country, he supposed he would have to learn to live without sherry. Theoretically he knew that life is possible, may even be pleasant, without joy, without passionate griefs. But it had never occurred to him that he might have to live like that.

This crisis, which supplies the climax to the book, is precipitated by several factors, but none of them, nor even all of them together, are sufficient in themselves unless we assume that the principal factor working in the Professor is that of Time's chemistry. That granted all is clear, notably the repeated yearning for the scenes of his childhood and his distaste for the love, work and honours of his adult life.

Nevertheless the book remains slight, or, rather, its various parts and phases are slenderly linked. The first *motif* is the reluctance of the Professor to move from his old and uncomfortable house to the lavish new one, a perfectly comprehensible emotion in itself; then his relations with his family, his wife, his daughters, his sons-in-law. And, most important of all in the attention the author devotes to it, the posthumous influence of a beloved former pupil, who had enriched the eldest daughter, his fiancée, by his bequest of a lucrative patent, and the Professor himself by the dearest friendship of his life. The whole part played by this pupil, Tom Outland, in the book is curious; at one time it breaks off altogether to become exclusively the narrative of Outland's archæological investigations in the southwest. This shifting of interest will bear only the one explanation, namely, that Miss Cather desired to reveal the Professor's mind as it swept over the wide panorama of his past before turning to make the last great descent which concludes the travels of every man on this earth. And considered this way, she evokes in her readers moods of perfect sympathy for the cultured, detached, delicately-minded man as he reflects upon the joys and sorrows of his full, well-employed life. No modern writer save Anatole France could have treated this mood of retrospection better nor more tenderly.

But Miss Cather, despite her rare talents and fine perceptions, has disappointingly allowed herself to fall in line with a tendency only too familiar in present-day American writers—to play the schoolmistress. There are already too many folk with not a tithe of her gifts ready and willing to teach their compatriots good taste, right codes of decency, proper manners or morals. Having made the Professor what he is, Miss Cather might have assumed that her readers would sympathise with his distaste of his exuberant son-in-law's exploitation of the memory of his wife's dead lover. But no, she must pause and insist by reiteration, from one side and another, how bad is Marsellus's taste so to act; and not in this case alone, but in others, she is not satisfied to let the man's acts speak for themselves and paint him, but she must rub it in that he is a vulgar creature, even if of good heart. At one time I literally thought that the authoress meant to give me a lecture on the proper instruments to use for eating. Miss Cather is far too good an artist, too important a figure in English letters, to let herself follow Mrs. Wharton in some of the less inspired tendencies of the latter's New England conscience.

Walter Millis, "Letters and Life," *Survey*, 55 (1 December 1925), 310–12

There are times when one wonders whether the complicated introspections of our present-day novelists can have any significance for the practical problems of society at all. Those comfortably objective days when one could follow Mr. Dickens in an attack upon the Courts of Chancery, drift with Mr. Hardy into the complete but conceivably remediable tragedy of the double standard, discover with Mr. Galsworthy the existence of the class struggle or even learn from Mr. Tarkington that the industrial age is an economic turmoil, seem very far away from this newer fictional world whose tragedies are chiefly characterized by the fact that there is never under any circumstances anything to be done about them. One wanders in vain through the fall book lists to find a point of approach. Willa Cather, it is true, can be detected in a half-hearted and parenthetical assault upon the Smithsonian Institute; but as a rule our institutions, even the institution of marriage as such, have ceased to interest. Under the most objective of methods, like that for example of Louis Bromfield's *Possession*, the conflict remains wholly an inward one; the adversary is not in the controllable facts of society but in what Edgar Saltus liked to call "the immedicable misery" of life itself. These books seem mainly to express that ultimate futility of any human organization to which the only answer appears to be an inactive fatalism. The novelists have no longer any concern with the weighted averages of prosperity or the incidence of the divorce rate. These things no longer matter.

Konrad Bercovici's *The Marriage Guest* is an essay in economic change; but as has been pointed out, it is not really economics, it is merely humanity struggling with its own limitations. And there is no moral—only a very gentle irony of fate....In America everything is possible—and nothing makes so very much sense.

That is perhaps why *The Professor's House* by Willa Cather is as satisfactory a summary as any of what appears to be the novelists' attitude. The point of the book lies in the fact that she leaves it perfectly pointless. Miss Cather assembles a vigorously interesting family out of the cultivated American middle class; they wander casually and fragmentarily through her pages; she pauses to comment upon the unsatisfactory nature of bureaucracy or to overhear her professor's critique of the force which Tom Outland's upsetting heritage symbolizes: "No, I don't think much of science as a phase of human development . . . I don't think you help people by making their conduct of no importance," but in the end nothing happens. Unless a truer statement is that in the end everything has happened. These are all very vivid human beings, involved in all of humanity's minor doubts and difficulties, but there are no heroes or heroines, no particular beginnings and no conclusions. Miss Cather is not interested in their passions but simply in their lives; and about life she finds it possible to say only that one lives it, and that when it is over it is over.

Both Mr. Van Vechten's [in *Firecrackers*] and Mr. Bromfield's characters [in *Possession*] consciously withdraw themselves from the claims of human relationships; Miss Cather's Professor on the other hand has accepted them all, he has given himself to his family, his friend, his work, his obligations, but at last he, like the others, is quite alone. For a time that discovery leaves him with a sense of helplessness, but then he looks back to see wherein he had made his mistake. The answer is that "he had never learned to live without delight. And he would have to learn to just as, in a prohibition country, he supposed he would have to learn to live without sherry." Miss Cather has the materials for a clash of civilizations, the forgotten Pueblo on the Mesa, the Spanish adventurers, the college town on the lake, and the impinging commercialization of science—but she leaves them at loose ends, like the lives of her characters.

Life in the Eighteenth Century novel was broadly an adventure; life in the Nineteenth Century novel seems very often to have been a public meeting. But one cannot go through these books without feeling that life with our contemporary observers has become a private, and generally unsuccessful, effort to escape. The authors are not engaging existence; they are rather in full flight from it. There are no longer problems to be solved; there are merely facts to be accepted or avoided. The escape may be into one's self, into ambition, into external beauty, into passion, or even (rarely) into rectitude, but it never quite succeeds. Miss Cather is willing to call it square and let things go at that. The kind of harmony at which she arrives may be the only possible one, it may even be a desirable one, but it has nothing to do with social dynamics. Objective preoccupations with the attainment of the good life are illusory—there is no great external misery or wrong or injustice that can command human enthusiasms, but neither is there in the end any way of overcoming the deficiencies of things as they are. If we are to take the word of the novelists, in all classes and sections of the community the fault, the real fault, is in ourselves—and

the sociologists can make what they can out of it.

Laura Benet, *Commonweal*, 3 (2 December 1925), 108–9

This book is a singularly constructed building. The reader must walk through many rooms to arrive at its lighted portion—the fantastic story of Tom Outland in the midst of commonplace chapters. Even the personality of the professor, drawn so keenly and delightfully in those first pages, cannot outweigh the conventional figures of his wife, daughters, and sons-in-law, who, like the furniture of his new house, are always on hand, modern in style and beautifully decorated. They appear and reappear with military precision until the risen ghost of Outland scatters them as papers are scattered before a fresh wind. They are fairly convincing; in Louis Marsellus there is even a trace of wistful eagerness. But they are as puppets beside that adventurous memory, symbolizing the pioneer America that civilization has strangled.

The professor who has become part and parcel of his ancient and uncomfortable study is, with Augusta, the sewing woman, the only other significantly human element. The romance that smouldered in his histories was kindled to living fire by the coming of a pupil who swept like a tropical rainbow across his narrow horizon. Tom Outland is nobody's son, a young cowpuncher who witnessed and adsorbed a tremendous experience. The story of the discovery of the remote mesa and the cliff city is as pure gold unrefined—"On that morning through a veil of lightly fallen snow . . . far up above me a thousand feet or so, set in a great cavern in the face of the cliff, I saw a little city of stone asleep . . . The tower was the fine thing that held all the jumble of houses together. It was red in color, even on that grey day. In sunlight it was the color of winter oak leaves."

Other parts of the book retreat before this picture. The hero of such an atmosphere could never have been the author of a great invention, the bequeathing of which makes his friends' fortune. It is too plausible. Even his shoulders are not broad enough for the load. Death for him in the war is natural—but not commercialization. In *My Antonia*, the heroine accomplishes her destiny in a setting which fits her. The disposal of Outland is false, especially in the pathetic, forgotten shadow of Doctor Crane.

As the story sweeps on, we realize Tom Outland's spiritual companionship is at one with the professor's forgotten self. Here is a man of middle age, the years of his prime behind him; his significant work accomplished; his disillusionment, as regards his family, complete. Memory holds him in a fastness. Next in beauty to the translucent image of the city, cut in the rock's face to challenge sun, wind and eternity, is the poignant description of the professor's dreaming. We pity him as we pity our own lost selves striving to return to us as old and valued friends—"The boy who had come back to St. Peter this summer was not a scholar. He was a primitive. He was not nearly so cultivated as the old cliff-dwellers must have been—and yet he was terribly wise . . . He seemed to know among other things that he was solitary and must always be so; he had never married, never been a father. He was earth and would return to earth."

Never even in the fine edged portrait of *A Lost Lady* has Miss Cather more profoundly sounded the depths of a lonely soul receiving the last kaleidescopic flash of its youthful ego as the curtain of life falls away from it.

The Professor's House is in parts, though not as a whole, a step forward in her art. It holds an element that is unexpectedly illuminating. The story could have been better told, the material more artistically arranged. But without the long draught of Lillian, Louie, Rosamond and the others, would we so keenly appreciate Augusta, earthbound, faithful to the end, the professor, eternal romanticist, and behind them, tall and lonely, a boy of twenty with a handful of unset turquoises?

Lloyd Morris, "Skimming the Cream of Six Month's Fiction," *New York Times Book Review*, 6 December 1925, p. 2

Miss Cather's *The Professor's House* is decidedly inferior to the best of her previous work, and, although it contains much that is excellently accomplished, it is defective in structure, inadequate in design and uncertain in effect. It is a significant book because it marks Miss Cather's first important attempt to portray an America that in civilization and culture has advanced beyond the status of a pioneer development. But, as a work of art, it is unsatisfying; it raises problems that remain unfulfilled, and it ignores both the implications and the significance of its central subject.

Edwin Muir, *Nation and Athenaeum* (London), 38 (19 December 1925), 440

P. C. Kennedy, *New Statesman*, 26 (19 December 1925), 306

. . . *The Professor's House* is not quite in the first class; it is not inevitably excellent; but it approximates continuously to excellence, and the thought, method, and style are such as to keep us, while reading, safely above the cheap and the fashionable, and to make us admire or disagree on intelligent and reasonable grounds. If less perfect in form than *A Lost Lady*, *The Professor's House* is both more intimate and less sentimental. As its title suggests, it is a study of an interior, for though we are shown the professor going about his work outside, in the university town and in Chicago, we always see him as if we were looking out through the windows of his house. Within everything is vivid, without everything is a little remote. The effect is admirably secured, and it has sometimes an intimate and purely feminine beauty. The defect of the book, as of *A Lost Lady*, is a certain coldness of characterization. Miss Cather is never quite intimate with her characters. She regards them seriously, but too rationally and too little passionately. Her insistence on verisimilitude sometimes actually comes between us and them; for verisimilitude would only be so absolute as she makes it if the human race were purely rational, and not, as they are, rational and irrational. Professor St. Peter is beautifully observed, and we admit him; but, after all, we wish to know him better. What Miss Cather does do, however, she does excellently; there is not a cheap or a careless line in the book. The style deserves all the praise it has been given.

After reviewing Michael Arlen's *Jericho Sands*, it is a relief to turn to such an entirely unpretentious book as *The Professor's House*. Miss Cather writes from the pure impulse of imagination. Her people are not in themselves exceptionally interesting, but they are of interest, of enthralling interest, because they *are* people; the most interesting fact about them is that they are not exceptional. There is the professor, a human being, which is more than one expects of a professor in fiction: he has a wife: they are middle-aged and reminiscent, and between them lies the faint hostility of habit. Then there are the two daughters, and their husbands, one a rich business man, one a journalist. And there is one overshadowing character, dead before the story begins, who was engaged to the elder daughter, and whose invention, bequeathed to that daughter, has given her husband the means of becoming rich. The story is told with an odd episodic brusqueness; we are switched suddenly, two-thirds of the way through, back to the early life of the dead inventor. There is no formal shape to the whole; and yet it has the very accent of truth. It would be difficult to convey, without seeming to exaggerate, the case and precision with which fine inexplicable shades of mood and emotion are rendered.

Carl Van Doren, "Desire Under All Desires," *Century Magazine*, 111 (January 1926), 379–81

"It is a question," I wrote about Willa Cather four or five years ago, "whether she can ever reach the highest point of which she shows signs of being capable unless she makes up her mind that it is as important to find the precise form for the representation of a memorable character as it is to find the precise word for the expression of a memorable idea. At present she pleads that if she must sacrifice something she would rather it were form than reality. If she desires sufficiently she can have both." Since that time she has published three novels which have greatly increased her eminence, but I still think that the moving reality of her work is hardly matched by the form she gives it. I no longer think, however, that she has as much choice in the matter as I formerly thought she had. It begins to look as if her imagination were not the sort which can always foresee or control the shape its materials are to take. And it is a somewhat striking fact, which I have never seen noted, that she is at her best in this regard only in every other novel. After *O Pioneers!* she relaxed a little in *The Song of the Lark*; after *My Antonia*, in *One of Ours*. Now again, in *The Professor's House*, she seems to me to have fallen off from the masterly order and structure of *A Lost Lady*. Between peaks, her imagination draws breath.

Miss Cather comes at so many points so near perfection that she invites a strict scrutiny to which more rough-and-ready novelists neither need nor deserve to be subjected. *The Professor's House* particularly invites such scrutiny because it is built on a scheme more complicated than any of her earlier novels. Each of those is in a sense a biography, delicately, austerely following the fortunes of a single character through a long curve of growth. This latest novel is essentially a situation. A net of circumstances, already growing, closes in around Professor St. Peter. Though his whole past is involved, and indeed is subtly indicated, the story deals with the moment in which he becomes aware of his plight. Not if the outcome were an actual surprise, of the type which ends comedies, could it have been kept more deftly out of sight nor could it have thrown more light upon all related events than it does here. The entire action lies within the spirit, but it is as positive as any train of swift adventures.

I suspect that the germ of *The Professor's House* came to Miss Cather from some momentary confession, some chance-dropped word, of some man who told her, whether he meant to or not, of the bleak hours through which all men pass when they first realize that youth is irrevocably gone, that the sense of being inseparably involved with other human beings is delusion, that they must henceforth endure the unavoidable loneliness which gradually prepares them for the one experience more lonely than birth. Perhaps the germ lodged in her imagination as a statement; perhaps it lodged there as an observation in flesh and blood. In any case, she was moved to exhibit it on a scale which would do justice to a mood so general. Around Professor St. Peter she created a family, friends, a university, a continent, a world, in order that his discovery of his isolation in the midst of them might have the fullest emphasis. To give it a dramatic touch which would sharpen the narrative, she brought in Tom Outland, picture and essence of youth, to furnish the needed contrast. Having left a fortune to one of St. Peter's daughters, Outland drops seeds of confusion in the professor's house. Envy springs up between the two sisters. The daughter is thrust further from the father, the wife from the husband. That friendship which has been the most charming thing in all St. Peter's life as a teacher is the thing which precipitates the situation. Yet the precipitation is but an outward matter. The gist of the theme is inward. Sooner or later, St. Peter must have reached his troubling conviction.

Now that the story has been told, it is easy to analyze its meanings and implications. Miss Cather, however, is better at representation than at analysis. She chose to tell her story in a way which is at once the most natural for the reader and the most difficult for the writer. When I, for example, began to read the book, I felt at first that it was thin. I did not see just what the situation was, nor did I get hold of the characters as rapidly as, from my previous acquaintance with Miss Cather's books, I expected to. Indeed, I was nearly through the story before I saw whither it was tending. Then suddenly it took hold of me, as it must of every reader. Without perceiving it, I had slipped into the secret, precisely as if these characters were real persons into whose circle I had come and among whom I had lived a good while before making out the drama in which their lives were arranged. The sons-in-law of St. Peter I comprehended first; then the daughters, Kathleen and Rosamond in the order named; then Mrs. St. Peter. Outland, dead before the story begins, hovered in the background till almost the end, when the professor was editing the younger man's diary. Finally he too became clear, only the next instant to step aside and let the light of comprehension fall upon the chief personage. And in that instant all that had gone before was focused upon the situation thus revealed.

The situation might have been made clear in a more downright manner, but it could never have carried the weight of impressiveness without this increasing revelation, this casual, gradual unfolding of the evidence.

Such a method lays a heavy burden upon the narrator, who must at every step prepare for the solution without carelessly giving it away too soon at any point and without yielding to the temptation to put in details which do not contribute to the whole. Miss Cather in *The Professor's House* does not seem to me ever to be premature, but I think she occasionally delays the movement by being interested in certain elements of her story for their own sakes. Looking back over the narrative, I have a feeling that she took longer to get started than was really necessary; the earlier chapters already have grown slightly dim in my memory, which I think they would not have done if they had not been diffuse. And I am sure there is too much of Tom Outland's history. It is a touching history, of a boy who found a lost cliff city in a romantic canyon, and who thereby was lifted to a long view of life by which to measure the world when he entered it. The scene, of course, is charming, and Miss Cather devotes to it some of the loveliest pages which she has written since she wrote the somewhat analogous pages in *The Song of the Lark*. But charm and loveliness Miss Cather can always command, and she could here have commanded those qualities in less space and not have let her story drag on the threshold of her dénouement. As in *One of Ours*, she has again fallen under the spell of a splendid youth, and she has let him have the center of the stage for a longer time than he earns by his services to the plot, however much he may have earned it by his undeniable intrinsic merits.

Some proof of the delay which Outland causes in the third quarter of the book may be seen in the rapid acceleration of the pace which comes the moment his history has been concluded. I then realized that I had from the first been primarily concerned with St. Peter, and that less of Outland would have explained why the professor was all of a sudden so overwhelmed with a sense of his lost youth. For though the adventure on the mesa is novel and exciting, it is not so novel or exciting as St. Peter's profound conviction that the boy he had once been still survives in the man he is now: "The boy was a primitive. . . . What [St. Peter] had not known was that, at a given time, that first nature could return to a man, unchanged by all the pursuits and passions and experiences of his life; untouched by even the tastes and intellectual activities which had been strong enough to give him distinction among his fellows and to have made for him, as they say, a name in the world. Perhaps this reversion did not often occur, but he knew it had happened to him. . . . He did not regret his life, but he was indifferent to it. It seemed to him like the life of another person."

The passage by itself is notable; in its setting it rises like a peal of bugles. Of course it would not do that unless the plot had been conceived with the beautiful lucidity which characterizes *The Professor's House*. I believe however, that it would bite even more deeply had the novel been shaped with a little more of the fierce economy which makes art perfect.

Alexander Porterfield, "Contemporary American Authors, Part V: Willa Cather," *London Mercury*, 13 (March 1926), 516–24

No figure of contemporary American literature is more interesting or more important than Miss Willa Cather. She is, in fact, that *rara avis*, an autochthonous American author. Born in Virginia and "translated" at an early impressionable age to the immense, astonishingly fecund prairie of Nebraska, where Pole and German, Slav and Czech and Anglo-Saxon with their varied and conflicting customs and traditions are being slowly merged into an indigenous whole, where "East" means Chicago and New York is as remote as New South Wales, her roots are deep in the soil. Her novels are remarkable for their exquisite economy, a charm of manner and a gift of fusing her materials into a single-minded and extraordinarily vivid narrative which derives little of its verisimilitude and beauty from the canon of an older prose. Her talent has had its nourishment and inspiration wholly in that section of the American scene which forms the subject of her novels. Unlike Mr. Sinclair Lewis, who finds the awkward age of the robust and probably too prosperous Middle West ridiculous and vulgar, Miss Cather seems to hang over her landscape with something of the tenderness of its own early summer sky. Indeed, alone among her contemporaries, she has pursued an independent path, abstaining rather from that criticism of American customs and American manners which has recently become so commonplace a characteristic of American fiction. It is possibly this fundamental difference, this sensitive and patient understanding that Miss Cather brings to her observation of the beginnings of a new civilisation, which make her more important, perhaps, and certainly more interesting than almost any other living American novelist.

For that, after all, is the American scene—that inarticulate conglomeration of a half-assimilated people moving steadily through the vicissitudes of life in the crude to a single destiny of racial culture and completeness. Not New York, not Boston or Baltimore, say, with their inherited traditions of leisure and aristocracy and learning brought over bodily from England three hundred years ago; no. The Republic which came into being on July 4, 1776, was admittedly a product of exactly those traditions, and it was the obvious intention of its gifted authors, moreover, to establish a Whig oligarchy in America without the inconvenient decoration of the Crown; but there is frequently a drawback to the very best intentions: they are apt to go astray. They went astray in this case somewhat sooner than usual, for the business geographically got out of hand at once, and, as the acquisition of territory rapidly exceeded even the most ambitious ideas of the birth-rate, the population had to be recruited from the more satisfactorily philoprogenitive races of Europe—the German, the Scandinavian, the Latin and so on. The character of the whole scheme changed, of course, immediately. Behind a narrow strip of the Atlantic sea-board the Republic took on an un-Anglo-Saxon aspect which was as vigorous as it was disconcerting, and, in that bewilderingly enormous expanse of country between the Alleghanies and the Rocky Mountains, innumerable communities sprang up and quickly prospered, which, cut off from

each other by differences in speech and vastness of distances, preserved almost intact the habits and traditions of a dozen fondly recollected European cultures. Viewing this scene, so apparently chaotic, Miss Cather has fixed for us the definite beginnings of another civilisation and brought into the focus of her exquisite, clear prose the varied differences, the confused but gradually uniting pattern and philosophy of American life.

Much of Miss Cather's best work, it is true, has been conceived in something of an atmosphere of placid reminiscence. In *My Ántonia* and *O Pioneers!* the reader finds himself in the Middle West of the United States some thirty-five to fifty years ago, when life, for all its hardships, still was leisurely, and, on the homesteads of the slowly conquered prairies, almost patriarchal. Her characters, however, have an authentic stamp of racial individuality. They reflect the reality of the present. In fact, it is possible to see in Miss Cather's novels the beginnings of a definitely American tradition evolved from a conflict of association and assimilation, as opposed to the European tradition, say, of Mrs. Wharton. Not that there is anything especially revolutionary about Miss Cather—the rules of punctuation are scrupulously observed; the manner can be best described as orthodox; in short, Miss Cather succeeds just where so many of her contemporaries fall down, and that is in the task of writing beautifully and well. The King Charles's head of psychoanalysis and experiment in *genre* does not keep continually turning up in her books as they do in those rather Mr. Dick-like compositions of Mr. Sherwood Anderson for instance. Exquisitely concise, restrained and orderly, Miss Cather has a freshness, an originality, which comes neither from imitation nor invention. She gets the sense and smell and spirit of the Middle West into her prose, and lets it go at that. As a result, her novels have compactness and proportion; they come to life, and make their points and end, each a definite accomplishment; and, like all works of art which manage to create the illusion of life, they convey the idea of mysterious and unwieldly forces operating, obscurely perhaps, somewhere underneath the surface of things which it would be impossible probably to treat in a directer manner. Miss Cather's Swedes and Germans have all the significance and symbolism which goes into the making of myths. There is something vast and contradictory about them. They represent humanity in a state of flux, a modern Babel, and it is especially this sense of contradiction and unwieldiness revolving slowly into some kind of perspective and design which gives Miss Cather's work so much of its importance and vitality. A breath of the "fresh, easy-blowing morning wind" and fragrance of the Nebraska prairie clings to her pages, but, more than that, Miss Cather has caught the stuff and spirit of a people taking root in a new soil, and made literature. Not that she has ever made the slightest effort to emphasise her local individuality by the use of peculiar words or idioms, or an aggressively conscious "Americanism." Her English is pure and simple, her cadence quietly melodious: in restraint, as sometimes in outlook and mood, she reminds us of Chekov: she is as carefully accurate as the most accurate of the French. The American quality in her is subtle and pervasive: a natural thing, not the result of a forced effort.

At first Miss Cather was distinctly influenced by Mrs. Wharton. Both *O Pioneers!* and *My Ántonia* suggest the technique of *Ethan Frome* in their hard, clear outline and concise proportions, their quality of frugal and arresting narrative. As a record of life in its more primitive aspect, divorced for the time being from those symbols and traditions by which man lives, both of these earlier novels, however, have a tendency to be pedantic. As stories, both are simple, even slight. The *dénouement* of *My Ántonia* is really a repetition of the climax in *O Pioneers!*: nevertheless a certain freshness of phrase and spontaneity of feeling is unmistakable; incidents and characters linger in the mind, infinitely brave and touching

[. . .]

My Ántonia is the better of the two books by far, and Ántonia the better character. She seems to symbolise the soul and spirit of the Middle West more clearly than Alexandra in *O Pioneers!* The story is itself symbolic but, for all its skill and beauty, its delicate perceptions, *My Ántonia* is distinguished chiefly by reason of its promise rather than its actual achievement, a promise which was fully kept in her next novel, *One of Ours*.

[. . .]

Verisimilitude and symbolism meet and intermingle, miraculously, like oil mixing perfectly with water; the beginnings of a new culture and a new tradition springing from and nourished by the soil of a new continent, the welter of conflicting tongues and ideals which is shown so sympathetically in *O Pioneers!* and *My Ántonia*, here burgeons into a clear singleness of beauty and originality which seems almost an emanation of the soil itself. The characters which people *One of Ours* have a disturbing actuality.

[. . .]

Claud himself, the central character of the story, is one of Miss Cather's most disturbing and illusive figures. Unlike his father, Claud "could ill bear disillusion." He is a dreamer, an idealist—the second generation. That his death, at the head of his men, seems for the best, that tragedy would have been living, is conclusive evidence of the extraordinary sympathy and skill with which Miss Cather draws her portraits. With Claud's mother, one feels that he is "safe, safe." And it is on that note that the story ends.

[. . .]

Miss Cather's next book is by common consent her best—a masterpiece. It is unfortunate that it is not better known in England. So far as plot goes, A Lost Lady is perhaps a little slender, but in it all Miss Cather's gifts have reached their full maturity and given it a quality of aching beauty unsurpassed in contemporary fiction, English or American. It is a story of the Middle West in the age of railway-building, of the charming wife of Captain Forrester, a retired contractor, and her hospitable and openhanded household seen through the eyes of an adoring boy. In nothing she has done before or since has Miss Cather managed to create so many striking minor personages; never has she created so adroit and accurate an atmosphere; never has she fused all her materials into so single-minded and exquisitely concise a narrative. Indeed, from the standpoint of construction, A Lost Lady is extraordinarily good. It has its beginning, its middle and its end. It is dramatic and arresting, a glamorous achievement. Through the eyes of the boy, Niel, the reader sees the Forrester house-hold—the Captain, on whom his wife depends, grow old and die; their friends and money disappear; the slow coarsen-ing of the lovely Mrs. Forrester and the life she had inspired about her crumble until she too disappears, to be heard of afterwards only by rumour. The reader watches the house-party at Sweet Water at the beginning of the story without the slightest suspicion of anything wrong till the man who has taken Mrs. Forrester out driving in a sleigh pulls off his gloves.

His eyes, sweeping the winding road and the low, snow-covered hills, had something wolfish in them.

"Be careful, Frank. My rings! You hurt me!"

"Then why don't you take them off? You always used to . . . "

And in that phrase Miss Cather fixes the attention with a dramatic skill it is impos-sible to admire or envy too completely. It is in the handling of such situations, however unpleasant, that she shows that restraint which makes her so superb an artist. Niel, for example, unable to sleep one morning, gets up early and goes out into the fields and comes upon a thicket of wild roses, just beginning to open.

"Where they had opened, their petals were stained with that burning rose-colour which is always gone by noon—a dye made of sunlight and morning and moisture, so intense that it cannot possi-bly last . . . must fade, like ecstasy. Niel took out his knife and began to cut the stiff stems, crowded with red thorns.

"He would make a bouquet for a lovely lady; a bouquet gathered off the cheeks of morning . . . these roses, only half awake, in the defencelessness of utter beauty. He would leave them just outside one of the French windows of her bedroom. When she opened her shutters to let in the light she would find them—and they would perhaps give her a sudden distaste for coarse worldlings like Frank Ellinger.

"After tying his flowers with a twist of meadow grass, he went up the hill through the grove and softly round the still house to the north side of Mrs. Forrester's own room, where the door-like green shutters were closed. As he bent to place the flowers on the sill, he heard from within a woman's soft laughter; impa-tient, indulgent, teasing, eager. Then an-other laugh, very different, a man's. And it was fat and lazy—ended in something like a yawn."

But this story, like all Miss Cather's work, is difficult to describe or quote from.

Beautifully developed to its end, it is something to read; and its haunting loveliness lingers in the mind afterwards with the delicacy of music. Miss Cather's gifts and fine perceptions, manifest in even her first novels, are here crystallised into a wholeness and harmony of narrative and feeling which has all the freshness, the vitality and understanding of her earlier work with a clear, added beauty of its own.

Good as *One of Ours* is, *A Lost Lady* is supremely better. It is supreme as a portrait, supreme as the record of inevitable incidents, one leading to the other, entirely and wholly free from blemishes of artifice and subterfuge; the culminating product of an unique and frugal talent which, indeed, borders at times closely upon genius. The characters with which Miss Cather peoples *A Lost Lady* stand out against their background in exquisite relief—the charming Mrs. Forrester herself; the Captain; Niel Herbert and his uncle, Judge Pommeroy; "Ivy" Peters with his hard, red face which "looked as if it were swollen from bee-stings, or from an encounter with poison ivy," and the unblinking hardness of his small, staring eyes; the Ogdens; and Frank Ellinger. They have the individuality of life, and if the central purpose of a novelist is the creation of characters who move and breathe, Miss Cather may be rightly considered something more than merely competent, or even gifted. Perhaps she is, actually, something much more than that. In addition to her rich, abundant sense of verisimilitude in drawing character, her sense of form and charm of style, she brings a deep and instinctive feeling for nature to the composition of her novels which has its roots and origin in the vast, rolling landscape of her Middle West. Always apparent in her work, this feeling has matured and deepened in each successive piece of writing she has done, till

in *A Lost Lady* it approaches positive wizardry, and she conveys an actual illusion of the passage of the seasons. As the reader watches Mrs. Forrester sip her port before the fire, her garnet ear-rings twinkling in the dancing light, for example, he is almost physically aware of the cold outside pressing against the window-panes, the snow and the bitter wind stalking under the black, frozen trees. Situations no less than character and descriptions are given an equally arresting beauty and reality. Slight as the whole thing is in substance, it has power and compactness, an intensity which makes the story linger in the memory afterwards with all the exquisite regret and glamour of a charming legend.

Miss Cather's next book, after this astonishingly touching and fine novel, seems almost in the nature of a descent, a disappointment. *The Professor's House* is a study in introspection, even slenderer than usual in story but conceived and treated with a tenderness and sympathy which is characteristic. It is not quite so compact in form as some of her earlier novels, with its shifting of interest in the middle and its rather uneventful climax. Briefly, it is the story of a scholarly professor at a Middle Western university passing through that critical, uneasy period between middle and old age—at least, it should be taken as a study of such, otherwise its meaning is difficult to perceive exactly. The Professor is reluctant to move into a new and more comfortable house and remains in the old room he uses to work in, despite the protestations of his wife and daughters. The reader finds him first a man in the middle fifties, a little dissatisfied and tired, if at the zenith of his intellectual powers, follows him through an emotional crisis which is hastened by several somewhat slender causes, chief of which is his relationship with his family, and leaves him at the end, worn out by his struggle but on the whole reconciled with his new attitude of mind.

He had never learned to live without delight. And he would have to learn to, just as, in a Prohibition country, he supposed he would have to learn to live without sherry. Theoretically he knew that life is possible, may even be pleasant, without joy, without passionate griefs. But it had never occurred to him that he might have to live like that.

It is this crisis which supplies the climax to the book. An important factor in its development is the connection between the Professor and a former pupil, Tom Outland, who had left one of the Professor's daughters, to whom he was engaged, a wonderfully lucrative patent on his death in France. At the middle of the book the narrative breaks off to become the story of Outland's scientific investigations in the south-west of the United States. It is not the best of devices, but it does allow Miss Cather to exhibit, in the Professor himself, that searching quality of introspection which comes with the termination of middle age to every reflective man on earth.

It is not nearly so disturbing nor so beautiful a book as *A Lost Lady*, but, like all Miss Cather's fiction, it is distinguished by a sympathy and fine perception so peculiarly her own. It is rich, too, in its characters and their conflict—Marsellus, the young Jew who married one of the Professor's daughters, the rich one to whom Outland has left his patent, is quite the best personage in the book. All the faults, the virtues, of his race are shown here with the delicate restraint and the reality which make Miss Cather so superb an artist.

[. . .]

Miss Cather has also published a collection of short stories, *Youth and the Bright Medusa*, which were loudly acclaimed at the time of their appearance. Some of them are earlier pieces, written when Miss Cather was engaged in teaching at Pittsburg, and which first saw the light of day in a volume called *The Troll Garden*. Most of them are good. "Coming, Aphrodite!" is hardly a short story at all, but it has a beauty and vitality which is not always found in stories reprinted from periodicals. The best of the lot, perhaps, are "Paul's Case" and "The Sculptor's Funeral," and they are interesting principally as the first indication of a talent manifesting itself in contemporary American letters which was not entirely derivative, notwithstanding the persuasive influence of classics shown in an imitation of Mrs. Wharton. The best in American letters is usually hailed in England as a projection of the European tradition, the rest is simply lumped together as a feeble effort to achieve some sort of individuality.

Nevertheless, there is a clear, unmistakable point of departure, which is neither feeble nor derivative, in the present trend of fiction in America, and it is for this reason if no other that Miss Cather looms so largely on the literary horizon of the United States. Her finest book quite possibly remains to be written; but, with her sense of the American scene, her exquisite perception of character and her freshness of style, Miss Cather will some day write a novel which will crystallise forever the distinct and definite American tradition which, with the exception perhaps of Mr. Sherwood Anderson and Mr. Dreiser, she has done more to establish than any other American novelist. In the romance and disillusion and rewards of the Middle West she has found the secret of a new and glamorous prose narrative.

Zona Gale, "My Favorite Character in Fiction," *Bookman* (New York), 63 (May 1926), 322–3

The best that I can do in naming a favorite character in fiction is to name the one which is occupying my thought at the moment. One has a new favorite character for every new favorite book. If I tried to name them all I should have to give a party. The character who occupies my mind at the moment is Tom Outland in Willa Cather's *The Professor's House,* and this is for the same reason that a little while ago I was thinking most of the protagonist in Johan Bojer's "The Great Hunger." And for years, still earlier, of the bishop who offered up candlesticks instead of candles. And in my little girlhood, of Sydney Carton who said "It is a far, far better thing that I do, than I have ever done." I suppose therefore that what I mean by my joy in Tom Outland is that he is one more who can set free whatever is in him by identifying himself with a great idea. Does not the slang phrase "What's the great idea?" seem, as many slang phrases seem, to voice a profound spiritual wonder. What *is* the great idea? The bishop found it, Sydney Carton found it, and the "Great Hunger" man found it in self identification with an idea. In every case, under whatever guise, the process was the same—the identification of self with some precious idea. To buy the soul of a "thief" with a gift of two candlesticks; to sow rye in an enemy's empty field; to ride off to the guillotine in somebody's place; and to develop a passion for the preservation of the her-itage of a desert and of a dead people—these are not so different, since by such things the provincial limitations of self give way to the universal field of group emotion. The provincial self about its own affairs is a fascinating field for literary research; but what *amour* or personal adventure which Tom Outland might have had could be so emotionally thrilling as the passion and the hope and the understanding which he puts into this quest? In him Miss Cather creates a living being, passionately pursuing an objective that has no personal taint. He expresses the love of the unknown which is the basic hunger of the race. He has caught "the Great Idea."

I. A. Richards, "Some Outstanding Novels," *Forum,* 76 (August 1926), 318–19

The Professor's House by Willa Cather [is] really two novels, both good, one set inside the other. The inset novel—a young cowboy-archaeologist's adventure on a mesa which holds the ruins of a vanished civilization—is an admirable piece of quiet, strong narrative. Miss Cather seems to lack invention, but to lack little else. Her young hero later becomes a physicist and a discoverer, is killed in the War and haunts the rest of the book as a memory and an inspiration. His great discovery—a "bulk-headed vacuum" which revolutionizes aviation and appears to be also a gas—seems oddly enough to come from Kipling's *With the Night Mail.* This is of course a trivial detail of no importance, unless it helps to indicate why Miss Cather is not yet the great novelist she should be. She has very little sense of action, and action and invention go together. Such observation, perspective, and balance as hers are rare, but all her work is strangely static. Her principal study here, the Professor, is an appealing and impressive figure, but more a statue than a man.

Helen E. Haines, "The House of the Professor Falls into Three Pieces" [clipping from unidentified newspaper, 1925–26, Willa Cather scrapbooks, Red Cloud, II-4, II-39]

That Willa Cather's artistry should fail seems impossible. That a structure, sound and balanced, rising apparently to proportioned completeness, should suddenly mushroom into three separate parts and collapse in disunity is the last thing to be expected of the work of a skilled architect. But that is what happens to *The Professor's House*, and the calamity leaves this reviewer sadly embarrassed. For how are you to convey the brilliance and significance of a work when you are still dazed by its collapse? How are you to consider the urgency and validity of a problem that suddenly effaces itself? And then, too, how do you know that with an artist of Miss Cather's calibre this apparent debacle may not after all be some sort of an achievement in symbolism or implicit meaning that you have been too obtuse to appreciate? Well, as I see no hope of being able to answer any of these questions, perhaps I had better tell as simply and directly as possible what the

book is about and why it leaves me disappointed and perplexed.

Undoubtedly, in her new novel, Miss Cather is preoccupied with a central purpose which she seeks to drive home from several different approaches. Quite obviously her purpose is, essentially, the purpose of Sinclair Lewis—to reveal the shallowness and sordidness of American ideals of success and achievement, based on money-seeking and personal aggrandizement. She reveals this through a series of contrasts in character, in experience and in accomplishment. The single-minded scholar, pursuing his ideal of scholarship without thought of gain is set in contrast with the young journalist of literary gifts and ambitions who makes more money by writing daily "prose poems" for a newspaper syndicate. The idealist discoverer and inventor, regardless of self, sacrificing ease and reward for the acceptance of the great discovery, the perfection of the scientific process, are set in contrast with the scientist whose first concern is degrees and decorations, and with the business man in whose hands the great invention, commercialized, capitalized and advertised, becomes an inexhaustible source of riches.

This theme is presented in three books. The first, "The Family," is the longest, filling more than half the volume. It is the novel itself, triumphantly launched and carried with skill and power into midstream. The scene is a Middle Western college town near Lake Michigan. The family is the family of Professor Godfrey St. Peter—the professor himself, his wife Lillian, their two married daughters and their daughters' husbands. All these people live; each one is distinct, individual, and entirely human. Then, there is Augusta, the sewing woman, the serious, faithful German Catholic, who for years has cut her patterns and draped her "forms" in the barren little attic study where, in alternation with her tenancy, the professor has found escape from his family and carried to completion his great historical work, *Spanish Adventurers in North America*. Augusta is a somewhat symbolic figure. She represents, I think, the solid reality of mother earth, the primitive simplicity, sympathy and strength that Miss Cather apotheosized in *My Ántonia* and that she regards as the basic attributes of woman. It is part of the theme that Augusta should offer the only rescue and the only solace that reach the professor in his struggle against submergence in a life that is tolerable to him. On the professor Miss Cather has centered her skill in the evoking of personality. He is not the absentminded, lovable stock figure of tradition, but a man of originality and force, to whom the rewards of scholarship and freedom of individual life are the only things that count. Enmeshed in the intricate web of family ambitions, maneuvers, jealousies, diplomacies and bitterness, he realizes his helplessness, but his perceptions are never blunted.

Almost instantly we are plunged into the drama of "family"—that inexhaustible drama that offers the ultimate in complexity and emotion. The professor's new house is just completed; the house that fulfills his wife's ambitions, that is the last word in comfort and equipment and artistic harmony. It has been built from the history prize of five thousand pounds awarded him in recognition of his life-work, the history of the Spanish adventurers. The old, ugly, square frame house, with its single archaic bathroom, is outgrown and discarded; the house that is part of the professor's inner life and from which that life can never be uprooted. He and his wife are established in the new house, and there his exterior life goes on; but he still rents the old house for the sake of that dark, dingy attic, with its hard couch, its makeshift desk and its rusty, leaky gas heater; here is the only raft on which he escapes family submergence.

For it is as family prosperity has increased, as family interests have multiplied, that the family atmosphere has become oppressive and electric. There is the professor's wife, Lillian, still beautiful, a woman of poise and charm and intelligence, absorbed only in the family well-being, luxuriating in the inflowing wealth, freshened in sex consciousness by the acquisition of sons-in-law and using all her charm and skill to hold and deepen their admiration and devotion. There are the two daughters and their husbands, Rosamund, dark and sumptuous, is married to Louie Marsellus, the opulently expansive young Jew, whose business acumen has developed a fortune from the invention bequeathed to Rosamund by her first fiancé, a genius protege of her father's, killed in the war. Kathleen, the younger sister, slight and fragile, is married to a young Scotsman, whose longing for a literary career is sacrificed to the daily grind of journalism and the money-making lure of "good cheer" articles and poems. The wealth that pours in upon Rosamond and Marsellus embitters and estranges Kathleen and McGregor, laps Lillian in complaisance, and inflicts a thousand pin pricks upon the professor's fastidious and independent spirit. What Miss Cather has set to trace is the mounting effect of materialism, blunting delicacy and good feeling, testing all things by cost, choking the springs of spiritual and intellectual growth and of simple contentment. And she sees the three women as the instruments and abettors of materialism, yielding to it, fostering it, frustrating all efforts to withstand or overcome it. Her keynote is struck when the professor, in a brown study before the open fire in his new house, is asked by his wife to tell his thoughts.

278

" 'I was thinking,' he answered absently, 'about Euripides; how, when he was an old man, he went and lived in a cave by the sea, and it was thought queer, at the time. It seems that houses had become insupportable to him. I wonder whether it was because he had observed women so closely all his life.' "

Thus we are drawn into a vital drama of temperament, of cause and effect; it moves with vigor and penetrates below the surface. We look forward to a working out of its complex problem that shall illuminate and convince. And then we pass to Book Two—and find ourselves confronted by a narrative utterly different in a subject, scene and style. The main structure of the book has broken down and in its disintegration this fragment has arisen. This interpolation is the story of Tom Outland, the inventor-fiancé, whose legacy had cast its golden pall over the professor's household. It is a narrative of archaeological discovery in New Mexico. Its origin is easy to trace in Miss Cather's own sojourn among the cliff-dwellings of the Southwest and her deep interest in those relics of aboriginal civilization. But this personal interest cannot justify a divagation so fatal to the unity and significance of her book. Tom Outland's story seeks to re-create the magic that Miss Cather herself has found on the New Mexico mesas, the magic of turquoise sky and electric air and the age-old brooding of primitive forces undisturbed by a modern age. But that magic, to me at least, is not conveyed in these pages; they give description of things seen, not immediacy of experience. Outland is a child of the Southwest, one of the rough diamonds not unfamiliar in fiction. While herding cattle in winter camp on a lonely range,

he explores the great Blue Mesa and discovers a hidden cliff-dwellers' city, perfect in preservation, rich in archaeological treasures. He carries the story of his find to Washington, confident that an enthusiastic government will promptly and joyfully act to guard and preserve this priceless acquisition.

The final segment of the novel, Book 3, covers just 25 pages. It returns us to the professor and his problem; but we find him no longer a living man, but a psychological simulacrum engaged in a struggle with his own consciousness until we turn the page and suddenly encounter "A Note on the Type in which this Book is Set." Life, of course, holds no finality; we do not demand an "ending" to a novel that recreates human nature and human experience; but we may fairly ask logic, cohesion and reasonable sequence in any rendering of life in art. What conclusion Miss Cather indicates for the professor's problem, I will not tell. And if you should remark that I will not tell because I don't know—Let us change the subject!

Checklist of Additional Reviews

Wisconsin Library Bulletin, 21 (October 1925), 231.
Pratt Institute Free Library Quarterly Booklist, Autumn 1925, p. 39.
Booklist, 22 (November 1925), 72.
Keith Preston, *Pot Shots From Pegasus* (New York: Covici Friede Publishers, 1929), pp. 233–8.

MY MORTAL ENEMY

MY
MORTAL ENEMY

WILLA CATHER

ALFRED A. KNOPF
NEW YORK
1926

Keith Preston, "Miss Cather's Prose Lyric," *Chicago Daily News* [October 1926], p. 14

In her novelette *My Mortal Enemy* Miss Willa Cather tells a romantic story in an old-fashioned setting with much deliberate charm of style. A great love turned to hate is the theme of *My Mortal Enemy*, not in itself a novel idea. If it seems new, the novelty lies in a somewhat high-blown conceit. "People can be lovers and enemies at the same time, you know. We were . . . A man and woman drawn apart from that long embrace and see what they have done to one another." So Myra Henshawe at the last explains how her husband came to be "her mortal enemy." The language is obviously exalted and poetic, suggesting that this book belongs to those commonly described as prose-lyrics.

Oswald Henshawe with his weakness and magnanimity, his enigmatic "half-moon eyes" and his suggestion of personal bravery unutilized is one sort of romantic character, a potential explorer confined in a railroad office. Myra, with her magnetic charm, her impulsive furies and generosities and her frustrated ambitions, is another. Miss Cather writes their story sometimes with the crisp and racy idiom that is so like a man's, as in old John Driscoll's warning to his niece: "'And I advise ye to think well,' he told her. 'It's better to be a stray dog in this world than a man without money. I've tried both ways and I know. A poor man stinks, and God hates him.'" More often, however, the writing has a studied and deliberate charm, as in the description of New York on a snowy day: "Here, I felt,

winter brought no desolation; it was tamed, like a polar bear led on a leash by a beautiful lady."

Such writing is effective and yet one is too conscious of the distinguished stylist picking her words and figures with judicial care. As compared with Miss Cather's earlier creations, Myra and Oswald Henshawe seem like story-book characters against a studio background, and this season's reprinting of *My Antonia* appears as much more of an event than the first printing of *My Mortal Enemy*.

"Pride's Bed," *Time*, 8 (18 October 1926), 38–9

. . . Sometimes, in a small U.S. town, even in no town at all, you come upon a great house alone in its grandeur. It will have been built by some man whose intensity raised him above his fellows to the position and estate demanded by an acquisitive nature. If the house is still owned by relations of the builder, you may not see in them many traces of the old blood. But should you find the builder's kin elsewhere, and fallen on hard days, mark how often some intensity of the old blood will have been its own undoing.

The house in this story of Myra Henshawe stood behind a tall iron fence in a ten-acre park at Parthia, Ill. Myra, an orphan, was John Driscoll's great-niece and he brought her up there, a forceful, coarse old Irishman and a vivid, a wild little girl. She had jewels and many gowns and a Steinway piano. She rode keen horses. The town band played at her parties and serenaded John Driscoll on his birthday; he had bought the bandsmen their silver instruments and when they played for him he treated with his best whiskey. He had wrung a great fortune out of contract labor in Missouri swamps.

Myra became a beautiful young woman, short, plump, like a dove in repose, in action very erect, vital, challenging. Her spirit and swift wit were of a sort that old John Driscoll could understand, "racy, and none too squeamish." He was probably proud of her the snowy night she left his house, penniless, after two years of intense, secret waiting, to marry the man whom she loved and he did not. He was certainly proud of her when, after willing his house to pale-handed nuns, founding a women's refuge in Chicago and providing that Myra could always go to that refuge free and have pinmoney, he knew that she would sooner go to the river.

It is Myra's story, but her young years with that illiterate, powerful old man made her much that she was. With such love as she and Oswald Henshawe had, another woman might have stayed happy. But ambition for him and hatred of their poverty ate her heart. Her wit sharpened when they called on his stuffy, kindly German business friends. She had been formed for distinction, for surroundings of ease and dignity and charm. Childless, she needed scope to spend herself without stint on her friendships, for she had that concentration of affection which makes individuals of its most commonplace objects and the constancy of spirit which keeps attachments with fine people inviolate in their highest mood. Deathly poor and dying bitterly, long after her bright New York days, she spent gold pieces, hoarded in an old glove, that masses might be said for her gracious friend, Madame Modjeska, years dead.

Dying of cancer in her sixties in a Pacific coast boom town, with loutish roomers clumping overhead and with no love left for her patient, tender, ineffectual husband, Myra was bitter over her self-defeat, until the end. Passion had made her a lowly bed; she had writhed on it for years. She still could laugh at some of life's absurdities. Some of its beauty was still warm to her—Heine's poems, her own lovely hands. But her steely pride was turned upon itself, her mortal enemy. Not even religion could resign her to the indignities of poverty. When she felt her time upon her, she stole off alone to a Pacific headland, to watch dawn break over the sea.

The Significance. This is a very short story; very complete, very intense, very subtle. A rare woman's whole life is told and her time etched in around her with a touch as sure as it is delicate. It adds immensely to the literature of places as well as of people, particularly with a violet, snowpowdered December twilight in old Madison Square, which once was "like an open-air drawing room." What the work represents spiritually, no reader will soon show another, save that the tragedy of a strong, restrained nature, devoid of falsity or baseness, is a moving thing to watch, to experience.

The Author. Willa Sibert Cather spends months on end riding over her brothers' ranches in the Southwest. Then she buries herself for more months, of writing, in New York. The emotional maturity of her characters, their frequent arrival at or tragic necessity for spiritual self-reliance (see *A Lost Lady*, *The Professor's House*), must be a reflection of their author's real acquaintance with solitude. Miss Cather is nearly 50 now; sociable when she likes; vigorous, cheerful, charming. But more and more she is a recluse who, having had experience as country girl (Nebraska), college girl (Nebraska State), reporter and editor (Pittsburgh *Leader* and *McClure's Magazine*), teacher and archaeologist, enough to "last a lifetime" is increasingly a subtle artist after the Wordsworth formula, "emotion recollected in tranquillity."

"Myra Henshawe, Another Great Portrait by Miss Cather," New York *Sun*, 22 October 1926

Willa Cather's first novels were on the large scale. *The Song of the Lark* was decidedly long, made up of six parts and running to nearly five hundred pages. Its method was leisurely, almost diffuse. The reader had to use the sort of patience required by fiction which, rather than active, is thoughtful, cumulative and a little intricate. If he used that patience his reward was sure. The story was there, a true story, almost the first, of a woman artist in the making. Like her first novel, *O Pioneers!* it was powerful in its American localism. Where else had (or has) been given so richly the very substance of life in our great midland country? Miss Cather's "Moonstone" had beauty in it. Thea Kronborg did not leave that Colorado town in order to be somewhere—anywhere—else but because she had to be elsewhere to fulfill her destiny.

Thea Kronborg, though, was always the main subject of the book, and the best later work of her creator has centered in the portraiture of women. Antonia, the Lost Lady, and now Myra Henshawe. *My Antonia* was still upon the larger scale: in that book also the story teller had certain aspects of the Middle West of her youth to interpret. *A Lost Lady* (five years later) showed a new concentration or distillation. The scene was the Colorado country of *The Song of the Lark*; the localism was

as firm and clear as ever, but now achieved with a few telling strokes. Mrs. Forrester became as singly our affair as any human being can be. It was all done with marvelous concision and economy. Within the last ten years Miss Cather has reduced her style to its essentials—distilled is the word.

This we feel even more strongly in the new novel (or novelette) *My Mortal Enemy*. It is shorter even than *A Lost Lady* because more highly concentrated. There is as much substance in it, and substance of a similar nature. Myra Henshawe, technically a "good woman," is not less complex of nature than Mrs. Forrester. Mrs. Forrester the faithless, the "light woman"—or at least the polyandrous woman—dies, you remember, in the lap of luxury, "well cared for to the end," and if she ever paid the wages of sin we do not know it. She seemed simply to have fulfilled her nature. With Myra Henshawe, on the other hand, virtue brings no reward of enduring happiness. She has given up the world, has given up certain wealth and position, to marry the love of her youth. Their passionate mating has merged into a long and, in the main, successful marriage. Henshawe has been always devoted to Myra, full of little romantic attentions. But she is compact of common sense and high emotion, while he is a sentimentalist, and she comes to hate the soft bonds with which he holds her. Toward the end, when, a nearly helpless invalid, she must depend on him as never before, her resentment finds momentary issue in a speech to the niece, Nellie, who tells the tale.

Nellie wonders how the older woman can be so hard on her devotee. ". . . She sighed, and looked at me wistfully.

"It's a pity, isn't it, Nellie, to reach out a grudging hand and try to spoil the past for any one? Yes, it's a great cruelty. But I can't help it. He's a sentimentalist, always was; he can look back on the best of those days when we were young and loved each other and make himself believe it was all like that. It wasn't. I was always a grasping, worldly woman; I was never satisfied. All the same, in age, when the flowers are so few, it's a great unkindness to destroy any that are left in a man's heart. . . . But I'm made so. People can be lovers and enemies at the same time, you know. We were. . . . A man and a woman draw apart from that long embrace, and see what they have done to each other." In the end she contrives not to die "alone with her mortal enemy." But Henshawe's sentimentalism protects him: he never knows.

A tale of deep emotion and understanding. Myra Henshawe takes her place at once in the cherished gallery beside Antonia, and Thea Kronborg (Tillie too) and Mrs. Forrester. A true and fine "Cather."

The publishers produce, after eight years, a new edition of My Antonia. It appears to be a reprint from the old plates, but for a revised introduction, which will doubtless give this issue the standing of a "first" among collectors. To own a "first" of My Mortal Enemy, as with all Miss Cather's recent work, means investing $15 in one of two hundred large paper copies on Japanese vellum, signed by the author. This revised introduction is an interesting item. The original five and a half pages have been condensed to three; and all the part of it that represented Miss Cather as having been at work on a version of her own of Antonia's story is cut out. The narrative of Jim Burden now stands unchallenged, even *in posse*.

Fanny Butcher, "*My Mortal Enemy* is a Masterpiece, by Willa Cather," Chicago *Daily Tribune*, 23 October 1926, p. 15

There is no doubt in the minds of some of us about the unique place which Willa Cather occupies in American literature. She is the predominant woman novelist of her day, and there is a completely unruffled integrity about her writing which is almost unbelievable in these days of vast and impressive lures to the novelist. She writes slowly, and all the king's horses and all the king's men (done up in glittering gold dollars) can't make her hurry. She needs just so much time to do what she is doing and she takes it, no matter how yearningly the magazine editors plead for stories or serials. She is as near to the realization of the *summum bonum* as any person I have ever met—and that is because she is realizing, in her work, the complete and whole joy of her life dream, and because she never allows that dream to be tarnished by adulation or visions of wealth. I don't mean that she is the only person writing in America today who feels that way about writing, but I do mean that she is as conspicuous an example of it as any one writing today, and the result of her fortitude (or her lack of interest in gain, if you please) is a glowing and beautiful piece of work.

I suppose that side of her work seems especially impressive just now because her latest book, *My Mortal Enemy*, on which she has been working for so long, is in reality little more than a short story. And yet that short story, that novelette, has not

286

only the whole of two lives in it, but perhaps the whole of life itself, as life is lived in marriage. And so exquisitely is the story told that it isn't until you have finished the book and have gone into that silence of thought which a really good book always sends you into that you realize how tremendously she has done something which is in reality a fragile, delicate tracery. It is the iron under the golden arabesques that you feel after you've finished *My Mortal Enemy*.

My Mortal Enemy is not an easy book to write about, because Miss Cather has removed from her story every unnecessary word, every thought that isn't germane, and the framework that is left is so wondrously beautiful a unit that you feel you must say, "There it is, a lovely, perfect thing. To take it to pieces would be like trying to take to pieces love itself. The moment you analyse it, it loses its magic. But accepted, it is lyric."

So it is with *My Mortal Enemy*. You say that it is the story of a man who loved a beautiful and vivid woman, who married him despite her family's cutting her off, that it is the story of a jealous wife, that it is the story of the disintegration of love as poverty seeps into its apparently water tight happiness, to say that it is any or all of those things is to do it an injustice, and yet it is to tell the truth. And under the flotsam of those lives there is the steady rhythm of the fundamental hatred of the sexes one for the other and their irresistible attraction one for the other. To say that, likewise, is to tell an untruth and at the same time a truth about the book.

You see, it is impossible to say exactly what you mean about *My Mortal Enemy*.

It is as fragile and delicate and simple a tale as *The Lost Lady*, and yet while that book had little of the undercurrent of human life and relationships, this one is vibrant with them. Without having any of the surface characteristics of a profound book, it is profound.

Miss Cather has chosen to tell the story through the lips of an observer, and the way in which she records the growth of the idea in her heroine's mind that her husband, who is the apotheosis of devotion, has always been, fundamentally, her mortal enemy and makes that idea communicate itself to the person who is writing the book, is tremendous. It is more convincing than any direct narrative could ever have made it. And yet the idea was a subtle one, which took years to come to flower.

Many readers will see in *My Mortal Enemy* only the story of a great and devoted love, and the querulousness of a sick old woman who regrets the luxuries which she forsook for her marriage. That is as it should be, for any book which is profound on the face of it you will find to be—probably—profound only there. This is a masterpiece of tragedy, a presentation of the great subcurrental rhythms of love and hatred, and yet it is on the surface a book with the lightest possible touch—slight, as nothing Miss Cather has ever done before is slight, and yet with roots so deep in human life and thought that it is wholly right.

A little over a hundred pages, printed with wide margins and in generous type, a book that you could read in less than an hour, and yet a book that leaves behind it deep conjecture and pictures which are realer than your own life. It is a really great book.

Lee Wilson Dodd, "Alone, With Ourselves," *Saturday Review of Literature*, 3 (23 October 1926), 234

A high-spirited, intelligent, socially gifted, and ambitious girl, with a generous dash of Irish malice and imagination in her, makes a runaway love match, thus renouncing (as she at first supposes) a very great fortune. Her young husband, who is not by nature adapted for business, yet forces himself to do fairly well to supply her somewhat extravagant needs as a brilliant and popular social being. But as they come to middle life good fortune deserts this pair. Through no obvious fault of the husband's they sink to a shabby-genteel poverty. The wife loses her health. The husband works for her and waits upon her with a selfless devotion. And the dying, tragically frustrated wife now knows that her heart has never renounced the great fortune that might have been hers. It was not in her really to renounce it, all that it must have meant to her; and this failure has poisoned her whole life, as well as her husband's.

This deceptively simple and unexpectedly poignant story comes to us only in glimpses through the eyes of another, younger woman . . . Miss Cather's name appears on the covers and on the title-page, but she is not otherwise supposed to exist for us as we read.

Nevertheless, Willa Cather is the most interesting person connected with this story, for she created it. It is either a very short novel, or a very long short story, of perhaps twenty thousand words; but whatever their precise number may be, it is precisely the right number, placed in the right order by an artist who knows what words are for and what can be done with them and how without seeming effort to do it. Miss Cather is a cool, scrupulous mistress of her medium, her material, and all its human, social, and philosophical overtones. She has no desire merely to stir our mere facile emotions. It is not our nerves she would trouble, but our minds—or whatever it is that we most deeply and personally are!

The art of this book is austere, a fabric of true renunciations, aristocratic, disdainful—perhaps even too disdainful of that slack-slippered, unblushing gossip who lurks at the heart of every born novel reader. I, for one, should have liked to know more of Oswald and Myra. I should like to have been permitted the privilege of spying upon them more fully, on less rigidly selected occasions. Yet almost I dread to admit it, lest this acknowledgment of human weakness encounter, by chance, the disciplined auctorial scorn it deserves!

One thing is certain. Miss Cather has given us neither more nor less than she meant to give; and, doubtless, if we still crave more, that too was thoughtfully foreseen and unpityingly ignored.

The heroine of this chiselled story comes to our common end, death, expressing in the presence of her husband a "strange complaint." "Why," she says, "why must I die like this, alone with my mortal enemy!" She is not referring to her husband, however! So, at the last, it is really a "mystery story" after all, as all honest and thoughtful stories are. It deals with that ultimate mystery lying close and cold at the heart of every woman and man. It is only because Myra, Miss Cather's heroine, had the insight and courage to speak out, that her complaint seems "strange." It is a complaint common to humanity. For we are all of us to die one day like that, alone with our mortal enemies.

Isabel Paterson, "When Desire Shall Fail," *New York Herald Tribune Books*, 24 October 1926, p. 3

Of all our contemporary novelists who are concerned with something more than the elementary aspect of fiction, the telling of a tale for sheer diversion, Willa Cather has been most ardent and single hearted in the pursuit of beauty, that essential beauty which Keats identified with truth. Not only has she striven to bring out by the selective alchemy of art the loveliness of common things and obscure lives; she has been chiefly preoccupied with idealism as a motive force. Almost all her principal characters have been moved by some purpose beyond their private and temporal prosperity. Consciously or unconsciously they seek for some larger fulfillment than worldly success can yield; and even when frustrated they are not wholly defeated—they have had the dream.

But it is observable, though it may be accidental and therefore not deeply significant, that the note of disillusion and bewilderment has been increasingly marked in Miss Cather's later work. In *A Lost Lady*, *One of Ours* and *The Professor's House*, all the omens were unfavorable to the luckless idealists; the net of circumstance was too strong and close for any hope of escape. Claude Wheeler, the inarticulate visionary farmer boy in *One of Ours*; Tom Outland and Professor St. Peter, of *The Professor's House*, were too fine and sensitive to win through; Marion Forrester was destroyed by the coarse and earthy streak which flawed her exquisiteness. Now, as if to sum up the lesson that all is vanity, Miss Cather shows a woman who was broken by life because she was too hard, too grasping and selfish.

To be sure, Myra Driscoll wanted both to have her cake and to eat it, which is platitudinously impossible. Reared in provincial luxury, as the prospective heiress of a wealthy uncle, she set her heart on the one man for whom her uncle cherished a rooted animosity. That there was no substantial reason for the old man's grudge only strengthened his determination. He was a self-made man of Irish peasant blood, a race which has been taught tenacity in hating. He gave Myra her choice between inheriting his fortune and marrying Oswald Henshawe. She chose her lover. But she never forgave Oswald for what he has cost her!

"She had wanted to leave (her uncle's house) without anything but the clothes she wore," and she did. But quite obviously she expected Oswald to make it up to her literally and materially. Oswald earned a comfortable living, and a woman of generous spirit would have been content. But the mere sight of another woman in a carriage while she was in a hired cab embittered Myra. She was lavish in giving, and Oswald paid the bills. People who have never earned anything are frequently open-handed and pride themselves on the fact. Myra would give away the shirt off Oswald's back if she didn't like the fit of it. It was up to Oswald to provide himself with new shirts, of course.

She also prided herself on her capacity

for friendship, but she expected a full return. Her idea of helping Oswald's career consisted in being rude to his wealthy business associates. Always her lofty pretensions ended in some act of petty malice. Of course, it was out of the question that they should save any money, and when reverses came with old age and Myra had no one and nothing left but Oswald she turned on him and accused him obliquely of having ruined her life. "Why must I die like this, alone with my mortal enemy?"

If this story—it is only a longish short story, not a novel, and to present it as such is to raise unwarranted expectations— were the work of any less distinguished author, one would call it admirable, but rather as promise than performance. It recalls Miss Cather's first little novel, *Alexander's Bridge*, rather than the glowing pages of *My Antonia*. To be sure, the easy and lucent prose is superior to that of the earlier work; but there is the same discrepancy between the author's apparent intention and the actual effect produced. Alexander and Myra are adumbrated as great natures ruined by the defects of their qualities; but they do not, of themselves, confirm the impression. Alexander was rather negative, unrealized. It is implied that Myra possessed "imagination, generosity and the flaming courage of youth"; but she appears simply wilful, obstinate and greedy. This spiritual insignificance of the principal character falsifies the emotion with which her story is charged; sympathy is overstrained and finally wearied. It simply doesn't seem to matter. Myra posed even in death.

It seems a hard rule that an artist such as Miss Cather must compete with herself; that all her work must be measured against her own highest attainment; but it is inevitable. The penalty of excellence is living up to it. And, of course, it cannot be done always.

Louis Kronenberger, "Willa Cather Fumbles for Another Lost Lady," *New York Times Book Review*, 24 October 1926, p. 2

For several reasons, some of them not altogether significant, Miss Cather's latest story will doubtless be compared with *A Lost Lady*. Both books are short. Both have something of the same framework, the same approach. Both carry us out of one age into another. And both have to do, though only one of them makes the fact explicit, with a lost lady. Again Miss Cather has taken a woman of charm, of rich personality, of sensitive intelligence, and shown how the attrition of circumstances and of temperament wears her down, brings her to an unfitting end. But this time, unfortunately, though it is only fair to suppose that her exact aims are different, Miss Cather has fallen short, rather far short, of her earlier level. Her lost lady is not so real, not so moving, not so delightful. Her background, if less ambitiously attempted, is much less significantly achieved. Her approach, through the eyes of a second person, is by no means as sensitive and significant as Niel's to Mrs. Forrester in *A Lost Lady*. And *My Mortal Enemy* is dangerously, destructively briefer.

Nellie Birdseye, who tells the story of Myra Henshawe, stands outside its limits. Miss Cather's method of giving us one character through the eyes of another is not, of course, new, but the interpreters of *My Antonia* and *A Lost Lady* had a real relationship to them, dwelt inside their plots. They gave them more verisimilitude than Nellie gives this. They gave them a viewpoint and an interpretation which Nellie does not give to this. She simply tells us about Myra Henshawe at two periods of her life when she knew her. As a young girl she spent a week in New York with Myra when she and Henshawe had been married some twenty years. Originally, deep in love, they had eloped and Myra, by that act, had given up a fortune. When Nellie first knew them their happiness was beginning to grow clouded. They lacked money. Myra needed wealth to live, to expand, to be happy, to be fine. She had pride and a generous but violent nature. There were quarrels, scenes, necessary adjustments.

Ten years later Nellie met the Henshawes again, in very reduced circumstances out West, with Myra an invalid. Her whole life spoiled by poverty and its annoyances, a beautiful love ended, a nature roused to bitterness and violence by self-denials and failures, she is but the wreck of her old self. She is slowly dying—face to face with her own dual nature, her "mortal enemy": alone with the husband she has ceased to love and with herself. She makes, just before the end, a deathbed revolt to freedom and peace by running away.

Miss Cather's methods are always as engrossing as her material, and a good bit of the effectiveness of her earlier novels lies in the individuality of their form. Most obvious are her use of a secondary character to interpret the chief character, which colors and enriches *My Antonia* and *A Lost Lady*, and her use of incident in place of situation or analysis for purposes of revelation. Both these characteristics are conspicuous in *My Mortal Enemy* and both, for almost the first time, largely unsuccessful. Nellie is a colorless, artistically meaningless character, and her impressions are correspondingly without color or meaning. The book is a succes-

sion of incidents, and they do not reveal enough. One seriously doubts whether, in its effect as well as in its form, it can be called a novel; it has no real continuity, forms no organic whole. We are given a woman's character and the end of a great love largely through incident and exposition, and we only get characteristic contours. We do not really know the woman. We do not really know her life. The book implies much but connotes little. That is its weakness, and it is a serious one.

One is forcibly struck by the increasing tendency toward brevity which Miss Cather's novels reveal—*The Song of the Lark, My Antonia, A Lost Lady, My Mortal Enemy*—each a study of a woman, and each shorter than the last. Compression and selection grow naturally stronger in most good writers as they master their medium. But in *My Mortal Enemy* they have been carried too far. All bones and no flesh is never a wise method. In this instance Miss Cather has done even worse—though she has used very little, she has not always used the bones. Significant things are left out, and the reader is left not only unsatisfied, but also puzzled.

Though in actual merit *My Mortal Enemy* is perhaps Miss Cather's least important book, it does have a certain value as regards Miss Cather's development. Immeasurably inferior to *A Lost Lady* that it is, according to every concrete standard by which it can be judged —style, for form, tone, lifelikeness, plot— it does impress one, somehow, as a "later" book. It belongs in the same period as *The Professor's House*. For with *The Professor's House* Miss Cather began delving into the innermost, fundamental nature of a character, into his mind and soul. One gets the feeling that she was trying to delve so here, and that in part at least, the groping and confusion of her character are responsible for the groping, the confusion, the incompleteness of her method. She seems to be finding life more complex, more elusive, more irreducible that she once did. The simplicity, the openness, the warmth of an Antonia no longer deeply interest her. She is absorbed by a sophisticated, troubled, neurotic woman here, a woman lost far less circumstantially than Marian Forrester was; and she is lost also. Marian Forrester lives. Myra Henshawe does not even begin to live; but Myra Henshawe is, without question, a "harder" character to realize. But if this book is greatly inferior to *A Lost Lady* for one reason, it is greatly inferior to *The Professor's House* for another. That book eluded her exact grasp also, but it had rich connotations, moments of depth, which *My Mortal Enemy* has not. This book fails in all ways to be prehensile. It does not coalesce. The whole is not a great as the sum of its parts, and it should be greater.

Walter Yust, "Rich Study of Woman Who Had Courage but Could Not Endure," *New York Evening Post, The Literary Review*, 30 October 1926, p. 3

In all probability, Miss Cather will be told by any number of critics that she has failed, in *My Mortal Enemy* to realize what she has set out to do. And the assurance with which critics decide that an author has failed is only equaled by the assurance which allows them to know what the author has intended to do.

Miss Cather is like no other novelist writing in America. She adheres to no standards but her own—and they may change. (This is very disconcerting, of course.) She has been known to write very short novels, and *My Mortal Enemy* is one of them. (This, too, is disturbing: "America's Greatest Woman Author" need not be so unconventional.) Besides, she neglects to post signboards pointing the way she is going in a novel. (The most distressing impropriety of all—allowing life, in *The Professor's House* and *My Mortal Enemy*, say, still a little mystery, still a few obscurities, reticences; and the reader to wonder over them as mortals, lacking omniscience, must do night and day.)

Which leads us to the statement that *My Mortal Enemy* is from first page to last a moving representation of a woman who could not endure, but who had courage. She is brave but embittered. She refuses her uncle's great wealth to marry a poor man, and lives in mounting regret.

Her end is noble—and wistful. The last page turned, and Myra Henshawe lingers to confound the critics—who, sure as shooting, will find her only indifferently summoned, because there is no apparent running comment on her every hour of life.

Myra Henshawe lives for the reader as events and personalities significant enough for investigation and some thought do in daily experience—intense for the glimpses, but no less vital and credible and glamorous, because they are not better, more intimately, known.

And this may seem to suggest Miss Cather's method. If it does, it is merely our interpretation, and may be wrong. The important point is that *My Mortal Enemy*, with Myra, and her husband, whose life is twisted and tortured—but who holds to kindness—is a story of a rich and rare flavor, of luminous prose, of lifting and momentous suspense.

Louise Maunsell Field, "What's Wrong With the Men?" *Literary Digest International Book Review*, 4 (November 1926), 761

Three novels now on my desk prompt me to repeat the question I asked some months ago in these pages: What's wrong with the men? Are we to accept the amiable ineffectuals in recent fiction as true portraits of the typical male of the day? Or do they merely represent a literary fashion which is being almost slavishly followed both by American and by English writers?

So far at least as these three novels are concerned, one might extend the question from the quite remarkably unheroic heroes, and make it include their creators. For Mr. Maxwell's [*Gabrielle*] and Mr. Swinnerton's [*Summer Storm*] . . . are both markedly inferior to many they have done in the past, while Miss Cather's slender volume, in length scarcely more than a novelette, is an exceptionally fine piece of work, a book which it would perhaps not be unduly extravagant to call a little masterpiece. Yet it must be admitted that she too presents a man quite notably lacking in those attributes we are accustomed to call "manly." Myra Henshawe is a thorough woman, both in her weaknesses and in her strength; but Oswald Henshawe, kind, amiable, constant Oswald, is more than a little feminine—unless one is willing to accept the

dictum pronounced more than once, that the masculine is at once the vainer and the more sentimental sex.

There is certainly nothing sentimental about this new novel of Miss Cather's. *My Mortal Enemy* is of the stuff of genuine realism, not of that pseudo variety which rakes out and displays the contents of garbage barrels and sewers, proclaiming it as the material, and the only kind of material, of which life is made. And it is sadder by far than such dredgings ever can be, sadder just because of the absence of any overt tragedy. There is in it nothing of extravagance; from first to last it remains within the bounds of ordinary human experience, showing the other side of romance, and that which happens when the high moment has come and gone, when the man and woman "draw apart . . . and see what they have done to each other." But it is only the woman who sees clearly. Myra, broken and dying, facing the truth sternly, implacably, has still something of splendor; that dreadful cry of hers, which enables the narrator, Nellie, "to sense how it was with her," has in it, for all its anguish, a something of magnificence; but there is no splendor nor any magnificence in Oswald, lying to his wife for the sake of a pair of topaz cuff-links.

In method, as in matter, the book is out of the ordinary. The story is told in the first person by Nellie, whose mother and aunt had been intimate friends of Mrs. Henshawe in the days when she was Myra Driscoll. Nellie, as a child, had often heard the romantic story of the petted, good-looking young girl who, one snowy night, walked out of her rich great-uncle's house to marry the man she loved, tho Oswald Henshawe was all but penniless, and she very well knew that her marriage entailed forfeiture of the wealth to which she was accustomed. Any number of sentimental tales have included such an episode as this, and conferred upon the lovers, after a due number of hardships, a future golden in more senses than one. But sentimentality is far removed from *My Mortal Enemy*. Miss Cather shows us the end of the romance; Myra's very heart and soul are revealed. These few pages do indeed record a life.

John F. Wheelock, "Miss Cather Recounts an Endurance Test," *Writer*, 38 (November 1926), 532–4

[The review included a fascimile of one page of Willa Cather's corrected typescript of *My Mortal Enemy*, p. 533.]

In *My Mortal Enemy*, a book shorter than the usual novel and longer than a short-story, Willa Cather deals with a man still in love and a woman out of love after years of marriage. The main character, Myra Henshawe, freely admits the death of a once great love, declaring that such is the inevitable end of all love subjected to marriage. Is it an implication of Miss Cather's personal optimism regarding the continuance of love after marriage that her heroine is made an extraordinary individual, while the husband is pictured without highlights or shades, the figure of an ordinary man? With considerable care, Myra Henshawe is presented as an acutely dominant woman, able to "do anything she wills," yet succumbing to minor circumstances and not willing to save her own life at the risk of her soul's salvation.

This novel is constructed in short-story fashion, detailing the characteristics of a woman and the circumstances surround-

ing her, showing how they influence her conduct so that at the climax of the story she can say, speaking of her husband: "Why must I die like this, alone with my mortal enemy?" The methods by which Miss Cather builds up the character of Myra Henshawe to the point where the disillusioned woman can make this remark and convince the reader that its utterance is plausible under the circumstances, are worth noting. In the first place, the man and the woman must be kept married. One does not usually remain with a mortal enemy even in marriage. Three reasons are provided for keeping Myra and Oswald Henshawe together through life, each painstakingly woven in to the course of the story, and each interlocking with the others. Myra's temperamental Irish nature has only one constant quality—her devout belief in the sanctity and efficacy of the Church. The idea of divorce, therefore, is by her untenable, although Miss Cather does not provide her with a recognized Church marriage, an omission which places this phase of her adherence to Oswald on a shaky foundation. Myra's depth of submission to the Church is brought out in her approval of the manner in which her Uncle had disposed of his fortune; by her providing money for a mass for her friend Modjeska; by her final turning for spiritual consolation to Father Fay; by the symbol of the ivory crucifix; and by various speeches affirming her belief in the power of the Church, although she was living outside it.

The second obstacle to the continuance of her unhappy marriage is, necessarily, her husband. Unlike Myra, he is not bound to marriage by any religious conviction, and under ordinary circumstances it is to be supposed that he would have sought relief from contact with Myra's hate by divorcing her or leaving her. To solve this problem, Miss Cather pictures

Oswald as particularly submissive and easy-going. Not only to Myra, but to all people and all happenings, he is yielding. Furthermore, in contrast to Myra's selfishness he is made utterly unselfish, and he is shown to be a sentimentalist who for the memory of blissful days long past can endure present unhappiness which provides reminders of the dead happiness. When it would seem that life with Myra would have become unbearable to him, his patience is explained by his remark: "These last years it's seemed to me that I was nursing the mother of the girl who ran away with me. Nothing ever took that girl from me." Still further, he is fascinated by Myra, and in that fascination was bred his love; her whims appear to have pleased him even when they were deliberately ill-intentioned. As a final tie to hold Oswald to his contract when Myra's fascination would have faded with age and intimate acquaintance, Miss Cather makes illness come. When she so desperately needs some one to care for her, how could Oswald leave the woman he had always cherished, remembering that she had once loved him?

As if these two reasons were not enough to insure the prolongation of Myra's marriage to her enemy, Miss Cather presents a third circumstance: poverty holds them together. Oswald is making only enough money to keep the invalid Myra in his own pathetic way; he cannot afford to put her in a hospital or sanitarium—he must even do most of the nursing himself. Myra has been cut off in her Uncle's will without a cent of her own, and having spent freely when Oswald was earning readily, she has no accumulation of funds which would allow her to provide for herself. And since by Myra's own confession, she is a woman who had always believed that what she needed above everything was money, she accepts her dependence upon Oswald.

These three reasons, however completely they cover the ground to prove that Myra and Oswald would have been found still man and wife when the opportunity came for "that strange complaint breathed by a dying woman into the stillness of night, like a confession of the soul," cannot be justified unless there can be shown a mutual overlapping, each with the other, which will be in accord with the general course of the story. This occurs when Myra shows that whatever contribution she could make to the alleviation of their physical poverty she conceals from Oswald, that she may employ it for "unearthly purposes"; when it is set forth that this same devotion to the Church, exhibited in another, was the original cause for her disinheritance when she married a Protestant; when Oswald's indulgence of Myra is offered as one cause of his financial misfortune; when it is made plain that she feels her husband was responsible for her break with the Church and the consequent loss of her fortune. The sense of futility in the attempted ordering of their lives is complete, in the face of Myra's disregard of human relations and her subservience to a spiritual relation which seems to be capable of challenging her will but not her wilfulness.

With all these details, Miss Cather's carefully-built story might still fall short of creating an illusion of reality were it not for another precaution which the author takes. Invading a field in which Mrs. Wharton has achieved peculiar success, Miss Cather adds authenticity to her narrative by introducing actual people as minor characters, notably Madame Modjeska. Again and again there is presented some man or woman, a book, an event, an idea, which bears the imprint of historical truth. These incidents, by placing Myra Henshawe in the last quarter of the nineteenth century, confirm her course of action by surrounding her with a society much more likely to have commended it than the society of today.

Joseph Wood Krutch, "The Modest Method of Willa Cather," *Nation*, 123 (10 November 1926), 484

A characteristic contemporary novel which lies open before me begins: "The door opened and the sunlight sprang into the hall like a great blond beast." Miss Cather, on the other hand, commences thus: "I first met Myra Henshawe when I was fifteen." Where the first would capture the attention by violent assault, the other asks only with classic courtesy for the loan of one's ears, and this beginning is characteristic of a certain modesty of method in which half the charm of Miss Cather's stories lies.

In a penetrating essay, "The Novel Démeublé," she has herself made a plea for a type of fiction less elaborate in its mechanics than the conventional novel, and she has put her preaching into practice by scrupulously avoiding in her best work any machinery more elaborate than her tale required; yet the modesty of which I speak is something beyond that—something which inheres in the very fact that her stories are frankly stories, events retained in the mind of, and recounted by, a definite person. At a time when novelists are seeking above all else "immediacy" of presentation and are employing not seldom fantastic means to attain it, she has sought no such illusion, has made no effort so to dramatize her narrative as to make it the equivalent of a contemporaneous experience. Events are seen frankly through the haze of distance; the thing immediately present is not these events themselves but the mind in which they are recollected; and the effect is, therefore, not the vividness and the harshness of drama but something almost elegiac in its softness. The knowledge of the narrator is both mellow and imperfect; he gropes, reflects, and tries (after the manner of a human, far from omniscient, spectator) to piece together the bits of his information and to extract from it as much as he can of its secret meaning. What we get is not that sense of present action for which novelists more commonly seek but rather a mood—the reverberations of wonder, of interest, and of pity which have lingered after many years in a sensitive, resonant temper.

Told in a different fashion the story of *My Mortal Enemy* might be almost lurid. Its central character, a somewhat spectacular woman who made in her youth a sacrifice of wealth for love and then found herself throughout life unable to maintain the high mood which would make of such sacrifice a success, is all but flamboyant. Yet told as Miss Cather tells it the effect is not of storm and stress but rather of a quiet and brooding sadness, because its center is the mind of the narrator. She has known the woman when she was still the heroine of a village legend, still a symbol of the love and youth that triumph over difficulty; she has seen her at intervals during the years that follow; and she has gradually divined how things stand, how what began as high romance has ended in the sordid impasse to which a wife who insists upon luxuries beyond her husband's income leads both him and herself. To the girl who tells the story, Myra was more than merely an acquaintance, she was one of those from whom life could be learned. In her she had hoped to see romance justified, young faith encouraged; but from her she heard instead: "People can be lovers and enemies at the same time, you know. We were:—A man and woman drawn apart from that long embrace, and see what they have done to each other. Perhaps I can't forgive him for the harm I did him. Perhaps that's it. In age we lose everything; even the power to love." And it was not, we feel, that Myra was worse than most; only that high resolution is an affair of minutes, life an affair of years. Only things founded in selfishness and prudence last it out—hence the *lachrymae rerum* for which there is no help.

This method of Miss Cather's—and she has never, I think, been entirely successful except when adhering to it—has its obvious limitations. It does not stir deep passions and it is, as Nietzsche would have said, to the last degree Apollonian. The mood is a minor mood, brooding and faintly melancholic, with an eye turned always backward. But in the midst of our strident literature its graceful ease has a charm not easy to overestimate. Whenever Miss Cather evokes memory there comes with it a lingering fragrance.

Independent, 117 (13 November 1926) 563, 568

Myra had beauty and Irish wit, a taste for salty stories, a love of luxury, and a will of her own. She forfeited her fortune—every penny—by running away and marrying the man she loved before a justice of the peace. But did she love him? A beginning as romantic and unworldly as that ought in all conscience to have but one conclusion: "They were poor, but she loved him, so what did it matter!" But

halfway through *My Mortal Enemy* one realizes that Myra Henshawe *is* worldly and quite unromantic; so wasn't it after all a mistake to give up the fortune and marry a man whom she would learn to hate? Not according to Myra's husband. His statement is that the youthful Myra who had run away with him and who had loved him was the *true* Myra. Well, did she love him or not, and if she did, why the awful tragedy of those later years when they lived in partial estrangement? Was it solely the humble rooms they were obliged to take in a hotel? Perhaps the key to the tragedy lies in the chance remark of Myra's that one could easily forgive one's enemies, but one's friends were a different matter. In the end, *My Mortal Enemy* turns out to be her own husband.

Critics have pointed out that each of Miss Cather's succeeding novels is shorter than the last. The instrument of her technique grows sharper at each trial, so that *My Mortal Enemy*, though a full-length portrait, is only twenty thousand words long. One can hardly find a fault in the perfection of the author's technique, or complain that it is inadequate to her subject; but now and then one is led to wish perhaps ungraciously that she had used another instrument occasionally or chosen a subject that required one.

One characteristic in Miss Cather impresses a reader of many American novels. She is perfectly acclimated to the American environment, but it never oppresses her. She always tells a story and unfolds character. So many novelists of recent seasons have newly discovered the American scene, Babbitt in the country or Babbitt in the city, and are so occupied in stressing his inhuman mediocrity, that there is little left. Miss Cather's novels could only be written in America, about Americans, but the story's the thing. And the story grows out of character.

R[obert Morss] L[ovett], "Thick and Thin," *New Republic*, 49 (24 November 1926), 22–3

Here are two of our most sensitive and sincere women novelists. Miss Cather's book is a long short story. Miss Gale's [*Preface to a Life*] is somewhat more than the regulation nine innings. Miss Gale, if not quite because she offers the fuller meal, gives us much more to think about, and her attempt, which does not altogether succeed, is more interesting than Miss Cather's more competent but thinner portrait. Each of them has done better before.

My Mortal Enemy, in a short space, tries for a full-length portrait. The story is implicit in the portrait. Neither story nor portrait can mean as much to us as *A Lost Lady*, nor the best parts of *The Professor's House*, for Miss Cather's work has a mineral quality which is at times solid, but at others—and this is one of them—merely smoothly polished. The lady in this case, Myra Henshawe, is a good deal of a "character," a fact of which Miss Cather is rather too conscious, for she invites us, as visitors to a gallery, to stand now here, now there, now forward, now back a few paces, so that the portrait's various lights and facets may change with the angle and the distance. A serious, considered painting, built up in browns and grays and the mellower ochres, but with one of those rather miscellaneous faces which hint that the artist has done better with separate traits than with the subject as a whole. Myra Henshawe, in spite of the careful evidence as to her nature, doesn't altogether add up.

There is perhaps no more difficult technical decision in writing a novel than the position of the narrator. Is he to be the author directly, or a third person within the book, and if so, will he also be within the action and the mood as well, or in a vague sort of liaison with the author, and not of character's rank and individuality? Miss Cather seems to have chosen clearly in her own mind, but I often feel that the choice subtracts considerably from her novels. Her narrators are within the book, usually an intimate part of what is going on, but their prime allegiance is to her: it is with her tongue that they speak, with her eyes that they see. They do not merely record, they manage, interpret, choose and feel, they are extremely important; they have power, delegated by the author, to rule the mood and the action completely. In fact, they are Miss Cather, under a thin disguise. Why the disguise? That Miss Cather is discovered talking to us, when we thought it was going to be someone else, is often disturbing. For her narrators are always the same. The person who guides us through *My Antonia* is supposedly a man, the guide through *My Mortal Enemy* is a young woman, and what each reveals to us suffers unaccountably from the fact that these so possibly dissimilar guides are exactly alike. A grosser instance: Tom Outland, manifestly the central figure in *The Professor's House*, is at first presented at second-hand, in absence, in recollection—distantly, with something of the mysterious clarity which the right amount of distance can lend to people in a book. But suddenly we are seeing his life through Tom Outland himself, and we are somewhat surprised by certain familiar ways of looking at things, a certain spacious, but for him rather feminine sensitiveness, which ceases to surprise us when we realize that Miss Cather has invaded Tom Outland, indeed ejected and extinguished him. So with *My Mortal Enemy*: the young girl becomes more and more palpably Miss Cather herself. I don't know why this should lessen the sharpness and validity of Myra Henshawe, but it does. . . .

If the whole were as good as many of the parts *Preface to a Life* would be a very distinguished book indeed. Miss Gale's minor characters, as I have said, are usually very well done, and there are a number of uncommonly lovely bits of description. . . . One misses, throughout, what one misses so much in most novels: anonymity; the author is so much about, or whispering in the wings. . . . Miss Gale has not solved the question, Where shall I stand in relation to my characters, within them, outside of them, half-way between them and the rest of their world?

There is a fundamental clarity in writing of fiction which can only be achieved by solving this intimate question. Before the more visible problems of the novel are solved, this obscurer question must be dealt with, plainly and satisfactorily. Failure so to deal with it does much to handicap the skill of gifted writers such as Willa Cather and Zona Gale.

Schuyler Ashley, "Willa Cather Rigs Up a Ship in a Bottle," *Kansas City Star*, 26 November 1926

Technically this last book of Willa Cather's is a considerable feat, a real *tour de force*. Yet twenty readers will admire where one will enjoy *My Mortal Enemy*. To press so much lonely bitterness and frustration into less than twenty thousand words, to portray a life's defeat so completely in miniature, is possibly beyond the skill of any other American writer. The book is a minute and tragic epic of egotism.

The mere outline of the story falsely suggests simplicity. Early in the 1880's, in a small Illinois town, Myra Driscoll renounced the fortune that would have come to her from her uncle, in order to marry the boy she loved. For some years she and Oswald Henshawe, steadily gaining foothold in New York, were reported to be happy, "as happy as most people." But as Nellie Birdseye, the stiff lay figure through whom Willa Cather has chosen to tell the story, remarks in a rare moment of penetration, "that answer was disheartening; the very point to their story was that they should be much happier than other people."

Even such ordinary bliss was not to last. The Henshawes encountered adversity, the enigmatic reversals of middle life, which do unquestionably bring down so many insouciant young couples of their sort. Oswald's career as a minor railroad official, a role for which he had never been inherently gifted, was terminated by a receivership and reorganization. Sickness laid a merciless hand on Myra and changed the gay, vital girl, the charming hostess to the world of the theater and the arts, into a bed-ridden, fiercely querulous invalid without hope and without solace. No longer, in the wretched combination of illness and poverty, was there room for any grace, any dignity.

Like so many happy people, Myra had been able to live generously and yet wholly for herself. In the natural flowering of her personality others were incidentally made happy. She had enjoyed helping bewildered young actors in their love affairs, sending queenly gifts to lonely friends and even patronizingly and charmingly entertaining country cousins like Aunt Lydia and Nellie Birdseye. From the easy, comfortable New York of the 1890's Myra Henshawe, with her splendid vital energy, drove her life along like a smart carriage and pair.

In this book, as in a Greek play, Willa Cather chooses that all the catastrophes shall take place off stage. So there is an interval of ten years between the fast incidents in New York and the discovery by the omnispective Nellie Birdseye of the Henshawes, shabby, lonely, weighed down by illness and indigence, in a shoddy apartment house of a West Coast city. Myra Henshawe is dying, daily withdrawing deeper into herself, as the defeat of her inordinate demands on life becomes more complete. Oswald is caring for her beautifully, tenderly, with the quixotic and the indomitable devotion of an idealist. His love, the one exquisite thing life has left her, only irritates Myra. It is the best stroke in the book that Miss Cather makes this credible and comprehensive. "Tout comprendre, c'est tout pardonner." Myra dies alone with herself, with that pitiless exorbitant self that she could never for one moment escape, truly, her "Mortal Enemy."

A somber tale, surely. It would be pleasant to escape the conviction that it is explicitly and uncompromisingly true. Miss Cather has deftly told Myra's story entirely through prosaic little incidents all taking place in a humdrum every-day atmosphere. This creates an infernal effect of realism, like the bleak light which streams into an ugly room through north windows at noonday.

By dwarfing the stature of her book and forcing her readers to see the entire drama through the eyes of a scarcely interested and certainly uninteresting spectator, Miss Cather has created difficulties for herself, which for the most part she conquers. But why create them? Surely classic restraint and tranquility do not demand absolute baldness of treatment.

Flaubert dreaded a word too much, but he equally abhorred an incident or a portrait too few. Here both Oswald Henshawe and Nellie, the teller of the tale, are sketches irritatingly incomplete. If the device of Nellie is to be used at all why should she not be decently accounted for, satisfactorily interwoven into the strands of the story?

Lonely sailors and prisoners of war have been known to produce models of full-rigged ships inside of bottles, but it is not recorded that their frigates were more perfect or more life-like for being so constricted.

Ethel Wallace Hawkins, "Atlantic Bookshelf," *Atlantic Monthly*, 138 (December 1926), n.p.

My Mortal Enemy is a brilliant study of temperament. Nothing that Miss Cather has written—not even *A Lost Lady*—has more vitality; and nothing is more relentless.

In its technique this short novel, with the swift, straight flight of its narrative, and its inimitable economy of detail, is at the opposite pole from its predecessor, *The Professor's House*. In its theme there is a likeness, but only a superficial one. The earlier novel shows a phase, a temporary dearth and disillusionment, in the life of a gentle and essentially reasonable nature capable of endurance and adjustment: *My Mortal Enemy* depicts, in its so small compass, the furious lifelong fight against disappointment of a fiery nature, gallant but not fine, clear-sighted but not just, and scorning acceptance as low surrender.

The story tells how Myra Henshawe, an ardent spirit greedy for romance and beauty, wrecks her life by an inauspicious love; for she is a woman who cannot be happy in poverty, or just in unhappiness. Her passion for her young lover passes into a distaste for her gentle, unsuccessful, incorrigibly loyal husband, and later into a deep rancor. Her thwarted but indestructible romanticism finds its outlet in her attempt to wring from friendship and from art something nobler than the humdrum of every day—as in her faithful worship of the great Modjeska; and again in the impulse that makes her, in straits of poverty, keep hidden away a sum of money "for unearthly purposes." But one follows her story, though with an intensity of interest, yet with a qualified sympathy; for if she has an indomitable spirit, a pungent wit, and a rather capricious generosity, she has also coarseness, littleness, and malice.

Myra Henshawe will stand among the most powerful of Miss Cather's creations. It is with great art that so few scenes are made to build up an effect of an entire life revealed, and again with great art that both the noble and the ugly elements of Mrs. Henshawe's nature are represented as intensified by the sharper stress of her miserable last days; the purer flaming of her sense of beauty and the strong upwelling of her almost forgotten faith are shown, and no less clearly the implacable injustice and unforgiveness that are less the derangement of mortal illness than the natural result of her years of rancor. Subtlest of all is the tracing of the process by which this spirit at war with itself externalizes the battle and simplifies conflict into hatred.

My Mortal Enemy shows Miss Cather's power at its most concentrated, and has passages of a clear, etched beauty. It is a fine piece of art, 'bitter as gall, and passionate and wise.'

"Culling the Sweet and Bitter Fruits of Six Months' Fiction," *New York Times Book Review*, 5 December 1926, p. 5

Willa Cather gives us, by her latest performance, no cause for doleful predictions, but *My Mortal Enemy* shows her in a period of transition which is fraught with danger. What there is of her story is finely done, but its over-skeletonized treatment causes one regret for the more full-bodied picture which might have emerged in this companion piece to *A Lost Lady* had Miss Cather chosen to be less frugal in her handling of the theme.

Sidney Homer, "Willa Cather and *My Mortal Enemy*," *Boston Evening Transcript*, 11 December 1926, p. 6

Miss Cather no longer finds life to be the simple thing she once thought it was. Existence takes on deeper meaning, it is more complex, possesses overtones with which the author of *My Antonia* did not concern herself. In her later period she senses the irreducible quality which life presents and attempts to solve it. She explores the shadowy realms of the mind and soul where things are so unreal and unbelievably fantastic. But when she returns from her search she leads by the hand a wraith, like Orpheus in the myth. In *The Professor's House* we viewed an effort to seek out the fundamental tone in a man's character. Then, as now, the attempt was not successful; such attempts rarely are. Miss Cather has led a real being back from her soul-searches but once—in *A Lost Lady*—an occasion when she was not really engaged upon a search into mind and soul.

My Mortal Enemy is quite like *A Lost Lady*, in length, form, and approach. Again we see a woman of intelligence and charm subjected to adverse environment and embittering circumstance, and we watch how they bear down upon her, tear her hopes and desires to bits, and finally drive her to a miserable end. But this time Miss Cather does not reach the heights she achieved in her former novel. The Myra Henshawe of her present story is never the living person that Marian Forrester was, the blood that pulses in her is not so red, does not color her complexion with the delicate tints of life. Marian moved us to pity as we watched her losing herself in life; Myra Henshawe affects our emotions but little. Mrs. Forrester moved against a real background of people and locale; life pulsed in Captain Forrester and Neil and Mrs. Forrester's lovers; one could feel the heat of the sun and hear the whistle of the passing trains as one sat on the broad veranda of the great white house which pioneer money had built and furnished in that lovely Western valley. But the characters in *My Mortal Enemy* do not live. The New York of Myra's day is an unconvincing picture—a posturing Diana atop the old Madison Square Garden, vague references to the Fifth Avenue Hotel, a Jersey City ferry, and Jean de Reszke's return to the Metropolitan after a season in London. The Pacific Coast town in which the story ends has neither name nor people moving in the streets; it has the municipal existence of a

sign in one of Shakespeare's plays at the Globe Theater announcing that the stage had suddenly become "Venice."

Perhaps the fault lies in the approach to the story. Miss Cather employs her usual method of telling what happens through a second person. But this approach lacks in sensitiveness. Nellie Birdseye stands to one side of the main current of action and calls off the events. But she does not explain them, nor does she give us the character she is supposed to give us through her eyes. She has not that living connection, that intimate knowledge of Myra's life, that sympathetic relationship, which the interpreter had in *My Antonia* or in *A Lost Lady*. The result is inevitable—the interpretation lacks the ring of truth; it is meaningless. Nellie Birdseye fails to interpret the main character, chiefly for the reason that she herself is colorless. Neil, who interpreted Mrs. Forrester, loved her and understood her: Nellie is the niece of a woman who was a girlhood friend of Myra's twenty years before the story opens. . . .

Miss Cather's story can by no stretch of the imagination be called a novel. It is so short that it is truly a soul portrait and an incomplete one at that. Miss Cather's novels have steadily become shorter. With *My Mortal Enemy* it seems that she has reached the danger point, if not passed it. She develops her story by incident rather than by analysis of situation as does Schnitzler in *Beatrice* and *Fräulein Else*. What results is something resembling a pencil sketch that an artist makes and in which he roughly marks out the outlines of his subject, vaguely hinting at the general form that the finished painting on canvas will take. Miss Cather achieves contours, gives us a hint of what may be in her mind and what she might have said had she written at 350-page length. But her sketch has no definite meaning, its lines are never so clear and suggestive as the lines in *A Lost Lady*. The story tempts us and invites up to guess at what sort of a life Myra Henshawe lived and what sort of a woman she was. Her husband is drawn far more clearly; he is the only one who in any degree stands out definitely in the puzzled groupings of Miss Cather. Myra Henshawe is a lost character rather than a lost lady.

Dial, 82 (January 1927), 73

My Mortal Enemy, by Willa Cather is a character study of such severity that even its rightful emotional quality has been denied it; it is presented with a creative tautness which robs it of warmth. The story is set down with unquestioned economy and skill; it has touches of swift discernment, but it would be a better work of art if the mind could fasten upon an occasional moment of relaxation in its unfolding. Although a work of imagination, it has the surface of glazed pottery.

John M. Kenny, Jr., *Commonweal*, 5 (9 March 1927), 499–500

A selfish, grasping old woman, whose husband has become her mortal enemy because in old age she cannot forgive him for the harm she did him in youth, is treated by Willa Cather in her latest sketch in a most astounding way. For the character-study of Myra Henshawe affords the author an excellent opportu-

nity to expound numerous and varied revelations through the medium of this demented old woman—especially so since Miss Cather apologizes for her in the early stages of her infirmity, by saying:

"She isn't people. She's Molly Driscoll, and there never was anybody else like her. She can't endure, but she has enough desperate courage for a regiment."

Miss Cather takes Molly Driscoll, petted and adored niece of an Irish immigrant who had become a middle-western town idol after he had made his fortune in convict labor, makes her elope with a German free-thinker, and then, after a glimpse of the couple in New York that should warn the reader of what is about to be expressed, she skips ten years and picks up the thread again in a ramshackle hotel in the West where she puts Myra Henshawe through her paces, finally leaving her to die "alone with her mortal enemy," propped up against a tree and gazing out over the sea.

With a firm economy of method, a wholly admirable subtlety, a technique that is none the less sure for being unobtrusively present in the simple, faultless unfolding of her story, the author accomplishes, without seeming effort, the goal of all novelists—the imprisoning of a soul between the covers of a book. The uneventful life-story of Myra Henshawe seems scarcely epic in its retelling, but Miss Cather's artistry makes of it a tragedy worth the knowing. To fashion a moving human story from the slender material of Myra's life, was an infinitely more difficult task than any of the author's other portraits of women. There was nothing of glamour about Myra, and to take a wealth of what appears at first to be trivial detail, and weave it into the pattern of a perplexed soul of a woman, is no mean achievement. Her understanding, which she conveys to the reader perfectly, is complete and never falters. She is never coldly unpitying in her attitude, and at no time is she sentimental.

We have Miss Cather's word for it that the mortal enemy of the title is Oswald, Myra's husband. But is seems rather ridiculous that this man who is at times the very sublimity of negation and is always the gentle, loving husband, should be a force of destruction to the turbulent Myra. Her own warped soul was her chiefest enemy. Oswald's very gentleness and his uncomplaining submission to his lot is enough to arouse the ire of the malignant Myra—but there the blame is more the woman's than her husband's.

"People can be lovers and enemies at the same time, you know. A man and woman draw apart from that long embrace and see what they have done to each other. Perhaps I can't forgive him for the harm I've done him. Perhaps that's it. In age we lose everything—even the power to love." Thus spake Myra.

If she was crushed by the forces of fate, then surely she was the mill of the gods, chosen to grind exceedingly fine the bitter-sweet of life for her unconscious victim, her husband.

Times Literary Supplement (London), 10 May 1928, p. 354

Miss Willa Cather has written a long short story on the theme of the hostility a woman may feel for the man she profoundly loves. Need and resentment, love and hate live with unfading vigour in the heart of Myra Henshawe, whose story is told in My Mortal Enemy. She makes a runaway match and loses a fortune, lives through prosperity and vicissitude, and dies after cruel suffering and poverty,

devotedly nursed by her husband who is still her lover and her enemy. He has not been strictly faithful, but at heart he has never failed her; he has been tolerant and admiring, and he is heroic in the end, when, entirely turned against him by her illness and misery, Myra bitterly regrets her marriage and denounces him in terrible words. The depressing moral of the book seems to be that whatever choice is made in youth will be regretted in age. If Myra had not married her story would have been that of a frustrated woman to whom money and luxury would mean nothing. Having brought poverty upon herself she could only think longingly of the comforts she had thrown away.

The story is told by the young cousin of the famous and wilful Myra, who has been brought up on stories of the brilliant, the only interesting member of the big Illinois family, and meets her for the first time when she is past her youth but still fascinating. Nellie, the young girl, feels her charm and sees her goodness and her selfishness, her subtly mixed qualities so contradictory, so intense. She sees, too, before she is old enough to understand them, something of the jealousy and hostility Myra displays toward Oswald Henshawe. Miss Cather places these three characters with beautiful clarity and precision before us. Years intervene; then, accidentally, Nellie, who is teaching in New York, finds that Myra and Oswald have a poor flat in the same building as hers. Their friendship is renewed, and she watches the drama of Myra's death. It is finely related, but the impression left is one of the pain and futility. Oswald, so endlessly patient and sensitive, goes off, to die years later in Alaska, and Nellie is left with her strange, bright and dark memories of their lives.

Sometimes, when I have watched the bright beginning of a love story, when

I have seen a common feeling exalted into beauty by imagination, generosity, and the flaming courage of youth, I have heard again that strange complaint breathed by a dying woman into the stillness of night, like a confession of the soul: "Why must I die like this, alone with my mortal enemy?"

Edward Shanks, *London Mercury*, 18 (July 1928), 207

My Mortal Enemy is slighter in substance than *A Lost Lady* and not perhaps so rich in evocations. The subject is perhaps a little drier. It is the gradual discovery by a young girl of the hollowness of a beautiful legend. Myra Henshaw in her youth threw away a fortune to make a runaway marriage and Nellie has always heard of her, and thought of her, as a figure of romance. But little by little she learns that the qualities which lead to a courageous elopement do not necessarily ensure a happy married life and that the romance of Myra and her husband is all in the past. It is as slight as it is short, but it is all done with Miss Cather's lovely economy and it is by no means unworthy of the author of *A Lost Lady*.

Checklist of Additional Reviews

Booklist, 23 (December 1926), 132.
Woman's Citizen, December 1926.

DEATH COMES FOR THE ARCHBISHOP

BY WILLA CATHER

Death comes for the Archbishop

"Auspice Maria!"
Father Vaillant's signet-ring

NEW YORK

ALFRED A KNOPF · MCMXXVII

Herschel Brickell, "The Literary Landscape: Miss Cather in New Mexico," *North American Review*, 224 (September–October 1927), front advertising section, n.p.

Willa Cather's *Death Comes for the Archbishop* has an eager audience waiting for it, as any novel by Miss Cather is certain to have by this time. It represents Miss Cather in a story-telling mood, offering none of the complicated pattern of *The Professor's House*, for example, and few "problems" to vex the critics and the public.

It is the fictional biography of a French priest who went to New Mexico in the mid-Nineteenth Century as a Vicar Apostolic and remained until his work had won him a post as Archbishop. With wholly admirable simplicity and economy, Miss Cather has done this priestly portrait against a pioneer background rich in many elements, a living tapestry to be seen through the limpidity of her prose without blur or distortion.

This is the sort of historical novel-writing that looks easy and is just the opposite. Weeks after one has closed the book, the story is there in sharp, clean outline and the personality of Father Jean Marie Latour lingers to be felt and understood. Miss Cather has given the younger generation who think the overtones of life can only be caught in murky, obscure, amorphous prose a lesson, if they will heed it. As a work of art, *Death Comes for the Archbishop* will inevitably take high rank among her novels.

Fanny Butcher, "Willa Cather's New Novel Is Simply, Beautifully Told," *Chicago Daily Tribune*, 3 September 1927, p. 8

Any season which includes a novel by Willa Cather is an important one in the history of American literature. She is one of our few really great woman novelists. To those of us who read books for a living the knowledge that she has done another novel is as much hay to old Dobbin as a Dempsey-Tunney bout is to the sport editors. It is always a contest, too, whether Miss Cather wins the public's acclaim or doesn't, and what makes it amusing and worthwhile is that we suspect—though we never could quote Miss Cather as saying so—that the public may be, so far as she is concerned, damned.

I don't mean that she doesn't appreciate the public's joy in her books, for she does—sort of naively and charmingly, especially when the public is a railroad conductor who recognizes her name and tells her all about his own excavations in New Mexico—but she has never written a line, so far as I know, to please the public. She writes her novels to please herself, or perhaps to satisfy some inner secret urge for writing, some impelling power to get something said. If they please the reviewers and the reading public, so good. If they don't, Miss Cather isn't bitter or she doesn't think the public is all wrong. She merely says she knew what she was trying to do and she did it as she thought best, and that's that, and goes on to another theme and another method.

Her last book, *My Mortal Enemy*, for instance, was, to my idea, one of the subtlest and most beautiful pieces of writing and criticism of life that she—or anyone else—has ever done. The world at large didn't think so. They liked *The Professor's House* better. Her new novel, *Death Comes for the Archbishop*, is one of the books that no one can say beforehand how it will affect the public. Miss Cather's admirers will see in it a tremendous piece of work—a vivid but calm portrayal of not death at all coming for the archbishop but of a long life lived bounteously and fully (though with its reservations) making the coming of death what the coming of death should be for all of us, the closing of a full life. They will see a novel done with such sparseness, such knowledge of the main character as to be a biography rather than a novel. Perhaps there was such an archbishop in the early days of New Mexico. But whether there was or not in the flesh there will always be one now that Miss Cather has created him. A man with delicate background, education, and an appreciation of fine things, he goes to New Mexico when that vast country was still a wilderness, taking with him a boyhood friend, and together they conquer not only a wilderness but a people. They take their religion into a country which was ridden by religions. They take their faith into the hearts of men and women who were living in a country still too young to admit of much faith in their kind. They live their lives in their separate ways, deep friends, but deeper lovers of the strange new country which has lured them.

The archbishop and his vicar are almost the only characters in the book. The others, unforgettable, vivid, but only a background for the two, and in reality the vicar is only a background for the archbishop. The book is a calm, beautiful portrait of a great man, who lived a full life and met death with a sense of a life well lived.

There is a great background for the archbishop to live against—the vital means, the tang of the air, the daily pulse of a new country—all are caught in Miss Cather's pen. Her writing is the most deceptive in the world to the ordinary reader, and never more so than in *Death Comes for the Archbishop*. To most readers she writes such an unadorned English as to seem a pale style. There is nothing ornate, nothing gestury, nothing flowery. And yet there is no one writing in America today who has a purer, clearer, more beautiful style than Miss Cather. It is the ideal toward which the flowery fingers of adjectives are really striving, or would be if they knew enough to snip off their purple patches.

Death Comes for the Archbishop contains some of the finest writing Miss Cather has ever done. But that very simplicity of style, the very meagerness of plot may make it less popular than some of her other books. Mind, I don't say that it will be. I say merely that there will be more of sport in watching the public's reaction to it than there would be if it were an out and out destined best seller. Any one who doesn't read it will miss one of the fine books of the year, however.

Henry Longan Stuart, "A Vivid Page of History in Miss Cather's New Novel," *New York Times Book Review*, 4 September 1927, p. 2

In *Death Comes for the Archbishop* Miss Willa Cather has given us an account of the episcopate of one of those devoted servants of the Catholic Church who carried its doctrines to the New World.

The Congregation De Propaganda Fide has had to face many knotty problems during the four centuries of its existence, but probably no single one where so many possibilities for mistake and disaster existed as that which confronted it after taking possession of New Mexico for the United States by General Kearny in the summer of 1848. The religious destiny of a new district "larger than Central and Western Europe, barring Russia" suddenly became a matter of urgent concern. And everything about the new territory was cryptic and unprecedented. Missionaries and enthusiasts such as accompanied the Spanish conquistadores wrote some of the most splendid chapters in the history of the Catholic Church. But to administrators of a later and more sober day they bequeathed some terrible dilemmas. Everywhere abandoned missions and ruined churches bore witness to Indian warfare as terrible in its character as the desert raids which wiped out the African Church in the fifth and sixth centuries. Even the character of the neophytes who had withstood the storm and the pastors around whom they rallied was a debatable question. There was too much reason to fear that for the former religion had become matter of a few pious practices grafted upon a paganism never really abandoned in the heart and that, for the latter, the corruption almost inevitable when isolation overtakes an infant church was calling for stern disciplinary measures if the seed sown in the blood of so many martyrs was not to be choked in thorns and brambles.

These are the times and conjunctures that seldom fail to produce extraordinary men, or, rather, that call forth from men who in normal times might have spent their lives blamelessly and anonymously, unsuspected resources of heroism and initiative. Such a one was Jean Marie Latour, successively Vicar Apostolic Bishop and Archbishop of Santa Fe for thirty-eight years.

At the very beginning of any consideration of such a book, a question of literary conscience poses itself. The newly aroused interest in American history as dramatic material of the first order is having many results, some good, some less so. But it is quite plain that it is producing and will produce in the future a type of book which falls under no category hitherto familiar. This new type may be roughly defined, not so much as an historical novel, as a superimposition of the novel upon history. And it is not taking the place among forms hitherto recognized without a certain accompanying mystification. No one who has followed current literature within the last few years will have any difficulty in recalling instances in which such outstanding landmarks in our history as the gold rush of 1848 on the Pacific slope, or the acquisition of Alaska have been dealt with in very lighthearted fashion. For the smaller fry whose mission is merely to entertain the question how far established fact is adhered to is hardly worth putting. But for a writer of Miss Willa Cather's calibre, it is in its place. The facts of the Santa Fe episcopate are accessible in any standard book of reference. We know that its first Bishop was John Baptist Lamy, that his life followed, chronologically at least, the limits given it by Miss Cather. We may suspect that, in the new setting she has given it, an enormous amount of tradition, collected upon the spot is enshrined. Nevertheless, the mere transposition of Latour for Lamy, for a man not forty years dead, is a little disquieting. Does it bespeak a resolution to have done with the tyranny of fact, an enfranchisement from the limitations hitherto accepted, more or less loyally, by those who make the historical novel their concern? And may not the new fashion quite possibly be laying down snares for the feet of generations to come, little versed in documentation and quite ready to take the word of so fascinating a writer in matters of fact as well as of fancy?

This reservation made, it is sheer critical duty to go and admit that Miss Cather has succeeded in producing a truly remarkable book. To begin with, it is soaked through and through with atmosphere, not of the facile sort acquired by the mere descriptiveness, but by the relation of every scent and sound to the senses and nerves of one who sees the barren upheaved land and breathes the intoxication of its barrenness for the first time.

Moreover, by an artistry that is as beautiful as it is rare, every perception of this fantastic diocese and of the violent and generous children who are his charge is allowed to reach us through the perceptions of a thoroughly civilized man, of gentle birth, but from the Province where feudalism lingered intact, and the stubbornness of whose sons is a French proverb, cultured, a little aloof and filled with pity for something vaguely fine and doomed to perish that he sees around him. Bishop Latour, though he accepts all hardships with equanimity and good grace, has no discoverable austerities. He likes good cheer, good wine and good architecture, shudders retrospectively, like Mrs. Trollope at the memory of frontier Cincinnati, and to the day of his death never loses a certain feeling of satisfaction as he washes his hands in the bit silver bowl that was the gift to him of a lordly Spanish parishioner. His Indian guides love him for his good manners, for his unostentatious courage and for the respect with which he listens to their tales of the old religion, satisfying himself with an "Our Father," recited together before pastor and neophyte roll themselves in their blankets. His hand is forbearing and patient, even when armed with the thunder of Rome, and ready to fall upon recalcitrant Padre Martinez, the bull-necked tyrant of Taos, who leads the life of a patriarch of the Old Testament amid his herds and women. His belief in God and his faith is crossed, as it is crossed among so many scholarly Christians, by a scepticism as to the power of average human nature to correspond with the message offered.

When officiating on the enchanted mesa of Acoma,

he had never found it so hard to go through the ceremony of the Mass. Before him, on the gray floor, in the gray light, a group of bright shawls and blankets, some fifty or sixty silent faces; above and behind them the gray walls. He felt as if he were celebrating mass at the bottom of the sea for antediluvian creatures, for types of life so old, so hardened, so shut within their shells, that the sacrifice on Calvary could hardly reach back so far. Those shell-like backs behind him might be saved by baptism and divine grace, as undeveloped infants are, but hardly through any experience of their own, he thought. When he blessed them and sent them away it was with a sense of inadequacy and spiritual defeat.

Many figures, some familiar, come into the story Miss Cather has to tell us. There is our childhood friend Kit Carson with his dignified Mexican wife. "There is something curiously conscious about his mouth, reflective, a little melancholy— and something that suggested a capacity for tenderness. The Bishop felt a quick glow of pleasure in looking at the man." There is Father Vaillant, blundering, warmhearted and enthusiastic, type of the older missionary school of Jogues and Laliement, who leaves his rich Denver parishioners ("men who owned mines and sawmills and flourishing businesses; but they needed all their money to push these enterprises") and goes back to beg among his poverty-stricken Mexicans who gave "if they had anything to give at all." There is the guide Jacinto, who takes his Bishop during a blizzard into an ancient haunt of fear and superstition, after first swearing him to secrecy, and lets him listen to the roar of a subterranean torrent moving in utter blackness under ribs of antediluvian rock. There are legends, beautiful and terrible, of Fray Baltazar, who made his rock bloom like the rose and paid for gluttony with his life, of Fray Junipero, who met the Holy Family at the foot of three cotton trees in the desert. From the riches of her imagination and sympathy Miss Cather has distilled a very rare piece of literature. It stands out from the very resistance it opposes to classification, in the authentic line, and at no great distance either, of such masterpieces of our literature as *Eothen* and *Arabia Deserta* [travel books by Alois Mucil and Alexander William Kinglake respectively].

Robert O. Ballou, "The Story of the West which Willa Cather Sees," *Chicago Daily News*, 7 September 1927, p. 14

Willa Cather has written another western novel. That is the truth of the matter. Yet when it arrives as a thought for the first time it is so shocking, so utterly unbeliev-

able, that it requires saying excitedly. The territory allotted long ago to those brawny penmen whose stories have been summed up in the line: "Ride, ride, ride, shoot, shoot, shoot, ride, shoot, ride, shoot, ride, marry the girl," has been invaded once more by an artist whose beautiful quiet prose has nothing in common with the roar of a .45 or a trail marked by the bodies of the slain.

There is really nothing surprising about it. For one of the most convincing evidences of a fine creative ability lies in that tendency of the true creative artist to tell of that which he sees about him, and Miss Cather is an American. For years she has been writing about America, unfolding bit by bit a scene of conflict and growth which is her country's own. She is (let it be said with deep satisfaction) "one of ours" more truly than the hero of her own novel which bore that phrase upon the cover.

She has clung consistently to a love for the rural districts. In *A Lost Lady*, *My Antonia*, and *One of Ours*, the best scenes were laid in the open country or a country village. And in her latest book, *Death Comes for the Archbishop*, published last Friday by Knopf, the scene is again far from the crowded cities, in New Mexico, a country which she has long loved.

She has gone back into history for her story, back to the middle of the nineteenth century, when Rome sent missionaries to evangelize the American Indians and Mexicans. She has followed two of these, Fathers Latour and Vaillant, into the southwestern frontier country, over the almost pathless mountains and into the simple hearts of the red men and Mexicans. She has made a vivid picture of a lifelong friendship between two priests and between the priests and their spiritual charges. With her you see Magdalena, the half-starved Mexican girl, cruelly exploited by a heartless American husband, risk her own life to save the lives of these two good friends; you follow Kit Carson over a long trail for an evening's visit with his bishop and see the old woman Sada stumbling through the snow in the night that she might worship a moment in the bishop's church, a privilege denied her by her employer. You feel Sada's need greatly when she weeps:

"Nineteen years, Father; nineteen years since I have seen the holy things of the altar."

When, leaving her, the bishop gives her a little silver medal with the image of the virgin on it, you agree with him:

" 'Ah,' he thought, 'for one who cannot read—or think—the image, the physical form of love.' "

Yes, it is a western novel. But in a deeper sense the scene is set in whatever place man is. It is excellent evidence to support Lenox Robinson's dictum, "If your art is local enough to be understood in Chicago, it is universal enough to be understood in Shanghai or Kerry."

Death Comes for the Archbishop is a supreme apologia pro vita of religion, of the Catholic religion, if you like, but of any religion surely.

Miss Cather's is an art of consummate gentleness, without loss of honesty, of complete sympathy without any bathos. Her prose is fashioned after the older traditions of writing in which speed (or I believe the later word is pace) is of little consequence. It is restful and satisfying. The old Navajo Indian whom she created in this book, telling the archbishop on his deathbed how he had come in one day by train over a distance which they had traveled together years before in two weeks, unwittingly makes the best comment possible on the manner of his own creation.

"Men travel faster now, but I do not know if they go to better things."

Dorothy Foster Gilman, "Willa Cather Writes a Fictional Biography," *Boston Evening Transcript*, 10 September 1927, p. 2

In the first place, this is not a novel. In the second place, it is one of the most superb pieces of literary endeavor this reviewer has ever read, regardless of language or nation. Third and finally, it is a piece of work that everyone may read with reverence and respect. Miss Cather gives us history. Yet she distills the fine essence of it so miraculously that we feel that the recorded events shaped themselves only a day or two before, that the saintly and clerical pioneers she describes might walk in our midst today were we willing to go forth into the wilderness and await them.

Nor are these words of ours the result of any previous admiration for Miss Cather's writings. We have never particularly appreciated the significance of her work until today. The art of the historian is something of which many historians know little. When Carlyle wrote his *French Revolution* the familiar and commonplace criticism by spiteful reviewers was unvarying. "Very little accurate information about the Revolution" they all declared bitterly, "but altogether too much about Carlyle." When Mr. Strachey wrote of Queen Victoria there was not a great deal of the author's personality in the biographical survey, but historical facts were selected for the express purpose of rendering ponderous, complaisant, feminine royalty a little ignoble. A fashion was thereby created. Men and women have risen who fancy themselves wrapt in the mantle of the historian when they are in actual fact merely wearing the drab blue smock of the professional literary scavenger.

We assert firmly that this is not a novel. It is technically an historical biography dealing imaginatively though accurately with the life of a Catholic missionary in New Mexico during the years following 1848, when the United States acquired considerable foreign territory.... Few writers in any language have elected this period in American history and have revealed such a capacity for making that history live. Miss Cather pays thus a tribute to all those unknown soldiers of the Catholic faith who, migrating from France or Italy, gave their lives eagerly for the glory of their church. Their form of warfare was more terrible in many instances than that carried on in Europe ten years ago. For these men entered the battle weaponless. Spiritual armor they may have had, but it is not always the protection tradition would make us believe. This story of Jean Marie Latour comes in the nature of a revelation to historians, to those who fancy they can write fiction, and to that multitude of readers who know little or nothing of that ardent fire kindled by Jesus Christ in the hearts of his apostles. "When the cathedral bell tolled just after dark, the Mexican population of Santa Fe fell upon their knees, and all American Catholics as well. Many others who did not kneel prayed in their hearts. Eusabio and the Tesuque boys went quietly away to tell their people; and next morning the old archbishop lay before the high altar in the church he had built."

N.E.A. Book Survey, "Willa Cather in Somber Mood as She Writes Story of Taos and Santa Fe of Early Days," *New Mexico State Tribune*, 10 September 1927, p. 6

Willa Cather's latest book, *Death Comes for the Archbishop*, is the story of an archbishop who builds a cathedral, and she has constructed it like a cathedral. It is dignified, slow, somber, lofty, beautiful: illuminated by altar candles rather than a glare of electricity.

There is no stirring high mass, however, no crash of the organ, none of the exalted drama of Holy Week. The plot is negligible, with no climax and no woman interest. No Beautiful Lost Lady with her fatal gift of promising joy adds color or complication. The major characters are two devout Catholic priests, Jean Marie Latour, Catholic bishop of New Mexico, and Father Joseph Valliant, his vicar.

The action is in the 1850's and the locale the Spanish American country centering in Santa Fe and Taos.

Against the background of Spaniards, Indians, early American traders and settlers, Willa Cather presents an unforgettable picture of the life of the time.

That the story is reverently conceived and beautifully written no one could question. It has an exquisitely sensitive quality, and a poignant tenderness. Perhaps one should not ask more. But there are many who will wish for more light, color, and drama in her cathedral, and who will find its somberness oppressive.

When an author can create such living, breathing, vital characters as Miss Cather has, the public is apt to expect them from her. Many will prefer her lost ladies to archbishops.

Lee Wilson Dodd, "A Hymn to Spiritual Beauty," *Saturday Review of Literature*, 4 (10 September 1927), 101

After reading *Death Comes for the Archbishop*, I indulged myself in a critic's daydream; and found myself not too patiently trying to explain this book—so reticent, so distinguished, so beautiful—to a rebellious young person in very short skirts who rather petulantly had asserted that she was an incarnation of Average Public Taste in America.

"You say, my dear child, that Miss Cather's novel has bored you; that you couldn't get through it; that it isn't really a novel at all. When I ask you why it isn't really a novel, you maintain there's no story in it—by which, obviously, you mean there's no 'love story' in it. In this as in most things you are wrong and—don't bother to forgive me, sweet child!—rather pathetically stupid. There is a great, a very great, love story in Miss Cather's masterly, quiet narrative. It is a severe, purely designed chalice of hand-beaten silver, filled to the brim with the white essential wine of love—love of man to man, love of God to man, love of man to God.

"True, it nowhere lures you to identify yourself with some fair, and conceivably frail, heroine whose neurotic organism is asquirm with sexual desire. In this respect, I am forced to admit, it fails your instinctive expectations pretty badly; and unless you can (temporarily) free yourself of these anticipatory longings, this book is not for you. But if you can manage to survive this disappointment and attune your mind (may I daringly presume you have one?) to less customary harmonies, harmonies both throbbing deeper and lifting higher than the common range, I venture to assure you that you will soon forget to be bored."

However, not even in day-dream could I longer continue, for my rebellious young person in very short skirts had already vanished, leaving behind her merely an echo of jazz and faint whiffs of perfumed lip-stick, aromatic chewing-gum, and synthetic gin . . .

Death Comes for the Archbishop tells how a young man, Jean Marie Latour, once a seminarist in Auvergne, rode with difficulty into the newly erected territory of New Mexico as Vicar Apostolic, and of the wise and good works he wrought there for many years, until, mourned by all his people, "the old Archbishop lay before the high altar in the church he had built." Is it a narrative of fact—biography in the guise of fiction? Or is it an independent creation, a fabric woven of many colored strands, sombre or brilliant, drawn from the annals of our Southwestern frontier? I do not know; and while I shall be interested to learn, if I am ever to learn, I do not greatly care. For this much is certain: by putting unforgettably before us the life (actual, wholly imagined, or partly imagined) of Father Latour, Miss Cather has also given us *truth*, has brought to us a quintessence distilled from a given region, with all its forms and modes of being, throughout a selected, unifying stretch of years. No artistic purpose is more difficult of fulfilment; and to indicate Miss Cather's stature as artist, it is enough to say that in the present novel one such staggering attempt has been serenely and triumphantly carried through.

But that is not all; it is far from all.

Range through the world's literature and ask yourself how many convincing portraits you can remember of a good and great man. You will not, I fear, recall many. . . . Well, here, at least, is one such portrait—winning, human, and complete. But no, there are *two* such in this extraordinary book, and they are finely differentiated! Father Vaillant and Father Latour . . . Both living men, and utterly unalike, except in their central shining goodness—for I can think of no other word to express their quality. It is the love of these two men for each other, for their God, their Church, and their body-breaking and often heart-breaking tasks which makes of this book a grave, uplifting hymn to Spiritual Beauty. It is nothing less than that.

Nothing less . . . and it has, perhaps, turned one astonished reader a little giddy in the head. The whole thing was so unexpected. Intellectual and Spiritual Futility Blues have been so much more in our modern line. So if there are any artistic faults in this book (as there well may be, man being what he is) I confess that I was far too stirred to note them.

Rebecca West, "Miss Cather's Business as an Artist," *New York Herald Tribune Books*, 11 September 1927, pp. 1, 5–6

The most sensuous of writers, Willa Cather, builds her imagined world as solidly as our five senses build the universe around us. This account of the activities of a French priest who was given a diocese in the Southwest during the late '40s impresses one first of all by its amazing sensory achievements. Miss Cather has within herself a sensitivity that constantly presents her with a body of material which would overwhelm most of us, so that we would give up all idea of transmitting it and would sink into a state of passivity; and she has also a quality of mountain pony sturdiness that makes her push on unfatigued under her load and give an accurate account of every part of it. So it is that one is not quite sure whether it is one of the earlier pages in *Death Comes for the Archbishop* or a desert in central New Mexico that is heaped up with small conical hills red as brickdust, a landscape of which the human aspect is thirst and confusion of the retina at seeing the past itself veritably presenting such reduplications of an image as one could conceive only as consequences of a visual disorder. When the young bishop on his mule finds this thirst smoldering up to flame in his throat and his confusion whirling faster and faster into vertigo he blots out his own pain in meditating on the Passion of our Lord. He does not deny to consciousness that it is in a state of suffering, but leads it inward from the surface of being where it feebly feels itself contending with innumerable purposeless irritations to a place within the heart where suffering is held to have been proved of greater value than anything else in the world, the one coin sufficient to buy man's salvation. This, perhaps the most delicate legerdemain man has ever practiced on his senses, falls into our comprehension as lightly as a snowflake into the hand because of Miss Cather's complete mastery of every phase of the process. But she becomes committed to no degree of complication as her special field. A page later she writes of the moment when the priest and his horses come on water in language simple as if she were writing a book for boys, in language exquisitely appropriate for the expression of a joy that must have been intensest in the youth of races.

Great is her accomplishment. That fear of making a composition out of the juxtaposition of different states of being, which Velasquez was so fond of practicing, when he showed the tapestry makers working in shadow and some of their fellows working behind them in shadows honeycombed with golden motes, and others still further back working in the white wine of full sunlight, is a diversion of hers also. She can suggest how in this land of carnelian hills that become lavender in storm, of deserts striped with such strangeness as ocher-yellow waves of petrified sand, of mesas behind which stand cloud mesas, as if here nature had altered her accustomed order and the sky took reflections as the waters do elsewhere; of beauty in which a quality of prodigiousness is perpetually present like a powerful condiment—the Bishop and his boyhood friend would find refreshment in going back in memory to the cobbled streets of Clermont, where ivy that is cool to the touch and wet about the roots tumbles over garden walls and horse-chestnuts

spread a wide shade which is scarcely needed, and simple families do explicable things and eat good food and love one another. Perfectly conveyed is the difference in palpability between things seen and things remembered; as perfectly as those other differences in palpability which became apparent to the senses of the Archbishop as death approached him. Then the countryside of Auvergne became a place too wet, too cultivated, too human; the air above it seemed to have something of the heaviness of sweat. The air that can only be breathed on land which has not yet been committed to human purposes, the light, dry air of the desert, is more suited to one who is now committed to them as little as it. He has now the excess of experience which comes to old age; since no more action is required from him, there is no particular reason why his attention should be focused on the present. So as he lies in his bed in the study in Santa Fe where he had begun his work forty years before, all the events of his life exist contemporaneously, in his head, his childish days in Clermont and on the coast of the Mediterranean, his youth in the seminary at Rome, his travels among the deserts and the mesas, the Mexicans and the Indians. That is well enough, but it could not go on. He longs, and one can feel the trouble in the old man's head as he wishes it, for this free wind that has never been weighed down by the effluvia of human effort to blow away his soul out into its sphere of freedom.

The book, it may be seen, though clear as a dewdrop, is not superficial. Miss Cather is inspired to her best because she is working on a theme that is peculiarly sympathetic to her. When Father Vaillant goes to administer the sacraments to the faithful on the ranchero of Manuel Lujon he bustles into the kitchen and, with scarcely less care than he bestows on preparations for the holy office, he rescues the leg of mutton that is destined for his dinner and cooks it himself so that when he carves it at table a "delicate stream of pink juice" follows the knife. It is an incident which Miss Cather relates with a great deal of sympathetic feeling; and it is, of course, a beautiful symbol of the effective synthesis which inspires the Roman Catholic Church to its highest activities. That Church has never doubted that sense is a synthesis of the senses; and it has never doubted that man must take the universe sensibly. The people, the suffering generations, deprived of material for the enjoyment of the senses, cry out for saints who shall sanctify their own fates by being holy, who court suffering, who deprive their sense of all material enjoyment. But behind them watches the Church to see that they avail themselves of this hungry sainthood only as one does of some powerful opiate, in small doses and not habitually. Not for long were the faithful to be allowed to abuse or miscall the body which has been given to them as the instrument with which they must perform their task of living. Those who claimed supersensual ecstasies were—as one may read in the life of St. Teresa— exposed to the investigations of persons who comported themselves like inspectors of nuisances. While it is untrue to say that Protestantism invented or even specially stimulated Puritanism—the type of mind which tries to satisfy an innate sense of guilt by the coarser forms of expiation is naturally attracted to whatever the current religion may be and emerges equally under Catholicism or paganism or Islamism or any other formulated faith— it is true to say that Catholicism has always suppressed with extreme vigor such heresies as led to unwholesome abstinences becoming the general practice. The Cathari, for example, were persecuted because although their ascetic teachings might have led to individual sinlessness, they would have wiped out the community, and there would have been so many happy villages the fewer. It would almost seem sometimes as if the Church burned heretics because it was afraid that if it did not, man would burn his soup.

And soup, as the Roman Catholic Church knows, as Miss Cather knows, is a matter of the first importance. "When one comes to think of it," said the Bishop, sitting over a meal prepared by Father Vaillant on one of their early days at Santa Fe, when they were gloomily discussing the possibility of maintaining a French propriety of diet in a country so basely ignorant that it knew nothing of the lettuce "soup like this is not the work of one man. It is the result of a constantly refined tradition. There are nearly a thousand years of history in this soup...." Doubtless he would, if pressed, have admitted that, while the introduction of good soup and lettuce was not the object of his labors in his diocese, they would at least afford a test of success. It was with no sense of trivial declension from his activities that, at the end of his life, he chose for the country estate of his retirement land on which he had seen an apricot tree with "two trunks, each of them thicker than a man's body," which was glorious with great golden fruit of superb flavor, and because of that indication of suitability planted orchards of pears and apples, cherries and apricots there, from which he furnished young trees for his priests to plant wherever they went, for their own eating and to encourage the Mexicans to add fruit to their starchy diet. In all his intermediate activities he has never really gone far from the earth that grows lettuces and apricots.

There is a chapter relating to the rebellious Father Martinez in which Miss Cather, with a blacksmith's muscle, has wrought into compendious form a prodigious deal of reading about the problem the Church has had to face in its effort to secure priests lion-like enough to maintain the faith on the raw edges of civilization against the paganism of lawless men and yet lamb-like enough to remain in loyal subjection to authority seated half the world away; it, too, is a demonstration of sense founded on a fusion of the senses. The Bishop, although fastidious almost to the point of squeamishness, tolerates this priest who rides at the head of a cavalcade of Mexicans and Indians like their robber chief, whose corridor walks are perpetually haunted with a shadow-show of servant maids fleeing before young men whose origin seems to be indicated by the tart disputations at the supper table concerning the celibacy of the clergy, whose past is stained with bloodshed arising out of a lecherous desire for certain lands as hot as the lands themselves. In spite of all this the Bishop does not deprive him of his parish. He looks around and marks the theatrical fervor of the landscape of "the flaming cactus and the gaudily decorated altars," of the gestures with which the women flung shawls on the pathway before him and the men snatched his hand to kiss the Episcopal ring; and perceives as in complete keeping with that world this passionate and devout scoundrel who gives his virility to the chanting of the mass as he gave it to murder, to the enrichment of his church with vestments and shining vessels as to the complication of his domesticity with amorousness. It is as if he tasted a chili con carne, judged it just as the Mexicans who were going to eat it would like it, and out of regard for the harmonies of life smoothed from his face all signs of what his French palate thought of the high seasoning. Though this may be an affair of importance, it is still an affair of the senses.

But there is more to life than this; St.

Teresa was greater than her investigators. The community that chose to die might know more in the moment when it went out to death than the neighboring unperverted community might know when it came in to supper. It is inconceivable that man was born of woman to suffer more forms of agony than there are kinds of flowers simply in order that he should make good soup. That complaint might be made against Miss Cather herself, in her own absorption in sense and the senses. She arranges with mastery such phenomena of life as the human organism can easily collect through the most ancient and most perfected mechanisms of body and mind. But must not such an art, admirable as it is, be counted as inferior to an art which accepts no such limitations, which deals with the phenomena of life collected by the human organism with such difficulty that to the overstrained consciousness they appear only as vague intimations, and the effort of obtaining them develops new mechanisms? Ought not art that tries to make humanity superhuman be esteemed above art that leaves humanity exactly as it is? One is reminded constantly of that issue while one is reading *Death Comes to the Archbishop* by its similarity in material to some of the recent work of Mr. D. H. Lawrence. Both writers come face to face with the Indian and find there is no face there but an unclimbable cliff, giving no foothold, like the side of a mesa; but each takes it so differently. "The Bishop," says Miss Cather, of a certain conversation by a camp fire, "seldom questioned Jacinto about his thoughts or beliefs. He didn't think it polite, and he believed it to be useless. There was no way in which he could transfer his own memories of European civilization into the Indian mind, and he was quite willing to believe that behind Jacinto there was a long tradition, a story of experience, which no language could translate to him. A chill came with the darkness," . . . and so on. There is no attempt to fit the key into the lock. That door will not open. But Mr. Lawrence cries out in his last book of essays: "The consciousness of one branch of humanity is the annihilation of the consciousness of another branch . . . We can understand the consciousness of the Indian only in terms of the death of our consciousness." There is nothing here to say he will not try it. Indeed, the querulousness of it, suggests a tired, brave man becoming aware of an imperative call to further adventure. There may be necessary a reentrance to the darkness of the womb, another fretful birth. He will try it!

The difference in their daring is powerfully suggested by a certain chapter of this book named Stone Lips. The Bishop and his Indian guide are on the desert when a snow storm breaks and covers the land with a white blindness. The Indian makes the Bishop leave the mules and clamber over rocks and fallen trees to a cliff in which there is a cave that has an opening, sinister enough in itself, with rounded edges like lips. It is large, shows signs of being used for ceremonial purposes, and is clean and swept; but it is icy-cold, and full of a faint but loathsome odor. There is a hole in the wall about the size of a watermelon. This the Indian guide fills up with a mixture of stones, wood, earth and snow. Then he builds a fire and the odor disappears. There is, however, a humming as of bees, which puzzles the Bishop till the guide takes him to a part of the cave where there is a crack in the floor through which sounds the roaring of an underground river. The Bishop drops off to sleep, but wakes up and finds the boy mounting guard over the hole in the wall, listening as though to hear if anything were stirring behind the patch of plaster. The episode owes its accent of course to the proximity of the cave to the pueblo of Pecos, which was reputed to keep a giant serpent out in the mountains for use in religious festivals.

Miss Cather passes through this experience responding sensitively and powerfully to its splendid portentousness, but she stays with the Bishop the whole time. Mr. Lawrence, on the other hand, would have been through the hole in the wall after the snake. He would have been through the crack in the floor after the river. Irritably and with partial failure, but also with greater success than any previous aspirant, he would have tried to become the whole caboodle. Does not such transcendental courage, does not such ambition to extend consciousness beyond its present limits and elevate man above himself entitle his art to be ranked as more important than that of Miss Cather?

To ask that question is our disposition today. It is the core of contemporary resentment against the classics. But one must suspect it. It leads to such odd preferences on the part of the young: for example, to the exaltation of James Joyce over Marcel Proust, although *A La Recherce du Temps Perdu* is like a beautiful hand with long fingers reaching out to pluck a perfect fruit, without error, for the accurate eye knows well it is growing just there on the branch, and *Ulysses* is the fumbling of a horny hand in darkness after a doubted jewel. Such a judgment leaves out of account that though a jewel is more precious than a fruit, grace also is one of the ultimate values, a chief accelerator of our journey toward the stars. It should, like all occasions when we find ourselves rejecting nontoxic pleasantness, make us examine ourselves carefully to see if we are not the latest victims to the endemic disease of Puritanism, to this compulsion to satisfy an innate sense of guilt by the coarser forms of expiation.

There is, after all, no real reason to suppose that there is less Puritan impulse in humanity than there ever was, since the origin and control of such infantile fantasies as the sense of guilt have hardly yet begun to be worked upon; and it would be peculiarly apt at this moment to express itself in the sphere of art. The Church no longer takes care of it among the literate, for during the last century they either ceased to go to church at all or have transferred their adherence to some faith which does not pander to those lownesses; but they found a new and disguised channel for the old impulse in reformist politics.

That again has been denied them, for the war has damped political enthusiasm just as the biological advances of the nineteenth century damped religious fervor. The weaker spirits are scared by the evidence that social change may involve serious hardship and have scuttled back to Toryism; the stronger spirits who can bear to envisage hardship are just as paralyzed by their doubt whether there is any economic system yet invented which is certain to justify by success the inconveniences of change. There has happened, therefore, a curious reversal of the position in regard to the gratification of the Puritan and counter-Puritan impulses in the last century. The young men who were Puritans in politics were anti-Puritans in literature. They were willing to die for the independence of Poland or the Manchester Fenians; and they relaxed their tension by voluptuous reading in Swinburne. Nowadays the corresponding young men gratify their voluptousness by an almost complete acquiescence in the political and economic status quo, an unremorseful acceptance of whatever benefits it may bring them personally; and they placate their Puritanism by demanding of literature that never shall it sit down to weave beauty out of the materials which humanity has already been able to collect with its limited powers, that perpetually it must be up and marching on through the briars toward some extension of human knowledge and power.

It is characteristically Puritan, this demand that the present should be annihilated. The churchgoers of the breed insisted that we should have no pleasures in this world, but should devote ourselves to preparation for the next. The political sphere made the same demand in many veiled forms, which one may perceive, in the phrase constantly used in propagandist literature that it is the duty of each generation to sacrifice itself for the sake of future generations.

It is, of course, pernicious. It makes man try to live according to another rhythm than that of the heart within him, which has its systole and its diastole. It deftly extracts all meaning out of life, which, if it were but an eternal climbing of steep steps, sanity would refuse to live. And esthetically it is the very deuce, for in rejecting classical art it rejects the real sanction of the revolutionary art it pretends to defend. For when Willa Cather describes in terms acceptable to a Catholic missionary society the two young priests stealing away secretly from Clermont to avoid saying goodbye to their devoted families, who would have been too greatly distressed by the loss of their sons, she is not as explicit as Mr. Lawrence would be in his statement that in this separation a creature as little Christian as a snake was trying to slough its skin, that a force as hidden from the sun as an underground river was trying to separate itself from its source. But by proving exhaustively what joy a man can have and what beauty he can make by using such material and such mechanism he already has she proves Mr. Lawrence's efforts to add to their number worth while. Since man can work thus with his discoveries, how good it is that there should be discoverers!

There is nothing here which denotes rejection of any statement of life fuller than her own. Her work has not that air of claiming to cover all the ground which gives the later novels of Henry James the feeling of pretentiousness and futility which amazingly coexists with the extremes of subtlety and beauty and which is perhaps due to his attempt to account for all the actions and thoughts of his characters by motives established well in the forefront of consciousness. Miss Cather is indeed deeply sympathetic to what the order of artist who is different from herself is trying to do, as can be seen in her occasional presentation of incidents that would be beautifully grist to their mill: as in the enchanting story of an El Greco painting of a St. Francis in meditation, which was begged from a Valencian nobleman by a hairy Franciscan priest from New Mexico for his mission church, who forced the gift by his cry: "You refuse me this picture because it is a good picture. It is too good for God, but it is not too good for you," and was, at the pillaging of the mission church, either burned or taken to some pueblo. How we can imagine that part of the spirit of El Greco which was in that picture, crying out while flames made it the bright heart of an opening flower of massacre, or while the smoke of the adobe dwelling discolors and stripes it like a flagellation, "It is just as I thought" . . . And how in the anguished accents of Mr. Lawrence's work that imagined cry sounds!

Miss Cather is not unaware of these fissures in the solid ground of life, but to be aware of them is not her task. Hers is it to move on the sunlit face of the earth, with the gracious amplitude of Ceres, bidding the soil yield richly, that the other kind of artist, which is like Persephone and must spend half of his days in the

world under the world, may be refreshed on emergence.

"Artist Astray," *San Francisco Chronicle*, 11 September 1927, p. D11

Willa Cather's capabilities in literary artistry have been proved beyond question in *A Lost Lady*. That early success has kept her faithful followers in hopes of more. Her latest story, *Death Comes for the Archbishop*, is not a fulfillment of their hopes; yet neither is it a failure. It is the beginning of many good stories, none of which is ever ended until, in natural course, death comes for the Archbishop, who is the noble hero of it all. It presents a series of episodes from the lives of two pioneering churchmen in New Mexico. They are good men to know.

Vera Beaton, *Chicago Journal of Commerce and LaSalle Street Journal*, 13 September 1927, p. 14

Willa Cather is one of the most distinguished and unpredictable names in American letters. Her versatility is unquestioned and the only reliable prophesy that can be attempted concerning her future work is that it will contain exquisite depths and that its simplicity and loveliness in style will touch the heart. Certainly by reading Miss Cather's former novels no one would have anticipated *Death Comes for the Archbishop*.

But in looking back, there is to be found an unmistakable hint of this latest book in *The Professor's House*. The New Mexican episode concerning the tragic mesa is a forerunner to the mass of legend and fact which Miss Cather has woven around the central figure of the missionary Archbishop, the builder of the second cathedral of Santa Fe. The book inspires conjecture on the part of the reviewer. It is easy to believe that the annals of New Mexico have been an insistent part of Miss Cather's imagination since first she felt the charm that is so unique of the Southwest. That insistence impelled her to insert the enchanted mesa into one novel. *My Mortal Enemy* followed *The Professor's House*, but Miss Cather was still haunted by the romance clinging to the earliest history of our civilization.

Clearly, *Death Comes for the Archbishop* is a novel that was written through some inner urge and was written for the author's own pleasure and satisfaction. It will have no popular appeal; it will, in fact, be entirely enigmatic to those readers who are unable to acknowledge the claim that can be laid upon the spirit by certain places and surroundings. New Mexico with all its strangeness and beauty has caught Miss Cather and she has tried to embody the mystery of its enchantment within the covers of a book. The one criticism which one might venture is found in the fact that mesa, cult and pueblo are so deeply engraved upon her mind that she forgets that many of her allusions will be unintelligible to the less fortunate who have not trodden the same pathway of travel.

Thus when she mentions the "Penitentes" she makes no explanation of that amazing and powerful and still existent order. Miss Cather does not worry over these omissions. She is writing a prose

poem, singing into it the blinding sun of the desert, the rites of a savage people, the shadows of the great Pecos forest and the greater Truches mountains, the compelling beauty of Taos, Zuni, Lagone, Isleta, of white Pueblo and green mesa and towering cathedral rock.

Edwin Francis Edgett, *Boston Evening Transcript*, 17 September 1927, p. 6

It is good to know that in her latest novel Willa Cather has abandoned the ultrasophistication of *One of Ours*, *The Professor's House* and *A Lost Lady* for the more simple formula of a straightaway historical novel. She has given it the somewhat formidable and pretentious title of *Death Comes for the Archbishop*. I have read the statement of an enthusiast that it is a wonderful title, but I think that in this instance, at least, it is an extremely foolish and inapplicable title. Death does come to the Archbishop, of course, but in the mildest of ways, for he dies peaceably in his bed after as a good man he has lived a good life of service to his fellow men. Miss Cather's story has to do with the work and personality of a French priest, one Jean Marie Latour who went to Mexico in 1851 as vicar apostolic, and became eventually an archbishop. With him went also to New Mexico Father Joseph Valliant, and together they labor in the cause of righteousness and religion. Lovers of stories of the earliest days of our primitive West may be interested to know that the redoubtable Kit Carson enters into the story, which is made additionally effective by the beauty of its writing. Miss

324

Cather has been a very highly praised and very much exalted novelist during recent years, and in my opinion her admirers have gone altogether too far in expressing their admiration of her. I thought *One of Ours*, for which Miss Cather was awarded the Pulitzer Prize in 1923, a very ordinary story, and as for *The Lost Lady*, well, I have no words with which to express my dislike of it. It was a preposterous attempt to make a bad woman seem to be a good woman. But now I am glad to say that in her latest novel Miss Cather is content to be a real story-teller, and not an apostle of modernistic fiction. For that, at least, we should be grateful to her.

William Whitman III, "Eminence Comes for Miss Cather," *Independent*, 119 (17 September 1927), 283

Death Comes for the Archbishop is a mature and beautiful novel by one of our great living prose writers. Serene and contemplative in manner, it is typical of Miss Cather's best work, symbolizing the fruition of her literary artistry. To me the three most significant novelists of the day are Theodore Dreiser, Sinclair Lewis, and Willa Cather, who, if she has not produced the impressive tones of Dreiser or the amazing portraits of Lewis, has at least equaled them in the profundity of her vision and exceeded them in her sensitive command of the English language. Moreover, like Dreiser and Lewis, she is an American in subject and expression.

With the publication of *O Pioneers!* in 1913 Miss Cather was hailed as one of the important novelists of American literature, and since then each book by her has been received with delight and praise, discriminating in its sincere enthusiasm. And yet, though Miss Cather must be considered primarily as a novelist, it is in novel construction that she is weakest. Her prose is sombre and beautiful, her delineation of character subtle and honest, but for the most part her books have been collections of short stories unified by a central character or scene. In *Death Comes for the Archbishop* this is particularly noticeable. Miss Cather's books lack the massive, moving unity of the "great" novel; her art is fundamentally that of a short-story writer. That she has recognized this herself is fairly clear after a survey of her earlier work.

She began her literary career as a poetess, short-story writer, and journalist biographer. Her first novel, *Alexander's Bridge*, was published in 1912, to be followed a year later by *O Pioneers!* Unlike *Alexander's Bridge*, which was in conception a long short story, *O Pioneers!* was a succession of scenes unified by a group of characters set against the background of Nebraskan soil. In this book is expressed that sympathy with the pioneer West, the prairie, and the homesteader which is the keynote to Miss Cather's best work, and which reaches in the opinion of many its most brilliant expression in *My Antonia*.

The Song of the Lark, published in 1915, is her most ambitious novel, and one which conforms most clearly to the requirements of the "great" novel. Thea Kronborg is the heroine, and *The Song of the Lark* is a record of her struggles to achieve a career as a concert singer. But under the pressure of this book Miss Cather seems to tire, and the story, overweighted with its own substance, lags and becomes confused.

Evidently conscious of failure, she returned to her earlier and simpler method employed in *O Pioneers!* and wrote *My Antonia*. The story of Antonia Shimerda is told in a succession of illuminating and interpretive scenes which contrast and harmonize the character of the Bohemian girl with the sombre background of the Nebraska prairies. Miss Cather's keen sense of life, of tragedy and hardship on an untilled fertile soil, is particularly adjusted to this subtle and impressive work of art. She has done for the West what Sarah Orne Jewett did for New England, but with a greater freedom, a richer fertility, a more moving splendor.

In *One of Ours*, which followed the war, Miss Cather tells the story of a young Nebraskan farmer, unable to find peace in the society of either his mother or his wife, who sought release in the war. Claude Wheeler's early life, the tilling of the soil, the clash of uncongenial personalities, is convincing and penetrating, but the two episodes, the farm and the war, fail to harmonize, and the conclusion of this novel left me with a sense of futility and impatience. Spiritual unity, inevitably a part of any work of art, seemed sadly lacking.

The story, *A Lost Lady*, is more successful. In this long short story Miss Cather's subtle craftsmanship is at its best, and this study in miniature is beautifully and almost completely satisfying. Technically, the shift in point of view during the telling of the story destroys the exquisite balance of charming Marianne Forrester's portrait, but here for the most part we surely have Willa Cather at her best.

The Professor's House is another example of the artist's failure to master completely narrative construction. The story of Professor St. Peter and the story of Tom Outland, killed in the war, are not sufficiently blended to relieve the "episodic brusqueness" of the narrative. But when Miss Cather returns to the miniature as she does in *My Mortal Enemy*, she is once more a master of her craft.

With *Death Comes for the Archbishop* Miss Cather has woven out of her experience and great ability a novel which takes advantage of her unusual and brilliant gifts, and avoids the pitfalls of construction which have been her greatest weakness. The story of Father Jean Marie Latour's gentle conquest of the Southwest for the Roman Catholic Church is a series of unforgettable and brilliant pictures of heroism and renunciation, of a flowering fruitful land. It is a prose poem of early New Mexico celebrating the tumultuous and sleepy soil, the undeviating and mysterious soul of its varied people.

In structure the book is a series of short stories relating the life of the bishop, his early struggles, his friendship and love for his comissionary, Father Vaillant, his journeys among the Mexicans and Indians through the wild and solemn grandeur of the country. Interwoven into the growth of the great diocese are incidents, stories in themselves, that suggest the customs and folklore of the people, their prejudices and passions. At the end death comes gently for the archbishop, and his holy work has ceased.

What stories these are! Miss Cather's prose has a purity, a moving serenity which transcends the pedestrian paragraphs of novelists greater than she. She is the priestess of the soil. Her heart and memory are concerned with the juniper and greasewood, the gray deserts and the cornelian-colored hills, and with the people who are growth of this soil. All her subtlety and artistry have been devoted to this romantic tapestry, intensifying, making alive and vivid the vision which she herself must have pondered over and deeply loved.

Miss Cather in remarking on the genius of Sarah Orne Jewett referred to unforgettable memories which, eventually finding expression, are the basis for enduring art. This quality above all others pervades her own work. Its strange quality of still intensity and fulfillment suggests a fresh and fertile soil. The archbishop lying at home in France: "When the summer wind stirred the lilacs in the old gardens and shook down the blooms of the horse chestnuts, he sometimes closed his eyes and thought of the high song the wind was singing in the straight striped pine trees up in the Navajo forests." In his declining years he longed for the "bright edges of the world," and so returned to New Mexico to die in exile for love of them.

I am grateful to Miss Cather for this figured tapestry. *Death Comes for the Archbishop* is an epic in which to rejoice. Against the feverish background of current literature, this romance enjoys the quiet of permanence and the benediction of understanding.

Lillian C. Ford, *Santa Fe New Mexican*, 23 September 1927, p. 4 [reprinted from the *Los Angeles Times*]

Willa Cather's new novel recreates a little-known period in American history, that of the missionary priests in the southwest shortly after New Mexico was taken over by the United States.

The story follows the lives of Jean Marie Latour, a young French priest sent out by Rome to New Mexico where he was the vicar apostolic and the bishop of Agathonica and of his lifelong friend, Father Joseph Vaillant, who in the end himself became a bishop.

Miss Cather talks with the simplicity of a contemporary chronicler of the difficulties the two priests encounter in the sparsely settled, desolate land, from the time of their arrival in Sante Fe, where the local clergy refuse to recognize their authority, through their long journey to Old Mexico and back after the necessary papers of authorization, and through their strange encounters with criminals, Indians, and with American pioneers and scouts, including Kit Carson.

One hastens to add what perhaps does not need adding, that this is no story of adventure in the wild west. The interest is in the characters, especially in that of Father Latour, with his old-world culture and ideals, his love of art and of music and of gracious living, and of how he developed spiritually under the law and trying conditions he found in early New Mexico. The story has charm and atmosphere, without excitement or suspense. So beautifully realized is the life depicted that it all reads like a document left by a contemporary, yellow with the passing of time and impregnated with the aroma of a by-gone age. Miss Cather seems to know every landmark in the country in which she writes and to appreciate all the complex elements out of which the New Mexico of today developed. Particularly strong is her recapture of the spirit of the proud and valiant Pueblo Indians whose civilization was so ruthlessly destroyed by hardier tribes, and her description of Acoma and Laguna, and others of their centers.

Francis Talbot, S. J., "Willa Cather Eulogizes the Archbishop," *America*, 37 (24 September 1927), 572–3

Several years have passed since an ardent admirer of Willa Cather first rubbed her into my attention. He was an unfeigned enthusiast, convinced that he had discovered an American who was, at the same time, a novelist and an artist. Though his persistence counted against my interest in Willa Cather, it did create some curiosity which first led to admiration and later to some disappointment. Without doubt, Miss Cather was an artist who wrote fiction. She handled all of her tools with the strong grasp of a master journeyman. She flitted over her material as delicately as a fly in a china shop.

No fault could be found with her technique, but a disconcerting trend of mind grew apparent in her last few novels. *A Lost Lady* and *The Professor's House*, for example, told the story of deteriorations. Though they were relatively reticent, compared to similar studies during the past few seasons, they were unmistakably frank in their larger meanings. They made one suspect that Miss Cather had lost faith in her fellow-man and believed that all flesh was as grass. Happily, she has now explored the road that leads upwards with as much keenness as she plotted the downward path. In her latest novel, *Death Comes for the Archbishop*, she discovered two good men, placed in surroundings that would ordinarily crush any high resolves; she follows them through arduous years; and, at the ending of their days, she finds them to be not men but saints. Her theme is purification and santification, rather than degeneration.

These two men who play hero in the novel are priests. It is no new thing for Willa Cather to speak well of Catholic priests. Whenever she had occasion to use them in her stories, she had shown a fine respect for them and their calling. She had, likewise, a reverent regard for their function and their Faith. But the passing references to people and things Catholic which she made in her earlier novels have now been developed into the main theme of a story. As a result, Miss Cather has written an undeniably true and beautiful Catholic novel.

The prologue is in violent contrast to the story. "One summer evening in the year 1848," she begins, three Cardinals and a missionary Bishop from the United States dined luxuriously in the gardens of a villa in the Sabine Hills, overlooking Rome. The Cardinals were witty and suave, cultured and elegant; the Bishop was plain American. At this dinner, a decision of import to the Church in the United States was reached. The American Bishop had obtained the appointment of a young French priest, then laboring in his diocese along the Great Lakes, to the vicariate of the territory newly acquired by the United States from Mexico. Jean Marie Latour was the priest named. His diocese embraced a territory "larger than Central and Western Europe, barring Russia." But no man could define its limits or say what was its condition.

From Rome, with its international character strongly stressed, the novel crosses to the vast, mysterious territory vaguely comprehended as New Mexico and Arizona. Father Latour, the new Vicar, leaves Cincinnati for Santa Fé; the journey consumes a year. Arrived at Santa Fé, he finds the clergy rebellious; and so he must travel some 1,500 miles down to Durango, in old Mexico, where lived the

Bishop from whose jurisdiction his diocese was carved. Obtaining his credentials, he rode his horse back to Santa Fé and began the life work among the deserts and the mountains, among the half-breeds and the degenerates, that obedience had assigned to him as his garden and his fruits.

Associated with Father Latour in his apostolate was Father Joseph Vaillant. While the Vicar was as handsome and as impressive as the humanistic stock from which he derived, the assistant was, in the words of an old native woman, so ugly that he must be very holy, and, in the words of Miss Cather, "homely, real, persistent, with the driving power of a dozen men in his poorly built body."

These were men of steel. Together they picked up, as though with naked hands, the embers of a dying Faith and fanned them with their heaving breath to a consuming fire. They rode their mules through the wind-swept deserts and across the beetling mountain trails; they rode incessantly through rain and snow and scorching suns; they slept under the trees and ate in the native huts; and their souls were desolated more than once as they shouldered their heavy crosses. But they spent their lives for God and they did not count the beads of tears and sweat. When death came for Archbishop Latour and Bishop Vaillant, for he had been separated with heartbreaks from his old friend and had been created the first Bishop of Colorado, God had already advanced to them a share of the wages that they fully deserved.

That a modern novelist, sophisticated to the finger tips, should take two men of God as the heroes of her tale, that she should comprehend their unworldly ambitions as fully as she did the psychology of a frail lady, is indeed surprising. It was surprising to me, from my viewpoint, as it seems to have been surprising to the reviewers of a diversely extreme viewpoint. They have been compelled to admit that Miss Cather is still the artist and the competent novelist; but they have been shocked to realize that she has actually found two Roman Catholic priests worthy of admiration. Accordingly, they have made stupid efforts to show that *Death Comes for the Archbishop* is not a novel.

It may be freely granted that there is no real heroine, with sharply defined sexual impulses, in the story. The two men do not help to form a triangle. Neither of the men whose souls are laid bare have a thought about a woman. Nevertheless, this is a love story, a story of a passionate, flaming, consuming love. It tells of the love of the two men, one for the other, of the devastating love of these two men for men, women and children, of the all-embracing love of God for these two men and of other men, and of their love for Him. If the theme of love be a requisite for a novel, this is a romance of the highest caliber.

For another reason, the classification of the book as a novel may be more validly questioned. Novelists of our day are interesting themselves more and more in the plotting of their stories in American history. In following the current fashion they are trespassing on the domains of biography and history. Willa Cather is thoroughly familiar with the land and the history of the Southwest. She has a kinship with its mountains and its mesas, its adobe houses and its pueblos, its red sand-hills and its mysterious caves. She has uncovered the newer history of its annexation by the United States, and has explored the later paganism that shrouded the rich Spanish Catholicism which had in turn supplanted the well-developed prehistoric culture. In idealizing the locale and in sensing its rich overtones and in dramatizing the events, Miss Cather has written an historical novel. Nevertheless, she has clung so closely to facts and has described actual persons so truthfully, that her novel may rightly be called history or biography.

Were one to investigate Miss Cather's notebook, he would find that Father Jean Marie Latour is none other than Jean Baptiste Lamy, that Father Joseph Vaillant is Rev. Joseph Macheboeuf, both drawn to the life. The Spanish Cardinal of the prologue is undoubtedly Cardinal Merry del Val, transported to the reign of Gregory XVI, and the blunt American missionary Bishop is the Rt. Rev. John Baptist Purcell. Thus, most of the people mentioned actually lived and are described really as they lived. In the same way, the events may be verified almost wholly in the history of the founding and development of the Santa Fé diocese. The novel, *Death Comes for the Archbishop* might justly be indexed as the biography of the first Archbishop of Santa Fé, Jean Baptiste Lamy, or as a sketch of the early history of the Catholic Church in New Mexico and Arizona. The plot follows fact minutely, and the fiction is merely embroidery of the plot.

The Catholic reader may possibly dislike certain incidents retold in the story, that of Padre Gallegos, for example, who was a gambler and a sportsman, who was a dancer and a drinker, and who contradicted in word and fact the Catholic practice of clerical celibacy; or that of Padre Martinez or of the miserly Padre Lucero, or the legend of Fray Baltazar. But these incidents had as much historical foundation as those more edifying ones of Padre Jesus and of Fra Junipero, of Father Latour and of Father Vaillant. One might have preferred Miss Cather to forego these old legends and tales just as one might beg a person not to speak of the corns on a beautiful lady's toes. But Miss Cather's concern is not so much with scandals as with the opportunity these scandals afforded to show the nobility of her two priest-heroes. They were untouched by them personally and they exemplified in their reformations the cleansing sanctity of the Church.

In her narrative, Miss Cather seldom falters in her description of Catholic doctrine or belief. Curiously, the only mistakes are to be found on two pages, in which she speaks of "the Blessed Sacrament of the Mass," of the Blessed Virgin as "divine" and of old Sada as "adoring" the little silver medal. Otherwise, Miss Cather speaks as accurately of our mysteries as would a Catholic author. Father Vaillant's signet ring carried the legend "Auspice Maria!" and this is also the motto on the title page of the novel. Whatever significance may be placed on this, *Death Comes of the Archbishop* is a sincere, artistic, distinguished fictional biography that is worthy of a Catholic novelist.

"Buckskin Beatitude," *Time*, 10 (26 September 1927), 38–9

A large part of Miss Cather's pre-eminence as a novelist is due to her ability as a scholar. Her offering for this season is more scholarly than creative—a reconstruction of the episcopal works of the first Roman Catholic bishop of her beloved New Mexico, Jean Marie Latour. She draws him with esthetic reverence, an immaculate conception of a missionary in buckskins who, lost and athirst in the desert, still retained elegance, distinction and "a kind of courtesy toward himself, toward his beasts, toward the juniper tree before which he knelt and the God whom he was addressing."

The juniper tree was cruciform. Some hours after his prayer, young Bishop Latour found hidden water. Brother Joseph Vaillant, the scrawny but indomitable baker's son with whom Jean Latour stole out of France to make comradely conquests for God in the New World, and who later became bishop of tumbled, rocky Colorado, might have greatly elaborated this miracle, introducing the Virgin in colored robes when he related it. But not Bishop Latour. He was not a visionary ascetic. He wrought humbly with Nature, not beyond her.

This spiritual politeness of her subject is doubtless what brought Miss Cather, who is not a Catholic, to write his story. His nature leaves her free to chronicle every aspect of the vast country in which he worked and where she, three quarters of a century later, annually repairs for enlargement of the spirit. Into his pious story she can bring a wealth of unchurchly anecdotes because, trekking around his desert diocese on his cream-colored mule, Bishop Latour was respectfully studious of its folklore. He was austere towards priests like Padre Martinez, the bison-shouldered Mexican at Taos, brazen in fleshliness. But when Jacinto, his Indian guide, led him through a blizzard to shelter in a secret, tribal, mountain cave, the Bishop honored the inscrutable and did not ask if the vibrant mystery of the place was, besides a buried river, some ceremonial monster, an infant-devouring serpent as legend said.

The book is filled with colorful people, rainbow scenery, amazing weather. The lean, kind, sandy figure of Kit Carson welcomes the Bishop at Taos. Navajos, Zunis, Acomas, remnants of the clearly pueblo tribes, move quietly about in smaller villages, vivid as their blankets and pottery, drawn with the patient accuracy of an archeologist. Cornelian hills circle Santa Fé, where the cathedral arises like a golden butte. Windstorms smother the bishop on the plains, cloudbursts drench him among the peaks.

Everywhere history is made to move in a living atmosphere, for that is the highest excellence of Miss Cather's writing, her mastery of intangibles. Just as the maturity of her mind has led her, in character-drawing, beyond the emotions of a spiritual emphasis, so the maturity of her senses has brought her to dwell upon qualities of air, shadow and faint fragrance in her objective scenes. When she paints a mesa, she remembers the cloud mesa above it. Two bronzed runners passing over some sand dunes remind her of the "shadows that eagles cast in their strong, unhurried flight."

It was the dry, aromatic lightness of New Mexico's air that drew Jean Marie Latour back, when his work was done, to die there "of having lived," instead of drawing out his days, as he might have done, in sociable comfort abroad. The New Mexican air is Miss Cather's necessity too. ". . . One could breathe that only on the bright edges of the world. . . . Something soft and wild and free, something that . . . released the spirit of man into the wind, into the blue and gold, into the morning, into the morning."

"Week By Week," *Commonweal*, 6 (28 September 1927), 486–7

Although Jean Marie Latour—the general figure in Willa Cather's memorable novel, *Death Comes for the Archbishop*, which is reviewed elsewhere in this number of *The Commonweal*—is, in the truest sense, a creation of Miss Cather, it would seem that her model was the Reverend John Baptist Lamy, a French priest of the Cincinnati diocese. He was appointed by Pope Pius IX vicar apostolic for the great territory of New Mexico, which was organized in 1850, having become a possession of the United States in 1848, following the war with Mexico. He was consecrated as a bishop in 1850 in Saint Peter's Cathedral, Cincinnati, by Archbishop Purcell. Accompanied by Father Joseph Projectus Machebeuf, Bishop Lamy left for his distant see shortly after the consecration. Father Machebeuf is evidently the model for the inimitable Father Vaillant of Miss Cather's book, for he later became the first bishop of Denver, after laboring for many years with Bishop Lamy in the religious development of the Southwest.

Bishop Lamy was of a literary turn of mind and wrote a series of long and interesting letters which, apparently, must have fallen under Miss Cather's interested observation. A writer in the *Catholic Women's News*, Theodore A. Thoma, speaks of these letters, saying that, in them, Bishop Lamy faithfully recorded the mode of life of the people of New Mexico, painting pictures that still fit the New Mexico of today. "He proved himself a real missionary for the betterment of temporal affairs as well as spiritual welfare, and today his name is known throughout New Mexico as the father of horticulture, which is one of the greatest resources of the state. The state has recognized its debt to Bishop Lamy by naming after him a town on the Santa Fé Railroad, where the branch line begins to climb to see the city of Santa Fé, the ancient villa resting in the lap of the foothills of the Rocky Mountains, named by the early Franciscan Fathers the Sangre de Christo, or Blood of Christ Mountains. Santa Fé itself has rewarded the memory of its saintly bishop and archbishop with a life-size bronze

statue which stands before the great Cathedral of Saint Francis." However much Miss Cather may have drawn upon Bishop Lamy's letters, these materials simply served her as clay serves the sculptor, or paint the artist; she herself breathing life into the splendid figure of her Bishop Latour. The alchemy of the artist in dealing with the material of his mystery—in this case the most stubborn of material, real characters and historical facts—has never, assuredly, been more triumphantly illustrated.

Michael Williams, "Willa Cather's Masterpiece," *Commonweal*, 6 (28 September 1927), 490–2

When Walt Whitman cried out on some page or other of *Leaves of Grass*, that who touched that book really touched a man, he said something that was true in its special sense not only of his book but of all true books. They are living things. They have in them not only the life, or something of the life, of their writers, but also they have a life of their own: individual, separate, unique. Like men, they are composed of body and soul. As in the case of man, we can recognize the palpable fact of their living quality, but we experience the same difficulty in any attempt precisely to define that quality as we experience in trying to define any man or any woman. "All things find their end in mystery," wrote some Schoolman long ago. Even the most convinced materialist: one to whom what we call the soul is merely the product or effect of mechanical processes of the blood, and nerves, and glands, when asked for his explanation of how matter itself began, can only say that all things, matter included, certainly begin in a mystery, however they may end. He may believe, or try to believe, that some day he will know it all; will be able to explain the beginning and foresee the end; but here and now he must admit the mystery.

All works of human art contain or partially express the ambient mystery of life, of which death itself is only an element. Among these works of art: temples, cathedrals, symphonies, peasant songs, sculpture, paintings, dramas, roads and bridges, ships (whether of the air or of the sea) books—true books, living books—are especially steeped in mystery. Criticism may usefully attempt to deal with such books for the sake of the value of incidental discoveries, helpful minor interpretations, though criticism never understands creation. But at least it may do it reverence. It may be its missionary, hunting out and bringing to the shrine of art all those who may be seeking beauty but who do not know where it is to be found.

It seems to me that it is the duty of criticism so to call attention to Willa Cather's new book, that all readers competent to appreciate a great work of literary art may have their opportunity to enjoy it. When I say "all readers competent to appreciate a great work of literary art," I have no intention of being supercilious; I do not address myself to any coterie of highbrows; I have no thought of those superior persons of Mallarmé's dictum, the inbred aristocrats of the mind, to whom only are the inner secrets of art revealed. For readers who delight in what is vaguely called "style," to whom the rhythms and the verbal coloring of "fine writing" are delight-giving things in themselves, there are indeed many wonderful pages in this book. For those who seek in prose fiction not only the attraction of interesting characters, places, events, adventures, but also the more subtle but no less real attraction of philosophy—which, broadly speaking, is surely the effort of the human intellect to examine deeply, and, if possible, to understand, the universe in which and through which the pageant of human life proceeds—there also is much and worthwhile stuff. And at the same time the simplest and most humble of readers may and surely will find this book acceptable and more than acceptable. I know few books so deep, even so profound, in subject matter, which are expressed in so simple a vocabulary.

The stylistic beauty of Willa Cather's book: beauty of the rarest, truest kind, is in her pages as perfume mingled with incense breathes from flowers on some altar: as color appears in those flowers, or in the sky at sunrise or sunset, or in a rainbow, or in the eyes, the lips, the cheeks of living men and women. In order to write this book, she has read a great deal in other books, she has studied books; she has observed the desert country of the American Southwest morning, noon and night, through all four seasons of the year; she has lived among and with its people; and she has thought, very deeply, very long, about all those things, and about life itself; moreover, she has brooded; she has been affected by movements of her soul, by intuitions and inspirations coming from beyond the frontiers of thought. Thus her spirit became mysteriously maternal; and this book was born, not made. Her words and phrases, simple, and nearly always words of common use, are so vivified by their association with her marvelous inner processes that they shine with their real meanings (which are so blurred and defaced in the hands of hasty or dishonest writers); they mix and mingle in rare combinations of color and music. A child could read this book without effort;

artists, philosophers and priests, may and will ponder it profoundly.

Is it a novel? I do not know. All depends upon what one's definition of a novel may happen to be. Is it history, or biography; rewritten, or rather, recreated? Historical characters, like Kit Carson; historical events, like the Gadsden purchase of Arizona, or the building up of the Archdiocese of Santa Fé, are dealt with in such a way that the book throws more light upon the southwestward sweep of the United States than many volumes of professed history. Yet the book decidedly is not—or certainly is not only—an exercise in the present-day habit or fad of "novelizing" history or biography. There is no "love interest" in its pages—at least, not of the kind that one ordinarily associates with novels, and perhaps even more with the new order of fictionized biographies. The love that glows in Willa Cather's book can never be put into the movies because it is the love that moves the universe and all its stars, the love of God for man, of man for God. It is one of the serenest, most mellow, most peaceful books ever written; but the peace, the serenity, the mellowness, are not shallow, not superficial. They are there as a starlit sky and a calm sea combine upon some perfect night of beauty; but the unimaginable depths and distances of space, the power and dread of the sea, are unforgotten.

One would have to be able to write as well as Miss Cather, and on the same subjects (and that is a highly improbable thing) adequately to pay tribute to one high merit of her wonderful book, namely, its descriptions of the colors, the sounds, the scents, the aspects of the southwestern desert. But "descriptions" is a misleading word; Willa Cather does not really describe the desert, she magically evokes it. Perhaps only those who know it by personal experience can fully appreciate her wizardry; but surely no reader can be insensitive to the enchantment of her crystalline prose; crystalline and limpid, yet at the right moments shot through and scintillant with colors, and ghosts of colors, and tones of color, and super-tones. Not even Mary Austin can bring the desert country into language with more success; and that is the highest praise, in terms of comparison, that I can give. I know that country; I have lived in it, many months at a time; I can remember; but I do more than remember, I live it again, in this book.

It tells the story of one Jean Marie Latour, a Catholic missionary priest who, when a young man, is sent to New Mexico as the Bishop of Santa Fé, after that portion of the country comes into the possession of the United States. With him is his friend from youth, Father Joseph Vaillant, now his vicar, and destined also to become a bishop in the turbulent gold fields of Colorado. Vaillant is the son of a peasant. Latour comes of an aristocratic family that in past centuries gave cathedral-building bishops to France; he is one who, without a vocation to the priesthood, might have been a typical man of the world, a somewhat delicate-minded, courteous, virile yet gentle person. But the vocation makes all the difference. It brings him to New Mexico, cuts him off from the sophisticated European culture and refinement of life which he so appreciates, to labor a long lifetime amid Indians and semi-barbarous white folk, living crudely, hardly, dangerously, and at last dying in exile. Vaillant, however, you cannot think of save as a priest, and a missionary priest.

. . . And always, everywhere, they give all their powers, their endurance, their courage, their strength, their culture, their riches of European experience, to the task that has brought them to this oldest, this newest of regions: the task of extending

334

the Catholic Church, the Faith; the task of saving souls.

It is in her treatment of this central motive of the life of Archbishop Latour and his companion, Father Vaillant, that Willa Cather succeeds most surely. Her book is a wonderful proof of the power of the true artist to penetrate and understand and to express things not part of the equipment of the artist as a person. Miss Cather is not a Catholic, yet certainly no Catholic American writer that I know of has ever written so many pages so steeped in spiritual knowledge and understanding of Catholic motives and so sympathetically illustrative of the wonder and beauty of Catholic mysteries, as she has done in this book.

There is one short chapter, or section, for example, entitled "December Night," which contains the quintessence of the meaning, the power, the consolation, the charm, the beauty, of Catholic devotion to the Blessed Virgin. . . .

I should like to quote the entire section, for the sheer pleasure of slowly savoring a most beautiful piece of prose; and for me also it is like repeating a most efficacious prayer. Well indeed did Miss Cather write on her title page, "Auspice Maria."

My colleague George Shuster has written one or two big books and lectured up and down the country trying to get people to understand the rich soil and background that American art, in literature, music, painting, sculpture, possesses in the shape of its Catholic element—the works and ways of the Spanish, Portugese, French and English explorers who came companioned by the men of the Cross, men of the same stuff as Willa Cather's Jean Marie Latour and Joseph Vaillant. It is not, in this connection, a matter of the truth, whether final and absolute, or provisional and relative, of the Catholic faith; it is a matter of the rich heritage of heroism, of authentic deeds and fascinating folk-lore, and of the solid, substantial contributions flowing from the work of the early Catholics for the enrichment and strengthening and beautifying of American life and culture. If the Spaniard came as a swordsman, with him also came the man of the Cross. The swordsman died losing to others the lands and power he had fought for; but from the blood-dewed paths of the missionary flowered the things that last—agriculture, the vine, arts, letters, lessons of the highest deeds of the human spirit.

Willa Cather is one of the few American artists who has perceived the great treasures lying in wait for art in the Catholic tradition of the United States. One of her books is called O Pioneers! She, too, is a pioneer. She will lead others to that treasure-trove. Let us hope that among them may be a few Catholics. American Catholics sorely lack, and even more sorely need, authentic artists. Producing rich men and politicians, a scattering of judges and a host of lawyers, isn't quite the proof that the nation needs of the civilizing influence of the Faith. The Church in the United States has never failed in its succession of splendid priests and even more splendid nuns. But the laity has not as yet flowered to any notable extent in the production of the finer works of culture and of life. Books like Willa Cather's may and should help to remedy the matter. At any rate, I consider it the duty of Catholics to buy and read and spread Willa Cather's masterpiece.

Burton Rascoe, "Miss Cather and Others," *Bookman*, 66 (October 1927), 214

Joseph Wood Krutch, "The Pathos of Distance," *Nation*, 125 (12 October 1927), 390

In *Death Comes for the Archbishop*, I take it, Miss Cather has taken a sabbatical in order to write a story outside her main line of interests because she wanted to describe the effect of the clear air and sunlight of Mexico and because she wanted to write about Catholic prelates. It is not a story, I think, which those who liked *My Antonia* and *A Lost Lady* will find especially thrilling. Enjoyment of it must come largely from her cadenced prose. It is a story of missionary work in Mexico in the middle years of the nineteenth century and of a young priest's efforts to introduce Christian morals and civilization into a community of heathenish and animalistic Mexican peasants. It seems to me a formless sort of novel in which only one character comes to life and that character only for a moment. That was when Father Vaillant shooed the Mexican cook out of the kitchen, and prepared a roast that he could eat. For the rest I read the novel with a constant satisfaction over the limpid prose and with a constantly disappointed hope of discovering a theme or a story in it.

In one of his literary essays Havelock Ellis drew a useful distinction between what he called the Nordic and the Celtic treatments of the past. The uninstructed reader of Homer might, he pointed out, very reasonably suppose that the poet was contemporary with the events which he described, whereas in the case of any Celtic epic it is always perfectly evident that the author is dealing with things which, for him as well as for the reader, are remotely picturesque. The Greeks, in other words, preferred to treat the past as though it were present because they were interested in a dramatic immediacy, but the Celts deliberately evoked the pathos of distance because that pathos was to them the essence of poetry.

Now I am by no means certain that this distinction upon the basis of race is valid; perhaps it would be safer to speak merely of the heroic and the elegiac moods; but certainly the distinction itself is of fundamental importance and it is, moreover, the one which serves better than any other to define the particular quality of Miss Cather's work. Though she is absorbed in what would be to another the heroic past of our continent, her mood is that which Ellis would call the Celtic. She has upon occasion evoked her own memories, and one would expect to find in them the softness of remembered things, but even when her stories are rather documented than recalled she manages to invest documents with the wistful remoteness of recollected experience and to make past things vivid, less because they are present in the heat and sweat of actuality than because some softened memory of them seems to be. Not Calliope nor Melpomene is her muse but rather she who was called the mother of them all, and she is always at her best when that fact is most clearly recognized.

Certainly her newest story—concerned with the life of a missionary bishop to the newly annexed territory of New Mexico —would be in the hands of another something quite different from that which she has made it. These were stirring, adventurous times; many writers might feel that they could be recaptured only in some exciting and dramatic narrative; but Miss Cather softens the epic until it becomes an elegy. In recounting the lives of her characters she chooses by preference their moments of calm reflection; when she wishes to throw the long tradition of the priesthood into relief against the primitive background of the new land, she seizes upon some contrast that is deep without being violent; and she sees everything as one sees it when one broods or dreams over the past. The tumult and the fighting reach us but dimly. What we get is the sense of something far off and beautiful— the picturesqueness and the fragrance of the past more than the past itself, pictures softened by time and appearing suddenly from nowhere.

In a garden overlooking Rome, a cardinal drinks his wine and discusses the appointment of a new bishop for a vague and distant see. That bishop, come all the way from the Great Lakes, struggles with the paganism of his priests, rides miles over the desert to perform a belated marriage ceremony over the Mexicans whose children he has baptized, or dreams of the cathedral which shall some day rise in the savage land; but at night he cooks himself a soup with "nearly a thousand years of history" in it and in the sense of these vanished contrasts lies the effect of the book.

After supper was over and the toasts had been drunk, the boy Pablo was called in to play for the company while the gentlemen smoked. The banjo always remained a foreign instrument to Father Latour; he found it more than a little savage. When this strange yellow boy played it, there was softness and languor in the wire strings— but there was also a kind of madness; the recklessness, the call of wild countries which all these men had felt and followed in one way or another. Through clouds of cigar smoke, the scout and the soldiers, the Mexican *rancheros*, and the priests, sat silently watching the bent head and crouching shoulders of the banjo player, and his see-sawing yellow hand, which sometimes lost all form and became a mere whirl of matter in motion, like a patch of sandstorm.

Even when Miss Cather strives most consciously to give to her books a narrative movement there is likely to be something static or picture-like about her best effects, and when she falters it is usually in the effort to carry the reader from one to the other of the moments which rise like memories before her. In the present instance she has nothing that could properly be called a plot, but she is wisely content to accept the fact and to depend upon the continuous presence of beauty rather than upon any movement to hold the interest of the reader. When things are recalled in the mood of elegy there is no suspense and they do not take place one after the other because, all things being merely past, there is no time but one. And so it is in the case of *Death Comes for the Archbishop*. It is a book to be read slowly, to be savored from paragraph to paragraph, and it is quite the most nearly perfect thing which its author has done since *A Lost Lady*.

Robert Morss Lovett, "A Death in the Desert," *New Republic*, 52 (26 October 1927), 266–7

Some years ago Miss Cather, in *My Antonia*, wrote a book which, as a straightforward record of experience, stands out in the mass of fiction which gathers about the advancing frontier and the conquest of the soil, an unquestionable masterpiece. In *Death Comes for the Archbishop*, she has returned to this type of simple, unaffected narrative of a human life, and again has produced a book which will remain an American classic. It might be thought that in exchanging the Nebraska prairies, the place of her own childhood, which made the background of *My Antonia*, for the desert of New Mexico, which she could have known only as a visitor, Miss Cather had sacrificed the immediate contact and life-giving connection with her theme which is the source of creation. This does not seem to be true. Miss Cather has entered fully into her background. She has lived into her New Mexican environment until the desert land, scarred by canyons and arroyos and swelling into mesas, with its people Mexican, Navajo, Hopi, are substantial to her as they became to the Archbishop. He was a stranger, a missionary. The experience through which he found his straying flock in their desert pasture can be best appreciated by another stranger. The character of the Archbishop remains a little remote and unapproachable, with something serene and ineffable about it, the true note of sainthood. Miss Cather does not try to enter into this mystery by the help of psychological analysis—she is content to present the Archbishop as he appeared to those about him, recalling with loving skill the lines of a noble presence, divining with delicate intuition his movements and words. After all, the careers of the Archbishop and his missionary coadjutor, Father Joseph, belong to America of only fifty years ago. One remembers this nearness with an effort. As he reads, he seems to be with the companions of St. Francis among the hills of Assisi, or with St. Francis Xavier on the shores of Japan.

The story so beautifully told is that of Jean Marie Latour, bishop of the vast tract which the United States acquired from Mexico in the last century by conquest and purchase. While a youth in the seminary of Montferrand, at Clermont, he and his friend Joseph Vaillant heard from the Bishop of Ohio the call to go overseas, to the new nation growing up between the Great Lakes and the Gulf; and early one morning, to forestall opposition by their families, the young men took the diligence for Paris, whence, after some weeks of preparation, they sailed for America. For ten years they labored in Ohio, and then, when the annexation of New Mexico made necessary the separation of its missions from the diocese of Durango, Father Latour was consecrated its first bishop, and Father Joseph was sent with him as his vicar. There followed years of missionary labor, of horseback journeys measured by thousands of miles, of struggles with the Mexican clergy, who, subject to a far-away bishop, had fallen into sloth and corruption, of reawakening faith in little communities and isolated families, of visits to the Indians in their pueblos and glimpses of their tribal mysteries and ceremonies to which the true religion was obliged to accommodate itself, of the planting of gardens and the founding of schools, and finally, the building of the cathedral of Santa Fe by a French architect whom the bishop brought to build a Romanesque church, similar to those which he had known in his boyhood among the hills of Auvergne.

The Bishop and his vicar illustrate the contrast, become traditional, between idealist and realist. Father Latour was of gentle birth and culture, a student and a philosopher, careful in habit and exquisite in manner. He gave himself to the discomforts of his missionary life with joy, but with effort. Father Joseph was the son of a baker, a true child of the French bourgeoisie, with a practical genius, a vast curiosity about people and a love for them. He threw himself into dangers and hardships because he enjoyed them. When they were on a journey together and a new passenger forced his way into the already crowded stage coach, Father Latour, repressing his irritation, would notice that Father Joseph took on new animation at the sight of another human being. Father Latour was abstemious; he could not help feeling the grossness of Father Joseph's fondness for the table—and yet he recognized the miracle by which food and wine were immediately converted into spiritual energy. The two men so different were necessary to each other, and the account of their brotherly companionship is full of charm. They were separated at length by duty. When the gold rush to the mining camps of Colorado opened a new and trying missionary field, the Bishop sent his friend to work in it. There Joseph Vaillant surpassed himself in the service of humanity and the Church. When he died, the first Bishop of Colorado, no building in Denver could hold the multitude that came to his funeral.

Miss Cather tells her story not with the directness of a chronicle, but with an interlacing of theme, a shifting of material, which breaks the flat surface of the narrative into facets from which the light is variously reflected. At times one sees into a past far behind the contemporary record, for this land had had three centuries of history before the coming of the French priests. There were the conquistadores, and the Franciscans who founded the first missions and were wiped out in martyrdom in the revolt of the seventeenth century. Stories of this earlier age of faith survive in Miss Cather's book, like the Flowers of St. Francis. Interspersed also are reflections of Father Latour, always so wise and so pointed. When traveling with the Navajo Eusabio he notices that his guide is careful to obliterate every trace of their passage through the desert.

Father Latour judged that just as it was the white man's way to assert himself in any landscape, to change it, to make it over a little (at least to leave some mark or memorial of his sojourn), it was the Indian's way to pass through a country without disturbing anything; to pass and leave no trace, like fish through the water, or birds through the air. . . . It was as if the great country were asleep, and they wished to carry on their lives without awakening it; or as if the spirits of earth and air and water were things not to antagonize and arouse. When they hunted it was with the same discretion; an Indian hunt was never a slaughter. They ravaged neither the rivers nor the forest, and if they irrigated, they took as little water as would serve their needs. The land and all that it bore they treated with consideration; not attempting to improve it, they never desecrated it.

How pertinent is the Bishop's observation to our eager, lavish race which ravages the soil which the Indians treated so reverently! And how finely perceptive is his discrimination of the appeal of the frontier, which kept him in New Mexico, when he might have returned to Auvergne.

He had noticed that the peculiar quality in the air of new countries vanished after they were tamed by man and made to bear harvests. Parts of Texas and Kansas, that he had first known as open range, had since been made into rich farming districts, and the air had quite lost that lightness, that dry aromatic odor. The moisture of plowed land, the heaviness of labor and growth and grain bearing, utterly destroyed it; one could breathe that only on the bright edges of the world, on the great grass plains or the sagebrush desert.

Miss Cather has recaptured for America an aspect of its history, in this story of the Church, venerable and rich in tradition, becoming primitive amid pioneer conditions, among childlike people, in the piety of its missionary saints. It is not a tragic or a pathetic tale, but one full of happiness and triumph; and yet it moves one to tears, by the picture of such goodness and beauty seen through the medium of a faultless art.

Frances Lamont Robbins, *Outlook*, 147 (26 October 1927), 251

Death Comes for the Archbishop, by Willa Cather, happens to be the first title in our list of the best-selling novels of last week. It was not selected for review for that reason. It is always possible that such a position is the result of chance. If it is not, here, then even more than Miss Cather are the book-buyers who have given it to be congratulated. For her, it can do little more than warm more glowingly the cockles of a heart already content with her work.

Some of the people who have bought *Death Comes for the Archbishop* have probably been among those constant admirers of Miss Cather's who hope always to find between the covers of each new book another *My Antonia*. They will be disappointed. This book is not a novel, whatever its publishers may choose to call it. Bishop Latour, his life, surroundings, friends, are true. In fact, his house in Santa Fé is, or was recently, a dude ranch.

Imaginative biography, you may choose to call it. Certainly Miss Cather corroborates with a wealth of imaginary detail the historical data concerning the Archbishop and his diocese. Imaginative biography, perhaps; written with complete and philosophical detachment, with loving understanding or setting and background, in a prose style, singularly appropriate to the subject, and of poignant beauty. For those to whom comparisons, so dear to the American reviewer, are not "odorous" one might say that Miss Cather's biographical method (that only) recalls those used by Marcel Schwob and André Maurois, in *Vies Imaginaires* and *Ariel*, or, to go further back and up, by Sabatier in his *Life of St. Francis*.

But *Death Comes for the Archbishop* is not biography. Out of the press of crowding biographers, Miss Cather emerges as a hagiographer, taught in the school of Gregory of Tours, from the books of the *Sacred Conversations*. In this book she has produced something sounding out from a thousand years ago. Only one paragraph of her book is of today, and that stands out harshly from the page like a typewritten sentence in an illuminated manuscript. The quality of the book is of the deep and simple tone of the Bishop's Angelus, the bell that set his France, his Europe, wise and wonderful, reverberating over cactus and adobe and red canyon walls. It is the ancient function of the bell to break up the natural vibrations and allow the entrance of the extranatural, to permit the incursion upon this world of another dimension. That is its immemorial, great rôle in all the rites of pagan and of Christian magic. Miss Cather's book, by some gift, sensible to feeling but inexplicable, rings. While its note lasts, life is broken up and held in suspension.

Arnold Ronnebeck, *Rocky Mountain News* (Denver) [Autumn 1927]

The exhibition of some 40 watercolors by Frank G. Applegate of Santa Fe, N.M. constitutes a well selected survey of his work. The fact that a number of his paintings, exhibited here in June in the collective show of the New Mexico painters, aroused quite unusual interest, and the fact that about a dozen of his watercolors are privately owned by Denver collectors induced us to invite the artist to this one-man show. The exhibition comes from Norman, Oklahoma, where one of the large landscapes has just been purchased by the Fine Arts gallery. Applegate counts without doubt among the important "modernists." That is why his work is so stimulating to some and so annoying to others. I won't even mention the too well known I-know-what-I-like kind that proudly asserts that they close their eyes when they enter a room with "such" an exhibit. I will only mention those who get angry because they sometimes see a perfectly plausible mountain or house or tree in Applegate's pictures and sometimes quite incomprehensible zig-zags and squares and warping rectangles as they, for instance, appear in "South Western Valley" and "Navajoh-Land." Curiously enough, similar geometrical designs appear likewise in the paintings of other Santa Fe artists, for instance in Dasburg's, Nordfeldt's and Bakos' pictures. Yet each of these men represent such a strong personality that the thought they might copy an idea is too childish to be considered. They do not copy an idea, but they copy the country! They are simply observant of what they see. With a strong feeling for design and organization of forms, they take from the country just those elements which are more clearly defined in the dry atmosphere of the high plateaus of the Southwest than in any other part of the world. The outline of a mountain range at the horizon of the desert 60 or 80 miles distant is sometimes just as sharply designed as the pattern of the nearby fields. It is this emphasis of design, pattern and solid composition of colorful shapes that annoys those who will not see that the old masters whom they adore were preoccupied with these elements. If so-called modern art as a reaction against impressionism had not started in Paris, its essentials would have been discovered in the American Southwest. This seems at least highly probable, given the character of the country and the sensibility for form and color of the handful of creative minds that settled there some six or eight years ago. They came too late for a discovery; but, being of this time, their vision fits well into the general artistic tendencies of our period. There is an astonishing parallel in modern literature. In Willa Cather's very beautiful latest book, *Death Comes for the Archbishop*, we have just come over some passages describing the landscape of the Southwest in a masterly way.

Words, chosen with the same care with which the painter selects the lines of his composition, succeed here in giving the most vivid picture of the country around Santa Fe. In the chapter, "The Vicar Apostolic," we read: "Across the level Father Latour could distinguish low brown shapes, like earthworks, lying at the base of wrinkled green mountains with bare tops—wavelike mountains, resembling billows beaten up from a flat sea by a heavy gale, and their green was of two colors—aspen and evergreen—not intermingled, but lying in solid areas of light and dark. . . . Below them, in the midst of that wavy ocean of sand, was a green thread of verdure and a running stream. This ribbon in the desert seemed no wider than a man could throw a stone—and it was greener than anything Latour had ever seen, even in his own greenest corner of the Old World. . . . Running water, clover fields, cottonwoods, acacias, little adobe houses with brilliant gardens, a boy driving a flock of white goats toward the stream—that was what the young bishop saw." And that is an amazingly congenial description of what we see in Applegate's water colors. Two artists gifted with high sensibility, but expressing themselves in different mediums, arrive at results so identical that Willa Cather's description of the country is at the same time a translation of Applegate's water colors into words. Those almost unbelievably green spots we see in his "Chimayo, New Mexico Springtime," in "Land of Manana," "Placita" and "Cordova." There are the black-green patterns of evergreen—"not intermingled, but lying in solid areas of light and dark." There are the "little adobe houses with brilliant gardens" and their stoic, wooden inhabitants, awkward and motionless like the carved boultos and santos, piously beaming before candles and flowers in the white-washed rooms inside. And of course there are always the "wave-like mountains," and always there are clouds. "The great tables of granite set down in an empty plain were inconceivable without their attendant clouds which were a part of them, as the smoke is part of the censor, or the foam of the wave . . . The desert, the mountains and mesas, were continually reformed and recolored by the cloud shadows. The whole country seemed fluid to the eye under the constant change of accent, this ever-varying distribution of light." Literature is one thing and painting is another. There is no literary aspect in Applegate's work, but its comparison with the word pictures of one of the greatest and most subtle novelists of this country might contribute to their understanding among those who do not take the time to study—but who judge and quickly dismiss an art form that is different from what they think is "right." The Southwest is different from New England or the Seine valley. And the vision of the creative artist of today is different from that of the impressionists or the cubists. Frank G. Applegate's work is one of the outstanding contributions to the artistic tendencies of our time and of our country. It grows and will continue to grow out of his profound understanding and love for its very soil.

S. B. J., *Catholic World,* 126 (November 1927), 275–6

A novelist who deprives herself of the factors usually relied on by those of her craft, and depends, for sustaining the readers' interest, on the adventures of two mission priests, undertakes a difficult task. There is no love story, in the usual acceptation of the phrase, in Miss Cather's novel, nor is there any intricate plot or baffling mystery to set our wits to work anticipating the conclusion. Linking together a number of otherwise unconnected episodes, are the personalities of Father Latour and Father Vaillant, two heroes of the Church engaged in attempting to revive an almost forgotten Catholicism in New Mexico. That is all, and yet *Death Comes for the Archbishop* manages to be a story of absorbing interest.

That is evidence of the artistic character of Miss Cather's craftsmanship. Her palette holds all the colors necessary for painting the wild, mysterious country and the different types of humanity with which she deals, but nothing is overdone. Weird adventures are related with a restraint that makes the narration all the more effective. The poet and the psychologist and, some may think, the preacher are there, but they are all held in the leash of the novelist. The story proceeds uninterruptedly through light and shadow to its end.

Undoubtedly one of the factors in the success achieved is the skill with which the writer has used the richly varied elements at her disposal. The society she describes is a curious assortment of racial types, including American ecclesiastics, Spanish *rancheros*, adventurers of the Kit Carson kind and Mexican Indians. Moreover, it was a society in a state of transition. Barbarism and civilization mingle on the same page, and, as though this was not enough, there runs as an undertone through the story of the two homesick priests, memories of rural France.

But even its fine craftsmanship does not wholly account for the fascination of the book. That must be attributed in part to the subject. In the lives of these two priests you have the real romance of that conflict the Church wages with hea-

thenism and the heroism which may be only obscured by mission reports and statistics. By men such as these, lonely, and very human in their perplexities and worries but endowed with supernatural heroism, have the foundations of Christendom been laid. In particular, it may be said, that *Death Comes for the Archbishop* bears a close resemblance, in the main outline of its story, to the course of events in the history of New Mexican Catholicism.

Mary Ellen Chase, "Atlantic Bookshelf," *Atlantic Monthly*, 140 (November 1927), n.p.

One who has followed with admiration the writing of Miss Cather through the past decade is impressed first of all by the evidence on every page of her new book of her own interest and pleasure. If Pater's dictum be true, that to know when one's self is interested is the first condition of interesting others, then the readers of *Death Comes for the Archbishop* should be absorbed from the meeting of the Churchmen on the terrace of the Sabine Hills to the quiet last paragraph which leaves the Archbishop lying before the high altar of his own cathedral in Santa Fe. For obviously the author *is* interested. And, fortunately for herself, she is in this book held by none of those criteria which in the writing of novels so nag and harass an author given by disposition to wandering from the straight and narrow way.

From the outset Miss Cather makes it clear that her book is not a novel. It is a chronicle, a piece of historical narrative, a biography, a sketch, a tale; and it quite justly affords her all those rights and privileges which the construction of the novel is bound to deny. Since she is concerned with the life histories of Father Latour and of his intrepid vicar, Father Vaillant, rather than with their destinies as determined by circumstance and situation, she may with perfect propriety and with entire charm indulge herself in character sketches for their own sake, in the recital of miracles and of saints' legends, and in the exposition of historical incidents. Thus the displeasure which many felt upon reading in *The Professor's House* the chapters dealing with Tom's discovery of the pueblo, chapters fascinating in themselves but certainly intrusive in a novel of situation, must be wholly absent from this new book. Indeed, one shares the author's delight in the quaint and the marvelous, the instructive and the curious, and gladly wanders with her into any of the bypaths she chooses to explore.

The style of the book is beautiful in its simplicity and orderliness. One feels that the author often restrains her desire to be lyrical or rhythmic in order not to obscure the impressiveness or the power of her narrative. This is especially well illustrated in the closing paragraph, which the reviewer, for one, immediately contrasted with a similar situation in an early chapter of *My Mortal Enemy*, the latter memorable for its gorgeous imagery, this more memorable for the very lack of it. The value of the book as a chronicle of the history of our Southwestern states, then "bright edges of the world," can hardly be overestimated. The characters of Jean Marie Latour, priest, bishop, and archbishop, and of Father Vaillant, vicar and bishop, hold tenacious sway over memory and imagination. Indeed, Father Vaillant with his zeal for souls and his practical faith in God, who gave him feather beds and an oxcart for his missionarying in

Colorado, recalls Parson Adams with his much-tried faith in human kindness, and should, with Fielding's parson and Goldsmith's vicar, complete a never-to-be-forgotten ecclesiastical trio.

But perhaps in this abundance of riches there will linger most clearly the beauty of the descriptive passages. Surely Miss Cather, even in *My Antonia*, has never surpassed them. The violet mantle of the purple verbena, which held within itself "all the shades that the dyers and weavers of Italy and France strove for through centuries"; the long lavender brooms of the old and twisted tamarisks against sun-baked adobe walls; the towers of the cathedral in Santa Fe, which seemed to leap out of the rose-covered hills—these with many others make for us Keats's "endless fountain of immortal drink."

Mary Ross, "Bright Edges of the World," *Survey*, 59 (1 November 1927), 164

To the pageant of America's making no novelist has contributed more than Willa Cather. One by one her sensitive lucid stories have built up the epics of the pioneer—that slow fruitful process of man, pressing forward in towns and cities or almost alone in the great plains to make, with his hands and his spirit, a life that is not only secure but beautiful. This latest novel is laid in a new country, among the towering mesas, the conical red hills and stunted junipers of New Mexico, in the decades following the annexation of that wild and unknown territory to the United States.

In 1851, when Father Latour came to serve as the Vicar Apostolic and Bishop of Agathonica, its bright landscape had been etched through centuries with the ways of men, the Indians of the ancient pueblos, the bold flashing-eyed Spaniards, the Mexicans who had pushed up across the deserts to the southward. Father Latour and his lifelong companion, Father Vaillant, brought with them the subtlety and sophistication of the French missionary priests, the mystic splendor of Rome. The dignity of Father Latour could look straight into the eyes of his friend, the Navajo chief Eusabio, or meet the piercing blue gaze of Kit Carson, gallant soldier under orders, who hunted the Navajos as a ferret hunts rats.

When death came to the archbishop thirty years later, after their story of hardship and visions and friendship, he had seen the dream of his life—the great simple cathedral of Santa Fé, in the Romanesque of his native Auvergne. The Navajos had been cruelly expelled, then allowed to trek back wearily to the country which was their birthright of centuries. In the towns, adobe houses were mixed with box-like frame dwellings with scrolled porches. Orchards had sprung from the dry switches he had brought in desperate journeys across the country; on his little pond, piped with water from the Santa Fé creek, a hundred lotus blossoms floated, progeny of five bulbs he had slipped into his valise in Rome. His vigil was ended, and with it a bright chapter in the history of his church and of that amorphous United States which was welding slowly the bonds of a nation. Something was passing forever with the life of the archbishop, something which Miss Cather makes so achingly beautiful that one must be thankful it will linger in her book:

Beautiful surroundings, the society of learned men, the charm of noble women, the graces of art, could not make up to him for the loss of those light-hearted mornings of the desert, for that wind that made one a boy again. He had noticed that this peculiar quality in the air of new countries vanished after they were tamed by man and made to bear harvests. Parts of Texas and Kansas that he had first known as open range had since been made into rich farming districts, and the air had quite lost that lightness, that dry aromatic odour. The moisture of plowed land, the heaviness of labour and growth and grain-bearing, utterly destroyed it; one could breathe that only on the bright edges of the world, on the great grass plains or the sagebrush desert.

That air would disappear from the whole earth in time, perhaps; but long after this day. He did not know just when it had become so necessary to him, but he had come back to die in exile for the sake of it. Something soft and wild and free, something that whispered to the ear on the pillow, lightened the heart, softly, softly picked the lock, slid the bolts, and released the prisoned spirit of man into the wind, into the blue and gold, into the morning, into the morning!

Sydney Greenbie, "Willa Cather in the Far Southwest," *Springfield (Massachusetts) Republican*, 13 November 1927, p. 7F

Death Comes for the Archbishop is the most puzzling of Willa Cather's writings, not so much because it will not submit to easy classification as because the author's purpose is wonderfully concealed. One approaches it as one would a novel, and though one finds from the very beginning that it is not merely that, one continues to read it as though it were. Yet one cannot rush off with the usual facile encomium that it is "more fascinating than most novels" because it is a novel, at the same time that it holds the most critical attention as a biography and a history. That a writer has such control of her technic that she can take out all the expected elements of fiction, leave the appearance of fact, and hold the interest of the story reader, is an achievement neither sought nor accomplished by the general run of writers of this time and before. The work is a novel; yet there are only two lonely priests in it, and a few devoted Mexican women and some Indians.

One is puzzled by Miss Cather's purpose. Of the vast scene that is America, she selects the least common types—two alien priests adrift in a desert world. Obviously she has selected characters as far from her own personal likes or dislikes as she could conceive. And she sits there with large, thoughtful eyes, and looks at them. We have heard of looks that kill, but here we have looks that bring to life. She conjures up realities that, while hardly existing, nevertheless record themselves on the film of her moving picture camera, and lo! when you develop the reel there is a picture. It may be thrown upon the screen, yet there wasn't any one really there when it was taken. Such conjuring even Houdini could not expose. And she works in a quiet, disinterested way.

Miss Cather lets you see two priests urging Mme. Olivares to lie about her age so that she and her "daughter" and the church may hold on to the vast fortune her husband left her which his brothers were trying to reclaim. And you see not a

moral guilt at all, but simply a woman who cannot get herself to say she is 52 when she is only 42. Whether or not the novelist believes it wrong to perjure oneself does not concern her. You simply see a human situation, and how people in any given situation may act, just as you would stand off to watch an enormous tree being blown down by a great gust of wind.

She lets you see a converted Indian save the life of his priest in a sudden snowstorm by leading him to a hidden cave sacred to the Indian, within which no white man ever stepped, and the entering of which, were it to become known, would mean certain death to the convert. And while a physical scene is portrayed, and the roar of a subterranean river is heard through a fissure in the cave, it is really the depths of a bronze man's faith that you peer into, and the rumble of a race's superstitions down in the bowels of antiquity.

The reader sees a ridge high over the Rio Grande, "covered with cone-shaped, rocky hills, thinly clad with pinions, and the rock was a curious shade of green, something between sea-green and olive." And in the description of that ridge one gets the sense not only of the grandeur of New Mexico, but also of its seeming uselessness to man. What earthly good can such a world be to civilized people? But Miss Cather finds a purpose for it. You see the bishop stand "regarding the chip of yellow rock that lay in his palm. As he had a very special way of handling objects that were sacred, he extended that manner to things which he considered beautiful. After a moment of silence he looked up at the rugged wall, gleaming gold above them. 'That hill, Blanchet, is my cathedral.'"

So it is throughout. The transforming power of her pen touches the base and the noble and turns them both into something more human, more God-like. The prejudiced will not find in this lovely narrative of the impersonal self-surrender of two priests anything to protest against. The "scientific historian," if he looks at history at all with human eyes, cannot possibly object to a novelist revivifying facts that in his hands are often only bones and remains. The artist who believes so much in art for art's sake cannot possibly criticize Miss Cather for making her art serve understanding. In *Death Comes for the Archbishop*, Miss Cather has proved that Havelock Ellis was right when he said that science and art are one.

Rachel Annand Taylor, *Spectator* (London), 139 (29 November 1927), 894

Death Comes for the Archbishop (by the author of that little masterpiece *A Lost Lady*), though a book of grave and gentle quality, seems slightly perplexed in its intention. It is not really a novel; and, since it seems left in a half-way condition, one wishes it were. The refined scholar-saint, whose Catholic diocese extends over the wastes of New Mexico and Arizona, is a noble figure, touched in with details both austere and tender; and his naïf friend and helper, Brother Joseph, is lovable in his own way. But these two merely make a kind of centre for a series of impressions of these strange inhuman landscapes, kneaded with the rituals of an older faith, and their stranger, more difficult inhabitants. The incidents are unusual, and keenly recorded. If they had been linked into a unity by more insis-

tence on their connexion with the history of the Archbishop's soul, the artistic effect would have been more satisfying. As it is, the dying Archbishop, gazing at his golden Romanesque cathedral, is remembered like a friend.

Gilbert H. Doane, "Willa Cather, '95, Fictional Biographer," *Nebraska Alumnus*, 23 (November 1927), 452

Death Comes For The Archbishop, Willa Cather's latest book, is one of the finest she has written. There is a finesse in the style that is rarely equalled. As one reads it, one almost exclaims: "How easily she writes!" Yet, she must work for such perfection. The story is that of Bishop Jean Latour, first bishop of New Mexico. Father Latour and his vicar, Father Vaillant, come out from France to take charge of the newly created see. We follow them through their daily life in and about Santa Fe, as they work in their diocese, and as they rest in the courtyard of the episcopal residence. It is a charming picture—the sensitive Bishop, an aristocrat of old France, with all his love for scholarly pursuits and his fruit trees, which he so carefully cultivates in his garden; and, in contrast to him, the beloved Father Vaillant, the son of a bourgeois baker, who worships his bishop, whose simple faith in the miraculous powers of the Virgin is a key to his character, and whose zeal in promulgating the Faith leads him out across the desert to the remote corners of the diocese. They are an interesting pair, whom we cannot help but love and revere. Father Vaillant ultimately becomes Bishop of Colorado, and dies at Denver, his old friend, Bishop Latour making the long and somewhat hazardous journey to that frontier city to attend his funeral. Bishop Latour lives to become Archbishop, and to retire to a small place outside of Sante Fe, where he tends his beloved fruit trees and takes young priests, newly arrived from France, for instruction in the ways of the Southwest. Finally, as the old Archbishop realizes that he is about to die, he goes back to Sante Fe, to die in the old episcopal residence, where his many friends and servants can come to his bedside. He dies at sunset, as he would have wished, and his body rests in state before the high altar of the cathedral he built.

One closes the book with a feeling of reverence and almost awe, for one has seen unfolding before him a life of great beauty. The book can hardly be called a novel, historical, or otherwise; rather it is what might be termed a fictional biography, for Bishop Latour really lived—under another name—and was actually the first Bishop of New Mexico.

Times Literary Supplement (London), 1 December 1927, p. 906

If Miss Willa Cather's new novel, *Death Comes for the Archbishop*, is in the least disappointing, it is only because she has abandoned that neatness of construction that made *A Lost Lady* so memorable a book. She has been content to let her mind wander over New Mexico as it was in the middle of the last century, leaving it free to browse among old Indian stories and to discover forgotten and beautiful legends, only occasionally jerking it into

memory of its duty of bringing Jean Marie Latour from his early manhood as a young missionary priest, to those last days when, as Archbishop, he lay in the palace at Santa Fe quietly awaiting death. Although Latour is much more a slight figure moving with other figures against a finely painted background of legend and history than what, in novels of plot and action, is called "the central character," he is a very definite person, a man of bravery, sensitiveness and courtesy, and his faith and his goodness envelop the disconnected pictures and incidents of which the book consists with a tranquillity, almost a holiness:

> At one moment the whole flock of doves caught the light in such a way that they all became invisible at once, dissolved in light and disappeared as salt dissolves in water. The next moment they flashed around, black and silver against the sun. They settled upon Magdalena's arms and shoulders, ate from her hand. When she put a crust of bread between her lips, two doves hung in the air before her face, stirring their wings and pecking at the morsel. A handsome woman she had grown to be, with her comely figure and the deep claret colour under the golden brown of her cheeks.

The picture is a simple enough one, but, to an imagination hypnotized by page after page of similar writing, there is a curious religious symbolism about it; it is easy to feel that under the patter of words lies another vision of which the woman with the doves is but the external form. Whether or not the reader sees in the missionary efforts of Latour and his life-long friend, Father Vaillant, any more than the story of hard, self-sacrificing work nobly done, or in the descriptions of the scenery any more than faithful and exact writing, he cannot fail to recognize in *Death*

Comes for the Archbishop a beautiful and unusual book.

[Henry Seidel Canby] "Notes of a Rapid Reader," *Saturday Review of Literature*, 4 (10 December 1927), 421

Miss Cather is growing restless in the old forms. The novel irks her. First she tried the *nouvelle*, or long short story, and wrote a masterpiece in *A Lost Lady*; then she built *The Professor's House* according to the structure of a concerto; now, for the *Archbishop*, she chooses the method of chronicle history. Instead of providing suspense and a climax, she depends, like history, upon interest in men and events. It is the honester way, if you can succeed with it. She has.

written by women [*There is No Return* by Elizabeth Bibesco, *Oberland* by Dorothy M. Richardson, *Helen and Felicia* by E. B. C. Jones, and *Death Comes for the Archbishop* by Willa Cather], but so unlike that they might be the work of four different sexes. All have merits much above the average, but none seems to share, to any great extent, the merits of the others. . . .

Miss Willa Cather's study of the life of a French Roman Catholic Bishop in Mexico in the middle of the last century is written with perfect taste and with perfect command of its subject. It also, unlike many historical novels, conveys a sense of the past: to me the sense of a remoter past, 1750 not 1850. *Death Comes for the Archbishop* is perhaps more admirable than interesting. It has the air of a biography, not of a novel, and one cannot quite see why Miss Willa Cather wrote it. It bears throughout the impress of a sensitive and distinguished mind: but it does not excite us as the account of a great missionary enterprise ought to do.

L. P. Hartley, "New Fiction," *Saturday Review of Politics, Literature, Science and Art* (London), 144 (10 December 1927), 828–9

The term "woman novelist," if it implies that there is some quality common to fiction written by women which is not to be found in fiction written by men, is most misleading. Here are four novels, all

Checklist of Additional Reviews

Frances Newman, "A Reservationist's Impressions of Willa Cather's New Mexican Catholic Missionaries of 1850," *New York Evening Post, The Literary Review*, 3 September 1927, p. 8.

Walden E. Sweet. "In Old Santa Fe," *Rocky Mountain News* (Denver), 25 September 1927, drama section, p. 7.

Booklist, 24 (November 1927), 67.

SHADOWS ON THE ROCK

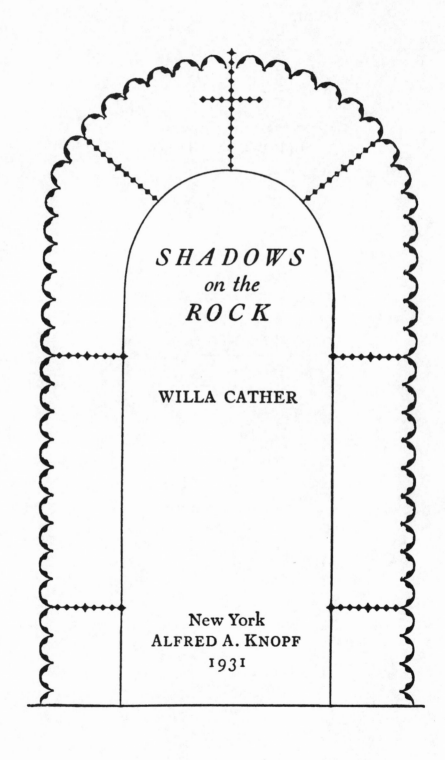

SHADOWS
on the
ROCK

WILLA CATHER

New York
ALFRED A. KNOPF
1931

Kenneth C. Kaufman,
Southwest Review, 16
(Summer 1931), xi–xiii

The Rock is the granite headland from which Quebec looks down on the St. Lawrence; the time is between October, 1697, and November, 1698; and the story is the awakening of a twelve-year-old girl to her heritage as one of the first of the Canadians. Her name is Cécile and she is the daughter of Euclide Auclair, apothecary to Count de Frontenac.

Through her eyes we see, as through a peep hole, a gigantic stage where Titans play their destined rôles and come to heroic ends: Frontenac, that stern old solider whose life has been a record of winning battles and losing fortunes, who knows how to serve his king but not how to flatter him, is her father's protector and her own friend. Bishop Laval, living in bitter poverty for the sake of his Seminary, forever busy with his plans for the Christianization of Canada, has time to pat her head and help her with modest charities. And Bishop de Saint-Vallier, friend of the King, enemy of Frontenac and Laval, courtier and man of the world, is a frequent visitor at her father's shop.

And in the dim background are the outlines of all the heroes who discovered and claimed for France that vast empire which sweeps in a great semicircle from Labrador to the mouth of the Mississippi, threatening to enfold in a strangling embrace the puny English colonies on the Atlantic.

The names of Champlain, Jolliet, Marquette, Tonti are a part of everyday conversation; the lives of the martyrs Brébeuf, Jogues, and Lalement are Cécile's fairy tales; and once the cobbler showed her the last on which he had made the shoes of Robert Cavelier de la Salle, dead now, murdered by his own men on the faraway coast of Texas. Shadows on the rock.

Minor characters, too, are here, drawn with the sharpness of outline and the justice of perspective which are an integral part of Miss Cather's art: Auclair, the philosopher-apothecary, quiet, mild, happy in his task of alleviating disease and pain, friend to the great, loved of the poor, simple, genuine; Blinker, the baker's handy man, a forlorn, kindly soul, bearing the secret of a terrible past locked in his bosom; Jacques, son of an abandoned woman, younger than Cécile, her playmate and protégé; Father Hector Saint-Cyr, the missionary, a man of noble birth and a cultured gentleman, spending his life in the wigwams of the Indians for the glory of God; and Pierre Charron, the trapper and trader, with his lost love and his gay, hardy, self-reliant manhood, whom Cécile was afterward to marry.

The story is slight.

[. . .]

In comparison with *Death Comes for the Archbishop*, and this comparison is inevitable, *Shadows on the Rock* is something of a disappointment. In both books we find a tremendous theater of action, an old order of life being overthrown and a new established, a clash of racial and national ideals; in both there are heroic, legendary figures; in both there is a similar religious preoccupation; and in both there is the same majestic austerity of style, and the same perfect assimilation of regional phenomena. But in the earlier book the protagonist is a major personality; we follow him through a lifetime of toil and watch that toil come into fruition; here the protagonist is a secondary character, and the limitation in time precludes the slow and inevitable evolution of destiny, the rich substance of character overcoming environment and merging with it into a new order of things. Here is a huge canvas with the major figures merely outlined and with the high lights playing upon the minor ones.

We are thrown back, then, upon the life of Quebec, compressed into these thirteen months, as the real interest of the book. We see it with the savage forest at its back and the blue river at its feet; with the trails of explorer and missionary leading off endlessly into the wilderness; locked in the merciless grip of winter for eight months of the year, madly rejoicing when the ships come in from France; with its old-world customs and limitations gradually yielding to the limitless new world; Quebec with its beauty and its sadness, with the spirit of the Church brooding over it; Quebec, that was the heart and soul of France in America. And that dream of New France was another shadow on the rock. This picture of Quebec is utterly convincing. There is no doubt that Miss Cather is the greatest of our provincial novelists, and her province is the world.

Ethel Wallace Hawkins, "The Atlantic Bookshelf," *Atlantic Monthly*, 148 (August 1931), 8, 10

The spell of Miss Cather's new novel begins with the beautiful title, *Shadows on the Rock*. This quiet chronicle is full of the pathos of humanity—the eagerness, the effort, and above all the transitoriness, emphasized by the mighty background against which the shadow-shapes come and go.

Simplicity and largeness characterize equally this story of old Quebec. It is one of the shorter of Miss Cather's novels, and one of the more beautifully constructed. It follows the cycle of a year, and is finished by an epilogue that shows the harmonizing work of time. Ordinarily it might be thought an odd tribute to an American novel to say that it seems like a perfect translation from another tongue; but it is high praise, I think, to say of a tale of seventeenth-century Canada that it sounds like the work of a Frenchman. And surely this is true of *Shadows on the Rock*, this story of simple lives that yet gives, as its author supremely knows how to give, the brooding sense of eternity.

As ably as Mr. Theodore Dreiser portrays naive ignobleness, Miss Cather portrays an instinctive fineness and magnanimity. The gentle soul of Euclide Auclair, apothecary of Quebec and personal physician to Count Frontenac, takes on stature as the story progresses. Auclair is a man both keen and kind in his judgments of men, both firm in his principles and tolerant. His nature is a generous one. Well aware of a certain timidity in himself, a reluctance to exchange things as they are for unknown conditions, he heartily admires the self-reliance and adventurousness of Pierre Charron, the woodsman, and the pertinacity of the count, his patron, in essaying enterprise after enterprise. The sense of Canada as an outpost, or a land where hearts are turning back with longing to another land, is given by the opening scene, in October, when the ships have sailed for France, and by the scene in the following fall when the ships sail up the river again, welcomed with an uproar of joy and with tears. But it is given quite as much by the silent yearning of the apothecary for his old home in France. Similarly, the sense of Canada as a well-grown young land with a life of its own is given by the ultimate resolution of Auclair's homesickness into contentment.

Infant excellence in fiction is all too likely to become a stench in the nostrils. But the child Cécile Auclair, with all her precocious piety of a well-taught little French girl, with all her precocious tact and selflessness and steadfastness, is an altogether fragrant little creature. Still more appealing is Cécile's protégé, the small good Jacques, son of La Grenouille the prostitute. I can think of few episodes in the chronicles of childhood more engaging than the little boy's proffering of his one treasure, his carved wooden beaver, to companion the *beau petit âne* and the *beau mouton* in Cécile's miraculous creche. "He isn't new," says Jacques. "He's just my little old beaver the sailor made me, but he could keep the baby warm." Pleasing, too, is the little boy's solemn wonder at Cécile's silver cup, engraved with her name. "To have a little cup, with your name on it . . . even if you died, it would still be there, with your name."

The author's work has always been marked by a trait without which no novelist, I think, reaches greatness—compassion. In *Shadows on the Rock* an example of this is found in the portrait of Blinker, the thickset cross-eyed drudge who tends the baker's oven fires at night and worships the apothecary's little girl as if she were an angel. Poor repulsive Blinker is a heartbreaking figure—secretly tormented, waking and sleeping, by memories of the horrible trade that his father had compelled him to practise in France; so softhearted that he has to creep from the room, shamed by his sudden sniffles, when Cécile, on Christmas Eve, tells Jacques once again how the kings and the shepherds came to worship the little weak Jesus.

I think that Miss Cather's power of feeling and rendering beauty has never shown itself more superbly. Nothing in the book is more living than the magnificent pictures of the city on the rock above the great river, in many seasons, hours, and weathers. The art of these passages is above praise. I believe that to many readers they will be the lasting impression made by the novel; as to others the enduring memory will be that of the human bravery seen afloat for a while on the mightier stream.

John Murray, "Promethean Fires," *Canadian Bookman*, 13 (August 1931), 167–8

This new novel by Willa Cather is not, as reviewers in the book sections of newspapers of widespread circulation have rather cruelly pointed out, a novel of action. But it seems to me that it is not quite fair to compare it unfavorably on that score, with Sir Gilbert Parker's *The Seats of the Mighty*, or other highly dramatic novels in the same setting, because *Shadows on the Rock*, quite evidently, was not intended to seek recognition in that field. In fact the book speaks for itself and may be depended upon to consummately satisfy those readers who in their reading of the book find themselves in tune with the spirit of its author.

With no flurry, hurry, dash, or emphasis on the rigorous hardships of pioneering, we are at the very beginning ushered into a home in Quebec that has been transplanted from Paris with all its essentials of what a home ought to be.

[. . .]

Another aspect which seems to me to be significant, although I question whether it has even entered the mind of any other reviewer, is the good that it may well do in promoting those bonds of brotherhood that should flourish to the full in the Canadian nation.

Religious bigotry, or at least a proscribed religious outlook, has shut out too many non-Catholics from the birthright of all Canadians—an unrestricted appreciation of all the elements of the early making of Canada in which Catholicism was dominant because that was the faith of those early Canadians.

Why should I, as a Protestant, allow that fact to color my reactions to an account of the lives of a group of people of a faith other than my own?

To me this book comes as a benediction upon those views and, as such, I believe it will do untold good and perhaps prove to be as significant an addition to novels of early Canadian life as would a tale embodying drama and action to the nth degree.

For those who appreciate an unfolding of the lives of its characters amid scenes of early Canadian history, there is much to entrance them in this latest of Willa Cather's novels.

William E. Harris, "Willa Cather and *Shadows on the Rock*," *Boston Evening Transcript*, 1 August 1931, p. 8

Willa Cather is no exception to the rule that most storytellers who take their profession seriously tend inevitably towards mysticism in the riper years of full-grown maturity. Having viewed man's struggles with himself and earthly matters, these authors gradually become increasingly fascinated by the inscrutable aspects of the universe, as well as the place therein of men in relation to an omnipotent godhead of some sort. Possibly Eugene O'Neill in the steady march from his early one-act plays up through such dramas as *The Emperor Jones* and *The Hairy Ape* to *The Great God Brown* and the later *Strange Interlude* is a more spectacular example. Nevertheless, Miss Cather as one of our most important writers of fiction—one hesitates to describe her work as storytelling—illustrates very handsomely the change that comes over authors.

Like *Death Comes for the Archbishop*, Miss Cather's latest book is a biography of a time and a place rather than a novel of men. More particularly does this seem true than in the case of Father Jean Latour, because both Auclair and his young daughter are essentially passive figures. Euclide has not the push of the New Mexican prelate, nor is he impelled by so strong a spiritual ideal.

And moreover, he is at the end of the arch of life. His love of a well-cooked dinner does not merely arise from his French inheritance; it seems a direct expression of the wistful longings that come to man as they pass out of the burning sunshine into the quieter, sadder shadows of dusk. Cecile, on the contrary, is but a child in her mind and heart, despite the maternal duties her dying mother has let fall upon her slim shoulders at so early an age. The picture of Kebec at the turn of a century and epoch, the sadness of a man outliving his time— these are the dominant qualities then, of Miss Cather's present work. Where *Death Comes for the Archbishop* showed the struggle of a great religious faith against the primitive growth of a wilderness refusing to be tamed or modified, *Shadows on the Rock* portrays a man, meek before the inspiring grandeur of those miles and miles of primeval forest, his needing that religion always so in danger of being trampled out. It is an eminently fitting sequence, entirely logical in its development.

As a matter of fact this progressive change emphasized the transition in Miss Cather's own personal growth. It also hints the danger she skirts as an artist with a stern, unrelenting desire to picture life as she sees it. Nearly all her early books, *Alexander's Bridge*, *O Pioneers!*, *My Antonia* and *The Song of the Lark* were tales of frontier men and women striving against the odds Nature set to attain the full run of their own potentialities. The atmospheric background was no less vivid, no less true than in *The Professor's House* and the two more recent books. But now the characters appear only incidental puppets in the hands of an austere, impersonal godhead around which Miss Cather's interest focuses. And this despite the immensely vivid quality of her writing, the keen effortless building up of a character such as Euclide Auclair or the blossoming Cecile. For almost any other American novelist today *Shadows on the Rock* would represent a triumph of difficult and imaginative resource. For Miss Cather it merely represents a successful continuance of her earlier endeavors to write history in terms of timeless, authentic fiction. The French background of old Quebec is far better known than that of the older Spanish civilization in New Mexico. It seems doubtful, therefore, sweet as has been Miss Cather's accomplishment, that it adds any notable progress to her art.

On the other hand, *Shadows on the Rock* presents more keenly than almost any of the author's earlier books the danger that has already been suggested. It has become very nearly a gesture with Miss Cather to avoid plot complication of any kind. In *The Song of the Lark*, which only a few of Miss Cather's admirers consider one of her finest studies of a character overcoming environment, she came within an ace of ruining a difficult task well done, by the stiffness of her storytelling. Since then accordingly she has more and more avoided all pretense of writing the conventional work of fiction. Now, however, a new element appears to be slowly entering in. As the author pursues with increasing intensity the mystical aspects of life, her tales take on an increasing air of romance. In *Shadows on the Rock* it is hard to lay one's finger upon a concrete example, so completely seems the whole redolent with this characteristic. But a passage from *Death Comes for the Archbishop* will perhaps point the meaning. "A priest in a thousand one knew at a glance," reads the author's description of Jean Latour. "His bowed head was not that of an ordinary man; it was built for the seat of a fine intelligence ... There was a singular elegance about the hands ... His manners, even when alone in the desert were distinguished. He had a kind of courtesy toward himself, toward his beasts, toward the juniper tree before which he knelt, and the God whom he was addressing." These words suggest the phrases of romance, a very high order of romance, rather than the tools of the realistic writer of fictional history or pioneer biography that Miss Cather once was. There exists just that subtle distinction the author herself pictures as separating Euclide Auclair from his neighbors in New France. He, a sentimental intellectualist watching for that last tip of white sail sliding behind the curving shore; they, plain, serious folk who went back to their "shops and kitchens to face the stern realities of life." In the same way one feels that Miss Cather at this stage of her career is dealing in sentiments where earlier she wrote of terse, rugged emotions. The fact remains none the less, that shining through every line of *Shadows on the Rock* is the author's quiet achievement of beauty in a work of art. Writing far more intensely than most novelists, or even out-and-out philosophers, she ever remains modestly impersonal. The beliefs, the emotions expressed are always those of her characters. The jewelled simplicity of her words are dedicated to the longings, the aspirations of all humanity. If in a mystical view of life her keen powers of observance appear to soften, to romanticize, it is because through nearly twenty years of active story-telling she has sought to comprehend and visualize on paper the sufferings of ambitious men and women in the phrase of Auclair: "The mind, too, has a kind of blood . . . and hence a life without security, without plans, without preparation for the future is terrible." Of such has been and is Miss Cather's preoccupation.

Carl Van Doren, "Willa Cather's New Chronicle of Virtue," *New York Herald Tribune Books*, 2 August 1931, p. 1

Almost alone among living novelists Willa Cather gives intelligent, even passionate comfort to those readers who believe in human virtue as something proud, rich and memorable. Her books are like generous vacations from the world which her contemporaries, as a rule, examine in their fictions with a harsh or feline scrutiny. Though she can be ironical, she denies herself the benefits of malice, and seldom stings. Individual enough, she is never paradoxical. Her characters live

in the sun, busy with actions which, however difficult, are not clouded with spiritual confusion. If she were a little less distinguished in her understanding and her comments, she might easily fall into a monotony of virtue. As it is, she is moving rather than exciting. Distinction saves her. She has, what is always rare, that distinction without singularity which goes with health of mind and heart. And with a fine self-knowledge she has generally chosen to tell such stories, about such men and women, as belong in the center of her field of vision.

Her variety has been conditioned by her growth. Her successive books, that is, have come from successive layers in her own actual or imagined experience. It took her three novels to say what she had to say about the figure of virtue which first held her imagination—the pioneer woman. Though Alexandra in *O Pioneers!* and Thea in *The Song of the Lark* and Antonia in *My Antonia* are not all literally the same person, they are all built upon the same model, and they differ chiefly in their special talents. Alexandra, a Nebraska Artemis, stays at home and manages her land. Thea, an Athena from the foothills, is driven abroad, to Chicago, to the Southwest, to Europe and New York, by the irresistible instinct which makes her, in the end, a great singer. Antonia, obscure Hera in a prairie township, lives for her husband and children. The talents of the three women being different, their careers are different. But they themselves, in their native essence, are as alike as so many goddesses. There is something partly archaic about them, as if they had survived from a cooler, clearer, stronger day. They are various aspects of one heroic image, and they must be taken together to fill out Miss Cather's record of the virtue which engaged her when she wrote.

A Lost Lady is a kind of afterpiece to this first cycle. Marian Forrester has been

358

touched by the heroic age, not created or molded by it. As it changes about her she declines. Her flaw is not that she takes a lover, but that she takes one who is trivial and base. Alexandra or Thea or Antonia would any of them have known that what is third-rate is good enough only for those who too are third-rate, that it is better to have no love at all than to have love and have to be ashamed of it. They would not knowingly have stooped. The story of the lost lady, lost because she accepts counterfeit, throws a backward light upon her more heroic sisters, who stand higher than ever in an integrity of which chastity is but an item.

That integrity which is the sum of all the virtues in these novels with women as their principal characters is stressed as much in the novels dealing primarily with men. Claude Wheeler in *One of Ours* and Tom Outland in *The Professor's House* are young men who spend their few years looking for a life which shall be full enough to call for all their powers and yet not so complex as to divide their natures. Tom, with a directing dash of genius in him comes nearer to what he wants than Claude, who has so much pioneer in his blood that he is bewildered by everything in the twentieth century except the war, in which he dies. But both are without the capacity for deft evasions or smooth compromises. They will not stop living while they are still alive. They keep on demanding whatever is most intelligible and most profound, most peaceful and most rapturous, best and truest. Without an opportunity for splendor in their fortunes or their deeds, they are quietly heroic, to be remembered for their virtues or not at all. They are pioneers modified but not denatured.

Yet Miss Cather is not an abandoned apologist for the frontier. As early as her second novel she sent Thea bruised by her conflicts in the world, not to the Colorado of her birth, but to the deeper calm of a desert canyon in Arizona. And in *The Professor's House* St. Peter feels his youth comes back to him in the presence of Tom Outland, who has absorbed the long past of forgotten cliff villages. Pioneer instincts, Miss Cather implies, are for pioneers. They can sustain an Alexandra or an Antonia, thinking and feeling with a peasant simplicity within the limits of a peasant culture, but they do not entirely suffice for Thea or Tom, and they fail Claude altogether. Though pure nature, such as the pioneers faced, will serve for a time, it ceases to affect them when they have mastered it. Something more ancient is needed, something more impregnable, something more fixed and lasting.

Outside the core of Miss Cather's imaginative devotion to the frontier the next layer of growth was concerned with the Indian Southwest, with its refuge and healing for Thea, its proportions and perspective for Tom. But Miss Cather's imagination could not perpetually feed upon ruins. It widened from them to something which still persisted in the Southwest, venerable and disciplined, and living; it grew another layer to include the Catholic Church.

When, or if, the Protestant schism becomes an episode in the lineage of heresies, and all Americans are Catholics, Miss Cather will deserve a blessed reputation for her prophetic sympathy, and *Death Comes for the Archbishop* may well be a canonical classic. Yet her sympathy seems not to mean conversion. She only extended her mind to round her art. Nebraska was too new and raw. The cliff villages were too old and dead. In the life of the Archbishop she had a chance to work with all the elements which had so far powerfully stirred her. He was, in many of his functions, a pioneer. He spent his effective years in the Southwest. He inherited, as a Catholic, a discipline able both to support and to renew him. Moreover, he was a priest, and possibly not quite so hard to make convincing as Miss Cather had found some of her heroes. She could write the chronicle of his virtues out of ripe accumulations of imagined experience.

In turning to Quebec for the scene of *Shadows on the Rock* she has surrendered some of the advantages which she had in *Death Comes for the Archbishop*. There were, of course, pioneers in the Canada of the seventeenth century, and there were Catholics. But the setting is remote from her familiar prairies and deserts, and her materials come from later, and naturally less abundant, stores of observation. As if she could not wholly trust her imagination to carry her through the full drama of the age and place, she has chosen to represent the last days of the Count de Frontenac as they appeared to a child, the shadows of events, not the events themselves. Her epic is consequently domesticated.

The method is, in a sense, the reverse of that in the pioneer novels. Whereas there Miss Cather puts into relief the heroic qualities which give dimension to the common lives of her chief personages, here she represents, with learned and delicate precision, the daily existence of Quebec. The administrative problems of Frontenac, the opposition of the bishops, the precariousness of the lonely winter between the departure of the annual ships for France and their alleviating return, the perils of the wilderness just outside the closed circle of approximate safety—these enter the novel as muffled news interpreted to Cécile Auclair by her father, the intelligent but not heroic apothecary. Pierre Charron, hero of the coureurs de bois, appears only as a guest in the neat Auclair household, where on ordinary evenings Cécile reads Plutarch aloud to her father. And even when the child is not in the center of the stage, she determines the tone of the drama. If the chronicle is to be all of one stuff, it cannot be viewed now through eyes twelve years old and now through eyes harder and closer to events. It must be simple and decent, and in the idiom of familiarity.

Obliged by her method to forego heroism at first hand, Miss Cather has had to run the risk of a certain lack of sinew, and her narrative does not have the force of that in *Death Comes for the Archbishop*. Her strength lies less in her movement than in her still life, less perhaps in the drawing than in the colors. She has employed a chronological scale new to her (though she once approached it in *The Professor's House*.) Except for a brief epilogue and various reminiscent digressions, she confines herself to the happenings of a single winter, spring and summer. When a short time must last through the whole of a novel, it has to be filled either with actions to recount or else with objects, opinions, sensations, moods to analyze or describe. In *Shadows on the Rock*, with its actions reported not exhibited, the moods and sensations are most of them uncomplicated, and the opinions are held too civilly to lead to strife. What gives the chronicle its body is the objects described—the accurate landscapes of the changing seasons, the river, the headland up which the city climbs, the streets, churches, markets, waterfront, houses, interiors, costumes, food and drink, whatever about the daily life of Quebec was customary enough to be set down or unusual enough to be pointed out. The novel has made the town and its inhabitants exquisitely visible.

Pictorially rich, *Shadows on the Rock* is dramatically somewhat thin. Its excellence must be discovered not in the weight and thrust of the major events to which it refs but in the idyllic or pathetic touches which make up the flesh of the actual story. Not even the luminous episode of Jeanne Le Ber, the recluse of Montreal, lingers more tenderly in the memory than the account of the excitement with which Cécile saw her first parrot, or of the satisfaction which the neglected child Jacques has in Cécile's cup with her name on it. "To have a little cup, with your name on it . . . even if you died. . . . Cécile had suggested that he drink his chocolate from it, and she would use another. But he shook his head, unable to explain it. That was not at all what her cup meant to him. Indeed, Cécile could not know what it meant to him. She was too fortunate." Such small strokes of nature, such quick glances into inarticulate hearts, occur in the novel again and again and almost take the place of heroism.

They do not quite take its place. Miss Cather, without the witty malice which can make genre-painting lively through a whole novel, works best when she has a strong thread on which to range her incidents. She is a chronicler rather than a dramatist, and needs time for her characters to turn around in. Only in this latest novel and in *The Professor's House* has she used less than most of the lifetime of her heroes and heroines to complete their records. She has been apparently skeptical about those hours of climax with which some novelists are content. Do not men and women after great hours descend to their accustomed levels? How can the truth be told about any human being unless it can be shown what time, with the repeated assaults of years, can do to him? The virtue of a moment is mere animal chemistry compared to the tested union of virtues which can weather decades of experience. Drama is not so credible as biography. Miss Cather has inclined in her novels away from dramatic and toward biographical devices. It may be that she does not feel as dramatists feel. Certainly she thinks as biographers think. But in *Shadows on the Rock*, a novel with no unmistakable hero or heroine, she has written, it might be said, a biography without a subject. Unless the subject is the Rock of Quebec, upon which the shadows of events fall how gracefully, yet how unwaveringly! The virtues which she chronicles are the virtues of a whole community.

Miss Cather has always been divided between her passion for heroic individuals and her admiration for ordered, fruitful comely societies. She has said that when she first learned the ways of Boston after Nebraska she would have given all she had or ever hoped to have if only she might be thoroughly at home in this new world which she found so bland and charming, so settled and so diversified. The writer she then particularly valued was Sarah Orne Jewett, who dealt hardly so much with the shadows of passing as with the wraiths of past events. Faithful to that enthusiasm, Miss Cather has now played Miss Jewett to Quebec, as she tended to play Miss Jewett to New Mexico in *Death Comes for the Archbishop*. Her admiration for a society has, at least temporarily, won her from her passion for heroes. It need not, of course, be an irrevocable attachment. The passion and the admiration are not contradictory. As Miss Cather has also said: "The history of every country begins in the heart of a man or a woman."

John Chamberlain, "Willa Cather's Tale of Canada," *New York Times Book Review*, 2 August 1931, p. 1

When, as a student, Willa Cather first looked upon the Puvis de Chavannes frescoes of the life of Sante Geneviève, she conceived the idea of trying "something a little like that in prose"; something with no accent, with no "artificial" elements of composition. In the Golden Legend, she goes on to explain, the martyrdoms of saints are no more dwelt upon than the trivial happenings of their lives. "The essence of such writing is not to hold the note, not to use an incident for all there is in it—but to touch and pass on. *** In this kind of writing the mood is the thing." The result of that wish to do work in fresco—nurtured through years that saw the production of novels that, if plotted by title on a graph according to merit, would result in a chart resembling a depiction of the fluctuations of the business cycle—was *Death Comes for the Archbishop*.

Miss Cather's latest novel, *Shadows on the Rock*, a fresco of seven panels showing various aspects of life in Quebec in the days of Frontenac, is a further venture into the same genre. There is no conflict in the book, no use of "incident for all there is in it." As prose the work is inordinately beautiful; it is full of softly flashing northern color, of descriptions of landscapes that, in the words of Elinor Wylie, are "drawn in pearly monotones"—with the emphasis on the "pearly." But there is not a really memorable incident in the book, and for this reason it falls below the level of *Death*

Comes for the Archbishop, which is not the novel that Willa Cather will be remembered for thirty years from now. Like the nun, Jeanne Le Ber, whose story Miss Cather tells as illustrative of a phase of French Catholic life in the Canada of the seventeenth century, Miss Cather has become a recluse in spirit—she has, for the time being at least, left her own world of Nebraska pioneers behind her, and gone in search of other and older and more myth-clouded pioneers of the American Continent. She is living, like her nuns, "in the world of the mind (which for each of us is the only world) ***" The salt, the sweat, the riot and the rigor of pioneering, present to some extent in the person of Father Joseph in *Death Comes for the Archbishop*, is conspicuous by its absence in *Shadows on the Rock*. The shrinking of her little heroine, Cécile Auclair, from country-style life on the Ile d'Orléans below Quebec, is symbolic of the book.

Shadows on the Rock is plotless. There is in it none of the fustian and romantic psychology of the historical fiction of Sir Gilbert Parker, but there is little characterization, for all that. What we have is, as has been suggested, a number of panels that take one around the clock and around the year in the Quebec which Louis XIV despaired of ever making a jewel in the French colonial crown. As Parkman says:

> There was one corner of the world where his emblem, the sun, would not shine on him. He had done his best for Canada, and had got nothing for his pains but news of mishaps and troubles. He was growing tired of the colony which he had nursed with paternal fondness, and he was more than half angry with it because it did not prosper.

From this colony Louis XIV had removed Frontenac seven years before.

The Count was now 70 years old, but the state of affairs in Canada required a man of Frontenac's capabilities, so Louis called the old Governor before him. "I send you back to Canada," he is reported to have said, "where I am sure that you will serve me as well as you did before; and I ask nothing more of you." It is after the return of Frontenac, in the last year of his life, that Miss Cather picks up the story. What she does is to colloquialize Parkman; she tells, as anecdote, what Parkman tells as history. The trouble is that she sticks to the citadel on the rock, Quebec, and lets the coureurs de bois go for the most part. There are references to LaSalle, to the attack of Sir William Phips on Quebec, to the life in the woods, where the Indians often eat boiled dog; to the fur trading life, where "*** o'est un mariage, / Espouser le voyage ***"; but there is precious little of actuality, of the bite of black flies and the fear of the redskin.

Miss Cather prefers to stick to the transplanted amenities of Catholic civilization; what we get is a household chronicle, an evocation of quiet tradition. Thus we are taken into the apothecary's shop and home of Euclide Auclair, who has cast his lot with Frontenac, his patron; we learn of Auclair's fondness for wood pigeons preserved in melted lard, of his preference for the older medicine of a time before the court physicians tried every sort of purge on the tough old Sun King, who lived out his natural life in spite of the barbarities practiced upon him. We learn, too, of the upbringing of a girl of good family under the French system; Cécile is rigorously trained in the tradition which makes the family sacrosanct, the table and wines a matter of art, and the daughters demure and reclusive until marriage at last gives them a chance to go out into the world. The wilderness to the west and south of Montreal, which has swallowed up the brave La Salle, comes into the shop of M. Auclair only as anecdote; Pierre Charron brings stories of the life of the fur trader, of the long portage and the starvation, the cold and the heat, but it is a tale told of another country. Michilimackinac is far away. Except for occasional fears, Cécile might be living in Rouen, in Dijon, or in Toulouse.

Of course this is Miss Cather's intention; she says as much. What she has tried to do is to give one a sense of the way of life that follows the French Catholic emblem. But the lack of conflict in the method is almost fatal to continued enjoyment of *Shadows on the Rock*; once one has got the flavor—and it is the flavor of wine of a good vintage year—there is little excuse for going on. The incidents which Miss Cather takes out of Parkman and his sources—such as the story of the recluse, Jeanne Le Ber—are good, but they are not the best that is in Parkman. The clerical conflict between Mgr. de Laval and the new Bishop, Saint-Vallier, is in Miss Cather's hands faithful to history. Parkman says that "the conflict lasted for years, with the rancor that marks the quarrels of noncombatants of both sexes"; and Miss Cather endeavors to reproduce this rancor of the non-combatants who talked the matter over. But this ecclesiastical quarrel is, too, not the best of Parkman. One can only wish that Miss Cather had chosen a more dramatic method, and more vital eye-witnesses and participants; one can only wish that she had selected for her reflection of pioneer history a "live" body with poetic eyes such as Elizabeth Madox Roberts's *Diony Hall*. A reasonable objection might be that the French, lovers of tradition that they are, have never been ardent colonists. Even so, this does not justify a substitution of static description for drama throughout a novel of 280 pages.

Shadows on the Rock, it must be confessed, is not the highest point on the graph of Miss Cather's work. Superbly written, with that sensitivity to sunset and afterglow that has always been Miss Cather's, it still shows that good prose is not enough. It would be rash to say that Miss Cather had come to the end of her rope, for in the past she has followed indifferent work (*Alexander's Bridge, One of Ours*) with excellent work (*The Song of the Lark, My Antonia* and *A Lost Lady*). But perhaps her experience, the "feel of the rock" that the novelist must have, has run out. Lack of experience has seemed to show in much of her work; it will be remembered that her most vital stories have been told by the mechanism of providing onlookers. Niel, idealistic boy, gives us his eyes; and Jim Burden, a fictional "friend" of Miss Cather's, goes back to see the battered but unbeaten Antonia. There is a disturbing gap, which affects characterization in *The Song of the Lark*, and the war sections of *One of Ours* are unreal in the light of Remarque. But the experience has usually been there, however refracted, in the early Cather books. In *Shadows on the Rock* there is little of the stuff of life that makes memorable fiction; there is nothing but the two-dimensional life of the fresco—beautiful, pale and rightly alien to the novel form.

World-Herald (Omaha), 2 August 1931

A new book by Willa Cather is an event of importance in the literary and cultural world. She is one of the few who are writing today of whom it is believed some permanent value attaches to their work.

A new book by Willa Cather is also an event of importance to Nebraska and the middle west, for she is of us. It is true that she left us; that she sought elsewhere for both inspiration and for glory, yet she cannot take away from us a glow of pride, that this, our daughter of small-town Nebraska, our graduate of our own state university, has challenged the world and won its applause.

Shadows on the Rock represents the work of a subdued and calm artist. There is in it none of that crude and earthy strength which made *My Antonia* one of the best of books about the early settlement of the prairie.

Nor is there, in this new book, that shrewd and sharp and devastating analysis of a woman such as gave *A Lost Lady* rank as one of the best Cather novels—some think the best of all.

There is in *Shadows on the Rock* a contemplative study of individuals and of a time, such as marked *Death Comes for the Archbishop*, the last previous work from the pen of Willa Cather, appearing four years ago.

Once more a pioneer time and country wins Willa Cather's interest. And again the quiet service of the Catholic church has seized her imagination. . . .

When one has finished he is conscious of having read a book charming and strong for the very simplicity and lucidity of its even force of language; rising to poetry at times because of the warm sympathy for and keen perception of nature Miss Cather has. But this is a novel with plot and suspense, not action; this is a quiet, restrained, finished piece of work, done in love, not heat; in humility, not daring.

"Home-Grown Parnassian," *Time*, 18 (3 August 1931), 47–8

This week Publisher Alfred A. Knopf is proud. Well he knows that the U.S., leading nation in bathrooms, does not lead the world in books. He knows that U.S. readers generally prefer magazines to books, that U.S. publishers issue fewer books proportionately than their European colleagues, that many a U.S.-published book is foreign-born. He realizes, too, that out of the 10,000 titles published annually in the U.S., few stand out as obviously Good Books, fewer still are home-grown. So this week, when Publisher Knopf issues Willa Cather's *Shadows on the Rock*, he is pleased and proud to be purveyor of what is sure to be acclaimed as a Good Book written by an obviously home-grown author.

Like its predecessor, that great & good seller *Death Comes for the Archbishop*, *Shadows on the Rock* is concerned with the American scene, colonial times. But Authoress Cather has moved from Spanish Southwest to French Northeast: the rock her story shadows is Quebec, at the turn of 1700. If you expect to encounter shades of Wolfe and Montcalm, of the storming of the Plains of Abraham, you will be disappointed; the story does not move that far (Quebec fell in 1759). There is not so much as an Indian fight and even the deeds of pioneering derring do are all messengered action. Explorers Daniel du Lhut, Robert Cavelier de la Salle are mentioned, but they are only names. Heroine of this quiet tale of a quiet time is a little girl, Cécile Auclair, and nothing happens to her except that she and her apothecary father do not return to France after all.

Papa Auclair, family apothecary to the Frontenacs in France, followed his patron to the New World when Frontenac was made Governor General of New France. In Quebec he lived as far as possible the quiet bourgeois life he had known at home. A philosopher, Papa Auclair believed in good manners, good cooking; well-behaved Cécile adored him, cooked beautifully. She liked Quebec and its people, made friends with many of them. ...It does not sound very promising, perhaps. But Authoress Cather is better than her implicit word: if she does not hold you breathless, she never lets you nod. And when you have finished her unspectacular narrative you may be somewhat surprised to realize that you have been living human history. Willa Cather's Northeast passages are never purple. Captious critics might complain that she sometimes simplifies too far, that her people are sometimes so one-sided as to be simply silly, that she sometimes, for one who can write like an angel, gives a fair imitation of poor Poll: "When Pierre had made a landing and tied his boat, they went up the path to the smith's house, to find the family at dinner. They were warmly received and seated at the dinnertable. The smith had no son, but four little girls. After dinner Cécile went off into the fields with them to pick wild strawberries. She had never seen so many wild flowers before."

But quotation, often unjust, cannot do Willa Cather justice. Her manner of writing has little in common with her noisy day. Characterized by an English critic as "that *rara avis*, an autochthonour American author," she is most conveniently classified by negatives. Says the same critic: "The King Charles's head of psychoanalysis and experiment in *genre* does not keep continually turning up in her books as they do in those rather Mr. Dick-like compositions of Mr. Sherwood Anderson for instance." Unlike Sinclair Lewis, she does not bite her country's hand: unlike Edith Wharton (whose example influenced her early work) she casts no nostalgic backward glances toward Europe; unlike Ernest Hemingway, she carries no gnawing fox in her devoted bosom. Her simple, colloquial language obeys the canon of good prose (she rereads *Pilgrim's Progress* annually), and in that is unremarkable. But she has an individual quality, positive attributes which hide their light under a phrase or even a paragraph, but which shine through her pages like moonlight under water. When she was much younger (she is 54) she used to read Henry James and try to write "beautifully": experience has rescued her writing from self-consciousness and quotation marks.

Frances Lamont Robbins, "Three Novels by Women," *Outlook and Independent*, 158 (5 August 1931), 440

[Reviewed with Daphne Du Maurier's *The Loving Spirit* and J. E. Bockrose's biography of George Eliot entitled *Silhouette of Mary Ann*]

Willa Cather has, I believe, been touched and exalted by the studies of the pioneer Catholic church in America which she must have made in connection with *Death Comes for the Archbishop*. She has seen among the shadows that lie about the rock on the St. Lawrence the majestic shapes of churchmen and martyrs and soldier governors and the stirring shapes of Indian fighters and *coureurs de bois*, and the dim, crowding shapes of lesser men and women, the thousands who made French Canada. She has caught them with keen, devoted eyes and sought to make them tangible as they are visible—sought, because I do not find that she has succeeded. The great archbishop of the southwest and his fellows, saints or sinners, came to life in Miss Cather's hands and joined the company of those whom novelists have made immortal. Euclide Auclair, follower of Frontenac, and his daughter Cecile, Jacques, son of La Grenouille and who knows what wandering sailor, Father Hector, Antoine Frichette, Pierre Charron, the shoemaker and his mother, the drummer boy and the recluse of Montreal remain shadows; lovely ghosts, but ghosts. And if Bishop Laval and Frontenac are living and will live on, it is not Miss Cather but other, older writers who have made them so. There is no plot to *Shadows on the Rock*. It is a sensitive record of two years in Quebec, precisely what life was like just before Frontenac died, what was the spirit of it, what people did and believed, and how Frontenac's life and death affected Auclair, the advanced and liberal-minded apothecary whose patron he was, and Auclair's young daughter, a true Canadienne. It is made up of such scenes as lend color to bare history and such incidents as give hagiographers their material. Its characters are beautifully presented; its descriptions rich. It has great charm. It is written in a warm, living and carefully restrained prose, soothing and enriching. But it has no theme. The shadows have no souls. *Death Comes for the Archbishop* was a bell, ringing between heaven and earth, its deep reverberations going on and on and on into space. *Shadows on the Rock* is a bell, too, a pure, thin tinkle in a sanctuary; beautiful, but not great.

George E. Brooks, "A Story of Early Days in Quebec," *Times-Dispatch* (Richmond), 9 August 1931

Ever since the publication of her previous work, *Death Comes for the Archbishop*, the name of Willa Cather on the cover of a book serves as a guarantee of a certain standard of workmanship that causes her readers to anticipate with pleasure any of her publications. In her newest book, *Shadows on the Rock*, Miss Cather has contributed another volume which may be used as a valid argument to justify a pardonable pride in some of our American writers, even in competition with those of literary England.

The average person who might be asked to tell something of Quebec might draw upon his knowledge of travel posters and describe it as one large hotel labeled "The Frontenac," or he might draw upon his geography and describe it as a mountain of snow and ice. Again, remembering his history, he might describe Quebec as a large rock that rises majestically above the St. Lawrence, on the top of which are the Plains of Abraham. Quebec is all of these and much more, and to call it any one is to do an injustice to the accomplishments of the Creator in His work.

To Miss Cather Quebec is much more than a rock: it is old France on a pedestal, on which is reflected through the lives of its quaint inhabitants the laws and customs, religion and industry, of the homeland across the sea.

Modern Quebec is alluring. But it is in the Quebec of the seventeenth century, in the days of the early arrivals from France, that Miss Cather places the setting of this story. And the events and activities of the lives of the people portray the shadows that register against the rock.

The chief characters of the story are Auclair, an old apothecary, and his motherless daughter, Cecile; Pierre Charron, a trapper, who eventually marries Cecile; Jacques, a childhood playmate of Cecile, and several new world representatives of the old world church and state. These, as well as the other characters in the book, are genuine: they live and breathe and have their being. Each seems to contribute his mite to the total effect produced, that of a charm and quaint appeal which only the people who live on the big rock know.

The story of *Shadows on the Rock* is divided into six parts and an epilogue. To say that this is simply a story of old Quebec would not be quite accurate, for the plot seems to be one of the minor elements of the book. Suffice to say that the plot provides a thread by means of which the people find their way through the pages.

The plot, in general, deals with the simple events in the everyday life of these people, subject to the vicissitudes of the king who rules over them, and the elements which play so vital a part in the long journeys of the ships that bridge the gap between the homes and friends on either side of the ocean. Since the plot plays such an inconspicuous part in this work, the major interest must be found between the lines rather than in them.

Miss Cather's style is decidedly intellectual as well as charming. To catch the spirit of an era and a people is no small task. Yet Miss Cather has done both. She has caught the spirit of an era because the reader sees to how great an extent the events of the times played a part in the lives of the people. The tremendous influence of church and state, the absolute domination of the people by institutions, and the submission of the individual to authority are all clearly depicted by the author.

Moreover, Miss Cather has given us some very good reasons for the courage and strength of our modern Canadians since they are only reproductions of those early people who cast their influence upon history.

As a picture of the Quebec of yesterday, *Shadows on the Rock* is well worth while. As a means of understanding the Canadian of today the book is of even greater value.

Only through travel and reading can the various peoples of the world come to a means of common understanding. The latter is a less expensive way of acquiring a broadened outlook. All things are not possible of presentation in vivid colors; some things have to be etched. Such is the accomplishment of *Shadows on the Rock*.

Dorothy Van Doren, "A Study in Comeliness," *Nation*, 133 (12 August 1931), 160

No American writer writes more beautifully than Miss Cather, with more care for the just word, for the pure phrase, for the noble and elevated idea. It is no longer necessary to say that she is in the very front rank of American novelists. There would be plenty of persons to put her securely in first place; but comparisons of this sort are unnecessary to establish her quality. Wherever her place, it is hers and hers alone. She can claim undisputed title to it by virtue of her unceasing labor in the cause of fine writing. She has given herself to it with the ardor of one of her own *religieuses*, and the results

have been altogether worthy of her devotion.

Her latest novel is a triumphant series of examples of her talents. Laid in the Quebec of the late seventeenth century, it paints the life of that passionately French colony with broad, smooth strokes. If it centers around the apothecary, Euclide Auclair, and his daughter Cécile, it draws within its strong light many others of the colonists: Jacques, the son of the village prostitute; Count Frontenac, Auclair's patron, proud, reserved, defeated; the old Bishop, spending his body and his soul for Christ; the young Bishop, proud also, and unsure of his powers, reckless, extravagant, broken by life before he leaves it; Pierre Charron, the colonial adventurer of the best type, full of life and strength and gaiety; and the recluse, Jeanne Le Ber, giving the last second of her time, the last ounce of her strength, the very drops of her blood, in undeviating and passionate zeal for God.

With this group and several others only a little less clear, Miss Cather recreates the Quebec of 1700 and the France of the same time. In the apothecary's household are assembled all the virtues that the French can claim. It is a comely household; twelve-year-old Cécile, with her cleanliness, her piety, her skill at cooking and housewifery, her sweet and childish ardors, makes it so; and the apothecary, wise, calm, loyal, makes it so also. In the little shop and the sitting-room behind it dwell order, peace, and love. It is Miss Cather's particular gift that when she writes of these virtues she makes all other characteristics seem unnecessary. If this is not in fact a comely world, her world is altogether comely and convincing. Cécile, back from a visit to sluttish, disorderly people, reflects on her own cleanly home. "These coppers, big and little, these brooms and clouts and brushes, were tools; and with them one made, not shoes or cabinet work, but life itself. One made a climate within a climate; one made the days, the complexion, the special flavor, the special happiness of each day as it passed; one made life." Miss Cather has made life of the complexion she likes it to be, she has made her own special flavor and happiness and climate. It is not romance, it is surely not realism. It is something more; a kind of undubitable piety and goodness which warm the heart and refresh the mind and occasionally bring tears to the eyes.

Having said all this, I can say that I think a certain quality of coherence and growth has gone out of Miss Cather's writings. She becomes increasingly disparate and episodic. In her best books, which I should say were *The Song of the Lark*, *My Antonia*, and *A Lost Lady*, she builds up her episodes into a tightly knit and meaningful whole, not wholly because they are built around a central character—*Death Comes for the Archbishop* and *Shadows on the Rock* move around central characters—but because Thea and Antonia and Mrs. Forrester actually live their lives before our eyes, because we see them not only accepting life but wrestling with it, trying to mold it to their own desire. They are strong and they do not always succeed; they try to shape their destinies and in the end are shaped by them. This struggle with life is fainter in *Death Comes for the Archbishop*; in *Shadows on the Rock* it has almost disappeared. One feels that the characters in the latter book completed their earthly existence before the tale began and are engaged in shadowy and painless struggles with their past, struggles in which no blood is spilt because the blood has gone out of them into the color of the Quebec sky, into the red of Cécile's curtains drawn tightly over the windows to keep out the wind and the sound of the rain.

My only objection to this sort of soberly splendid landscape painting is that Miss Cather is still in the height of her middle years and it is not time for her to become reminiscent or resigned. Archbishop Latour, at seventy-five, could write: "I am enjoying to the full that period of reflection which is the happiest conclusion to a life of action." If one may say so without being impertinent, Miss Cather is two decades away from such a period. I should like to see from her hand another novel with more edge to it; one that was no less shapely or beautiful or wise, but one in which her characters were presented in process of learning all that she knows about life. But if she will not do it, we may be well content with what we have.

Newton Arvin, "Quebec, Nebraska and Pittsburgh," *New Republic*, 67 (12 August 1931), 345–6

This is a very delicate and very dull book. There is not a page in it that is not consummately written, and scarcely a page that leads one irresistibly on to the next. No doubt Willa Cather recaptures in it, as Mr. Knopf says on the jacket, "the very tone and feeling of the seventeenth century in this old French city [Quebec]": indeed, there is no denying that *Shadows on the Rock* is exquisitely and artfully evocative. Willa Cather would not be Willa Cather if she did not make you feel that Quebec was like this, exactly like this, in the last year of Frontenac's life— from the quality of the winter sunlight on the St. Lawrence to the décor of an apothecary's shop and the relations between the old bishop and his successor. As in *Death Comes for the Archbishop*, moreover, there is a group of historical and imaginary characters—a skeptical apothecary, the aged Governor-General, a dashing young fur-trader, a somber old bishop and a haughty younger one, a shoemaker, a Jesuit missionary, a reverend mother—all of whom have that curious literary charm that comes from talking more or less like real people and acting more or less like historical celebrities. Auclair and Charron and Saint-Vallier combine the accent of reality with the tender blur of distance; and the product, to a certain taste, is captivating. At the very least, it argues both insight and craft.

But it is not enough to make a good novel, and *Shadows on the Rock* was born dead. Whatever beauty it may have is not the kind of beauty that expresses life. The book is as lovely, as fastidious, as lacking in movement and perspective, as if Puvis de Chavannes had painted it on the walls of some public building. Miss Cather does not believe deeply in this material; she gets into no serious relation with it: it appeals to her literary taste, to her fancy, to her mood of elegy and reminiscence, but not to her convictions or to her imagination. As a result, it has no center and forward drive. One is not allowed to focus one's interest in any single character, in any single situation, in any single development. No doubt it may be said that the center of the book is not this character or that, but the place itself, Quebec. Then there is something wrong, for Willa Cather, with the very subject. She herself once remarked that a writer gets his real material from the experiences he has before he is—I believe it was twelve: at any rate, some early age. In writing about Quebec in 1697, then, she pays the penalty for dealing with material that does not have and cannot be made to

have deep significance to herself: it fails to enchain the reader. Is this why one of the characters in the book says, with some bitterness: "You see, there are all those early memories; one cannot get another set; one has but those"?

At any rate, there are not many things in *Shadows on the Rock* more striking, to an admirer of Willa Cather, than this speech. It could be made the theme of an essay not only on her whole work but, with the right changes, on work of her literary generation. Why do three or four of her best books have a genuine largeness of contour, a genuine density of implication, and why, nevertheless, has she written so many weak books, in proportion, and, at last, so disappointing a book as this? She is a writer of distinguished gifts and austere purposes, yet she is a writer who apparently has never come to grips with the real life of her time, whose triumphs have been too often the triumphs of what seems like judicious evasion, who at all events writes as if mass production and technological unemployment and cyclical depressions and the struggle between the classes did not exist. The answer to the riddle is in Pierre Charron's words: one cannot get another set of early memories; one has but those.

The best of her books embody an individualism, an atomism, a fissility, as well as her worst. Her theme has aways, it is true, been the theme of loyalty, of fortitude, of fidelity to certain values or purposes; but it has always been the loyalty of "self-reliance," and the values have always been conceived as endangered, not as fostered, by the society roundabout. Society, for her as for Emerson, is in a conspiracy against the manhood of each of its members. So Alexandra Bergson, in *O Pioneers!* succeeds in her struggle with nature in spite of her family, not because of it; and even her triumph is overshadowed by the hostility and the meanness of her neighbors, so that she never really escapes from isolation. Thea Kronberg, in *The Song of the Lark*, devoting herself to a singer's career, has first to overcome the cultural handicaps of life in Moonstone, Colorado, and, later, the obstacles offered to any such career by life in Chicago and New York. It is only nature and "fate," in *My Antonia*, but misunderstanding and pettiness and a sort of social drought that play havoc with Antonia Shimerda's life; and the mellowness she wins through to at the end, grand as it is, is envisaged as a purely private victory. And so that tale runs on: the corruption of Mrs. Forrester, in *A Lost Lady*, by surrender to the cheapness of the life about her; the contrast between the dead sculptor and his erstwhile small-town congeners in "The Sculptor's Funeral"; the frustration of Claude Wheeler, in *One of Ours*, by his family's lack of understanding, his wife's bigotry and selfishness and his neighbors' dullness; St. Peter's sense of separation from his wife and children in *The Professor's House*; Latour's conflicts with his superiors and with his superstitious flock in *Death Comes for the Archbishop*—always the struggle between an individual and his group; always the separatism of the pioneer; always a personal triumph or a personal defeat.

In any event, the impressiveness of Willa Cather's best work remains untouched. Her individualism had its roots deep in a social earth, and hence it is emblematic and expressive. It was really composite, indeed, for it represented not only the decentralization of the frontier, but—more indirectly and unconsciously—the abandonment by American writers, of the elder generation, of the class to which they technically belonged, the middle class. And certainly the conflict between the individual and the group is a permanently valid theme both for comedy and tragedy. But everything depends on the way in which it is looked at; and the writers of Willa Cather's period never arrived at that individualism which is enriched and pointed by allegiance to purposes embodied in a social group or class. Their juniors, too, indeed, with a few honorable exceptions, have not yet passed beyond the phase of disloyalty for its own sake. But they cannot long postpone "the moment to decide": they will do well to remember the dismal circle, on the margin of hell, populated by the disconsolate shades of the angels who, in the great rebellion, were too "detached" to take either side—*questi sciaurati che mai non fur vivi*. For a generation, American writers have had a holy horror of taking sides positively: they have regarded their responsibility as discharged by their not taking the side of the directing class. That is why their individualism, like Willa Cather's, has had its day, and now more and more betrays its incurable sterility.

Fanny Butcher, "Willa Cather Writes a Novel of Old Quebec," *Chicago Daily Tribune*, 15 August 1931, p. 10

Often enough in the life of a reviewer to keep one keenly interested in every package of books which arrives, but so seldom as to be a single blessing of a year or perhaps two, there comes a book which is so authentically the work of genius, so immediately perceptible as a masterpiece, so emotionally beautiful in style as to be great even to the untutored reader—to the trained critic, superb. Such a book is Willa Cather's latest novel, *Shadows on the Rock*.

There is something so intensely beautiful about the actual writing of *Shadows on the Rock* I cannot remember its equal in any prose of the last years. It touches the emotions, it nourishes life in one, just as sheer writing. No matter what it might be about, the inherent exquisiteness of the words, their design in sentences, their pattern in paragraphs is something which deeply stirs the mind. It is almost impossible to put into words the kind of mental joy that the writing in *Shadows on the Rock* induces in a sensitive reader. It has something of the same effect mentally that great love has emotionally on one. It digs at the roots of one's mental being. It nourishes one's mind. It restores it to the rhythm of life. It makes one's mind feel as if it had come alive after coma. Why it should do that is what is inexplicable.

The words are the same words that every one uses. The sentences are merely words put together, the paragraphs an arrangement of sentences. And yet in those words and in that arrangement there lies one of the great magic beauties of life.

Mind you, I am talking about the writing of *Shadows on the Rock*, not at all about the content. What it is about is of little matter compared to how it is set down. It is not the shifting panoramas of Quebec in the seventeen hundreds, when it was a rock in the wilderness and a little band of French planted their culture in its seamy and unwelcoming crevices that thrill you. They are simple pictures of heroism, tenderness, intrigue, sickness, death, thirst for power, quiet acceptance of fate . . . pictures of human life in its relation to the march of man through the ages—which are the pictures of human life at all times—with a deep reality. Their magic power over the reader is not in the essence of their facts but in the essence of their fancy, as it were. It is not what Miss Cather records that stirs the reader to the depths of his or her emotions, but the way in which she records it.

In speaking of little Cecile's cooking a dinner for a voyageur she says: "These coppers, big and little, these brooms and clouts and brushes, were tools; and with them one made, not shoes or cabinetwork, but life itself. One made a climate within a climate; one made the days—the complexion, the special flavor, the special happiness of each day as it passed; one made life."

In that sentence, describing the little heroine of her book, Miss Cather has set down the whole fact of *Shadows on the Rock*. With her coppers, big and little, her brooms and clouts and brushes—with the simple tools which every one has to use, with the words which are the common heritage of her race, Miss Cather has made life itself. She has made, in the truest sense, a climate within a climate, she has given the complexion, the special flavor of a period of life itself. It is the supreme magic of writing.

Shadows on the Rock tells exactly what the book is. Across the rock of Quebec, eternal, pass the shadows of a generation of human beings—a gentle apothecary, his little daughter who grows so to love her adopted land that the thought of returning to her native soil is a torture to her; his wife, who is dead before the book starts, but who lives so vividly and so beautifully in the little tenderly lovely home which she had made, and in her little daughter's sweetness and motherliness as to be one of the main characters in the book. Shifting shadows also are the two bishops, the old one who lives in poverty and homeliness, the young one who is an arrogant courtier before he is a churchman. Another shadow, vivid but fleeting, is little Jacques, the son of a prostitute, whom the heroine mothers with a touching devotion. The recluse at Montreal, a shadow of a shadow; Pierre

Charron, who loved her and in his despair became a bold voyageur; Blinker, who had been a torturer and hated the thought of himself—all of them shift and weave their shadowy form into the record of Quebec. As individuals they are shadows against the rock of human life that manifest itself in one way one day; in another, an outwardly different way, but is always firmly, eternally the same. That quality of the permanence of human life and the vitality of human effort is the burthen of *Shadows on the Rock*. And in some magic way Miss Cather has put that flow, that eternal rhythm of life into her prose, superbly.

To me *Shadows on the Rock* is a more beautiful piece of work than *Death Comes for the Archbishop*. It is one of the most excitingly exquisite bits of prose in the English language.

R[obert] M. C[oates], "The Art of Willa Cather," *New Yorker*, 7 (15 August 1931), 49–50

I often feel a little shamefaced to think how slight a background I have for reviewing contemporary fiction. Before I started this job, I was a pretty random reader, devoting my attention to books that interested me, without regard to their publication dates, and turning to the up-to-the-minute things only when I found one lying around—say on a guestroom bedside table. As a consequence, I could name a sizable list of present-day authors, and pretty well-known ones, too—Alec Waugh, Eddie Cantor, Louis Bromfield, Chic Sale, and so on—with whose works I am totally unfamilar.

The rub comes, of course, when I am faced with a book by a person of the prominence of Willa Cather—whose *Shadows on the Rock*, published by Knopf, has just reached me—and realize suddenly that I have never read a line of hers before. What I did in this case, naturally, was to dig up a copy of *A Lost Lady* (which I've been told is her best book) and give it a hasty reading, get a friend to tell me the plot of *Death Comes for the Archbishop*, and try to remember what I'd heard about *My Ántonia* in the days when it was a best-seller. I now feel qualified to speak in the capacity of an expert on the art of Willa Cather.

At any rate, quite apart from my pleasure at adding Miss Cather to the list of People I Have at Last Read, I found *Shadows on the Rock* a very delightful book. To be sure, I liked *A Lost Lady* even better, as being more compact, having a more finely organized structure and a surer character portrayal. But that is beside the point. In her new book, Miss Cather succeeds quite well enough to please almost anybody.

The story itself is a rather rambling affair, wandering from one personage to another, and alighting on each only long enough to recount in detail some significant episode in his career. This method gives the book, as the author probably intended, rather the discursive value of a volume of memoirs of the period—which is roughly that of Quebec in the closing years of the Comte de Frontenac's rule as Governor of the Province—than the hard and fast matter-of-fact air of the historical novel. . . .

The value of the book, then, lies not in the power of the narrative but in the tender and slightly wistful recital of humdrum, homely incident, and this I take to be Miss Cather's peculiar forte. Without questioning the beauty of some of her passages, I couldn't, however, help feeling as I read on through the book that the quality of wistfulness, unlike mercy, can be strained. There are moments of delicate pathos ("Papa," little Cecile pauses to call back to her father as she is being carried off for her outing on the river, "you will not forget to keep the fire under the soup? It has been on only an hour") that almost bring tears to the eyes, but they are a little too like the tears one occasionally feels pricking one's consciousness at a musical comedy, when the lights and the music and the heroine's forsakenness all conspire for an instant to touch the emotions, but in a manner as mechanical as tickling to produce laughter. In the book, as at the play, one soon gets to looking forward to such exit lines, and discounting in advance the method by which the effect is produced.

For myself, I think a good part of the reason for this lies in the thinness of the story itself. In *A Lost Lady* (that's the other one of hers I read, you remember), Miss Cather had a central character whom she understood profoundly, and the portrait was rich and warm indeed. In this, one gets rather the impression of a series of paintings on glass—brilliant, lit by a kind of transparent glow, but so frail, so very insubstantial.

Wilbur Cross, "Men and Images," *Saturday Review of Literature*, 8 (22 August 1931), 67–8

Sometimes a novelist's art may be summarized in a happy title. Twice Edith Wharton thus betrayed her art. *The House of Mirth* was in the end anything but a house of mirth.

The Age of Innocence was anything but an age of innocence. As in these novels, Mrs. Wharton's attitude towards persons and things has been consistently ironical. Likewise, Sinclair Lewis's *Main Street* and *Babbitt* by their very titles forecast the drab life of Middle Western towns, with satirical intent.

Willa Cather's art has passed through several phases. In *O Pioneers!* and *My Ántonia*, her subject was mainly the early settlers on Nebraska plains among Yankee, Bohemian, French, German, Scandinavian, and Russian immigrants. There they are as she saw them in the flesh in her childhood and youth. Subsequently, she moved her scene south to Colorado and eventually to New Mexico also, where she sojourned later. But of gross observation there is little or none. Everywhere she selects significant incidents, rarely working them too hard, for bringing out the characteristics of the men and women whom she depicts. When as in *The Song of a Lark* she becomes more liberal with incident, she succeeds less well. The novel which she can best manage is comparatively short, like *A Lost Lady*, which in the opinion of many, still remains her masterpiece.

Outwardly, Miss Cather has moved far in her method. At first she adopted the traditional form of the novel, rather loose in construction. Then, as in *The Professor's House*, she began to experiment with the biographical manner, which she has come to like best of all. *A Lost Lady* is her one study of a situation such as we almost always have in the novels of Edith Wharton. But throughout all of Miss Cather's work there is a lyrical quality which at times rises to genuine poetry. You see it in her earliest work. No one, for example, can ever forget the way she brings into *My Ántonia* the plough magnified to a great black image against a glorious sunset as a symbol of the life on the Nebraska prairies. The lyrical mood, which climbs to its height in *Death Comes for the Archbishop*, is the prime characteristic which separates Miss Cather from her two outstanding contemporary novelists.

Her title, *Shadows on the Rock*, the happiest one yet, seems to have behind it a philosophy of life and of art too. Are we but shadows projected upon a scene, whether the scene be on the plains or on the slope of a fortress? Or are the men and women, whom we observe and watch everyday or whom we read about in old books, but shadows to us after all? Can we penetrate the inner consciousness and tell the world what is going on in the mind, as Virginia Woolf and others profess to do? Well, Miss Cather will do the best she can and leave it to her readers to determine whether she ever gets behind the shadows. She does not fall into the old fallacy of thinking that she sees things as they are. Nobody knows what they really are. She renders them as they appear to her, well knowing that they may appear to others differently. Nothing quite exists outside the mind that perceives, infers, reasons. Miss Cather's mind has a romantic glow.

In the time of which she writes in her latest novel, Quebec was not much more than a village of two thousand inhabitants living on the slope of the fortress and down by the river. For its economic existence, it relied upon trading with the Indians; too often, furs for brandy. It was, too, the outpost for missionary work with them, along the St. Lawrence and far back in the woods. Vast domains were explored and claimed for France. It was a New France north of a New England. Miss Cather's purpose is to tell about the life of the people on the rock, far from home. Most of all she dwells upon the mentality of the immigrants who brought into the wilderness with them the ideas of a well-ordered universe which had become fixed in their minds by the teachings of the Catholic Church when they were children in France. God and the angels were always near them in the beauty of the landscape, in the sun and the moon and the stars, and in the many miracles God wrought for their happiness. So there was little or no sickness for the home they had left beyond the sea. What was tragic in their lives is kept well in the background. Everywhere the colony is invested with a poetic glamour by beautiful descriptions of the rock through the changing seasons of the year.

> It was the first day of June. Before dawn a wild calling and twittering of birds in the bushes on the cliff-side above the apothecary's back door announced clear weather. When the sun came up over the Ile d'Orleans, the rock of Kebec stood gleaming above the river like an altar with many candles, or like a holy city in an old legend, shriven, sinless, washed in gold.

There is no study of character in detail. There is nothing comparable to the great missionary priests in *Death Comes for the Archbishop*. The tone is subdued to a poetic atmosphere which must be maintained. Purposely the sketches are slight and delicate like the pastels of Latour or Watteau. Action is reduced to a minimum. Of political history just enough is given to fix the time and the scene; no more. Characters come and go in glimpses. Here and there is comment or an anecdote or a short strip of biography. Quarrels are indicated rather than described. The clash between Bishop Laval and his successor, Saint-Vallier, is but a clash of temperaments. The hardships of Pierre Charron, the fur trader, who subsisted in the woods with the Indians on dried eels and dog meat boiled with blueberries, are toned down by a half-humorous narrative. So throughout. So far as the story is held together, it is by Auclair, the apothecary and medical advisor to the Count de Frontenac, and by Auclair's charming daughter, Cécile, about whom we learn most as we see them in their daily routine or on an evening reading aloud Plutarch or La Fontaine. Indeed, the apothecary's shop, where men and women of all classes go for herbs to cure their ills, is the center towards which the tale drifts, until we come to the lyrical afterglow in the death of Frontenac, who as he lies dying waves a feeble gesture with his left hand as a silent command that the priests and nuns kneeling by the bedside rise and draw back. The last battle must be fought alone. The great shadow passes on and leaves the rock in full splendor. A new age is at hand.

A novelist who tries an unaccustomed form must expect that many readers will be disappointed. It is always a risk. Why not another *Lost Lady* or another *Death Comes for the Archbishop*? Miss Cather willed otherwise. *Shadows on the Rock* is quite of another kind. In some respects it resembles Sterne's *Sentimental Journey*, where scenes and characters separate and coalesce at the command of the author, and at last fall into an exquisite harmony of tone and atmosphere. The characterization, because it is brief, must be deft. Necessarily, much is left to the imagination. Miss Cather loves particularly the eyes. Of Saint-Vallier, Auclair remarks to his daughter: "What restless eyes he has, Cécile; they run all over everything, like quicksilver when I spill it." And Cécile's eyes, when her heart was touched, grew dark "like the blue of Canadian blueberries." In other instances, it is a hand or a gesture or a movement of the face that subtly reveals character. It is all a delicate art, more difficult than the art of the traditional novel. Few have ever measurably succeeded. Miss Cather is among these few.

C[amille] McC[ole], *Catholic World*, 133 (September 1931), 752–3

At the end of the past three decades of crude realism, Freudism, inchoate English, shallow philosophy, and "sophistication," the work of Willa Cather, because she has seen such high stars and so ably and unswervingly followed them, must now stand as one of the most eminently encouraging literary signs of that outmoded period. Remote from her age in that she has subscribed to none of its more meretricious phases, she is by that very fact a most enduring part of it.

And so it is with her latest novel, *Shadows on the Rock*. On the surface the book would seem to be little more than the story of Euclide Auclair, the French apothecary, who with his motherless daughter Cécile, lived out his own life and a great share of the lives of his fellows, under the patronage of the Count de Frontenac in the early days of the settling of the Quebec country. But the book is more than that. In this story, as in all of Miss Cather's novels, it is the undertone of feeling, the delicate and artistic shading of mood, the perfect fusion of style and subject—in one word, the shadows—of the story which one will remember long after he has forgotten the historical background of these hardy characters so stoutly facing the stern realities of life on the Kebec Rock itself. . . .

No living novelist, with the exception of Miss Cather, seems to possess the comprehensive sympathies so necessary in the handling of such material and perhaps the surest test of this is that a Catholic can read this book and feel so very strongly the very pulse and tradition of his Faith running through it.

When an adventurer carries his gods with him to his new country, the colony is bound, Miss Cather assures us, to have rich graces and blessings and a bright life, "where the great matters are often as worthless as astronomical distances, and the trifles dear as the heart's blood." And when Cécile one day suggests to old Blinker, that sad and mournful neighbor of theirs who had come to Canada to forget his part as an executioner in France, "that the angels are just as near to us here as they are in France," he replies, "Ma'm'selle, I think they are nearer." No one should miss reading this book. And Catholics, especially, should be reminded of the wealth of tradition which is our heritage. For the angels are always very near in this story and the strong religious spirit which made old Euclide give not only drugs for the body but sound advice for the heart has a permeating and fine influence here in Kebec where the people had not forgotten to bring their God with them.

Granville Hicks, "Bright Incidents," *Forum*, September 1931, pp. vi–viii

"When," writes Miss Cather, "an adventurer carries his gods with him into a remote and savage country, the colony he founds will, from the beginning have graces, traditions, riches of the mind and spirit. Its history will shine with bright incidents, slight, perhaps, but precious, as in life itself, where the great writers are often as worthless as astronomical

distances, and the trifles dear as the heart's blood."

It is with "bright incidents, slight, perhaps, but precious," that this story of Quebec in 1697 and 1698, the last year of Frontenac's life, is concerned. For the most part they are incidents that illustrate the paradox of life in such a settlement: the men and women that they introduce are poised between the vast uncertainties of frontier isolation and the unshaken, very real, very consoling certainties of their faith. As we see them—the apothecary Auclair and his daughter, Bishop Laval and Bishop de Saint-Vallier, Father Hector, Pierre Charron, and Frontenac himself—they move in two worlds, both far removed from modern experience and for that reason romantically attractive to many modern minds. Tenderly, delicately, Miss Cather presents these precious incidents of hers, thus recreating, in a not at all unconvincing fashion, a cultural and spiritual situation glamorous in itself and made doubly glamorous by the magic of her pen.

Especially when taken together with *Death Comes for the Archbishop*, this new novel helps to define Miss Cather's position among contemporary writers; indeed, it makes quite clear why she is and always has been a minor artist. She has always, it will be remembered, been interested in local color, and her own estimate of her debt to Sarah Orne Jewett is perhaps not exaggerated. In her best books, *O Pioneers!* and *My Antonia*, the characters so completely reflect and represent the background that her talents for description lend themselves to the purpose of the stories, and the books are vitalized and at least superficially unified. In other works, however, notably *The Song of the Lark* and *The Professor's House*, she introduces long passages of her favorite kind of description, chiefly, so far as can be discerned, for their own sake. And now, in these two latest books, she devotes herself, with no apologies and no other purpose, to the re-creation of picturesque phases of the remote American past.

But what, someone may ask, is the harm of engaging in such an enterprise? Since Miss Cather writes with beauty and presents her characters with insight, since she extends our experience in at least one direction, what more can we ask of her? These are reasonable questions, but there is an answer to them that *Shadows on the Rock* inevitably suggests. Like *Death Comes for the Archbishop*, the novel is diffuse; Miss Cather lets her imagination play over a variety of her bright incidents but never focuses it sharply upon any centralizing theme. Like *One of Ours*, it evades many problems that the material logically raises. Like most of her books, it is elegiac, beguiling its readers with pictures of a life that has disappeared, and deliberately exploiting the remoteness of that life in order to cast a golden haze about it.

In other words, whatever its virtues, *Shadows on the Rock* betrays a failure of the will. Even its style, effective and appropriate though it is, suggests a kind of passivity; and the characters have the appearance of life chiefly because the author persuades us that it is natural to see them through a glowing mist. In short, Miss Cather is a highly endowed craftsman, but her endowment does not include the kind of disciplined resolution that must guide the imagination of a great writer. To-day, perhaps even more than in the past, it takes stern stuff to make a novelist. Miss Cather, one is forced to conclude, has always been soft; and now she has abandoned herself to her softness.

Arthur Dygert Bates, "History and Romance in Old Quebec," *Christian Century*, 48 (9 September 1931), 1118–19

The writer recently had one of those evenings when he became so engrossed in the story that he could not lay it down until he had finished it. After it has been read, the reader can do nothing but sit back in his comfortable chair, and with a mighty heave, wish there were more to read of that exquisite beauty and romantic past into which it has projected him. . . .

Of course the professional critics are not as happy about this book as many others are. No longer does one expect them to be really enthusiastic about anything. Their sole business is to look for flaws and magnify them many fold; or to treat a thing of beauty like this in an historical survey, and show how it represents a decline, like a downward curve on a graph depicting the business cycle. But read it anyway, and enjoy it. You will probably want to visit and re-visit old Quebec, and see for yourself the old Hotel Dieu, or the site of the old chateau where the old count lived and died, because fate perverse would not let him die in the land of his fathers. Or you may want to see the old Hopital Général, where the old Bishop de Saint-Vallier lived in his later years, and died, finally, somewhat broken and repentant. Or you may even want to see once again the old chateau at Versailles, and see the descendents of the old carp to which Louis XIV threw whole loaves of bread, while the country starved.

Helen Cowles Le Cron, "*Shadows on the Rock* Is Not a Poor Book; It Merely Shows that Genius Can Be a Trifle Dull," *Des Moines Register*, 27 September 1931, section 10A, p. 4

I have now finished Willa Cather's new book, and sit here wondering whether to call it "a delightfully successful historical novel," "a hauntingly poetic narrative of life in old Quebec between 1697 and 1713," or merely "a quiet tale of long ago, rich in simplicity." It is most emphatically all of these good things, and might truly be described in exactly such pleasant, if somewhat shopworn, phrases. In fact, that is just the trouble. Twenty other able American authors could have turned out the same book as easily and competently (and not too differently) and deserved more credit. For Miss Cather, having once excited our brains, nerves and hearts with *My Antonia* and *A Lost Lady*, now leaves those same brains, nerves and hearts cruelly flattened and disappointed when she offers us less. And we can somehow forgive a genius or near-genius more easily when he or she lets us down by being inartistic, careless, or even flagrantly ill-bred than when he or she does the same trick by being pleasantly ordinary and agreeably obvious. No, I mustn't give you the wrong impression. *Shadows on the Rock* is not a bad book. It is distinctly readable but not very important.

Some years ago (I have said this before on the book-page) Willa Cather wrote a preface to a new edition of the stories of Sarah Orne Jewett in which she said, "To note an artist's limitations is but to define his genius. A reporter can write equally well about everything that is presented to his view, but a creative writer can do his best only with what lies within the range and character of his talent." *Shadows on the Rock* is not commonplace exactly, but nowhere does it draw blood or even scratch skin deep beneath the surface. It seems to me that Willa Cather does not here exhibit or in any way hint at those sharp and glorious limitations that certainly do define genius. At her best she is gentle and wise; at her worst she is only a trifle dull. And I cannot believe that this rather remote historical story falls within the range and character of her very definite talent.

I shall hasten to return the book to Donald Murphy; if I were still editing the book-page I should probably wrap the volume neatly in blue and silver paper and give it to one of my relatives or friends for Christmas. I should choose some critical and fastidious lady of the older school (I do not refer to age but merely to a preference for good writing of the traditional sort) who would appreciate it for its wholesome and idealistic qualities and enjoy it all the more because it fails to deal with provincial Nebraska.

Michael Williams, "Quebec in Pastel," *Commonweal*, 14 (30 September 1931), 528

This is so rich a book, so full of life, yet so simple that criticism of it is difficult because there is so much to be said about so many important things, that I scarcely know how to express my sense of its beauty, its truth, and its goodness, within the limits of a brief review. It has a quality similar to that of the best folk-lore, in which a story that is almost naive is yet so deeply rooted in the ultimate mystery of human life, and the simple incidents are yet so suggestive of inner meanings as to become mystical in the best sense of the word, full of haunting undertones and overtones of spiritual values, like a parable in Scripture. Or its quality might be likened to the effect produced by pure music: some composition loyal in every note to the almost mathematical laws of music, yet in which the individual genius of the composer is unmistakably present, stamping it with the seal of a unique character, and through the channel of its originality opening up a way into the spiritual world of ideal things.

Willa Cather always remembers that the primary virtue of art is what Blake called "the bounding line"; the design, the form; unlike Blake she does not break her own rule anywhere—certainly not in this book—so that her vision never becomes vague, or confused. So she has written a story, full of many stories; all human, which may be read by simple souls or subtle souls alike, and which many among both types will undoubtedly return to over and over again. It is a permanent addition to literature; it belongs to the very small group of novels which triumphantly proves the innate worthiness of that badly abused art form.

Quebec, when the great governor, Frontenac, was ruling over the forests and rivers which the Kingdom of France was attempting to colonize, and the great bishop, Laval, was ruling for the Church which among those rivers and forests was seeking to colonize in behalf of the eternal kingdom; Quebec, a French town transplanted to a barbaric wilderness, bringing the law and order, the arms, the civiliza-

tion, the culture of the dominant race of old Europe—this is the scene of the book. The reader enters the governor's mansion or the bishop's austere palace rarely; mostly we are in the house or the shop of Auclair, the apothecary, in company with Cécile, his little daughter, who cooks the chicken and prepares the salad for her widowed father, and chats with him about their relatives and friends in far away France, or about the ships that will come from there, and the things that are happening in the town. There is a hunter and woodsman, Pierre Charron, who loved, one who became a nun—but not a gentle teacher in a school, nor a nursing Sister, nor even a cloistered contemplative, but rather a hermit, practising frightful austerities, like the legendary figures of the days of Antony of Egypt; yet she does not seem fantastic; she expresses the quintessence of that spirit of ascetic mysticism which in all ages exists in the Church. This woodsman in the end marries Cécile, after episodes and scenes in which priests and soldiers, woodsmen and nuns, and all the characteristic types of the French colony come and go, with the seeming haphazardness of every-day life, without a trace of artificial arrangement, yet in their totality they illuminate and explain old Quebec as volumes of history could not do.

I think this book is the fruit of a long period of brooding. Obviously, years of study went into it. Miss Cather knows her period thoroughly; better still, she understands it; moreover it is from today, in the spirit of modernity, that she looks backward; and looks forward as well. For although this story happened in the past, it could happen, indeed it is happening today, as it will tomorrow, and the morrow after that. For its sins, and sorrows, but especially its virtues: courage, fidelity, kindness, courtesy. It is humanity conscious of its source and its end in divinity. The shadows on the rock of Quebec are those events, and those living men and women, all quite real, moving and acting in time and space, yet shadows of eternity, at once symbols of and actors in the endless story of life everlasting.

Louis Kronenberger, "Willa Cather," *Bookman* (New York), 74 (October 1931), 134–40

If one were asked to name, not the most brilliant, nor the most influential, nor the most original, nor the greatest American novel of the past twenty years, but the most human and solid, surely one would answer with something by Willa Cather— with *My Ántonia* or *The Song of the Lark*. Nothing else is quite like these books in their associations with the American (although a vanished American) scene, or in their solid, deep-coloured human strength. And at the time they were written they were all the better by comparison with what other novelists were writing. Willa Cather gained recognition when a period of patently shoddy literature (1905–15) had given way to one of consciously better writing—an age which, with its Hergesheimers and Cabells and Imagist poetry, now strikes us as one of romantic escape. The sense of art, striking America with all the force of a new idea, struggled, in the novels of that period, to get itself expressed; and the sense of art far outweighed the sense of life. Willa Cather, at the moment of Poictesme and art-photography old Salem, by recreating the Middle West of her childhood with sturdy vigour, and setting living women against a living background, seemed by contrast with romancers a peculiarly valuable American novelist. She seemed native without being crude, womanly without being feminine, cultivated without being refined. She was picturing, it is true, an America of an older, a more idealistic day, but it was an America she had known and seen and honestly loved; and her work seemed, quite apart from its own merits, a start in the right direction.

More than ten years have passed, romantic dozing has lost its savour, the American scene is now considered worth studying, and Miss Cather with the publication of a new novel offers us the chance of ascertaining how far she has kept moving in the right direction. Has she, who while writing of pioneers was once a pioneer herself, kept pushing on; has she found fertile acres and settled down to plow them, or has she drifted back to civilization and settled down in a comfortable arm-chair in a firelit, book-lined room? Now that she has a long career behind her, we may begin to search out the direction it has taken and the importance it has achieved.

The novels of Willa Cather may roughly be assigned to three periods. Passing two early experiments, we may say that the first period begins with *O Pioneers!* and ends with *My Ántonia*; that the second begins with *One of Ours* and ends with *My Mortal Enemy*; that the third begins with *Death Comes for the Archbishop* and continues—one cannot say whether it terminates—with *Shadows on the Rock*. There is, of course, nothing absolutely decisive about these three periods, and one period is likely to provide us with a partial throwback into an earlier one or an adumbration of a later. But it is equally evident that each of these periods has its own special feeling about life, and even its own special approach to life. *The Song of the Lark, The Professor's House* and *Shadows on the Rock* all have something, I suppose— the flavour of the author's personality, perhaps, or something else equally vague—in common; but they have very little else. The dominating spirit of *The Song of the Lark* is affirmation; of *The Professor's House*, unrest; of *Shadows on the Rock*, tranquillity.

[. . .]

The book is beautifully written; it has fine finish, and harmony of tone. Much more, even, than *Death Comes for the Archbishop* it breathes tranquillity, and like its predecessor, it is gently bathed (rather than passionately steeped) in the atmosphere of the Church. It is pervaded by the feeling that piety is not only noble but also efficacious, the feeling of

> . . . More things are wrought by prayer
> Than this world dreams of.

Little Cécile, throughout, seems en route to sainthood; in the epilogue, however, one finds her married to the tender *coureur-debois*. The idea of the goodness in life which runs through the book does not disturb us aesthetically—there is no undue sentimentality; the book is simply never real. It is without life, without even that semblance of life which can sometimes pass temporarily for reality. There is no blood in it, no muscle, no bodily emotion. It does not dispense with the commonplace to create the heroic, to give us the feeling that life is purer than doubtless it is, but also larger; there is plenty of commonplace, but it is commonplace flavoured with lavender, domesticity without domestic strife, old Quebec swept clean and fresh by human hands, but unpeopled by human beings. It is a genteel book; but since no other book of Miss

Cather's has deserved that epithet in the past, we must look further to find out why this one does.

We need not look too far. One can scarcely mistake the reason for this period of what I have called tranquillity, which began with *Death Comes for the Archbishop* and continues in *Shadows on the Rock*. Miss Cather, in her past few books, has less and less conveyed to the reader a sense of life, a sense of reality. One can see now, with her long career falling into perspective, that the only novels of hers which contribute genuine experience are those concerned with childhood and girlhood or with the Middle West of a vanished generation. She has herself confessed that an artist's experiences as a child are the most valuable he can have; she has approved, in *The Song of the Lark*, Wagner's dictum that all art is merely a way of remembering one's childhood; and on this theory she went legitimately and successfully back to the past and produced *O Pioneers!*, *The Song of the Lark* and *My Ántonia*. This world, that she knew so well, she has managed with great success to make the reader share; he believes in it, he participates in it. Trying other milieus thereafter, Miss Cather has been far less convincing, her picture has far less reality, her treatment far less significance. In *Shadows on the Rock* this lack of reality becomes more noticeable than ever before, and for a very definite reason.

For the world of *Shadows on the Rock* is a purely idyllic one. It is a world of serenity, indeed, but not of serenity after storm, with "all passion spent"; storm is not admitted to that world. Reality has been deliberately ruled out; being an idyll, the book takes a quiet happiness for granted; it depends, for its very existence, upon the right to ignore those things in life which upset harmony; it presupposes charm of expression, grace of gesture. In terms of the idyllic Miss Cather has done a pleasing job, and an almost but not quite consistent one—for here and there, with an incident, an allusion, a minor characterization she brings us, for just a moment, into touch with reality. But on all important counts, *Shadows on the Rock* establishes a pretty and placid world of its own.

Obviously, in the hierarchy of fictional art, the idyll occupies a low place. Not even pretending to treat of real life, it can teach us little about human character, can penetrate to little permanent truth, can stimulate few really deep emotions. It can never be, in other words, much more than charmingly untrue and aesthetically pleasing. A certain type of writer may succeed with the idyll form though he fails with more ambitious fiction, but a novelist of Miss Cather's stature, who in the past has triumphed on so much larger a scale, must inevitably disappoint us by making use of it. She adds nothing to her reputation with *Shadows on the Rock*: not quite perfect enough of its kind to survive in its own genre, it merely strengthens our feeling that Miss Cather is moving in the wrong direction. For, to answer the question raised at the beginning of this essay, she has not gone forward, she has gone back; she has preferred to construct an orderly, gracious world of her own rather than to deal with life as men, in their collective experience, understand it. It can safely be said that the only environment which has permanently interested first-rate novelists is that of their own day; but passing this by, it is still true that a novelist may write "historical novels" and make them true and important chronicles of human experience. In our own time Sigrid Undset, in her two imposing novels of the past, has treated of people whose lives, like those of Miss Cather's men and women in *Death Comes for the Archbishop* and *Shadows on the Rock*, are penetrated by the Church, and has charged them with a humanity and strength it would be difficult to overestimate. But Miss Cather's break with reality is not in her mere choice of the historical novel; it is in her using the historical novel as the vehicle for an altered point of view—as a way of permitting distance all the more to suffuse the dream with light, soft, serene colouring. This makes it impossible for her to give any sort of valid interpretation to life; and as vision it never captures our imagination nor stirs our emotions; it is simply pretty.

It seems a pity that Miss Cather's recent books, so much better written, so much shapelier in form, so much surer in aesthetic sensibility than her early ones, should give us nothing beyond good style, shapely form, delicate sensibility. All her later work is distinctly minor, pale beside the rich earthiness of the earlier novels, thin beside their vibrant sturdiness, sterile where they were fecund. This sterility cannot, of course, do damage to her past achievements: she remains, by past performance, the best American woman novelist of her time. *The Song of the Lark* and *My Ántonia* are books that one will want to read tomorrow; and *A Lost Lady*, real and romantic both, with its bouquet compounded of evanescence and frailty and regret, is well-nigh perfect: one of the few distinguished novelettes written in America.

Horace Gregory, *Symposium*, 2 (October 1931), 551–4

By this time a great deal of Willa Cather's ability to write a distinguished novel may be taken for granted. Perhaps her two short novels, *A Lost Lady* and *My Mortal*

Enemy, represent the climax of her mastery over form. Her stories are reduced to the lowest common denominator; plot and character development run to a common end. Her later novels have the authenticity of a folk tale, beautifully retold. There are no surprising revaluations of human conduct to trap the unwary reader. Her moral problems are written large and in words of one syllable. And now, by her own confession, she has set forth on a long journey, "a return to childhood, to early memories."

The danger of Miss Cather's position lies not so much in her taking "a happy vacation from life" but in her refusal to express a moral issue in terms of adult experience. Her latest novel is a logical step backward from *Death Comes for the Archbishop*. We are given an orderly society, dominated by the Roman Catholic church. The scene is seventeenth century French Canada. The choice is deliberate and carefully planned. So far there can be no quarrel with Miss Cather's selection of material. But when we realize that the story is told from the vantage point of a thirteen-year-old child, the issue becomes significantly simplified. We are warned in advance, as it were, that there will be no conflict of full-grown emotions or desires. Miss Cather's world has become very small indeed—a study in still life, transfixed by a stream of moonlight pouring through a stained glass window of a cathedral. At best her present work must be taken as an example of reaction against the tendency of the American novel to gain sociological importance. At worst, it is a romantic if not completely sentimental dream of a lady novelist yearning for an ideal home in which all the elements of a pioneer tradition are refined beyond ultimate conviction.

It has been said (particularly by Mr. Carl Van Doren) that Willa Cather has become interested in problems of abstract virtue. If this is true, then *Shadows on the Rock* contains a curious paradox. Miss Cather's anatomy of virtue is clearly outlined in her story and is noticeably concrete. What is more, it is fully justified by the accepted tradition of the Catholic church in French Canada and nineteenth century New Mexico. It is a primer of human conduct, each point decisively illustrated by an anecdote, a living example of right and wrong. One learns that physical dirt is a symbol of evil. Extreme poverty or the circumstances of living on the Frontier cannot be offered as an excuse for the lack of personal cleanliness. Since this lesson is made one of the major problems in the novel, Cecile, the heroine, becomes a model of cleanliness and industry. We are told again and again of her ability to keep her father's house neat and shining with soap and water. Her conversion of her little friend, Jacques, son of the town prostitute, is a matter of continually washing his hands and face. Whenever he repeats a coarse word, learned from sailors in his mother's bedroom, Cecile washes his mouth, inside and out. It is a sign of virtue, if one is poor and a servant (witness Cecile's father, apothecary to Count Frontenac), to remain a loyal (and poor) servant to your temporal master and to your church, in good times and bad, in sickness and well-being. We must remember that Cecile is not merely a child, but the perfected conception of a virtuous childhood. The details of the story are presented in the light of her duty to her father, her priest and to her God. Her articles of faith are absolute. Jacques, in a moment of doubt asks a question and we hear her answer:

"Cecile, all the saints in this church like children, don't they?"

"Oh, yes! And Our Lord loves children. Because He was a child Himself, you know."

Here we recognize a strange misalliance of two distinctly opposing ideologies, which accounts, perhaps, for a lack of belief in Miss Cather's characterizations of Jacques and Cecile. On one hand, the two children are perfect examples of Rousseau's natural man-the-child whose instincts lead quite naturally toward the Good Life. On the other, they are embodiments of a consciousness of guilt and a sense of the original sin.

As for Miss Cather's seventeenth century Quebec, it is evident that she has drawn upon the historical sources of her novel with the greatest care and accuracy. Whatever we are permitted to see of the old bishop, Laval, his successor, Saint-Vallier, and Count Frontenac, we are willing and prepared to accept as genuine. But it is also evident that she has omitted much. The effect is that of an ingeniously contrived distortion of pioneer life. The characteristic hardships of living in a new land are deftly eliminated—and this at a time when very nearly all of our present standards of comfort were unknown. The cleanliness of the apothecary's shop and household seems almost an anachronism. One would say (since the apothecary and his daughter lived alone) that the poor child was a hopeless drudge or a phenomenon of extraordinary physical vitality. The conviction with which we read O Pioneers! and My Ántonia does not enter into a reading of Shadows On The Rock. In Miss Cather's early work there is no sense of thin or incomplete detail; there we find her structural material as solid as the sustained cadences of her prose.

Miss Cather's particular value as an artist has long been associated with the characteristic phenomena of American life. It may be argued that her interests have always been controlled by a traditional America, rather than the actual and contemporary scheme of existence. Throughout the body of her work one may grant a strong undercurrent of nostalgia for the past, but there was also to be found in Willa Cather an unmistakable relationship to the soil from which she sprung and a celebration of its unique tradition. Her first three novels were of pioneer stock and whatever may be drawn from their cultural background is of Puritan origin. It may be that Puritan culture drained through a Western or Middle Western environment grows singularly weak. In Willa Cather's case, however, there is a curious deflection from the main stream. There are pioneers of a kind in Shadows on the Rock, but emphasis is laid upon their devotion to a society in the old world. One remembers that this particular society developed far more rapidly on the Continent than in French Canada.

In general, the tradition of the Catholic church in America has run counter to the tradition of Puritan culture on North American soil. With notable exceptions of missionary work in Canada and New Mexico, its career has been and still is distinctly urban. To appreciate fully the naivety which colors the atmosphere of a novel like Shadows on the Rock, a sophisticated, urban, if not downright decadent imagination is required. It is perhaps inevitable that the surface qualities of the book should be enjoyed by a large public. Certainly, the adventures of Cecile are as appealing as Cinderella's—less terrifying, but far more reassuring. One has only to be good and one is rewarded with a proper husband and a generous supply of small children. As for Miss Cather, she is a tired woman in a large city looking backward wistfully from an apartment house window to the past, to a civilization as remote as Keats's dream of St. Agnes' Eve.

James Southall Wilson, *Virginia Quarterly Review*, 7 (October 1931), 584–90

I do not know that it has ever been told of Sainte-Beuve that once he visited a dear friend soon after the birth of her child, and the mother, remembering his penchant for discussing a new book in terms of its origins, said, lifting her boy to him, "Maître, review for me the latest edition." "Hélas! ma chérie," he responded, "this is life, not art."

When Willa Cather presents the world with a new novel it is somewhat in the spirit of abashed humility that a self-respecting critic should approach her work; for she is of the true faith in that, as God created Man in His own likeness, she creates men and women in the likeness of the creatures He has made. She has not developed for herself a form for her novels, or a formula of workmanship that makes it easy to fit each book into a discussion of her growth as an artist. Each of her novels has its own existence quite apart from any of her other books, whatever family resemblances there may be. We admire the firm, sure modelling, the quick, fresh, lovingly laid-on coloring, and step back the better to wonder at the beauty of the statue in its entirety—and lo, Hermione steps down from her pedestal.

There is less story to *Shadows on the Rock* than to any other of Miss Cather's novels. Yet it is full of incident and full of characters. . . . The method seems episodic but the effect does not seem episodic. It is true that nothing much happens in the story proper except that

Auclair and his little daughter live before our eyes for a year and some days in the apothecary shop and that the great Count de Frontenac dies: it is from the Epilogue that we learn that little Cécile later married. The unity of the book is partly through tone and partly by means of the exquisite skill with which Miss Cather has interwoven her materials of life. France and Canada, memories, legends, the fabric of faith and the traffic of the heart and mind to-day, affairs of Count, bishops, nuns, fur trader, shoe-maker, apothecary, little maid, harlot, sailor, and saint are all of one stuff, in one picture, shadows on the same rock. There are strength and strife, more by implication than by narration, but out of them—as in the riddle of Samson—comes forth sweetness.

If in particular the book is an embodiment of the spirit of old Quebec, like all true and intense art that has its roots in a place, it has universality too. It is pervaded by the spirit of humanity. The attitude toward all things in the book is one of the tenderest compassion. And this, we understand, springs from no soft sentimentality but as the flower of something hard and bitter. It may be recalled here that of the poor creature, Blinker, who in France had been born to the trade of the torturer, it was said that having known misery, he had learned to pity the miserable. Though its people are French, *Shadows on the Rock* is in a tradition, in that it exalts three qualities that have been three of the cardinal virtues in English literature since the time of Beowulf: courage, loyalty, and kindness. But the book does not generalize; Miss Cather keeps to the human, the specific, the concrete, the little—not for her "unremembered"—acts that make life; for what she is doing after all is bringing alive "a little group of Frenchmen, three thousand miles

from home, making the best of things."
...There will be much comparing of *Shadows on the Rock* with *Death Comes for the Archbishop*. It is inevitable; yet they are books that ought not to be compared, though her most recent novel is in many respects more like the one that preceded it than is any other book that Miss Cather has written. The *Shadows* is a more intimate book; the other casts the larger shadow. One might love the newer book better, but it will not be so greatly admired. By its theme and inception, *Death Comes for the Archbishop* had a wider scope. The world of *Shadows on the Rock* is a rounded world, bound in by the trackless forests and the sea. We enter into the circle of a hearth fire and we come to feel that every family is the Holy Family. We know our little world lovingly. But we have not as in the other book the illusion of distances that lure us on, vistas of romance and uncertainty. We get from the one book—the figure is stolen from Miss Cather—"a warm sweet odour— very like the smell of ripe strawberries" which is the "aromatic breath of spruce and pine, given out under the hot sun of noonday"; from the other we get the savour of the more mysterious scents that the winds brought from those same shores to the early explorers, which they described as "the smell of luscious unknown fruits, wafted out to sea." In saying which, it is not meant that *Shadows on the Rock* is any the less a novel to be crowned and welcomed with the ringing of bells.

Alexander Woollcott, "Miss Cather Speaks Again," *McCall's*, 59 (November 1931), 20, 101

On a summer's night in 1918, astray in the once pleasant valley of the Somme, which the collective folly of mankind had recently turned into a blighted wilderness, I wandered about in quest of some shelter not already preempted, and, by a bit of luck, found what I wanted in a fragment of a house, still standing after years of bombardment had reduced most of the habitations in that part of the world to rubble. In temporary possession were two Australian soldiers who had come up from the railhead after dark with the letters from home for their regiment. Graciously they allotted a corner of the plaster-strewn floor to me. One of them, a lean and scornful young veteran of Gallipoli, brewed me a cup of tea and even loaned me the Melbourne mail bag as a pillow for the night. For his own use, he was reserving the sack from Sydney, and cherishing a bit of candle-end. Thus equipped, while the guns boomed away at the evening routine of destruction, and with the gap where the window had been now blanketed to keep the contraband light from shining into the night, he read himself to sleep in the pages of William Morris' *The Sundering Flood*.

I remember my twinge of admiration at the quiet steadfastness of that procedure. There he was, imperturbable at Armageddon, too strong to be decivilized by the collapse of the world around him, too much himself to be unmade by any external force on earth. And curiously enough, the picture of his tawny, tousled head, bent over the pages in the flickering candlelight, has been brought back to me across the years by Willa Cather's new novel. For, like her *Death Comes For the Archbishop* which preceded it, this latest work of hers sings and serves and celebrates just that spirit—the spirit of the unswerving priests who, in the earlier work, carried the Word into the parched wilderness of New Mexico a century ago; and now, in her new book, the spirit of the little stubborn French colony of Quebec, that held the fort and kept the faith on a rock in the St. Lawrence a hundred years before. This new book is called *Shadows on the Rock*. It is a sure, tranquil, fond evocation of a day gone by, and it has been put down on paper with a serene art, which, to my way of thinking, no other American writer can match.

When the advance copy arrived on my doorstep I found, imprinted on the jacket, the following solemn utterance from the publisher:

"Seldom has any novel been as widely bought and as dearly loved as *Death Comes For the Archbishop*. I assure Miss Cather's readers that *Shadows on the Rock* is of the same superb vintage. (Signed) Alfred A. Knopf."

Now, of these two sentences, the first is a piece of arrant and deleterious nonsense. For the exquisitely wrought and nobly imagined book called *Death Comes for the Archbishop* was neither addressed to, nor embraced by, the multitude, but was (and still is) the darling of a haughty minority. Mr. Knopf's second sentence, however, is justified by the event. For *Shadows on the Rock* does prove to be a companion piece to the book which preceded it. It was made for the same customer. It was cut from the same lovely fabric.

Here, as in the earlier book, are staunch, undaunted exiles, and the tale of

their adventures in the new world has, as its counter melody, their nostalgia for, and their loyalty to, the one they left behind. What imparts to each quiet narrative a gentle radiance is Miss Cather's own relish of their steadfastness.

Into the wilderness they carried the fineness of French life, guarded like a flame cupped by the hand in a storm, and they never were more French in all their home-bound lives than when, as in some sunburned outpost beyond Santa Fe, or in some snow-besieged Canadian fort, it took a bit of doing.

Do you remember the Christmas dinner of the two priests in *Death Comes For the Archbishop*—the onion soup with croutons which Father Vaillant, shifting from cassock to cook's apron, made with his own gnarled hands as no one could make it in all the vast unpeopled empire from the Mississippi to the Pacific? The thoughts of the two, as they sipped it, were far from the endless sand and cactus of their bleached frontier. Meeting silently, their thoughts were in a little town on the other side of the world. Coming together, their thoughts loitered in a certain gray, winding street paved with cobbles and shaded by tall chestnut trees on which, even on Christmas day, some few brown leaves would be clinging, or drooping, one by one, to be caught in the cold green ivy on the walls.

Well, in *Shadows on the Rock*, a tale of old, sweet folkways and small homely pieties in the Quebec of Frontenac's time, we watch the same flame cupped against other winds by other hands. This time the central place is no mission, but an apothecary's shop. There on Monsieur Auclair's shelves are found bay leaves and camomile flowers, senna and hyssop and mustard, brought from France by the doughty square-riggers that braved the battering Atlantic every eight months to keep Quebec in touch with home. And in the house behind the shop one found the apothecary's little daughter, faithful to the ritual of orderly home-making which her mother had taught her.

So sure is Miss Cather's skill that you follow with her own deep interest the fond minutiae of life on that river-girt, forest-encircled headland, sharing its modest joys, and feeling a lift in your own heart when, at last, a joyous shout goes up that hails the first sail of the storm-beset ships arriving from France. In honor of the great occasion, Pierre Charron, the trapper, gave a dinner on shore for one of the captains, and over the wine, as the evening waned, there were many tall tales of sea and forest. Coming out of the chateau, Father Hector Saint-Cyr spied them.

"Down yonder by the waterside, before one of the rustic booths, he could see a little party seated about a table with lanterns. He could not see who they were, but he felt a friendliness for that company. A little group of Frenchmen, three thousand miles from home, making the best of things—having a good dinner. He decided to go down and join them."

And now you and I, too, may draw up our chairs. I do not know a table in any land, in any time, where we could do better.

"That Final Sacrifice," *New Mexico Quarterly*, 1 (November 1931), 419–21

When, in 1927, Willa Cather, hailed by some critics as the greatest of living novelists, published *Death Comes for the Archbishop*, New Mexico laid claim to her as one of her own. The novel had its setting in New Mexico and dealt with episodes taken from the history of the state. It won world recognition. Now, when Miss Cather writes a novel, it is with an especial interest that it is read by New Mexicans.

There are other elements which make *Shadows on the Rock* of unusual interest to New Mexico. Although its setting is a great distance from this state, in Quebec, it might have been written of New Mexico. Its background of the isolated colonial settlement, where homeloving colonials looked longingly back across the sea toward their sunny fields in France; its ecclesiastical flavor, with martyrs blazing a glorious trail for the church, these things recall our own history of the same period, the late seventeenth and early eighteenth centuries.

The rock of Miss Cather's new novel, is the great rock on the edge of the St. Lawrence upon which Quebec was founded. The shadows are the people who strangely have picked this spot for the founding of a town, to which ships each summer make their way across the treacherous Atlantic to bring dispatches and supplies. The story is that of an apothecary, who came to Canada with Count Frontenac as his personal physician, and spent nine years of virtual exile with the aging governor-general, living for the time when he would return with the Count to Paris. But the time never came. The expected summons from the king was never received by the Count, who finally released the apothecary to return with his daughter to France, and offered gold to pay his passage. The apothecary, born and nurtured in old feudal France, at that time makes the "final sacrifice," places his life's dream of returning to France behind him and decides that, like the Count, he will remain and die in the colony.

The plot is not strong; it is a mere thread running through the episodes and shifting seasons of the book. It was the last year of Frontenac's life. The last ships returned to France, and through the long, hard winter, the colony lived on its memories and hopes, till the first ships came from France in June.

Miss Cather does not need strong or swift action to make her novels grip and hold attention. She has a subtler and a finer art. She can conjure up before the reader, scenes more vivid and real than any his eyes have seen. She can make her characters live and breathe and walk, rejoice and suffer. Hers is a finished art. Each line, each sentence, each paragraph in itself is a thing of beauty to be enjoyed. As in each of her novels, *Shadows on the Rock* has many passages which cling to the memory, passages filled with beauty and meaning, words which, like the characters of the book, are alive. Thus:

"*Inferretque deos Latio.* When an adventurer carries his gods with him into a remote and savage country, the colony he founds will, from the beginning, have graces, tradition, riches of the mind and spirit. Its history will shine with bright incidents, slight, perhaps, but precious, as in life itself, where the great matters are often as worthless as astronomical distances, and the trifles dear as the heart's blood."

And again:

" 'Listen, my friend. No man can give himself, heart and soul, to one thing while in the back of his mind he cherishes a desire, a secret hope, for something very different. You, as a student, must know that in worldly affairs nothing worthwhile is accomplished except by that last sacrifice, the giving of oneself altogether and finally. Since I made that final sacrifice, I have been twice the man I was before.' "

Donald R. Murphy, "Willa Cather's Admirers Defend Her Quebec Novel," *Des Moines Register*, 1 November 1931, section 10A, p. 6

Willa Cather's latest book has its shock troops of admirers. Several phalanxes of them advanced to the assault after three reviewers had placed the story of Quebec in the second rank of Miss Cather's novels.

Zella Wallace of Des Moines insists that while *Shadows on the Rock* may have been disappointing to Mrs. Le Cron, it was far from that to her. She writers:

"It is a novel that glimpses the quiet joy, the depth and sanctity of home and family life, where love and order dwell. There are characters whom we love and honor. There are also authentic historical glimpses of early Quebec when it relied largely for its economic existence upon trading with the Indians. This novel makes us see the sterling qualities in the character of these early French settlers who combined the high French traditional art of living with the rigors of the Canadian winters; and felt, all the while, that God was leading them toward their racial achievement and destiny.

"To people who feel that this novel pictures life too idealistically to be true, and the girl, Cecile, as too perfect in her character; I would say that this kind of writing is not realism. This is not the type of art that is done in bas-relief, it is a subdued oil painting of shadows. So far as I know, this type of artistry is original with Willa Cather.

We may not care for it but it is well to recognize it, nevertheless. To me this novel is like organ music that is faint and far away; yet deep, beautiful and inspiring; and the strains of the melody linger on in the heart and memory— long after the book is closed."

Kathleen M. Hempel of Elkader even more emphatically remarks: "*Shadows on the Rock* reminds me of one of those days in winter when the whole world is transformed into a fairy land of beauty. There is a sort of soft grayness, a magic calm, that thrills one. Some critics are blind to this loveliness and can see only the wet tracks the snow will make on the rug!"

Miss Hempel goes on to give her opinion of a tabloid in which it was humorously suggested that *Shadows on the Rock* might be more of a "menace" to Protestantism than Al Smith.

"Religion," says Miss Hempel, sternly "was so closely interwoven with the every day life of all the early colonists, that to confuse this realistic portrayal with religious propaganda is not only ridiculous but amusing. Should Miss Cather ever write a story with ancient Rome for a background one would feel confident that Mrs. Little would hasten to assure her readers that she was leading them back to paganism. An account of colonial Pennsylvania would bring a warning that we were trembling on the brink of Quakerism. And to write of Salem would mean that witchcraft was being thrust down our unwilling throats. Probably my metaphors are a bit mixed but so is Mrs. Little's reasoning!"

Leon Whipple, "Gold in What Hills?" *Survey*, 67 (1 November 1931), 150–1

Willa Cather's fine art paints pictures of old Quebec in the one year 1697 to 1698, measured by the sailing of the ships for France one summer and their return the next. This shuttle weaving from the old land to the new is her motif. The pioneers are always dependent on the mother land not only for material things but for cultural standards and the sense of continuity in life. On the contrary, they are always breaking up the inherited forms and ideas under the disciplines and spiritual stresses of their adventure. So the gentle-souled daughter of the exiled apothecary, motherless at thirteen, strives to keep house and live graciously as the mother taught her they lived in old France. But in the end she marries the far-ranging woodsman who is Canadian and represents all that is new. This historical implication is scarcely stressed; the story moves with a kind of pastoral sweetness and beauty through the year's events as revealed to the eyes and heart of the little Cécile while the grim old Count Frontenac ebbs to death in the chateau on the grim rock. The apothecary, Euclide Auclair, imports drugs and comfits for the homesick, and likewise the philosophy and spiritual mood of the elder land. He is beautifully drawn as are half a dozen characters, Bishop Laval, the trapper, Charron, Frontenac, and the recluse who has her cell built behind the altar of the church in Montreal. It is like a gallery of old and mellow pictures. The tale is slight, the motif an undertone, but the people and the moods of the grim rock make the novel memorable.

"The Library of the Quarter," *Yale Review*, 21 (Autumn 1931), viii

Miss Cather's title invites figurative extension. These shadows on the rock are not the sharply blocked patterns of clear morning or mellow afternoon. They fall in the hour between sundown and moonrise. They are cast by old men's reveries, the faith of those who have renounced the great world, and the wonder of children—delicate wavering images of life apprehended rather than seen, on the enduring background of nature that may be lovely or terrible but is always unmindful of the brief frailty of man.

The title is more important than with most novels, for it reveals the direction and the mood of the narrative, which is tender and musing rather than directly dramatic and active. The drama is stated by implication and symbol. As the story begins the sun of the great day of Old France was about to set. It was never to rise to full height on New France. The period of which Miss Cather writes proved to be a time of dreams. The heroism of the famous French explorers, the hardihood of the trappers, the endurance of the pioneer settlers, the daring of the seamen who manned the fleets that came and went through the Gulf of St. Lawrence were followed by no commensurate fulfilment. The author justly gives them the remoteness of things remembered from a dream world, or, to use her own phrase, from "the world of the mind." This she accomplishes both through her choice of materials and through her way of approach. In the materials of the story, the sense of insubstantiality is produced by the bringing into the foreground of old age and childhood and the foreshortening of all that belongs to tumultuous maturity.

To enforce the impression she uses the method of description and the relation of little everyday events. Thus she illustrates her own observation that in the history of a colony as in life itself, "great matters are often as worthless as astronomical distances and the trifles dear as heart's blood." This is true and finely said, and some of the slightest incidents in *Shadows on the Rock* are to be treasured. But the method as Miss Cather applies it does not seem to have in the end the cumulative effect that a novel, by one means or another, should communicate to the reader—the cumulative effect of mounting event and emotion. There is compensation, however, in the weight of reflection that the book gathers, as it goes its quiet way, on the true values in French civilization and on what values are worth saving in the movement of any civilization from an old to a new world, from the past to the present. It is the work of a humanist—a persuasive plea, in the form of an historical idyl, for what distinguishes human living from the life of the brute.

Charlotte M. Meagher, *Quarterly Bulletin of the International Federation of Catholic Alumnae*, 14 (December 1931), 25

The announcement of a new novel by Willa Cather has come to be an event to be acclaimed. No one questions her authoritative handling of a setting, the intrinsic interest of her theme, the quality of her craftsmanship. Since the publication of her earliest novels in the second decade of the century Willa Cather has held her place in American literature; when in 1922 her *One of Ours* captured the Pulitzer Prize, that place became a literary shrine; and in 1927 when her matchless story of the South West, *Death Comes for the Archbishop*, left the presses, new hosts of devotees were gathered to that shrine. This year in *Shadows on the Rock*, Miss Cather gives her readers an exquisite companion volume, an idyll of the North.

For this latest novel, if novel it can be called, its author has chosen the youthful colony of Quebec in the closing years of the seventeenth century. "When an adventurer", says Miss Cather, "carries his gods with him into a remote and savage country, the colony he founds will, from the beginning, have graces, traditions, riches of the mind and spirit. Its history will shine with bright incidents, slight, perhaps, but precious, as in life itself, where the great matters are often as worthless as astronomical distances, and the trifles dear as the heart's blood." This is what the story gives us—French-Canadian *graces, traditions, riches of the mind and spirit*, and again *trifles dear as the heart's blood*. Here on the river bank we watch the play of colony life, the shadows cast by youth and age, artisan and peasant, statesman and churchman, great and small.

Lovers of Quebec will revel in the touches of description which flash back to them the city at different seasons of the year: "It was the first day of June. Before dawn a wild calling and twittering of birds in the bushes on the cliff-side above the apothecary's back door announced clear weather. When the sun came up over the Ile d'Orléans, the rock of Kebec stood gleaming above the river like an altar with many candles, or like a holy city in an old legend, shriven, sinless, washed in gold.

The quickening of all life and hope which had come to France in May had reached the far North at last." But it was in the autumn that Cécile, through whose eyes we see it all, best loved her Quebec. "Why should she spend the golden afternoons indoors? The glorious transmutation of autumn had come on: all the vast Canadian shores were clothed with a splendor never seen in France; to which all the pageants of all the kings were as a taper to the sun. Even the ragged cliff-side behind her kitchen door was beautiful; the wild cherry and sumach and the blackberry vines had turned crimson, and the birch and poplar saplings were yellow."

Standing out against these backgrounds we have all the centers of the people's life—the Ursuline Convent where Cécile had gone to school; the new Seminary of Bishop Laval; the cathedral, the Hotel Dieu where the apothecary, always accompanied by his little Cécile, went to care for the sprained ankle of the Reverend Mother; the little church of Notre Dame de la Victoire, later to be known as Notre Dame des Victoires. Here we have too the mystic beauty of the Laurentians, and the "sunny fields that ran toward Beaupré."

It is this Quebec of 1697 and 1698 that Miss Cather so graphically paints for her readers. Whether she shows it to us on market day down in the square, or on "the most important day of the year," the day the ships from France are sighted down the river; whether we see its life radiating from Count Frontenac, or blessing the saintly Bishop Laval, or endeavoring to understand the difficult Monseigneur de Saint-Vallier, it is a richly colored pageant vibrant with the throb of the colony heart.

The story has no plot; it is simply a series of episodes in the life of Cécile Auclair, the little twelve-year-old whose mother dying would think fearfully of how much she was entrusting to that little shingled head. Cécile's housekeeping in the home at the apothecary's shop in Mountain Hill; her long walks with her father; her motherly care and solicitude for the tiny Jacques, grandson of one of the King's Girls of the days of the marriage marts; her naive friendship with the great and humble Bishop Laval; her short, troubled sojourn on the farm over on the Ile d'Orléans; her gay little efforts at acting hostess to her father's guests, guests as widely different as Father Hector, the missionary, and Pierre Charron, colonial free lance, all kindness and French tact, these interests and activities are all set out before us in a series of pastels of exquisite tracery and color. The book closes with an epilogue which lets the reader look in upon these interesting people fifteen years later, to find Cécile the mother of a merry family, the saintly Laval gone to his reward, Saint-Vallier, chastened and mellowed and successful in his diocese, and the apothecary enjoying the fulness of days.

It is platitudinous to offer praise for the literary method of Willa Cather. Her wide background, her understanding of the epoch in France as well as in the new world—parenthetically one is led to hope for a Willa Cather novel centered in Mme. de Maintenon—her keen analysis of human motives and human actions, her rare ability to capture a mood, whether of a character or of a city, all these, together with the incomparable lucidity as well as the simplicity of her style, make the book a joy to any reader.

To the Catholic *Shadows on the Rock* brings added delights, for in it Miss Cather has given a most sympathetic picture of Catholic life in all its completeness. And it is complete: the tares are there with the wheat, the garment has its seamy side: the mother of little Jacques remains "irreclaimable"; the churchmen carry on

their feud; but it is life permeated with Catholic tradition. It is difficult to understand how one not of the Faith could so comprehendingly portray the spiritual life of the people. Her touch is sure from such a minute detail as little Jacques' "untraditional" beaver in the Christmas crib to the greatness of the vow of "perpetual stability" of the sorely tried missionary, or the solemnity of a French-Canadian All Souls' Day. The passage in which the early nuns of the colony are characterized deserves to be quoted in full:

"The cheerful faces were those in the convents. The Ursulines and the Hospitalières, indeed, were scarcely exiles. When they came across the Atlantic, they brought their family with them, their kindred, their closest friends. In whatever little wooden vessel they had labored across the sea, they carried all; they brought to Canada the Holy Family, the saints and martyrs, the glorious company of the Apostles, the heavenly host.

"Courageous these Sisters were, accepting good and ill fortune with high spirit—with humor, even. They never vulgarly exaggerated hardships and dangers. They had no hours of nostalgia, for they were quite as near the realities of their lives in Quebec as in Dieppe or Tours. They were still in their accustomed place in the world of the mind (which for each of us is the only world), and they had the same well-ordered universe about them: this all-important earth, created by God for a great purpose, the sun which He made to light it by day, the moon which He made to light it by night—and the stars, made to beautify the vault of heaven like frescoes, and to be a clock and compass for man. And in this safe, lovingly arranged and ordered universe (not too vast, though nobly spacious), in this congenial universe, the drama of man went on at Quebec just as at home, and the Sisters played their accustomed part in it. There was sin, of course, and there was punishment after death; but there was always hope, even for the most depraved; and for those who died repentant, the Sisters' prayers could do much,—no one might say how much."

J. C. Squire, "Far Away and Long Ago," *Times* (London), January [1932]

Rupert Brooke, travelling through the vast spaces of Western North America, wrote, "At a pinch one can do without gods, but one misses the dead." It was this hankering for a historic background, doubtless, which led so many Americans of the last century to write Baedeker literature. The Coliseum, the Bay of Naples, and the castled Rhine had ancient and picturesque associations which America could not parallel: America had no Roman Empire and no robber barons— at any rate of the right kind.

Time, which devours all things, to some extent creates as it devours; the present fact vanishes, and history and legend take its place. As generation succeeds generation the patina of age comes over the memory of events, and more and more scenes become remote enough for imagination to find exercise in reconstructing them in their main outlines, and for the heart to find in them whatever illusions it desires.

Hawthorne, I suppose, was the first American to turn early American history to great artistic use. Some later men, notably Longfellow, strove hard to find in Salem and Acadie the interest that was so evident in Nuremburg and the Drachen-

fels; but it is only in our own time that the poets and novelists of America have begun to feel that the historical background of the Continent is rich and varied enough for systematic—if I may use the horrid word—exploitation.

Not only have they discovered South America, but they now see through a haze of romance the Spanish and French settlements, the opening up of the West, the Gold Rush, and even the Civil War. I suppose that the most finished prose written in America in this generation has been written by Miss Cather, Mr. Wilder, and Mr. Hergesheimer, and they have all been at their best when brooding over the past of America.

Miss Cather is developing as an artist, and she can be trusted not to repeat herself in any way. But I am not sure that her line of development will be welcomed by those who admired her earlier novels, which culminated in that enchanting book, *A Lost Lady*. *Death Comes for the Archbishop* was a perfect thing in its way, but everything in it was, as it were, seen at a distance, a distance too far for sounds to be audible.

In this new book the same quality is more noticeable still. The scene is Quebec (Kebec), under French rule, at the end of the seventeenth century. Miss Cather exhibits, with an apothecary and his daughter at the centre of the scene, representatives of all sections of the little population, from Governor and Bishop down to the dregs of the waterside. The strands of personal relation are cunningly and naturally interwoven. The descriptions are excellently clear and economical. We are always kept aware of France over the sea and events there, of the contrast between the French-Catholic civilisation of the small town and the savage-haunted wilderness around it; we even gradually become aware of the growth of a specifically Canadian sentiment.

But that far-away feeling persists. We see the characters, but their voices are muted. They live, but we never forget that they have long been dead. It is an exquisite achievement, but not a book for those who want excitement.

Perhaps it may best be defined as a quietist poem inspired by Catholic religion and morality at their purest. The prime motive of the book is indicated by the frequent references to tradition and loyalty; and emphasised in a beautiful passage about the carriage of gods overseas. In many a short sentence is more said of the spirit than many can say in whole books: as, for instance, of Frontenac, the Governor:

> He would die here, in this room, and his spirit would go before God to be judged. He believed this, because he had been taught it in childhood, and because he knew there was something in himself and in other men that this world did not explain.

But a longer passage will better indicate both the atmosphere and the style:

> By many a fireside the story of Jeanne Le Ber's spinning-wheel was told and retold with loving exaggeration during that severe winter. The word of her visit from the angels went abroad over snow-burdened Canada to the remote parishes. Wherever it went, it brought pleasure, as if the recluse herself had sent to all those families whom she did not know some living beauty—a blooming rose tree, or a shapely fruit tree in fruit. Indeed, she sent them an incomparable gift. In the long evenings, when the family had told over their tales of Indian massacres and lost hunters, and the almost human intelligence of the beaver, someone would speak the name of Jeanne Le Ber, and it again gave out fragrance.

> The people have loved miracles for so many hundred years, not as a proof or evidence, but because they are the actual flowering of desire. In them the vague worship and devotion of the simple-hearted assumes a form. From being a shapeless longing, it becomes a beautiful image; a dumb rapture becomes a melody that can be remembered and repeated; and the experience of a moment, which might have been a lost ecstasy, is made an actual possession, and can be bequeathed to another.

That flow of placid melody is never much changed. All good writers to some extent colour dialogue with their own styles: one of the most difficult things about story-telling is to leave some individuality in the speech of various persons while still preserving some continuity of prose. Miss Cather's style envelops all: she, as it were, quietly intones through the mouths of everybody, giving the whole picture a tinted glaze, which intensifies the feeling of remoteness. There are many compensations. The charity of her heart is as uniform as the movement of her style. She never comes near the soft or the mawkish, but there are times when she is nothing less than Franciscan. In an age addicted to "hard-boiled literature" she is like the evening star over a turbulent sea.

"New Novel," *Times* (London), 15 January 1932, p. 6

Miss Willa Cather has been to Quebec for inspiration, and her new novel is about the life of the colonists in the days of

Bishop Laval and Count Frontenac, whose names are inseparably connected with the city and environs. She lets us see the daily life of the philosopher-chemist Auclair, the friend of the Governor and the Bishop, whose shop has clients of all classes, and whose profession keeps him in touch with the whole community. His young daughter, Cecile, is his house-keeper, a charming little figure, who mothers the little boy Jacques and the ex-torturer Blinker with natural and uncon-scious goodness. The great personages of the story, Frontenac and Laval, are depicted, with their responsibilities and difficulties, as very human and accessible guardians of the colony, and from a wealth of detail Miss Cather has selected, with brilliant judgment, what is most sig-nificant. Her miracles and wonders, her tales of the saints and martyrs of New France, are skilfully woven into the talk of the people and invested with new live-liness and grace by her pen. So clear and unaffected is her story that it is almost as if an authentic journal kept 200 years ago in Quebec had come to light. She owes something to the vivid example of Father Dollier de Casson, and like that vigorous writer she emphasizes the isolation of the colony for the eight months between the departure of the sailing ships in October and their return in July. This is perhaps the first really interesting novel that has yet been written in or about Quebec. It misses nothing of the natural beauty that still distinguishes the place, and it makes the reader realize that there is a very great deal to be said in favour of pioneering days and a "new" world in the making.

Times Literary Supplement (London), 21 January 1932, p. 42

A second American invasion of Quebec is taking place at present, this time a peace-ful and advantageous invasion. First there was Miss Agnes Repplier with her excel-lent study of Marie de l'Incarnation, the foundress of the Ursulines, standing out against a vivid background of history and heroic figures. Now comes Miss Willa Cather, who chooses a later period and reconstructs the daily life of the people of the rock in the days of Frontenac and Laval. *Shadows on the Rock* is an imagi-native effort to see Quebec as it may have been two hundred years ago, made by an artist who has steeped herself in tradition and history and who has closely observed the untouchable loveliness of sky and river and forest round the year.

There is no particular drama in the quiet history of the chemist, Auclair, and his little daughter, Cecile, but their rela-tionship with the Count and the Prelate, who were rather more than passing shadows and who have left their indelible impression on the rock, is delightfully vivid. Miss Cather has avoided any attempt to be French or archaic and has made her people talk pleasantly and nat-urally with the commendably modern touch. From Dollier de Casson, the Sulpician priest who wrote the history of Montreal, she has borrowed the idea of making the sailing of the ships from Canada in the autumn of the year and their return in the summer the high peaks of her narrative. They were, indeed, the events of greatest moment in the lives of the colonists, and the desolation of the empty river waiting for the hand of winter

397

to seal it for endless months is conveyed with acute feeling that is matched by the thrill and wonder aroused by the sight of the sails beating back when summer has released the waters. Townspeople and woodsmen, fishers, farmers and prelates play their parts in the tale, but the outstanding figure is that of the rugged Bishop Laval, who disciplined himself so severely to enrich the Church, living in poverty and even ringing the bell of the cathedral himself for Mass. Contrasted with him is the younger and suaver bishop, St. Vallier, for five years a prisoner of State in England, who returned to Quebec after a long detention at home and founded the General Hospital, became its humble chaplain and died within its walls. Frontenac's portrait is lifelike and touching, and Miss Cather provides an authentic thrill of horror when Blinker, the cross-eyed servant, tells Auclair the truth about his earlier life in France. Miss Cather has made a book full of life and brilliance out of material that has become sentimental and unreal in other hands. This rivals the best novels that have been written about Quebec, a lively book and full of beauty.

M. MacC., "Willa Cather's Novel: Pioneer Days in North America," *Irish Press* (Dublin), 22 January 1932, p. 5

A few years ago Willa Cather stormed her way straight to the reader with one of the best modern novels in the English language, *Death Comes for the Archbishop*. Hitherto, we had not heard of her here in Ireland, presumably because her work, differing so much from the psychological novel in vogue, did not appeal to the reviewers.

Miss Cather goes back for her subjects to the valiant spirits and the great personalities of pioneer times. Her new book, *Shadows on the Rock*, just published by Cassell is a story of French Quebec—the Quebec of Laval and Frontenac. The characters in this book are, most of them, French born colonists who have emigrated out of duty or necessity, bringing with them the ordered life and gracious ways of their own land. Miss Cather's is a memorable picture of the world which these French *émigrés* make on this rugged rock in a land so different from their own. A convincing but sad picture it is. Indeed, the objection might be made to *Shadows on the Rock* that it is a picture of defeat.

But there is heroism in it, the heroism of the apothecary following his patron into dreaded exile out of a sense of duty, the heroism of his little daughter taking up and carrying on the ordered life which her dying mother had taught her, the heroism of the missionary taking a perpetual vow that he will minister to the natives in their wigwams to the end in spite of his eternal longing for the gracious ways of home.

And what writing it is! Miss Cather is one of the very few living novelists who make of their books works of art. Her style is worthy of her theme. It has the simplicity and naturalness of first rank work. Her language is in perfect harmony with her subject. It is perfectly harmonious without flourish or emphasis. It has no glitter or gaudiness. It is not "clever." She never seeks effects. Her writing is measured, quiet, beautiful and of a great restrained power. There is a grace and sweep in her prose which captures the reader's attention in the first paragraph and holds it to the last word.

Then, she is on the side of beauty and simplicity and against vulgarity and shoddiness. Moreover, she is not concerned with the construction of her novel in the conventional mould; she dispenses largely with plot. Her books contain no big scenes. Rather she is interested in great character and in significant events.

Archer Winsten, "A Defense of Willa Cather," *Bookman* (New York), 74 (March 1932), 634–40

With the publication of *Shadows on the Rock* by Willa Cather this novelist who has been singularly free from attack in the early and middle reaches of her career suddenly experiences the bite of critical disfavour. Although it is by no means unanimous, the instigators, including Newton Arvin, John Chamberlain, Horace Gregory, Granville Hicks, Louis Kronenberger and Dorothy Van Doren, constitute a group well above the ordinary run of reviewers. If, as I think, there is an answer to the assertions, both they and Miss Cather deserve it.

Miss Cather is granted, for the most part, some good work in the past. By one she is celebrated as the defender of the individual against the petty influences of society; by another as a master of form, one whose ability to write a distinguished novel should be taken for granted; and by a third as the author of the "most human and solid" American novel (*My Antonia*) of the past twenty years. These kind prefaces to complaint follow in beaten paths of critical and lay appreciation. Miss Cather has often been praised, and for a variety of qualities and achievements. She has been spokesman of the soil for

Nebraska; she has made articulate the Scandinavians, Germans and Bohemians of that country as well as the older American stock to which she belonged as a girl. For the late Stuart Sherman she was first and last expressing a sense of values. He demonstrated it in all her novels up to and including *The Professor's House*, which was her most recent when he wrote. A few years later, with *Death Comes for the Archbishop* before him, T. K. Whipple summed up Miss Cather as an extremely sane, capable and conscious artist. In those qualifications he suspected her of falling short of the very highest achievements. Her perfection came from pruning rather than from the white heat of an imagination that blazed an errorless way. Even so, he regarded her as an exemplar of the pure artist, possibly our best, and marvelled at the intelligence and will which had made so much out of her original gift. There has been little enough in the sources of these brief summaries to prepare us for the blast that followed her last book.

For she has become "a tired woman in a large city looking backward wistfully from an apartment house window to the past". Her novel is a logical step backward from its predecessor; it refuses to express a moral issue in terms of adult experience; it is comparable to the fairy-tale of Cinderella. From another point of view she is berated as a writer who "has never come to grips with the real life of her time," who "writes as if mass production and technological unemployment and cyclical depressions and the struggle between the classes did not exist." Her book is exquisite, it is consummately written, it is very delicate and very dull. When she wrote of Nebraska and its settlers she had a valid theme having to do with the development of America. It was not of our time, to be sure, but there were social problems for readers with that sort of thing on their minds. When the scene changes to Quebec and the social problem is merely the preservation of an old order, of a remembered feeling, rather than the struggle for a new one, the reviewer speaks of sterility.

Another gentleman sees Miss Cather's work as falling into three periods. There is the first, one of affirmation of life. Thea Kronborg, Alexandra Bergson and Antonia Shimerda carry that bright standard. Then comes the period in which life is frustrated, and Mrs. Forrester, Professor St. Peter, Claude Wheeler and Myra Henshawe show it. Finally we come to the point where life does not figure at all. Archbishop Latour, Father Joseph Vaillant, Euclide Auclair and Cécile prove that, and what was fondly taken to be Miss Cather's "noble vacation" from life in *Death Comes for the Archbishop* becomes almost complete unemployment with *Shadows on the Rock*.

No, it is not a novel at all. It is two-dimensional, like a fresco (cf. Miss Cather's own statement in connection with the Puvis de Chavannes frescoes where she speaks of writing "something without accent, with none of the artificial elements of composition"). It is splendid landscape painting. Miss Cather now "has abandoned herself to her softness." Frail and thin, her work. Shadows is the word; and the word was at hand, being on the jacket, the covers, and the title-page. "This makes it impossible for her to give any sort of valid interpretation to life; and as vision it never captures our imagination nor stirs our emotions; it is simply pretty."

These are the conclusions of our critics. If they have been rudely torn from context, at least the impression they make is not false, for the attack has been unusually violent. It is as though a tea-pot no one suspected of simmering suddenly blew its top off. And Miss Cather, obvi-

ously taken aback, said in her recently published letter that she had made an honest try and got pleasure out of it, if nobody else did.

It would be tedious business to try here to argue the merits of these criticisms individually, just as it would be useless, though personally satisfying, to dispute matters of taste. For instance, they are mistaken who make so much of Miss Cather's statements about the connection between childhood and art. One critic sees her as wholly successful only when she is remembering her childhood, and he recalls her use of Wagner's opinion in *The Song of the Lark*; another, seeking a reason for failure, takes her letter of Nov. 23, 1927 to *The Commonweal* and states that she says she *has* returned to childhood, when what she said was, "Writing this book . . . was *like* a happy vacation from life, a return to childhood, to early memories." In each case Miss Cather referred to the feeling, to the clearer, more vivid emotion, not the facts nor the narrow world of childhood. Not to recognize this is distortion of a dangerous sort because it departs from truth in the guise of quotation. As for questions of taste, one of our critics says "the book (*Shadows on the Rock*) is simply never real." My disagreement is tepid beside that of a Catholic writer who refers to the characters as "those living men and women, all quite real, moving and acting in time and space, yet shadows of eternity, at once symbols of and actors in the endless story of life everlasting." For a reason I shall take up later I do believe that taste, more than any other factor, has made such a wide divergence of opinion possible. I mean taste in the sense of the preconceived notions which form our likes and dislikes.

But let us turn to the source without further delay. The line of Miss Cather's development is in its general contours a clear one. Although she is not given to self-revelation, the few times she has spoken have been very much to the point. First, we have her reference to things she wrote while in college. She was trying to tell the story of some Scandinavian and Bohemian settlers she had known. She brands her "honest" attempts as "bald, clumsy and emotional." Doubtless they were; but the point of importance is that even then she was turning towards the subjects that had made their deep imprint on her emotions. Sarah Orne Jewett's subsequent advice was merely the confirmation of an earlier instinct. She was objective in her desire to take what she had seen and known, subjective in following the path marked by her own emotions. She was not successful on either count. The fault lay not in her material, not in her emotions, but in her method. It is not hard to believe that she felt it, for she turned to a master, Henry James, than whom no one was more full of method. That was her beginning as a conscious artist and she has never once gone back on it.

In fact, the first few years found her so preoccupied with artistry she could hardly break through to the fulness of her expression. She was not, as is so often asserted, treating material which was not her own, and she was mistaken, at least partly, when she said so in her 1922 preface to *Alexander's Bridge*. The collapse of Bartley Alexander in Boston was as much her material as were Mrs. Forrester's derelictions in Sweet Water, Nebraska. The difference in quality of those two books lay in the treatment, in a background limitation of Miss Cather which will be taken up in detail later, and in that invaluable something the significant artist adds out of his own spiritual resources.

An addition must be made to the Whipple interpretation of her as an artist. She was not merely the artist dealing with the land, the society, or a person. These things vary in her books; the other is never stinted. She is always the artist of the idea. She has expressed it through the mouth of Fred Ottenburg when he spoke of Thea Kronborg. The quotation is long but worth its length. "It's the idea, the basic idea, pulsing behind every bar she sings. She simplifies a character down to the musical idea it's built on, and makes everything conform to that. . . . Instead of inventing a lot of business and expedients to suggest character, she knows the thing at the root, and lets the musical pattern take care of her. The score pours her into all those lovely postures, makes the light and shadow go over her face, lifts and drops her." After making the obvious substitutions, it becomes clear that Fred in his cups was telling the truth about Miss Cather as much as about Thea.

That this connection is not fanciful is amply proven elsewhere. Her last two books have been notable examples of simplifying character to what seems to her its most significant aspect, of doing away with expedients and wholesale invention. And in her letters dealing with them she has made still more explicit her attempt. Is not there something about them reminiscent of musical tone-poems? Also, the preface to *Alexander's Bridge* mentions "the essential matter" of the story, which is "the basic idea" under another name. This, she asserts, is not arguable. The artist has seen it, felt it; it has come to him with an immediacy comparable to that of life itself. The only debatable point, for the artist, is one of presentation.

Bearing these things in mind, we can, perhaps, summarize them as follows: Miss Cather started with a deep feeling for her experiences. For expression she turned to the art of writing. The struggle with new forms tended to submerge her feeling. At the same time, she was moving forward to her conception of the "basic idea" as a unifying principle of whatever she might write. It was fully formed when she wrote *Alexander's Bridge*. Still there was something lacking, the depths and realities of her emotions. And so, she turned back to her original subjects which had always been associated with deep feeling. They had first call, so to speak, on her loyalty to the past. Later, having answered the call, she could extend the same loyalty to more distant, though not too distant, realms. She turned also from artifice to the art of simplicity. *O Pioneers!* was written, and the rest is the story of her gradual strengthening of the power of her art and of her choice of scene and "basic idea."

It is not necessary to spend much space on Miss Cather's art because there cannot be any question about it. True, from the time she turned away from artificiality in composition until the past few years, her novels showed a certain looseness of structure and unevenness of pace. But that certainly could not be said of her last two books. In them there is a marvellous fidelity to mood, and the structure is no less faithful to its purpose. They are the undeniable climax to Miss Cather's long search for mastery of her art. On their grander, more complex scale, they are as perfect as *A Lost Lady*. As for their not being novels, this is an especially poor time, in the midst of almost fantastic experiments in form, to draw the line at their comparatively mild departures. They are fiction, they create character, and they tell a story. To regard them simply as chronicles or inspired historical work is to miss the better part of what was put into them.

That brings us back to Miss Cather's "basic ideas." They are things known within her spiritual and imaginative existence. They have to do most often with values, with ways of living, with the peace, whatever it may be, that a man makes with his god before he dies. She gives them to us for all they may be worth, not with a hand that shatters what it offers. She does not hate or scorn the matter which obsesses her. Is not this just a little strange and original among serious writers today? Or is it, after all, that her calmness comes from having failed to grasp any sort of reality?

It comes down to this: are these things of no importance, are they divorced from reality now that we have big cities, "mass production," "technological unemployment", and critics in whom the knife must be turned twice in the wound before it is felt? In *Alexander's Bridge* we have a question of loyalties. Shall a man live out his fullest potentialities when to do so means the rejection of all that his life has been and the flouting of his established responsibilities to persons and to society? The answer is "No." Stuart Sherman said that later Miss Cather would have answered differently. At any rate, she did in *A Lost Lady*, although the book is less an answer than a presentation. In *O Pioneers!* and *My Antonia* we are given the full measure of a woman's strength, the lifelong heroism of daily living. The struggle of an artist towards expression is *The Song of the Lark*. *One of Ours* is the quest of a boy to find his own spirit. *The Professor's House* is the way a man learns to keep on living when he knows the best things are past. The price that life can and sometimes does exact from a too impetuous person, that is *My Mortal Enemy*. The establishment of one of the great systems of living and the agents of that establishment are *Death Comes for the Archbishop*. And *Shadows on the Rock* represents the endurance of a civilization which is dear to its possessors, the transplanting of a way of life to alien surroundings.

These have been very rough approximations of things so deeply imbedded in these books that they cannot be taken out whole. Even so, I cannot feel they are matters in any way affected by political, social, economic or philosophical considerations of today. I cannot see that their strength is vitiated by being set in the past or that they are made to seem better than they actually are by the use of a nostalgic atmosphere. Their source is life itself and if in them, life is somewhat simplified for the idea, Miss Cather's extraordinarily vivid sensuous imagery binds us again to the world of sight, sound and feeling that we know. She defined her work for us in writing of *Death Comes for the Archbishop* that it was "a conjunction of the general and the particular, like most works of the imagination." Again the "basic idea," again her art fleshing the general with experience, remembered or imagined. If that flesh be composed of significant minutiae, said to be a characteristic of feminine writing, so much the better for feminine writing when the concept still unifies the whole as in the best of Miss Cather's work.

We should not, on the other hand, overlook definite limitations which led, at times, to partial failure. In *One of Ours* the last part of the book fails, especially when contrasted with the first. If Miss Cather had been less magnificent in the beginning, her war scenes would not have suffered so much. They were adequate enough descriptions which might have been written by someone who had been there; someone, but not Miss Cather. She certainly would have brought back scenes less easily forgotten. And with that failure the mood broke down. It was recaptured at intervals behind the lines in old houses and among people with whom the author was familiar. The story might have been successful, it almost was. It was not supposed to be a war story in any strict sense.

It was Claude Wheeler's uncertain quest made successful through the accident of war. That quest was certainly Miss Cather's material, but the war got in the way, just as the artificial form, and the unfamiliar scene, too, detracted from *Alexander's Bridge*.

The idea can be thoroughly consistent with her usual preoccupations, but let her try to place it in surroundings with which she is not exceedingly intimate, and it suffers. She can know perfectly, but it is not enough. It was not enough that she knew so much about Professor St. Peter and his family and the college community; Tom Outland carried the book off to New Mexico, one of her beloved lands, and it never really came back. Her own emotional realization of the story seemed inhibited, and with the failure of her mood, she became just another intelligent writer. This dependence on certain scenes argues a limitation but not a fault. A similar narrowing of the possibilities can be traced in the choice of her chief characters. As one would expect, it goes back to her "basic ideas" which are always concerned with values and a way of life. She does not always confine herself to values which are entirely her own, and thereby she achieves some variety; but they must be associated closely enough to engender the lyric feeling which is one of the distinctions of her work. For the writing of each book she must run a difficult gauntlet. She is dedicated to the consideration of values; she is dependent upon the type of scene that moves her; the choice of a protagonist is limited by her values; and she must write so that a mood reinforces what she says.

From one point of view these are limitations. From another, they become the ground on which, the material with which, she rears her structure. The western plains, Santa Fe, and Quebec are used (she has to have them), but with an honest eye on their own reality. One test of her creativity as opposed to mere photography is that after her we see and feel more in those places. Her characters also are used, though never by tampering with their reality. They are chosen because they represent her idea, or possibly her idea occasionally flows out of them. But a character is never twisted to her purpose. The idea, the character, the scene—with how consummate an art the balance among these factors is achieved in her several faultless works. She is a great artist in her field, and that field is not small, though its boundaries may be clear.

It is my contention that *Shadows on the Rock* demonstrably falls into the direct line of Miss Cather's work and is by no means the least important. Had it no deeper merits, it could stand as *a tour de force* demonstrating the sustained magic of a mood, the perfect fitting of style to content, the choice of incident proper to mood, and the carrying strength of a quiet voice. For years Miss Cather has been working towards this unobtrusive art. There are levels of existence which cannot be touched by the dramatic and comparatively strident technique of both the conventional and unconventional novel as we know it. And in this novel we have one of those levels brought to a beautiful realization. Had there not been a paleness as of silver, a thin note of something so delicate and fine that it must be carefully guarded, the whole job would have fallen through. In *Death Comes for the Archbishop* Miss Cather, working with a more generous theme, did not bind herself to quite so subtle a task. And for that reason this book is her greatest triumph as an artist.

But she has not stopped with artistry, though certain of her critics did, and some of them did not get that far. As in her previous books, she had a solid foundation, a new change rung on her old and persistent theme of a way of living. This time it was a culture brought by a few Catholic-French families to Quebec. Had I not seen this point persistently ignored in the reviews, I should have thought it impossible to miss. Early in the book there is a description of Madame Auclair shortly before her death which says everything. "Then she would think fearfully of how much she was entrusting to that little shingled head; something so precious, so intangible; a feeling about life that had come down to her through so many centuries and that she had brought with her across the wastes of obliterating, brutal ocean. The sense of 'our way'—that was what she longed to leave with her daughter. She wanted to believe that when she herself was lying in this rude Canadian earth, life would go on almost unchanged in this room with its dear (and, to her, beautiful) objects; that the proprieties would be observed, all the little shades of feeling which make the common fine. The individuality, the character of M. Auclair's house, though it appeared to be made up of wood and cloth and a little silver, was really made of very fine moral qualities in two women, the mother's unswerving fidelity to certain traditions, and the daughter's to her mother's wish." There is the gist which the book develops in full. Those qualities, fidelity, loyalty, that feeling about life.

To say that these are copy-book maxims, the stuff for a fairy story, it absurd. They lie too close to a present-day reality; they are reinforced by the fact that Quebec is much more like a bit of France than any other part of Canada is like a section of England. Does it not seem strange to us, even unreal, that today, twenty miles out of Quebec there should be a famous shrine of great healing power and a small town slowly building a huge cathedral? How does it happen? It happens because there was a beginning made two or three hundred years ago of which *Shadows on the Rock* is the expression. How easy it is to imagine our sturdy critics faced with a flesh-and-blood Auclair or Cécile. "But this man is incredible," they exclaim. "This little girl is a paragon of virtue," and turning away together, snicker her out of existence.

I can understand how some people could find this book foreign to their beliefs and, taken personally, distasteful. But I should convict those who attacked Miss Cather's latest work in the way they did of a serious lack of imagination. Faced with a way of living that was strange, or insignificant, or obnoxious to them they failed to see their reactions as marking their own limitations. Instead, it was Miss Cather who was getting soft, whose characters lacked reality, whose book was simply pretty, but never moving. As a matter of fact, she has said that although she could admire, she could not wholly accept the feeling about life and human fate which was her subject. Acceptable or not, she did it justice. It seems to me that her imagination succeeded admirably where those of her critics failed. In extenuation it can be said that some of their failures were not ignoble. They too had ideas about a way of living; and what could be more natural than that Miss Cather's presentation and everything connected with it should suffer in the contrast? And what could be more annoying to one like myself whose emotional bias, as strong as that of the reviewers, was formed by what I consider the perfect art and moving theme of *Shadows on the Rock*.

Walter L. Meyers, "The Novel Dedicate," *Virginia Quarterly Review*, 8 (July 1932), 410–18

. . . I ("we" and "you" and "the reader" no longer seeming adequate) find Willa Cather's *Shadows on the Rock* . . . like Virginia Woolf's *The Waves*. It is high emprise. In both books there is an attempt to liberate the "breath and finer spirit" of what, from other hands, would have been a full-bodied novel. *The Waves* is the wraith of a fiction streaming up toward the unattainable; *Shadows on the Rock* seems to me a patient walk in the valleys with head bared, a waiting for unimaginable, silent rays of stellar energy. In this book, Willa Cather has indeed carried her "novel démeublé" to the point where it must be regarded as dedicated. *Death Comes for the Archbishop* was something of a lingering farewell to the world of varied fictional delights; *Shadows on the Rock* is almost a complete withdrawal from all the mechanic lures, an abnegation, an exercise of high spirituality like that of the religious devotees whom the author has sympathetically depicted.

I am relying here not merely upon impression but upon Willa Cather's abundantly declared and demonstrated sincerity and aspiration in her chosen art. From this viewpoint *Shadows on the Rock* appears rather less than great save as an aspiration. Yet that is much. One may well be but moderately stirred by the permanent artistic accomplishment in the book and yet glow with admiration of its method, of all that can underlie it, and of what might come to pass if it could be more frequently employed.

Possibly it is being applied more widely than we know. Some approach toward it may have denied publication to many a worthy and dull first novel. Perhaps it has tempted many a successful novelist, to be regretfully abandoned out of practical considerations. In truth, to employ it happily one should be a clear spirit indifferent to fame and an author assured of wide circulation for everything he produces.

Briefly, the method, in its most rigorous application, requires denial of nearly all the obvious strategems of either the conventional or unconventional novel. There must be no dramatic moments. Also that sense of some imminent change, physical or spiritual, affecting vitally people whom we wish well or ill, must be rejected or sternly minimized. There must be little of the progressive quality, the attempt to forward understanding of an intricate, many-sided theme or of complicated personality. In truth, there should be no easily phrased concept or impression of the life depicted. With like severity, all gusto in the treatment of any part or detail will be repressed. Characters will not be permitted to display themselves too engagingly. Descriptive bravura will be throttled down. There should be no conscious attempt to reveal the recondite quintessence of anything; even conventionalities of expression, figurations somewhat moribund, may be used if they come naturally and gratefully to the pen, as— "the mighty St. Lawrence, rolling northward toward the purple line of the Laurentian mountains, toward frowning Cap Tourmente which rose dark against the soft blue of the October sky." There will remain, then, as more obvious devices, merely a gentle reiteration of properly vague master purpose and, in each element of the novel, a mildly literary exactness of specification.

All this, I know, has a rather perverse air and reads like a plea for drabness, flaccidity, and laziness. It is offered, however, as an acknowledgment of restraint and perchance of fine technique in the selection and collocation of materials. I see dimly a possible and not fully recognized development of the art of fiction—details chosen not only with reference to the major purpose but with reference to their interfluence: in short, a subtle refinement upon such devices as contrast and upon dramatic intensification; and withal a dependence upon the readily discernible and commonly felt value of materials unheightened save by the most restrained of literary phrasing. Thus, if it were the description of a market day in Old Quebec, there would be no metaphysicizing, and no agonized search for the *mot juste*; but there would be the utmost care as to what images lingered in the reader's mind and what his mood when he approached the market place, and what the mental state in which he quitted it for the cathedral or the water front.

In this manner, a reader might be roused to that creative activity which we are finding more and more essential in living literature. He would not be flogged to it or shocked into it or vulgarly enticed. He would be offered familiar, easily manageable material upon which the author had done just enough work to indicate the possibilities, a fireside scene, perhaps; and straightway he might be given a characterization so sketched that the faculties stimulated by success with the fireside scene would gain values which the characterization would hardly yield if otherwise approached. Thus the reader might be made to come a progress without the aid of narrative or expository propulsion, and what might seem to one thumbing the novel casually a rather aimless and low-toned work, might prove upon careful reading quite the reverse and might end with a veritable climax in some such mild sentence as that with which Willa Cather concludes *Shadows on the Rock*: "While he was closing his shop and changing his coat to go up to his daughter's house, he thought over much that his visitor had told him, and he believed that he was indeed fortunate to spend his old age here where nothing changed; to watch his grandsons grow up in a country where the death of the King, the probable evils of a long regency, would never touch them."

But these references to *Shadows on the Rock* may seem to reverse my judgment upon it and to imply that it is a triumphant illustration of the technique I have outlined. I repeat that I do not think it is a triumph of execution; nor do I think it was written throughout in the manner I have designated. I do not know of any novel so written. I have been postulating. Doubtless *Shadows on the Rock* was composed merely with the determination to avoid all excess or strain and to produce only what gave pleasure to the author and seemed to her sanative and reassuring in a distracted world.

I hope, in truth, that Miss Cather put her faith in something above technique. At any rate, there is in writing of the sort she has recently done much that calls to mind Wordsworth's "wise passivity," his waiting, as Pater has phrased it, for "a power not altogether his own, or under his control, which comes and goes when it will" and endows him at moments "with a creative language which carries the reality of what it depicts directly to the consciousness."

Checklist of Additional Reviews

"Cather Pageant of Quebec in the Sixteen Hundreds," *Kansas City Star*, 1 August 1931, p. 14.

William Soskin, "Willa Cather's Poetic Tale of Olden Quebec," *New York Evening Post, The Literary Review*, 1 August 1931, p. 10.

Booklist, 28 (September 1931), 26.

The Roamer, *Baltimore Catholic Review*, 11 September 1931.

Pittsburgh Monthly Bulletin, 36 (October 1931), 68.

Wisconsin Library Bulletin, 27 (November 1931), 255.

Pratt Institute Free Library Quarterly Booklist, Autumn 1931, p. 36.

Margaret Ruth Taylor, *Epsilon Sigma Alpha Sorority News*, December 1931, p. 5.

William Lyon Phelps, "A Literary Mystery," *Delineator*, 120 (January 1932), 12, 59.

John O'London's Weekly, 26 (23 January 1932), 659.

J. B. Priestly, "Rousseau—and a Slapdash Biography," London *Evening Standard*, no. 33524 (28 January 1932), 9.

Ludwig Lewisohn, *Expression in America* (New York: Harper Brothers, 1932), 538–43.

OBSCURE DESTINIES

WILLA CATHER

OBSCURE DESTINIES

New York ALFRED·A·KNOPF *Mcmxxxii*

Margaret Cheney
Dawson, *New York
Herald Tribune Books*,
31 July 1932, p. 3

If the quality of Miss Cather's writing were of the kind that settles willingly within a definition, it would be possible always to respond flatly to her work with delight or coldness, appreciation or disapproval. But for all the analysis that has been expended to discover and describe the essence of her books there seems to be something so elusive about their character that not only do we fail to name it, we sometimes fail to know whether or not it is present.

About these new stories, for instance, it is hard to be sure. Reading over passages from the older books that deal with the Western scene, to which these stories all return, it seems to me that now something is lacking, some emanation which came from sentence no more complex or stylized than the clear, pleasant one in *Obscure Destinies*, some intensity of feeling which once raised characters rather like these to an importance the new portraits do not attain. Yet there is so much of the same cadence and the same temper that one hardly dares say "This is so."

Anton Rosicky, the Bohemian farmer, settled in the West, has a close kinship to Antonia and to many of the Cather pioneers whom one remembers with joy. Rosicky, proud and affectionate father of five good sons; Rosicky, with his "queer triangular-shaped eyes" full of a merry sweetness, doing with wisdom the thing that would brighten his son's fretful wife, ignoring misfortune to his cornfields, not out of stoicism but out of enjoyment of

life as a whole, telling the story of his boyhood's privations with wonder at his final escape—Rosicky is an appealing person. Old Mrs. Harris, too, in the second story, is touched with that special love which Miss Cather has for people who achieve character without arrogance. "Grandma" moves in an atmosphere more complicated by divers personalities than that of the Rosicky family, where a common respect for the land is dominant. Grandma came from Tennessee, following her daughter and her daughter's husband and her daughter's many children, perfectly content to abide by the tradition of her upbringing that every young matron should have an old woman somewhere in the background to take over the cares and duties of the household. In the West people did not understand her status. They pitied her and criticized Victoria for letting her work so hard. They could not believe Mrs. Harris wanted it so, and offered little kindnesses to her which irritated and humiliated her. Her belief in her function was incorruptible, and it was without any sense of self pity that she performed her tasks, working patiently, not humbly, for every member of the family until she died.

"Two Friends" is rather apart from the preceding stories, and although it is by far the shortest and least substantial, it has some claim to be called the best . . .

This last piece is even simpler than the others, yet seems to have more of an underpinning. The other two drop away from you; there is a quick spurt of emotional response to Rosicky and Grandma Harris and then it is all over. In the little picture of the two men who sat in big chairs outside the store of an evening looking down the powder-soft roads and talking or keeping quiet with mutual respect, there is something finer than sympathetic portraiture, something which makes you feel, as Miss Cather often does, that you have perceived one of the subtler implications of a commonplace fact. And again, as always, Miss Cather's sentences seem to bear themselves with an incomparable grace, and reading them is a pleasure it would be hard to spoil.

John Chamberlain, "The Return of Willa Cather," *New York Times Book Review*, 31 July 1932, p. 1

In these three long short stories—in the form, by the way, of the Henry James whom she once made her apprentice model—Willa Cather returns, quite literally, to the scenes of her childhood—to the Western country of *O Pioneers!* and that nostalgic poem of *April Twilights* written from a train window on the Burlington route. And it is better that Miss Cather should return—better for the tensile strength of her art, which had gone soft in *Shadows on the Rock*. Miss Cather, in her life-time, has had two sources which have fed her: a set of heroic youthful memories, and the remembrance of the artist's struggle in the America of before the World War. From the wellsprings of her childhood recollections have come the splendid figures of the Alexandra Bergson of *O Pioneers!* and of Antonia Shimerda, figures thrown, in a symbolic sense, against the setting sun of an older West. The motif of the artist's struggle has played through work as diverse as *The Song of the Lark*, *The Professor's House* and *A Lost Lady*—stories respectively of Thea Kronborg the singer, Professor St. Peter, an artist at evocation of the past, and Marian Forrester, who attempts to arrange her life in a pattern of personal triumph only to fail because her second-generation Nebraska environment makes success impossible. All of the stories, no matter from which of the two sources they may have sprung, have been paeans to the tenacious individual will struggling to "live out its potentialities," and only once, in the case of Professor St. Peter, giving up when incentive is gone. In *Shadows on the Rock*, however, there was no will; there was simple acceptance of a quiet French Catholic world miraculously and incredibly insulated in seventeenth century Quebec from a wilderness running 3,000 miles west to the Pacific and north to the Pole. The lack of any human galvanizer showed in the texture of the work, which might have been called, with little exaggeration, by a girl's book title of *Cecile of Old Quebec*.

But here, in at least two of the stories of *Obscure Destinies*, we have the Willa Cather of old. The first tale in the book is of "Neighbor Rosicky," a Bohemian who has gone West, to Nebraska, to escape the meanness of cities, where, if one is poor, one can only, in Rosicky's philosophy, "choose between bosses and strikers, and go wrong either way." The story of this old Bohemian, whose weak heart ultimately carries him off, is one of earth hunger, but it is not the hunger of a petty nature. Old Rosicky loves the soil, even with all its terrors of drought, parching winds and spreading thistles, because "in the country, if you had a mean neighbor, you could keep off his land and make him keep off yours ... [while] in the city, all the foulness and misery and brutality of your neighbors was part of your life." Forty years ago, long before Rosicky's time as a paterfamilias, this might have been news to the oppressed Middle Border farmer in Hamlin Garland's story of the human incidence of a brutal mortgage—the story called "Under the Lion's

Paw." It might even be news today to countrymen who have looked in vain to the Farm Board. But Rosicky is a Bohemian, with a "scarcity economy" tradition behind him which enables him to get more satisfaction and sustenance out of a given plot than his neighbors of New England Protestant derivation can get—even as the Czech and the Pole in Massachusetts and Connecticut today can gain a satisfactory living from land long deserted as sour by the Yankee stock. . . .

The second and longest story of *Obscure Destinies*, "Old Mrs. Harris," conveys far more than it seems to on first acquaintance. . . . What makes "Old Mrs. Harris" a genuine work of art is its subtle dissection of any American town in which "infinitely repellant particles" from all over the map have met and mingled and worked out a temporary adjustment. It is a more brooding *Main Street* in petto, marred somewhat by a didactic close. To judge from the tone of Miss Cather's prose the Colorado town in which the Templetons attempt to gain a footing is in the pre-radio stage of American culture, for the raucous note of the late 1920s is not to be found in Miss Cather's sentences.

The final piece of *Obscure Destinies*, "Two Friends," is not up to the standard set by "Neighbor Rosicky" and "Old Mrs. Harris." . . . She has mishandled material that, potentially, promised much. It promised much because Miss Cather is kin to her "J. H." and "R. E." in that she cannot abide the civilization of the "Yes-man," the constricted institutionalized world of today in either its Communist or potentially Fascist phases. Her own atomic and fundamentally escapist psychology should have enabled her to make a fine story as "Neighbor Rosicky" or "Old Mrs. Harris," which are very fine indeed.

Fanny Butcher, "Willa Cather Called Leading Woman Writer," *Chicago Daily Tribune*, 1 August 1932, p. 17

There is no doubt in the mind of this reader that Willa Cather is the greatest living woman novelist of the United States. She has won that distinction by an adherence to the canons of superlative writing aided by a genius which is as pure and natural as the fresh dew on a spear of grass in the early morning.

She has never once in her writing career compromised with the exigencies of time or fortune. If it took her three years to write a novel, sobeit three years were spent on it. If she might have made a small fortune on the serialization of another novel, that small fortune was looked upon as a heavy price to pay for the publication in an alien form of a work of art, and she refused.

She literally did deny herself a pile of gold by refusing to have *Shadows on the Rock* serialized, and the piles which she cast aside by not allowing (after one unsuccessful attempt) her novels or stories to be made into movies might pay the national debt of one of the Balkan states.

One thing of which any reader may be absolutely certain when he reads anything from the pen of Willa Cather is that what he is reading is something that the author had to write from some inner urge and that, in so far as it lies in human power to do so, Miss Cather has written exactly what she meant to write.

If, as in the case of *Death Comes for the Archbishop*, she has done a religious epic and the world asked for a novel, the world has received what Miss Cather chose to give it, not what it demanded. And if, as also in the case of *Shadows on the Rock*, she chose to do an ecstatic soul-picture of a period instead of a lifelike chromo of a time, and thus disappointed some of her readers again, as in the case of *Death Comes for the Archbishop*, she followed her own genius and gave to the literature of her language a masterpiece.

I call attention to Miss Cather's straight, arrowlike literary flight to her own goals because in *Obscure Destinies* it seems to me that the most marked joint characteristic of the three short stories which make up the volume is that she has chosen—as always—to say what she set out to say in her own way and not in any sense in the traditional way.

Of the three stories, one, "Two Friends," is unimportant in the sense that it neither adds to nor detracts from Miss Cather's position. It is the story of two middle aged pillars of a small town who quarreled over politics. It has the flavor of the period in it and there are two or three pages of superb writing at the beginning. But neither in the characters nor in the setting does Miss Cather surpass herself.

Of the other two stories one, "Neighbor Rosicky," has the same beauty of character and solemnity of peace that has made *My Antonia* one of the classics of American literature. If you do not know that simple tale of a Bohemian servant girl you do not know one of the great tales of literature.

The same quality is inherent in Rosicky, the same tenor of character and the same inspired recounting of his life in the prose of the author. It is the most unadorned of tales—of a Bohemian farmer, father of a family which admires as well as loves him, husband of a woman who is known throughout the countryside for her wholesome happiness, the story of a successful human being who has found life worth living despite hard times, de-

spite hunger, despite strange languages and strange lands. It is so simple a tale and so simply told that many will find it almost casual as they read it for the first time. But they will not forget Rosicky.

But of the three stories "Old Mrs. Harris" is the gem of the most brilliant, the most precious, beauty. It is in its few pages a commentary on all of life, on a whole culture. On the surface it is merely the brief story of three generations of women living in one crowded house; the grandmother, who is overworked, who carries her comb in her pocket because there is no other place to put it, and who finds compensation for any hardship in the love which her grandchildren bestow upon her; the mother, pretty, spoiled, who manages to keep her husband and her children gay through misfortune by a sheer lack of understanding that they might be anything but completely happy in the mere acts of devotion to her, and the granddaughter, who has a passionate urge to go to college, to be something other than her mother.

As sharply and as clearly as any three lives have ever been pictured for the reader those three lives live in Miss Cather's pages. Tragedy, irony, and the sheer unquestioned beauty of human devotion are all caught there.

There is nothing in *Obscure Destinies* to tarnish even the tip of one of Miss Cather's immortal golden laurel leaves, as there sometimes is in the volumes of short stories from the pens of novelists, and "Old Mrs. Harris" will add new and shining leaves to her crown.

414

Clifton Fadiman, "Misted Memories," *Nation*, 135 (3 August 1932), 107

Obscure Destinies is comprised of three long short stories of the pre-war West. "Neighbor Rosicky" is a simple, low-toned account of the life and death of a Bohemian farmer living on the Nebraska prairie. "Old Mrs. Harris," a character-study of three women, depicts as many generations in the life of a family transplanted from the old South to the new West. "Two Friends" draws a pastel portrait—which the Sherwood Anderson of *Horses and Men* might have signed—of a pair of late nineteenth-century small-town business men. Of these the first, conceived somewhat in the mood of *My Antonia* and *O Pioneers!*, is the most successful. Its idealized peasant types, as her readers know, dwell close to the heart of Willa Cather. Her warm sympathy and simplicity of outlook are exactly suited to such an idyll of quiet sentiment as "Neighbor Rosicky." The remaining two stories are less effective. "Old Mrs. Harris" should have been a short novel of the length, perhaps, of *A Lost Lady*. At any rate, it seems to require a more complicated, a fuller treatment than has been accorded it. The shortest of the trio of tales, "Two Friends," suffers from the opposite defect. It is little more than an anecdote of character into which Miss Cather has infused her beautifully misted memories of the old populist West, as she imagines it to have been before Sinclair Lewis made his way down Main Street. It is too slight for forty pages. On the whole, *Obscure Destinies* will please Miss Cather's admirers; and even those who are bewildered at the jacket blurb which ranks her with "the greatest of living authors" will note with satisfaction that for the moment the artificial, ivory-tower mood of *Shadows on the Rock* has been abandoned. These stories are drawn naturally and without manipulation from that same store of memories which produced those excellent books, *My Antonia* and *O Pioneers!* . . .

With these memories it would be discourteous to quarrel. Every adult is entitled to hold his childhood inviolate. But one should, I think, bearing in mind the natural kindliness of Miss Cather's temperament, swallow her West with at least a few ounces of citric acid. She prefers to remember kindly, patient, intelligent peasants like Rosicky; manly, generous, wholesome farm children like the young Rosicky; gentle, educated, beauty-loving couples like the none-too-credible Mr. and Mrs. Rosen (Miss Cather really should not bother with Jews; her Bohemian touch is surer); and picturesque, democratic, heart-of-gold business men like the two friends, Dillon and Trueman. All her characters dislike pushing, boosting, "progressive methods." The author conceives them as belonging to an era "when business was still a personal adventure." They are her pioneer West. But when one remembers what kind of "progressive methods" were actually used in the winning of the West, one wonders whether these people of Miss Cather's were not entirely eccentric to the period rather than representative of it, as she appears in all honesty to believe. Her West was not built up by the exercise of the nicer Christian virtues, but by blood and iron. The government troops, the railroaders, the packers, and the monopolists of the latter half of the nineteenth century were only by courtesy of Miss Cather's idealism engaged in "a personal adventure." The old West had its humble peasants, its kindly small-town bankers; but for the most part it was the joint creation of masters and slaves.

In the opening years of this century there flourished a now almost forgotten New England writer, Sarah Orne Jewett. While she was far from lavender-and-old-lace, she was hardly what one would call a realist, even for her time. Preferring always to stress their finer and more endearing qualities, she wrote poignant little tales about simple New England people. She was in her way a skilful and honest writer. When Willa Cather was a young girl, she knew and loved and was encouraged by Sarah Orne Jewett; and of recent years she has done much to rescue her from ill-deserved neglect. The two women as artists are much alike, though Miss Cather is far stronger, more full-blooded and more sophisticated. In both is a foundation of Christian idealism. Both possess a sweetness and a sympathy which are not quite fit for large themes or any very resolute confrontation of life. Both prefer humble and patient people as against "important" or masterful people. While never sticky, they are both what the book trade would call "wholesome." In years to come, I believe Miss Cather will be recognized as a greater Sarah Orne Jewett of the West. She strikes lovely notes, but they are minor. To her better books (and they are her earlier ones) one may turn for a very moving kind of country sentiment, but hardly for a large, true, realistic picture of the time.

Dorothea Lawrance Mann, "Willa Cather Returns to Her Beloved West," *Boston Evening Transcript*, 6 August 1932, p. 2

Something over a year ago in the Hudson Theater in New York J. B. Priestley, speaking of contemporary American writers, paid high tribute to the genius of Willa Cather, and instantly the whole great audience broke into tumultuous applause, offering as fine and spontaneous an ovation as has ever been given to a serious novelist in this country. That acclaim was important because it testified so surely to the fact that—no matter how pessimistic critics may seem at times—there does exist in this country a fine and discriminating audience ready and eager to appreciate the best work. Whenever we are prone to doubt the taste of American readers we have only to remember the secure place which Miss Cather holds. Not all her books are of the same quality, but it is certain that she has never pandered to popularity, never relaxed her standards, and at her best she has done as fine work as has ever been produced in this country.

This new book is a collection of three long short stories. All of them are stories of the West, the country Miss Cather knows best, and to which she oftenest returns. All of them are written with a deceptive simplicity. So it seems she might sit down beside you and tell of people whom she has known intimately and whose stories have interested her. Each is a narrative built, we feel sure, about real persons. They are definitely real to us, even though we might be told that they are creations of Miss Cather's imagination. Our first spontaneous interest is in these people as real people. We want to know their stories precisely as we want to know the stories of persons we have met and who have appealed to our interest. It is not until later that we reflect on such facts as that every one of these characters is a man or woman who has come to the West from some other country or from some other section of this country. In other words, this West of which she writes is still the West of the transition period. People are there because they have chosen to live there, not because they have been born there or because the tradition of their families exists in those places. As time passes there come to be in all communities generations who know no other homes, but all of these people of Miss Cather's belong to an earlier period.

Rosicky is a Bohemian exile who at the end of his days looks at the alfalfa field, seeing not only his own alfalfa crop, but a color familiar to him in the fields he knew in his childhood in Europe. Rosicky has come to Nebraska by slow stages. There has been London first of all, where he was excessively poor and always hungry and dirty; hungry because there was no money to buy food and dirty because when all water must be carried by pitcher up four flights of stairs to one room which is occupied by a whole family, and two lodgers as well, bathing is by no means an easy matter. After the misery of London, New York has for several years offered all the comfort and enjoyment which Rosicky could ask. He could earn money, eat well, live comfortably, hear good music frequently, and for a time it seemed all he should ask of existence. Then comes a day when Rosicky realizes that the growing discomfort in his mind comes from the fact that he is shut away in a city from the good earth which

should belong to man. Then it is that he finds courage to follow other Bohemians out to Nebraska and in the course of time own a farm and marry and bring up a fine family of children in an easy affluence far indeed from the experiences of his young manhood. On those rare occasions when any one of Rosicky's children knows discontent, the old man will remind them that no one who owns his land, has food to eat, room to live comfortably in, plenty of water and plenty of sunshine, has a right to complain.

Those readers who place *My Antonia* among the books which never grow old will find this story belonging to that same mood. It is like a welcome breath from that earlier period of Miss Cather's writing. It is impossible to read of the Rosickys without feeling warmly toward them. You know what Doctor Ed feels when he turns into the farmhouse for breakfast after a hard night. You know why it is worth driving eight miles over snowy roads for the welcome given him there. Nor is it the welcome alone, for there is such at breakfast as makes the reader hungry even to read about, while round the table is the whole Rosicky family, full of content and good feeling. Small wonder that it is hard for Doctor Ed to tell Anton Rosicky that he is a sick man. There are plenty of stories written about farming communities, but there is something different in the rich warm humanity of this tale of people who have put human values above getting on in the world, who love each other and love the particular piece of ground which belongs to them.

"Two Friends" Miss Cather tells in the first person, making it seem a reminiscence of her own childhood. It is the story of the two men who stand out in a small Western town because of their prosperity and because of the breath they bring with them of larger worlds known to them intimately but known to their fellow towns-people only by hearsay. They are American business men of the older West, of the days before big business took the romantic personal adventure out of the affair. One is a big cattleman, the other a banker. The two sit of evenings on the sidewalk in front of the bank and the child lingering near by is fascinated by their conversation, whether they talk of the outlying farming community which must borrow money from the banker, or whether they tell of the plays and the actors they have seen in St. Joseph and Chicago. In the other two stories in the book the end is the end of all human destinies. In this story the end is otherwise, for these two perfect friends finally quarrel, and quarrel strangely as it seems to us now, over that vital issue of the middle nineties—Bryan and free silver. Curiously it is the banker who has attended the famous Democratic convention at which Bryan made his speech about "crucifying mankind upon a cross of gold." It is the banker who has thrilled to the impassioned orator's arguments about the curse of gold, and it is he who organizes Bryan societies and drives through the farming districts securing votes for Bryan. It is the cattleman who refuses to be convinced, and who on a memorable day goes so far as to change his bank—an act symbolic of the utmost breaking of a friendship. To the listening child, it seems that these two great men each lose something when they are parted from each other. Neither is ever so impressive again. In this story there are reminiscences of the atmosphere of *A Lost Lady*.

The supreme story in the book is "Old Mrs. Harris," a story whose overtones and undertones are so poignant with tragic human meanings that it must stand among the best things Miss Cather has ever done. The setting of the story is a Colorado town in the sandhill country,

whither have come the Templeton family from Tennessee because "young Mr. Templeton"—who is still young Mr. Templeton though his daughter is old enough to enter college—has brought his family because he has the idea that Colorado is a better place to bring up children than Tennessee. Old Mrs. Harris has come along with the Templetons because she cannot imagine any life for herself that is not bound up with the life of her children and grandchildren. Back in Tennessee, old Mrs. Harris's fate had been like that of many other old women. The family had lived in her house and though she had taken charge of the house there as she takes charge in Colorado, the Templetons had been aristocracy in Tennessee and there had always been plenty of help on all occasions. The whole countryside was filled with women all too glad to be called to the Templetons to help out.

There, old Mrs. Harris had presided over a household of helpers. In Colorado everything is quite different, but still we find old Mrs. Harris determined to keep up the traditions of the family and only hurt because the middle western women who did their own housework believed that Victoria was ill-treating her mother. To old Mrs. Harris a household was not properly run unless there was an orderly parlor and a lady of the house always dressed and ready to entertain her friends in that parlor. In Tennessee, life had flowed in a certain mold. Young girls were spared hard work because as soon as they married, it was understood that their lives would be full enough with children. The young mothers must be spared in order that they might give themselves to their children. It was the way of life that the old women should take upon themselves the brunt of existence. So out in Colorado, it is Grandma Harris who sleeps in the dining room on a hard couch, who rises early and gets breakfast for the children and later takes another breakfast in for Victoria and young Mr. Templeton. It is Grandma who is at the beck and call of the whole family at all hours, but despite all this hard work there is never a moment when old Mrs. Harris would have Victoria resemble those women who are her neighbors.

The story is told both from the standpoint of Grandma Harris herself, and from the standpoint of her next-door neighbor, Mrs. Rosen, the well-to-do Jewish woman who loves children and old people and whose house is as different as possible from the bareness and disorder of the Templeton house. Mrs. Rosen pities Grandma Harris and does her best to rouse various members of the family to lighten her lot. Not till the end of the story are we permitted to realize how much the friendliness of Mrs. Rosen means to Grandma Harris even though her principles will not allow her to agree that Victoria or Vickie should help with her work. Almost every page of this story is fraught with hidden meanings. Bit by bit we discover them just as we find our way behind the dignified exterior of old Mrs. Harris, who has prayed unceasingly that she might never have a long sickness and never be a burden and who feels her own death approaching with only joy that it all seems destined to fall out just as she might have wished it, could it have been given her to plan her end. There is very skillful art in the way in which all these shades and implications are made clear to us till it seems that the whole philosophy of women is fitted into this one short story.

R[obert] M. C[oates], "The West of Willa Cather," *New Yorker*, 8 (6 August 1932), 46

In her new book, *Obscure Destinies*, Willa Cather has collected three stories of the West of plains and prairie—of Omaha, Colorado, and Kansas—and so, having made a long journey from the Mexican border up to Quebec, she returns to the scenes of her earlier writings. It must be said, I think, that the scenes themselves are not so vivid now as they once were: the landscapes against which the figures in these stories move are as if etched, not colored, but perhaps that is because Miss Cather's art has grown more subtle, more sparing of emphasis with the passage of years. To have seen too bright the garishness of the prairie in "Neighbour Rosicky," to have felt too intensely the heat of the sandy plains in "Old Mrs. Harris," might have marred for the reader the quiet precision of the stories themselves.

For the characters are always delicately, beautifully alive, and yet there is a kind of phantom quality about them, too. Mrs. Harris, slaving at kitchenwork so that her lovely daughter may remain cool and unflurried, dying as it were hastily to keep the volunteer nurses of the neighborhood from learning the poverty of the household; Anton Rosicky, the little Bohemian farmer, working blithly in his cornfields, dying too in his turn, but with a patriarchal contentment, knowing that his son has made a happy marriage—one sees them all, clear-moving and yet somehow remote. The stories are laid in a time some thirty or forty years ago, and a kind of nostalgic sadness hangs over them all: it is as if, before beginning to read each story, one had been forewarned that all the characters in it were long since dead.

Henry Seidel Canby, "This Is Humanism," *Saturday Review of Literature*, 9 (6 August 1932), 29

These "three new stories of the West" make the reviewer pause. Here is no bold experiment in a new type of fiction such as has characterized Miss Cather's novels, nor any new terrain studied closely for a texture of life refreshingly different from our own. This is the West of Miss Cather's early novels, a country where roads are ankle deep in summer dust, incredibly beautiful by moonlight, a country where the corn will burn up in a single torrid day, or it is the high sage brush plains of Colorado, familiar to us before. It is a country where many people are mean and commonplace, where there is little generosity of living; and into it her imagination plunges deep for recollections of great souls that make a contrast and a salvation.

"Great souls" sounds a rhetorical description of Miss Cather's unfaltering realism, but this, nevertheless, is what distinguishes these stories. They contain all the elements of that country of disillusion which the sociological novelists have made wearisomely familiar. In "Neighbour Rosicky," the work is hard, the family does not get on, the American town girl who marries the Bohunk's daughter longs for cheap amusements. In "Old Mrs. Harris" the little Colorado

town has every horror of prying neighbors and cheap convention. The family's pride is to keep up appearances, and the husband's easy shiftlessness, and the spoiled wife's selfish egotism, are only euphemisms for the exploitation of a poor old grandmother who believes that after forty the old should go to the kitchen and youth have its way. In "Two Friends" a dose of political claptrap breaks down a life-long friendship which was a symbol of the possible excellence of human values in a town where everything else was commonplace.

Yet, while it would be most misleading to say that Miss Cather views these dreary possibilities as an optimist might, a difference, but no such crude difference, distinguishes her work from the passionate drabness of the school which sees America only as a lost opportunity. She looks with keen eyes and unafraid, a little deeper. In "Neighbour Rosicky" she has drawn a full-length portrait of a good man, good in the sense which takes little account of principles but much of character and personality. It is so much harder to write of such a character, to make him live, to make you love him, without one concession to tricks of sentiment or appeal to conventional reactions. Rosicky, the ex-tailor's boy, happily at home at last on the land, would be to you just a Bohunk with a pleasant face. He is never anything else through the story, and yet a great soul is manifest. Grandma Harris is a pure essence of that stiff conventionality which holds itself fast in the respectable just above the level of the poor white. Beside the warm flexibility of temperament of her neighbor, the Jewish Mrs. Rosen, she is crystallized prejudice. The grandchildren that love her, and for whom she drudges without understanding the meaning of sacrifice, will be ruined, one feels, by just such ideas as she lives by, when their hearts, like the oldest's, grow harder. A bare difference of a degree of angle, a shift in the lens, and she would be a ridiculous old woman, killing herself to keep the house respectable, a stupid martyr to selfishness. The lens is not shifted. She remains a stupid old woman, a victim of selfish and futile respectability, but she is a great soul. Mrs. Rosen sees that.

And in the last story, "Two Friends," something still more difficult is attempted. Mr. Dillon and Mr. Trueman—the Irishman and the old American—are themselves characters of depth and color. Dillon with his imperious head on a small, wiry body, his musical, vibrating voice, and his air of superiority amounting to arrogance; Trueman who made you feel solidity, "an entire absence of anything mean or small, easy carelessness, courage, a high sense of honor"—these two men represented success and power in the community. But it was not their souls that were great, it was their friendship. As they sat in their chairs at night on the brick sidewalk it was a "strong, rich, outflowering silence between two friends, that was as full and satisfying as the moonlight. I was never to know its like again." And it was precisely that friendship which gave solidity and meaning to the little town which would have seemed so commonplace to others, which *was* commonplace, except for this node of influence.

It is remarkable how easily and surely, like all the really competent novelists, Miss Cather builds up these stories, without one trick, without one undue emphasis, with every signfcant detail, not sparing the human weaknesses, never flattering, never ignorant of cruelty, ugliness, disappointment, never afraid of humor, as of Trueman's rear that "looked a little like the walking elephant labelled 'G.O.P.' in *Puck*," nor of beauty, as of "the soft, dry summer roads in a farming

country, roads where the white dust falls back from the slow wagon-wheel." And this is perhaps why, in an unsentimental period, she can make great souls where others deal in stereotype, caricature, or studio photograph. The West is a little more human, and our imagination a little richer, for Grandma Harris and Neighbour Rosicky.

Majl Ewing, "Willa Cather Writes Three Pioneer Tales," *Times-Dispatch* (Richmond), 7 August 1932

Obscure Destinies is a group of three stories which mark a return both in setting and technique to Miss Cather's earlier work. The stories are set on the Western plains at the end of pioneer days when the land has yielded somewhat to man's ways and before the pioneers of various races and sectional cultures have begun to be integral parts of the community.

"Neighbor Rosicky," the first story, might well be a chapter from *My Antonia*. Old Anton Rosicky, after a starved boyhood on a Bohemian farm and years of labor in the sweat-shops of London and New York, had settled on the Nebraska prairie, reared his family, and found the happiness for which, for nearly forty years, he had been hungering. In this last winter of his life, after Doctor Ed tells him he has a bad heart and must put the heavy farm work aside, he gives us glimpses of the cruelty of life in cities and makes us feel his abiding satisfaction in the life of the soil. He feels that it is not hard even to die, to lie in the tall grass at the edge of the hay field where a man could look up at the complete arch of the sky over him, hear the wagons rattle by, and be among the friendly people he had known. I can only suggest to you the quiet beauty of "Neighbor Rosicky" in which the common places of life are illuminated for us by his gentle humor and rich understanding of what happiness consists.

"Old Mrs. Harris" has more in it than the story of a pretty selfish woman who allows her mother to become a drudge so that she can play lady in the parlor. Underlying the surface story is another more tragic one which we are not told but which we deeply feel. Old Mrs. Harris wore out her life for Victoria and her children. She gave up her comfortable, shaded farm home in Tennessee to follow this daughter and her ne'er-do-well husband to a raw community in the Colorado sand hill country. She did not regret having spoiled Victoria; she was so pretty, the sort of woman people would go on spoiling. She did not rebel at her lot, nor would she even voice her regret that they weren't back home.

But the town, like all new Western towns, was Democratic. Its people neither understood Victoria Templeton's ways nor liked her manner, and Mrs. Harris knew they felt sorry for her. None of this does Miss Cather tell us directly. We see it through kindhearted little Mrs. Rosen, who, being Jewish, wondered at the difference in the treatment of the old by this race and hers, but did not criticize. By little kindnesses and short visits she tried to make Mrs. Harris more comfortable. Mrs. Harris silently and gratefully accepted her friendship.

No one in the family but Mandy, the black girl, noticed the old woman's failing. Victoria, when she learned of it, was provoked that ma would be useless just when Victoria was going to have another baby. Still Mrs. Harris went slowly about the work. One morning Mandy found her uncounscious. The doctor was sent for and Mr. Templeton and inquisitive Mrs. Jackson came in to nurse. Mrs. Harris was put into Victoria's best night gown and made comfortable in Victoria's feather bed. But Mrs. Harris was out of it all, never knew that she was the center of so much attention.

I regret that Miss Cather did not conclude her story here, allowing us to draw our own conclusions. The paragraph of moralizing which concludes this distinguished chapter in our social history is obtrusive. We do not have to be told that Victoria and Vickie will grow to understand old Mrs. Harris as they become burdened with life. But this is petty criticism of a very fine study of character and the temperament of a new Western community of the nineties.

The third story, "Two Friends," is much shorter and less distinguished because of the motivation of the quarrel between the two big men of a Kansas river-valley town, but the atmosphere of the town and the vitality of those characters make this an inferior story only in comparison with its two distinguished companions.

Hazel Hawthorne, "Willa Cather's Homeland," *New Republic*, 71 (10 August 1932), 350

Willa Cather here returns to her earlier and happiest theme, the remembered West. And yet the quality of clear country daylight and prairie sweetness does not flood these three stories as in *My Antonia* and *A Lost Lady*. Some of the more recent novels have been historical narratives, which with a turn of the hand could have been excellent boys' books of the Henty type, since her source materials, the facts of true adventures, lie on the surface. Her work, to be sure, has the strong purity of bare rock, but sometimes one wishes for more, for the subtler interest of plant and branch and foliage.

The first of the stories, "Neighbour Rosicky," seems to be of the going on to his death of the husband of *My Antonia*. He is a Bohemian exile, who has suffered various experiences of cities—Cheapside, Vesey Street—and now finishes out his life on a prairie farm.

The story "Old Mrs. Harris" contains the detail of middle-class life which Ruth Suckow also knows and repeats so well. It is the best of the three, and less of a literary task than they, less an assuagement of the conscience of the writer become completely professional, who must contemplate with words as much as feeling, all she has seen and heard, until finally the words come along before the feeling has matured. . . .

"Two Friends" is frankly nostalgic. . . . Here in good measure is exhibited Willa Cather's deep feeling for dusty country. It is only when she is concerned to express this feeling that she makes the best use of her material.

D[onald] R. M[urphy], "Through the Haze of Years Cather Again Writes of Midlanders," *Des Moines Register* [21 August 1932]

Very probably it is impossible for a midlander to be an impartial judge of Willa Cather's novels. The three novelets in this new book seem to me as fine as anything she has done, but that may be because she is talking to me in my own language about my own people, the farmers and the small town dwellers of the middle-west.

This new book descends directly from *O Pioneers!*, *My Antonia*, and *A Lost Lady*.

"Neighbor Rosicky" leaves you with the same feeling *My Antonia* gave you. . . .

"Old Mrs. Harris" is the story of three women. Mrs. Harris herself was the grandmother of the Templeton family. They had all come from Tennessee. . . .

Mrs. Harris knew that it was the part of the older women to look after the household. Back home in Tennessee, it had been easier. There had been a big house, and plenty of help. But it couldn't be helped. That was the way things happened. So Mrs. Harris looked after the children—they were nice children and they loved her enough so she often forgot how tired her feet were.

Perhaps you can say more when you write about old people. They've been through it; they know, as much as anybody knows, what it's all about. . . .

"Two Friends" is a slighter story, the tale of a child remembering the two big men of the little town, a banker and a cattleman. . . .

The charm of the story is the charm of events recollected long afterward, soon hazily through a luminous veil of years.

Willa Cather remembers the giants of her childhood and makes us remember the great men of our little world in our day, great men whose memory is gone from the streets they once dominated, and who live only in the chance recollection of some small boy or girl who once long ago looked up at them in an awe that time has tempered to an occasional and mildly melancholy recollection.

Michael Williams, "Willa Cather," *Commonweal* 16 (31 August 1932), 433–4

It has always seemed to me that much of the critical discussion aroused by Willa Cather's fiction during the last few years has been a waste of interest, since it was a rather futile sort of controversy concerning the merits of her "historical" novels—*Death Comes for the Archbishop* and *Shadows on the Rock*—as contrasted with her stories of "modern" life, particularly the stories of Middle Western characters and conditions with which Miss Cather is thought to be, in the real sense of the words, most at home. The controversy was further confused, and needlessly complicated, by the fact that in her historical tales Miss Cather took up times, places and persons dominated by Catholicism, and thus necessarily dealt with influences absent (or apparently absent) from her modern stories. So successfully did she deal with these subjects that many of her

Catholic readers were more than inclined to believe that she herself must be at heart a child of the Faith, a member at least of the soul of the Church if not of the visible organization. How else—they thought—could she so truly understand the subtle power of supernatural things, and so wonderfully interpret and depict them? On the other hand, readers, and particularly reviewers, to whom supernatural influences and beliefs are at best picturesque or romantic features of a vanished era, or outmoded anachronisms when they appear today, while quite willing to recognize and at times even praise Miss Cather's art in rendering such things, were inclined to regret her preoccupation with them, and to wish that she would return to the world more native to her knowledge and her skill. They have had their wish fulfilled by her new book, containing three stories of the Middle West. Yet I think that in these tales, fully as much as in the books that dealt with the Archbishop of Sante Fe, or the French colonists of Quebec, Catholic readers will find a spiritual beauty quite consonant with the more explicit treatment of their religion to be found in the historical tales. Neither Catholic readers, or readers to whom Catholic themes are unrealities, need concern themselves with praising or deprecating Willa Cather's choice of subjects, or her mode of treating them, on grounds extraneous to her own intentions as an artist. For the great secret of Willa Cather's work is a simple one, yet remains, like many other simple truths, a mystery. It is the secret of creative art. She possesses in a degree that seems to me unique among all contemporary American writers two supremely important qualities of the creative writer: sympathetic imagination, and mastery of language.

The object of a fiction writer's imagination must, necessarily, be human beings. When such a gift is as powerful as in the case of Willa Cather, no Catholic who has a true understanding of the truth-finding power of an artist's understanding and sympathy should wonder at (although heartily they should be thankful for) Willa Cather's grasp of spiritual values. Of her almost magical power over words, nothing adequate could be said except by those possessing a similar gift—and the recipients of that particular gift are few and far between. Nevertheless, nearly all readers who can recognize and appreciate the evidences of that power when they come upon them, are well and sorrowfully aware how degraded, and vulgarized, and distorted, and cheapened, and battered, and enfeebled, has become the medium of words—as a result of their maltreatment by the purveyors of commercialized fiction and hasty journalism.

How marvelously Willa Cather has restored the virtue of words to serve in the conveyance of an artist's sense of the wonder, and pity, and beauty, and mystery of human life is most amply demonstrated in her latest book. If there is a bookcase in any literate household in which a copy of *Obscure Destinies* does not stand (but, well-worn, often taken down for use), then such a household is to be pitied, and should be immediately rescued from its poverty.

I do not intend to describe the three tales of *Obscure Destinies*. In a sense, it could not be done; any more than one could describe the content of a piece of Mozart, or of Wagner. This does not mean that the stories are at all obscure, even if the men and women they deal with are. Each story is quite plain and straightforward, full of details, but always significant details, telling about real persons, on a farm, or in a small town, amidst the immensity of the plains of the West; all of whom (so far as the main characters are concerned: Mr. Rosicky, the Bohemian farmer; old Mrs. Harris; and the two friends who at last quarrelled) die as the stories end. Only, they do not die. They live in this book, and will continue to do so as long as authentic literature possesses any power in America. For there can be no stinting of one's statement concerning Willa Cather's work. She is permanently great. If challenged to prove this, I could only point to the scene where Mandy, the Negro drudge, the bound girl, washes Grandma Harris's swollen feet. If that page does not belong to immortal literature, I know not where else to look for it. Yet, while that passage is particularly illuminated by the purest light of beauty, throughout the whole book that light glows and gleams, a living light, like candles on an altar in a shrine dedicated to human pity and love; and also like sunshine on a field of corn, or like the moonshine which transmuted the dust of the roadway where the child watched the two friends talk, and part at last, their friendship wrecked so unnecessarily, and die. Yet still they live—as Willa Cather's work will live.

"Three Stories of the West," *Christian Science Monitor*, 17 September 1932, p. 12

The three long short stories in Miss Willa Cather's *Obscure Destinies* are character studies. They show no attempt to diagram a plot. They simply tell of the last years of the chief characters. The first two stories—"Neighbor Rosicky" and "Old Mrs. Harris"—are records of unconscious heroism in dealing with two different problems of age: the remaining story, "Two Friends," tells of a lifelong friendship broken.

Of the three, "Old Mrs. Harris" strikes deepest and is most admirably executed. It is done tenderly, without sentimentality, but with a sharp realization of the code that governed the life of Grandma Harris.

. . . Old Anton Rosicky, with his gentle ways, his twinkling eyes, his nice broad curved back like the shell of an old turtle, is the natural product of the pen that wrote *My Antonia.*

"Two Friends" is entirely different. In it are two middle-aged men, prosperous and respected, who have long been friends and are separated by a political quarrel. The story verges on the commonplace and were it not for the wistful undercurrent supplied by the child who admired their friendship and grieved over "something delightful that was senselessly wasted," the story would hardly belong with the other two. "Neighbor Rosicky" is delightful. "Old Mrs. Harris" will find fit place in any collection of Willa Cather's best work.

Helen MacAfee, "The Library of the Quarter," *Yale Review*, New Series, 22 (Autumn 1932), vi, viii

---

A great deal of nonsense concerning "escape" and "escapists" applied to contemporary fiction has lately gone the rounds. There is only one escape from life—death. To leave the conduct of business affairs for religious exercises, to turn from politics to physics, or from talking to reading, is not to flee from the reality of the world but merely to move from one of its expressions to another. Miss Cather has been especially interested to inquire which of these expressions, for the people whom she depicts, make existence all the way up to death seem supportable or intelligible; which activities afford them sustaining pleasure, satisfaction, or comfort against its confusion or disasters. Sometimes she has sought to push the inquiry on a broad front, as in *Shadows on the Rock*, where she raised the question of what keeps a national culture, as well as an individual, going. I think she has been most successful when she has dealt, as in *Obscure Destinies*, with a small self-contained group.

The longest and best of the three pieces in the volume takes its place among novels rather than amplified short stories. Bearing properly the title of one character, "Old Mrs. Harris," who holds the key to the narrative, it nevertheless gives admission to several others, living through a variety of events and over a considerable period of time. It is a model of compactness and lucidity. In its hundred pages, never crowded, never hurried, there seems scarcely a line to take away. Equally, I think, there is nothing that need be added to them. The clear completeness of the story appears the more remarkable when one considers that it rests not on a big scene but entirely on homely details closely observed and objectively put forward. This is a method that has yielded some of our bulkiest and most redundant modern novels. One of Miss Cather's special gifts, here well illustrated, is the power of selecting just enough features or acts, and of sketching in just enough of the background, to give the whole an effect of the expansiveness of nature, and at the same time to communicate the sense of a creative impulse ruling the design.

Archer Winsten, *Bookman* (New York), 75 (October 1932), 648–9

These three stories are composed of nothing which is not familiar in Willa Cather's previous work. The Western scene, the small town, the people, the mood, the ambitions, and the problems are essentially the same. The similarity is so striking that one gathers an impression of paraphrase, although, of course, the plots differ from their predecessors. For instance, it is impossible to read far in "Neighbor Rosicky," the first story in the book, without being reminded intimately of Mr. Shimerda and his family in *My Antonia*. Similarly, Dillon and Trueman in "Two Friends" recall the business men who were friends of the Forresters in *A Lost Lady*. Both facts are noted with some pride on the publisher's jacket. Nor can the third tale, falling into no such obvious similarity, be said to strike a new note in a Cather story. The enlightened, helpful family next door (this time Jewish), the wrong-headed, unsuccessful Templetons pursuing a mode of living brought from a "feudal society" (the Old South) and suffering condemnation in the democratic West, the ambitious daughter, the self-sacrificing grandmother—all these are landmarks among many others along the well-used Catherian way.

Regarded simply as a story, "Neighbor Rosicky" stands forth as the best. At the end of it, the story is finished and becomes as "complete and beautiful" as Rosicky's life seemed to Doctor Ed. The contrast of country and city, damning the latter, has been achieved, and the sons will remain on the farm where, as their father thought, they belong because they are not "mean" types who would do well for themselves in cities. "Old Mrs. Harris" is less conclusive. The grandmother's death leaves too many questions unanswered, too many important characters moving on into a doubtful future. It is more like the first section of an unfinished novel which is too good to remain unpublished, but which would have been better if completed. Miss Cather's method, developed in her two "chronicle" novels, of "touching and passing on" is less effective in a long short story. Not that she has attempted that method here, but rather that its previous use may have led her to believe that such characters as Vickie and Victoria Templeton could be left hanging in mid-air. "Two Friends" is extremely slight. Take from it the beauty and feeling which Miss Cather is able to put into anything she writes, and there would be left only an unconvincing quarrel between old friends who suddenly found themselves disagreeing on Bryan and free silver. Unconvincing not because such things are impossible, but because the author seems to treat the quarrel so perfunctorily. She is more interested in the mood.

This book, then, is a demonstration that Miss Cather is capable of doing again, and just as well, what she has done before. It is difficult to tell how soon her work will lose its vigour and freshness if this course is pursued, but certainly she has nothing new to say on these matters. In several volumes she has preserved that period of the West, its deeds and its sense of values. If she wishes, and is able, to document it further, no one can deny her. But the task, though no one can do it as well as she, is a comparatively small one; our first raptures gone, they will return only when she begins discovering again.

Howard Mumford Jones, "Battalions of Women," *Virginia Quarterly Review*, 8 (October 1932), 591–2

On the principle of setting a thief to catch a thief, literary destiny has set our women novelists the task of delineating the monstrous regiment of women. In *The Sheltered Life* a female battalion clings about General Archbald, and his granddaughter, Jenny Blair, brought up by indirections to find directions out, is the occasion of the ultimate tragedy. Two of Miss Cather's three stories in *Obscure Destinies* turn upon analogous situations. In one ("Neighbour Rosicky") the good Rosicky, despite medical warning, dies as a result of working his son's fields in an effort to create happiness for a city-bred daughter-in-law, and in the other ("Old Mrs. Harris") Grandmother Harris sacrifices her existence to a daughter brought up a southern belle. There are other female figures in these books, but it is curious to observe the cruel precision with which two distinguished American women novelists delineate the damage women do.

Miss Cather's volume will not greatly increase her reputation. "Neighbour Rosicky," it is true, a return to the earlier manner of *My Antonia*, is a charming genre picture of immigrant Bohemian farm life, gentle and penetrating and beautiful. But "Old Mrs. Harris," the longest of the three tales, seems to betray labor, and though Mrs. Harris herself is a remarkable creation, the other personages are not well-rounded. Miss Cather seems to have had difficulty with Mrs. Rosen, the Jewess who serves to interpret the story, and whose conversation does not

ring true; and, what is more awkward, the story wavers between being a tale and being a short novel without quite satisfying the conditions of either genre. The third sketch, "Two Friends," is merely a slight essay.

Miss Glasgow's book, on the other hand, is rich and full, with those inimitable touches of wit and wisdom which only Miss Glasgow can give. . . .

C[lare] A[rmstrong], *Catholic World* 136 (November 1932), 246–7

Announcement of a new book by Willa Cather gives rise to pleasurable anticipation; one settles down to share Miss Cather's versatility, her deep, broad wisdom and her sympathetic understanding of human values. In the present volume this anticipation is fully realized. It consists of three long short-stories. "Neighbor Rosicky," the opening story, has the flavor of *My Antonia*. Here is a hero in homespun. . . .

The second story deals with grandmotherhood as a vocation, in telling the tale of "Old Mrs. Harris," who lived quite simply and entirely for others. . . . Miss Cather's portrait of Mrs. Harris is so fundamental and convincing that we do not need her final paragraph to realize the deathlessness of such a life.

In the last story, "Two Friends," we have a Remington-like canvas of a "little wooden town in a shallow Kansas river valley, long ago, before the invention of the motor-car." We get only a glimpse of this scene and these people, but it leaves a strong vivid impression. There is at once a sculptural quality and a poetry about these figures, and the tragedy of their interrupted friendship rouses in us, too, the feeling "of a truth that was accidentally distorted—one of the truths we want to keep." All in all then this pleasant volume, if it is not Miss Cather's best work, is nevertheless, honest, delightful, satisfying.

H. L. Denman, "People's Safety Valve," *San Francisco Chronicle*, 10 November 1932, p. 10

Editor *The Chronicle*—Sir: In a new story by the famous author, Willa Cather, occurs this passage:

> He spent the rest of his life among the golden hills of San Francisco. He moved into the Saint Francis Hotel when it was first built and had an office in a high building at the top of what is now Powell street . . . there . . . he used to sit . . . watching the bay and ferry boats across a line of wind-racked eucalyptus trees.

The golden hills, to my knowledge, stop outside our city limits. We have hills, all sorts, but not golden ones. Then that spelling of St. Francis—why, we hardly were able to recognize the hotel. And find a high office building at the top of Powell street, if you can. Also, why "what is Now Powell street?" What did it use to be? I have called it Powell street ever since I can recall, and so has everyone else. And last, but not least, how can anyone look toward the bay from Powell street, through a line of eucalyptus, when there are none in the vicinity nearer than, well, say Telegraph Hill, which perhaps figured somewhere in the impressions that the author evidently had concerning our city and its locations.

Times Literary Supplement (London), 1 December 1932, p. 920

Three short stories of the West is not a very generous allowance for a full-priced novel; but as the stories are by Miss Willa Cather there will be nothing scamped or hasty in their workmanship and every page will be well worth reading. *Obscure Destinies* reveals her sympathy with humble folk, farmers in Omaha, an old woman exiled from Tennessee and taking hardly to the cruder West, two unsophisticated business men in a small Kansas town who meet daily and take all their holidays together. These are important and lovable people to Miss Cather, who sees their foibles and their virtues and can envisage their whole lives from birth to death; and for the time being she succeeds in making them important and lovable to us. . . .

Miss Cather's ability to depict a whole community with clarity and distinction is evident in this tale of the emotions of one old woman and a young girl. It is through old Mrs. Harris that Vicky the second is enabled to go away to "get learning." There is more charm in this story than in the other two, and a pleasant warmth and glow in the picture of the Templeton family. The final tale tells of the friendship between two very ordinary men in a little town and how it was destroyed quite inadvertently but beyond any hope. Mr. Dillon and Mr. Trueman, the "Two Friends," are admirably handled, and if this tale has less colour and variety it does not lack humour.

Peter Quennell, "New Novels," *New Statesman and Nation* (London), 4 (3 December 1932), 694, 696

Obscure Destinies . . . is an uneven work. The first of the three short stories that compose it is sentimental in a not unpleasant manner, and left me with no very distinct impression. The second is a beautifully constructed tale. It describes the life and death of an old woman, who has followed a selfish daughter and her daughter's family from the southern states of America to a western town. Here she feels that her daughter is misunderstood. It is quite natural, according to Southern notions, that old women should make way for "the young folk," should work hard while their children sit in the sun; and the sympathy of a well-meaning Jewish neighbour is not only hurtful but also offensive.

But the third story is probably the finest. This is a sketch of two prosperous business men, whose evening amusement was to sit on the wooden side walk, cheek by jowl, with some spitting and tilting of chairs, and talk politics and watch the passers-by:

> The road, just in front of the side walk where I sat and played jacks, would be ankle-deep in dust, and seemed to drink up the moonlight like folds of velvet. It drank up sounds, too; muffled the waggon wheels and hoof beats; lay soft and meek like the last residuum of material things. . . . Nothing in the world, not snow mountains or blue seas, is so beautiful as the soft, dry summer roads in a farming country, roads where the white dust falls back from the slow waggon wheels.

The "Two Friends" quarrel about "free silver" and one realises that a memorable intimacy has come to grief.

Clifton Fadiman, "Willa Cather: The Past Recaptured," *Nation*, 135 (7 December 1932), 563–5

Dates tell us that Willa Cather is the contemporary of Dreiser, Anderson, and Lewis. She received her first official recognition in 1922 when the Pulitzer Prize was awarded to *One of Ours*. And it was about this time that the ascendancy of what is now the older generation of living novelists became a historical fact. Yet from this entire group Willa Cather has always stood somewhat apart. Their interests, their attitudes, were not hers. Her calm pulse did not throb in time with the hurried beat of the rebellious decade. The great post-war revolt against philistine values agitated her but mildly. The sex manifesto of Anderson and his followers apparently never reached her ears. In her thirteen books there is hardly a trace of the crusade against respectability waged by Mencken, Lewis, and Masters. Though deeply American in tradition and outlook, she has no report to make to us on the America of her time.

Let us commit no easy or ungenerous errors in the attempt to account for this. I am sure there is in her no conscious desire, stemming from fear or defeat, to evade the saliencies of her own period. Nor is Willa Cather, perhaps the least cynical of our important writers, impelled by any Cabellian disdain for the current scene. Yet it remains indisputable that—except in the case of *One of Ours*, to which we shall revert—she has detached herself from contemporary interests. Though she has stirred her readers' hearts, she has never changed their minds. And that is essentially what most of her compeers have done.

Frequently a writer's influence can be gauged by the rapidity with which his followers popularize his ideas and ingest them into their daily conduct. Thus the critical attitude of Lewis begot the Babbitt-baiter. The amusing snobbery of Cabell produced the college-boy aesthete and fantast. Today we find the Hemingway pose reflected in the monosyllabic conversation of young journalists, or perhaps even in the iron-visaged small fry of Mr. Steig's inimitable drawings. But there have been no Catherians. We have read and admired her, but drawn nothing from her to make part of our own conduct. Whatever her influence may have been, it has not been "educational."

To understand this detachment, and particularly to understand the reasons for its recent intensification, we must grasp the basis of her mental outlook. Though its roots lie in the Nebraska prairies, it is Vergilian in its grace, its aversion to confusion and violence, its piety, its ancestor-worship, its moral idealism, its gentle stoicism, its feeling for the past, and its sense, touching rather than tragic, of the tears which lie in mortal things. There are lines of hers whose grave, simple sentiment and purity of rhythm actually echo the cadences of the more reflective passages of the *Aeneid*.

For Ántonia and for me, this had been the road of Destiny; had taken us to those early accidents of fortune which predetermined for us all that we can ever be. Now I understood that the same road was to bring us together again. Whatever we had missed, we possessed together the precious, the incommunicable past.

These sentences were composed in 1917. At that date Willa Cather's mind was already formed.

Of all conceivable temperaments the Vergilian is perhaps the least suited to portray an epoch like ours, darkly colored with brutal struggle and mass disaster. Only once has Miss Cather attempted an interpretation of a living issue. We need not be surprised that it was foredoomed to failure. Several of her books, notably *The Professor's House* and *My Mortal Enemy*, merely miss their effect; only one is today quite intolerable. *One of Ours* is intolerable because, while its subject matter is large, its point of view is petty, or at best unsophisticated. This novel deals with two very serious things: the frustration of American youth and the war. To these tragic and many-rooted problems, calling for the sternest and most masculine analysis, Miss Cather brought a gentle Vergilian heart. She yearned over her silly, sulky boy, Claude Wheeler, striving to extract from the dull lead of his career the silver of tragic beauty. Today Claude merely annoys us; there is no other way of putting it.

The crucial test was Miss Cather's treatment of the war. She put her limitations on record in her eulogy of Claude: "He died believing his own country better than it is, and France better than any country can ever be. *And those were beautiful beliefs to die with.*" (Italics mine.) This note of regretful acceptance of an imperialistic carnage that left a mountain of bones on a hundred European battlefields implied in Miss Cather a simple inability to see her own time realistically. Even the Pulitzer Prize Committee must

431

have known this to be true. It awarded the annual prize to *One of Ours* as the novel which "best presents the wholesome atmosphere of American manners and manhood." Miss Cather, perhaps unconsciously realizing that her talents were not adapted to a convincing interpretation of contemporary life, abandoned the field. She has not since returned to it, for *The Professor's House* is only in fact, not in spirit, a post-war novel.

One of Ours may be viewed as the only book Willa Cather ever wrote in accordance with a literary fashion. This revolt-from-the-village novel has acquired prestige from the authority of her name, but actually it is no better than similar books by Floyd Dell, Duncan Aikman, and others even less memorable. It were best forgotten, for it is by far different work that its author will live.

To classify the novels of Willa Cather is to make clear her remoteness from the problems which engaged most of her contemporaries. First there are the novels dealing with the Western pioneers of foreign birth or ancestry, and with the generation which directly followed them. Her finest works (*O Pioneers!*, the first half of *The Song of the Lark*, *My Ántonia*, *A Lost Lady*, and *Obscure Destinies*) fall roughly into this class. Then there are those less successful novelettes, influenced by Edith Wharton and Henry James: *Alexander's Bridge*, some of the stories in *Youth and the Bright Medusa*, *The Professor's House*, and *My Mortal Enemy*. Possibly in reaction to the earthy simplicities of her Western novels, these treat isolated emotional conflicts in the lives of the well-bred. Finally, we come to the two recent novels—legends would be more correct—of outright withdrawal into a kind of dream history.

These three interests bound the field of her artistic activity. Reflect upon them and it becomes clear why, in satisfying them, Willa Cather has been led farther and farther away from contemporary life, deeper and deeper into the past. There is a way of treating the past so that it links with the present and illuminates our own lives. The novels of Evelyn Scott, for example, dynamic and forward-looking, have this power. Miss Cather's mind is basically static and retrospective, rich in images of fixed contours. Her evocation of the past can be beautiful and moving, and even at its most ethereal can transport us to a world of pleasant reverie. But few will affirm that it bears any relationship to our present-day conception of history.

One recalls at once Miss Cather's West, which she has made so wholly real that many have taken it to be wholly true. It is a West filtered through a very special and selective temperament. It is not false; it is merely partial. She decks her scene with a narrow range of good people—stoical, warm-hearted peasants, Christian souls like Alexandra and Ántonia and the mild, likable Ray Kennedy. Her business men are always gentlemen. Railroading is romantic—and it *was* romantic, no doubt, except that it was also other things. Although her finest book tells the story of a servant-girl, she prefers ordinarily to place her characters in comfortable middle-class surroundings. Thus *O Pioneers!* is not about pioneers at all, except for the first fifty (and best) pages. It deals with the second generation of prosperous farmers far removed from the sweat and toil and heartache which went into the conquest of the soil. In general, Willa Cather sees her West through a lovely haze, abstracting those qualities in people and even in landscape which lend themselves to her special idealistic bias.

Those who have studied the winning of the West in its less picturesque and Rooseveltian aspects may find little interest in Miss Cather's treatment. On the other hand, if one accepts her very special point of view, it cannot be denied that *The Song of the Lark* and *My Ántonia* are as moving today as when they were first published. No one has better commemorated the virtues of the Bohemian and Scandinavian immigrants whose enterprise and heroism won an empire. These books are safe for many years. Can one name another modern American novel whose emotional quality is so true, so warm, so human as that of *My Ántonia*?

Such books as these spring from their author's admiration for the quality of moral courage. But it is usually—and here too Miss Cather is at variance with her contemporaries—a moral courage acting in harmony with convention. It never takes up arms against the social order. The idealism which was so full and fruitful in *My Ántonia* shows its weaker side in a kind of reserve which of late has come perilously close to gentility. In part this may be due to Miss Cather's religious faith. Her allegiance limits the moral problems she may face and imposes upon her an attitude of submission. Catholicism lies quite openly at the heart of her last two novels. They are books from which the very idea of moral conflict is excluded. Not that there is any deliberate falsification of life in them—naturally, one does not expect moral struggle to enter very intimately into the lives of archbishops and fourteen-year-old girls—but they reveal a growing tendency to select from the great array of human emotions those which do not call up conflicts that are difficult to resolve. If this tendency is indulged, Miss Cather's remarkable and precious talents may end in a cul-de-sac; and we shall have to fortify ourselves against works of piety dressed up as novels.

It is perhaps in her treatment of the relationship between men and women that this emotional caution is most clearly revealed. When in 1915 *The Song of the Lark* was published, the Victorian compromise, at least in intellectual circles, had already broken down. But its hold, probably against the author's own will, was strong in this book, and has grown stronger in her later ones. When Miss Cather tries to project a vigorous male character she is hardly convincing. Fred Ottenburg is a case in point. By an overemphasis on his feats of eating and drinking and his general physical vitality, she tries to compensate for her inability to present him as a complete male. The love relationship between Fred and Thea is faded and unreal, though the opposite effect is intended. To tell the truth, the unspoken, non-sexual, half-unconscious love between Thea and Dr. Archie is, in comparison, warmly and vividly portrayed. Relationships of this order, loves from which the body is barred, are common in Miss Cather's writings: Jim Burden and Ántonia, Dr. Archie and Thea, Captain and Mrs. Forrester, Mrs. Forrester and Neil come readily to mind.

In *The Song of the Lark*, Harsanyi, referring to Thea, says: "Her secret? It is every artist's secret . . . passion. It is an open secret, and perfectly safe. Like heroism, it is inimitable in cheap materials." Miss Cather's conception of passion is broad. It includes passion for one's work, one's children, one's friends, one's land, one's memories, and for beautiful objects and experiences. But it does not extend, except formally, to sex. There is something very oblique, sparse, overdelicate about her infrequent treatments of even the slightest sexual irregularity. This is not so true of her early work— *O Pioneers!* for example—but it has become increasingly evident. Her most recent stories are constructed so that such matters will not naturally intrude. The love affair in *Shadows on the Rock* has no more substance to it than a fairy-tale romance. Though Miss Cather cannot be accused of prudery, there is unquestionably in her a strong vein of puritan reticence. In a book like *My Ántonia* this may be transformed into an artistic virtue. But it can also too easily degenerate, as *Shadows on the Rock* shows, into mere sweetness and twilight.

The characteristic quality of Willa Cather's mind, however, is not its puritanism or its idealism, but something deeper in which these are rooted. She is preeminently an artist dominated by her sense of the past, seeking constantly, through widely differing symbolisms, to recapture her childhood and youth. A sort of reverence for her own early years goes hand in hand with her Vergilian ancestor-worship; and out of this has flowered her finest work. *My Ántonia* is one long gesture of remembrance. The most remarkable parts of *The Song of the Lark* describe Thea's childhood, especially her friendships with Spanish Johnny and Ray Kennedy. Once Thea reaches Chicago, she becomes the heroine of a novel. The more she triumphs as a mature artist, the less interesting she becomes as a personality. Only at the very end, when she returns to her childhood home to sing in church, the book suddenly breaks once more into beauty and reality. *A Lost Lady*, too, owes much of its quiet emotional power to this same Vergilian quality of reminiscence. All her books are filled with throwbacks of the memory. Give one of her characters half a chance and he will begin to recall his youth. Pierre Charron in *Shadows on the Rock* says: "You see, there are all those early memories; one cannot get another set; one has but those."

Although this preoccupation with the past bore fruit in two beautiful and significant novels, it has also been responsible for Miss Cather's continuous diminution of vitality since *A Lost Lady*. For while it is the fountain of her inspiration, it may also function as a chain limiting her freedom of movement. The greatest novelists, such as Proust, draw simultaneously from both worlds, that of the remembered past and that of the fully realized present. The purely retrospective artist is faced with a simple difficulty—his material begins to lack significance unless it is constantly renewed by contact and comparison with the life about him. Soon he may find himself telling the same story over and over again. This Miss Cather has not done, though she has frequently repeated characters. But once she had fully exploited her early Western recollections, there were only two courses open. She could go forward into the present—or she could retreat even farther, call history to her aid, break contact with contemporary minds, and evoke rather than create. She has taken the latter path, one hopes not irrevocably.

Somewhere Miss Cather speaks of "the world of the mind, which for most of us is the only world." It is a perilous phrase. That world of the mind can be a small or large one, depending upon the depth and frequency of its meetings with other minds. It may be a closed world or an open world. Of recent years Willa Cather has been pensively drawing the shades and fastening the shutters. It is quite true that her prose, considered solely as an instrument, has gained in precision and a certain minor poetry of phrase; but it has lost, many feel, some of the fresh morning vigor and warmth of her earlier work. In sheer power of invention the last two novels are inferior to her earlier ones. They have fewer characters, no changes of scene, no richness. *The Song of the Lark* is too long, but one has an admiring sense that it could easily have been longer, that the author had all she could do to keep a rein on her imaginative faculty. But in *Death Comes for the Archbishop* and

434

Shadows on the Rock there is something precious, over-calculated. The effects are somehow parsimonious. Life is gently set in a sanctuary and viewed through a stained-glass window. They are, indeed, hardly novels at all, as we understand the word, but reworked legends, acceptable additions to the lives of the saints.

No one may dictate an artist's subject matter or his point of view. His own feeling for what is vital and important, his own sensitiveness to the forces which move his fellow human beings will point the road for him. There is a very real danger that Miss Cather may, quite simply, lose contact with life. Her hypertrophied sense of the past may permanently transport her to regions where minor works of art may be created, but major ones never. And this is a sad thing to contemplate, for the author of *My Ántonia* and *The Song of the Lark* was not a minor writer, but a major one. These books will remain classic in our literature and stir the imagination of Americans when her archbishops and her shadows have long vanished from memory.

L. A. G. Strong, *Spectator* (London), 149 (9 December 1932), 844

Miss Cather possesses a union of qualities denied to most of her contemporaries; simplicity, a philosophy based on spiritual values, and a serene control of her medium. In her last novel these were somewhat discounted by an exceedingly slow-moving story, and it is good to be able to chronicle that in the three Western stories here presented here she is once more at her best. The first chronicles the

life and death of a Czech tailor who has become a farmer, married, and reared a large family.

"It was as if Rosicky had a special gift for loving people, something that was like an ear for music or an eye for colour. It was quiet, unobtrusive; it was merely there."

"Neighbor Rosicky" is suffused with beauty, pity, and goodness of heart. Miss Cather handles with perfect tact a story which other hands could easily have sentimentalized. The other two are, if anything, even better. Her work is a quiet and steadfast music in a noisy age.

T[homas] M[oult], *Guardian* (Manchester), 16 December 1932, p. 7

Miss Willa Cather's new book contains three long stories, and at the end of each we encounter death. But if the sensitive reader allows this fact to turn him from them he will do so at his peril, for there have been few lovelier contributions to the art of fiction in recent years, few nobler tributes to the essential goodness of human life—and if we were challenged to name one lovelier or nobler it might easily be an earlier novel by Miss Cather herself. With flying colours she passes the test by which writers of fiction stand or fall, so far as their quality as artists is concerned—that of portraying the world's quieter people, the humble men and women of uneventful lives. After all, brutality and sensationalism are for the coarse brush. The delicacy and tenderness of the story entitled "Neighbour Rosicky" are perfect. . . . The picture is like music in its complete harmony. And when the old man dies the end is like music fading. The principal figure in the second story is a feminine counterpart of Rosicky, the ancient Mrs. Harris, a grandmother who is loving, kind, unobtrusive even as he. The remaining story, "Two Friends," is more rugged in theme, although just as exquisitely written. It tells of two commonplace business men who quarrel over politics, in spite of their mutual affection, and never meet again. From the technical standpoint the best impression left by this book is of a complete avoidance of overemphasis, a complete absence of so-called fine writing.

Helen Moran,
"Fiction—II," *London Mercury*, 17, no. 159 (January 1933), 272

After an eclipse, during which her books were at best pastels, Miss Willa Cather has emerged with three long short stories, written with the clear strength of *My Antonia* and *A Lost Lady*. They are unfortunately described as stories of the "West." Maps should be supplied with all American books published in foreign countries. The "West" is too wide and varied a territory; too vague a term. These stories have nothing to do with cowboys, or the search for gold in the films or the hills of California. Miss Cather creates people, not types. These are homely, quiet people who seem so real that when old Rosicky dies one feels a pang of regret because now it is too late ever to know him, forgetting for the moment that he is a character in a book. Even old Mrs. Harris, in the story of that name, an unlovely, unappealing old woman, finally wins our sympathetic admiration. . . .

Granville Hicks,
"The Case against Willa Cather," *English Journal*, 22 (November 1933), 703–10

In her first representative book, *O Pioneers!*, published in 1913, Miss Cather clearly indicated the subsequent development of her career. After experiments, some fortunate and some not, in the short story, and after the failure of *Alexander's Bridge*, her one book that betrays the influence of Henry James, she found her distinctive field of literary activity and her characteristic tone. *O Pioneers!* contains all the elements that, in varying proportions, were to enter into her later novels.

We observe first of all that the very basis of *O Pioneers!* is a mystical conception of the frontier. At the turning point of Alexandra's career, when, after an examination of the river farms, she decides to remain on the high land, she looks at the Divide with love and yearning: "It seemed beautiful to her, rich and strong and glorious. Her eyes drank in the breadth of it, until her tears blinded her. Then the Genius of the Divide, the great, free spirit which breathes across it, must have bent lower than it ever bent to a human will before." This exultation sustains Alexandra throughout the book, and at the end she says, "The land belongs to the future. . . . We come and go, but the land is always here. And the people who love it and understand it are the people who own it—for a little while." Miss Cather's final comment is, "Fortunate country, that is one day to receive hearts like Alexandra's into its bosom, to give them out again in the yellow wheat, in the rustling corn, in the shining eyes of youth!"

But, though Alexandra speaks of the future, her mind is fixed on the past, on the days of the Bergson family's struggle, before ease had corrupted her brothers. Miss Cather, too, is concerned with that past era, and she looks back at it with nostalgia. "Optima ides . . . prima fugit" might as well be the motto of *O Pioneers!* as of *My Ántonia*. Alexandra retains to the end the spiritual qualities of the pioneer, but the novel depicts the general disappearance of those virtues after the coming of prosperity. The coarsening of Lou and Oscar Bergson and the confusions of Frank Shabata and Emil are the fruits of change. Carl Linstrum, who has lived in cities and learned to hate them, looks with apprehension at the new developments. He tells Alexandra,

> This is all very splendid in its way, but there was something about this country when it was a wild old beast that has haunted me all these years. Now, when I come back to all this milk and honey, I feel like the old German song, "Wo bist du, wo bist du, mein geliebtest Land?"

Even in little things *O Pioneers!* is prophetic. We find, for example, in her depiction of Amédée's funeral service, the same fondness for the colorful ceremonies of the Catholic church that dictated so many passages in *Death Comes for the Archbishop* and *Shadows on the Rock*. We find, also, in her scorn for the agrarian radicalism of Lou Bergson and Frank Shabata, the political conservatism that is implicit in all her works. And we find the episodic method, the reliance on unity of tone rather than firmness of structure, that is so marked in the later novels.

The two successors of *O Pioneers!*— *The Song of the Lark* and *My Ántonia*— closely resemble it, especially in the qualities we have noted. Both depend upon a mystical conception of the frontier, and both look back longingly to the heroism of earlier days. The more successful portions of *The Song of the Lark* are those portraying Thea's girlhood in Colorado and her visit to the cliff-dwellings. Both of these sections are developed at greater length than the part they play in Thea's life warrants, as if Miss Cather could not resist the temptation to expand upon her favorite theme. *My Ántonia* is exclusively concerned with the frontier, and the heroine retains the pioneer virtues in poverty and hardship, even as Alexandria and Thea do in success. All three women are triumphant products of the pioneering era; in them the mystical essence of a heroic age, now unfortunately passing, is embodied.

But if these three novels were merely mystical and nostalgic we should have less to say about them. After all, Miss Cather saw at first hand the Nebraska of the eighties and nineties, and her accounts of the life there are not without authenticity. However much she emphasizes the heroism and piety of the pioneers, she does not neglect the hardships and sacrifices. And heroism and piety did play their part in the conquest of the frontier. Miss Cather's proportions may be false; she may ignore motives, conditions, and forces that are altogether relevant; but there is nevertheless a basis in reality for the picture she gives.

That is why *O Pioneers!* and *My Ántonia* have their importance in American literature. Although the story of *My Ántonia* is told by Jim Burden, with his concern for "the precious, the incommunicable past," the book does create credible pioneers in the Burdens and Shimerdas and does give convincing details of their life. In the latter part of the book there is a passage in which several daughters of immigrants tell of their

437

homes in the first years in Nebraska, and we realize that Miss Cather can appreciate the bleakness and cruelty of this land for the travelers from across the sea. She can understand their eagerness to escape to the towns, and she knows, too, the monotony and narrowness of the prairie city.

Against this background Miss Cather presents the unforgettable picture of Ántonia, more human than Alexandra because of her weaknesses, more likeable because of her defeats. Though the reader never doubts that Ántonia is exceptional, though he realizes how much bitterness and tragedy the frontier brought to many of its daughters, he accepts Jim Burden's account of her:

> She was a battered woman now, not a lovely girl; but she still had that something which fires the imagination, could still stop one's breath for a moment by a look or gesture that somehow revealed the meaning in common things. She had only to stand in the orchard, to put her hand on a little crab tree and look up at the apples, to make you feel the goodness of planting and tending and harvesting at last. All the strong things of her heart came out in her body, that had been so tireless in serving generous emotions. It was no wonder that her sons stood tall and straight. She was a rich mine of life, like the founders of early races.

From the first, it is clear, the one theme that seemed to Miss Cather worth writing about was heroic idealism, the joyous struggle against nature sustained by a confidence in the ultimate beneficence of that nature against which it fought. In her own childhood she had actually seen such heroic idealism in the lives of Nebraskan pioneers, and in writing of those lives she achieved not only personal satisfaction but also fundamental truth. One may feel that she deals with the unusual rather than the representative, and that what she omits is more important than what she includes. One may be conscious that the haze of regretful retrospection distorts innumerable details. But one cannot deny that here is a beautiful and, as far as it goes, faithful re-creation of certain elements in the pioneering experience.

But after *My Ántonia* was written there came a crisis in Miss Cather's career as an artist. She obviously could not go on, painting again and again the Nebraska she had once known. The West was changing, as she had been forced to admit in *O Pioneers!* and the others. Could she learn to depict the new West as she had depicted the old? The story of this new West could scarcely take the form of a simple, poetic idyll. Heroism and romance, if they existed, had changed their appearance. Characters could no longer be isolated from the social movements that were shaping the destiny of the nation and of the world. She would have to recognize that the life she loved was disappearing. Could she become the chronicler of the life that was taking its place?

At first she tried. The earlier chapters of *One of Ours* describe a sensitive Nebraskan boy in the years before the war. Claude Wheeler, who as a youth flinches before the coarseness and materialism of his father, suffers almost as much from the narrow religiosity of his wife. The joy and beauty that are so prominent in the lives of Alexandra and Ántonia have vanished from Claude's Nebraska. Though he seems capable of a heroic idealism, his life is miserable and futile. Then the war comes, and he enlists, goes forth to battle in heroic mood, and dies a hero's death. Thus Miss Cather, thanks to a romantic and naive conception of the war, was able to approximate her favorite theme. But the second part bears no relation to the issues raised in the account of Claude's unhappiness in Nebraska. For Miss Cather, as for Claude, the war provides an escape from apparently insoluble problems.

Insoluble indeed, Miss Cather found these problems, and as she looked at the life about her, her despair grew. Once she had created symbols of triumph in Alexandra, Thea, and Ántonia, but now she concerned herself with symbols of defeat. Of all the books between *My Ántonia* and *Death Comes for the Archbishop*, *A Lost Lady* is the most moving. Why Marian Forrester is lost Miss Cather never explains, contenting herself with a delicate and pathetic record of that descent. Captain Forrester has in him the stuff of the pioneers, but his wife, though one feels in her capacities for heroism, is the product of changed times, and she abandons her standards, betrays her friends, and encourages mediocrity and grossness. She is the symbol of the corruption that had overtaken the age.

But *A Lost Lady* is merely a character study, and Miss Cather felt the need for a more comprehensive record of the phenomena of decay. St. Peter in *The Professor's House* is alienated from his wife and family; he has finished the work that has been absorbing him; he realizes that he must learn to live "without delight, without joy, without passionate griefs." That, Miss Cather seemed to feel at the moment, was what we all must learn. Heroism and beauty and joy had gone. For St. Peter these qualities had been summed up in Tom Outland, dead when the story opens, and perhaps fortunately dead: "St. Peter sometimes wondered what would have happened to him, once the trap of worldly success had been sprung on him." But Tom lives in St. Peter's memory, and his story occupies much of the book. Tom is the pioneer, vital, determined, joyful, sensitive to beauty. In telling his story Miss Cather escapes from her gloom and writes with the vigor and tenderness of her earlier work. But in the end the animation of the Outland narrative only serves to accentuate her melancholy, and she is left, like Professor St. Peter, in a drab and meaningless world.

The university, his new house, his old house, everything around him, seemed insupportable, as the boat on which he is imprisoned seems to a sea-sick man. Yes, it was possible that the little world, on its voyage among all the stars, might become like that: a boat on which one could travel no longer.

Her despair increased, and Miss Cather made one more study of defeat, in *My Mortal Enemy*. But obviously she could not continue with these novels of frustration and hopelessness. One may risk the guess that, while she was writing her studies of despair, she personally was not particularly unhappy. Her reputation and income were both established on a reasonably high level. As a person she could be as contented as anyone else who enjoyed comfort and security, and as indifferent to the woes of the world. But as a writer she had that world as a subject, and the contemplation of it filled her with sadness and regret. It was not a world in which her imagination could be at ease, for her imagination still demanded the heroic idealism of the frontier. She could deal with that world only by portraying, in a few tragic lives, the corruption and defeat of what she held dear. She could not understand why evil had triumphed or how good might be made to prevail. All she could express was her conviction that something of inestimable value had been lost. She could only repeat, "Wo bist do, wo bist du, mein geliebtest Land?"

Miss Cather has never once tried to see contemporary life as it is; she sees only that it lacks what the past, at least in her idealization of it, had. Thus she has been barred from the task that has occupied most of the world's great artists, the expression of what is central and fundamental in her own age. It was easy for her, therefore, to make the transition from *My Mortal Enemy* to *Death Comes for the Archbishop*. If she could not write as she chose about her own time, she could find a period that gave her what she wanted. The beauty and heroism that she had found in pioneer Nebraska and that seemed so difficult to find in modern life could certainly be attributed to life in mid-nineteenth century New Mexico. And thence she could turn, in *Shadows on the Rock*, to Quebec about 1700. Once more she could show men and women who were neither awed by the savageness of nature nor unappreciative of its beauty. Once more she could deal with "the bright incidents, slight, perhaps, but precious," that are to be found whenever "an adventurer carries his gods with him into a remote and savage country."

Death Comes for the Archbishop, which describes the life of two Catholic missionaries in the Southwest, is highly episodic, and the episodes are so chosen as to make the most of the colorfulness of the country, the heroism of the characters, and the contrast between the crudeness of the frontier and the religious and cultural refinement of the archbishop. As one reads, one seems to be looking at various scenes in a tapestry, rich in material and artful in design. At first one is charmed, but soon questions arise. One asks what unity there is in these various episodes, and one can find none except in Miss

Cather's sense that here, in the meeting of old and new, is a process of rare beauty. What significance, one goes on to inquire, has this beauty for us? Does it touch our lives? Is this really the past out of which the present sprang? Did these men and women ever live? Is there anything in their lives to enable us better to understand our own? We ask these questions, and as we try to answer them we realize that we are confronted by the romantic spirit. Miss Cather, we see, has simply projected her own desires into the past: her longing for heroism, her admiration for natural beauty, her desire—intensified by pre-occupation with doubt and despair—for the security of an unquestioned faith.

What is true of *Death Comes for the Archbishop* is also true of *Shadows on the Rock*. Miss Cather has again created her ideal frontier and peopled it with figments of her imagination. The construction is even weaker, the events even more trivial, the style even more elegiac, the characters even less credible. The book has a certain sort of charm, for Miss Cather's dreams have beauty and are not without nobility, and it has brought consolation to many readers who share her unwillingness to face the harshness of our world. But for the reader who is not seeking an opiate *Shadows on the Rock* has little to offer. Compare Cécile with Alexandra and Ántonia; compare Pierre Charron with Tom Outland. What Miss Cather chiefly tries to do is to throw over her Quebec the golden haze of romance, and she succeeds so well that her characters are, to the reader's vision, obscured and distorted almost beyond recognition.

Apparently it makes little difference what Miss Cather now attempts to do. The three stories in *Obscure Destinies* are more or less reminiscent of her earlier work, but the honesty and enthusiasm have disappeared. As if she were conscious of some lack, she finds it necessary to rely on direct statements. In "Neighbour Rosicky" she underlines the harshness and rapacity of the city and exaggerates the security of the country, and she introduces Doctor Ed to point the moral of the tale: "Rosicky's life seemed to him complete and beautiful." "Old Mrs. Harris" is so lacking in unity that its point has to be explained in the closing paragraph: "When they are old, they will come closer and closer to Grandma Harris. They will think a great deal about her, and remember things they never noticed; and their lot will be more or less like hers." "Two Friends," concerned with two "successful, large-minded men who had made their way in the world when business was still a personal adventure," teaches that politics is much less important than friendship. Twenty years ago Miss Cather had no need of exposition, for her themes were implicit in her material, but now her romantic dreams involve the distortion of life, and she cannot permit the material to speak for itself.

The case against Willa Cather is, quite simply, that she made the wrong choice. The nostalgic, romantic elements so apparent in her recent work were present in her earlier novels, but they were at least partly justified by the nature of her themes, and they could be introduced without the sacrifice of honesty. But once she had to abandon the material her Nebraskan childhood had so fortunately given her, she had to make her choice. She tried, it is true, to study the life that had developed out of the life of the frontier, but she took essentially marginal examples of modern life, symbolic of her own distaste rather than representative of significant tendencies. And when time had shown how certainly that path would lead to impotence and ultimately to silence, she frankly abandoned her efforts and

surrendered to the longing for the safe and romantic past.

Willa Cather is by no means the only contemporary author who has fallen into supine romanticism because of a refusal to examine life as it is. One thinks, for example, of Elizabeth Maddox Roberts, whose first novel, *The Time of Man*, was worthy of comparison with *My Ántonia*. It is easy to understand why many writers turn from our industrial civilization. On the one hand, they cannot accept the cruelty and rapacity that are so integral a part of it and its inevitable destruction of institutions and ways of life they cherish. On the other hand, they are so much bound up in it that they cannot throw themselves, as the revolutionary writers have done, into the movement to destroy and rebuild it. Flight is the only alternative. But flight is and always has been destructive of the artistic virtues, which are rooted in integrity. If, to the qualities Miss Cather displayed in *O Pioneers!* and *My Ántonia*, had been added the robustness of a Dreiser or the persistence of an Anderson, not only survival but growth would have been possible. But the sheltered life seldom nurtures such qualities. She has preferred the calm security of her dreams, and she has paid the price.

Checklist of Additional Reviews

Open Shelf (Cleveland), July 1932, p. 16.
Time, 20 (8 August 1932), 31.
Edward Weeks, "The Atlantic Bookshelf," *Atlantic Monthly*, 150 (September 1932), 16.
Booklist, 29 (September 1932), 17.

Pratt Institute Free Library Quarterly Booklist, Autumn 1932, p. 40.

Pittsburgh Monthly Bulletin, 37 (October 1932), 59.

"Three Books Picked for the Prix Femina," *New York Times*, 18 May 1932, p. 19.

Frank Kendon, "The New Books at a Glance," *John O'London's Weekly*, 28 (3 December 1932).

"Miss Cather Wins French Book Prize," *New York Times*, 13 February 1933, p. 15.

LUCY GAYHEART

BY

WILLA CATHER

LucyGayheart

ALFRED A. KNOPF *New York* 1935

The Times Literary Supplement (London), 25 July 1935, p. 476

In her new novel, *Lucy Gayheart*, Miss Willa Cather seems to be writing the lightest and slightest of records of a short life: the obscure life of a young girl in an American village who goes to Chicago to study music, falls in love with a middle-aged singer, knows a brief moment of deep content and then the pain of a separation that is final—but the impression left on the reader is not slight. This is not a story of blighted love or damaging passion, any more than it is a village chronicle with "characters" scattered through it like plums in a boiled pudding. Haverford and its quiet continuous life are presented in glimpses, merely as the background against which Lucy Gayheart's enchanting figure stands out, but in the end we know the town and the river and the houses and gardens and the people that matter to Lucy. The unity of Miss Cather's design, the clarity and distinction of this book should put it beside her first great success, *My Antonia*. Lucy, in her fashion, is as lovely and as tragic as Juliet, and the lasting impression she makes—not that they know it until long afterwards—upon those who knew her well or casually is conveyed with the full measure of Miss Cather's art.

The German watchmaker who sells and plays musical instruments as well, the plump, half-jealous, half-maternal elder girl, Lucy's father and sister, Lucy herself, remembered as "a slight figure always in motion; dancing or skating, or walking swiftly with intense direction, like a bird flying home," are extremely alive in their shabby house with its fruitless orchard.

Harry Gordon, the rich young man of the town who loves and tries to master Lucy, believes the sudden lie she tells him and becomes indirectly responsible for her death, is by no means a stock figure; and his knowledge that he has pronounced his own life-sentence because of his brutal vanity is as moving as Lucy's vain efforts to insist on an explanation. It is a subtle story of motives and accidents, infinitesimal in themselves but carrying lasting consequences. There is no emphasis on love or death or the terrifying premonition of disaster and coldness, but one recognizes the experience of a life-time, a sure knowledge of young passion and old grief in this simply related tale. Lucy Gayheart, beautifully expressed by her name, stands poised like youth itself on a hill, flying yet fixed in the mind.

K[enneth] C. K[aufman], "Truncated Destiny," *Christian Science Monitor*, 31 July 1935, p. 12

Willa Cather's latest book, *Lucy Gayheart*, is a definite return to her first love— the prairie small town on the edge of the great West; its protagonist the daughter of an immigrant, German this time—but scarcely a return to the affirmative mood of *My Antonia*, *The Song of the Lark*, or even of *O Pioneers!* For although Lucy Gayheart faces the world from her small-town environment with somewhat the same glorious courage and capacity for living as Thea, and with a similar talent (she is a pianist), her ill-advised love affair turns out disastrously. The object of her infatuation is a concert singer, much older than Lucy, whom Miss Cather makes impressive as a great artist, but not especially convincing or admirable as a person; the affair scarcely passes the platonic, is not much more than a case of school girl hero-worship.

Artistically, no doubt, Miss Cather is justified in her refreshing reticence—often remarked upon—in the treatment of themes into which most of the writers of her particular generation have rushed gleefully and rashly; certainly she aligns herself thereby on the side of the angels. And she may be justified artistically in removing the singer from Lucy's life by an accident so abrupt, so outside of the picture that it smacks of the *coup de theatre*. Not, however, before Lucy, in a pique, has helped Harry Gordon, her childhood, home-town sweetheart, to put the worst possible construction on the situation, and allowed him to contract a loveless marriage. . . .

But she is not justified artistically, and it does not seem that she plays fair with her heroine, in cutting short her career within less than a year by a very similar accident. And especially just as she was at the point of recovering from her shock, of being saved by her art for a happy and useful life. Lucy's love affair is real enough, but it is not important enough; it should, by all the canons of experience, have faded into a fragrant memory; whereas Miss Cather attempts to develop it into a major tragedy. And it is simply not the stuff of which tragedy is made. Lucy should have the right to work out her own destiny; instead, her story merely stops. It is not tragic, it is only pathetic. This second part of the book is altogether too brief, too episodic; in compensation a third part, a sort of epilogue, shows us Harry Gordon, twenty-five years after, remembering Lucy with poignant regret, as a glorious symbol, a silent influence remolding his life. Such a splendid, vital,

talented creature deserves better than to survive only as a symbol, an influence.

For the rest, the book shows Miss Cather's usual excellences. It deals again with the past, the scenes of her girlhood. It portrays the frontier town in a sort of nostalgic glow; it is real enough, but certain of its uglinesses are omitted. There is no touch with the present. The minor characters are clearly and effectively drawn. Lucy's father, gentlemanly, inefficient, neglecting his business for his music; her unlovely, hard-working, managing sister; her fusty Chicago music teacher; the great singer's valet; Harry Gordon, who under his mask and in spite of his mistakes, is a man: all these give a more effective impression of reality than Lucy. And the prose is the same serene, beautifully cadenced instrument.

One does not get the impression that the hand of the potter shook, but only that it grew weary, and rounded off the work in haste, instead of drawing it out to its full, graceful and gracious outline.

William Plomer, *Spectator* (London), 155 (2 August 1935), 200

Lucy Gayheart is carefully and plainly written, there is nothing in it that could offend anybody, and some people may find it charming, but like many a novel it seems to me hopelessly ill-adapted to the tastes of any fairly alert contemporary reader. One is not asking for a "Marxist ideology," but a certain perspective, a certain critical attitude, irony, a sense of the fantastic. Imagine a film of Chicago in 1901—the big hats and busts and frilly, bell-shaped skirts; the moustaches, collars, and Norfolk jackets; the strange vehicles and furniture; the remote, spasmodic, and self-important behaviour. Miss Cather writes of that place and time, but gives us no sense of the period at all, a sense very highly developed in M. de Montherlant, and one which might, I think, be shown to make for the durability of fiction.

Dorothea Lawrance Mann, "The Supreme Art of Willa Cather," *Boston Evening Transcript*, 3 August 1935, book section, p. 3

The quality which sets Willa Cather apart from almost every man and woman writing today is that she is supremely an artist. She is so truly an artist that she has reached the point where she is free. In her work we discover not one art alone, but the unity of the arts. It would be easy to describe this novel in the terms of pictorial art—its lights and shade, its masses, its line, its pattern, the harmony of the whole. Miss Cather is so great an artist that she has created her own way of writing. We can imagine quite easily that her work would be recognized even if it were issued without her name. It is one of the most hopeful signs of the growth of taste in America that Willa Cather's work is appreciated so widely. A few winters ago J. B. Priestley spoke in a theater in New York concerning American writers of the present day, and when he referred to the supreme art of Willa Cather, the audience, which had listened with interest to his evaluation of others writers, burst into a storm of applause which seemed to shake the house—a spontaneous ovation to a truly great novelist.

Lucy Gayheart is in the authentic Cather tradition. It is part of what Miss Cather has sometimes referred to as her "own material." Lucy comes from one of these small mid-Western towns Miss Cather herself no doubt knew, and knew at about the same period she describes Lucy as living there. Lucy goes to Chicago to study music, not with any very lofty ambition at first. She expects to learn more about music than her town can teach her, and then perhaps to come back and teach the children of the town. Lucy has no initial scorn of the town or her old friends. She does not fight against its restrictions. It is probable that she does not realize in the beginning that it has restrictions. The awakening of Lucy to wider horizons, to greater potentialities in life, is perfectly natural and simple. Lucy is at heart an artist and here again she is Miss Cather's own material for Miss Cather has frequently described for us the growth of an artist. Once aroused, it is equally natural that Lucy should see only one future—to live out all her potentialities. Lucy is too young through the whole story to differentiate entirely between what part of those potentialities are music alone and what part is bound up with Clement Sebastian, who opens her eyes and ears and heart to a larger world than any of which she had dreamed.

It is interesting to observe the way in which Lucy is portrayed to us. There is little emphasis on Lucy's features. We realize her almost entirely through motion. The people of the town remember how Lucy walked. It was generally considered a long way out to the Gayhearts' but Lucy covered the distance a dozen times a day and never seemed tired. In Chicago Sebastian discovers that it makes him happy and starts his day well to see Lucy's way of walking, and so he forms the habit of watching her walk through the cold air toward his studio. When Lucy returns home after the tragedy she still walks swiftly but the old lady who had been fond of her reflects that before this Lucy had always walked as though she were hurrying toward something delightful while now she walks as though she were hurrying to escape from something.

Lucy's love has a delicate, wistful, almost unworldly quality about it. It is natural to ask what part is music and what part Sebastian. Sebastian himself with his artistic perceptions, his knowledge of the world, seems to understand her very truly, and he is very gentle and very understanding with her. Those months of association in Chicago when she plays his accompaniments are a large mass of light. There are moments when she had presentiments of sadness, but they scarcely touch the clear light of the whole. Even the passage with Harry Gordon scarcely troubles Lucy at the time. It is only those older, Auerbach and Sebastian, who can guess that Harry really means something to the girl. At the moment she can throw aside without regret anything out of keeping with her mood of the moment. Then the shadow falls swiftly, irrevocably, the dark and light serving to emphasize each other. Still we feel that there is a pattern in the book. Lucy is too strong, too true an artist, not to learn by suffering. Not that Miss Cather moralizes about it. That is never her way. She merely shows us that music and life are not over to Lucy. Bit by bit she is coming to an understanding of herself, to a knowledge that nothing she has lived through has been without its purpose.

Fanny Butcher, "Willa Cather Writes Idyll of Spiritual Love," *Chicago Daily Tribune*, 3 August 1935, p. 11

Apparently there is something lucky for me about Willa Cather's books. The last one, *Shadows on the Rock*, I read on a heavenly lonely voyage back from Europe. Her newest one I read on a heavenly and far from lonely voyage to Quebec. It is really on account of *Shadows on the Rock* that we are on our way now to Quebec. It made me know that some day I must see Quebec . . . must approach it just as it was approached in that lovely record, from the sea.

And just so I shall see it for the first time, looming from the great river that loves the sea so deeply that it carries its salt savor for five hundred miles inland with it.

And how more appropriately could one approach Quebec than with *Lucy Gayheart*? Not that she ever approached it. Chicago was her city of dreams. From the soil of Nebraska to Chicago and back to the soil of Nebraska she made her beautiful and tragic way. Truly gay at heart, the gayety of youth essenced in her smile, the toss of her head, the eagerness in her eye, Lucy came to Chicago in 1902 to study music. She heard a great singer in concert and left the hall uplifted. By chance she became his practice accompanist and such love and passionate happiness in the relationship which grew up between them is rarely chronicled in a book, as it is rarely existent in life.

Sebastian, disillusioned as he neared 50, saddened in love and in life, had a renascence of all of the things that make life worth the living in Lucy's love. Something delicate, fragile, and yet incomparably powerful joined their spirits. In the technical sense of the word they were never lovers. In the spiritual sense they were immortal ones.

The idyll of Lucy and Sebastian is one of the few real ones in modern literature. But it is not as an idyll that *Lucy Gayheart* will be read, loved, and remembered, but as a statement that the loveliest things are those which die . . . and also as a statement that it is not what one does about life so much as what one thinks that is indelible.

For the last third of the book is concerned with twenty-five years in the life of Harry Gordon, who had walked away from Lucy in the Auditorium hotel in 1902 because he believed her to be the mistress of Sebastian, and who had walked straight into a marriage which had given him material but not spiritual comfort. But for him Lucy Gayheart might not have died and, although he never admitted it to any one, for twenty-five years his life had been fundamentally influenced by that fact. The subtle power which Lucy exerted over him was not lessened by time, never would be until he, too, died the reader knows.

There probably will be criticism of Miss Cather's technique in *Lucy Gayheart*. It is composed of three books, the first of which is concerned with Lucy in her natural and unawakened youthful joy, the second with her romance and its tragic ending and her listless and futile struggle to find something to tie to in life, her discovery that life, not Sebastian, was destined to be her lover, and the sharp cutting off forever of that destiny. The third book is concerned with the deathless power which the dead Lucy exerted on Harry Gordon, who had loved her.

It is a daring technique, but, as Miss Cather said to me when I saw her a few weeks ago, "I see no reason why one cannot write a novel as a composer writes a symphony," and that is almost exactly the form of *Lucy Gayheart*.

I find Miss Cather's technical experimentations highly stimulating. Oddly enough, although she always has written books which are so characteristically her own as to be recognizably Willa Cather whatever her theme or technique, she has done more actual experimentation in technique than most of the so-called experimentalists.

That she writes a beautiful and classic prose does not mean at all that she uses always the classical novel form. She has taken the technique of music before for her model, notably in *The Professor's House*. Even in *Shadows on the Rock*, for it is such sheer ecstasy of prose as to be like a lovely, pure, clear melody. *My Mortal Enemy* is a tense contrapuntal exercise so deft that it is startling. *A Lost Lady*, an aria echoed, re-echoed, worked over in overtones.

Lucy Gayheart is, like all of Willa Cather's books, written with distinction and beauty. In my opinion Miss Cather will be remembered in that mythical hundred years as the outstanding woman novelist of her generation.

Cyril Connolly, *New Statesman and Nation* (London), 10 (3 August 1935), p. 11

The more titles that head a reviewer's column, the less merit will be found in the books. Here is a holiday eleven with a very long tail. I am going on a holiday myself, and it is typical of the cocytus of English fiction that it is almost impossible to fish out of it even a couple of books to read on the train. There is a real paucity of good trash. My advice to anyone going on a holiday is to get detective stories. That is where some of our best brains go. When I reviewed novels in the late twenties there was still an aesthetic interest in the process, Gide, Forster, Huxley, Hemingway, Wyndham Lewis, Garnett, Thomas Mann, James Joyce, Virginia Woolf—these wrote novels one could write a whole page about. At present reviewing novels is like living in some decaying idiorrhythmic community in Crete or Mount Athos. When one of the brothers is gathered, there is no novice to take his place, when one of the luscious cobwebby bottles is empty there is no one to press the new wine. Willa Cather, however, is a real link with the past; she has always interested me as the unique American writer to owe nothing to Europe; like Whitman and the early Mark Twain, she has realised the great truth that indigenous American literature must be non-European, must be Middle West. Of course American literature need not all be indigenous; wholly American writers like Hemingway and Fitzgerald are steeped in European influences and European manners and are not jeopardised by the fact. But there are always people who believe that a writer must remain saturated in the primal regional element, and to them Willa Cather must be the great argument against expatriation. The apostle of what Henry James called "The thin, empty, lonely American beauty."

And yet, I think, to some extent its victim, for her talent does not seem to have really ripened; the lush summers and enormous winters of Michigan and Wisconsin have not enriched her to the extent she has enriched them. A Lost Lady and My Mortal Enemy are early American masterpieces, like Mrs.

Wharton's Old New York and Ethan Frome. Lucy Gayheart, though a beautiful and firmly written book, is lacking in the quality of the others. Lucy Gayheart goes from "Haverford on the Platte" to Chicago, where she becomes accompanist to a brilliant baritone, Clement Sebastian; she falls in love with him and throws over her stupid, conventional, graceless, money-making and conceited young beau from Haverford, Harry Gordon. Sebastian goes to Europe and is drowned, and she goes back to Haverford, where Harry has married someone else, and is drowned too. We are then shown in an epilogue that Harry's love was really greater, that his whole life was determined by her death, that his clumsy patronising American emotion was something finer than Sebastian's polished European appetite. But the two deaths seem introduced from laziness and a desire to round off the story rather than as the inevitable consequence of choosing such a subject. This is a book well worth taking out of the library, a story perhaps rather skimped psychologically, but told with a real artist's exquisite touch.

Clifton Fadiman, "Miss Cather's New Novel," *New Yorker*, 11 (3 August 1935), 46–7

On page 32 of *Lucy Gayheart* Willa Cather, in her habitually quiet tones, poses the novel's theme. "Some people's lives," she remarks, "are affected by what happens to their person or their property; but for others fate is what happens to their feelings and their thoughts—that and nothing more." Accordingly, the measure of her success with the individual reader is a simple one. If the people in *Lucy Gayheart*—particularly Lucy herself—seem to you to have interesting feelings and thoughts, their fates will move you. If not, not. And that, I am mortified to confess, is about all I can discover I have to say about Miss Cather's first novel since *Shadows on the Rock*.

The setting of *Lucy Gayheart*—a small Nebraska town on the Platte River in the years 1901 and 1902—will be familiar to Miss Cather's admirers. Lucy herself recalls the wonderful heroine of *The Song of the Lark*. But she is an expurgated version. Indeed, the whole book is gentler, milder. It has little of the fine, I had almost said masculine, vigor of the Willa Cather of twenty years ago. Lucy is meant to be sensitive and alive and strong, but for the life of me I cannot see that she is anything but sweet to the point of dewiness, though I would not go as far as Fairy Blair, one of Miss Cather's minor characters, who considers Lucy "frightfully stuffy and girly-girly." As I am not greatly interested in Lucy's feelings and thoughts, I do not care about what happens to them, and hence her tragedy can be no more than ephemerally touching. Some good people are moved by Ophelia's fate. Others, doubtless not so good, feel drowning was far too comfortable an end for the treble-voiced little nuisance.

Lucy's home-town admirer is Harry Gordon, a self-confident, rising young businessman who possesses an underside of sensitivity and nobility. But this underside, we are told, is glimpsed only by Lucy; and I fear it is true. For me there is little in his behavior to distinguish him from the average pushing young commercial Puritan of his time and place. Hence, one fails with Gordon, too, as one fails with Lucy. One can't connect with him. His twenty-five-year repentance, after the death of Lucy, seems merely vaguely irritating.

Though Lucy is happy amid the simple verities of Haverford, she also has, like many of Miss Cather's heroines, intimations of "another kind of life and feeling which did not belong here." When she comes to Chicago and is chosen as accompanist to Clement Sebastian, a famous middle-aged baritone, these intimations assume concrete form. She falls in love with Sebastian. There is a short idyllic period in which Lucy worships genius, and the aging singer inhales the fragrance of youth, and not a breath of the carnal enters to turn their romance into something with three dimensions. It is the bodilessness of the affair—but, of course, this was 1902, when bodies were unfashionable—that makes it so easy to forget. We are told that Lucy's feeling for Sebastian was "a faith, an ardour," that was "a revelation of love as a tragic force, not a melting mood, of passion that drowns like black water." But we must accept this on faith. As portrayed, the relationship is pretty sweet and gentle. Lucy's is so typically the feeling of the impressionable country virgin for the nobly melancholy man of the world that some readers, at least, must be forgiven a mild sensation of ennui.

We are told, and very beautifully, that "if you brushed against his [Sebastian's] life ever so lightly it was like tapping on a deep bell; you felt all that you could not hear." But this, too, we must take for granted. Sebastian's character is too casually studied. Indeed, all the characters, while clear, are touched in so delicately that they seem to have no depth—and yet it is precisely their depth which we are invited to feel lies at the base of their tragedy.

The sudden death of Sebastian introduces a note of novelty which the pattern situation rather badly needs; but the death of Lucy, just a few months later, is a little hard to accept. It offers Miss Cather a chance, however, to do well what she has done so wonderfully in some of her other books. Twenty-five years after the death of Lucy, the events are reviewed in the mind of Harry Gordon, and we are given one of those typically Catherian elegies in silverpoint, so well written as almost to make us forget the slightness of the story and the people in it.

There is nothing that would more delight any reviewer who respects his craft and the beautiful art of Miss Cather than to be able to call her new book worthy of *My Antonia*, *O Pioneers!*, or *A Lost Lady*. But *Lucy Gayheart* is not in their class. Miss Cather is handling material remote in time and in appeal. The trouble, however, is not that she is writing about 1902 but that she is writing about 1902 somewhat in the manner of 1902. There is the rub. So simple a village tragedy needs, if it is to be made real to us today, deeper probing, wider sweep, more copious detail. These are not supplied. Instead we are offered an art so refined that it seems almost devoid of content and a point of view which, in its idealistic piety, is—Jove strike me if I slander!—unhappily reminiscent at times of ladies' magazine fiction. There is not one of us who will not at the end of the book sympathetically murmur, "Poor Lucy!" But this is not the reaction to an adult novel. It is the easy and momentary sympathy one feels at the recital of any pathetic happening.

Howard Mumford Jones, "Willa Cather Returns to the Middle West," *Saturday Review of Literature*, 12 (3 August 1935), 7

The American novel is in danger of becoming a prose pamphlet. Mr. Dreiser has employed it as an instrument to prove that we live like carnivora; Mr. Lewis has used it to show that we live like fools; Mr. Hemingway and Mr. Faulkner have written to indicate on the one hand that life is futile and cruel, and on the other hand that it doesn't make any difference anyway. Seduced by the plausible simplicities of what they regard as Marxian doctrine, a younger group is striving to transform the novel into a sociological treatise with fictional attachments. Being what it is, the most hospitable, the most Protean of literary forms, the novel has lent itself to all these didactic purposes, but in so doing, though it has made technical advances, it has failed to enrich itself artistically. It is an obvious truth, wrote Henry James, that "the deepest quality of a work of art will always be the quality of the mind of the producer. In proportion as that intelligence is fine will the novel . . . partake of the substance of beauty and truth. To be constituted of such elements is, to my vision, to have purpose enough." It is the special glory of Miss Cather to have the quality of mind which, to the highest kind of criticism, is purpose enough. If others, in the strong language of Scripture, go whoring after strange gods, she has held to the simple and perdurable principle that the primary business of the novelist is to create a work of art, which, arising out of human experience, returns through the long arc of the writer's shaping power, to enrich human experience. *Lucy Gayheart* is such a book.

The two qualities of Miss Cather's fine intelligence which especially appear in *Lucy Gayheart* (not that they are absent from her other works) are her intuitive insight into the most opposite personalities, and the perfection and beauty of her style. In it she returns to the Middle West—to Nebraska and Chicago—for the scenes and characters of her latest fiction. The plot is of the slightest. . . .

But when did any one ever read Miss Cather for the "plot"? A novelist less skilled would have created a sentimental romance; a novelist less wise would have satirized the singer, the heroine, and the stuffy little town; a novelist less humane would have denounced bourgeois morals and sent his heroine off on a career of hard-boiled episodes. Miss Cather does none of these things. Unlike George Sand, she is never maudlin; unlike Charlotte Brontë, she is never melodramatic. She holds the disparate elements of her story together through the unity of the heroine's life and through her experienced and disciplined prose. The little episode is told in a mood of sympathetic retrospection, but without denunciation, without nostalgia, without sentimentality. Only the coda, in which we are asked to believe that the banker's son keeps the Gayheart house as a sentimental souvenir, is momentarily touched with falseness. Elsewhere Miss Cather is, as she usually is, miraculously right.

Stylistically, Miss Cather is the most classical of contemporary novelists. The simplicity of her style would be austere, except that it is informed with delicate verbal and emotional beauty. She is incapable of writing a false or blundering sentence. Wiser than most of her contemporaries, she knows that sentiment is not to be confused with sentimentality; and as a consequence her pathos, like her lyricality, is never forced, but always sincerely felt and adequately, because economically, written. It is only in the larger strategy of structure that she occasionally fails—seldom in the smaller tactics of situation or scene. She shows us what the novel can be, and what it so seldom is, a flexible artistic form productive of a rich esthetic experience.

Paul Jordan-Smith, *Los Angeles Times* [4 August 1935]

If, as John Powys and many others maintain, the Middle West is the heart and soul of America; and if, as not a few intelligent critics affirm, Miss Cather is the surest interpreter of that soul, then it should be a matter of no surprise that some 50,000 American readers have possessed themselves this week of a first edition of Miss Cather's latest novel, *Lucy Gayheart*.

Save only the collectors (a piggish and snobbish minority), none of these admiring purchasers will have reason to deplore Miss Cather's steadily widening popularity; nor will the faithful find any evidence of waning powers.

True, the novel is without Marxian significance; it ignores the class struggle, the theory of surplus value, and gives no hint of the materialistic interpretation of history. It is, I fear, not proletarian. Miss Cather senses pains and problems that have other than economic and class origins. Yet, without any seeming awareness of these matters, she has contrived to create a romance of modern times, with a setting in the very center of agricultural America.

It is to the world of *A Lost Lady*, rather than to those of *Death Comes for the Archbishop* or *Shadows on the Rock* that we are invited. And there we meet, in Haverford and Chicago, the Gayhearts, Harry Gordon, Paul Auerbach and Clement Sebastian. We are taken to the outsides of Chicago; in Haverford, we get to know the patterns on cottage walls, the treacherous, meandering river, the orchards; the gestures and secret longings of a Main-street people.

But Miss Cather is not telling the story of a town; she writes this romantic, tragic history of Lucy Gayheart and of the two men who gave her their love; of Sebastian, famous singer, and Gordon, a provincial banker.

And I have no intention of disclosing any particle of that poignant history. The framework is slight. The story may be read between dinner and early bedtime; but the reader will know that he has touched life; that he has been introduced, ever so skilfully, to living people.

Miss Cather uses nothing that is not necessary to the telling of her story; and the story loses nothing by reason of her economy. But she is more than a craftsman. She can take a block of common sidewalk concrete and an ordinary country banker, and from these humble elements (see page 229) she can extract more truth, beauty and sentiment than can most any modern sculptor you can name.

Stephen Vincent Benet, "The Artistry and Grace of Willa Cather: Even in Lesser Books She Is a Superb Stylist," *New York Herald Tribune Books*, 4 August 1935, p. 3

This is neither the best nor the most solid of Miss Cather's novels, but we are always grateful for anything she chooses to give us—particularly when she writes of the middle country and of that pre-war America which she can make so curiously romantic. In our particular literary scene, she occupies a position as individual as it is strong. She has written nothing from *Alexander's Bridge* to *Lucy Gayheart* which is not unmistakably marked with her own seal. Yes she has dealt with a number of different worlds from the Santa Fe of *Death Comes for the Archbishop* to the New York of *My Mortal Enemy*. And she has dealt with them so much on her own terms that to praise her for her style, her scrupulousness and her integrity is like praising the Empire State Building for its height. She is, in certain ways, one of the most French of our writers, with the order, lucidity and grace of fine French prose—she is also, certainly, one of the most American. Speaking as a reader, I don't know any of her books, except *One of Ours*, that I haven't read and reread— and three of them at least seem destined to survive beyond our time—and to those I myself would add a fourth in *The Professor's House*.

And that is why I come to this review in a quandary. For *Lucy Gayheart* seems

454

to me one of her rare failures—and yet both the subject and the setting would seem admirably suited to her gifts. There is the Middle Western town in the 1900s, and the girl growing up in it. There is the world of music which Miss Cather knows and understands. There is love and the memory of love, and an old man, at the end, remembering youth and tragedy. And yet the book is not convincing—it only gives at rare moments that illumination, that heightening of life which is one of Miss Cather's great and individual gifts. The settings are real enough; they live on the page. You know the town by the Platte, with its frozen river in winter, its tree-shaded streets in summer. The music studio is real and the little bakery in Chicago above which Lucy Gayheart lives—even the train that takes her away to the city is real, the locomotive with the hoar-frost on its flanks. But the people—even Lucy Gayheart—are the people of a dream. . . .

It is perhaps natural that in a narrative of this sort, the characters should become symbols rather than human beings. But even symbols, in fiction, should have a certain amount of flesh and blood on their bones. There is no particular point in saying that Lucy, as drawn, seems to lack any trace of common sense—neither Romeo nor Juliet was distinguished for that quality. And, admittedly, the particular passion from which she suffers is exceedingly difficult to depict and yet keep from falling into a school girl's sentiment for a matinee idol. But Lucy, in spite of the occasionally very beautiful prose with which Miss Cather has clothed her, remains a symbol of a phase of youth—and a rather special and passing phase—rather than youth itself. It is hard to feel the significance of her tragedy because it is hard to feel significance in her.

Were she more strongly and sharply surrounded, were the chief male characters vitally alive, her dreamlike quality and her humility of love might shine by contrast. But unfortunately, with her male characters, Clement Sebastian, the singer, and Harry Gordon, the banker, Miss Cather has done what she does very seldom but will do occasionally. She will draw the outline of a male character with her usual scrupulous care, and then, somehow, completely forget to animate him. There are his hat and his shoes, but he has gone somewhere else—into another book, perhaps.

It was so with Claude Wheeler—it is so with both Sebastian, who is little more than a voice, a regret and a velvet jacket, and with Harry Gordon who is, until the last section, little more than a Claude Wheeler in reverse. In the last section he begins to come alive but by then the book is ending. Guiseppe and Mrs. Ramsay are real enough, but they are minor characters. The main figures move in a mist. And it is my personal misfortune that, having seen the Footprints of the Stars in front of Grauman's Chinese Theater in Hollywood, Lucy's own footprints, in cement, produce on me an effect not intended by the author. It may not be so with others.

"What is left?" There is a great deal. There are little perfections of observation and a sense for mood and landscape that are rare in any writer. There is the feel of a bygone America, seen through a clear glass. . . .

There is one of our finest stylists, writing. I am sorry not to like this book of Miss Cather's as I have liked others. But I am very grateful to her for having written any.

J. Donald Adams, "A New Novel by Willa Cather," *New York Times Book Review*, 4 August 1935, p. 1

"Art," Miss Cather has somewhere observed, "should simplify." It is a principle to which she has faithfully adhered, and in its practice she has grown increasingly adept. The principle is sound but hazardous. As applied to the novel, the point to which it can be carried without sacrifice of body is especially difficult to fix. And it has its obverse side; if you simplify, you must also intensify, for the act of selection will not of itself insure conviction and depth. These difficulties Miss Cather has admirably surmounted in *Lucy Gayheart*. Her new novel is not an expansive reading of life; it has not the scope of a major work of fiction, but within the confines she has set for it her story achieves a rounded quality, a substance, that only a disciplined art could give.

In setting, time and mood, *Lucy Gayheart* belongs with those earlier novels in which Miss Cather recalled the Nebraska of her youth. Her central character is again a girl whose quality of spirit sets her apart, a shining figure in a commonplace environment. The two motivating themes of the story, passionate desire to win something deeply satisfying from life, and the grasping back at youth in middle age, are themes which have attracted Miss Cather before. Their threads are interwoven in the story of Lucy Gayheart and her love for Clement Sebastian. . . .

It is an old situation, that of the middle-aged, disillusioned but distinguished man, unhappy in his personal life, hungrily reaching out for something that will bring back the freshness of youth, and the young girl who feels her life enriched and deepened by knowing him. Miss Cather handles it delicately and persuasively, so that one believes in it as something more than a mere girlish infatuation on Lucy's part, something less simple than physical attraction on that of Sebastian. . . .

One naturally regrets that Miss Cather did not choose to tell a story of wider implications, or one composed of elements that she had not fully utilized before, but the story she has told is done with all the distinction, all the quiet grace of style that have long marked her work.

R. H. P., "Willa Cather's Newest Effort," Omaha Sunday *Bee-News*, 4 August 1935, p. 20

Miss Willa Cather brings to the bookstalls this week her first full length novel since *Shadows on the Rock* was published in 1931. And in so doing she returns to the present and comes back to the Nebraska locale that was used in her earlier volumes.

It is difficult to appraise this work with justice and understanding. A conscientious reviewer must preserve a nice balance between enthusiasm generated by local pride and a critic's duty to judge this novel against a background of other—and, I suspect, finer novels by the same author.

A further difficulty with Miss Cather is an inability to get your teeth into something tangible. I do not wish to imply that Miss Cather is a second Winnie the Pooh, or even a Barrie whimsy. But there is no denying to her work an elusive, haunting quality hard to pin down and analyze. It is something like judging a fine piece of needlepoint of lovely, but not intricate pattern. When you say "beautiful" you have said almost all that may be said; but you can hardly claim to have exercised a very critical judgment in so doing.

So it is with *Lucy Gayheart*. It is a beautiful book, but it is not an epic. Neither is it a great tragedy, nor a great comedy. In fact it is not even a novel in the narrow sense, but rather two carefully drawn character sketches portrayed with that nice understanding of word values for which Miss Cather is most famous.

I know nothing of Miss Cather's favorite color, but were I to guess I should say gray. She writes in middle tones. There is pathos in *Lucy Gayheart*, but not tragedy; there is humor but not laughter. . . .

Frankly, this reviewer was disappointed. One has come to expect a great deal of Miss Cather and *Lucy Gayheart* is not another *Shadows on the Rock*, or *Death Comes for the Archbishop*. Emphatically it is not another *My Antonia*.

Yet no admirer of Miss Cather can disregard this novel. It must go on the shelf, with the rest of the Catherana to mark the progress of Nebraska's foremost author.

Joseph Henry Jackson, "Youth's Valorous Way with Life is Theme of Willa Cather's Latest," *San Francisco Chronicle*, 4 August 1935, p. 4D

For a quarter of a century Willa Sibert Cather has been unquestionably America's foremost woman novelist. Honored abroad as well as at home—she was, you remember, awarded the Prix Femina Americaine in 1933—Miss Cather has never disappointed readers who appreciate and admire her simplicity in style and her firm grasp of whatever theme she pitches upon. Or, rather, she has only disappointed such readers once, with the latter half of her novel of the war, *One of Ours*; and the most carping critic should make allowances for the effect of war's alarms on the emotions of even the coolest artist.

Nor will this new novel, her first in four years, disappoint them. A sort of spiritual cross between a modernized *My Antonia* and *A Lost Lady*, this story will please almost any reader by its simple directness, its gentle depiction of youth, unhappy youth, trying so hard to adjust itself to the world as it is, and not quite knowing how. . . .

You may wonder for a moment why I spoke of this as a small-town tale, rather than a story of universal significance, of striving and living and love and disappointment and sadness which might have been placed anywhere. It is true that Miss Cather's implications reach much farther than the actual setting of her story; she would not be herself if they didn't. But in the final analysis, this tender little story is really a story of another lost lady—lost in a different way from the author's earlier heroine, but lost none the less. Lucy was not for the great world, the big town. She wanted Life, yes. She was like her name—gay and bright and brilliant too. But she was lost from the beginning; you'd know, even if Miss Cather had not suggested it at the very commencement of her story, that Lucy would not quite escape into the kind of life and the kind of world in which she wanted so much to be. Certainly it was Harry she should have married. But, being Lucy Gayheart, she could do nothing else but what she did. She was a creature made for a different kind of happiness than the kind she could have found at home. Yet she was also a creature who would never find it.

Naturally nothing needs to be said about the way the story is written. If you have read so much as a line of Miss Cather you know already that she cannot write other than strongly and well. For all the simple delicacy of her style, there is the power of directness behind it; she knows how to use words better than nine out of ten novelists writing today. And it is this as well as the moving story that will win you to *Lucy Gayheart*. It is the kind of novel that, because of the way it is done, becomes—slim little story or not—a part of the one who reads it.

her characters. She gives us the world of music and sophistication in Chicago, and she gives us the small town. There is something bitter, perhaps, in this paragraph:

"In little towns, lives roll along so close to one another; loves and hates beat about, their wings almost touching. On the sidewalks along which everybody comes and goes you must, if you walk abroad at all, at some time pass within a few inches of the man who cheated and betrayed you, or the woman you desire more than anything else in the world. Her skirt brushes against you. You say good-morning, and go on. It is a close shave. Out in the world the escapes are not so narrow."

George Grimes, "Willa Cather Returns to Nebraska to Write a Simple, Tragic Tale," *World-Herald* (Omaha), 4 August 1935

Willa Cather returns to the Nebraska scene for the greater part of her new novel. But she is not so much concerned over Nebraska as she is preoccupied with the tragedy of life. Her new novel, a very simple story, beautifully told, is tragic. It is not a happy book. It reflects, perhaps, its author's conviction that one must seize what happiness he can in life, seize and treasure it dearly when it is offered, for it may soon be lost. . . .

Such is the story, a fragile, tender, sympathetic story. It is done with that expert writing which enables Willa Cather to give us an insight into the inner hearts of

"By Willa Cather," *World-Herald* (Omaha), 7 August 1935, p. 6

Those who read novels for enjoyment have been subjected to some rather harrowing experiences of late. When they pick up a new book, they run into the danger of finding it either a sheer propaganda piece on behalf of the American "proletariat," or a study of human degradation and depravity utterly shocking (Faulkner and Caldwell), or a clinic on sex and death (Hemingway), or a slap at us all as idiots (Sinclair Lewis), or a meaningless mumble-jumble of words (Gertrude Stein). The harassed reader either retires to the older, gentler novelists for a second glance at former favorites, or immerses himself in the more decent and less shocking tales of murder.

On August 1 a new novel appeared, and under the title was the phrase "by Willa Cather." The novel has its deficiencies, and will not be likely to displace in favor among her many warm friends in Nebraska her earlier books, like *My Antonia*, which bit down hard into life. But the new book, *Lucy Gayheart*, is distinguished, as all of Willa Cather's books are distinguished by a magnificently beautiful prose, handled with fine intelligence. There is nothing in it that is sordid for the sake of making a reader ill. There is nothing in it that savors of propaganda. There is no obvious attempt to reach a certain market by sensationalism. The novel is the product of a mind of rich quality, and so it is a book that can be read and enjoyed by intelligent people as a work of art.

Miss Cather can't write a bad sentence. She has the gift of sheer beauty of phrase, and she makes prose a medium for simple and lovely English. One may quarrel with her conception of the emotion of love—and she makes it rather austere and tame—but one rejoices that she doesn't make it unqualified sensualism. Reading her books affords the great satisfaction one has in contemplating the work of any artist who is in complete control of his medium.

Miss Cather rarely visits Nebraska. Yet her ties with this state are many, because of her long residence here, her education here, her use of the Nebraska scene for her strongest novels. Nebraska may legitimately claim her as its own. So a new novel from her pen is an event of importance to Nebraska as well as to the literary world. Even though maturity has mellowed her outlook and tamed, to some degree, her interpretation of life, it has not reduced in effectiveness a style of writing that has not many equals in the field of American literature.

L. M., "Miss Cather's First Novel in Four Years," *Kansas City Star*, 10 August 1935, p. 14

Among American writers of sensitive and beautiful fiction, Willa Cather sits on the dais. From *Alexander's Bridge* (1912) to *Lucy Gayheart* (1935), hers has been twice distilled prose. In twenty-three years, eleven novels. As one of her readers who have been profoundly entertained, we are grateful to Miss Cather for this slender output.

Four years have elapsed between the appearance of *Death Comes for the Archbishop* and her next novel, but the archbishop contained literary gold enough to last the reader four years. And when *Shadows on the Rock* was published, again there was treasure to span four years, to *Lucy Gayheart*.

Lucy Gayheart, however, is in some ways disappointing. True, it possesses its mine of literary gold, and our emotions were keenly engaged. But there is an anticlimax. Not even an artist of Miss Cather's stature can drown both hero and heroine mid-book and continue her story successfully in their shadows. We felt let down. With Lucy under the ice, our interest in a minor character's agonizing over one of her childhood footprints in a concrete sidewalk was not warm. We also perceived faulty character development in the case of Harry Gordon. Introduced as a boor, he is presented eventually, for no good reason, as a post-mortem knight. . . .

The book has a worth-while idea in it; it is planted in the earlier sections but is not cultivated to the end. This idea is that a woman may lose her greatest human love and yet not necessarily lose her happiness; that her most satisfying sweetheart may be, not a man, however fine and great, but life itself. The seed of the idea is sown on page 11, when an early star signals it into Lucy's understanding while she rides homeward at dusk in Gordon's sleigh. On page 184 it comes into full flower.

"Suddenly something flashed into her mind, so clear that it must have come from without, from the breathless quiet. What if—what if Life itself were the sweetheart? It was like a lover waiting for her in distant cities—across the sea; drawing her, enticing her, weaving a spell over her. She opened the window softly and knelt down beside it to breathe the cold air. She felt the snow flakes melt in her hair, on her hot cheeks. Oh, now she knew! She must have it, she couldn't run away from it. She must go back into the world and get all she could of everything that had made him what he was. Those splendors were still on earth, to be sought after and fought for."

Lucy is ready to go back to Chicago and carry on bravely in that philosophy. The reader applauds; he becomes eager for the remainder of the story that will portray Lucy as a great figure of the concert stage, enriching the world with her talent, a talent now all the finer because it blossoms from a scarred heart.

Instead of which, the author violently interferes with her character; she pushes Lucy Gayheart under the ice of the Platte. The reader is shocked, and he is not much interested in watching a sad country banker take the spotlight for a closing scene that disrupts the unity and purpose of the novel.

Having recorded our severest criticism, we must reassure any reader who would hesitate to read the book. Miss Cather writes too richly to be disqualified on the points of unity in plot development and consistency in characterization. Whatever the scene she is presenting, it is projected with the vividness that makes the reader feel himself present. Her descriptive touches bring the reader moments of beauty. Her picture of life in Chicago among genuine artists of the voice, the piano and the violin are colorful and convincing. *Lucy Gayheart*, in spite of faults, is one of the fine works of the summer.

William Troy, "Footprints in Cement," *Nation*, 141 (14 August 1935), 193

Years after the heroine of this novel has been found entrapped by a tree stump beneath the icy waters of a Middle Western river, her former admirer, now sole owner of the old Gayheart place at the end of town, gives instructions to one of his retainers: "Those marks there in the cement were made by Gayheart's daughter Lucy, when she was a little girl. I'll just ask you that nothing happens to those two slabs of walk—in my time, at least." Such a sentiment of the past, with its special commingling of the sacred and the commonplace, is actually all that Miss Cather's new work, despite its elaborate preparation of character and background, finally manages to communicate. The book has been only another and less memorable rendition of the theme that has occupied this novelist from the beginning. Like the heroines of *The Song of the Lark*, *O Pioneers!*, and *A Lost Lady*, Lucy Gayheart is one of those exquisite "sports" that were thrown up at the close of the period of pioneer expansion in the West. She is too lovely, too intelligent, too responsive to the call of what is rhetorically designated as life to be content with anything which that period had to offer. Unlike Marian Forrester, however, she is unable to compromise, and that is the pathos of her situation. For a few hours she has known dangerous release in the arms of an aging and unhappy baritone in a dimly lighted studio in the Fine Arts building in Chicago. After such a taste of abandonment, with all that it holds of music and continental passion and romantic sorrow, the daily bread of Harry Gordon's too well-disciplined affections loses all its savor for her. After such a revelation, as a matter of fact, there can be no future for either Lucy or the book. Miss Cather would be hard put to it to dispose of such a character as Clement Sebastian elsewhere than in the picturesque depths of Lake Como. And Lucy Gayheart has made a choice which leaves her only the life-in-death of continued existence in the Platte valley. For Harry Gordon and the reader there can be only the perennial, if somewhat unsatisfactory, consolation of the footprints in the cement.

The outline of Miss Cather's story as given is of course reducible to something that one has already seen many times and will see again in the Hollywood cinema. But to complain of its hackneyed simplicity is not to take account in this book of that other element of the novel form for which Miss Cather has been considered especially notable. The following is offered as a fair example of the style that is used to indicate or render subjective states on the part of the characters:

She had never loved the city so much; the city which gave one the freedom to spend one's youth as one pleased, to have one's secret, to choose one's master and serve him in one's own way. Yesterday's rain had left a bitter, springlike smell in the air; the vehemence that beat against her in the street and hummed above her had something a little wistful in it tonight, like a plaintive hand-organ tune. All the lovely things in the shop windows, the furs and jewels, roses and orchids, seemed to belong to her as she passed them. Not to have wrapped up and sent home certainly; where would she put them? But they were hers to live among.

That this is not the best writing that has come to us from the author of *My Antonia* and *A Lost Lady* is as evident from the sentimentally relaxed rhythms as from the stereotyped imagery. What it reveals even more profoundly than the naively romantic pattern of her newest book is how completely this writer now permits the *élans* of her sensibility to conquer over her intelligence. Where a Flaubert, troubled by much the same conflict between imagination and conscience, was able at the end to attain to the high detachment of *L'Education Sentimentale*, Miss Cather surrenders to the temptation of facile sentimentalism which has been her greatest temptation from the beginning. For those who had hoped that the archeological holiday of her last two novels might be followed by a return to the clearly envisaged experience of her earlier books about the West, this most recent novel can only be a source of grave discouragement.

Frances C. Lamont
Robbins, "The New
Fiction," *American
Mercury*, 36 (September
1935), 113–17

Lucy Gayheart by Willa Cather has
recently appeared, the first novel in some
years by this careful writer. It is short, and
in places very lovely. By no means the
equal of some of Miss Cather's earlier
books, it is quite in tune with the mood
of tender and delicate retrospection which
has been growing on her. For the scene,
she has left heroic New Mexico and faint,
picturesque New France and returned to
the Nebraska of thirty years ago. This is
a time and place which she loves. Her
central figure is such a girl as she has
created before, in greater detail and to
greater emotional extent. It has interested
her, hitherto, to carry her immigrant girls
through the conflict of Old World ideals
and New World vulgarity to a triumphant
self-realization based upon the traditional
feminine virtues. In *Lucy Gayheart*, she
sets down, in a sustained mood of pitying
tenderness, the story of short life, an
incident only, and of a fulfilment purely
mystical.

Lucy Gayheart is the daughter of a
mild German watchmaker, band leader
and half-hearted farmer, who would
rather play the flute than hoe the corn.
Lucy is in love with life and with the
natural world about her. The longing for
identification with life and beauty is
strong in her. When, in being, and later in
memory, she walks down the street of her
little town, clean window panes sparkle
and birds sing, syringa smells sweeter and
people sitting on porches feel pleased
about things. Pure in heart, Lucy sees
God, and the reflection of her vision
shines from her eyes upon those who
know and touch her. Music is Lucy's
second life: movement and sound put into
lovely order. Already a successful student,
she goes to Chicago where she becomes
the assistant accompanist of Clement
Sebastian, a great singer. Her rich spirit
and high-hearted innocence are charms to
attract and solace a disillusioned man,
and armor to protect. In love without
passion, Lucy's life is made complete and,
after a parting which is the foreshadow-
ing of tragedy, she returns to her village.
When the immutable loss comes, Lucy's
silver bells are stilled. Sweetness remains,
but the gay heart's gaiety is gone. There is
only death left for Lucy, not a pitiful child
gesture in imitation of tragedy, but death
as love's perfect consummation.

Poetic symbolism is at the heart of all
the Cather novels. The flaw in Alexander's
bridge paralleled the flaw in his character:
the Professor's new house illustrated the
confusing intrusion of new standards
upon old faiths. And in *Lucy Gayheart*,
the black ice over which Lucy loved to
skate, lying over still waters that run deep,
becomes the thin ice of life over which the
soaring spirit skims. When truly the ice of
the River Platte breaks under Lucy's swift
feet, it is because she chose that it should
break, letting the waters of love lost close
over her.

Order and simplicity have always been
Miss Cather's great virtues of style. Her
work is another proof that order is prose's
first law. She believes that writing is
meant, first of all, to be understood, and
that creative talent, burning and turbulent
though it may be, is strong or weak in
effect in proportion to the clarity of the
sentences in which it expresses itself. Miss
Cather is blessedly unaffected by fashions
in writing. She has always followed her
own bent; written of things she knows,
and told the truth as she sees it. So,

because her vision of truth encompasses human nature, which has its strengths as well as its weaknesses, she is not afraid of embroidering what is called sentiment into her novels. In *Lucy Gayheart*, she is as sentimental as the Schubert songs which Lucy played and Sebastian sang. She knows that a girl could love a middle-aged artist she being life and he resignation, and that he could love her, and that their love could be made real without a seduction scene. In a vulgar generation, she has remained dignified and courteous in speech. She can suggest perversion without recourse to the psychoanalyst's jargon, and can describe meanness and cruelty without the use of invective. She understands the value of selection and knows that a line will often tell as much as a page. But, although it has been part of her expressed theory that style should be subservient to content, the fact is that it is by their beauty of style that her recent novels have captured their audience. This is particularly true of *Lucy Gayheart*.

Miss Cather's sympathies have sometimes been with the enthusiasm of youth, sometimes with the courage of middle-age. Here they are poised between the two. Youth's dream and maturity's memories blend in this book, and I think it is this particular fusion of dream and memory which accounts for the novel's lack of vitality. Miss Cather, especially since the publication of *Death Comes for the Archbishop*, has been classed by reviewers with the escapists. If escape means escape from vitality, she belongs with them. Vitality is of the moment—inhale, exhale, throw a brick, eat your dinner and curse the cook. But Miss Cather seeks no escape from truth when she dwells on memory and dreams. Nothing was truer than dreams; nothing is truer than memory. The instant of life which lies between dream and memory is probably only a very noisy lie; and when it finds its way into books, it is rather more of an escape, for most of us, than any amount of remembering and dreaming.

Ethel Wallace Hawkins, "The Atlantic Bookshelf," *Atlantic Monthly*, 156 (September 1935), 10

Willa Cather has not chosen to add another great calm painting—or, if you will, another great calm piece of music— to *Death Comes for the Archbishop* and *Shadows on the Rock*. For a partial likeness to *Lucy Gayheart* one must go as far back as to *A Lost Lady*—for a matching fleetness of narrative, a matching concentration and vehemence of emotion. In the opening paragraph, Lucy Gayheart is described as her fellow townsmen used to see her: "walking swiftly with intense direction, like a bird flying home." With the same swiftness and direction the story moves.

Lucy Gayheart is in a modest way a darling of the gods. She is the loveliest girl in her small town, the most gifted, the most admired. The "biggest" young man in the community is inclined to believe that she will do nicely for him. Music, her passion, is also her talent. After she has studied the piano for a time in Chicago, she is found able enough to be recommended as his accompanist for his hours of practice, to the great baritone who is her idol. Thrilled and scared, she enters into what proves to be an unimagined heaven. But the gods' darlings are traditionally in danger.

I do not know whether Miss Cather's power of rendering the emotional under-

463

currents of a situation show better in those scenes in Clement Sebastian's studio in which Lucy's artistic and personal ardors expand so rapturously, or in the episode of Harry Gordon's advent from the hometown for opera week with Lucy—Harry Gordon, all ignorant of the change in her, superfluously reinforced in spirit by three new suits and a pocketful of opera tickets, but rather touchingly resolved that this time he will not be as funny as he can in the art museum.

The author's rare sense of form shows once more in this novel. The narrative, compact as it is, follows a beautiful design. A strong sense of actuality is given to the persistence of Lucy's spirit, with its "belief in an invisible, inviolable world," in the place where she is not, and to the evolution of the bumptious and supremely self-satisfied Harry Gordon into a man very much a man and at the same time touched with a fanciful tenderness that in someone else he would once have shouted down with mighty laughter. I am inclined to believe that what will persist longest in memory from a reading of the book is its swiftness, and the intense reality of the visual images.

Catholic World, 141 (September 1935), 763

When a book by Willa Cather proves disappointing, that is news indeed. Reluctantly we admit that her latest novel is so, despite frequent evidence of the charming and delicate Cather touch. The heroine is a memorable personification of youthful longing, "a slight figure always in motion; dancing or skating, or walking swiftly with intense direction, like a bird flying home." Lucy's typical small-town routine would doubtless have ended in marriage

with Harry Gordon, the most suitable of the local swains, had she not gone to study music in Chicago. But there she came in contact with Clement Sebastian, a famous and lovable concert star with a nostalgia for his vanished youth, and to him Lucy tendered a youthful adoration which was, in reality, a falling in love with art and romance. The characters of Lucy and Sebastian have a hauntingly permanent quality, although they are not much more than vividly sketched, but the book as a whole is thin and dotted with flimsy patches.

John Chamberlain, "The World in Books," *Current History*, 42 (September 1935), iv–v

Willa Cather's novel is about the love of a small town girl from Nebraska in the Nineties for a middle-aged concert singer who she meets in Chicago. The subject is a timeless one, but it is doubtful if even the Nineties and the American Middle West could have conspired to produce such a bloodless romance. *Lucy Gayheart* has the quality of a ballad of the "nicer" type as Clifton Fadiman has said, one finishes reading it with a sigh of "poor Lucy." But this tribute of momentary pity for the pathetic is certainly not the mood that is generated by great art. It is as if Willa Cather, after a lifetime of brave experimentation in fiction, had decided that the mood and methods of the genteel tradition in novel writing were good enough. And this, in itself, is pathetic.

Lucy Gayheart is saved somewhat by the incidental characters, who are acutely observed and etched, and by the prose, which, however freighted with melancholy images, has a flow and a glow that only Willa Cather can manage. The epigrammatic evocation of small town life is good too. But none of these virtues can compensate for feeble portrayal of the main characters and failure to plumb the depths of a situation involving two really far from bloodless human beings. One feels that the shadowy quality of Lucy and her singer, Clement Sebastian, are the fault of Miss Cather, not of nature or of the Creator. When we first meet Lucy at the skating party on the Platte River she is anything but shadowy. And her father and sister and Harry Gordon, the small town banker, regarded her as vital enough.

Newton Arvin, "Sweet Story," *New Republic*, 84 (11 September 1935), 138

The charge of thinness or insubstantiality is one that could long ago have been urged against the fiction of Willa Cather at its least distinguished, but until *Lucy Gayheart* appeared it would not have seemed quite just to tax it with sheer banality. Almost the only interest *Lucy Gayheart* has is the melancholy interest it derives from showing that Willa Cather can be almost unrelievedly commonplace. It would not be quite literal to say that any one of twenty or thirty American writers of the last two generations, especially women writers, could have written this identical novel; but its materials are as standardized and its ethical implications as conventional as such a remark would indicate. . . .

Personal distinction, the fine artistic temperament, sensibility and elegance are at a discount in a dull, barbarous and malignant world; they struggle briefly, but they are carried under, and they survive only as exquisite ghosts in the memory of the appreciative: this is what the fable only too evidently enforces.

It is a moral that, with qualifications, was once worth enforcing, and when Willa Cather wrote "Paul's Case" or *A Lost Lady*, one felt that the prevailing ikons, to which even men of letters said their prayers, were being quietly flouted. It was much that a gifted writer, at that time, should tacitly repudiate the philistine values that many of her fellow writers accepted and propagated. But the repudiation was always strongly temperamental; there was a minimum of critical thought behind it; and it has long been clear that Willa Cather is incapable of seeing the predicament of the superior individual or the artist in anything but a softly reflected and sentimental light. Her imagination takes in the individual instance, the specific wrong; but it has a terribly narrow reach, and is helpless in the presence of large historical forces. In personal terms she has disliked some of the morals of her class, but she has never dreamed of challenging them fundamentally, and as a result her celebration of the Lucy Gayhearts and the Clement Sebastians has become merely the reverse of a cultivated superciliousness toward the rest of mankind.

Sebastian himself betrays this interestingly in a remark he makes to Lucy about his worldly and self-seeking accompanist, Mockford. After we have been told that nothing ever came near Sebastian "to tarnish his personal elegance," so that he must use silver toilet articles and have rose-colored blankets on his bed, it is somewhat disagreeable to hear him say: "Jimmy is rather brassy at times—fault of his early training. He came out of the slums, really." The coarseness of which self-styled aristocrats are capable is no novelty to the observant eye or ear, but this speech accounts, almost by itself, not only for the tenuity but for the triteness of *Lucy Gayheart*.

Charlotte M. Meagher, "Romance at Noonday," *Commonweal*, 22 (27 September 1935), 534

The publication of a new novel by Willa Cather has come to be an event anticipated. This latest of Miss Cather's output fully justifies all expectations. *Lucy Gayheart* is a slender novel of 231 pages, reminiscent of *The Song of the Lark* in its Middle West setting and its use of a musical background, reminiscent of *A Lost Lady* in its eddyings of passion; but it surpasses either of these in compression, in power, in depth, in emotional value.

Lucy Gayheart, the lovable, talented daughter of the watchmaker-musician, is the center of a deep maelstrom of love and pride, ambition and frustration. Harry Gordon's love for Lucy, the girl's passionate devotion to the great Clement Sebastian for whom she played accompaniments during her student days in Chicago, the tragedy that enveloped not only her own bright visions but Gordon's as well—these form the texture of the plot. The story opens with her townspeople still remembering Lucy "as a slight figure always in motion . . . like a bird flying home"; it closes with these same townspeople thinking of her as "like a bird being shot down when it rises in its morning flight toward the sun." (The jacket carries a bird in downward flight.) It has to do with "youth, hope, love—all the things that pass," as Sebastian is made to express it;

with "having one's heart frozen and one's world destroyed in a moment," as Lucy saw it.

The novel has all the excellencies one expects in Miss Cather's work. The plot, slender though it is, moves on unswervingly and with force. The background merges with the story as readily and as naturally as one's own garden compasses one's friends and familiars. What Alice Meynell taught us to call the "spirit of place" is evoked here as magically as it was made to dominate *Shadows on the Rock*. One meets it everywhere—in the valley of the Platte with its scrub-oaks and its cottonwoods, as well as on the Chicago lake front where "even the grey gulls flew by on languid wings."

Of all the characters, Harry Gordon is perhaps the best drawn. It is in his portrayal that the reader discerns the author's keenness of insight, her understanding of human nature, her gift of delineating character in all the subtle changes which the years carry with them. The middle-aged Sebastian whose "personality had aroused her even before he began to sing, the moment he came upon the stage," is always a breathing, living figure. Lucy herself in her vivacity and sparkle, or in her deep sorrow, is thoroughly alive. And even the minor characters stand out, none more so than the German music teacher Auerbach, in his beautiful understanding. The reader will not soon forget such characters nor the scenes in which they figure. Poignantly moving pages are those which tell of Lucy's pleading for the sparing of the Gayheart orchard, of her afternoon in that orchard living over in memory the year just closing, and of Harry Gordon sitting alone in his private office late into the evening of the day on which Lucy's father had been buried. Such pictures live long in the memory.

Miss Cather's simple, crystal-clear style would seem to have gained in that rare power to achieve even the slightest nuances of impression, of emotion—of anything for which head and heart struggle for expression. One could make a long list of the striking, apposite similes and metaphors which give clarity, force and beauty to every page of this entrancing novel.

Dorothea Brande, "Willa Cather and the Sense of Life," *American Review*, 5 (October 1935), 625–9

Sometimes it seems that Willa Cather is an artist doomed not to be understood by her own times. Those who were young when the stories were written which later appeared in *Youth and the Bright Medusa* can never read her without a reminiscent recapturing of the excitement and joy to which they were once stirred, nor, sadly, without an unjust feeling that some tacit agreement between themselves and the author of those stories has not been fully met. Even less can the younger reviewers, handicapped by having been taught by the new psychology to criticize fiction by standards more suitable to the psychiatrist's laboratory than the artist's workroom, understand an author who uses only the materials which seem to her pertinent to her subject, refusing staunchly to handle those which her newest critics invariably try to thrust upon her. It is probably fortunate for all of us that Miss Cather goes quietly along her own way, offering book after book which we cannot fail to recognize and receive as the work of a true artist, although—some for one reason, some for another—seldom quite so generously as we should like.

That is what makes reviewing such a book as Miss Cather's *Lucy Gayheart* a thankless task. More than probably she fulfilled her own intention, and we have had evidence before this that her intention was often better than any we could have dictated to her. In addition, Miss Cather is unsurpassed in craftsmanship. Few novelists can do what she does so unerringly: she brings her *story* unobtrusively to a full circle; her characters then go on, truly created, alive independently even for us, who so often and so inconsistently complain that they were never fully living. Surely no author ever had a better right than Miss Cather to paraphrase Sargent's bitter epigram: "A portrait is a picture that has something wrong with the mouth." Miss Cather in her solitude must feel that our definition of a novel should be "A book which has something wrong with the end ... or some character, or a motive."

At least she must have the satisfaction, for what it is worth, of knowing that her books are a vital element in the lives of her readers. While *Lucy Gayheart* was still running serially, it already had the importance that gives rise to living gossip: "She killed off her hero at the end of the first part, and her heroine at the end of the second," we said; "what's left for the end?" No insignificant book raises such a question as that.

Well, what was left for the end is justification enough for a dozen novels, and yet I too want to join in the chorus of scolding and complaint, and say in my turn that if the book had been much shorter, if, indeed, it had been kept to the dimensions of a long short story, not even the most obtuse reader could have failed to see the pertinence of every element in it to that ending. Of course she did not "kill off" the hero or the heroine of her book at all, although the character who gives her name to the novel does drown at the end of the second section. For the hero—or heroine, as you choose—is none of the characters of the story, but the sense of life; and Miss Cather says so as openly as she can without bustling into the middle of her own scene. But since she did spend so much time in drawing Lucy, and in drawing the singer, Sebastian, they come to have at once too much and too little presence: too much if they are to be seen as vehicles of life, too little if we are intended to feel them as individuals.

Since the story of the book is well enough known by now, I shall only summarize it briefly. . . .

The pattern of the book is at once subtle and clear: only Tolstoi's use of the railroad station in *Anna Karenina* returns to me at the moment as so surely handled as Miss Cather's scenes on the icy river. Every element of the opening pages is used again at the scene of Lucy's death, and yet there is not an obvious item among them. And then, with the generosity of the artist, there comes that added gift of the footprints, withheld until it can bring its own relief and comfort: "Was there really some baffling suggestion of quick motion in those impressions, Gordon often wondered, or was it merely because he had seen them made, that to him they always had a look of swiftness, mischief and lightness? As if the feet had tiny wings on them, like the herald Mercury." And, when the book closes: "As he was leaving the Gayhearts', he paused mechanically on the sidewalk, as he had done so many thousand times, to look at the three light footprints, running away."

Since the book has its successful pattern, since the closing section is no anticlimax, but embodies the very feeling of continuing life that its author intended, what possible complaint can there be against *Lucy Gayheart*? Yet the chorus of wistful complaint arises, however much it has been set off with appreciation and praise. Because Miss Cather knew so much about her Lucy, took us so close that we heard her breathe and knew her thoughts, she seems arbitrarily to have denied us some deeper knowledge that we needed, and which Miss Cather herself must have had. The relation between Lucy and Sebastian is ambiguous, not merely subtle; Lucy's sense of life—that central focus of the book—is never convincingly vivid for all the author's reiteration of it. Lucy's father and sister are stock figures, and Lucy herself too oblivious to them to lend them any part of her own rather fitful reality.

That is the type of complaint her readers must make against Miss Cather—surely the most satisfactory captiousness a writer can be asked to bear: that she does so well, we want her to do better, to give us what she herself has taught us to expect. And that is something as near perfection in art as the novel has been able to come.

Edith H. Walton, "The Book Parade," *Forum and Century*, 94 (October 1935), v

Returning once more to Nebraska, Miss Cather relates in delicate, muted tones the story of a young girl who was betrayed by her ardent impulsiveness. . . . With the best will in the world one cannot claim *Lucy Gayheart* as one of Miss Cather's major works. It is pathetic rather than tragic; its wraithlike, legendary quality cannot be measured against the robustness of *My Antonia*. One must accept it for what it is, a brief tale, with a gentle subdued charm, which is written as flawlessly as its more substantial predecessors.

James Southall Wilson, "Two American Novels," *Virginia Quarterly Review*, 11 (October 1935), 620–6 [reviewed with Ellen Glasgow's *Vein of Iron*]

Everything or anything that Willa Cather has written or may write is precious. *Lucy Gayheart* is the story—the very simple story—of a young girl's life. Two men loved her, and the last section of the book is told through the thoughts of one of these men. The people of her village, Haverford on the Platte, still talk of her, "still see her as a slight figure always in motion—like a bird flying home." That is what Willa Cather does for you: she makes you see to remember forever the figure of a beautiful young girl with two ends of a crimson scarf floating behind her on the wind; as a poem might make one remember it—or a painting. When she was a girl of thirteen, Lucy had stepped on the fresh cement of the sidewalk and the three footsteps she left there were for one man who loved her the tangible record of her personality. "Three light footsteps running away,"—that is the lasting impression *Lucy Gayheart* leaves upon the reader.

Like all of the other novels of Miss Cather, this book is beautifully expressed through vivid pictures and firm, cool language. It has not the power and loveliness of *A Lost Lady* or *Death Comes for the Archbishop* or *Shadows on the Rock*. In spirit and manner it suggests more *My Antonia* and the earlier stories. It is not one of the most successful of her books; but for those who think her the greatest writer of prose in America to-day, it is enough that it is for all that characteristically a Willa Cather novel.

Randall Jarrell, "Ten Books," *Southern Review*, 1 (Autumn 1935), 407–8

Lucy Gayheart is very unpretentious, a quiet book on a small scale. The book depends on two accidental deaths—the death of Sebastian, the singer with whom Lucy Gayheart is in love, and Lucy's own death. This is a structural flaw; as de Maupassant said, people are killed every day by bricks falling from scaffoldings, but you mustn't write novels about them. Everyone knows the statement (with which, of course, one may disagree violently) that the best style is one which the reader does not notice at all. Miss Cather's style and general treatment almost satisfy this demand; or at least, one notices the faults of her style more than its virtues. This is not intended to be ironic; I mean that it is only by careful re-reading that one sees all the virtues of Miss Cather's style; her faults, on the other hand, are of a sort that our age particularly notices. Her style has very distinct limits, but inside these limits she writes with ease and grace. (The last sentence in Book II is the worst sentence in the book; it was probably just bad luck, one of those unaccountable lapses during which we forget our names, that kept Miss Cather satisfied with it.) Miss Cather's style and sensibility are not those of a first-rate writer; but she does not strain them, and there is nothing false about *Lucy Gayheart*.

You know Lucy Gayheart only in the way you might know yourself, if you were badly forgetful, and not very introspective. Sometimes things people say about you surprise you a good deal, and one or two of the things other people say about Lucy surprise you almost as much. Very few people know their own characteristic locutions, or turns of thought; you do not know Lucy's. She is made a rather general and lyrical figure throughout, and this prepares you for the way in which she is regarded near the book's end. In telling you, very beautifully and sensitively, about her footprints, Miss Cather compares them to those of "the herald Mercury"; and Miss Cather has written so gently and restrainedly, what she has said seems so just that they have that much significance for you, too.

Miss Cather's treatment of Lucy's grief seems unsuccessful; she tells only the general things everybody knows, just the things she could have taken for granted. She writes of emotion better than of sensation; yet she frequently describes an emotion so that you remember having felt the one she means, but decide that her description of it is not good enough. I do not say that Miss Cather is rather romantic and sentimental, and that she pays no attention to economics and sociology. Mr. Hanley is very much interested in the economic implications of *his* story, and it is a good story; but there is no reason to hold him up to Miss Cather and say, "Go thou and do likewise."

Miss Cather is especially good in the cultural levels she gives to her characters in the speeches she has them say; there is no mistake to hurt your confidence in her. Her attitude toward music, her great singer, are very convincing and satisfying. Besides Miss Cather knows so much about writing; you do not need to look at the list of "other books by this author" to realize that she has written a great many books, and learned a great deal while she was writing them. Miss Cather is

somehow so sympathetic, and so interesting, that *Lucy Gayheart* demands both liking and respect. *Lucy Gayheart* is not an "important" book at all; but surely, if it affects one so it has enough of virtue.

Helen MacAfee, *Yale Review*, New Series, 25 (Autumn 1935), viii

Willa Cather's latest novel is an airy rectilinear creation. Looked at in retrospect it appears twice stepped back, like a modern building. Its main stage encloses the experience of a young woman leaving the constrictions of a small community that had made up its mind about her past and future to explore in a big city the possibilities of love and work of her own choosing. Before these were fully explored, both came to a pause through the sudden death of the man who had awakened equally her mind and feelings. Then the reader is drawn back with her from this experience to her old home; and, when she herself suddenly dies, is drawn back still further. The city was exciting to Lucy Gayheart not only because it conferred anonymity with the freedom "to spend one's youth as one pleased, to have one's secret," but also because it gave a stimulating sense of nearness to artists with exacting standards—those who "strove after excellence" for its own sake. But while it has praise for the city, the book is far from being an apology for footloose bohemia. The alien singer, whom Lucy loves and admires, regrets having "missed the deepest of all companionships, a relation with the earth itself, with a countryside and a people." This novel does not seem to me to establish such a relation for the reader so closely as do *A Lost Lady* or "Old Mrs. Harris," but it has a different function, perhaps, to present a memory seen in "a long perspective."

John Slocum, *North American Review*, 240 (December 1935), 549–50

At first appearances, Miss Cather seems to have written a novel which corrects all the minor faults of her previous successes. The time is the twentieth century rather than the nostalgic past, and the main scene is Chicago rather than some overworked small community. Her style shows the same sure mastery which can be found in such diverse novels as *My Antonia* and *Death Comes for the Archbishop*, though she occasionally slips, as in ". . . one's blood coursing unchilled in an air where roses froze instantly."

The story is based on the life of the charming and talented Lucy Gayheart. She goes from her small town into the music world of Chicago, where she meets and falls in love with a famous concert singer. Because he gives her a glimpse of a world that she has never imagined, she spurns her girlhood sweetheart. She lives in bliss, finding it hard to wait between their meetings. Then the singer is drowned in one of the Italian lakes. Lucy returns broken-hearted to her home town, almost recovers her happiness, when suddenly she is drowned herself after a quarrel with her sister. The last section of the book is devoted to the sorrowing of the sweetheart who realized too late how much he loved her. She leaves a gay and vivid memory in the hearts of the people who knew her.

With this absurdly mid-Victorian plot Miss Cather has done extremely well. Her characters seem genuine, especially Lucy, whose gaiety infects the reader. The town boy is a perfect prig, though not to be compared with Levin in Anna Karénina, who is also lovable. The key situation—Lucy's reaction to the singer's death—is handled by the author with great delicacy.

The fault of this novel lies not in what it includes, but in what it excludes. There is no complete picture of Lucy's small town background, nor of the development of her personality beyond the statement that she was a very simple person who was always gay. There is no evidence that Chicago had any effect on her. In fact there is no feeling for existence in twentieth century America rather than nineteenth, or eighteenth, except for Lucy's slight emancipation. There is little finality to the presages of her death which shocks the reader and does not convince him of its inevitability.

The wistful nostalgia of the last section of this novel fully counteracts the relative modernity of the setting and leaves the whole hanging on a blurred edge of time. One wonders if Miss Cather has a positive sense of values strong enough to withstand the present.

Robert Cantwell, "A Season's Run," *New Republic*, 85 (11 December 1935), 149–50

. . . [Among current trends,] there is the lamentable collapse of a number of those writers who, only a few years ago, were being hailed as the creators of masterpieces and the leaders of American culture—novelists of the type of Willa

Cather, Ellen Glasgow, Elizabeth Madox Roberts, whose latest books have revealed their inability to deal with the emotional and practical problems of the contemporary world in even the most elementary terms. The works of Willa Cather have always seemed to me to have been taken more seriously by the critics than was absolutely necessary; but *Lucy Gayheart* is simply a maudlin book, peopled with stock characters who move through stock situations and who die, unexpectedly and accidentally, to bring the story to a ramshackle conclusion. At one point Miss Cather does attempt to face the modern Middle West—one of her characters is a banker who is presented as being ruthless with the farmers as a result of his disappointment in love—but after five of the six characters die he has a change of heart. Ellen Glasgow's *Vein of Iron* is a much more durable work; her people are more vital and varied and interesting, and they come up against problems—the War, unemployment—that force them to reach into the reserves of their experience and understanding for strength to keep going. But that—to keep going, even if it is in hopelessness and misery—is evidently all they want; and when at the last Miss Glasgow pictures her impoverished family retreating to the hills to start over, the vein of iron in them seems considerably less heroic and admirable than she tries to make it.

The gap between these writers and the younger novelists is as great as that between the post-war and pre-war generations. The literary life is full of scandals, but it has witnessed few more awkward spectacles than that of eminent critics attempting to bolster up such fatigued writers as, in particular, Miss Cather and Miss Roberts, for whom the crisis has obviously been so much too much. Since most of these critics have already been compromised by the clumsiness of their log-rolling, these attempts have lost them the influence that they might have maintained with the younger generation. It is significant that the first attack upon them, written by Mary McCarthy and Margaret Marshall in *The Nation*, came from two young writers who merely quoted their own words to expose them. But the immediate effect of this discrediting of the elders—for these instances are merely illustrations of a general development—has been a break in the continuity of culture whose consequences are already apparent. The debauching of critical standards by the log-rollers and publicity men, a general disgust with the "vulgar and desperate scramble" of the literary life, a resulting skepticism as to the value of criticism, has produced a kind of modern nihilism that Erskine Caldwell summed up when he explained that the value of his novels arose from the fact that he did not read any books. . . .

E[dward] K[illoran] Brown, "Willa Cather and the West," *University of Toronto Quarterly*, 5 (July 1936), 544–66

The appearance of *Lucy Gayheart* (1935) marks Miss Cather's return to her greatest subject—the West, the clash in the West between the grandeur of the land and large natures in sympathy with it, on the one hand, and, on the other, the meanness of the towns and those among their people who are provincial and shrewd. The three short stories collected in 1932 under the title *Obscure Destinies* indicated that Miss Cather was preparing to return to the

West. When in one of these stories she refers to a little Colorado town as "a snappy little Western democracy, where every man was as good as his neighbour and out to prove it," we recognize the comment as by the same hand which drew the town of Black Hawk in *My Antonia* (1918); and when, in another, she presents a Bohemian family in which the prevailing spirit, warm, generous, magnanimous, had been created by a man who had suffered in London and New York and then found serenity and harmony on a Nebraska farm, we recognize even more clearly the author of *O Pioneers!* (1913). A full-length novel was needed to assure us that the return was not merely episodic; and *Lucy Gayheart* is as similar to the early Western novels as any one of these is to any other.

From the West—that is, from Nebraska and Colorado—Miss Cather broke away in *The Professor's House* (1925) and moved farther and farther in *Death Comes for the Archbishop* (1927) and *Shadows on the Rock* (1931). Closely considered, these three novels disclose important points of contact with the earlier works: the same formula of heroism, the same subtle and illuminating sense of a relation, a fundamental likeness, between the influence of the frontier in its purest expressions and the influence of mellow traditional civilizations. Still the later works, for all the quiet richness of their emotion, or the perfect movement of their narrative, are not completely satisfying to one steeped in *The Song of the Lark* (1915), *My Antonia,* and *A Lost Lady* (1923). It is not because they are historical novels and their glamour seems less substantial, less vigorous, than the subdued glow of the earlier novels. It is not because their style has been refined and modulated until it is a little artificial. What is dissatisfying is that New Mexico and New France are not Miss Cather's

country as Colorado and Nebraska are. The mysterious but sustained power of the earlier Western novels was an emanation from the land. When Miss Cather parts from this land, "the grand passion of my life" as she calls it, she retains much, her style, her art, her sense of heroism: but the essence of her power, an essence so fine that it almost resists definition, she cannot retain.

Lucy Gayheart is an attempt to recapture this essence: here once more we find a close and subtle presentation of distinguished and fine character and a poetic evocation of the Western land. The heroine is brought before us as a person whose essence, a fine animated charm, is less an individual thing than an expression in a human character of the electric air and broad vivid spaces of Nebraska. Her voice had in it "a ring of truth" that not even so great a singer as Clement Sebastian could define; even her laugh had an intense reality; in both something deeper than the girl herself found expression. All in her life that really mattered— and in this she represents the whole company of Miss Cather's heroic characters—occurred on a level so far below the surface of visible successes and failures that to most observers nothing at all seemed to occur to her until Clement Sebastian was drowned in Lake Como and Lucy in the little river that ran just beyond her Nebraska town. "Some people's lives," as Miss Cather says, "are affected by what happens to their person or their property; but for others fate is what happens to their feelings and their thoughts—that and nothing more." On the deep level of her real life two experiences befall Lucy Gayheart, each of them infinitely more important than Sebastian's death or her own—she loves Sebastian and she loves Harry Gordon.

For both men the love she feels is almost impersonal. Sebastian's voice, as he sings a mournful song of Schubert, reveals to her an aspect of reality for which no words, no colours, could be an adequate medium. The subtlest of all arts is the appropriate vehicle for its communication. "She was struggling with something she had never felt before. A new conception of art? It came closer than that. A new kind of personality? But it was much more. It was a discovery about life, a revelation of love as a tragic force, not a melting mood, of passion that drowns like black water. As she sat listening to this man the outside world seemed to her dark and terrifying, full of fears and dangers that had never come close to her until now." Sebastian's love for Lucy is impersonal in the same sense. In a restless, wandering life he had lost beyond recovery "the deepest of all companionships, a relation with the earth itself, with a countryside and a people. That relationship, he knew, cannot be gone after and found: it must be long and deliberate, unconscious. It must indeed be a way of living." In Lucy's simplicity and animation he finds an expression of what he has missed, so powerful that companionship with her can give, at least for a time, the serenity and balance which she had acquired in her long, unconscious relationship with the Western land.

The land is not so vividly described, its formative power is not so emphasized, as in *The Song of the Lark* and *My Antonia*: it will, accordingly, be proper to explore the full meaning of the land rather in touching on these novels than at this point. In *Lucy Gayheart* the meaning of the land is most clearly revealed in the character of Harry Gordon. In Harry there are coarse and mean elements, the shrewd calculating hardness of the pioneer turned banker, the cocksureness of the successful provincial, the streak of moral vulgarity which allows him to reduce the relation between Lucy and Sebastian to a common flirtation between music teacher and pupil, the naïve realism which makes him insist that "facts are at the bottom of everything." It is late in the novel before Lucy or the reader appreciates the element of greatness in Harry, perceiving that: "He knew the world better than anyone else here, he had some imagination. He rose and fell, he was alive, he moved. He was not anchored, he was not lazy, he was not a sheep. Conceited and canny he was most days of the month; but on occasion something flashed out of him. There was a man underneath all those layers of caution: he wasn't tame at the core." By his moral vulgarity, by being at a critical moment a small-town soul, he lost Lucy. Not even that loss, not even a tedious marriage of convenience and spite, not even year upon year of hard-fisted banking, could destroy the deeper, purer element of greatness. Nothing could spoil and tame him completely; indeed the purer, authentically Western element flashed out more and more frequently as he grew older. In the closing scene of the novel, at the Gayheart house from which all the Gayhearts have passed to the cemetery, Harry's cashier "was unpleasantly reminded that there was and always had been something not quite regular about his chief; something fantastic, which he was secretly afraid of." The fantastic something which inspired fear in the perfect provincial, which had survived and grown and vanquished, is the elusive spirit which scarcely bears speaking of and which is at the centre of all the Western novels of Miss Cather, and the source of their greatness.

[. . .]

In a recollection of her childhood in Nebraska, Miss Cather remarks: "I have never found any intellectual excitement more intense than I used to feel when I spent a morning with one of these pioneer women at her baking or butter-making. I used to ride home in the most unreasonable state of excitement. I always felt as if they had told me so much more than they said. . . ." The feeling that a character has suggested so much more than he has said is the highest pleasure to be derived from Miss Cather's fiction. The feelings at the base of her fiction are always feelings that language is ill adapted to express; and she seldom makes the error of trying to state them in the clarity of conceptual terms. She prefers to leave them in much of their appropriate mystery, allowing them to insinuate themselves subtly, naturally, into the minds of those readers who are attuned to receive them. The most mysterious and the most powerful of all her feelings is her feeling for the West. "When I strike the open plains," she says, "something happens, I'm home. I breathe differently. That love of great spaces, of rolling open country like the sea,—it's the grand passion of my life." The New France of *Shadows on the Rock* was marked, as she says, by "a kind of feeling about life and human fate that I could not accept wholly;" and that novel inevitably lacks the strange intensity of conviction of the great Western novels that preceded it—and of *Lucy Gayheart* which is, one hopes, but the first of a new series of explorations of the Western land and soul.

Checklist of Additional Reviews

Wisconsin Library Bulletin, 31 (July 1935), 84.

Open Shelf (Cleveland), August 1935, p. 16.

"Willa Cather's Tale," *Springfield* (Massachusetts) *Sunday Union and Republican*, 4 August 1935, p. 5E.

Time, 26 (12 August 1935), 56.

Booklist, 32 (September 1935), 14.

Alfred Kazin, "Symbolic Tragedy," *Scribner's Magazine*, 98 (September 1935), 2, 4.

Carlton Wells, "*Lucy Gayheart*," *Scribner's Magazine*, 98 (November 1935), 313.

Pratt Institute Free Library Quarterly Booklist, Autumn 1935, p. 37.

NOT UNDER FORTY

Not Under Forty

BY

WILLA CATHER

1 9 3 6

NEW YORK

ALFRED A KNOPF

Edward N. Jenckes, "Miss Cather's Impressions," *Springfield* (Massachusetts) *Republican*, 21 November 1936, p. 6

Willa Cather's *Not Under Forty* has a title which, according to the author, means that "the book will have little interest for people under 40 years of age." It is to be hoped that "people under 40" will disappoint Miss Cather of her gloomy prophecy. If they do not they will miss a collection of sketches and essays that, while unpretentious, convey pleasantly mature thoughts in language that has sufficient youth and zest for all but the consciously and rambunctiously young.

Nor do the settings of these reminiscences seem very ancient. The "chance meeting" in Europe with a niece of Flaubert was in 1930. It was 10 years earlier that Miss Cather met on a transatlantic steamship the elderly New Englander who communicated personal reminiscences of Katherine Mansfield. These serve as an introduction to comments on Miss Mansfield's life and writings, but the reader will perhaps wish that Miss Cather had exploited this New Englander as a "last of the Puritans."

He would have answered requirements as well as—if not better than—Mr. Santayana's types. . . .

Or, if one were meditatively inclined, one might ask what will be the attitudes and mental interests of people now under 40 when they get to be 65. Much writing today seems intended for persons under 40 and especially under 30. That is natural enough; but the writers sometimes seem to imply that in their opinion the persons whom they are addressing are incapable of getting any older. Yet minds will probably mature and mellow much as they always have, even if modern life has decreed the banishment of "crabbed age"—and perhaps no loss, either.

Miss Cather's "backward" look goes farther into the past when she tells of visiting Mrs. James T. Fields at 148 Charles Street, Boston in 1908, accompanied by Mrs. Louis Brandeis. Mrs. Fields, though still young in mood and spirit, "seemed to reach back to Waterloo. As Mr. Howe reminds us, she had talked to Leigh Hunt about Shelley and his starlike beauty of face. She had known Severn well and it was he who gave her a lock of Keats' hair." Miss Cather also writes an appreciation of Sarah Orne Jewett. Indeed, New England receives a generous allotment of space in this honest and refreshing little book.

Apart from the reminiscences, or incidentally thereto, Miss Cather talks about the writing of fiction. And if there is any "message" in the book it is to be found here. For Miss Cather, like Virginia Woolf, is a modern novelist who is capable of seeing the novel in historical perspective and has pondered the qualities which make a work of fiction a work of art or at least a fresh creation of genius comparable to Nature itself.

The younger generation in letters has not been heedful of criticism, and it may be thought that some of these best fitted to criticize have either sought current popularity as expounders and promoters of "contemporary" output (an indispensable function of journalism, but not the goal of criticism) or else have adopted an ill-humored and dogmatic attitude of rejection, bolstered by formulas derived from social theory. There has been need—and there is still need—of simple discernment and hard-headed deduction, such as is to be found in these remarks of Miss Cather's: "A novel crowded with physical sensations is not less a catalog than one crowded with furniture.... Characters can be almost dehumanized by a laboratory study of the behavior of their bodily organs under sensory stimuli —can be reduced, indeed, to mere animal pulp."

Some of Miss Cather's observations about style and the contents of fiction may be less definitely pointed. The field of fiction is so broad that some of its greatest achievements probably lie outside the purely artistic achievement of "inherent, individual beauty." Miss Cather recognizes this when she says that Balzac's vitality survives bad translation. But she adds: "Also it implies the lack in him of certain qualities which matter to only a few people, but matter very much." This, too, is true, though one may doubt whether it makes Flaubert a greater novelist than Balzac. Style is a great preservative, and yet style, to the novelist, may be a delusion and a snare. C. E. Montague's *Rough Justice* is a completely "artful" work, yet Anne Douglas Sedgewick in her letters names it as the novel which she most intensely disliked— "among novels on the plane of taking seriously." And while it seems probable that Flaubert will continue to be read, it seems even more certain that C. E. Montague will not.

In spite of her pessimism, Miss Cather can be confidently claimed as a writer in whom persons under 40 will feel interest even when she chooses to talk about standards or the personalities of the past. Undoubtedly any writer who professes to be "one of the backward" takes a chance. Yet, outside certain coteries and doctrinaire bands, Miss Cather will be accepted as a mentor both gracious and wise.

Elizabeth Clarkson Zwart, "The Writings of Willa Cather 'Can Only Be Experienced,'" *Des Moines Register* [22 November 1936]

"The qualities of a second-rate writer can easily be defined, but a first-rate writer can only be experienced. It is just the thing in him which escapes analysis that makes him first-rate. One can catalogue all the qualities that he shares with other writers, but the thing that is his very own, his timbre, this cannot be defined or explained any more than the quality of a beautiful speaking voice."—Willa Cather

The above paragraph does not appear in Willa Cather's book of essays until the 134th of its 147 pages.

Through those first 134 pages, I was groping constantly for words in which to say what I was feeling about Miss Cather. And then she herself explained to me why I could not find them.

Earlier in this all too short book Miss Cather says: "Whatever is felt upon the page without being specifically named there—that, one might say, is created. It is the inexplicable presence of the thing not named, of the overtone divined by the ear but not heard of it, the verbal mood, the emotional aura of the fact or the thing or the deed, that gives high quality to the novel or the drama, as well as to poetry itself."

She says of Katherine Mansfield: "She communicates vastly more than she actually writes. One goes back and runs through the pages to find the text which made one know certain things . . . and the text is not there—but something was there, all the same—is there, though no typesetter will ever set it. It is this overtone, which is too fine for the printing press and comes through without it, that makes one know that this writer had something of the gift which is one of the rarest things in writing, and quite the most precious."

Some one should have said all that about Willa Cather. I wish that it might have been I.

The six essays in *Not Under Forty* are all concerned with literature. Discussions of the work of Flaubert and Balzac are made possible by her description of "a chance meeting" with an old French lady who turns out to be "Caro," the beloved niece to whom Flaubert wrote the *Lettres à sa Nièce Caroline*.

Again Miss Cather uses the portrait of an old lady—this time it is her friend, the late Mrs. James T. Fields of Boston—to speak of Dickens, Thackeray, Matthew Arnold, Henry James, and others.

Her discussion of Thomas Mann's *Joseph and His Brethren*, is perfection.

Miss Cather's essay, "The Novel Demeuble," should be read by all of our younger writers, among whom Miss Cather sees "hopeful signs" that "they are trying to break away from mere verisimilitude."—She still sees this hope in spite of the fact that "The Novel Demeuble" must contain this line: "If the novel is a form of imaginative art, it cannot be at the same time a vivid and brilliant form of journalism."

There is just one wrong note in Miss Cather's new book and that is her title. Of it she says: "The title of this book is meant to be 'arresting' only in a literal sense, like the signs put up for motorists: 'ROAD UNDER REPAIR,' etc. It means that the

book will have little interest for people under 40."

If I could believe that to be true I would resign my job tomorrow and never again read a book published after "1922 or thereabouts," the time at which Miss Cather says "the world broke in two."

Isabel Paterson, "Remembering Happier Days," *New York Herald Tribune Books*, 22 November 1936, p. 6

With nice discrimination, Miss Cather explains in a prefatory paragraph that she has chosen the title of this volume to indicate the type of readers she is addressing. "The book," she says serenely, "will have little interest for people under forty years of age," because it is allusive and marginal to a vanished order of life. "The world broke in two in 1922 or thereabouts, and the persons and prejudices recalled in these sketches slid back into yesterday's 7,000 years." She excepts one of her subjects, Thomas Mann, as belonging also to the future, but here she considers mainly that aspect of his work which "goes back a long way."

Mostly the pages are pleasantly nostalgic for the nineteenth century, and the effect is deliberately conveyed by making the particular memories derivative. She calls up, not the shades of the great, but of their kin or friends, relicts, survivors.

In the essay entitled "The Novel Démeublé," Miss Cather speculates on the permanence of detailed, physical

481

"realism" for its own sake, with no animus toward contemporary fashions, as she is discussing the eminent Victorians; but the principles may be applied at large.

A sketch of Sarah Orne Jewett and a glimpse at second hand of Katherine Mansfield complete the tale of chapters. Though slight in substance and deliberately withdrawn from the present in theme, they are all informed by the urbane quality which marks all Miss Cather's work. The reader who fails to find pleasure in these pages because of chronological incompatibility is the loser.

William Soskin, "Willa Cather's Excursions into the Literary Past," *New York Times Book Review*, 22 November 1936, p. 2

Persisting in her quite understandable search for quiet and contemplative peace off the main concrete highways, Miss Willa Cather gives us a small book of literary essays. In them she cultivates an atmosphere of calm in which the melodies of her special tastes will not be drowned out by the blatant concerto of contemporary criticism.

The personalities and the special points of view recalled in Miss Cather's sketches slid back into yesterday's 7,000 years, she writes, about 1922, when "the world broke in two." She is content to be a backslider and to avoid crowds. Her essays are staged in such effectively quiet backgrounds as the old-fashioned Grand Hotel at Aix-les-Bains, or the Boston drawing room of Mrs. James T. Fields, where linger the spirits of Matthew Arnold,

Emerson, Whittier and Holmes. They are intended, she warns us, for readers "not under forty."

In such settings it is not necessary for Miss Cather to make important critical statements or define large issues of literature. She is interested in dramatizing philosophical experiences, moments of divination she has actually lived through. She describes that sort of experience in relation to her reading of Flaubert's *L'Education sentimentale*: "one is 'left with it,' in the same way that one is left with a weak heart after certain illnesses."

At Aix-les-Bains Miss Cather came upon a fine old lady, spirited, keenly alive to the music and the culture of her time, a very old lady who turned out to be the niece to whom Flaubert wrote his famous letters—Madame Grout. It gave the author an opportunity to kiss the old lady's lovely hand "in homage to a great period" and to discuss that moment of the refinement of the senses in which one is graduated from a taste for Balzac to a taste for Flaubert. Balzac, like Dickens and Scott, "has a strong appeal for the great multitudes of humanity, while Flaubert, Stendhal, Conrad, Brahms. . . ."

Beyond this distinction and a few entirely fascinating facts and memories regarding Madame Grout—her friendship with Turgenieff, her communion with Flaubert, her taste for Scriabin and Stravinsky—there is no extraordinary wealth of material in this essay. But how impressively is the material exploited under these romantic, almost theatricalized circumstances!

In Mrs. Fields's drawing room the nicely adjusted dramatization of atmosphere is continued. Here we are in the presence of a very, very old lady who talked to Leigh Hunt about the starlike beauty of Shelley's face. Occasionally Miss Cather seems so tremendously impressed with these physical circumstances that we are inclined to wonder just what, specifically, Mrs. Fields said to Leigh Hunt, and whether it was an enlightened conversation. But the sheer factual texture of the chapter is undoubtedly impressive—the provincial New England snobbishness of Dr. Holmes addressing the actor guests, Jefferson and Warren, as "you gentlemen of the stage," and the visits of Dickens and Thackeray and other luminous figures.

Miss Cather grieves that a modern, prosaic garage now stands on the site of the house where in softly lighted drawing rooms and dining rooms "Learning and Talent met, enjoying good food and good wit and rare vintages, looking confidently forward to the growth of their country in the finer amenities of life."

For those to whom this nostalgic note seems altogether out of tune with the ideals, artistic and social, of a generation under 40, Miss Cather has even more irritating words. Discussing the gleaming stream of present-day journalistic fiction, she finds a vast futility in literalness and material cataloguing. To her the work of D. H. Lawrence "sharply reminds one how vast a distance lies between emotion and mere sensory reactions." And the rude heckler who may think that the sensory reactions of Lawrence are infinitely more emotional than the arty hush of a Boston drawing room whose guests worship a vaguely formulated esthetic theory and retire to a good dinner would be immediately put in his place by Miss Cather.

In Sarah Orne Jewett, Miss Cather finds a native artist with an individual quality of voice that is more important than the work of the realists. She wants a writer to be rooted in the beauty of her home soil as Miss Jewett was on the coast of Maine. She found in Miss Jewett's person the stamp of "a lady, in the old, high sense." And the critics who find an insignificant, pleasant provincialism in Miss Jewett's homely writings are, Miss Cather thinks, probably "of foreign descent: German, Jewish, Scandinavian. To him English is merely a means of making himself understood, of communicating his ideas. He may write and speak American English correctly, but only as an American may learn to speak French correctly. It is a surface speech."

The surfaces of Miss Cather's speech are undoubtedly velvety, and the velvet is draped shrewdly and mysteriously about her meanings. Behind the drapery one finds a sincere worship of the best in Continental, rather rapidly aging artists (the age, mind you, is Miss Cather's premise at the outset), a sentimental fondness for inferior artists who have the social or racial solidity Miss Cather admires, a deep admiration for the prophetlike moments of Thomas Mann, whose writing in *Joseph and His Brothers* wakens the deep vibrations of her soul.

Mr. W. A. Dwiggins has designed the little book of essays in rather a bizarre manner that does not seem to me to suit the mood of Miss Cather's disciplined writing. The type in which it is set, also designed by Mr. Dwiggins, blurs the eye because the letters are condensed and tall and seem to bend in a text page. But Mr. Dwiggins explains his design elaborately in a note at the end of the book, and his aims are specific and sensible, whatever the result.

Kansas City Star
[28 November 1936]

Willa Cather, in the first collection of essays she has published, studies several personalities and certain aspects of literature and reveals some of her convictions about the art of fiction writing.

One of these convictions—an important one by the measure of her emphasis—is that literalness must give way to suggestion if fiction is to be art instead of journalism. She blames Balzac for the vogue of literalness that passes as realism.

"We have had," she writes, "too much of the interior decorator and the 'romance of business' since his day. The city he built on paper is already crumbling. Stevenson said he wanted to blue-pencil a great deal of Balzac's 'presentation'—and he loved him beyond all modern novelists."

As superior to this method, the enumerator's method, Miss Cather places the artistic suggestion of a Flaubert or Merimee. "Where is the man," she asks, "who could cut one sentence from the stories of Merimee? And who wants any more detail as to how Carmencita and her fellow factory-girls made cigars?"

Literalness in the presentation of mental reactions and physical sensations is no more effective, she continues, than literalness in presenting material things. Selection and suggestion still are the best tools of the artist. . . .

Therefore she can imagine nothing more terrible than, say, the story of "Romeo and Juliet" rewritten in prose by a cataloguing writer such as D. H. Lawrence.

As the title implies, *Not Under Forty* is intended for older readers; it does not deal with the younger school of authors, the "moderns." Flaubert, Tolstoy, Hawthorne, Sarah Orne Jewett, Katherine Mansfield and Thomas Mann are figures she discusses with admiration and understanding.

"The world broke in two in 1922 or thereabouts," she writes in a prefatory note, "and the persons and prejudices recalled in these sketches slid back into yesterday's 7,000 years. Thomas Mann,

to be sure, belongs immensely to the forward-goers, and they are concerned only with his forwardness. But he also goes back a long way, and his backwardness is more gratifying to the backward. It is for the backward, and by one of their number, that these sketches were written."

The most charming, and the longest, sketch in the collection, "A Chance Meeting," gives an account of Miss Cather's contact with a fine old lady, Mme. Franklin Grout, niece of Gustave Flaubert. Mme. Grout was the "Caro" of the *Lettres a sa Niece Caroline*, and Miss Cather forgot the discomfort of overly warm summer days at Aix-les-Bains in a prolonged discussion of the famous French writer in whose house Mme. Grout had been brought up.

Henry Seidel Canby, "Powerful Slightness," *Saturday Review of Literature*, 15 (28 November 1936), 7

I wonder whether Miss Cather is right, whether this criticism which insists so much upon discipline, upon fineness of perception, upon the strength which comes from real knowledge, will not be read with interest by people under forty? She is, I think, too pessimistic. If vigor at all costs, doctrine of any kind, and behavior to the nth degree is now in fashion, this may be more a reaction against the genteel and the vacuous than a permanent policy.

It would be well, however, for any one to read this little book if only to see the importance of taste in criticism. Miss

Cather's method is the personal and the narrative. She has a story to tell about most of her authors, but the story would not be told if the participants had not shared a subtle appreciation of what makes durable literature. In her first essay it is a favorite niece of Flaubert, his "Caro," whom she meets by chance at Aix-les-Bains. A New Englander who had known Katherine Mansfield as a child, opens the discussion of the "powerful slightness" of that remarkable student of "the major forces of life" approached "through comparatively trivial incidents." "No. 148 Charles St." is the account of a meeting with the elderly widow of James T. Fields of Ticknor and Fields, the famous publishers of the great New Englanders. And quite as personal is her admirable study of Sarah Orne Jewett. In all of these essays, so familiar, so personal on the surface, Miss Cather's continuing stress upon what impresses her in really good literature is evident. It is the immense pains of learning to write, the long struggle to escape from the tyranny of mere words, from the shows and affectations of approximate renderings of reality into the calm assurance of truth, which seem to her the stairway to greatness.

T. V., "Essays about the Art of Writing," *Los Angeles Times* [29 November 1936]

The title of Miss Cather's first book of essays is meant to serve as a warning, she says, to people under 40 who will not be interested. "The world broke in two in 1922 or thereabouts, and the persons and

prejudices recalled in these sketches slid back into yesterday's 7,000 years." Miss Cather's subjects are Flaubert and Madame Grout; Sarah Orne Jewett, Thomas Mann, Katherine Mansfield and the furniture of the modern novel. And only those bowed down with the weight of years will be interested?

Surely the title and foreword of this distinguished little volume were creations of a passing melancholy. For in the first place, the reviewer is quite confident (experto crede) that today's young men and women of intelligence are more concerned with Flaubert than were those of yesterday. As for Thomas Mann and Katherine Mansfield, it may be that they are not as fashionable, but they receive more serious attention than they did a decade ago.

And even if this were not true, Miss Cather's happy informality of manner, her sure critical instinct make this volume of essays on the art of writing as essential and as interesting to forward-goers as to the weary army of backward-lookers. Whatever Miss Cather touches becomes a work of art and acquires a new significance.

"American Essayist," *Times Literary Supplement* (London), 5 December 1936, p. 1007

Willa Cather is one of the best known of the older American novelists—older not in mental outlook but in the sense that she writes in a quiet, careful way, with no eccentricities of style or subject-matter. The whole tone of this little book of literary reminiscences and criticism indicates her preferences; there is much, for instance, about Balzac and Flaubert, and of the two she estimates Balzac far the more highly, for her tastes run more to the classical than to the exuberant. She has tried to narrow her field by the title she has chosen, deliberately dissociating herself from "modern" trends. She says in her preface that "the book will have little interest for people under forty years of age." But here she may well be wrong, for she reveals a thoughtful appreciation of authors one already loves which will tend to bring one back to others she mentions who may be less familiar.

This small collection of essays is a very personal one, containing not only critical impressions of Thomas Mann's *Joseph and his Brethren* and of that almost neglected writer, Sarah Orne Jewett, but recollections of people who have played interesting though minor parts in literary history. There is the story of the old gentleman who had met Katherine Mansfield as a little girl, and remembered her: of old Mrs. Fields, sitting in her house in Boston recalling the giants of her youth: and, most charming of all, the sketch of Flaubert's niece as a very old and very determined and delightful lady going to the Opera at Aix-les-Bains.

Thomas Moult, *Guardian* (Manchester), 11 December 1936, p. 10

Not only does Miss Willa Cather stand alone among present-day practitioners in the art of fiction across the Atlantic; she is also a critic and essayist of exceptional discernment, and to the reader with a sense of proportion her new book will be as welcome as though it were a novel or a group of short stories. As a matter of fact, some of the brief studies in this collection are almost to be described as short stories, for the author makes a personal, intimate, semi-dramatic approach to her subject, notably in her study of Katherine Mansfield, who has not previously been revealed in the light thrown upon her by Miss Cather's New Englander, a fellow-passenger on her way home from Naples, who had met Katherine as "a little girl with thin legs and large eyes who wandered away from the family and apparently wished to explore the steamer for herself." It is this elderly stranger's recollection that enables Miss Cather to interpret the author of "The Garden Party" afresh—and, as her admirers must admit, with uncanny rightness.

We do not feel, however, that we have simply been reading an essay on how the artist sets to work, which is what Miss Cather suggests in her closing paragraphs that she has really intended. Such a contribution to literary technique, written in such a style—serene, superbly confident—is but one of several "object lessons," as we may call them, that are included in a book whose title, *Not Under Forty*, is briefly explained in a preface: "It means that the book will have little interest for people under forty years of age. The world broke in two in 1922 or thereabouts, and the persons and prejudices recalled in these sketches slid back into yesterday's seven thousand years."

But we would urge our novelists and short-story writers under forty to read the essay on "The Novel Démeublé," which begins with the declaration that "the novel for a long while has been overfurnished." Miss Cather's argument, which includes the reminder that every writer who is an artist knows that his power of observation, his power of description, form but a low part of his equipment, should do something towards bringing about the dismissal of the "actualistic" novelist's excessive furniture—yes, even at the cost of much of Balzac himself—and, with it, "all the meaningless reiterations concerning physical sensations, all the tiresome old patterns, and leave the room as bare as the stage of a Greek theatre." It would be highly interesting to see how our successful modernists fared if we made such a drastic revision of the commonly accepted literary standards.

G. K.'s Weekly (London), 17 December 1936

After enjoying the new approach to literary criticism contained in these delightful essays one is left with the feeling that there is only one critic who could deal really adequately with them—and that is Miss Cather herself. Had she for instance chanced upon some relative of Miss Willa Cather, the authoress, in a French hotel, or some acquaintance of hers in a transAtlantic steamer, what an insight we should have had into the subtleties of her style and the fineness of her perceptions!

We have most of us admired at least one or two of Miss Cather's novels, and those critical essays are, most of them, novels in miniature. Characters appear and talk, and out of their conversation and their actions there grows (it would seem almost unconsciously) a delicate vignette not only of the persons, but of their work or that of their friends. At the end of the story one knows a new author or a familiar author in a new light. And the appreciation appeals to us as both true and discerning. On finishing the book one is irresistibly drawn to the bookcase to find a volume by one of the authors we have suddenly come to know—not least one of Miss Willa Cather's.

Louis Kronenberger, "In Dubious Battle," *Nation*, 143 (19 December 1936), 738–9

Miss Cather, explaining her title, says that this book of literary comment "will have little interest for people under forty years of age" because "the world broke in two in 1922 or thereabouts." Reading on, one finds this note stressed again and again, until one feels it has acquired an excessive significance in Miss Cather's mind—as though 1922 stands for one of the Ten Decisive Battles of the World, and people must greet one another, even today, with a peremptory "Friend or enemy?" As a result, the book has a propagandist smell, and one's first job is to discount its overtones—overtones of smugness springing from uncertainty, of an odd feeling of guilt, of a deep feeling of regret for the past and a self-righteous loyalty in going to the past's defense. But if Miss Cather is writing, as at heart every good writer must, for her equals and not for her classmates; if she is trying to say what is true and not what is comforting, it is scarcely for her to name her audience in advance.

Of course this book is a confession of what needs no confessing. Every American reviewer who asks for more in a novelist than charm of style and responsiveness to atmosphere has attacked Miss Cather in recent years for running out on the present to hide in the past and for rejecting even such portions of the past as had the poor judgment to be unsavory or ungovernable. That the author of *My Antonia* and *A Lost Lady* should have turned squeamish and at length genteel, that she should have broken with the vibrant tradition in which she achieved so much, is a great misfortune; it is perhaps an even greater one that she should regard her defection as a virtue, and be somewhat holier-than-thou concerning it. Faced with the choice, I think most of us would have preferred having her deal with life as she used to, even if she stopped from time to time to recoil in ladylike fright, to her refusing to deal with life at all. But it is presumably too late; the only noise of battle with which Miss Cather chooses to be concerned is its cadenced echo.

When Miss Cather comes to sum up a lifetime of reading, she reverts to Sarah Orne Jewett and Katharine Mansfield, to a niece of Flaubert's, whom she met at Aix-les-Bains, to the widow of James T. Fields, whom she visited at Manchester-by-the-Sea. To these she adds a curiously intense paper on Mann's *Joseph and His Brothers* and an essay entitled "The Novel Démeublé." The pieces on Mansfield and Jewett do not rise from appreciation to criticism, and must be dismissed. The memoir of Flaubert's niece makes delightful reading—one shares in the excitement of casually encountering a remarkable old lady who revivifies a great and brilliant period. The memoir of Mrs. Fields, on the other hand, is just too, too delightful, assuming you care for those great ladies whom certain playwrights are always creating along with mellow, middle-aged art connoisseurs from Vienna.

In "The Novel Démeublé" Miss Cather, still fighting the Battle of the Books, gets down to saying something. She argues forcefully against the use of so much unimportant baggage in the modern novel: so much cataloguing, so much parading of mere observation, so much

displaying of physical sensations for their own sake. What she argues for is the sovereign play of the emotions, the restitution of the valuable and lasting elements in the human drama. She is perfectly right of course; literature always needs to be decoded from a passing jargon into a universal language; consequently it needs what Miss Cather implies it lacks—a sound sense of tradition and cultural integration. But need she sniff and purse her lips as though the fate of literature lay with her alone? And dare she think that all we mean by tradition is more important than all we mean by experience? She meanwhile has become a little too fond of high-sounding, evocative words; a little too prone to imbue her work with the sense of good breeding. Much the same thing has happened to her in her way as has happened to T. S. Eliot in his. Each has mistaken a hothouse for a garden; each has forfeited much power, much understanding, in exchange for the consolations of a measured, formal attitude toward life. The critic may lack the right to question such decisions, but he cannot help commenting on what harm they have done, artistically, to those who made them.

Fanny Butcher, "Willa Cather's Book Intended Not for Youth," *Chicago Daily Tribune*, 16 January 1937, p. 15

Willa Cather, America's most distinguished woman novelist, has published her first volume of essays, *Not Under Forty*. "The title of this book," she declares in a prefatory note, "is meant to be 'arresting' only in the literal sense, like the signs put up for motorists: 'Road Under Repair.' It means that the book will have little interest for people under 40 years of age."

Miss Cather has, of course, a right to her opinion but so do her critics, and mine is that if only for the jewels of literary criticism set in her delicately golden prose, those under as well as over 40 will find joy in these papers.

To be sure they have a somewhat nostalgic quality, but that is because they are all concerned with writers (or in the case of Thomas Mann, with material) that are past, though only in the physical sense dead.

The first of the six papers is one that was originally published in the *Atlantic Monthly* and cut out and treasured by Miss Cather's admirers. It tells of "A Chance Meeting" at Aix Les Bains with the niece of Flaubert, the "Caroline" to whom the famous letters were written.

It is at the same time a brilliant and beautiful picture of a sturdy and determined old woman whose life was lived for, and then for the memory of, a genius; a critical analysis of the work of that genius; and a swift, clear sketch of a lovely spot on earth. Her analysis of Flaubert's art and his place in French literature is sure and exact. And the portrait which she draws of her heroine has much of the perfection of *A Lost Lady*. "A Chance Meeting" is, it seems to me, a small masterpiece.

"148 Charles Street" and "Miss Jewett" do not seem to equal it—perhaps, because they are records of emotional memories, while "A Chance Meeting" was a record of an intellectual one. They are concerned with Mrs. James T. Fields, wife of a famous Boston publisher who knew all of the great and gave them, in her rich memory, to Willa Cather when she needed them most, and with Sarah Orne Jewett who was, I believe, the greatest influence in Miss Cather's literary life.

The short "Novel Démeublé" is the only paper in which irony is more than hinted at. In it one finds outspoken disgust at the "over furnished" modern novel and a simple but memorable statement of the business of the novelist. The writer of any age will find in *Not Under Forty* something as refreshing as a spring in a cliff side.

W. J. Simon, "Willa Cather Addresses Herself to Mature Minds," *San Francisco Chronicle* [31 January 1936]

Since the war, world literature has taken a decided turn to—shall we say?—the left. A new prose, a new idea of realism, a new and frequently distorted technic have quite definitely taken the place of the calmer, more grammatical and more retrospective writing of the pre-war era. There are few of that other generation's representatives left—who have continued serenely into the present turbulent world of letters. Willa Cather is one of the few.

Miss Cather occupies a place that is decidedly unique in the modern literary maelstrom. Although she is America's foremost representative of the mauve decade, she is absolutely not a back-number. Instead, she has kept right up with the moderns without giving in to any of their more superficial ideas. In fact, Miss Cather has made a splendid success in her recent books in interpreting the tempo of today to those of her generation who are not as apt as she in orienting themselves to the changes that occur yearly about them. . . .

Willa Cather has little time or patience for the young man or woman, born and raised in the city, "violently inoculated with Freud," who finds no emotional depth in American English. Of him she says, "he can see what these Yankees have not—hence an epidemic of 'suppressed desire' plays and novels—but what they have, their actual preferences and their fixed scale of values, are absolutely dark to him." For she herself is intensely American and is proud of the traditions of American literature, the finest of which are embodied in every piece of work ever done by her. She writes with sincerity, and clarity, and with good taste without being too feminine, and she can be subtle without being obscure.

In a publicity minded book selling age when half a dozen "great new novels" by "truly great writers" are issued every week to a somewhat jaded reading public, one hesitates to use that adjective to salute excellence; it has become almost a stigma. Of Willa Cather, however, it might be said she is one of the foremost writers of English prose in America today; and *Not Under Forty*, which is more or less an expression of her literary convictions, will prove a joy to those who love good reading and to those who love Willa Cather. The two groups are synonymous.

Ellery Sedgwick, "The Atlantic Bookshelf," *Atlantic Monthly*, 159 (February 1937), n.p.

Now God be praised for prejudice, for it is prejudice which makes predilections what they ought to be. Genius it sometimes thwarts and oftener deflects. But to talent, prejudice is a friendly guide, shaping it after its natural bent.

Miss Cather was born with prejudices of her own. She dislikes all that Walter Scott used to call the Big Bow-wows. She admires not power but perfection. She shuns the crowd, and the things the crowd care for. She loves to watch—but always from a distance. For her fastidious talent America has especial need.

Neither Miss Cather's prejudices nor her predilections have undergone much change since she came out of the West. The formless prairie, the sandy sluggish streams, the windy landscape, and the wind-blown people formed a background at once too ample and too inchoate for her fancy. One knows instinctively that she was never happy till she escaped to the land she has made her own, a land of quiet where manners are made by tradition and the spirit never escapes from the mould which defines its excellence. The country of her allegiance is far from the land of her inheritance, and for its past she feels an alien nostalgia which those "under forty" can never know.

It is in praise of this past that she has written this slender volume in reverence and love. The most delightful of her essays is that in which she approaches the greatest of her gods, Flaubert, whose clairvoyance means hardly more to her than his intolerance of imperfection. Rather than to presume to stand directly before his altar, she makes her oblation vicariously, sitting at the feet of his niece, Madame Franklin Grout, the Caro of the *Lettres à sa Nièce*. They met by merest chance, but to sit beside one who had held an immortal hand was thrilling to Miss Cather, and the electricity of that touch lights the chapter. That she declined to press so fortunate an accident is wholly characteristic. She refused an invitation to visit her friend at Antibes. She put away from her the proferred gift of an authentic Flaubert letter. Sweetest to her are distant perfumes. She loves to live remotely, protecting herself from too common an admiration, and ever half afraid to draw near divinity lest she discover some touch of clay.

It is the same oblique approach she makes to the New England tradition. Old Mrs. James T. Fields lived on in Boston at 148 Charles Street. Not a mote in the sunbeam which floated through the windows of the long parlor but had danced there in the great days when Holmes, Lowell, and Longfellow had routed the incredulity of Thackeray and of Dickens as to the existence of American culture. The Fields legend went back past the demigods to the gods themselves, and as Miss Cather sat beside her hostess, reclining as ever on her sofa, the past became present, and the present had no being. From Nebraska to Charles Street, Miss Cather had come far, but it was her road home.

To anyone who, in those ancient days, walked up the carpeted stairs, past keepsakes and mementoes, tall octavos of Dryden, Donne, and Herbert, turning right through the long quiet parlor to draw a chair beside the sofa where, in lace cap and rustling silk, Mrs. Fields lay under the portrait of Dickens,—not yet cynical and bearded, but in his twenties and glowing in the confidence of genius, —Miss Cather's memories stir a thousand others.

To Miss Cather we are already indebted for a distillation of Miss Jewett's stories, wrought with a precision unknown elsewhere in American Letters. She now adds brief memories of their author. How handsome Miss Jewett looked in those days, the epitome of New England inheritance, a little formal, not free from self-consciousness, but a work of art quite as truly as her stories are a work of nature.

Slighter papers make up the volume, illuminated by flashes of intuitive understanding. Katherine Mansfield, she remarks, has "a powerful slightness." How excellent the phrase! When Miss Cather says that a second-rate writer can be defined, but one first-rate can only be experienced, she codifies a law of universal criticism.

Lionel Trilling, "Willa Cather," *New Republic*, 90 (10 February 1937), 10–13

In 1922 Willa Cather wrote an essay called "The Novel Démeublé" in which she pleaded for a movement to throw the "furniture" out of the novel—to get rid, that is, of all the social fact that Balzac and other realists had felt to be so necessary for the understanding of modern character. "Are the banking system and the Stock Exchange worth being written about at all?" Miss Cather asked, and she replied that they were not. Among the things which had no "proper place in imaginative art"—because they cluttered the scene and prevented the free play of the emotions—Miss Cather spoke of the factory and the whole realm of "physical sensations." Obviously, this essay was the rationale of a method which Miss Cather had partly anticipated in her early novels and which she fully developed a decade later in *Shadows on the Rock*. And it is no less obvious that this technical method is not merely a literary manner but the expression of a point of view toward which Miss Cather had always been moving—with results that, to many of her readers, can only indicate the subtle failure of her admirable talent.

If we say that Miss Cather has gone down to defeat before the actualities of American life we put her in such interesting company that the indictment is no very terrible one. For a history of American literature must be, in Whitman's phrase, a series of "vivas for those who have failed." In our literature there are perhaps fewer completely satisfying books and certainly fewer integrated careers than there are interesting canons of work and significant life stories. Something in American life seems to prevent the perfection of success while it produces a fascinating kind of search or struggle, usually unavailing, which we may observe again and again in the collected works and in the biographies of our writers.

In this recurrent but heroic defeat, the life of the American writer parallels the life of the American pioneer. The historian of frontier literature, Professor Hazard, has pointed out that Cooper's very first presentation of Deerslayer, the type of all pioneers, shows him a nearly broken old man threatened with jail for shooting a deer, a pitiful figure overwhelmed by the tides of commerce and speculation. In short, to a keen observer, the pioneer's defeat was apparent even in 1823. The subsequent decades that opened fresh frontiers did not change the outcome of the struggle. Ahead of the pioneer there are always the fields of new promise, with him are the years of heartbreaking effort, behind him are the men who profit by his toil and his hope. Miss Cather's whole body of work is the attempt to accommodate and assimilate her perception of the pioneer's failure. Reared on a Nebraska farm, she saw the personal and cultural defeat at first hand. Her forebears had marched westward to the new horizons; her own work is a march back toward the spiritual East—toward all that is the very antithesis of the pioneer individualism and innovation, toward authority and permanence, toward Rome itself.

The pioneer, as seen by a sophisticated intelligence like Miss Cather's, stands in double jeopardy: he faces both the danger of failure and the danger of success. "A pioneer . . . should be able to enjoy the idea of things more than the things themselves," Miss Cather says; disaster comes when an idea becomes an actuality. From *O Pioneers*! to *The Professor's House*, Miss Cather's novels portray the results of the pioneer's defeat, both in the thwarted pettiness to which he is condemned by his material failures and in the callous insensitivity produced by his material success. "The world is little, people are little, human life is little," says Thea Kronborg's derelict music teacher in *The Song of the Lark*. "There is only one big thing— desire." When there is no longer the opportunity for effective desire, the pioneer is doomed. But already in Miss Cather's Nebraska . . . the opportunities for effective desire had largely been removed: the frontier had been closed.

A Lost Lady, Miss Cather's most explicit treatment of the passing of the old order, is the central work of her career. Far from being the delicate minor work it is so often called, it is probably her most muscular book, for it derives power from the grandeur of its theme. Miss Cather shares the American belief in the tonic moral quality of the pioneer's life; with the passing of the frontier she conceives that a great source of fortitude has been lost. Depending on a very exact manipulation of symbols, the point of *A Lost Lady* (reminiscent of Henry James's *The Sacred Fount*) is that the delicacy and charm of Marian Forrester spring not from herself but from the moral strength of her pioneer husband. Heavy, slow, not intelligent, Forrester is one of those men who, in his own words, "dreamed the railroads across the mountains." He shares the knightly virtues which Miss Cather unquestioningly ascribes to the early settlers; "impractical to the point of magnificence," he is one of those who could "conquer but not hold." He is defeated by the men of the new money interests who "never risked anything"— and the perdition of the lost lady proceeds in the degree that she withdraws from her husband in favor of one of the sordid new men, until she finds her final degradation in the arms of an upstart vulgarian.

But though the best of the pioneer ideal is defeated by alien forces, the ideal itself, Miss Cather sees, is really an insufficient one. In her first considerable novel, *O Pioneers!* she already wrote in an elegiac mood and with the sense that the old ideal was not enough. Alexandra Bergson, with her warm simplicity, her resourcefulness and shrewd courage, is the essence of the pioneering virtues, but she is distinguished above her neighbors because she feels that, if she is to work at all, she must believe that the world is wider than her cornfields. Her pride is not that she has triumphed over the soil but that she has made her youngest brother "a personality apart from the soil." The pioneer, having reached his goal at the horizons of the earth, must look to the horizons of the spirit.

The disappearance of the old frontier left Miss Cather with a heritage of the virtues in which she had been bred but with the necessity of finding a new object for them. Looking for the new frontier, she found it in the mind. From the world of failure which she portrayed so savagely in "A Wagner Matinee" and "The Sculptor's Funeral," and from the world of fat prosperity of *One of Ours*, she could flee to the world of art. For in art one may desire illimitably. And if, conceivably, one

may fail—Miss Cather's artists never do— it is still only as an artist that one may be the eternal pioneer, concerned always with "the idea of things." Thea Kronborg, of the breed of Alexandra Bergson, turns all the old energy, bogged down in mediocrity, toward music. Miss Cather rhapsodizes for her: "O eagle of eagles! Endeavor, achievement, desire, glorious striving of human art."

But art is not the only, or a sufficient, salvation from the débâcle of pioneer culture. For some vestige of the old striving after new worlds which cannot be gratified seems to spread a poison through the American soul, making it thin and unsubstantial, unable to find peace and solidity. A foreigner says to Claude Wheeler of *One of Ours*, "You Americans are always looking for something outside yourselves to warm you up, and it is no way to do. In old countries, where not very much can happen to us, we know that, and we learn to make the most of things." And with the artists, Miss Cather puts those gentle spirits who have learned to make the most of things—Neighbor Rosicky, Augusta and, preëminently, My Antonia. Momentarily betrayed by the later developments of the frontier, Antonia at last fulfills herself in childbearing and a busy household, expressing her "relish for life, not overdelicate but invigorating."

Indeed, "making the most of things" becomes even more important to Miss Cather than the eternal striving of art. For, she implies, in our civilization even the best ideals are bound to corruption. *The Professor's House* is the novel in which she brings the failure of the pioneer spirit into the wider field of American life. Lame as it is, it epitomizes as well as any novel of our time the disgust with life which so many sensitive Americans feel, which makes them dream of their pre-adolescent integration and innocent community with nature, speculate on the "release from effort" and the "eternal solitude" of death, and eventually reconcile themselves to a life "without delight." Three stories of betrayal are interwoven in this novel: the success of Professor St. Peter's history of the Spanish explorers which tears him away from the frontier of his uncomfortable and ugly old study to set him up in an elegant but stifling new home; the sale to a foreign collector of the dead Tom Outland's Indian relics which had made his spiritual heritage; and the commercialization of Outland's scientific discovery with its subsequent corruption of the Professor's charming family. With all of life contaminated by the rotting of admirable desires, only Augusta, the unquesting and unquestioning German Catholic seamstress, stands secure and sound.

Not the pioneering philosophy alone, but the whole poetic romanticism of the nineteenth century had been suffused by the belief that the struggle rather than the prize was admirable, that a man's reach should exceed his grasp, or what's a heaven for? Having seen the insufficiency of this philosophy Miss Cather must find another in which the goal shall be more than the search. She finds it, expectably enough, in religion. The Catholicism to which she turns is a Catholicism of culture, not of doctrine. The ideal of unremitting search, it may be said, is essentially a Protestant notion; Catholic thought tends to repudiate the ineluctable and to seek the sharply defined. The quest for Moby Dick, that dangerous beast, is Protestant; the Catholic tradition selects what it can make immediate and tangible in symbol and Miss Cather turns to the way of life that "makes the most of things," to the old settled cultures. She attaches a mystical significance to the ritual of the ordered life, to the niceties of cookery, to the supernal virtues of *things*

themselves—sherry, or lettuce, or "these coppers, big and little, these brooms and clouts and brushes" which are the tools for making life itself. And with a religious ideal one may safely be a pioneer. The two priests of *Death Comes for the Archbishop* are pioneers; they happen to be successful in their enterprise, but they could not have been frustrated, Miss Cather implies, because the worth of their goal is indisputable.

From the first of her novels the Church had occupied a special and gracious place in Willa Cather's mind. She now thinks with increasing eloquence of its permanence and certainty and of "the universal human yearning for something permanent, enduring, without shadow of change." The Rock becomes her often repeated symbol: "the rock, when one comes to think of it, was the utmost expression of human need." For the Church seems to offer the possibility of satisfying that appealing definition of human happiness which Miss Cather had made as far back as *My Antonia*—"to be dissolved in something complete and great," "to become a part of something entire, whether it is sun and air, goodness and knowledge."

It is toward that dissolvement that Miss Cather is always striving. She achieves it with the "sun and air"—and perhaps few modern writers have been so successful with landscape. She can find it in goodness and in society—but only if they have the feudal constriction of the old Quebec of *Shadows on the Rock*. Nothing in modern life, no possibility, no hope, offers it to her. She conceives, as she says in the prefatory note to her volume of essays, *Not Under Forty*, that the world "broke in two in 1922 or thereabouts" and she numbers herself among the "backward," unaware that even so self-conscious and defiant a rejection of her own time must make her talent increasingly irrelevant and tangential—for any time.

"The early pioneer was an individualist and a seeker after the undiscovered," says F. J. Turner, "but he did not understand the richness and complexity of life as a whole." Though Miss Cather in all her work has recognized this lack of understanding of complexity and wholeness, and has attempted to transcend it, she ends, ironically enough, in a fancier but no less restricted provincialism than the one she sought to escape. For the "spirituality" of Miss Cather's latest books consists chiefly of an irritated exclusion of those elements of modern life with which she will not cope. The particular affirmation of the verities which Miss Cather makes requires that the "furniture" be thrown out, that the social and political facts be disregarded; the spiritual life cannot support the intrusion of all the facts the mind can supply. The unspeakable Joubert, the extreme type of the verity-seeker, says in one of his *pensées*: "'I'm hungry, I'm cold, help me!' Here is material for a good deed but not for a good work of art." Miss Cather, too, is irked by the intrusion of "physical sensations" in the novel.

Miss Cather's later books are pervaded by the air of a brooding ancient wisdom, but if we examine her mystical concern with pots and pans, it does not seem much more than an oblique defense of gentility or very far from the gaudy domesticity of bourgeois accumulation glorified in *The Woman's Home Companion*. And with it goes a culture-snobbery and even a caste-snobbery. The Willa Cather of the older days shared the old racial democracy of the West. It is strange to find the Willa Cather of the present talking about "the adopted American," the young man of German, Jewish or Scandinavian descent who can never appreciate Sarah Orne Jewett and for whom American English

can never be more than a means of communicating ideas: "It is surface speech: he clicks the words out as a bank clerk clicks out silver when you ask for change. For him the language has no emotional roots." This is indeed the gentility of Katherine Fullerton Gerould, and in large part the result, one suspects, of what Parrington calls "the inferiority complex of the frontier mind before the old and established."

Yet the place to look for the full implications of a writer's philosophy is in the esthetic of his work. *Lucy Gayheart* shows to the full the effect of Miss Cather's point of view. It has always been a personal failure of her talent that prevented her from involving her people in truly dramatic relations with each other. (Her women, for example, always stand in the mother or daughter relation to men; they are never truly lovers.) But at least once upon a time her people were involved in a dramatic relation with themselves or with their environments, whereas now *Lucy Gayheart* has not even this involvement. Environment does not exist, fate springs from nothing save change; the characters are unattached to anything save their dreams. The novel has been *démeublé* indeed; but life without its furniture is strangely bare.

Peter Monro Jack, "The Sense of the Past," *New Republic*, 90 (10 February 1937), 25–6

Miss Cather's little book must be the saddest of fall reveries. Elegiacally and sentimentally, it commemorates the past, the immediate Victorian past, tranquil and traditional, bookish and complacent and, looking around now, she finds little enough left of it. "The world broke in two in 1922 or thereabouts, and the persons and prejudices recalled in these sketches slid back into yesterday's seven thousand years." Flaubert's niece, the Caroline of the Letters, a very old lady when Miss Cather met her by chance at Aix-les-Bains, has her great moments when Turgenev's name is mentioned and she can say with a sigh, "Ah, yes, I knew him well at one time," and continue, "my uncle also was a man of letters, Gustave Flaubert, you may perhaps know. . . ." Mrs. Fields (the widow of James T. Fields, of Fields and Ticknor, publishers, of Boston) reclines in her widow's lavender on a green sofa directly under the portrait of Dickens and reads Arnold's "Tristan and Iseult" and Miss Sarah Orne Jewett exclaims that she didn't believe the poem had been read aloud in the Charles Street house since Matthew Arnold himself had read it there. Mrs. Fields had talked to Leigh Hunt of Shelley, heard of Keats from Severn, entertained Dickens, Thackeray, Arnold, Salvini, Modjeska, Booth, Longfellow, Emerson, Whittier, Hawthorne—as Miss Cather says "the list sounds like something in a schoolbook." They belong with the past, their sympathies lay with their elders, and Miss Cather's sympathies lie with them.

Nothing of great importance is said on either side. The tone of regret, the delicate tinting, the affectionate memory is all. A stray murmur from Mrs. Fields, awaking from a long reverie, seems just right: "You know, my dear, I think we sometimes forget how much we owe to Dryden's prefaces," and the murmur hangs there, timeless and incontrovertible, with no argument to spoil its cryptic finality. It is the Victorian world, in its domestic interior and on its best behavior, seen through the tender memories of niece and widow, hushed and reverential, "the peace of the past where the tawdry and cheap have been eliminated and the enduring things have taken their proper, happy places."

An indirect glimpse of Katherine Mansfield makes the most critically interesting of the six essays. A New Englander of taste and good sense had delighted in her as a child. Years later he read one of her stories, " 'artificial and unpleasantly hysterical' [he said], 'full of affectations; she had none as a child.' He spoke rather bitterly: his disappointment was genuine." Miss Cather pays an elaborate tribute to Miss Mansfield's art, but the New Englander may stick longer in our mind. A long, sympathetic review of Mann's *Joseph and His Brethren* is included as looking sufficiently backward for Miss Cather. But the slight general essay on "The Novel Démeublé" is disappointing: it reminds us how much more critically, alertly and intelligently Mrs. Woolf had done the same thing—the protest against materialism in the novel—in "Mr. Bennett and Mrs. Brown" (published in 1924, but then Mrs. Woolf's English world had changed "on or about December, 1910"). Miss Cather is happiest with her memories of the past and better in praise than in blame, and she almost persuades that not to be born after 1890 was the best of fortune.

J[oseph] J. R[eilly], "New Books," *Catholic World*, 144 (March 1937), 754–5 [reviewed with Agnes Repplier's *In Pursuit of Laughter*]

The simultaneous advent of a volume by the foremost living American novelist and by the most stimulating living American essayist is cause for rejoicing, for Miss Cather proves that a sense of style is not lost among us and Miss Repplier provides consoling testimony of the fact that civilization and its expression in literature existed before 1900.

Miss Cather offers us six essays, rightly described as studies in literary personalities and certain aspects of literature, while Miss Repplier surveys with wit, irony, humor, and a coolly appraising eye laughter among men—chiefly in England and America—from the Middle Ages when laughter was spontaneous, through the Tudor days when it was silenced, on down through the periods (Caroline, Hogarthian, and the rest) when our fathers and now we ourselves, realizing how precious is this thing we have lost, have sought to recapture it. Laughter to Miss Repplier as to Chesterton is the outer manifestation of something within, sanity, poise of mind and soul, equanimity, or if you prefer George Meredith's term, "the Comic Spirit."

The difference between these two books is the difference between two dissimilar interests. Miss Cather is essentially a creative artist who in musing mood occasionally turns an appraising glance on other artists in the field of fiction past and present and reveals her answer to the question: "What *is* great fiction?" Miss Repplier is essentially a social critic whose mind, whether concerned with movies, tea, or laughter turns, like a magnetic needle to the pole, toward the question: "What is wrong with current society?"

Both women are alert and penetrating, both are in command of distinctive styles, each perfect of its kind, the interests of both are wide and their erudition striking, even though Miss Cather records that somewhere between 1908 and 1915 she asked her accomplished hostess, Mrs. James T. Fields: "*Who* was Dr. Donne?" There is an opalescent quality in Miss Cather's writing, a sparkle and point in Miss Repplier's. Miss Cather writes in musing mood; Miss Repplier's pages are quick with challenges. One senses in Miss Cather a nostalgic yearning for a more leisurely day, a more savorsome existence, a truer literary art than are discoverable now, such as was known to those gracious women whom she brings to exquisite life again, Sarah Orne Jewett, Mrs. J. T. Fields, and Madame Grout, niece of the great Flaubert. She rebels against the contemporary accent on "the material investiture" of the novel done as by "the gaudy fingers of a showman or the mechanical industry of a department-store window dresser," and against that parallel iniquity the crowding of our novels with catalogues of physical sensations. "Can anyone imagine anything more terrible," she asks, "than the story of *Romeo and Juliet* rewritten in prose by D. H. Lawrence?"

Miss Repplier on her side also leaves us a matter to ponder. If we must believe that with the Middle Ages the careless laughter of human delight passed forever then, she says gravely, "On the preservation of the Comic Spirit depends in some measure the ultimate triumph of civilization."

The lover of beauty and wisdom in literature must call that a golden day in which these two books come to his hands.

Receive," *Yale Review*, New Series, 26 (Winter 1937), vi.
Booklist, 33 (January 1937), 149.

Checklist of Additional Reviews

Time, 28 (14 December 1936), 95.
Helen MacAfee, "Books to Give and

SAPPHIRA AND THE SLAVE GIRL

BY

WILLA CATHER

Sapphira
and the
Slave Girl

ALFRED A. KNOPF *New York* 1940

Dorothy Canfield Fisher, *Book-of-the-Month Club News*, December, 1940, pp. 2–3

The people of our times are turned towards embittered skepticism by calamity almost beyond human imagining. Helpless spectators of the horrifying spread of human slavery, readers of 1940 are forced into a suspicion that a happy ending to any story can be no more than a cheap and sleazy veil thrown over but not hiding the ugly figure of truth. To such saddened readers, aching with shame for humanity, Willa Cather presents a lovely story of escape from human slavery, which is not only literally and factually true, but deeply and symbolically the truth.

The book is very quiet in tone, slight and short—about half the length of the usual novel, with a good deal of space given to minute, affectionate and enchantingly detailed descriptions of the background of life in a rural district of Virginia, near Winchester, in 1856. Hardly a page in it is without a thumbnail vignette, clearly drawn, of the exact aspect of place or person, as they were on the date of the story:—"A short, stalwart woman in a sunbonnet, wearing a heavy shawl over her freshly ironed calico dress"—there is a plain, pre-Civil War country woman, every item chosen to make her different from a modern country woman visually vivid.

The home of the miller, where the action takes place, is like an old, finely-executed, pen-and-ink drawing with every tree, every walk, every plant set precisely in its place. Nor are all these details visual ones. The story of how the miller's wife happened to own the land in Back Creek, is told from 1747 to 1759, long before the birth of any of the characters of the book. The annual mowing of the meadows by eight scythe-swinging Negro field-hands is as brilliant with carefully selected detail as the best Breughel painting of peasant life. The talk of the Negro slaves is almost startlingly real, every shading preserved, the difference carefully marked between the language used by house servants when speaking to their white masters and when talking together in their own cabins.

But, although all this is utterly charming, Miss Cather's book is no period piece. Vivid as it is, the background is, outdoors and indoors, in its proper place back of the characters, back of the action. It is not in the book for its own sake, in spite of the loving care lavished on it. The reader's attention is wholly fixed on the story, one of the many variations on one of the oldest of human themes, a prison, a human being in it, the effort to escape, the uncertainty as to whether escape is possible. The use of the wonderfully described background is the sound legitimate use of setting a real world around real human beings.

And yet, although the story is on the always exciting theme of attempted escape from prison, although the men and women, black and white, are profoundly human and living, one feels a relaxed, mellow lack of intensity which, although it is agreeable in the extreme, seems at first rather odd in a story made up of the crudest and most violent elements. The tale is of the cruelly ruthless attempt made by a jealous elderly wife to use the unrighteous power over other human beings given slave owners, to wreck and blight a blooming, dewily innocent, and virtuous young girl, hardly more than a child.

Mrs. Colbert, the wife of the miller, complacent with the stupid self-esteem of the provincial over-valuation of material possessions, cold, calculating, relentless, is an appalling old woman of exuberant Elizabethan wickedness. Portrayed by Faulkner, in livid purples and bloody reds, she would have had the reader, his hair standing on end, shouting for help. But in Miss Cather's book we accept her as those around her accepted her, without heroics.

The same sort of almost dreamy quality is found in the portrayal of Nancy's tragic situation. Her danger, her trapped struggles to escape from the doorless, windowless prison in which slavery kept her, make an exciting story. But we are not excited by it. We believe fully in the stealthy, threatening footsteps which so terribly frighten Nancy: but Miss Cather does not try, as Hemingway does, to make us, too, hear them with a physical shudder. We follow the plot with the closest, most sympathetic attention, but—we realize at the end of the book—almost as though we knew all along, that Nancy was sure to be saved from the villainous plot to destroy her, that the nobility, integrity, sense of the sacredness of human dignity, felt by the miller and his magnificent daughter, cannot but conquer the forces of evil, as right cannot but in the end be stronger than wrong.

As soon as we begin the exquisitely written Epilogue, we see why the book has, for all its savage story, a lovely mellow bloom, why, as we read, we half knew that it is all going to come out all right. We see that it is not just a story, it is poetry, poetry in the sense of emotion remembered in tranquillity. We see that it is, and has been all along, a tale told to a little girl, held in her memory for a lifetime, recurring to her mature mind with the special moonlit, seen-in-a-mirror quality of stories remembered from childhood. And as we realize this, we see how it frees us from the turbid, immediate, imitation-emotion of literally

realistic stories, and permits us calmly to see in perspective the golden human values of the tale.

Those values are infinitely consoling and comforting to us, shocked as we are by the recurring, ever-nearer dangers to our own freedom. The book bids us have faith.

Elizabeth Shepley Sergeant, "Willa Cather," *Book-of-the-Month Club News*, December, 1940, pp. 4–5

In a letter of the year 1908, Sarah Orne Jewett wrote to a young Westerner in whom she was vitally interested: "To work in silence and with all one's heart, that is the writer's lot; he is the only artist who must be a solitary and yet needs the widest outlook on the world." Miss Cather was then using the fire and dynamic energy she had brought from the prairies to edit *McClure's Magazine*, and making a great success of it, as she had of teaching in Pittsburgh before that. But she had published *The Troll Garden*, a book of short stories in which the New England elder sensed a gift inborn and true. Such writing needs "one's first working power." It needs maturing, and that means another level of living. The bohemia of newspaper and magazine office life is too exciting. Backgrounds must be deepened—"your Nebraska life," "a child's Virginia."

Not long after this the author who now stands in the forefront of American novelists did give up her job and in solemn earnest start writing novels. Since then she has always lived in a quiet and

502

withdrawn way. Her private life has been as removed as she could make it from the gods of the marketplace. Who has heard her on the radio, seen her signing copies at a Book Fair, or at one of these meals where authors' personalities are publicized? Simple tastes, followed together with a passionate devotion to the literary art have kept her destiny to a single, unwavering line. Her life stream has thus flowed deep, as if cut in a canyon, unfrittered by the ten thousand charms of the bank. This pattern of life, so at variance with the custom of the twentieth century, has had its penalties, but it has enabled Miss Cather to be herself, and to fulfill the promise she brought from the West.

No biographer has yet ventured on terrain so reserved. But those who care to may find a quasi-autobiography in the novels, worth any amount of "publicity." It has taken thirty-eight years to give us "the child's Virginia"—to reveal, through the last chapter and the footnote to the new novel that the little girl who was carried to the window to witness the return of the slave girl, long after the Civil War, was, indeed, Willa Cather, born, not in Nebraska, as many assume, but under the Blue Ridge.

Now look back twenty-two years, to *My Antonia*, published in 1918; it starts right in where the Virginia childhood ended, with "an interminable journey across the great midland plain of North America. I was ten years old then." The narrator, a boy (who might be the girl still known to Nebraska folks as "Willy"), got out of the day coach at night, at Black Hawk (which might be Red Cloud) at the same moment with the Shirmerdas, a Bohemian family from Central Europe, who came in the immigrant coach. Their little girl, Antonia, was to reveal to the author in later years the meaning of the country, the conditions, the whole new adventure fate had in store. Riding now in the wagon box in the dark the Virginia child looked for creeks, rivers, fences, a mountain ridge against the sky. All she made out was "land, not a country at all, but the material out of which countries are made ... the dome of heaven, all there was of it ... I don't think I was homesick."

Next morning, the Western world came to view. "More than anything else, I felt motion in the landscape; in the fresh, easy blowing wind, and in the earth itself, as if the grass were a sort of loose hide and underneath it herds of buffalo were galloping, galloping." The markedly pristine, fresh and free element in the author's own nature is evoked by such a passage. Her instinctive relation to the American earth, and to those humans, often of foreign birth, who are extracting a living from it, is a major relationship, and lends something rich and lusty, nobly impersonal to the almost monastic pattern of a writing life. Places where wind and weather sting the blood, transfuse beauty to the veins, have given Miss Cather the perspective needed for long vistas into the Past—her most treasured realm. But Canada, the Mediterranean shore, the Southwest have never broken the heart's bond with old Nebraska neighbors like the Shirmerdas—they are, as it were, the extension of a family connection also fondly cherished. How long ago, without even meaning to, Willa Cather proved to us that the melting pot really melts!

Metropolitan life has never satisfied her, blunted her impatience with its more cheap and intrusive aspects. One might expect to meet her, any time in winter, on the windiest corner of Fifth Avenue, rebellion in her grey eyes, every hair of her fur coat standing on end. But once indoors, down town or up, her windows look inward. When France fell, she was reading the great French historians. She has always preferred old books to new, had George Sand (by Courbet) over her mantel, an orange tree hard by. Always enjoyed fine food and wine and great music, and taken such pleasures, as a European might, with the spaciousness they deserve. Her morning's work, her early lunch, her solitary walk have had a leisurely quality, too. Reading, reflection bring insight into the human destiny and the human heart, and are never omitted from an ordered day. Though Time is what Willa Cather most misses, as she has grown more famous, there is the claim of the young to meet, especially the gifted young artist or the beloved relative; and she does not forget older friends among writers, musicians, singers, and plain Americans you would not have heard of. Maybe homesickness for Eastern culture brought her here, but surely natal longing for Nebraska and Virginia created her books.

Morton Dauwen Zabel, "The Tone of Time," *Nation*, 151 (7 December 1940), 574–6

The boy who told the story of *My Antonia*, finding himself transported from Virginia to the prairies of Nebraska, said "I had the feeling that the world was left behind, that we had got over the edge of it, and were outside man's jurisdiction. I had never before looked up at the sky when there was not a familiar mountain ridge against it." For thirty years Miss Cather found her clue to the heroic values of life in that Western world of open plains and pioneer struggle; now she goes back, for the first time in her literary career, beyond her Nebraska girlhood to

the Virginia of her earliest memories, to a country of older laws and severer customs—to Back Creek Valley west of the Blue Ridge and to the house of Henry Colbert, the miller, and his wife Sapphira, a Dodderidge of Louden County. The story offers the familiar features of her earlier books: there is the retreat to the past—here 1856—when human dignity and honor were not yet outlawed by the cheap principles and vulgar comforts of modern times; there is the idealizing pathos of distance and lost beauty; there is an epilogue that brings the story twenty-five years nearer—but only to 1881—when time has dissolved old conflicts, clarified their mystery, and healed old wounds by its touch of grace and humility. There is a stoic husband, asking no questions of an unkind destiny; there is an imperious wife who finds herself exiled in the backwoods as earlier heroines like Marian Forrester and Myra Henshawe were exiled in the rough country of the West, self-confounded by her pride and fear of truth, defeating herself rather than allow victory or happiness to others, yet who must finally say, like the woman in Katherine Anne Porter's story, "I was right not to be afraid of any thief but myself, who will end by leaving me nothing"; there is also a young girl, the Negro slave Nancy, on whom Sapphira vents her defeat and jealousy, another embodiment of the spirit of youth and natural grace which appeared before in Alexandra, Thea, Antonia, Tom Outland, and Lucy Gayheart—the pure in heart whom no evil can ever defeat wholly and on whom Miss Cather fixes for her faith in experience in an age of warring egoisms and debasing ambition.

Miss Cather has risked not only a repetition of characters and effects in which her expertness has already passed from mastery to mere formulation; she has duplicated her matter and pathos so narrowly as to make unavoidable the sensation that what was once a sincere and vigorous theme has been subjected to a further attenuation of sentimental argument and special pleading. This effect is emphasized by the insistent plainness and simplicity of manner to which she adheres—that conscious simplicity which at times (in *My Antonia, A Lost Lady,* and *Death Comes for the Archbishop*) she has raised to a point of intensity and lyric poignance that forms the only real approximation to Turgenev and Gogol in American fiction, but which on other occasions (*One of Ours, Shadows on the Rock, Lucy Gayheart*) has lapsed either into an inert and nerveless dullness or into a sentimentality that begs the whole question of creating and substantiating characters by means of words, sensation, and observed detail.

Her devotion to the past and its perished beauty has been sincere but inevitably limited by a didactic principle and threatened by the inflexibility of an idealistic convention. Only when her sentiment is toughened by psychological or atmospheric realism has she brought off her pathos successfully, and only when her idealizations have been grounded in a hard sense of physical and regional fact have they missed banality and abstraction. To reread the whole of her work, as I have just done, is to realize how deliberately she has faced her risks in order to win her prizes. It is to see that the subtlety and scope of her themes (*The Professor's House, My Mortal Enemy*) have often failed to find the structure and substance that would give them life and so must remain at the level of a sketch; it is to realize that her novels reduce to a single motive and pattern whose sincerity is undeniable but rudimentary and soon becomes threadbare, repeatedly exposed by a meagerness of texture and sensible realization; but it is to admit at last that

in her finest books Miss Cather has brought to a kind of heroic climax and genuine epic meaning the work of the American women who preceded her (Rose Terry Cooke, Sarah Orne Jewett, Mrs. Freeman) and that she has sublimated to its elements a conception of pioneer life which in other hands has generally lapsed into vulgar romanticism and blatant American eloquence.

Sapphira, by recovering the gravity and lyric ease of her best work and by avoiding the flat prettification of history that nullified *Shadows on the Rock,* is Miss Cather's best book in thirteen years and one of the five best of her production. It shows in its central character the tangible passion and struggle, in its secondary characters the honest virtue and credible humility, and in its general atmosphere of fear and obsession a dramatic force that lift the tale out of its exaggerated moralism and dramatic simplicity into its own kind of truth and power. Its people rise above the flat dimensions of moral humors, and there are passages—Nancy's terror, Henry's struggle with his first consciousness of love for her, Sapphira's final surrender—that remind us how much integrity of word and effect is required to justify the hairbreadth compromises with melodrama and sentiment which Miss Cather risks and how she is one of the two or three masters who remain to us in this kind of art. They also remind us that in defining the spiritual forces that have gone into the making of our culture she has performed with dignity and profound honesty a service that usually falls into the hands of spellbinders and literary demagogues. At a moment when our spiritual riches, at best not too plentiful, are put to every possible test of confusion and debasement, the part she has played in saving them from the misuses of theory and from the fatuous complacency that easily converts them into a means of conceit and violence is not to be mistaken or underestimated.

Charles Poore, "Books of the Times," *New York Times*, 7 December 1940, p. 15

Willa Cather lives outside the literary stream of the moment as completely as Maude Adams lived outside the theatrical stream of her day. You will never see Miss Cather at any of the strange folk festivals of contemporary letters. And yet, while the writings of those who are constantly on view may sometimes be forgotten, the precise contrary is true of Miss Cather's, so that the appearance of *Sapphira and the Slave Girl*, her first novel in five years, is an eventful celebration of her birthday.

The story of *Sapphira and the Slave Girl* is very simple, so simple, as a matter of fact, that it would probably take any one as slow-witted as your reviewer years to trace out all its implications and counterpoints.

On the surface it is a novel about the jealous persecution of a beautiful mulatto slave by her mistress, who suspects a liaison between slave and master, and who goes about her skillful, devious efforts to destroy the slave with a stately, feline cruelty.

Around that sultry, slowly burning episode Miss Cather has created in a small backwoods community the fabric of three clashing ways of life: the way of those who believe in slavery, the way of those who do not, and the way of the slaves themselves. The men and women who personify these ways of life are drawn with all Miss Cather's mastery, so that each stands out as a true person in a living world.

The scene is the countryside near Winchester in Virginia and the time is the Eighteen Fifties, still unshadowed by the Civil War, with an epilogue a quarter of a century later.

Miss Cather was born in that country, though you may associate her life far more with the horizons of *My Antonia* and *O Pioneers!* and *A Lost Lady* and *The Professor's House* and *Shadows on the Rock* and *Lucy Gayheart* and *Death Comes for the Archbishop*. Yet you will find the epilogue returning to a childhood wonderfully remembered, and the whole story is steeped in the scenes and the names and the prejudices and the customs of Virginia from a Virginian's point of view. . . .

A good many contemporary novelists are apt to look like industrious apprentices or superficial romancers when their work is compared with Miss Cather's. And certainly a great many of them have been resoundingly overpraised for work that cannot hold a candle to *Sapphira and the Slave Girl*.

In reading Miss Cather's books it would always be well to remember that she leaves out enough unessential material to fill an ordinary novel. Indeed, I have seen historical novels that seemed to be made up largely of exactly the kind of material which Willa Cather, with her amazing discipline of selection, would leave out.

In *Sapphira and the Slave Girl* she examines the question of slavery without any portentous fanfare, entirely through the lives of her characters, without the editorializing that might have pointed up the discussion, but would have been fatal to the novel as a creative work. Nevertheless, you see the various points of view

506

as they operated in Virginia in that time. Sapphira believed in slavery. It gave her a chance to be contemptuously kindly, and well served. Her daughter Rachel, a ministering angel of the country-side, a visiting nurse of the days before there were visiting nurses, hated it. The people who helped Nancy along the Underground Railroad hated it to the point where they were actively doing something about it.

Henry Colbert, who did not like it and yet accepted it, nevertheless saw that while Sapphira's slaves were "better clothed, better fed and better cared for than the poor whites of the mountains," none of those ragged, hungry mountain men ever came down and asked to trade places with the best-cared for, best clothed and happiest of the slaves. In the end it was the slave girl who triumphed over Sapphira.

Miss Cather's triumph, on the other hand, I think, is that she has been able to write a fine novel about slavery and the South in which the Civil War itself is dropped out as an irrelevance to her work of art.

Clifton Fadiman, *New Yorker*, 16 (7 December 1940), 103–4

Willa Cather bucks the trend, swims upstream, walks by herself, and does very nicely, thank you. *Sapphira and the Slave Girl* (a peach of a title, by the way) is about as remote from the main stream of current fiction as you can well conceive. For one thing, it's brief. Miss Cather is the sort of writer who says to herself, "To tell this story as I want to tell it should require

no more than three hundred pages"—and no more than three hundred pages it turns out to be. Such self-control practically puts her in a class by herself these days.

Her work is spare, even austere. As a careful housewife chooses one skein from a basket of yarn, Miss Cather selects the single right detail from the mass at her disposal, and lets it go at that. Accuracy rather than richness of imagination is her hallmark. She has another quality shared by few of her contemporaries. Most writers, some of them greater than Miss Cather, make up their stories; she seems to remember hers. (Thomas Mann, though his arc is much wider, gives you the same feeling.) Perhaps the scenes of her novels are set in the long ago not because she wishes to evade the present but because the motor of her imaginative power can be set going only by throwing the switch of memory. For her, narrative *is* recollection.

Sapphira and the Slave Girl will not, I think, rank with her finest books, such as *My Antonia* and *A Lost Lady*, but it has more edge and vigor than its predecessor, *Lucy Gayheart*, which, on laboratory analysis, showed more than a trace of sugar. The scene is a new one for Miss Cather: the hamlet of Back Creek, just west of Winchester, Virginia. The time is 1856, and there is an epilogue—a favorite Cather device—dated twenty-five years later. The characters are in no way startling or dramatic, nor is their story unusual. Yet the relationship which binds them is studied in such a way as to give the reader a fresh insight into an old problem—in this case, the problem of master and slave. Do not expect from Miss Cather's cool and level art the black-and-whites of Margaret Mitchell's hot partisanship, much less the melodramatic *Uncle Tom's Cabin* view of slavery. Her book is not a study of servitude as a system but a consideration of the different ways in which different, very different, human beings act when that system impinges on them. . . .

Sapphira and Henry are both well done, the sense of the social distance between them being especially neatly conveyed. Though, as indicated, the rakish seducer Martin is straight out of the stockroom, the other whites—Rachel, the Colberts' daughter, an unconfessed abolitionist; and Mrs. Ringer, who "was born interested"—are clearly drawn. But the main effectiveness of the characterization rests upon Miss Cather's ability to do Negroes. The special clarity with which they stand out comes, I think, from the circumstance that she is not trying to prove anything through them. She shows the Lutheran conscience of Henry wrestling with the problem of how to be a good man and a slaveholder at the same time. But she herself does not pass judgment, except by quiet implication, and her Negroes are therefore allowed to be persons rather than shaped up to be object lessons.

Each of the blacks, whether it be the passive Nancy, or her genteel mother Till, or Till's "capon man," Uncle Jeff, or the fat, malicious cook Lizzie, or the self-respecting head millhand Sampson, or old, jungle-born Aunt Jezebel, who, as death nears, desires nothing but a taste of a pickaninny's hand—all these are not only separate and distinct characters but their relationships to their master and mistress vary subtly, as the relationships of children to their parents would vary in a large family.

One reads *Sapphira and the Slave Girl* with pleasure and admiration, never with any great heightening of interest. The emotion, as is true of many of Miss Cather's later books, has been recollected in too much tranquillity. But this undercharging of the atmosphere bears with it

its own compensation. Out of this book, designedly minor in tone and content, is exhaled a flavor rare nowadays, when the rhetoricians seem to dominate—a flavor of cool, almost austere gravity. I do not know how long this flavor will persist in the mind and memory of the reader. I know only that as you read, you cannot help sensing it.

Mary Ross, "Willa Cather's First Novel in Five Years," *New York Herald Tribune Books,* 8 December 1940, p. 1

In *Sapphira and the Slave Girl* Willa Cather again shows the beauty and distinction that long since gave her a preeminent place among contemporary novelists. In this, her first novel in five years, there is once more the grace, the clear, luminous perspective, the measured emotion and the perfection of carefully chosen detail for which thousands of readers have looked eagerly year after year.

Characteristically Miss Cather's novels bring the tale of a time that is past. Looking back at it, one can see in the harmony of perspective, the design and meaning of coursing events which buffeted and confused those who participated in them. Through her books, as through an open window, you look out. Whether the scene is Nebraska, Quebec, the Southwest, or, as in the present novel, Virginia, it has a quality of spaciousness, of sunlit distance, that often has seemed to me akin to that of a Perugino landscape.

Miss Cather is unlike many of her contemporaries in that she does not plunge her readers into the hurly-burly of living, the stream of consciousness, if you will. Her books are, rather, the essence of things remembered, washed clear of the unessential and polished to beauty by slow time, like stones cast up on a beach. We have, unfortunately, no English equivalent of which I am aware for the French word *juste*, that scrupulous fidelity to a shade of thought or feeling of which the integrity of Miss Cather's work is compounded. For out of her ability to listen and to ponder there comes not aloofness from the bygone lives of which she writes, but the poignancy of seeing them whole. She thus is able to communicate in terms of common lives, the quality of which Aristotle spoke when he wrote that beauty depends on order and a certain magnitude. . . .

It is . . . Nancy, the product of two races and the link between two eras, about whom the story turns. And it is [Sapphira] Colbert's growing jealousy of this girl that motivates it.

Nancy is the touchstone through whom the characters of the others are revealed: Henry's integrity and idealism; the courage and kindness of Rachel; the devotion and disciplined resignation of Till; and, above all, the pride, resourcefulness and undaunted determination of Sapphira. Through them, also, are revealed, without moralisms, the mixed values of a crumbling civilization. Nancy's flight to the North, and her return twenty-five years later, in a black silk dress and with a gold watch and chain, have the quality of a legend.

The story of Sapphira echoes in many ways the theme of the "lost lady" which recurs in Miss Cather's other novels as well as in the book with that name. That theme is the basic stuff of tragedy, the struggle of the individual to maintain personal integrity despite dissonance within and attack from without. In *Lucy Gay-*

heart, probably the "softest" of Miss Cather's books, the outcome was tragedy. *Sapphira and the Slave Girl* follows more closely the main stream of Miss Cather's work in that the story works out to the only endings that would have been satisfying for these individuals, without personal defeat and without the fortuitous interruption of circumstance. Readers will find it difficult to harmonize the conclusion of the story with the main body of it. This, I think, is due to a flaw in Miss Cather's ordinarily flawless technique. For here, to the confusion of the unprepared reader, Miss Cather, as a child of five, steps into the narrative in the first person.

New, insofar as I am aware, to Miss Cather's work and distinctive in American fiction is her delineation of the black men and women in this book. No preconceptions and none of the ingrained platitudes that typically beset accounts of racial interrelationships mar her portraits of Jezebel, Till, Nancy, Sampson, Bluebell and the rest. Observed with her scrupulous fidelity, they are appealing human beings to whom the Colberts owed much of the richness of life as well as the framework of their existence. With this clarity and justice, it would not be surprising if this proves to be a book with which readers in both the North and the South can sympathize in the portrayal of individuals who happen to be Negro.

The setting also brings to another region Miss Cather's beautiful precision. Read, for example, of the Virginia woods in spring:

> . . . On the steep hillside across the creek the tall forest trees were still bare—the oak leaves no bigger than a squirrel's ear. From out the naked gray wood the dogwood thrust its crooked forks starred with white blossoms— the flowers set in their own wild way

along the rampant zigzag branches.
. . . In all the rich flowering and blushing and blooming of a Virginia spring,
the scentless dogwood is the wildest
thing and yet the most austere, the
most unearthly.

Like nearly all Miss Cather's earlier
novels, *Sapphira and the Slave Girl* is a
brief book. Only in retrospect do you
realize how much is conveyed in less than
three hundred small pages. Here, in a
story as rounded as it is simple, is the life
of a household, in a given place and time;
of master and servant, of neighbors like
the postmistress who read the *Tribune*
surreptitiously and the little mountain
woman who was "born interested," of
the cousins "back home" for whom life
meant horses, and those who found their
place in Winchester's town decorum.
Only a very high quality of art can convey
the fullness of beauty that Miss Cather
has given time and again in a brief and
simple novel.

J. Donald Adams,
New York Times Book Review, 8 December 1940, p. 4

As a writer whose place in American literature is assured, Miss Cather claims our
eager attention whenever she publishes a
new book. Always there is the hope that
she will again strike a major chord, but
this she has not done since *Death Comes
for the Archbishop* appeared in 1927.
Shadows on the Rock, which followed it,
was notable chiefly for its descriptive
writing, one of Miss Cather's gifts that
never fails her. And *Lucy Gayheart*, which
she published five years ago, had the

quality of a diminishing echo. The voice
was distinctly hers, but we had heard it
before in fuller and deeper tones.

It is harder to recognize her in the
novel she has now written. Nor does this
seem to be so simply because Miss Cather
has here employed material she has never
used before. In writing *Sapphira and the
Slave Girl* she has gone back to her earliest memories, to her childhood life in Virginia, but these, it seems, have not the
same intensity that came out of her
removal to Nebraska and later, from the
strong impact which the history and physical presence of the Southwest had upon
her imagination. They, apparently, were
the great fructifying influences in her creative life. Her adolescent years among the
immigrant pioneers, and, in maturity, the
spell of the Southwest, kindled fires in her
mind out of which came her most deeply
felt work.

But Miss Cather is too accomplished
an artist ever to give us work which has
not some distinction of its own. *Sapphira
and the Slave Girl* is a subtly done, if not
completely satisfying, study of a domestic
situation. The story, set in the period
immediately preceding the Civil War,
revolves about a wife's suspicion of her
husband. Sapphira Dodderidge, aristocratic and well-to-do, was generally
regarded to have married much beneath
her when she chose for her husband
young Henry Colbert, four years her
junior and a Virginian of immigrant
stock. . . .

Henry Colbert, in spite of the circumstances of his marriage, was an upstand-
ing man, who gave himself unremittingly
to his work, and autocrat though she was,
Sapphira could not keep him in any mean
dominance. It is because Miss Cather
makes the quality of sturdy integrity so
apparent in drawing her picture of
Colbert that it becomes difficult to accept
her resolution of the conflict between

them upon which the story hinges. And that is why, although the elements in the situation are subtly presented, the final impression with regard to its outcome is an unsatisfying one. . . .

Apart from that crucial point, the story has validity. The strange relationship between the miller and his wife is admirably presented, and there is as always Miss Cather's limpid and seemingly effortless prose.

B[everly] L. B[ritton], "A Sentimental Journey to Virginia," *Times-Dispatch* (Richmond) 8 December 1940, section IV, p. 12

Willa Cather has taken a sentimental journey in this, her first novel in five years—a journey which brings her back to her native Frederick County, Va. and which utilizes the stories of the countryside which she heard as a child. Her epilogue, in fact—which occurs 25 years after the story's beginning—presents the author herself at the age of 5, as an observer of the recorded events.

But Miss Cather's sentimentality goes only as far as her choice of background and characters. In her treatment of them she remains the impartial, dignified storyteller, and in these traits she is as gifted as she has always been. *Sapphira and the Slave Girl* is no monumental work for the ages, but neither is it dull nor flat; her story is admirably framed and incisively told.

Sapphira Dodderidge was a Virginian of highly-placed and wealthy English ancestry who had surprised her blue-blooded family and friends by marrying sober, homespun Henry Colbert, a miller whom she knew but slightly either before or after her wedding. Instead of living in worldly Winchester, she chose to take over a tract of land on Back Creek deeded to her father by Lord Fairfax. There Henry set up his mill, and there Sapphira took with her a fairly large contingent of personal slaves—in days before the War Between the States, and in a section where slave-owning was mostly frowned upon.

The contradictions in Sapphira's nature were revealed more fully at Mill Farm, where she showed genuine concern and a remarkable amount of patience for Negroes, but little warmth or intimacy for her husband and daughters. When this story opens in 1856, she has "turned agin" one of the Negroes in particular—a beautiful mulatto girl called Nancy. . . .

Sapphira's sudden hatred for Nancy springs from her belief that the girl is sleeping with Henry, who usually occupies a small room at the mill rather than the big house. The invalid Sapphira, who has dropsy, becomes increasingly ruthless in her persecution of Nancy, even to the point of inviting down from the city a scapegrace nephew, and throwing Nancy constantly in his path.

Nancy being a good-hearted girl who worships her master, but is innocent of cohabitation with him, immediately senses the plot against her, and in desperation turns to her mistress' widowed daughter, who, too, has always been a stranger to Sapphira. Through Rachel Blake, Nancy escapes to Canada by the help of the "underground railway," which aided slaves in those hectic times.

Probably the most interesting of Miss Cather's characters are the Negroes, from lissom Nancy to her fiery old grandmother, Jezebel, who bit off a sailor's thumb when he threatened to punish her on her way from Africa to be sold in the States. There is Till, whose aim in life is to serve her mistress well: there is fat, gossipy Lizzie and her lazy daughter, Bluebell: there is the head millhand, Sampson, who intercedes with the master for frightened Nancy, and many others who will prove more memorable than any of the white characters drawn here.

Sapphira and the Slave Girl, then, is a slight story but a well-knit one, done in Willa Cather's best stately manner. It offers what is no doubt an authentic picture of Virginia in prewar days, and if it adds nothing in particular to its author's literary stature, it just as surely upholds for her that high place.

George Grimes, "Willa Cather's Scene Her Native Virginia," *World-Herald* (Omaha), 8 December 1940, p. 4C

This is the first novel from Willa Cather's pen since *Lucy Gayheart* was published five years ago.

Then she returned to the Nebraska scene, where she grew up, for the most part, in a story of a girl seeking beauty and success and love in her life. Now, in the story of Sapphira and Nancy, her slave girl, Miss Cather has drawn from the Virginia where she was born. She has told a story of Virginia four or five years before the civil war.

It is the Virginia just west of Winchester—a Virginia where not many of the families were wealthy, where the one that owned 20 slaves was the exception; a backwoods Virginia.

She has not told a story of the

approach of war, or attempted to paint upon a large canvas the conflicting currents of thought at that time. Her scene is more simple, for she has drawn only a few characters of the time, and the incidents she relates are intimate and personal.

Yet, so sure is her touch and so delicate her art that this scene, these characters, are of intense interest throughout. . . . It is a tale told with the simplicity that distinguishes the prose of Nebraska's most distinguished (although now expatriate) writer. It is a tale which reveals, with clarity and understanding and sympathy, relations between mistress and slave in pre-war Virginia. It is a tale which provides us with understanding of life of the times such as never comes from the big bold "historical novels" which flow from publishers' presses. It is a tale which helps to an understanding of all life, by the clarity with which Miss Cather can paint a character.

Sapphira we understand and sympathize with, even as we may condemn her conduct toward the slave girl. Nancy is made real; so are other Negroes on the farm; so is Henry, alone with his thoughts in the mill.

Sapphira and the Slave Girl is a novel close to Miss Cather's best.

"Pre-War Tale," *Time*, 36 (9 December 1940), 88

This week appeared Willa Cather's first novel in five years. It is an immaculately written account of a few months in the life of a family in Virginia. The year is 1856. The family is that of sober, plebeian Henry Colbert and his subtle, suffering, tony wife, Sapphira. They live, well-supplied with slaves, a little beyond the edge of civilization, within the fringes of the mountains. Sapphira's widowed daughter, an abolitionist at heart, does good among the mountaineers and the slaves. Sapphira's husband, another, spends most of his time at the mill, earnestly reads Bunyan's *Holy War*. Sapphira herself manages the household from her wheel chair (she has dropsy), yearns for the good life in Winchester. Mainly the story is of her more & more elaborate persecution of the young mulatto Nancy, whom she wrongly suspects of bedding with her husband. At her lowest she invites her rakehell nephew Martin for a visit, assigns him Nancy as his personal servant. Colbert and his daughter help Nancy escape, unscathed, into Canada. In an old-fashioned epilogue Willa Cather, aged five, sees Nancy's return as a middle-aged woman.

Willa Cather could not possibly write a bad novel; but *Sapphira and the Slave Girl* bears witness that she can write a dull one. This dullness, though, is the sum of many honest virtues: a nicely formed story, characters drawn with delicate authority, sharp, evocative vignettes of Virginia living & landscape. The whole work has the well-made, healthful, sober clarity of a Dutch interior. And like many unexceptionable people who inspire neither more nor less than respect, *Sapphira* is not too dull to be pleasant reading.

Henry Seidel Canby, "Conversation Piece," *Saturday Review of Literature*, 23 (14 December 1940), 5

It is a pleasure for a reviewer who has long followed American fiction with interest to find in this novel that delicate yet powerful art of brief and significant narrative, where all that is needed is included, and all that is needless is left out. There is much to be said for a novel made long by the very profusion of life,—but very little in praise of the skill of the hundreds of contemporary novelists who take nine hundred pages to accomplish what Miss Cather, with great craftmanship, does in less than three hundred. It is the French art of the *nouvelle*, in which Voltaire triumphed, and the Russian Turgeniev excelled. Miss Cather has triumphed in it also.

For this new novel of hers belongs to a notable trio, of which *Shadows on the Rock*, and *Death Comes for the Archbishop*, are the two other members. In these three books particularly, she has with deceptive simplicity evoked the quality of a life, a faith, and a region—of Quebec and French Canada; of our Roman Catholic and Spanish Southwest; and now of the hill country of Virginia and a slave-owning society just before the Civil War.

Sapphira and the Slave Girl is one of those quiet narratives which build up characters and situations with such easy brush strokes that the reader is not aware of the intensity of the situations developing until they take over the story. The reason is that Miss Cather is not writing a melodrama of slavery and seduction, but recreating, with subtle selection of incident, a society and a culture and a sociology in which a conflict of morals and of philosophies produces an inner, ever more tightly-coiled spring.

Sapphira is an aristocrat from Winchester, not adjusted to the environment of the hills, but easily dominating it. Her husband is Henry Colbert, a miller, who comes from plain people, and who is Sapphira's inferior in taste for fine living, her superior in everything else but courage. Nancy, the slave girl, offspring of a wandering painter or Henry's brother—no one knows—is the coiling spring. Lovely and gentle herself, devoted to Colbert whom she tends with the affection he has never had from his wife, she is the cause of jealousy which Sapphira is too proud to acknowledge. She is the cause of a vicarious crime, for Sapphira—with purpose clear or unclear—brings the seducer to the house, a seducer whose lack of scruple is itself a product of a social situation really as dangerous for the white as for the black.

Such a situation provides an opportunity for Miss Cather, with her well-known aptitude for subtle characterization, to recreate a Virginia of the last of the old days. Sapphira is eighteenth century; Martin, the seducer, is soft, early nineteenth; Henry Colbert and his faithful slave . . . belong to the future of utilitarian labor, and a bourgeois morality. Back of them all is old Jezebel, who had been born a cannibal, and is nearest to Sapphira's heart. Around them is history—the escape of Nancy to Canada, the oncoming Civil War, the wreck of a slave-owning society, the far-off survivors of which, seeming from another world, are seen by a little girl a whole generation after.

This is the kind of book that is sure to be tested by time. But, in any case, a retrospective ending is part of a seemingly informal chronicle, of seemingly unsensational happenings, accomplishing, what lesser novelists fail to achieve with three times the length. In the gradual evoking of the American past, where this American generation of writers has been so successful, *Sapphira and the Slave Girl* adds something unattempted yet by any one with Miss Cather's mature authority of art.

M. K. K., "Willa Cather Tells a Tale of a Human Freed," *Lincoln Journal and Star*, 15 December 1940, p. 4C

Willa Cather, after five years of silence, has written another book. In *Sapphira and the Slave Girl* Miss Cather returns to her early childhood memories of Virginia, where she lived until she was 9 years old. It is possible these memories are not so strong as the recollections from the formative years she spent in Nebraska—from 9 until her graduation, at 20. However, it must be said that in this book she has manifested herself as the great writer she is.

The story is a tale of a strange marriage, and of how the jealousy of the mistress, Sapphira, is taken out on the mulatto slave girl, Nancy. . . .

Henry Colbert had become Sapphira's husband in spite of his coming from "imported" non-English stock and being four years her junior. They have been married so long that they have a widowed daughter who lives nearby with her two little girls.

It is not until the mistress becomes jealous of Nancy and without foundation

—that things really begin to happen. Sapphira makes life very hard indeed for her young slave girl, so hard that her own daughter, who is an abolitionist, steps in and with financial help from the father finally transports Nancy out of the country via the "underground railroad."

The story has an epilogue where the author—rather unexpectedly—steps down to her own childhood 25 years later, and relates how Nancy returns to a free South visiting in grand style. She has made good in the North.

This latest book, like Willa Cather's other works, is relatively short. But the action is so masterfully condensed that the reader feels there is hardly a superfluous word. And the brush that is applying the colors is in the hands of the accomplished artist who knows how to compose in order to achieve the right effect.

Frederic R. Gunsky, "An Awaited Novel by Willa Cather," *San Francisco Chronicle*, 15 December 1940, p. 14

There is a distinctive quality in the novels of Willa Cather which you will not find duplicated anywhere in literature. It lies partly in the measured harmony of her supple prose, partly in her unique sense of the values of personality and setting. It is a pronounced quality, yet a subtle and elusive one. Critics have long admired it, and been grateful to Miss Cather for the once frequent bestowal of her artistry, but the problem of defining or describing it has baffled them. To know the writing of Willa Cather one must go directly to her books, preferably to *The Song of the*

Lark, My Antoina, A Lost Lady, The Professor's House, and the high point of her achievement, *Death Comes for the Archbishop*.

Many of us have suffered a sort of homesickness in recent years, longing for the reassertion of this great talent which appeared to have declined and been given its quietus. After *Death Comes for the Archbishop*, published in 1927, Miss Cather produced only two novels, *Shadows on the Rock* in 1931 and *Lucy Gayheart* in 1935. The former, a romance of old Quebec, is a lovely pattern of tapestry which is nevertheless disturbingly vague and remote. The latter tells the story of a girl who wanted to be a musician, as Thea Kronborg did in the early *Song of the Lark*, and it is by a comparison of these two novels that one sees how feebly Miss Cather's creative flame had begun to flicker. *Lucy Gayheart* seemed to be the faltering last work of an artist who had nothing more to say, possibly because the values she held dearest were everywhere being denied or stultified in an increasingly hostile world.

The publication of *Sapphira and the Slave Girl* comes therefore as a piece of very good news. This latest novel by Willa Cather is neither faltering nor remote. It proves that one of the nation's leading authors of fiction has not lost hope, that she retains her faith in the fundamental worth of common American people, and that despite the passage of years and youth she is still a fine craftsman in words who feels that there are things left to be said.

True enough, *Sapphira* is set in the past. Nothing could be farther from the contemporary scene, even from modern Virginia, it would appear, than the rural Virginia of 1856. The drama with which Miss Cather is concerned is involved in an outwardly calm yet actually intense conflict of wills, and a clash of personalities

515

which is striking but not spectacular. *Sapphira* is indeed a rather quiet story, and its bearing on the calamitous world of 1940 is a matter of contrasts which are only implicit.

Again, while there are slaves in the book, and Southern aristocrats and "Abolishers," there is little of the fury of opinion or violence of action which one associates with historical fiction of the period. The author does not take sides. This almost unprecedented impartiality in a novel of Southern life is particularly noticeable in her treatment of the Negroes. As Mr. Knopf remarks, "They are attractive to the writer as individuals, and are presented by a sympathetic artist who is neither reformer nor sentimentalist."

Simplicity of plot is one of the essences of the Cather bouquet. . . . Nancy Till, the slave girl, was probably intended to be the heroine of the novel, although her benefactor, Mrs. Blake, tends to supplant her in that function. In outline, at least, it is the girl's story, and the concluding chapter deals with her return, after an absence of 25 years, to the home which was the scene of the narrator's childhood. Earlier, Nancy was gentle, sensitive, and rather timid; her flight and the responsibilities of an independent life in Canada have given her poise, assurance, distinction— the "presence" so much admired by the author. The metamorphosis takes place, however, during the years not covered by the novel. If this were only the tale of Nancy Till, Miss Cather might be considered to have failed, by choosing to omit the most important part of her story.

But one must not forget Sapphira: forceful, proud Sapphira, the miller's wife, a suffering invalid who refuses to be pathetic, and at immense cost of energy and spirit maintains her genteel role as mistress of the estate. Sapphira, though she lacks their warmth of human appeal and possesses a most unlovely capacity for malice, probably belongs with Marian Forrester and Antonia Shimerda among the dozen finest portraits in the gallery of Cather women. Neither should one forget Rachel Blake, Sapphira's generous, homely, humanitarian daughter, a sister of mercy among the farm folk, whose duel of wills with her mother is one of the book's most interesting elements; or Henry Colbert, the miller, and his conscientious struggle against a love he would never have discovered save for the exaggerated suspicion of his wife; or Till, Nancy's mother, a figure in the classic tradition of Negro body servants; or Martin Colbert, the gay, friendly, unscrupulous young Southern gentleman, who later "got to be a Captain in the cavalry" before the Yankees made him eligible for a monument.

Of these memorable characters, the numerous fine sketches of subordinate figures (notably Old Jezebel, the African captive), the authentic historical milieu, and a vividly imagined Virginia countryside for background, complete with oak, dogwood and honeysuckle, the author has composed an admirable period piece, which, though episodic, is in general a sustained narrative of real people who might inhabit any age. Her characters convey a lively appreciation of those individual virtues and relatively restrained vices on which so high a premium has now been set. That is the important thing to say about *Sapphira*, together with the thought that Willa Cather remains a novelist of the greatest integrity and distinction. Her new book is not her best, but she is still capable of a masterpiece.

"Willa Cather's Study
of Virginia Woman,"
Springfield
(Massachusetts)
Republican, 22
December 1940, p. 7E

Willa Cather has written a novel after five years. But *Sapphira and the Slave Girl* . . . is rather an extended sketch, or a "long short story," dealing with an episode in a Virginia small town. Miss Cather, who lived in Virginia when she was a small girl, has delicately and beautifully reproduced the atmosphere of this bit of Southland. . . .

The book teems with characters, rather than situations. There is Sapphira herself, a woman who believes that she has married beneath her; almost a cripple from dropsy, she has a complex nature compounded of generosity, dignity, intelligence, maliciousness and unreasonableness. Her husband is the one sturdy member of the Colbert family, for the other brothers have all gone the way of dissipation. He is silent, steady, upright and a keen businessman. He makes his business pay by constant oversight, while other mills under lazy management have failed. His wife resents his constant attendance at the mill, but realizes it is necessary for success.

Nancy is a mulatto who adores her master, keeps his mill rooms immaculate, and is deft and conscientious in all she does. There is a real thrill for readers in her avoidance of and struggle with the dissolute Martin, and another thrill in her escape. Mrs. Blake, the daughter, lives partly in the past, mourning for her departed husband, and taking on all the burdens of the people around her. Her character is rather lightly sketched in.

Then there are Negro servants of the time before emancipation. They are a picturesque lot, sometimes shiftless, sometimes stern, but always devoted to their mistress. There is Aunt Till, who nearly sacrifices her daughter, Nancy, through her devotion to Mrs. Colbert. And the irresponsible Bluebell, who can sing like a lark. And Jezebel, who is dying at an age well past 90, a woman who had been captured in Africa and won her name because of the ferocious fight she had put up against her captors. Jezebel had had a wild existence before she came to Sapphira Colbert, an existence which could well make another story. Indeed, the Negroes of this book hold one's attention rather more closely than the "white folks," and Miss Cather shows that she understands thoroughly the colored people of slavery.

In some respects Sapphira reminds one of Willa Cather's "Lost Lady," for she has the charm of the "Lost Lady," and also a "yellow streak" which prevents her from becoming a noble character. There is material in this book for a long novel, but Miss Cather has chosen to present it on the scale of an expanded episode. It is written with Miss Cather's exquisite sense of shadings and in beautiful prose.

M. W., "Miss Cather's
New Novel," *Christian
Science Monitor*,
28 December 1940,
p. 11

One wonders a little, just at first, how Miss Cather came to write such a novel as this. Then it grows clearer that the threads of her story are closely knit with certain experiences which her own family had in the Virginia from which they moved when Miss Cather was a small child. In an Epilogue, she explains that while she has used surnames familiar among people living in Frederick County, "in no case the name of a person whom I ever saw or knew." Perhaps her vision of these people, half-memory, half-hearsay, so pressed itself upon her imagination that this tale became a necessary outlet. Possibly the history of her heroine, Nancy Till, because of authentic associations, is to Miss Cather more rewarding than it is to her readers.

However, to some of her readers at least, *Sapphira and the Slave Girl* will prove strangely disappointing. It will leave them baffled and disillusioned. For little remains, upon closing this book, other than a sense of sadness, of defeat, of the savor of slow decay. That, together with the penetrating melancholy of the scene and of characters set before Miss Cather's readers by a skill which is masterly. That Miss Cather is an artist, one knows from memory of such novels as *My Antonia*, as *One of Ours*, as *Death Comes for the Archbishop*. Because of these, one expects much, and one has the right. Yet this story of Sapphira and of Nancy, the slave girl whom she subjected to slow mental torture, leaves one full of regret.

The portraits of these people are able and most convincing: the gentleness and tolerance of the Negroes, the patience and increasing tenderness in the person of the miller, Henry Colbert, in effective contrast to the subtlety and hardness of Sapphira. One believes in these people; one admires the courage of Nancy, the faithfulness of her old slave mother, the indomitable quality of Rachel. Because of the skill with which Miss Cather depicts them and their pre-Civil War world of the South, they are difficult to forget; and, because of this same skill, the book becomes more sad and haunting.

Robert Littell, *Yale Review*, 30 (Winter 1941), x

... Now at last we are safe from books that may ride one's dreams, or one's waking moments with uneasy recollections. For Willa Cather has given us another novel, *Sapphira and the Slave Girl*, a story of the Old South, and quite unlike the many things, perfumed or war-torn, or nostalgic, which that battered phrase implies. There are characters here whose bare description would make them sound like stereotypes, incidents the blueprint of which is familiar—but Miss Cather melts it all down, alloys it with her own rare but not showy metal, pours it into the shape of a new mould, does something else to it the secret of which she alone knows, so that at last there is on it a patina in which reality and remoteness, austerity and life are curiously mingled.

Harry Lorin Binsse, *Commonweal*, 33 (10 January 1941), 306–7

What a relief it is to read something written by an author who regards her trade as a craft, as something involving care and polish and refinement. Most books of the day seem to be thrown together with a maximum of regard for content and a minimum for that content's presentation. After all we know that however good the content may be, it needs skill in its presentation or it is likely to remain still-born in its unread printed pages.

To say that Miss Cather is a craftsman is almost to insult a reader's intelligence with a truism, yet one cannot help feeling that it needs saying, if only by way of precept and in the hope that it may inspire others to be likewise. *Sapphira and the Slave Girl* ranks, I believe, with *Death Comes for the Archbishop*, *My Antonia* and *A Lost Lady*. It is several notches above *Shadows on the Rock*. Which means that all amateurs of her writing will consider the book a "must."

This time Miss Cather turns to a setting which played a part in her own life—western Virginia—and a period which has recently been greatly in vogue, the years immediately preceding the Civil War. Her story is really a study in the psychological effect of slavery on both slave and master, an almost geometrical demonstration of the proposition that whatever good things may result from slavery, it is bad and humanly perverting *in itself*, in the unnatural relationship it establishes between two children of God. And I don't care whether or not Miss Cather goes to church: she again demonstrates herself as steeped in Christianity: *anima naturaliter christiana*. . . .

One thing may be said, and with justice, against Miss Cather's way of writing. It can, on occasion, seem mannered and even a little thin. Sometimes her people are very close to being lay-figures, and seem to lack any particularizing touch. This is, of course, never true of her main characters: in this case Nancy, Sapphira, Henry Colbert. And perhaps there is genius in this simplifying emphasis on one or two persons, leaving the rest of the *dramatis personae* to serve as accessories

to the main action and study. Yet the effect is, indeed, somewhat less than full-bodied.

But to object on this ground is to object unfairly. Miss Cather, if anyone, defines her problems, sets her own limits. And what she produces is so incomparably better than what most novelists produce that we should all be grateful.

E[dward] W[eeks], "Atlantic Bookshelf," *Atlantic Monthly*, 167 (February 1941), n.p.

A cameo novel whose brevity is misleading, since it will not be taken in by the quick glance. Outwardly it lacks the tumult and temptation of *A Lost Lady*—the surface is unruffled, the conflict suppressed. But the antagonisms, the loyalties are there, sensitive and perceptible beneath the surface: You feel them with increasing force in the relation between Henry and Sapphira Colbert, and as the story kindles your curiosity you feel them in the less familiar relationship between Missy and her slaves. In the beauty of line and the almost perfect selection of detail this novel does Miss Cather proud. To me it recalls the neglected but equally lovely story, *The Trader's Wife*, by Jean Kenyon Mackenzie.

Catholic World, 152 (February 1941), 634

Not since *Lucy Gayheart*, published in 1935, has Miss Cather published a novel, but her followers will gladly excuse her sparse productiveness and consider the waiting worth while, for her intermittent books, when they do appear, have a chiseled beauty that is lacking in most modern stories. In *Sapphira and the Slave Girl* Miss Cather uses the directness of the fairy tale and the fluidity of poetry to depict the refined cruelty that Sapphira employs against the little slave girl, Nancy. With lucid description and subtle suggestion she gives a three dimensional quality to Sapphira Dodderidge Colbert, the owner of great wealth and many slaves; to her husband, Henry Colbert, a fine man of a lower social class; but most of all to the Dodderidge slaves—Jezebel, the African grandmother, Till the devoted servant, and little Nancy of the third generation of Virginia slaves. The one flaw in this delightful book is the Epilogue; it could so well have been devoted to a satisfying completion of the exceptionally well-drawn characters. Instead, Miss Cather confuses her readers and leaves them greatly exasperated. The beautiful format of *Sapphira and the Slave Girl* makes it even easier to read Miss Cather's beautiful prose.

Michael Williams, "Views and Reviews," *Commonweal*, 33 (7 February 1941), 399–400

Willa Cather's quality as an artist is tested by the spirit of our age; as all things, and all persons, are, or must be, before that spirit has done its work ("that all nations who have merited by faith the privilege of the children of Israel, may be born again by partaking of God's holy spirit"). Her newest novel, *Sapphira and the Slave Girl*, comes like a clearly articulated utterance of that still, small voice which bears its message lucidly, yet with the overtones of mystery, when the great tempests (of the "Build-up") and the earthquaking shocks of publicity are hurling other novels, by other kinds of writers, through vast and evanescent editions, which pass into the silence, leaving no word to be remembered. But Willa Cather is memorable; and will long be remembered—even if the Huns destroy the society she describes and adorns.

Mr. H. L. Binsse has admirably reviewed this exquisitely powerful work of fiction for *The Commonweal*'s readers. I wish only to add a few footnotes to his study: of a personal kind, perhaps, yet not, I hope, without a general interest— at least for those readers, few yet fit, to whom the aristocratic genius of Willa Cather is one of the fine flowers of a truly democratic American spirit. For I can think of no words more suitable than "aristocratic genius" to suggest (of course I am aware that they do not define) the quality of this creative novelist whose craftsmanship is almost commensurate with her high—her almost supreme— powers of imagination, of intuition, of intelligence, of self-control. I say "almost" is her technique equal to the full expression of her visions of reality, glimpsed down vistas of romance; fortunately—or rather necessarily—there are moods of her own temperament, there are certain of her intuitions so profound that they cannot be more than hinted at; or which no phrases at her command can do more than suggest. This fact is no limitation of Willa Cather's place among major novelists; indeed, it validates her certificate of mastery—granted not by any chair of criticism (which, if it be truly discerning, can but confirm it), but given to Willa Cather as a gift from the world above the world she moves in, and of which she relates her chronicles.

Steadily, as is the way of all wholesome, organic things, her artistry through much practice and fostering has grown. So, of course, has her knowledge of the realities of human life; and, concurrently, her appreciation of the fathomless atmosphere of the mystery in which all human beings live and move and by which they are—without which, in a sense beyond all language, there is nothing. To far too many artists—on becoming conscious of this ineluctable factor in life—like Till, in this story by Willa Cather, "the heavy atmosphere brings a heaviness of heart." And, as Nietschze truly tried to say before he passed into the darkness of the mere shadow of mystery, the artist must be a dancer: he must master, or anyhow practice as best he may, the "gay science" of life. But many novelists, and poets, again like hapless Till, "suffer a frightful shock," as Nietscheze did; and forevermore thereafter are incapable of treading the dance of life, and of singing of its ecstacies, or of relating such wholesome, mysterious tales as Willa Cather's, about Sapphira and the slave girl in which all her main characters, sinners and saints alike, know a life that burns with a steady flame—with leaping gusts of passion now and then. None of Willa Cather's characters are citizens of Laodicia.

Only true aristocrats can know and love, understand and appreciate the heights and depths of poor and humble souls—so specially open and hospitable to the indwelling of God. Without an aristocracy of artists, of genuine scientists, of statesmen, of soldiers and of priests, no free and democratic society can live, flourish and develop.

For always it is a law of life that *quality* must leaven and transmute mere *quantity*—or at least, quality must give

leadership, which must be obediently followed in democratic nations, or else there will be sickness and decay, as there has been with us since the miserable national failure to do America's bounden duty, after the World War, to support the other free nations with whose armies our armies so splendidly fought, only to be betrayed by the politicians and the money-changers. The consequent degradation of our press is only the most obvious proof of this degenerative process. With Willa Cather, and a number of other elect spirits, however, there was no surrender to the idolatry of mass production, of vulgarization; of Democracy *à rebours*. With the Willa Cathers who may be granted to us in the future, literature again may flourish in a soil of freedom and religion.

Alain Tarn, "Books of Southern Interest," *Southern Literary Messenger*, 3 (March 1941), 146

It has always been a question whether or not to call Willa Cather a Southerner. Certainly, until now, one could not call her a Southern writer for she had used neither Southern characters nor locales in her eleven preceding novels. Perhaps because she left Winchester, Virginia, her birthplace, so young, there was little lingering impression. Her ignoring of the South, although her novels have stepped into Canada, has been conspicuous. At last, in *Sapphira and the Slave Girl* she has made a book out of an old slave-and-the-underground-railway story. Had the book appeared anonymously, one's first guess as to its author might have been Ellen Glasgow, although Miss Glasgow would have presented a more sophisticated and finished piece of work.

This is not a great book. No characters emerge to be remembered. Occasionally Nancy, the slave girl, steps out for a realistic impression and then she becomes of a color with the autumnal shades of the tapestry—a loosely woven tapestry. At the very highest point in the story, where Sapphira's reactions and Martin's to the runaway slave are awaited with the first show of eagerness by the reader, there are blank pages and then the unconvincing note of Sapphira to her daughter and a rather flat paragraph on how the neighbors would whisper—but not a look at Sapphira. In short, one feels that Miss Cather missed the highest emotional spot in her own story.

The finest part of the story is the relationship between Henry Colbert, the miller, and Nancy, which Miss Cather keeps on such a beautiful plane that there is never a false note sounded or anticipated. In Henry's and his daughter Rachel's attitudes toward slave-holding, one sees George Washington's and Robert Lee's views and actions on the subject. Henry and Rachel might have been written as characters to be remembered but the author employed pastel colors where she might have used strong and lasting oils. Even in her attitude toward the country, which is sufficiently beautiful to merit some reaction, the enthusiasm is missing.

As the publisher says, "The theme is moving and dramatic and is treated with sensitiveness and imagination," but the "master" hand that Miss Cather used in many of her other novels painted weakly here. However, it is questionable if any other than Willa Cather—or Ellen Glasgow—could have handled this theme so beautifully and delicately.

Times Literary Supplement (London), 2 August 1941, p. 369

The story Miss Willa Cather tells in her latest novel may be considered slight, but the telling is delicate, suggestive and beautifully just. Hers is a warm and limpid style of narrative that gives unfailing pleasure; things seen or felt, large or small, are recorded in what seems a glow of candour. The scene, painted with lingering affection for a landscape evidently filled with personal and family associations, is the back country of Virginia in the last years of slavery. In delicately thoughtful fashion Miss Cather describes the relationship of owner and slave, the best and the worst sides of the old southern scheme of society, the way of life in which food and linen, horses and piety held a traditional place of ceremony, and in which a coloured girl of twelve, wearing a stiffly starched red calico dress, in summer walked barefoot round and round the master's supper table waving a long flybrush made of a peacock's tail.

When Sapphira Dodderidge, who in choosing Henry Colbert for a husband had married beneath her, came out with him to Back Creek Valley and the new mill house she had built there, she brought with her a score of negro slaves. The settlers from Pennsylvania in that remote region between Winchester and Romney did not believe in slavery, and owned no negroes. Sapphira had been born and bred to a belief in slavery and had only a cool contempt for those of different mind. She had sold most of her slaves to provide her husband with money to improve the mill; to those she retained she was a model mistress of the south, firm, authoritative, scrupulously fair and kindly. She took part in all the festivities and celebrations the coloured people loved; she indulged her favourites and was patient with the rest; she doctored the sick and sent linen for the new babies. With all that she had not hesitated to assure herself of the services of a personal maid who would remain trim and presentable by marrying her off to a shrivelled old darky. Henry Colbert did not interfere with her in these matters; the mill was his affair, the farm was hers. It was when an elderly Sapphira, almost crippled by dropsy, could no longer manage the farm that her southern justice—and not justice alone—failed her. Jealousy gave proof that a relationship in which both sides had implicit belief could nevertheless be inherently evil.

The story turns on Sapphira's calculated persecution of the mulatto girl Nancy, the daughter of her faithful Till by a visitor from Baltimore to the mill house. Her jealousy, mingling with all sorts of obscurer impulses, reaches the point at which she does everything she can to enable a rakish nephew to seduce the girl. The result is that her own daughter, the widowed Rachel, and eventually her husband are drawn into a conspiracy to secure Nancy's flight across the Potomac and into Canada. That is the entire story, and Sapphira's penitence and the indomitable spirit with which she meets the approach of death form a touching conclusion. The whole thing is done very quietly and with admirable strength. The miller and the religious minded Rachel are both very real, and the portrait of Sapphira, which at one stage threatens to become over-coloured, in the end takes on eloquent balance and proportion.

Checklist of Additional Reviews

Isabel M. Turner, *Library Journal*, 65 (15 November 1940), 982.
Booklist, 37 (15 December 1940), 154.

THE OLD BEAUTY AND OTHERS

The Old Beauty
and Others

BY

WILLA CATHER

1 9 4 8

NEW YORK

ALFRED A KNOPF

Helene Scherff Taylor, *Library Journal*, 73 (September 1948), 1192

Hardly more than sketches, these three short stories, "The Old Beauty," "The Best Years," and "Before Breakfast," contribute nothing to the stature of Miss Cather as a distinguished artist. Her admirers may possibly be embarrassed to note here the lack of literary maturity and the grace of expression that have created lasting eloquence in her best work.

Fanny Butcher, "Three Long Short Stories by Willa Cather," *Chicago Sunday Tribune*, 12 September 1948, section 4, p. 5

Willa Cather stipulated in her will that no unfinished work of hers should be published after her death. We know that she had just started the first draft of a fourth story to make up the volume, and that it was to have been, like "The Old Beauty," a long short story in the genre of a *A Lost Lady* and *My Mortal Enemy*, one in which Willa Cather was acknowledged supreme.

No one has been able to give more vividly, more tenderly, more truly the essence of a life in what for want of a more accurate definition is called short story, novelette or novella.

"The Old Beauty," like Willa Cather's previous short novels, is one of those works of literary art in which not only the whole life of an individual but the whole spirit of a period is caught in so few words that the reader can and often does remember most of them. In it, without telling actual minute details, she has recreated the essential past of Madame de Coucy, the former Lady Longstreet, a great beauty of a period when great beauty was considered something more than mere physical comeliness, and its possession and life itself held beauty and carried responsibilities as well as privileges.

"The Old Beauty" lies dead as the story opens, and 55 year old Henry Seabury, an American who had known her in his, not her, youth, is courteously evading the questions of reporters who are only routinely curious about the long forgotten toast of London society—ironically not even a name to them, only a newspaper assignment.

Henry Seabury and the Old Beauty make an incongruous pair, but together they echo the whole era.

In a sense "The Old Beauty" also embodies an era in writing which seems sadly past, a day when truly great authors shunned both haste and waste; when an author's output was judged not by quantity but by quality; when the skilled author implied much more than was set down in words.

Willa Cather's prose had, and still has in "The Old Beauty" the quality of music and magic truly fine prose always has. Compare her work with the work of some popular writers, who take ten pages to say what she says in a sentence, who fill their paragraphs with words as well as ideas whose sole function is to shock, not to enlighten the reader. The difference is apparent to the most casual reader. That reader may think the minute details and the four letter words and purple passages are titillating, but he will declare that he knows one of Willa Cather's characters with an intimacy with which he has never shared the board and often the bed of some of the heroines of popular fiction.

The other two stories in the volume are slighter: a nostalgic tale of a young Nebraska school teacher, who in a very real sense gave her life that others might live, called "The Best Years"; and "Before Breakfast," in which the hero's joy in the beauty of a beloved little north Atlantic island is threatened by science. "Before Breakfast" is one of the few faintly satirical things that Willa Cather ever wrote. It was unquestionably inspired by some incident on the Canadian island where Miss Cather used to spend her summers, as was "The Best Years" by her youthful years in Nebraska. Both stories have the tenderness of long, affectionate association with a background.

What the fourth side of the literary edifice which Miss Cather had planned in this book was to have been we shall never know. But that she had planned it, and patiently and skillfully; that it would have been an aesthetic balance to "The Old Beauty" and that it would have been a beautiful work of artistic restraint we can be sure. When Willa Cather died last April we lost one of our most distinguished creators.

Lloyd Morris, "Willa Cather's Valedictory to Lost Ideals," *New York Herald Tribune Books*, 12 September 1948, p. 1

This slender volume, terminated by her death, contains the last three stories which Willa Cather wrote. She had intended adding to these a fourth and much longer tale; she was still working on its first draft when she died in the spring of 1947. But although it does not fulfill her design, *The Old Beauty and Others* makes an appropriate valediction. "It is always hard to write about the things that are near your heart," she said, many years ago. "From a kind of instinct of self-protection you disguise and distort them." The things that were closest to Willa Cather's heart stand revealed, once again, in this final book.

On the American literary scene she impressed one as a curiously solitary figure. She seemed to be outside the main current of her time and also to be apart from the tradition which that current was displacing. This appearance was, of course, deceptive; a result perhaps of the late flowering of her talent. She was nearing her fortieth year when she published her first novel; the earliest of her major books did not appear until just before the first world war. Of the writers of her own generation, all but two had already produced their best books. Hers were to be published simultaneously with those of a new school of American novelists. Her work showed little kinship with that of Theodore Dreiser or Sherwood Anderson, her real contemporaries. It showed even less with that of the rising stars among her juniors: Sinclair Lewis, Scott Fitzgerald, John Dos Passos, Ernest Hemingway. Of the brilliant constellation that appeared in the 1920s, only Glenway Wescott resembled her somewhat, as might a younger relative belonging to a collateral line.

But Willa Cather's literary affinity was obvious in her neglected first novel. And her career is rounded to a perfect symmetry by its reappearance in the title-story of this book. In *Alexander's Bridge* she paid homage to Henry James by borrowing his fictional method. In "The Old Beauty," as if in deliberate piety, she chose a subject which he might have dealt with fondly. Her intervening books owed almost nothing to his method or his subject-matter; but the likeness existed, at a deeper level. They had in common an intense preoccupation with craftsmanship, a reverence for tradition, an attraction to exalted ideals. Both made a cult of "distinction, that unmistakable thing"—the phrase was hers, but might have been his. Both set an inordinately high value on sensibility, on fastidious discrimination. But far more important than these resemblances was another. For Willa Cather inherited the plight of Henry James, and it shaped her work as decisively as it had his. Like him, she felt herself an alien in the America of her maturity. But her isolation, like his, was illusory; she was as firmly joined as he to the taproot of native and contemporary experience.

Sometimes it seemed that a distate for what confronted her vision determined the things that came to be nearest her heart. While the younger writers of the 1920s were effecting (as Walter Lippmann said) the dissolution of the ancestral order, Willa Cather was celebrating the past whose authority they undermined. Not that she was any less exasperated than they by the America of Harding and Coolidge—or, for that matter, of Wilson and Taft; it was the intensity of her moral repugnance that dictated her retreat to a quarter they were too young to remember. In retrospect, the pioneering America of her Nebraskan childhood, the New York and Europe of the 1890s where she had made her excited youthful discovery of art and music and the theater, of good talk and a many-shaded society—these seemed immeasurably superior to the forms of life with which the twentieth century had replaced them. So they became the focus of her affections, the cynosures she held up to youth adrift in an era of complacent prosperity, an era lost to high purposes in its squalid obsession with money-making.

She held them up sadly: they were irrecoverable, and their equivalents were not to be anticipated. Her disenchantment with modern America was no more extreme than that of Dreiser and Anderson, Lewis and Fitzgerald, but whereas their skepticism laid down a ringing challenge and a summons to fight, hers was hopeless. The United States—as she said of the American tycoon whose progress she examined in "Before Breakfast," one of her last three stories—"had got ahead wonderfully . . . but, somehow, ahead on the wrong road." The course of the future, she felt, had been inexorably decided. Unable to envisage any nobler tomorrow, she composed, in her best books, an elegy on American yesterdays. These novels erected a memorial to a brief, heroic dream. In her childhood she had known those who cherished it; she had seen it frustrated by the conquering evangel of materialism and the triumph of an industrial civilization. In other stories she celebrated later victims of that triumph, men and women in whom (as she put it) the old belief flashed up with an intense kind of hope, an intense kind of pain—the conviction that there was something splendid about life, could they but find it. Mostly, they belonged to the past. In the present, they became rebels, or misfits. Twentieth-century America, condemned to free play of individuality as dangerous, and society conspired to extinguish any burning reckless vision of a superior way of life.

Did she fall into the trap which she herself detected—the disguise and distortion of times and people and experiences which compelled her affection? Youthful readers today are likely to think so. They will be surprised to find her in "The Old Beauty" extolling the "security, the solid exterior, the exotic contradictions behind the screen" that she found characteristic of "the deep, claret-colored closing years of Victoria's reign." They may question her admiration of women like the exorbitant heroine of *My Mortal Enemy*, who made Christmas for the lonely Polish actress, Madame Modjeska; like Marian Forrester in *A Lost Lady*, whose fastidiousness was so cheaply overcome; like Lady Longstreet in "The Old Beauty," who needed to be nothing more than lovely. And were the pioneers and builders of towns and railroads what she represented them to be—dreamers, enthusiasts spurred to action by no greater certainty than their own grandiose hopes? Economic and social historians have lately given a somewhat different account of them, and contemporary youth may prefer it to Miss Cather's. If they do, older readers will have the privilege of thinking them misguided. For it was not history that Willa Cather wrote, at her best, but a kind of poetry with moral implications. "Ideals," she said in one of her books, "were not archaic things, beautiful and impotent; they were the real sources of power among men." So, for an era that she judged to be meanly devoted to mean objectives, she tried to salvage the memory of a life that had seemed freer, more hazardous, more prodigal and more passionate.

The three tales that make up her final book are not among her best. But in them, as always, she was a skillful craftsman, exercising her finest gift: the power of evocation. If for no other reason than this, *The Old Beauty and Others* commands respect.

Charles Poore, "The Last Stories of Willa Cather," *New York Times Book Review*, 12 September 1948, p. 3

Willa Cather was born a Virginian and died a New Yorker and wrote most memorably about Nebraska and the West. The three stories in this, her last book, suggest those places in point of view or mood or setting. One is a wreath for an international enchantress of the Nineties. One is the soliloquy of a Western rich man facing his mortal enemy at last. In the pleasure they give and the mastery they show they belong with her finest and most characteristic work, with *My Antonia,* and *A Lost Lady*, and *Death Comes for the Archbishop*. Yet nothing in them, true fragments though they are, tells us so much, perhaps, about Willa Cather as a choice she made not long before her death a year ago last April.

That was when she unexpectedly answered a question. The question—put by an industrious anthologist—was: What, among the works of others, do you wish you had written? It went to a lavish variety of literary celebrities. Upton Sinclair chose a bit from Isaiah; Henry Canby chose a bit from his bible, *Walden*; Irwin Edman went straight to George Santayana. Miss Cather said she wished she had written the ballad of "The Mary Gloster," by Rudyard Kipling.

Why, of all things, did she choose that? Why didn't she choose something from Turgenev or Henry James or the Sarah Orne Jewett who had counseled her: "One must know the world so well before one can know the parish," or the Walt

Whitman who had given her the title for *O Pioneers!* ? Miss Cather used explanations as sparingly as she used words in writing *Shadows on the Rock* or *My Mortal Enemy* or *Sapphira and the Slave Girl*, or *Lucy Gayheart*—or the stories in *The Old Beauty and Others*.

And, on the rare occasions when she did explain, she did so with a glowing asperity that sometimes burned middle-class critics hell-bent on being as proletarian as all getout.

"Literalness," she said in an essay called "The Novel Démeublé," "when applied to the presenting of mental reactions and of physical sensations seems to be no more effective than when it is applied to material things. A novel crowded with physical sensations is no less a catalogue than one crowded with furniture."

Also these words, which might well be above every writer's desk and in every school that tries to teach writing:

"Whatever is felt upon the page without being specifically named there— that, it seems to me, is created. It is the inexplicable presence of the thing not named, of the overtone divined by the ear but not heard by it, the verbal mood, the emotional aura of the fact or the thing or the deed, that gives high quality to the novel or the drama, as well as to poetry itself."

All her later books are true to that principle. In some of the earlier ones, such as *The Song of the Lark*, there is too much archaeological furniture. Perhaps in *The Professor's House* and *One of Ours*, too. It was, then, the conciseness of Kipling's "Mary Gloster," as well as the fortitude in the deathbed portrait of a tough and picturesque old titan—like the titans of her West—who got things done, who scorned the soft and the cheap, the rust that tarnished the scabbarded blade, that appealed to her:

Never seen death yet, Dickie? Well,
    now is your time to learn,
And you'll wish you held my record
    before it comes to your turn.
I've made myself and a million; but
    I'm damned if I made you.

It has what Unamuno called "the tragic sense of life" that you will find in all Miss Cather's books. It shows "the inevitable hardness of human life," which, Thea Kronborg said toward the end of *The Song of the Lark*, all real artists must learn. It is not out of key with the spirit of the Marian Forrester of *A Lost Lady*, who "mocked outrageously at the proprieties she observed, and inherited the magic of contradictions." And it would not be despised by Father Latour, in *Death Comes for the Archbishop*, who went over the splendor of his memories tranquilly, and who said with a smile: "I shall not die of a cold, my son. I shall die of having lived."

All of a piece throughout, then, Miss Cather's stories return again and again to her themes: youth lost and fortitude maintained, daring and art and valor. The old values, she frequently likes to suggest, are better than the new. The giants lived yesterday; pygmies rule today.

Now that is a bracing stand to take. The trouble with it is that it really won't stand an awful lot of discussion. For what is a fine old value to me, may have been a pretty shocking and revolutionary notion to my crusty great-grandfather. As Anon has said, there must once have been people who thought that romance went kiting out of the sea when those new-fangled things called sails took the place of the good old paddles and the dugout canoes of the good old days.

Yet you know very well what Miss Cather means when Gabrielle Longstreet, the heroine of "The Old Beauty," living out her last days at Aix-les-Bains, in 1922, a significant place and date to Miss Cather, says: "I think one should go out with one's time."

And, like Yeats' dying lady, "with the old kindness, the old distinguished grace," mourning what Ezra Pound called "the old men with beautiful manners," who will come no more. Gabrielle, once the toast of two continents, is soon on her way to her final resting place. Where? Why, at Pere-Lachaise cemetery in Paris, of course. Hadn't it also been fashionably chosen by "Adelina Patti, Sarah Bernhardt and other ladies who had once held a place in the world"?

There is a faint ghost of absurdity to trouble us here. But please don't think Miss Cather wasn't aware of it. Her use of the word fashionable indicates that, without specifically naming it. What she was doing here was what she once said in a letter to *The Commonweal* a novelist should do—presenting "the experiences and emotions of a group of people by the light of his own [experience] whether his method is 'objective' or 'subjective.'"

Incidentally, that mention of Patti and Bernhardt is itself a quintessence of Catherism, a touch of the Willa Cather whose stories frequently show how much she admired great old-time singers and actresses as well as the ruins of the Southwest.

In the second story in *The Old Beauty and Others*, called "The Best Years," there is a wonderful picture of the Nebraska country at the turn of the century, when Miss Evangeline Knightly, the young school superintendent, was on her way to see a promising youngster who died young before finding the bright Medusa. Years later Miss Knightly, who had long since married and gone away, as Miss Cather's characters so often do, comes back for a postscript visit, in homage to nostalgia and the tidy ending (as Miss Cather's characters so often did).

A pert young modern, "a wide-awake, breezy girl with blond hair and crimson lips," is now the district superintendent. We are told that the former Miss Knightly "liked young people who were not in the least afraid of luck or responsibility," though the liking does not seem to be overwhelming. Anyway, when she explains that she would prefer a horse and buggy rather than an automobile to visit the schools again, the red-lipped blonde brightly says:

"I get you. You want to put on an old-home act. You might phone around to any farmers you used to know. Some of them still keep horses for haying."

To which Miss Cather's heroine answers nothing—nothing whatever— though you can feel the air quiver with what must have been her reaction to that bit of jazz-age sauciness. And again something is felt on a page without being specifically named there.

The story's explicit moral is that "our best years are when we're working hardest and going right ahead when we can hardly see our way out." But there is no comment on that, either. The commentary, if any, comes in the last story, "Before Breakfast," when the self-made Henry Grenfell, in his island retreat designed for peace of mind, goes back over the years and finds their climax singularly disturbing.

In a preface to a new edition of *The Song of the Lark*, written at New Brunswick, Canada, in 1932, not far from the scene of "Before Breakfast," Miss Cather had said: "Success is never so interesting as struggle—not even to the successful, not even to the most mercenary forms of ambition."

After revising *The Song of the Lark*, she was still critical:

"The interesting and important fact that, in an artist of the type I chose, personal life becomes paler as the imaginative life becomes richer, does not, however, excuse my story for becoming paler. The story set out to tell of an artist's awakening and struggle; her floundering escape from a smug, domestic, self-satisfied provincial world of utter ignorance. It should have been content to do that. I should have disregarded the conventional design and stopped where my first conception stopped, telling the latter part of the story by suggestion merely. What I cared about, and still care about, was the girl's escape; the play of blind chance, the way in which commonplace occurrences fell together to liberate her from commonness. She seemed wholly at the mercy of accident; but to a person of her vitality and honesty, fortunate accidents always happen."

Finally, in "Before Breakfast," we have a perfect Cather touch when Grenfell recalls saying to his wife and son, who have grown away from him, that while they are at the symphony, he is going to hear John McCormack sing "Kathleen Mavourneen." And his wife in her "innocent, well-bred way," says:

"Dear me! I haven't heart McCormack sing since he first came out in Italy years and years ago. His success was sensational. He was singing Mozart then."

There are few shouts in Miss Cather's writing. But the murmurs are incomparably clear.

Victor P. Hass, "Willa Cather's Last Stories Are Flawless, Oddly Empty," *World-Herald Sunday Magazine* (Omaha), 12 September 1948, p. 28

The three short stories published here are the last we shall have from the pen of Willa Cather. At the time of her death in 1947 she was working on a fourth, and much longer story but she did not live to complete it. In accord with her wishes, it will not be published.

One could wish—certainly I could wish—that these three stories had not been published either. They are unmistakably the work of the fine writer that Miss Cather was but they are also unmistakably inferior. To put it brutally, she had little left to say in her declining years though, as these slight stories prove, she said it well.

By the time she had retreated from lusty, gusty Nebraska to her native Virginia, Miss Cather's style had become detached and severely impersonal. This was evident in her novel, *Sapphira and the Slave Girl*. There is a story written on so high an intellectual plane that it seemed Miss Cather was forbidding the reader to invest his emotions in it. Certainly no reader could become part of the book as he could with the beautiful and moving *My Antonia* and the other-worldly but wonderfully compassionate *Death Comes for the Archbishop*.

That, as I see it, is the trouble with these last short stories—there is no room for the reader to play a part, to live the stories, to participate emotionally in the experiences of the characters Miss Cather has created. The flawless technique is there but there is no blood, no living tissue. It is as though Miss Cather had nothing more of herself to give save the fading brilliance of her mind and this was not enough without heart and sinews.

Yet I believe that those who have loved—and still love—the work of Miss Cather will want to read these three stories if only as a sort of farewell to a beloved friend.

The first story, "The Old Beauty," tells of the life and death of a once-celebrated belle. You meet Lady Longsteet as she dies but through an old friend, Henry Seabury, who was present, you learn how she had been the toast of Britain and of much of the continent and of how misfortune had overtaken her and of how, finally, she had come to a little French watering place to die quickly and serenely. That is the whole of it.

"The Best Years" I like best by far and it is somehow fitting that this story, the last Miss Cather wrote, should be of Nebraska in an earlier day.

Perhaps Miss Cather was homesick for this Nebraska of ours where she had spent so many happy years. This is the old Cather in these lines. It is the story of a girl who wanted to be a teacher and who did become a teacher in one of our country schools and of how she died during a blizzard when she was helping her pupils to survive.

Surely there is nostalgia and deep love in these lines about "dusty, sunflower bordered roads" and "the great blue sky, smiling, cloudless—and the land that lay level as far as the eye could see. The horizon was like a perfect circle, a great embrace, and within it lay the cornfields, still green, and the yellow wheat stubble, miles and miles of it."

It is absurd to wish, and yet I still could wish that Miss Cather had left the old beauty and the financier in the third story,

"Before Breakfast," and written a short novel around that theme of "our best years" being those when we were "working hardest and going right ahead when we could hardly see our way out." For "The Best Years" is a story that rings solid and true—but there is so little of it.

As for "Before Breakfast," I completed it only with difficulty. It is brief and it is sometimes brilliant, but it seemed to be a failure with Miss Cather's picture of the success and failure of a man scarcely emerging beyond the idea stage.

These stories will add nothing to Miss Cather's reputation but then they need not. That reputation rests upon a foundation of novels that will be read and loved for a very long time to come.

John Farrelly, "Fiction Parade," *New Republic*, 119 (13 September 1948), 24–6

The death of Willa Cather last year came as a surprise to many people who had forgotten she was still alive. Although she had published earlier and later, her work seemed finally identified with the twenties, and her reputation a lush growth of the boom years. But if she was originally overrated, she has now suffered the reverse fortune, and as an almost insuperable obstacle to any interest in her work, two of her flimsier novels have become established "safe" reading for adolescents. I refer, of course, to *Shadows on the Rock* and *Death Comes for the Archbishop*.

The three stories in this posthumous volume are certainly no occasion to revive her name. They are tired pieces, reworking old themes. The title story recalls Miss

Cather's concern for a "society whose manners, dress, conventions, loyalties, codes of honor, were different from anything existing in the world today." Unfortunately the peevish memories of a faded demimondaine are scarcely an effective tribute to the "old order." And the most memorable lines in the story refer to a man who has just threatened the heroine with his gymnastic attentions: "That was not an English-speaking man. . . . He is an immigrant who has made a lot of money. He does not belong."

The second story in the book returns to other "old days," the Nebraska farm life of the author's youth. A hard-working mother of a large family embodies what Miss Cather calls (but in the third story) "the ginger to care hard and work hard." The tone is indicated by such complacent defeatism as "I don't think schooling gives people any wisdom. . . . I guess only life does that."

This is the pessimistic tone of a nostalgic primitivism; it enforces a doctrine of struggle, but the struggle of crude energy as an end in itself. All the "ginger" is spent from the simplest success, and, characteristically, the mother reflects in an honorable and peaceful old age: "Our best years are when we're working hardest and going right ahead when we hardly see our way out."

Horace Reynolds, "A Bit of the Old Gleam," *Christian Science Monitor*, 15 September 1948, p. 22

The pathos of a character who finds herself living in a different and less con-genial world than the one of her youth is the theme of Miss Cather's "The Old Beauty." In her salon, Lady Longstreet had been the young friend of great men, older men, who had passed on, leaving her behind to read their memoirs and dream of their greatness. She is a relic as well as a relict—a woman looking backward not forward, an old lady who says, "I think one should go out with one's time."

The story has mood; in it whispers the immemorial and useless regret of the present for the past.

The scene of "The Old Beauty" is Europe, the ceremonious old Europe of Henry James; that of "The Best Years" is young Nebraska. This story, too, has mood, but it is the ebullient spirit of youth, not the reminiscent regret of age. Its characters are gay with the eagerness of young people enjoying the adventure of life in a new country. The piece suffers a bit from formlessness, lack of an abiding center of interest. It's like smoke in the wind. The reader's attention shifts from Miss Knightly, a charming young woman with the grim title of County Superintendent of Public Instruction, to the gallant wisp of a young girl schoolteacher, and then, from there, to the midwest country which produced them. After the wisp of a girl is frozen to death in a great blizzard, halfway through the story, her memory is hardly strong enough to sustain the weight of some twenty pages of aftermath.

The third and last piece is a not very clear character sketch. It's the story of a man who has achieved money, position—everything but happiness. His perturbations, vanities, satisfactions are not very convincing, nor is his hazy need to put his soul in tune with the illusion, through which, as Coleridge said, we reach the highest truth.

These stories make two things clear:

535

firstly, that rarely does the posthumously published work of any writer add materially to his reputation; secondly, that after the vigor of *My Antonia* and the romantic beauty of *One of Ours*, Miss Cather's later work fell off in both power and insight. The first two of these stories have a bit of the old gleam, but is often obscured by vague and tenuous narrative. Individual bits have the old clarity and brightness. Romantic sadness—the sense of ruthless change rolling over the precious and rare—speaks in the first story. The tiptoe eagerness of the young schoolteacher Lesley, and the picture of the pioneer children happy in their private attic, brighten the second. These first two stories are well worth reading, but they are not Miss Cather at her best.

William Peden, "Willa Cather's Legacy," *Saturday Review of Literature*, 31 (18 September 1948), 25

Admirers of the late Willa Cather will find this volume of three hitherto unpublished pieces of short fiction much to their liking. Two of these stories, "The Old Beauty" and "The Best Years," are among the finer productions of a highly skilled craftsman and deeply perceptive observer of life whose work at its best is a real contribution to the literature of the American short story.

Since the publication of her first volume of stories over forty years ago, Miss Cather's primary interest has been in character. A realist in the tradition of Henry James and Edith Wharton, her approach to the short story has been dis-tinguished by high seriousness and artistic integrity. Resembling the naturalists in her interest in the effect of heredity and environment on the development of the individual, she broke with them almost completely in her sympathetic attitude towards her characters. It is this mature and sympathetic understanding of men and women which is one of Miss Cather's most valuable literary assets, and which brings her work closer in spirit to that of Irish writers like Michael McLaverty and Frank O'Connor than to the stories of many of her younger American contemporaries—such as James Farrell, Eudora Welty, or Truman Capote.

Nowhere is this attitude towards her characters better illustrated than in Miss Cather's treatment of Gabrielle, the heroine of her title story. Gabrielle, daughter of a Martinique mother and an English colonial, had come into the England of the 1890's as fresh and unspoiled as a quiet country dawn. The delicacy of her beauty, its harmony of modeling and line, gave her an air of "having come from afar off" to conquer London as she did. With the passing of this beauty, she became a ruin. Unrecognizable, she muffled her face in furs, shrank from the eyes of the curious, hardened into scorn. She lived in the past, with the memory of the great men who had loved her, loving them more than when they were alive because now at last she understood them better.

It is interesting if fruitless to contemplate what some of Willa Cather's major contemporaries—Dreiser, perhaps, or D. H. Lawrence—would have made of Gabrielle; presumably, we might have been presented with the case history of a somewhat damaged biological specimen, the victim of suppressions, frustrations, or an arrested emotional development. Miss Cather's Gabrielle, however, is depicted with sympathetic understanding as both victor and victim of the times and circumstances which shaped her destiny. Gabrielle is the result, almost indeed the creation, of a romantic tradition already obsolescent in her youth, and of an "attitude in men which no longer existed" in her maturity. With dignity, restraint, and an unerring selection of the significant incident and detail, Miss Cather has captured the essence of an individual and a way of life. Gabrielle, like her ruined face in death, becomes regal, calm, and victorious.

"The Best Years" is the story of Lesley Ferguesson, a young girl school teacher in Nebraska's horse-and-buggy days. Like "The Old Beauty" it is an evocation and a romantization of the past, made memorable by its characterization of Lesley and her mother. In the final analysis, however, its chief virtue lies in its quiet beauty of language and nostalgic recreation of the past rather than in character or incident. In effect it is a tone poem, praising the "home place" and family ties, the abiding pleasures of simple life and people who "for some reason, or for no reason, back from the beginning, wanted the blood to continue."

The third and final story, "Before Breakfast," adds little to the value of this volume or to the many studies of the misunderstood man unappreciated by his family. The central character, Henry Grenfell, is a puppet rather than a human being; the author fails almost completely to enlist the reader's sympathy or interest, and weakens what little is left of either by an obviously contrived ending. In idea and execution, it is far inferior to "The Old Beauty" and "The Best Years" and hardly seems to merit inclusion in the same volume with them.

The three stories in this volume are the last to come from the gentle pen of one of America's greatest writers. They are each written with the reserve and detachment which distinguished Willa Cather's writing from that personal indentification with the author so characteristic of much modern fiction.

The title story, "The Old Beauty," portrays with economy and an intense focus of emotion the last few months of life of a beautiful woman who was once the toast of international society. The sadness that tinges the portrait of this fading beauty stops short of tragedy; yet is none the less memorable because of this restraint.

There are two other stories: "The Best Years" sketches vividly a rural tragedy that has its setting in the Nebraska country of the author's youth, "Before Breakfast" is a succinct, sophisticated penetration of the mind and heart of a successful man who cannot believe in his own success.

These quiet tales will be, by terms of Miss Cather's will, the last of her work to be published. In them her genius is well remembered.

Joseph Henry Jackson, "Willa Cather's Last," *San Francisco Chronicle*, 21 September 1948, p. 24

Willa Cather was so long associated with Nebraska and the plains country that it is difficult to remember she was born a Virginian, and, further, that she put in a six-year apprenticeship in New York, working on the old *McClure's Magazine* as an editor.

I make the point because Miss Cather's talent was one which matured relatively slowly. She was 31 when her first book appeared, 33 when *O Pioneers!* her first really important novel was published. This is significant, it seems to me, since writers who mature late have a way of continuing longer in the full and worthy exercise of their powers.

Miss Cather, as you will remember, died something over a year ago at 71. After her death it was learned that she had left firm instructions that none of her letters and no unfinished work—writers always have partly finished manuscripts lying about—should be published. However, she did leave three completed stories, one of them almost a novelette, and these three, the last work of Miss Cather's that will see print, are now brought out as *The Old Beauty and Others*.

In the title story, "The Old Beauty," you will find, I think, more than a few echoes of Miss Cather's unforgettable short novel, *A Lost Lady*. As the publisher notes there is much in the marvelously compressed story to remind you of the author's *My Mortal Enemy*, too. But if you remember Mrs. Forrester (and if you read *A Lost Lady*, you will), there are flashes here in which you must recognize traces of that earlier lady of Miss Cather's. In this tale of age and death and memory—and indirectly of youth and loveliness and a quality that men could never define but which drew them to the young Gabrielle in spite of themselves—Miss Cather exhibits almost precisely the aspect of her genius that made *A Lost Lady* the remarkable book it was.

In the second story, "The Best Years," you find the author using a setting more like *My Antonia* for instance. Here she gives you the rich farming countryside she knew so well, and against that background the beauty of two lives, one short and the other long, dedicated to youth. Barely a story in the strict plot sense, it is more a fully developed episode, a picture in which the untimely death of a young country schoolteacher is framed by the long career of her superior, a woman in whom resides the same love for and understanding of children. . . .

The final tale, "Before Breakfast," is again one of youth and age and the contrast between them, with the wise comment that "plucky youth is more bracing than enduring age." At the same time it is a story of a successful man's way of compensating for the private failures of which, like all intelligent human beings, he is fully conscious.

It is the first story which is most like the Willa Cather her readers know and admire for her ability to write pure, melodious, simple English and, by the use of this finely tempered tool, to create again and again the illusion of truth.

But the other two tales are by no means to be ignored. I should not be surprised if this unexpected last book sent many a reader back to the earlier Willa Cather. If it does, may I suggest the four titles to read first? They are *O Pioneers!*, *My Antonia, Death Comes for the Arch-*

bishop and the volume of short stories, *Youth and the Bright Medusa*. I do not include *One of Ours* for the reason that I've always felt the Committee awarded this novel the Pulitzer Prize when it was in a fine warm finish of admiration for (a) Miss Cather and her work and (b) the young man who fought the First World War—a thoroughly justifiable state of mind, to be sure but not necessarily one well adapted to judging fiction.

Hamilton Basso, "The Lost Lady," *New Yorker*, 24 (25 September 1948), 102, 105–6

The Old Beauty and Others, by Willa Cather who died a year ago at the age of seventy, contains the author's three last stories. The one that gives the book its title is an almost perfect thing of its kind; the others, while not quite so impressive, are good enough to warrant our gratitude; and the book, as a whole, is a sort of brief summing-up of Miss Cather's viewpoint as she came to the close of her long life and career. First for the stories:

"The Old Beauty" is a portrait, done in water color rather than oil, of a once enormously attractive woman, now grown old and plain, who has hidden herself away in Aix-les-Bains. The time is 1922. There, after many years in China, comes one of her former acquaintances, a "slender, fair-skinned man with white moustaches, waxed and turned up at the ends," who is looking for a place, the author explains, "that was still more or less as it used to be." At first he does not recognize the lady, and when he discovers who she is, he can scarcely believe that she

is the Lady Longstreet who had been the rage and toast of London. Upon renewing their acquaintance, which isn't difficult, he learns, from her and from her companion, a former music-hall performer who has lost none of her bounce and cheer, those details of her story that, because of his absence in China, he did not know. Then, driving in the mountains one afternoon, these three survivors of a forgotten regime have an automobile accident: their driver has to turn sharply in order to miss a car occupied by two women. They happen to be Americans— "bobbed, hatless, clad in dirty white knickers and sweaters." The three friends are badly shaken up, but the aged, faded beauty is unmoved by their narrow escape. "It was natural, wasn't it, after such a morning?" she says. "After one has been *exaltée*, there usually comes a shock. Oh, I don't mean the bruises we got! I mean the white breeches." She has been through a greater ordeal than she realizes, however. She has to be carried from the car to her room, and that night she dies in her sleep. When next her friend sees her, "the face that had outfaced so many changes of fortune has no longer need to muffle itself in furs, to shrink away from curious eyes, or harden itself into scorn. It lay on the pillow regal, calm, victorious—like an open confession."

But Miss Cather's story has an excellence that no outline can hope to indicate. By the time she is through, we have a full-length portrait of her central character, done with precision, economy, and the utmost purity of line. It is so good that the two other stories suffer by contrast. The one called "The Best Years" is more diffuse, slightly less sure; "Before Breakfast" is even thinner, in certain respects, than some of the stories Miss Cather published in *The Troll Garden*, her first book of fiction.

"The Best Years" begins in Nebraska

in 1899 (the locale is that part of the state between the Platte River and the Kansas line), and comes down to around 1920. The events of the story are seen through the eyes of a Miss Evangeline Knightly, who, when the tale begins, is a County Superintendent of Public Instruction. ("A grim title, that," Miss Cather observes, "to put upon a charming young woman.") One of the teachers under her supervision is a sixteen-year-old girl named Lesley Ferguesson. After driving out in a buggy to visit Lesley in her one-room school and see how things are going, Miss Knightly takes her to her home, in the neighboring town of MacAlpin. Lesley's mother is the back-bone of the family; their house, near the railroad tracks, belongs to her. Lesley's father is so lost in his veneration of William Jennings Bryan, and other preoc-cupations, that his four sons, as well as his daughter, hardly know him. A few months later, a blizzard sweeps over Nebraska. Lesley is trapped in her school-house with her students. She is eventually rescued, but she dies of pneumonia. Twenty years afterward, Miss Knightly, now married to a Denver architect, returns to MacAlpin for a short stay. She finds everything changed, including the fortunes of the Ferguessons. The four sons are all successful, the father has been rewarded with a well-paid job with the Democratic administration, and the house by the railroad tracks has been aban-doned for a brand-new one uptown. But Mrs. Ferguesson, as Miss Knightly finds out when she calls on her, is unhappy in her surroundings. "Folks in middle age make a mistake when they think they can better themselves," she says. "They can't, not if they have any heart. And the other kind don't matter—they aren't real people—just poor put-ons, that try to be like the advertisements. . . . This I know: our best years are when we're working

hardest and going right ahead when we can hardly see our way out." On that note, and Miss Knightly's final leave-taking of MacAlpin, the story ends.

"Before Breakfast," the third piece in Miss Cather's collection, seems to me an unsuccessful attempt to repeat what was done so expertly in "The Old Beauty." The author was a magician at working in a small compass and illuminating whole segments of a character's thought and experience with a line, but this story, to my notion, doesn't quite come off. The story concerns a prosperous, self-made business-man named Henry Grenfell, who goes every year for a solitary vacation on the remote island off Nova Scotia. Having worked hard all his life and become a des-perate prisoner of success, Grenfell fre-quently wonders if his life is worth the candle. Now, because of a conversation with a scientist vacationing on the island with his pretty daughter, he is compelled to wonder if *anything* is worth the candle. "What was the use?" he asks himself. "Why tear a man loose from his little rock and shoot him out into the eternities? All that stuff was inhuman. A man had his little hour, with heat and cold and a time-sense suited to his endurance. If you took that away from him you left him spine-less, accidental, unrelated to anything." Full of such doubts and bewilderment, Grenfell goes for a walk before breakfast. From a distance, he sees the scientist's daughter swimming in the icy water, and wonders why she has been so foolish as to brave the deathly chill. "There was no one watching her, she didn't have to keep face—except to herself," he reasons. "That she had to do and no fuss about it. She hadn't dodged. She had gone out, and she had come back. She would have a happy day." Grenfell's spirits are restored; he is chuckling as he returns to his cabin. "Anyhow," he thinks, "when that first amphibious frog-toad found his water-

540

hole dried up behind him, and jumped out to hop along till he could find another—well, he started on a long hop."

Aside from their merit as literary performances (though not even "The Old Beauty," mind you, is apt to be remembered as one of the world's masterpieces, for all its technical perfection), these stories of Miss Cather's have a special value in that, as I have said, they give us a good idea of the way the author saw things, and felt about them, in her final years. There is not a great deal that is new; this is, rather, a restatement and a recapitulation, although in "Before Breakfast" there seems to be a note of defiant affirmation that may not have been there before.

There are two themes, not always side by side, in nearly everything Miss Cather has written: the absolute necessity to follow one's life through, as in *My Antonia*, and the gradual crumbling away of the standards and values of the pioneering society that went down under the clanging material of the industrial age, as in *A Lost Lady* and *The Professor's House*. One of the things that is sometimes overlooked when Miss Cather is under consideration is that while she is generally included in the Theodore Dreiser–Sherwood Anderson generation of writers, she belongs to the earlier era of Henry James and Edith Wharton. (Her first book of fiction appeared in 1905, the year Mrs. Wharton's *The House of Mirth* came out, and about the time that James was publishing such short stories as "The Beast in the Jungle" and his later novels.) Then, too, growing up in Nebraska when that state was still really in its infancy, she was a part of the frontier society whose values she was always to celebrate, a little too elegiacally at times, perhaps, and occasionally a trifle sentimentally, but with a continuous sense of participation

and first-hand knowledge. In her own lifetime she saw this society disappear, and, equally important, the effect and influence it had on the national culture. The subsequent order, which she rejected almost as completely as did James, without making so much fuss about it, forever appeared cheap, vulgar, and mean.

"The Old Beauty" is a reworking of this theme. Against the world that has gone down, and is as faded as Lady Longstreet, are opposed those dirty white knickers; they are at the core of the shock that does her in. In "The Best Years," as in "The Old Beauty," Miss Cather again goes back to an old order of things—this time to the Nebraska of her childhood. The elegiac note is sounded again, as in so many of her books, and in Mrs. Ferguesson's speech about the best years, the need and importance of fortitude are underlined once more. Here, too, the new society is presented as less worthy than the old; the house in uptown MacAlpin, in which Mrs. Ferguesson finds so little happiness and so much to regret, is as much a symbol of fatality as the white knickers. Mrs. Ferguesson, in whom we can see the pioneer virtues thinning out and running down, is hardly less a captive of success than Henry Grenfell in "Before Breakfast." In this story, Miss Cather looks our modern material straight in the eye, and, in the person of Grenfell, tells it what she thinks of it. But, again, in Grenfell's consideration of the frog that hopped along to find another hole, she stresses the need to persist; the meaning of all life, perhaps, is simply to endure. This is a lean philosophy, certainly, but it is the one, I feel, that Miss Cather managed to live by. The tradition she saw disappear was her tradition, and the pioneer world that went down was her world, and the shelf of books she left us is the record of a lost lady—cultivated, poised, talented, and forever burdened

541

with grief. She opposed such standards as she found shoddy with the impeccable standards of her art, to which she held, as her last volume shows, to the very end. In short, she endured. For that alone she would deserve our homage.

Margaret Marshall, *Nation*, 167 (2 October 1948), 376

Willa Cather's last three stories have been published in a volume entitled *The Old Beauty and Others*. The third and shortest, "Before Breakfast," though it is very slight, at least has the fiber and articulation of a created work of art. The other two, the title story and "The Best Years," give the impression of being mementoes rather than new thrusts of Miss Cather's talent. So much so that one feels that they might almost have been written by a devoted understudy. The familiar visible elements of the Cather atelier are here: the style, the attitudes, the subject matter. But the invisible mysterious element, the creative energy which is necessary to quicken a given set of materials into life and entity, is missing. As a result the materials lie about, inert. And reading these stories is a little like walking among the ruins of a once loved house played upon by a mild sighing wind laden with the fragrance of nostalgia.

"The Old Beauty," which is the more ambitious of the two, is interesting, however, for the very reason that it does contain all the visible makings of a significant work of art, and shows so plainly what happens, or does not happen, when the essential invisible element is missing.

Miss Cather's talent shows forth in both her conception and her portrait of the central character, Madame Gabrielle de Coucy. As the beautiful young Lady Longstreet she had presided over a drawing-room in "old London" to which the more important men of the time, and particularly the older men, had delighted to come. She is ending her days at the Hotel Splendide at Aix-les-Bains. This is something of a stock character in fiction, yet Lady Longstreet, as Miss Cather distinguishes her for us with delicacy and subtlety, is at once untypical and very convincing. The settings and the situations are likewise handled with insight and a fine unobtrusive skill. The theme—Madame de Coucy's hatred of the new world which has replaced the old and her refusal of its furniture and its values which is symbolized by her actual death—is authentic and inherently moving. Here, as I have said, are the makings of a significant piece of fiction. But as the story moves to its dénouement, one becomes more and more aware that it has been written, not out of the passionate yet detached interest of the artist going about his business, but out of the much feebler partisan impulse of an individual with preferences.

The curious result is the betrayal, so to speak, of the very character, Madame de Coucy, and of the very values to which Miss Cather is, as a person, obviously committed. In the climactic scene the "old beauty" is confronted with the ugly new world when the car in which she is riding in the mountains stops short to avoid hitting another car. The women who spring from the other car are Americans. They have driven this car twelve thousand miles and never had an accident. They are "bobbed, hatless, clad in dirty white knickers and sweaters," and they call each other Marge and Jim. Shortly afterward, as a result of the shock, Madame de Coucy, already an invalid, dies of a heart attack. The ending is entirely believable, and the double nature of the shock which brings on Gabrielle's death is skilfully played upon. The trouble is that in the context Madame de Coucy's violent rejection of the new world appears, not as it might have, as a grand and even tragic refusal, but merely as a gesture of distaste and impatience toward two individuals.

Miss Cather would have done better with her story, one reflects, in her untired days. And one can't help thinking of what Henry James would have done with this rather Jamesian theme. (Why Miss Cather tired and James did not is another and very interesting question.) Like Miss Cather, he would, as an individual, have shared Madame de Coucy's preferences. As an artist, however, he would have maintained the detached position: both worlds, not merely Gabrielle's, would have stood before us—consider his adumbration of the new world in "The Reverberators"; the confrontation would have taken place between these worlds, not merely between their chance representatives; and the two sets of values being given, Gabrielle's rejection would have had a dramatic and moral significance it quite fails to achieve in Miss Cather's personal, nostalgic, and tensionless version.

page of this exquisite little book, "the last three stories" of that greatly mourned novelist of our land and time. Miss Cather went abroad to Aix-les-Bains for her "Old Beauty," and delightful are the restraint and tenderness and understanding with which she is pictured. The story, so full of sentiment, never descends to sentimentality. It is a perfect gem in a setting without blemish.

The author's Nebraska homeland was the locale for "The Best Years," and here Miss Cather opens our vision to the glories of the western prairie and the character of its people as we jog along beside the little school superintendent in her buggy on her visits to her outlying charges. The last story, "Before Breakfast," takes us to a secluded Canadian island where the author herself sometimes went to work and rest. She has relinquished it in these pages to Henry Grenfell of Grenfell & Saunders, who has fled to its solitude as a respite from his busy life as a successful magnate, and who cherishes his privacy there so autocratically as to resent even hearing of the findings of a visiting archaeologist. This subtle bit of character drawing leaves its meaning somewhat obscure, but, like both the other stories, this too bears the sure touch of a master craftsman's hand.

A fourth tale remained unfinished and in accordance with Miss Cather's wishes will not be published.

Mary Elizabeth Brennan,
Catholic World, 168
(December 1948), 253

A nostalgia for the rare literary art that was Willa Cather's grips one with the first

---

Checklist of
Additional Reviews

Virginia Kirkus Bulletin, 16 (15 July 1948), 341.

L. S. Munn, *Springfield* (Massachusetts) *Republican*, 26 September 1948, p. 10B.

Orville Prescott, *Yale Review*, New Series, 38 (Winter 1949), 384.

"Collected Tales," *Times Literary Supplement* (London), 13 April 1956, p. 226.

Index

547